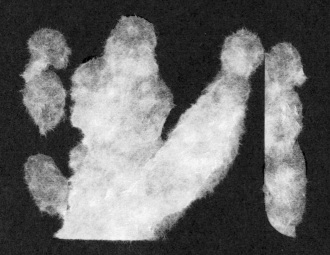

Big Business in the
THIRD REICH

by Arthur Schweitzer

INDIANA UNIVERSITY PRESS
BLOOMINGTON 1964

Second printing 1965

COPYRIGHT © 1964 BY INDIANA UNIVERSITY PRESS

LIBRARY OF CONGRESS CATALOG CARD NO. 63-62857

MANUFACTURED IN THE UNITED STATES OF AMERICA

TABLE OF CONTENTS

v

P R E F A C E

For quite obvious reasons, many observers are reluctant to concern themselves with the Nazi system; but justified repugnance to the regime should not prevent us from getting at the carefully kept, secret facts and gaining an understanding of the inner workings of a one-party dictatorship.

The problems that arose during the first phase of the regime are surprisingly modern. Although the solutions adopted by the dictators are completely unacceptable to us, we can obtain a not insignificant insight into the nature of contemporary issues when we know about the mistakes made in another economic system. Lessons can be learned not only from our friends but also from our enemies.

A case in point is the controversial issue of the so-called labor monopoly. The Nazis destroyed the unions, halted any form of "creeping socialism," and restored the managerial prerogative in plants; but there was no return to a "natural" labor market. With collective bargaining eliminated, market forces had no effect on wage rates, since these were fixed by the state at the level of the preceding depression. These direct controls imposed by the state were not resisted by employers because they provided low and stable unit wage costs in a period of prosperity. In fact, the destruction of trade unions not only ended their influence in plants and labor markets but also extended the power of big business over the economic policies and agencies of the state. Hence, "industrial peace" was achieved through employer domination of the field of industrial relations.

Another important issue is the effect of an armament program upon private capitalism. The Nazi rearmament boom not only provided the opportunity for rising employment and profitable output but also led to the regulation of a few private markets. Instead of opposing such regulation, many of the business groups involved accepted direct intervention on the part of the state. As we discovered, the major reason for such behavior was that many of the detrimental effects of regulation were compensated for by new and attractive inducements, initiated or supported by business groups. Not the freedom of markets but the opportunity to increase profits became the central criterion for judging the desirability of direct actions by the state. Business leaders thus failed to recognize the incipient forms of statism at a time when they were still in a position to oppose it or limit it. Our own military program as well as the great volume of capital that has been leaving the country since 1958 have both contributed significantly to our gold loss and to the deficit in our current balance of payments, with the result that we have come very close to government regulation of capital outflow and security markets. Will our massive concerns continue to seek singlemindedly the higher profits expected from the investment of American capital abroad, even when this might—barring a drastic change in our military policy—make government regulation of markets unavoidable? The German experience could be instructive in helping our leaders to formulate more clearly the question confronting them: Is the unswerving pursuit of the biggest profits always the best policy for maintaining private capitalism?

Behind the monolithic front of the Nazi regime, there developed a battle royal between big and small business for leadership of the economy. The majority of the small-business groups had not only become Nazified but were also intensely anticapitalistic in feeling and action. Hence, they pushed for a program of economic counterrevolution with the intention of replacing the industrial economy with a modernized guild system. It required the marshalling of all the resources and power of big business, effectively assisted by the military leaders, to defeat this economic counterrevolution. Although not likely, it is still conceivable that a counterrevolutionary potential might develop in this country. If all forms of price support were abolished and extreme price gyrations restored, at a time when the American family farm is under severe pressure from the new technological revolution in agriculture, a strong "wind of change" (of which the militant protests of the National Farmers Organization would be only the first whiffle) could come up. Some aspects of the present process of automation also harbor a counterrevolutionary potential. If automation is permitted to run its course without limits and sensible direction, the resultant decline of unit costs and the increase in undistributed profits may lead to an enormous expansion of big business, with the result that small business will be subjected to a severe squeeze. The subsequent and increasing animosity could provide the soil for the growth of anticapitalist movements. It is only when this counterrevolutionary potential is recognized and understood that wise policies can be devised to circumvent or minimize a not inconceivable danger.

Khrushchev has made it known that he wants to bury private capitalism. Being forced by American atomic power to rely primarily on the political power of the Soviet state, he counts upon the revolutionary potential of the impoverished masses in the less developed countries to assist him in reaching his goal. There are indications, however, that he also hopes for some unwitting help from the capitalist countries themselves. One is the counterrevolutionary potential that could undermine the internal cohesion and strength of the West. The other is the exclusively profit-minded—and politically short-sighted—capitalist who can be lured—by trade offers and other deals—to ally himself unwittingly with the Communist regime. The German experience provides an instructive example of how the profit lure can induce capitalists to engage (as did the collaborators considered in the last chapter of this study) in actions that must eventually tend to hurt the economic system for which they stand.

The rearmament boom of the Nazi regime, while providing a rapid increase in the volume of employment, took place under a set of deliberately created "un-Keynesian" conditions. The substantial increase in the money supply had a very small multiplier effect since the flow of new money was directed primarily toward the militarily important producer-goods industries. The reduction of interest rates was a result of direct actions on the part of the state and was not significantly related to the liquidity-creating effect of the new money. The rise in consumer purchasing power was deliberately retarded by pegging wage rates at the level of the depression. The share of taxes in governmental receipts was deliberately increased so that the income-creating effect of deficit financing was either minimized or counteracted. Having little confidence in the output-creating effect of deficit financing, the business groups pressured the government into placing orders with their own plants, even through this had the potential effect of significantly increasing the volume of public investments. In fact, the rearmament boom differed so basically from a genuine recovery that a Keynesian interpretation of the boom seemed impossible.

The Keynesian model—with its welfare state, competitive markets, undifferentiated structure of production, unorganized forms of business activity and economically and politically free labor force—implies an institutional setting that is diametrically different from the one that prevailed during the Nazi regime. In attempting to come to grips with the Nazi situation, we could not reason in terms of a pure economy but had to take the peculiar institutional factors as independent variables that were in need of explanation. The conceptual tools for such an analysis could be found only in the socioeconomic theory of Max Weber, whose work has been so sadly neglected by economists. Since his work remained incomplete and since his ideas have never been applied to dictatorial economies, we were forced to enter unmapped territory. How successful we have been in our attempt (which is necessarily tentative) to apply his theory remains for the reader to judge.

One advantage of social economics is its deliberate linkage with sociology and political science. The insight one can gain from knowing the noneconomic factors can be seen from our study of full and partial facism, of actual counterrevolution and potential fascism, of the class structure and the ideology of the various groups. Social economics becomes the appropriate mode of investigation when the political and social institutions cannot be taken for granted and when the economic institutions—themselves subject to change—influence the course of economic action.

The idea of this book originated during my tenure as research associate of the School of Business of the University of Chicago, when—encouraged by Dean Garfield V. Cox and Dean Neil H. Jacoby—I wrote six articles on the Nazi economy that were based on and limited to published documents. Major progress in this research was made possible by two travel grants and a faculty research fellowship from the Social Science Research Council and by a faculty research fellowship from the Ford Foundation. Subsequently, the research committee and the library of Indiana University provided funds for the purchase of a large number of microfilms, and the Graduate School granted assistantships to Claus Ruser, Gustav Schmid, Ivo A. Peko, Alexander Kondonassis, Horst G. Vitt, and Hans-Dieter Renning, who helped me to discover the relevant data in the huge volume of captured German documents. The sympathetic understanding of the successive chairmen of the Department of Economics—C. L. Christenson, William C. Cleveland, and Taulman Miller—relieved me of administrative duties and enabled me to devote more of my time to research than I should have been able to otherwise. I am indebted to my colleagues Albert K. Cohen, Henry M. Oliver, Jr., and to Joseph D. Coppock of Earlham College, for their critical reading of an earlier draft of the manuscript, and to Mr. Walter Albee, of the Indiana University Press, for editing the manuscript and designing the format of the printed book. The assistance received from many libraries, especially the U. S. Army Records Branch at Alexandria, Virginia, the German section of the Library of Congress (Dr. Fritz

T. Epstein), the microfilming team of the American Historical Association, the Berlin Documents Center, the Institute for Völkerrecht in Göttingen, the Bundesarchiv in Koblenz, the Midwest Library Center in Chicago and, last but certainly not least, the libraries of Indiana University, has been generous and most helpful. I am deeply grateful for all the support received in this extensive venture. The ideas and points of view expressed have been discussed with many scholars, too numerous to mention by name, but none of them shares responsibility for them.

The editors of the following periodicals have consented to the use of some of the material that was first published in their pages: *Journal of Political Economy, Journal of Finance, Political Science Quarterly, Journal of Business, Schmollers Jahrbuch, Zeitschrift für die gesamte Staatswissenschaft, Schweizerische Zeitschrift für Volkswirtschaft und Statistik.* The titles of the articles in question have been cited at the appropriate places in the notes and also appear in the bibliography.

Arthur Schweitzer

BLOOMINGTON, INDIANA
August, 1963

INTRODUCTION

Our generation has been burdened with one-party regimes. Nazi Germany and Fascist Italy, assisted by military Japan, determined the course of events in the 1930's and the 1940's. Soviet Russia and Communist China every day voice their intentions of remoulding the world in the image of their ideology. And the end is not in sight. There is every reason to believe that not only the present but also future generations will have to marshal enough strength and wisdom to resist and defeat dictatorial communism. Our knowledge of, and capacity to defeat, fascist regimes could and should furnish us with some significant lessons for coping with one-party dictatorships in the future.

An extensive examination of a large volume of documents (some formerly secret, but now public)[1] has led the writer to the new hypothesis that *no* single unified economic system prevailed throughout the entire period of the Nazi regime. A distinct shift in the economic policy of the regime occurred in 1936. There was not only a change in the economic goals of the rulers but also in the type of political and economic organization, in the distribution of economic power, and in the principles of market operation.

Once this shift had been clearly identified, it became necessary to investigate each period in terms of the goals and policies that the rulers imposed upon the nation. Since there was a good deal of divergency between aims and actions in the two phases of the regime, it seemed inadvisable to present both systems in the same volume. The purpose of the present book, therefore, is to trace the development and analyse the significance of the major economic changes in the German economy that took place during the first period of the Nazi regime.

Concentrating upon the economic actions of the rulers, we discovered that their policies were guided by four economic goals. These included (a) economic rearmament, (b) the suppression of trade unions, (c) the invigoration of capitalist institutions, and (d) a semi-guild form of economic organization that favored small urban and rural business. Our task then is to see how these ideas originated, by whom they were promoted, and how they were translated into definite policy proposals. Once accepted and implemented, what were the consequences of the adopted policies both for the ruling groups and for the economic system as a whole?

Clearly, such an analysis could be handled only if we could find a theory that would perform two important functions. As a starting point, we needed to find the essentials of the German economy as it existed at the beginning of the Nazi regime. We also required a thesis as to what the mutual relationships were between the private groups in the economy and the economic policies of the state. Given such a thesis, we could examine the impact of the four economic policies upon the positions of the various economic groups as well as upon the nature of the economic system.

Max Weber's theory of capitalism has been most useful for our purpose. In comparison with other approaches, Max Weber's theory has two great advantages. He distinguished carefully between industrial and commercial as well as between financial and political capitalism. Each type is represented by specific groups of businessmen who promote different interests and ideologies. In each case, physical means of production are appropriated and utilized as fixed capital by autonomous private enterprises, which engage in profit-making and capital-accounting.[2] Yet each kind of capitalist uses his capital differently and operates in a different environment. The industrial capitalist employs his capital primarily in production and supplies goods for sale in commodity markets. The commercial capitalist invests his trading capital in the purchase and sale of goods at a profit. Financial capitalists place loan capital with borrowers via money and capital markets. Political capitalists, however, operate outside the market nexus because they sell goods, provide loans, and furnish services to political bodies, especially governments.[3] The advantage of such a theory is that it permits us to examine changes in the capitalist system by tracing the goals and actions of each of these capitalist groups.

In addition, Weber places the four kinds of capitalist enterprise not only in their economic but also in their social and political environments. Each group occupies a definite but slightly different place in the capitalist property structure. In their internal as well as external activities, capitalist enterprises are alike in seeking to accumulate power as well as capital and thereby to gain positions of strength in the power structure. The difference arises in their relationships to the economic activities of the state. On the one hand, industrial capitalists are interested primarily in a predictable legal order that protects and enforces their legal claims against other concerns. Industrial capitalism aims at a minimum of economic functions performed by the state. On the other hand,

political capitalists cater to the wishes of the state by selling
goods and providing services to its agents. Thus, as the number of economic functions assumed by the state increases, the
volume of its purchases also increases, and the profit chances
of the political capitalist become larger. It is this principle
of elective affinity between capitalist groups and the state that
constitutes the second advantage of Weber's theory for our
investigation.

Accepting this well-rounded concept of capitalism as our
frame of reference, we then had to analyse the new phenom-
ena of the Nazi party and anticapitalist small-business groups.
As will be shown in the first part of this study, small business
not only became Nazified ideologically but also developed
an economic program of counterrevolutionary anticapitalism. This new aim ran counter to the cherished goal of big
business of employing the power of the state for the invigoration of capitalist institutions that had suffered during the
Great Depression. The resulting conflict of goals, largely
overlooked in previous studies of the Nazi economy, produced a fierce struggle for economic leadership between big
and small business. This fight penetrated into all economic
issues that arose during the earlier Nazi regime. In order to
come to grips with this anticapitalism, we have to narrow the
scope of Weber's capitalism by introducing a distinction between big and small business and to limit the concept of
capitalism to big business.

To account for the political position of the Nazi party as
a holder of power, we must give up the notion of the state as
a unified fiscal, military, and political entity developing an
economic policy that is clearly distinct from the economic
policy of private capitalism. Instead we must see who stood
behind the state and who originated each economic goal and
supported the subsequent economic policy. As for the suppression of trade unions, the German generals and the Nazi
party as well as big and small business supported the policy

of using the power of the state to fix wage rates in labor markets, whereas the Nazi party alone destroyed the old, and prevented the rise of new, independent trade unions. Economic rearmament was demanded and implemented by the generals, the Nazi party, and big business, whereas the economic policy promoted by Nazified small business was partly in opposition to economic rearmament. The invigoration of capitalist institutions by state action was originated by big business, effectively supported by the generals, tolerated by the top Nazis, but furiously opposed by Nazified small business. Finally, the anticapitalism generated by small business was tolerated to a certain degree by the Nazi party but strongly rejected by big business as well as by most of the leading generals.

During the first period of the regime, the Nazis not only failed to develop a uniform economic policy which might have been imposed upon the state and the economy but, for various reasons which will be specified and described, were forced to accept the generals and big business, as well as small business in the first two years, as partakers in the power of the state. This holding of power by all four groups calls for a modification of Weber's principle of elective affinity. It was not simply the case that economic rearmament enlarged the sphere of political capitalism at the expense of industrial capitalism.[4] The suppression of trade unions abolished the principle of free association for labor and at the same time, in combination with the invigoration of capitalist institutions by state actions, enlarged the sphere of capitalism controlled and enjoyed by big business. The defeat of the anticapitalist goals of Nazified small business by the use of instruments of the state produced the same effect. Rather than promoting the development of one capitalist group by minimizing the chances of others, the state in the first period simultaneously increased the profit opportunities of political capitalists and most other capitalist groups. As a result, what had been a privately controlled capitalism was transformed into an organized capitalism effectively assisted by the state.

In a study of economic systems, we thus have to consider two possible interpretations. Was the German economy in the first phase of Nazi rule a kind of political capitalism? Or did the interaction between a one-party dictatorship and a modern industrial economy give rise to an organized capitalism? Whichever thesis is supported by the relevant evidence, we are in a position to find a way through the impasse in the currently accepted theory of economic systems, which insists upon the dogma that all observable systems must be a variant either of an idealized market economy or of a villainous, centrally administered economy.[5]

In his recent study of the political system of the Nazis, Mr. William Shirer tells us that "the Nazi revolution was political, not economic," that the Nazi period was characterized by a war economy from the beginning to the end.[6] It would seem, however, that Mr. Shirer did not examine the economic documents. In doing so, one not only discovers the economic counterrevolution and its struggle with a reinvigorated capitalism but one is forced to the conclusion that the Nazi party did not determine military and economic policies in the first phase of the regime. If this is a correct view, and the reader is invited to examine the evidence given in the following chapters, then there must have existed during the early years, a kind of partial fascism in which big business and the generals functioned as equal partners in power. It is precisely because both these non-Nazi groups acted according to the notion of a partial fascism that they entered into an alliance with the Nazi party, that they were so cocksure of their ability to "tame" the Nazis. Thus, having facilitated the origin and growth of partial fascism, big business and the generals bear the additional responsibility of having failed to take the appropriate actions that would have tended to forestall the subsequent development of a full fascism.

If the evidence on partial fascism is accepted, our thesis calls for a revision of the current political theory of fascism. On the one hand, total fascism is only one phase of a fascist regime, requiring as an antecedent a phase of partial fascism. It is only in this preliminary period that there can arise the conditions for the possible—but not inevitable—evolution toward total fascism. On the other hand, the evidence on the specific features of partial fascism casts doubt on the thesis that fascism must necessarily be postdemocratic and postindustrial. Not only are the preconditions for partial fascism less formidable but some of its features are not limited to industrial countries. Some elements of fascism may thus be lifted out of their industrial setting and transplanted into the environment of countries undertaking the formidable task of industrialization. Military or one-party dictatorships in less developed countries may thus imitate some features of European fascism—especially the suppression of other parties and independent trade unions by some sort of secret police. If so, a revised theory of fascism is needed to explain the origin and results of the transplanted elements as well as the operation and effects of partial and total fascism.

Finally, our analysis leads to the conclusion that the defeat of the Nazi armed forces has not exterminated all political movements—in contrast to regimes—of a fascist nature. The recent anti-Semite agitation in West Germany and the formation of Nazi parties in Great Britain and New Zealand cannot be regarded as the last convulsive expressions of a dying movement. Having been repressed by big business and the generals in the first phase of the regime, the incipient ideas of the Nazified middle class—the so-called middle-class socialism and the anti-labor ideology—may well be reasserted in modernized form and used to furnish the goal for a Neo-Nazi movement, as has already been done by the Neo-Fascists in Italy.

Two different kinds of action seem necessary if incipient

Neo-Nazism is to be rendered harmless. We must know the meaning and history of the economic counterrevolution in the first phase of the Hitler regime so that we can meet and defeat Neo-Nazism on the intellectual level. We must also be ready for the political actions which are certain to set in when the new fascist movement turns again into a dictatorial party, builds up new para-military organizations, and again starts a defamation campaign against other persons, groups, and ideologies.

Obviously, in view of the suffering created by the Nazis and the price paid for the violent destruction of their regime, it behooves us to prevent the rise of new fascist movements and to minimize the influence of new regimes of partial fascism wherever they may arise.

WHO CONTROLLED WHOM?

CHAPTER ONE

The relationship between the Nazi party and various business groups has long been a topic of speculation and interpretation. The whole range of possible answers has been suggested at one time or other. One group of thinkers saw the Nazis as creatures of the capitalists, whereas another believed that the Nazis were freely dictating to the various groups of business. Numerous intermediate interpretations were also advanced. The large volume of formerly secret documents enables us to say that both big and small business were active participants in the new dictatorship. What was their role in the Nazi regime?

As a preliminary step one has to indicate the meaning of the terms "Nazi party" and "business groups." It is not enough to see one as political and the other as economic in nature. In addition to their central economic activities, business groups had developed organizations that were capable of engaging in specific political activities. The Nazi party was not only a distinct political organization but had built up the Labor Front and the Estate of Food, both of which could perform economic functions. It will thus be necessary to examine first the political aspect of business and then deal with the nature of the Nazi party as well as with its quasi-economic organizations.

In order to get our problem into proper focus, we will not only have to consider the Nazi party and the business groups at one particular time but investigate the changing relationship between these organizations over a number of years. This will be done in two distinct ways. In the present chapter we shall contrast the political aspects of business prior to the Nazi regime with the political aspects of the Nazi party as they existed at the end of 1936. The reason for selecting these different periods is not only to indicate the time span to be covered but also to bring out the discrepancy that prevailed in the types of organization at these two times. This discrepancy helps us to formulate one of our problems: How could the quasi-political organizations of business, adequate for exerting business influence in a political democracy, cope with the problems posed by the dictatorial Nazi party?

In the five chapters following this one, our study of economic and political organizations will proceed more or less chronologically. Our guide will be the issues of conflict and cooperation that developed in the various fields of action. The evidence presented will enable us to state in Chapter VI the kind of power structure that had developed during the first phase of the regime. Given this power structure, the subsequent chapters will analyse the nature and extent of the rearmament boom, the character of the labor markets and the functions of the Labor Front, the meaning of government assistance of private business, and the significance of direct controls in some specific markets.

POLITICAL ASPECTS OF BUSINESS

At the time of single proprietorships or small-scale partnerships, business concerns employed primarily one method for exerting their political influence: political influence was purchased directly. Either administrators were granted favors of various kinds in return for certain franchises or other privileges, or funds were made available for the election of candidates to specific offices whose holders felt obligated to give first preference to their financial backers. Later, however, the direct purchase of political influence seems to have declined in relative significance. The reason for a shift to the indirect exertion of influence has to be sought in new political, as well as economic, events. The purchase of time on radio and television has greatly increased the volume of funds necessary for waging and winning a national campaign. In addition, politicians and political parties have become more sensitive to the charge of "bribery" and exhibit a distinct preference for non-specific contributions to their campaign funds. At the same time, as the size of the concerns has increased, and the inter-business organizations have become stronger, there has arisen a tendency to establish quasi-political organizations for exerting political influence continuously. By the same token, the involvement of business concerns in political decisions has ceased to be merely an intermittent affair and requires the steady attention of specialists or specially devised organizations.

The growth of business enterprise has led not only to a greater degree of political involvement but to the formation of more plants of the same kind and, in addition, to an increase in the over-all variety of industrial establishments. The greater the number and size of plants and the larger the number of products produced, the greater have become the contacts with political agencies, and the greater the political involvement of massive business concerns. This expansion of economic interests has induced the controllers of large concerns to develop a program of political action of their own. In Germany as well as in the United States, such action has three goals. There is first the effort to keep political parties and governmental bodies out of the sphere of production and management, and also out of marketing and investment, which activities are usually regarded by business concerns as their private and exclusive domain. There is secondly the drive to "make room" for the "legitimate" expansion of large concerns by supplying a great variety of favors, gifts, and privileges that business has come to expect of political parties and governments. There is finally the determination to "keep the lid" on unions by harassing the stewards within the plant, by obtaining anti-union legislation from the government, and by reducing the rights of laborers and unions through reinterpretation by courts or other government agencies.

Aside from the last goal (of keeping the unions pliable), the political goals of business require a twofold organization for their implementation. One device is to rely upon politicians, political parties, and "friends in influential circles"— to use a phrase of the American businessman, Mr. Goldfine— for realizing the political goals of organized business. The other is the quasi-political organization of business itself through which economic power is translated into political influence and policies favorable to business.

Within the concern, the department of public relations has become increasingly significant. Its first task is to obtain public approval of what business leaders are doing. The second function of public relations, and one which is of growing importance, is to change and mould public opinion in the direction which business desires. A significant portion of the undistributed profits is used to finance these activities which are often called euphemistically the "social responsibility of management."

The methods employed by the departments of public relations differ. They may aim at influencing the opinion-leaders of other groups—free information is supplied to teachers; grants or fellowships are provided to colleges and universities. In the United States, educational institutions and policies have been given an increasing share of managerial attention, and a new organization of executives has been formed to determine the policies for corporate aid to educational institutions. Departments of public relations also seek to create mass effects. In using the methods of advertising for the promotion of business interests and ideology, by subsidizing all the means of mass communication, big business has obtained the power to change the attitudes and opinions of millions on an increasing number of issues.

The managing and moulding of public opinion have a significant effect upon the relationship between business and political parties or governments in all industrialized countries. If a public "desire" for a certain business policy has been created, politicians and parties will find it to their self-interest to act according to these wishes. This activity of the public-relations department is then an alternative to making financial contributions to political parties. In other cases, which may very well constitute the majority, large concerns have taken over the task of either preparing the public, or supplying supplementally needed mass support, for a certain policy of business which, however, has still to be carried through the political processes by friendly politicians and parties. Managing public opinion tends thus to be more successful in the promotion of ideologies than specific economic interests, provided the ideals suggested can be plausibly presented as instances of competition, freedom, and liberty.

The promotion of specific business interests is accomplished within the framework of the prevailing political institutions. Rather than establishing control only over markets or over an industry by inter-corporate understanding, quite often the market position can be secured (e.g., in regard to tariffs) and the future expansion (e.g., of a new federal highway system) facilitated only if certain political decisions favoring business interests are made. This requires the cooperation of administrators, legislators, and commissions or courts. Three organizational devices are employed (often outside the usual corporate organization) to achieve the desired policy.

Presenting business interests before courts and commissions is usually the function of the corporation lawyers. Both the members of the legal department and of separate law firms jointly prepare and present the corporation's case. In legislative matters, the representation of interests is either the task of the hired lobbyist—as the second "device"—or of the staff of the trade association. These men are not only specialists in the economic matter under discussion but they are also on friendly personal terms with the legislator and his staff, as well as with party officials. Knowing the personal and especially the financial worries of these officials, lobbyists are in a position to place funds "where they do the most good." The supposedly discreet contributions in 1958 to the campaign funds of members of Congress by the oil lobby is a case in point. Finally, there is the device of negotiation and consultation between representative business leaders and leaders of government. The former either participate in the hearings of legislative committees or visit the head of the government department concerned. In these consultations the points under dispute are discussed in detail, and a compromise is usually effected that incorporates most of the business interests.[1]

Only in the case of the lobbyist is there a fairly clear connection between values received and given. Yet the "consideration" is hardly paid directly into the pockets of the cooperating politicians. Any expert in the political promotion of business interests will pay for the services received indirectly so that no investigating committee can surprise him with damaging evidence. Successful promotion of interests via litigation and consultation calls increasingly for non-specific contributions to party treasuries or to committees financing the election of friendly politicians. Although an outright privilege bestowed upon a concern or industry as the result of a political decision will always call for specific payments in some form,[2] the increasing size of concerns and the steady involvement of business in politics have created a preference among business groups for dealing with large political organizations. Rather than aiming at, and paying for, specific deals, the tendency is to get and maintain a friendly political party in office through massive campaign contributions. Policies are then negotiated on the highest level and opportunities for steady consultation are then so institutionalized that a partnership between business and the party or government arises. Rather than shopping in a political "department store" for many small, unrelated items, big business, when it attempts to influence political affairs, can arrange over-all economic policies jointly with the government or party and pay for the favors in lump-sum campaign contributions.

The third political aspect of business, in addition to public relations and the promotion of special interests, can be seen in the development of economic class organizations. These organizations usually have arisen for two reasons. The manifold trade associations tend toward an amalgamation of many business interests into one national organization. Soon after the turn of the century such amalgamated groups of business were formed in the United States; yet their influence remained insignificant mainly because business did not unite behind these organizations. An outside stimulant was necessary. This was provided when governments assumed the responsibility of formulating and directing national economic policy. The *Reich* Association of German Industry was formed in 1919, and a spokesman was appointed to represent the association in its dealings with the new democratic government. Comparably, the National Association of Manufacturers was revived shortly before the New Deal government came to power.

In trying to represent the major and most articulate portion of business as a whole, the national organizations usually seek to perform two functions. In addressing themselves to the formulation of the over-all economic policy of the country, the leaders usually negotiate among themselves in order to arrive at a general policy that is agreeable to business. The national meetings are thus usually productive of policy announcements that state the point of view of business. On the basis of this over-all policy position, a series of committees are organized that formulate business policy in regard to specific issues. The policy adopted is usually translated into a specific proposal or bill that guides the representatives of the national organization in their consultations with top governmental administrators and strategically placed legislators. Consultation is usually the preferred form of policy implementation. Yet the policies under discussion are not industrial but national in scope, and the power brought to bear entails the pooled resources of big business as an economic class.

Prior to the Nazis' rise to power the *Reich* Association of German Industry was perhaps the best example of a class-oriented organization of business. This voluntary association comprised almost all industrial and territorial business organizations in the country. Not less than twenty-nine industrial and fifty territorial organizations belonged corporatively to the national association. Their combined membership represented about 80 per cent of all industrial enterprises in November of 1932.[3] Yet the leadership of the organization was not in the hands of its participating organizations. The controllers of the largest concerns were given the privilege of individual membership. The top leaders of the association, including the annual officers, the members of the executive committee as well as the heads of the standing committees, were usually selected from among those private members. The association was thus under the domination of big business. Its resolutions contained the proposals of big business, which were usually backed up with the power of all the large concerns of the country. It was generally recognized that the association operated as the organized power bloc of German big business.

In the last years of the Weimar Republic, German business had fully developed the political aspects of its organization. In comparison to American business, much more emphasis was placed upon formal representation and consultation with political parties and government officials. Lobbying was usually performed by trade associations, and public relations took a more subdued form since the radio was beyond the control of business concerns. Many trade associations had specific connections with certain political parties. The associations not only functioned as regular contributors to the party treasuries but several of them had some of their leaders elected as party representatives to parliament, in which body they represented also the economic interests of their trade association. The *Reich* Association of German Industry exerted a strong influence upon the economic policies proposed by most of the nonsocialist parties or upon many of the economic agencies of the government, except for the Ministry of Labor.

Since the associations were fully organized for political action, the question arises as to what was the specific capacity of German business groups in regard to manipulating political parties or governments. Being well organized, corporations or business groups possessed the demonstrated ability (*a*) to act as partners in special deals negotiated with politicians or administrators, (*b*) to provide financial backing for particular political campaigns or elections, (*c*) to enter into an alliance with a political party by having business leaders elected to political office, (d) to arrange for a definite but not publicized partnership with a government either by naming the ministers of economics and finance or by influencing decisively the economic policies of the government. Through these four lines of action, business groups had wielded great political influence in the Weimar Republic.

After the fall election of 1930, corporations and business groups were confronted with the existence of the Nazi party and had to decide what policy they should adopt toward it. Were the four proven lines of political action appropriate in handling a dictatorial party? Or was it desirable for the financial backers to join the Nazi party, accumulate power within its organizations, and thereby influence or determine its economic policy?

NAZI POLITICAL MONOPOLY

Six months after Adolf Hitler had become Chancellor, the Nazis had eliminated all other political parties. In law as well as in fact, Germany went through a political counterrevolution in the process of which the multiple-party system was replaced by a one-party system. The effect of this change was a centralization of political power, on the level of partisan activity as well as in the distinctly political offices of the state.

This exercise of centralized power called for an expansion of party activities and an expressly hierarchic organization of the party. Briefly, a fourfold organizational division developed within the Nazi party. The top leaders formed an oligarchic clique known as *Reichsleitung* that laid down the division of functions and determined the policies for the party. The political machine comprised the minor leaders, their staffs, and the unpaid functionaries who implemented the instructions of the top leaders on the national, regional, and local levels of action. Attached to the party were the integral organizations, called *Gliederung*. Each party member had to join a special occupational or professional organization for the purpose of permitting the party to build up leadership organizations that could be used for controlling non-party members. Finally, there were compulsory mass organizations, such as the Labor Front. These *angeschlossene Verbände* were affiliated with the party and led by the integral organizations of the party.

These organizations operated on distinct principles. The oligarchic clique and the party machine lived up to the principles of centralization and exclusion. Integral and affiliated organizations implemented the principles of organizational totality and domination. The two sets of principles reinforced each other and enabled the Nazis to establish for themselves a comprehensive political monopoly.

In their effort to be the sole political rulers, the Nazis achieved centralization through the device of singleness. Within the party, there was only one leader, one ruling clique, one party line. There was asserted to be no place for rival leaders, different political factions, diversity of political opinion. Each member of the oligarchic clique controlled one area of activity. The territorial jurisdictions were carefully defined; there was just one responsible leader for a region, a county, or a city. Singleness of command called for a multiplicity of offices held by the top leaders. Political monopoly for the party thus meant that centralized power was enjoyed as a personal privilege by the top leaders of the party.

Singleness of purpose and organization prevailed also in the external activities of the party in the political sphere. No opposition, in word or deed, was tolerated. The party alone nominated candidates for political office and presented a single ticket in elections. All candidates for appointive office had either to be members of the party or to receive the approval of the party. All legislation in any governmental body had to be submitted either to the deputy leader at the national level or to the designated party leader at the corresponding lower level of government. Legislation was thus subject to the veto power of the party.[4] Acceptance or rejection of ideas or policies in administrative offices of the state had to conform to the single party line. This line, formulated by the top leaders, was pronounced to the public, and interpreted in its application to daily events, by the party's propaganda leader. Ideas and theories taught in any of the academic institutions had to be in harmony with the political ideology of the party. In external affairs, centralization of power produced thus the single party candidate for office, the specific party line, the uniform public opinion, and the predominant ideology. All these attributes of singleness were necessary features of the party's political monopoly.

Exclusion accompanied singleness. Not only were Jews and non-Germans excluded from membership in the Nazi party, but also those who did not possess a fully documented Aryan ancestry, who were not regarded as politically reliable, who were not believed to be ideologically trustworthy, or who were not otherwise beneficial to the party or its leaders. The great increase in membership after the party's seizure of power was soon regarded with suspicion. An embargo was imposed which established May 1, 1933, as the dividing line. Anyone who had joined the party after this date was expelled. The preferred way of becoming a party member was to rise from the Hitler Youth into the para-military organizations and, if proven worthy, into the party. Keeping the party numerically small became a necessary condition for centralizing power in the party.

Exclusion also attached to the process of nominating candidates for elected offices and of selecting applicants for appointive offices, and served to transform party membership and the holding of political office into distinct privileges that entailed many political and economic advantages. It was even within the power of the top leaders to determine who should be excluded from government office and who should be exempted from the otherwise operating rule of exclusion.

Singleness and exclusion, interacting in various ways in specific situations, were the two means by which political power was centralized in party and state. This leads us to the first principle that governed the political actions of the Nazi party. As the party became increasingly hierarchic internally and as more and more potential members were excluded from the rights and privileges associated with membership, the centralization of political power within the party became correspondingly greater.

Centralized power was institutionalized and exercised through an extensive apparatus. After seizure of power, the Nazi party was twice reorganized. The political machine was reorganized internally, and a large number of sub-organizations were attached to the reorganized party. Broadly speaking, the party machine was subdivided into four functional divisions: one dealt with political matters (Rudolf Hess), another was responsible for administration (Robert Ley), the third handled financial affairs (Xaver Schwarz), and the last, under Walter Buch, served as the party court. Functional division was followed by departmentalization of each division. Each division was assigned tasks aiming at effective control over all forms of political life. The departments of the political division concerned themselves with all the problems that came up for legislative decisions. The administrative division divided the party members according to their occupations and professions and established departments for determining the party line that should be followed in each type of activity. The party thus enlarged the concept of political action by including the quasi-political aspects of occupations and professions within its range of political control.

The expanded party apparatus included two types of subordinate organizations. The integral organizations, headed by the chief of the respective department, trained their party members for future leadership positions. The affiliated organizations—comprising the nonmembers of the party—were dominated by the appropriate integral organization. Thus, the departmental headquarters of the party controlled both the integral and affiliated organizations attached to the party. In making the mass type of organization compulsory, in reserving all positions of leadership for Nazis, and by imposing one party line in each respective organization, the top leaders succeeded in establishing monolithic control over all quasi-political integral and affiliated associations.[5]

Being controlled by the party, the integrated and affiliated organizations became linked with the respective agencies of the state, provided the ministry involved was also headed by a leading Nazi. Propaganda and education indicate the two kinds of links that existed between the party-dominated associations and the respective ministries of the state.

The propaganda department and the Ministry of Propaganda were both headed by Joseph Goebbels. He employed both the party and the state agencies in exercising his centralized power. Journalists, editors, writers, broadcasters, and actors were all herded into mass associations, which were dominated by the respective integral organizations of these professions. Business concerns in the fields of journalism, printing, and radio broadcasting became the property either of the party or the state; owners of theaters, movies, concert halls, recording studios, tourist offices, and advertising agencies were pressed into compulsory business organizations. They were all responsible to the Ministry of Propaganda and Enlightenment. Finally, the ministry supervised, directed, or censored all "cultural" activities through its central or regional propaganda offices.[6] Through this interlocking of party and state organizations, the ministry controlled all official news, established a monopoly over political information, and presented and interpreted the party line to the public.

In the field of education, where the head offices of party and state were not occupied by the same man, youth indoctrination took place through an interlocking control of three forms of organizations. All schools and their officials became uniformly responsible to the Minister of Education. All teachers on the three levels of education were pressed into their respective compulsory associations, which were controlled by the corresponding integral organizations of the party. Gradually, the whole youth of the country from ten to eighteen years of age was pushed into the Hitler Youth. Its membership rose from 107,000 in 1932 to 7.0 million in 1938.[7] The party organizations of pupils, students, and teachers collaborated with the Ministry of Education in indoctrinating the minds of the young people with Nazi ideology.

There thus existed four types of organizations. At the center was the administrative division at headquarters. Each of its departments controlled the integral and affiliated organizations, and the latter two were connected with the respective state agencies, which came under the effective control of the leading Nazis. All these organizations became subject to the political line and discipline of the party; they also collaborated in fulfilling the specialized functions of the respective state agencies. The result of extending party control over this network of organizations was a monolithic form of domination over members and nonmembers alike.[8] In effect, the party succeeded through this control in establishing a political, informational, and educational-ideological monopoly in Nazi Germany.

This manifold political monopoly was foremost a product of the principle of interlocking political organizations. The following list includes the most important organizations.

The organizational network operated as a monolithic power structure within the party. The lines of power went from top to bottom and the lines of responsibility from bot-

Organizational Network of the Party*

Party	Integral Party Organization	Compulsory (Affiliated) Association	Government Agency
1) Head Office	NS Teacher's League	Association of German Teachers	Ministry of Education
2) Press Leader	NS Journalist's League	Association of German Journalists	Ministry of Propaganda
3) Head Office	NS League of Government Officials	Association of German Officials	Ministry of Interior
4) Youth Leader	NS Cadre Youth†	Hitler Youth	Hitler Youth
5) Labor Service Leader	NS Labor Service	German Labor Service	Labor Service Administration‡
6) Women's Leader	NS Frauenschaft	German Frauenwerk	National Health Office
7) Student Leader	NS Student League	German Studentenschaft	Ministry of Education
8) Dozenten Leader	NS Instructors' League	Organization of German Instructors	Ministry of Education
9) Peasant Leader	NS Peasant League	Reich Food Estate	Ministry of Agriculture
10) Leader of Culture	NS Propaganda Agencies	Chamber of Culture	Ministry of Propaganda

* For details see Organisations-Jahrbuch der NSDAP (München: Eher, 1936, 1938, 1940). Numbers at the left of the table have been added to permit identification with the diagram on p. 25.

† The Cadre Youth was not established until 1939.
‡ The Hitler Youth and Labor Services were recognized as compulsory associations and governmental agencies at the same time.

tom to top. Diagrammatically, the structure of power took the following forms, with the lines of power and responsibility indicated by downward-moving and upward-moving arrows, respectively.

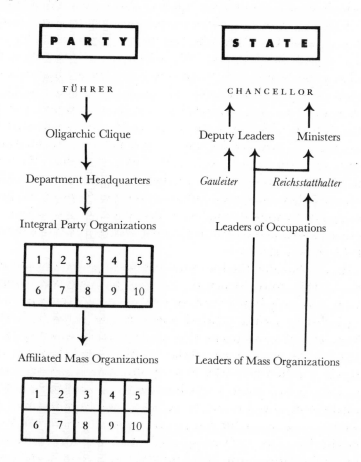

Although at the beginning Hitler was accessible to all members of the clique, who could present their departmental, integration, or affiliation problems for final approval, an elaborate chain of command was later set up. The deputy leader built up a centralizing office that gave instructions to the leaders of subordinate organizations. The latter, in turn, centralized power by simultaneously heading departmental, integral, and affiliated organizations. Eventually, the same principle of centralization applied also to the relationship between party organizations and ministers of the government. Even Joseph Goebbels, who had most of the work of his departmental, integral, and affiliated party organizations done within the Ministry of Propaganda, needed the approval of Hess or Hitler whenever he made significant political changes. The same centralizing influence prevailed also in the districts, since each *Gauleiter* could give instructions to the regional heads of the integral and affiliated organizations who, in party matters, were under his jurisdiction. Many of the *Gauleiter* were also the provincial heads of state, in which capacity they were responsibile to the ministers of the government. In spite of functional division, the interlocking of organizations and centralizing of responsibility led to a monolithic power structure.

In emphasizing the four interlocking organizations and the monolithic power structure, we seem to come into conflict with a recently stated thesis of totalitarian government. The rationale of such a political system is said to be "a double hierarchy of government that places a party functionary at the side of every major official" in the state.[9] Actually, the thesis of a dual hierarchy of party and state is sufficient only as long as one limits one's interest to an understanding of totalitarian government. If we take into consideration the whole range of totalitarian power, especially the domination of the formerly "private sphere," then the idea of a dual hierarchy turns out to be an incomplete version of one-party rule. For an understanding of all features of the one-party monopoly, in its political, informational, and educational aspects, it is necessary to examine all elements of the party apparatus. When this is done, the thesis of a dual hierarchy becomes a part of the interlocking organizations but fails to modify the principle of centralized power.

The Nazis explicitly expounded the principles of centralized power and interlocking organizations. The former was called the *"Führer* principle"; the latter was known at first as coordination *(Gleichschaltung)* and then as organizational totality *(Totalitätsanspruch)*.[10] Both principles were implemented with a high degree of success in the political, educational, and ideological-informational spheres of action.

VIOLENCE AND ORGANIZATIONAL FUSION

The power of the oligarchic clique would never have been so great, the three monopolies could never have been so stable and monolithic, if the party and its network of political organizations had not been intertwined with para-military organizations. It was through the Brownshirts (SA) and Blackshirts (SS) that violence became as indispensable for the party as for its ideology. In terms of actions, the task of the oligarchic clique was not only to reconcile violence with Nazi ideology but also to integrate the party and its political network with the para-military organizations. How then was organizational integration achieved?

The Nazis formed not one but two para-military organizations. The Blackshirts were formed as Hitler's bodyguard. Relatively small in number, the SS comprised 50,000 men in 1933 and 210,000 men in 1936.[11] In contrast, the Brownshirts, formed by Hitler as a potential mass organization, were trained in the strong-arm tactics of street fighting and received military drill in the use of small arms. The Nazi party thus had control over two para-military formations. Yet they differed so much from each other, in their functions as well as their future development, that only the SS will be analysed in this section.

In the formative years, the SS operated primarily within the party and its attached organizations. Its original function was to guarantee the personal safety of the leader. Its second function, of assuring Hitler's political control over the party, was not performed adequately in all situations. Gregor Strasser had received an offer to join the von Schleicher cabinet as Vice-Chancellor in December of 1932, and there was an actual mutiny within the ranks of the Führer's bodyguard when Hitler removed Strasser from his positions in the party.[12] The third function of the SS was to serve as the most disciplined and rigidly organized unit of the Nazi party. It was in the SS that the principle of hierarchic organization found its first and most efficient implementation within any Nazi organization.

When Hitler became Chancellor, the most crucial question for the top Nazis was: How can this newly gained power be so consolidated that no other person or group can successfully force us from our positions in the government? The Nazis found two answers to this question. On the one hand, they replaced the social force of the democratic state with the tyrannical force of the dictatorial state. Social force had performed the function of bringing the internal law to bear against actual violators whose antisocial actions were checked in the last resort by the police, acting under a procedure that conformed to the principle of a minimum exercise of force.[13] In promoting the principle of tyrannical force, the Nazis abolished the difference between social force and violence. Violation of a law was no longer an indispensable condition for the use of force. The police in applying force against partisan enemies of the Nazis were urged to employ unlimited violence against any enemy of the Nazis.[14]

On the other hand, since the exercise of unlimited force could not be entrusted to the former regular or political police, Göring temporarily established an auxiliary police in which units of the SS and the SA were assigned the task of intimidating voters in the terror election of March, 1933. Within a year, the SS was able to absorb the function of the new political police. In 1936, the function of the regular police was also allocated to the SS. There thus arose in the first phase of the regime a tyrannical police organization that (*a*) administered extralegal violence as a party organization, and that (*b*) simultaneously acted as a legalized force of the state.

How could the terror organization of the party act simultaneously as a police organization of the state? During the years of opposition, the Nazis did not find an appropriate organizational place for the SS. Officially, the SS was a subdivision of the SA. Actually, Heinrich Himmler—as head of the SS—was responsible to Hitler. Soon after the Röhm purge, the SS was established as an organization independent of the political and administrative control of the party. Himmler became one of the highest officials (*Reichsleiter*) in the party, reporting only to Hitler. The *Gauleiter* and other political leaders in regions and districts could not give any instructions to the corresponding leaders of the SS.[15] In order to coordinate their activities in particular campaigns, most of the *Gauleiter* became honorary officials in the SS. As a result of this organizational arrangement, the SS—although actually included within the party organization—stood on the same level of authority as the party itself. Both were directly responsible to Hitler.[16]

As an organization of the Nazi Party, this para-military organization was divided into the general and specialized SS. Three distinct sub-organizations grew out of the specialized SS. The first was the intelligence service, formed in 1931 and known as the SD, whose function it was to investigate the methods and aims of the Nazis' political enemies. The purpose of this search was to know the plans of enemy groups who were fighting against the Nazis. This investigation of alien ideologies was supplemented by the task of collecting political information vital for increasing the power of the party. On June 9, 1934, all intelligence functions within the party were merged in the SD, whose sphere of investigation was extended from political enemies to any potential opposition group within or outside Germany.[17]

The establishment of concentration camps gave rise to the Death Head Units, the second division of the specialized SS. Organized in groups of 100 men each, and comprising 3,500 men at the end of 1936, these units were in charge of the concentration camps, which were run officially as institutions of the SS. Well-equipped with small arms and machine guns, these units had to administer "discipline" to political and other prisoners. Finally, there was the preliminary armed SS, which in 1936 comprised four regiments that were motorized and equipped with modern weapons. Its original task was to be readily available for any uprising or other emergency in which military formations would have to be employed.[18] The original task of these militarized regiments, which grew later into the fully militarized SS, was to exclude the regular army from any police-like actions within Germany.

Soon after the Nazis came to power, the SS also became an agency of the state. This step was inevitable for two reasons. First, the power of Nazi ministers in a coalition government was only temporary. In order to make such power permanent, it was necessary to give the SS the authority of the state, yet keep that new state agency exclusively in the hands of the party. Second, the fact that the Nazi party had the legal privilege of being the only political party in the country did not assure its political monopoly. All the open and disguised enemies of the state had to be placed under an actual or potential threat of terror. From the point of view of the party chiefs, the suppression of other political organizations and the torture of their active leaders and functionaries could be accomplished only through legal and extralegal

violence on the part of the para-military organization. Extralegal violence was above the law.

Administering violence created for the state the new task
of providing for an armed establishment to assure internal
security. The Gestapo became the new "security" force. By
April of 1934, Himmler was head of all the agencies of the
secret police in the various states. Rather than limiting itself
to the elimination or detention of former political enemies,
the Gestapo increasingly enlarged its definition of, and actions against, "political crimes." As a result, a conflict arose
between the Gestapo and the other law-enforcing agencies.

In 1935, Wilhelm Frick, who was Minister of the Interior
and in charge of the regular police, presented a detailed report on this conflict. He emphasized especially three points.
The Gestapo had entered into "an untimely religious struggle" with the churches for which it had no specific legal
authority. The restrictions placed upon the use of "protective
custody" had been wantonly disregarded by the Gestapo.
While it was legal for lawyers to accept the defense of persons
accused of political crimes, the Gestapo had repeatedly arrested such lawyers. Even state officials, including those of
the regular police, had been investigated or put in concentration camps when they possessed the courage to report to
their superiors on the abuses of power by the SS. Frick concluded his memorandum with the proposal that it should "be
settled once and for all who should bear the responsibility . . .
in all matters appertaining to the political police."[19] Either a
new ministry of political police should be established under
Himmler, or Frick as the Minister of the Interior should
have exclusive jurisdiction over the political police.

One year later Frick's proposal was accepted in a modified
form. Himmler was granted full authority in all police matters, both for the regular and the political police, and remained officially responsible to Frick as Minister of the In-

terior. This policy of keeping the police within the Ministry of the Interior was intended to establish a close administrative relationship between the reorganized political offices and the other agencies of the state. A decree was issued which instructed the directors of the Gestapo to inform the heads of the regional state offices (usually high party officials) of all matters of political interest. The former became subordinate to the latter, so that any police action not acceptable to the head of the regional state office could not be immediately executed but had to be forwarded for final decision in Berlin.[20] In assuring co-responsibility between the regular administration and the Gestapo, the leaders of party and state tried to assure themselves that the local and regional police offices did not abuse their power and acted only in accordance with the synchronized interest of the SS and the leaders of the Nazi party.

At the end of 1936, there existed a parallel organization of the party and the state. Such an arrangement seems to confirm the thesis of a dual hierarchy. In terms of authority and personnel, however, there were fusion of organization and union of leadership rather than duality. In regard to the SD and the concentration camps, organizational union was complete. Both were state agencies and party organizations simultaneously. The reorganized Gestapo and criminal police, while not having an organizational counterpart in the party, were staffed almost exclusively by members of the SS. These two organizations of the state were thus the exclusive property of the SS. Finally, the officers and many of the men—but by no means all—in the regular police force were recruited from among members of the SS.[21] In this last case, personal union between leading positions in the state and in the party organizations prevailed.

The SS as a para-military organization and state agency for the administration of violence thus gave rise to the principle of organized fusion. Either there was one organization that belonged simultaneously to party and state, headed and staffed by the same Nazis in every respect, or the particular organizations were not identical but the state agency was exclusively headed and staffed by members of the para-military organization of the party. In each case, the principle of organizational fusion implied (a) that the para-military organization of the party possessed a monopoly over all the police forces of the state, and (b) that the two types of either completely fused or parallel organizations were headed and staffed exclusively by members of the SS. It was because of this parallel organization and subsequent fusion that the one-party regime was simultaneously a party-police state.

The principles of centralized power, interlocking organization, organizational fusion, and systematic use of extralegal violence secured a monopoly of power for the Nazis. To be sure, the implementation of these principles created many kinds of difficulties,[22] but they were all overcome without forcing the leaders to make significant concessions, whether to the generals or to the leaders of big business. In professions and in the areas of politics, information, education, and law-enforcement the Nazi monopoly was virtually complete by the end of 1936. Full fascism prevailed in all these fields of activity.

PARTIAL FASCISM

Strangely enough, the political monopoly of the party did not extend to either the military or the economic fields of action. What happened to those Nazi organizations that had developed extensive programs for a military as well as an economic counterrevolution which was supposed to accompany or follow the political counterrevolution, and why did the four principles of full fascism not also apply to economic and military affairs?

There can be no doubt that the Nazi party did everything

in its power to build up a genuine counterrevolutionary mass movement. The characterization of mass movements as "societies in miniature"[23] fits fully the Nazi case. In fact, the Nazis had developed their embryonic society to a greater extent in 1933 than had the Bolsheviks in 1917 or the Italian Fascists in 1922. The Nazi movement could encompass more types of activities, including the economic and military, and could organize each more effectively because the party was able to utilize the opportunities for democracy that had existed under the Weimar Republic.

Various attempts were made to limit the growth of the mass movement to the purely political sphere. One of the goals of the conservative politicians and business leaders who participated in the conference at Harzburg in the fall of 1931 was to benefit from the mass ferment, either at the expense of, or by a mutual gain with, the Nazis. Most important for economic matters was the formation of the Keppler circle, through which certain business leaders were given the opportunity to influence the economic policy of the Nazi party. The revision of the party program, especially on the issues of property and the nationalization of banks and trusts, contributed decisively to the revolts of Otto Strasser and Walter Stennes. While these concessions to business groups facilitated the departure of the quasi-socialist wing, the new policy of some business leaders of worming their way into the groups of advisors surrounding party leaders did not in any way slow down the rise, or alter the nature, of the counterrevolutionary mass movement.

Even more unsuccessful were the various attempts to reach an agreement with Röhm for transforming the SA into an auxiliary militia of the regular army. General von Schleicher's attempt to split the Nazi party by appointing Gregor Strasser as Vice-Chancellor in his government was a dismal failure. The valiant effort of General Wilhelm Gröner to oppose the para-military organizations of the Nazis was sabotaged by leading generals of the regular army. When Hitler was appointed Chancellor, the mass movement of the Nazis was not only intact but comprised economic and military components that were ready, if not overly eager, to proceed with the counterrevolution in their own spheres of action. Why then did the party fail to realize its goals in these areas?

The answer to this question is to be found in a complex of circumstances and conflicting interests involving the paramilitary organizations, the party, and the three groups of big business, the landowners, and the generals. The attempts of the SA to achieve organizational supremacy and totality are of primary importance in this connection and will be considered here in some detail.

While of great political value as street fighters and organizers of parades in the formative years, the SA became a political liability for the party leaders after the terror election of 1933. Events during the first eighteen months of the Hitler government demonstrated that there was no place for two para-military organizations in the earlier period of the Third *Reich*.

Two different conflicts arose in which the SA either collided with the organizations of big business or with the officer corps of the regular army. The issue of the conflict was that the SA claimed "organizational totality" in the same way that the other organizations of the Nazi party had. Rejection of this claim led to the violent elimination of the top leaders of the SA.

After Hitler had authorized the suppression of the trade unions (having already rejected two previous requests of the SA)[24], the SA and the party office for economic affairs adopted the policy of occupying the headquarters of the employer associations and some trade associations. Officials of the central employer association came to the conclusion that if the majority of the SA men could be given employment, the danger of a "second revolution" would vanish.

Gustav Krupp von Bohlen, as the spokesman of all business organizations, informed Hitler that all trade associations would be willing to collect funds for the Nazi party provided that all campaigns to collect funds from business firms were cancelled and the self-installed commissioners in business organizations withdrawn. The result was the so-called Hitler Donation, which provided the party leaders with ample funds to finance the extended organizational activities of their sub-organizations, including the SA and SS.[25] As a result of this financial support, party leaders regained control, and *Gauleiter* became more powerful than the leaders of the SA. Business concerns cooperated with the Nazis in finding jobs for the "old fighters," especially those in the SA. Business leaders thus could claim that they had successfully eliminated the danger of a violent economic counterrevolution by granting the party a subsidy. Yet this financial backing was not a payment for services expected or received; rather, it was a form of protection money, voluntarily offered and readily paid for being exempted from the violence of the SA as well as from the spy system and concentration camps of the Gestapo.

It was much more difficult to reconcile the conflicting interests of the regular army and the SA. In the summer of 1933 Hitler permitted the SA "to train 250,000 leaders and men within a year who should be at the disposal of the *Reichswehr* in case of an emergency."[26] This permission led to a series of negotiations with the regular army concerning the pre-military training of the SA. An agreement was signed in February of 1934 which authorized the SA to engage in pre-military training. A training office was set up, with an officer of the regular army acting as chief of staff, working out the plans, and approving the specific instructions for such training. The expectation of the army leaders was that in return for this concession the SA would refrain from building up military units of its own, but the SA thought differently. General Werner von Blomberg informed Hitler on March 2, 1934, that several divisions within the SA were busily engaged in training a so-called staff guard, including one company with heavy machine guns.[27] Ernst Röhm, chief of the SA, agreed only that the armed staff guards would not be permitted to appear in public. The generals were willing to assign to the SA the task of pre-military training if it were kept under strict army supervision. The SA had undertaken the task of building up a new military force, outside and independent of, the regular army. There were thus the beginnings of two rival military organizations, the continued existence of which would necessarily have undermined the Hitler government. Not realizing the danger of a civil war, Röhm is said to have presented to the cabinet a proposal for a new Ministry of Defense which would comprise the regular army as well as the SA.[28] Röhm, if the report is correct, would have been acting on the principle of organizational fusion. The SA thus tried to absorb the regular army in the same way that the SS had taken over the political police.

Although the events leading to the murder of Röhm and his cohorts cannot yet be documented, there is little doubt as to why the SA failed in a task that was so successfully accomplished by the SS. There was first a conflict between the SA and the Nazi party. Circumstantial evidence suggests that Hitler felt threatened by a "second revolution" in which the SA would take over not only military but also political leadership. It was this threat to the party and to himself that seems to explain Hitler's craftiness as well as the ferocity with which his former comrades-in-arms were murdered. If one can trust his statements, the slaying of the SA leaders was one of his "historical missions." The effect of these actions was, of course, to put a brake upon the Nazi revolution.[29]

There was, secondly, a conflict between the SA and the SS. The latter had achieved its goal of organizational fusion, whereas the SA had been denied an opportunity to achieve the same goal. In applying the techniques of murder and terror to his own comrades, Hitler did not lose any appreciable amount of his power. Using one para-military organization to destroy the leaders of the other turned out to be an effective device for controlling the extent of the counterrevolution. The principles inferred from previous experience—(a) that counterrevolutionary movements arise only on the basis of an immediately preceding revolution, and (b) that most counterrevolutionary movements tend to transform themselves into restorative movements that seek to re-establish a pre-revolutionary order[30]—did not apply to the Nazi movement. Not only did the Great Depression and the resulting social disorganization give the Nazis the opportunity to build up a counterrevolutionary movement, independent of any directly preceding revolution, but the coexistence of two para-military organizations enabled the oligarchic clique of the party to eliminate the military counterrevolutionists without having to rely for such action upon the regular army. Self-limitation avoided restoration.

Finally, there was the conflict between the SA and the generals of the regular army. The generals were the immediate beneficiaries of the destruction of the SA leadership. In presenting an ultimatum to Hitler that the threat of a military counterrevolution had to be removed,[31] von Blomberg and the other generals bore the ultimate responsibility, and also picked the time, for eliminating the Nazi element which favored a military counterrevolution. Even so, they did not directly participate in the purge. The temporarily disturbed relations between the top leaders of the party and army could be re-established, and the coalition government under Hitler could continue after the purge, because the political monopoly of the party was undisturbed and the right of the regular army to be the sole bearer of arms was reaffirmed.

Yet the SA as an organization was not liquidated. Under new leaders, who were fully devoted to the oligarchic clique, the SA became an integral part of the party and was assigned a twofold task. On the one hand, the reorganized units were subjected to intensive political indoctrination, so that, as future soldiers, these men would eventually infiltrate the regular army with Nazi ideas. On the other hand, the militarily organized units concentrated upon military sports and basic physical training for all SA members. The aim was "to keep them in condition to bear arms."[32] In addition, a series of specialized units were organized which received intensified training from officers of the signal corps, engineers, naval navigators, and cavalrymen in the regular army.

The reorganized SA thus gave rise to a new type of auxiliary organization. Politically, the new SA had to perform the same tasks of indoctrination and domination as any other integral organization of the Nazi party. Militarily, however, the new SA became an auxiliary organization of the regular army. In preparing men for military service and in keeping the reservists in physical readiness, the SA performed a service that was important for, but auxiliary to, the main military activity of the regular army. It is important to note that the nature of this service, in respect to any plans or instructions that might be formulated or carried out, was defined and supervised by officers of the regular army.

The purge of the old leaders and the reorganization of the SA gave rise to the new principle of partial fascism. This principle combined three formerly distinct ideas. First, the SA ceased to be an autonomous organization that was administratively equal to the party; reorganization introduced the distinction between integral and affiliated para-military organizations. The integral organization provided the leadership and was given the task of indoctrinating the affiliated organization. Full submission to the party and its leader was thus the slogan of the reorganized SA. Second, the strictly military sphere was beyond the control of the party as well as its para-military organizations. Any intention of taking over the regular army had to be excluded from the minds of the SA leaders. Those who planned to seize control anyway were physically eliminated by order of the party leader. Third, a distinction was introduced between military and pre-military training. The latter became the function only of the reorganized SA. Military sports and pre-military instructions had to conform to the military plans of the generals of the regular army. A party organization thus performed a service that did not directly contribute to an increase of the party's monopoly of power but served the goal of the coalition government, headed by Hitler.

While the principle of partial fascism was established by violence in the military field, the same principle was being imposed upon other party organizations. A political dispute arose within the party and its integral organizations about the tempo that should be adopted for realizing the counter-revolutionary goals. The intransigents among the Nazis demanded the speedy seizure of the various organizations of state and economy. The temporizers insisted that the Nazi movement aimed only at a political and ideological counter-revolution, which could not be extended to other spheres of action. This schism in the party had already appeared in 1930, when Hitler eliminated Otto Strasser from his positions in the party.[33] In 1933, the intransigents made extensive proposals for economic reform, and some of them appointed themselves as commissioners of business organizations. All these attempts were systematically opposed by the oligarchic clique of the Nazi party.

The temporizers employed the party machine as well as their positions in the state to resist the economic counter-revolution. A letter written by Dr. Frick, Nazi Minister of the Interior, was typical of such resistance. In July of 1933, he

sent to the state officials of districts and counties the following instructions:

The victorious German revolution has entered the phase of
evolution; that is, of normal legal reconstruction. Any sabotage
of the German revolution, such as illegal interference in the
economy and violation of the prevailing laws, must be suppressed
forcefully, whoever shall be involved. . . . I beg you to see to
it that the appointment of commissioners will cease . . . because
the new state, completely under National Socialist leadership, is
now in a position to solve by legal means any problems that may
arise.[34]

Göring issued similar instructions to the police commissioners of Prussia, and Hess gave the same directive to all
party members. The purpose of these directives was to make
it plain that the method of violence and the practice of putting commissioners over independent trade unions could
under no circumstances be applied to private concerns and
business organizations.

While the economy was being declared immune to the violence of the para-military organizations and the economic
counterrevolution was being opposed, a number of party and
mass organizations were being reorganized. Within the party,
jurisdiction over economic matters was taken away from the
commission of economic policy *(Kommission für Wirtschaftspolitik)* and granted, on June 13, 1933, to Wilhelm Keppler,
who was also appointed as Hitler's personal economic advisor.
In this instance, a state official of the Chancery obtained the
power to formulate the party line on economic policy and
impose it upon party agencies.[35] As head of the political organization of the party, Dr. Ley dissolved all the "fighting
organizations" of the industrial middle class into which the
small-business groups had been organized by the Nazis. The
former members of these organizations were permitted to
apply for membership in the party, and, if admitted, to join

the new integral organizations of leaders, known as the NS Hago. All other small urban businessmen had to become members of the new Estates for Handicraft and Trade. The principle of interlocking organizations and party domination of the mass of urban small businesses was thus established within the first year of the regime.

At the same time, party domination of the organizations led or pressured by the intransigents did not give rise to organizational totality. Certain integral and affiliated organizations either could not extend their power to the respective agencies of the state or were prevented from comprising all economic organizations in their areas of activity. The result was a set of party-dominated organizations that could not extend their influence beyond the political and ideological sphere of action.

"Incomplete" Party Organizations

Party Department	Integral Organization	Compulsory Association
Leader of Jurists	NS League of Jurists	Association of German Jurists
Welfare Leader	NS People's Welfare	German *Winterhelp*
Veterans Leader	NS League of War Veterans	
Labor Leader	NSBO	German Labor Front
Leader of Handicraft	NS Hago	Fighting Organization of the Middle Class

Each of these "incomplete" organizations tried mightily but failed to gain organizational totality and to realize its particular version of the counterrevolution.

It is thus our thesis that there was a coexistence of full and partial fascism during the first phase of the regime. The fields of strictly political, educational, informational, ideological, and police action were fully dominated by the Nazi party, but this monopoly did not extend to the military and economic spheres of action. Party-dominated organizations certainly existed here, too, but they could use neither violence, party fiat, nor state power to impose their will upon the military or business leaders of the country. The military and economic counterrevolutions were defeated before their supporters could muster all their resources to realize their goals.

It is our second thesis that the fight between the proponents of the merely political-ideological and the other forms of counterrevolution, between the leaders of the "complete" and "incomplete" organizations, created a major schism in the Nazi party. The monolithic party did not enjoy internal unity. The fight between the temporizers and the intransigents lasted throughout the first period of the regime. The issues involved in the struggle ranged widely and also extended to economic policy.

It is our third thesis that the cause for the failure of military and economic counterrevolution, and for the rise of partial (instead of full) fascism in these fields of action, lay primarily with the German upper class. Its three groups—big business, the landowners, and the generals—utilized their power to resist the plans of the intransigent Nazis and eventually were able to defeat them.

Our fourth thesis is that there existed a coalition between the upper class and the Nazis during the first phase of the regime. Economic power was primarily in the hands of the big business concerns and landowners, while military power was almost exclusively exercised by the generals of the regular army. The Nazi party was largely limited to the sphere in which its interlocking and complete organizations enjoyed a monopoly of power. The result of the coexistence of the two blocs was a bilateral structure of power, in which both holders were of more or less equal status. The incomplete quasi-military and quasi-economic organizations of the party representing partial fascism were tolerated only because they functioned as auxiliary organizations that provided services beneficial to the leading groups of the upper class. By the same token, terror, violence, and continual spying by the Nazi organizations were kept outside the sphere of the upper class so that oppression was not felt by the majority of its members during the first period of the regime.

How valid are these four hypotheses? In the following chapters it will be our task to examine the large volume of evidence in order to see whether the facts confirm the four theses. If not, we will have to discover in which way the facts differ from our expectations and which more adequate explanation can be given for the coexistence of full and partial fascism, for the interactions between business groups and Nazis.

A SPLIT IN NAZI IDEOLOGY

Confirmation or refutation of our hypotheses requires the use of the typological method, as it was simultaneously developed by Max Weber and Arthur Spiethoff.[36] As our starting point, we take Max Weber's proposition that "material and ideal interests directly govern men's conduct."[37] In applying the typological method, we will have thus to compare Nazi ideologies with business ideologies as well as political and military with economic interests. In each case a special effort has to be made to ascertain that the ideals and interests were held by a specific group and that the interests and ideals functioned as intentions for specific actions. When and how were the ideals and interests of the party and the business groups compatible with each other? If they came in conflict, what were the issues involved in the subsequent struggle and who was victorious in each of the major fights?

Use of the typological method presents some difficulties. One may be inclined to specify the comparison by saying that there was a fundamental conflict between business interests and Nazi ideologies. Or one may question the wisdom of confronting interests with ideologies because in this way the investigator is forced to compare incommensurables. If cor-

rect, both these arguments would gravely damage the usefulness of the typological method. It is therefore necessary to
show that the so-called fundamental conflict and the alleged
incommensurability are not inherent features of the typological method.

One version of the conflict between interests and ideologies
was given by Max Weber in his theory of political parties.[38]
His question was: How can an ideological party gain political power? And his answer was that it must transform itself
from a minority into a majority party. Such a task is possible
only if the ideological party builds up a party machine, accu-
mulates sufficient funds for winning elections, and is able to
shift to itself additional blocs of votes. Building up a political
machine means handing over the running of the party to
professional politicians who see as their task the technical
job of political management rather than of winning believers
to the party's ideology. In trying to collect funds from the
wealthy, the politician must give assurances that his party
will support not only general interests but also some specific
economic interests of the financial backers. Shifting the votes
of not-yet-attached groups to the party will require a watering
down of its ideological goals and the acceptance of another
set of economic interests that tend to be in conflict with the
party's ideology. In making these concessions, the ideological
party has a chance of obtaining political power only at the
price of giving up its ideology.

Whatever may be the validity of this theory in a democratic setting, it certainly does not correctly interpret the
situation of the Nazi party. On the one hand, the Nazis built
up a large and effective party machine, received substantial
funds, and came to power not as a majority party but by
entering a coalition government, as we shall see presently.
Getting into the government did not involve an explicit surrender of their ideology for the Nazis, although many of the
financial backers or political allies tried to secure such a surrender. On the other hand, in realizing their goal of a po-

litical counterrevolution (while giving up the aim of an economic and military counterrevolution), the Nazis did not abandon their whole ideology. What actually happened was that in establishing their monopoly of power the Nazis realized a part of their political interest as well as a part of their ideology. In turning against those party organizations that promoted military and economic counterrevolutions, the oligarchic clique surrendered the political and material interests of the SA leadership and diminished the material chances of the quasi-economic organizations of the party. This opposition to the undesired forms of the counterrevolution also suggests the possibility of a split in the Nazi ideology. One of our tasks then is to ascertain the specific features of this ideology and see whether the rejection of the economic counterrevolution did produce a split within the party ideology.

It is at this point that we must ask whether the Nazi ideology can be in one way or another tested. Various writers have given a negative answer. One comes from historians of Nazi ideology.[39] In investigating the origin of Nazi ideals, the historians came to the conclusion that the leading Nazis were not original thinkers. "For when the theory of national socialism is viewed in relation to political thought of the last century and a half it is seen to be stale stuff, stale and adulterated."[40] This is true but hardly relevant to our purpose. What is crucial is the fact that the Nazis succeeded in the depth of the depression in giving these stolen ideas a new meaning and relevance and thereby gained an increasing number of followers. Thus, we are not interested in the originality of the Nazi ideals. Our problem is to locate those aspects of the Nazi ideology through which the Nazis expressed motives and intentions that aroused millions and created their will to action.

It has also been said with much justification that Nazi ideology was loose, indefinite, inconsistent. When Hitler came to power, Nazi ideology included the racialism of H. St. Chamberlain and his followers, the extreme nationalism of the radical conservatives (e.g., Oswald Spengler, Möller van den Bruck), the romanticism of the rightist youth groups, some of the ideas of the national-revolutionary groups of ex-soldiers (Ernst Jünger and Ernst von Reventlow), and the ideas and sentiments of the extralegal soldiers fighting in Finland and Poland after World War I as well as the ideas and demands of the radicalized urban and rural middle classes.[41] Having this variety of ideas at their disposal, the Nazis selected freely those that proved most effective in propaganda and party-forming activities. Internal inconsistency is no handicap from our point of view, since we have no intention of testing the ideology as a whole but only those economic elements that came close to or overstepped the threshold of action.

In trying to discover the split in the Nazi ideology and ascertain the fate of its economic parts, we can confront ideals with actions only if the following conditions are given:

1. The Nazi ideology must be subdividable into its parts, and a definite meaning must be attributable to each.
2. Of these ideological parts, some must be economic in nature so as to become comparable with specific economic interests of business.
3. The comparable elements of ideals and interests must be ascertainable at the threshold between thought and action so that we shall be able to confront two lines of policy.
4. It must be possible to locate the originator and bearer of the testable ideological parts if we are to place the respective ideals and actions in their contexts and study them as expressions of group activities.

Given these conditions, the testing of our four hypotheses reduces itself to a confrontation of policies that have been derived either from certain interests or from certain ideologies. It will then be seen that the realization of both types of policies can lead to a clash between interests and ideals as well as to a conflict over the use of the same economic re-sources—and over control of the same state agencies—or pro-duce a struggle for the authority to make the relevant decisions.

What then were the components of the Nazi ideology? If we accept only those ideals that were limited to the Nazis and that governed their actions, we come to a more limited but also more specific list of items than is usually recognized. In taking only those goals that motivated a substantial num-ber of Nazis in their policy proposals, the Nazi ideology in-cluded (a) fascist imperialism, (b) extreme racialism, (c) rule of the oligarchy, (d) Nordic religion, (e) middle-class social-ism, and (f) social harmony in industrial relations. The many other ideals expressed by the Nazis and by other groups as well do not qualify for inclusion because they did not become part of the ideology of the party and its organizations.[42]

In regard to the relative significance of these six compo-nents of the ideology, we should like to advance three hypo-theses. In the period prior to the Röhm purge of June, 1934, the majority of the party leaders and their staff regarded all features of the ideology as of equal significance. Apart from merely tactical considerations, the party leadership on all levels behaved as if each element constituted a genuine part of the accepted ideology.

After the purge, the first three party goals were given priority over the last three. Those murdered by order of Hitler had violated the rule of the oligarchy. In refusing to accept unquestioningly the authority of the leader and thereby of the party, the actually disobedient members had to die, while the potentially disobedient were thrown into concentration camps. Extreme racialism called for the purity of all party and SS members and was then incorporated into the first marriage laws of 1935. Fascist imperialism became binding for everyone with the adoption of the Four Year Plan of 1936. These three ideologies became the dogma that could not be doubted at any time, that had to be accepted and lived up to by the members of the party, and that eventually had to be admired and outwardly adhered to by all groups of the population. There is no reason for attempting to determine to what extent big business or any other group succeeded in foiling the realization of this threefold dogma. All attempts in this direction did not change the party leaders' course to any appreciable extent.

The fate of the other three features of Nazi ideology was quite different. From the middle of 1933 onwards, middle-class socialism, social harmony, and Nordic religion were beliefs that were accepted by the top leaders only if they did not endanger the coalition government. The three ideals were useful because important groups of their mass following firmly adhered to them, but these ideals became expendable as soon as they pushed the leaders into undesirable policies or came into conflict with any particular aspect of the dogma. Our thesis thus is that the ideology of the party became divided, that Nazi practice produced a division into two distinct types of ideologies, one doctrinal and the other in one degree or another expendable.

Middle-class socialism and social harmony constituted two distinctly economic ideals of the Nazified middle groups. The actions proposed for the realization of these ideals were directly or indirectly detrimental to the interests of big business. A conflict therefore arose between economic policies derived from the expendable Nazi ideology and the policies promoting the economic interests of big business. It is this situation that calls for a confrontation of the two policies by our typological method.

Our comparison of the two opposed policies will be introduced by a study of the relative positions of big business and of small business, and of the relations of each to the Nazi party. We shall then compare the respective policies of small and big business in regard to the banking system, the types of economic organizations, the methods of market control, and the reorganization of handicraft business, as well as vocational training, the resettlement of farmers, and the building of residential houses. It is our thesis that on all these issues there arose specific conflicts between big and small business that had to be resolved within the framework of the Nazi regime.

It will be instructive to discover how and why these disputes arose and how they were resolved in a one-party dictatorship. Naturally, if our analysis shows that in economic affairs the Nazi ideology was flouted and defeated all along the line—we shall have to conclude that there was an aspect as well as a period of partial fascism in which the power of the Nazi party was limited to the political sphere while big business was largely in control of economic affairs.

POLITICAL VERSUS INDUSTRIAL CAPITALISM

If business interests could be actively promoted, what then was the relationship between partial fascism and capitalism? If business groups could formulate and implement economic policies, we cannot assume a passive capitalism that was modified and remoulded by an economically active Nazi party. Since the party, the generals, and big business were political allies and had formed a coalition government that pursued a very active economic policy, we have to ask: What were the actually promoted goals of the coalition government?

Gaining national independence was the self-proclaimed aim of the coalition governments.[43] Military and political, as well as economic, independence was to be re-established relative to other powers. The ultimate goal was thus the restoration of Germany as an imperial power. At home, not only was the depression to be overcome but also "national discipline" had to be imposed in industrial relations. As a result, the specific goals of the coalition government fell under five headings: (*a*) military equality with other powers; (*b*) national independence from the world economy; (*c*) the regaining of military strength through economic rearmament; (*d*) the suppression of independent trade unions; and (*e*) the invigoration of capitalist institutions that had suffered during the Great Depression. While the last goal was not specifically accepted by Hitler and the party, both tolerated the invigorations whenever they came into conflict with the policies proposed by Nazi intransigents. The other four goals were equally cherished by all groups of the coalition, which all desired a greater Germany and were determined to rule dictatorially at home.

The five policies ushered in the rearmament boom, which constituted a distinct and self-contained phase of the Nazi regime. The distinctiveness of these policies derived from four facts: The size of the public investments—5.4 billion marks for public works and 21 billion marks for military outlays—was small relative to the expenditures in the subsequent period of the Four Year Plan;[44] the financing of these public tasks was essentially non-inflationary; the policy of invigorating capitalist institutions had reached many of its targets by the end of 1936; finally, a dual power structure had developed in which almost all purely political power positions were held by party leaders, while the economic and military positions of leadership were in the hands of businessmen and generals. As a result, the policies of the coalition governments from 1933 to the fall of 1936 contained a high degree of unity. It is thus our last problem to ascertain the combined impact of these policies upon German private capitalism.

Of the various writings on the Nazi regime, many have dealt with the nature of its economy and the mutual relationship between fascism and capitalism; but only a few have recognized that the economy prior to 1937 was of a different character from what it was after 1937. For those concentrating upon the earlier phase, the nature of the rearmament boom has been the most interesting question. One view still holds that in spite of its military intention, the rearmament boom in its economic meaning was essentially a "genuine recovery" because its essential four features of money-creation, public investments, subsequent private savings, and a rising volume of employment could be observed in Nazi Germany.[45] It has been our task, in Chapter VII of this study, to test the thesis that the rearmament boom was economically identical with a genuine, governmentally primed recovery. For the present, we may say that this asserted identity was based on an untenable comparison between a hypothetical model and an actual cyclical upswing. A comparison is therefore required between the patterns of recovery and rearmament as they actually existed in different countries during the 1930's. In making this comparison, we shall attempt to show that the rearmament boom was not only motivated by the power goal of rising military and economic strength but entailed also: (1) a rising share of the public investment in total investment, (2) the creation of money primarily for military purchases, (3) a delay in the reduction of interest rates, (4) the exclusion of private parties from capital markets, (5) a tax policy that deliberately restricted private consumption, and (6) a steady relative decline in the production of consumer goods, (7) the freezing of money wage rates and an actual decline of real wage rates, (8) an extensive foreign-exchange control, and (9) a selective restriction of militarily nonessential imports. Although the four features of the hypothetical model of a primed recovery were present, the greater number, the specific form, and the relative weight of these characteristics were such that we shall have to see whether the actual pattern of rearmament was not distinctly different from that of a recovery.

If a genuine recovery did not exist, Keynes's main conclusion—that deficit financing increases private welfare and is beneficial for private capitalism—would not hold. The increased number of jobs would then have been purchased at the price of slightly declining real wage rates and a relative decline in real consumption. The increase in total output would have been partly marred by the fact that excess capacity remained chronic in most consumer-goods industries, while new capacity was built up for war-essential industries. Although total profits would have increased, the rate of increase would necessarily have been very uneven among firms and industries. If priority was given to public investment for the purpose of increasing the armed forces and their military power, it follows that warfare, rather than welfare, must have been the main beneficiary of the rearmament policy.

How did a rise in military power affect the nature of private capitalism? Since modern economic and political theory does not tackle this timely problem, we shall employ Max Weber's distinction between political and industrial capitalism.

Industrial capitalism is characterized by the appropriation of the physical means of production by autonomous industrial enterprises. These concerns engage in capital accounting and apply modern machine technology in the production and distribution of goods. Since profit-making depends entirely upon the sale of goods in markets, industrial capitalists seek to mould the desires of their buyers through mass advertising. Prices are either set by cartels or spring from a power struggle among massive firms that seek to translate open markets into their private domains. Industrial capitalism is thus necessarily market-oriented but does not require effective competition for its operation.

Obviously, the extension of markets requires a large measure of law and order. All private use of physical force must be suppressed and the police powers must be centralized in the hands of the state. Yet this power must be used only for the protection of private property and the enforcement of private contracts. Industrial capitalism thus develops best in situations in which the state guarantees private economic relationships but does not engage in any significant forms of economic activity. In modern states, however, such economic abstinence can hardly ever be expected. As political structures, they usually operate according to the dynamics of power. Being possessed of power, the state and its representatives usually pretend to a special prestige, the most important bearers of which are usually military leaders. Many of them make it their business to translate the prestige of power into a glorification of the state. The more important and larger the military establishment, the easier and more effective are the personification and glorification of the state. In the process of maintaining military establishments, the state becomes a buyer of military equipment, a provisioner of modern armed forces. Since many of the products are not readily available and frequently have no civilian use, the military demand calls for capitalist enterprises that become specialized suppliers of state agencies. The payment of these military purchases calls for significantly large amounts of loan capital. Certain capitalist producers and bankers, while realizing handsome profits in the process of serving the state, become economically dependent on it and are in this way political capitalists.

Political capitalism may be defined in terms of certain characteristic operations and effects, as follows: (*a*) large, non-economically motivated projects are launched by the government; (*b*) special non-civilian products and services are supplied by private enterprises outside capitalist markets; (*c*) the prices charged for such products and services and the interest rates on loans used to pay for them are higher than those prevailing for similar goods and services in capitalistic markets; (*d*) suppliers and financiers servicing the state seek exclusive contracts with government agencies and other privileges; (*e*) taxes collected for the payment of products and services obtained by the state fall primarily upon noncapitalist groups. As long as the resources required for military and political purposes constitute a relatively small percentage of the gross national product, political capitalism can exist side by side with industrial capitalism. The latter determines the basic form of the economic order, whereas political capitalism is merely a minor modification that does not constitute a threat to the capitalist system.

This situation of mutual compatibility disappears when the internal, political power aspirations are enlarged by the external ones. Power competition among states produces armament races. Capitalist pressure for the exclusive control of foreign resources or markets intensifies the armament race. The combination of power competition and expansive economic pressure transforms the political into an imperialist capitalism.

The extent to which the interests of imperialist capitalism are counter-balanced depends above all on the profitableness of imperialism as compared with the capitalist interests of pacifist orientation, in so far as purely capitalist motives here play a direct part. . . . In general and at all times, imperialist capitalism, especially colonial booty capitalism based upon direct force and compulsory labor, has offered by far the greatest opportunities for profit. . . . The universal revival of "imperialist" capitalism, which has always been the normal form in which capitalist interests have influenced politics and the revival of political drives for expansion are thus not accidental. For the predictable future, the prognosis will have to be made in their favor.[46]

Max Weber's theory thus culminates in the prediction that industrial capitalism will be surrounded and eventually superseded by a modern, politically oriented, imperialist capitalism. Placing Weber's theory in the context of the first Nazi period, we obtain the following thesis: the coalition goals of the Hitler governments could be expected to produce a political capitalism at home and an imperialist capitalism in relation to other powers, and both together could be expected to diminish, greatly if not fatally, the chances of industrial capitalism in Germany.

It will be our task to marshal the available public and formerly secret information in order to test this thesis. Great care will be taken to discover whether the political power of the Nazis acted in the way required by Weber's "dynamics of power" of the modern state. We shall also have to see whether the suppressing of trade unions and the invigorating of capitalist institutions were neutral factors in regard to political capitalism, and we must determine their effect upon industrial capitalism.

VIOLENCE AND BUSINESS POWER

There arises the question of whether capitalist enterprises can operate effectively under the conditions of violence maintained by para-military organizations. Did violence reduce the efficiency of business operations? Did it even undermine and eventually extinguish business power altogether?

If our thesis of partial fascism is correct, business power must have coexisted with violence. Ways and means must have been found to make them compatible with each other. It is our belief that compatibility could be achieved only because business groups became extensively organized, because a partial conjunction arose between business and military power, because the party had sufficiently strong political and economic reasons to keep violence out of the economic sphere, and because even the ruling groups regarded violence as a non-legitimate power.

From this hypothetical point of view, we should expect pressure for a change in the type of business organizations to have come from two directions. The intention of the intransigent Nazis to transform business organizations into mass organizations of the party could be successfully countered only if there were just one integrated network of business organizations. In fact, big business must have been strongly tempted to accept the principle of compulsory organization, while at the same time recognizing the major difficulty of securing effective representation of their interests in a compulsory organization. The second pressure for a reorganization of business should have come from the unified power of the party. Business organizations could have met this pressure only if they possessed over-all leadership and were led by someone who would not only represent the combined industrial properties of big business but who would be empowered to speak in the name of the state. Our expectation is then that the Minister of Economics should also have acted as the leader of all industrial business groups in the country.

The ever-present danger of violence should have induced business organizations to create an incentive for party leaders to keep violence outside of business enterprises. We shall therefore have to search for cases in which violence was inflicted upon some concerns and to discover whether this extreme form of coercion was stopped by the combined actions of party leaders and business organizations.

Yet such protection could hardly have been sufficient. Some form of assurance was needed that would become effective if either the party or the para-military organizations applied coercion to business. A friendly military force had to be available to prevent such violence from being applied. The need for such an assurance as well as the desire for armament orders must have induced business groups to seek a friendly relationship with the generals of the regular army, with a view to reaching the understanding that whenever a fundamental conflict arose between business and the para-military groups of the party, the generals would support the business groups. In fact, such an understanding seems to have been an implicit precondition for forming a coalition government with the Nazis. Our expectation is that economic power on certain occasions had to be complemented by military power in order that the potential violence of the para-military organizations might be resisted.

If business was thus insulated from violence by self-organization, protection, and assurance, one would suspect that such an arrangement exerted its influence upon the structure of power in the regime. It seems likely that a distinction developed between jurisdictional and structural power. The former should have come into view in all matters that affected the scope of business power. One would expect business leaders to have defended the functions that had been under their control before the regime or that had been acquired as a result of their participation in the Hitler government. The jurisdictional authority of business should have been asserted especially in economic matters against any expansive tendencies on the part of the generals. Yet this independence of big business as a power bloc can hardly have been in evidence when disputes concerned the basic distribution of the instruments of power. Economic power should then have tended to be insufficient, and business leaders should have called for reinforcement by agents able to apply and control organized physical force. We should therefore expect big business to have been an independent holder of power in functional matters and a dependent power bloc in structural affairs.

There is reason to believe that partial fascism gave rise to a dual power structure in regard to the actual or potential use of force. In such matters, the combination of the generals and business should have opposed the party-SS bloc. In jurisdictional affairs, however, each one of these power groups should have sought to defend its own material and ideal interests against any other holder of power. As an organization, the SS became increasingly independent of the party and gradually developed into a powerholder in its own right. Hence, our contention is that in daily operations there were at first three and then four power groups, coexisting, collaborating, or quarrelling with each other. In case of fundamental conflict, these four groups re-allied themselves into two opposing blocs, when one had to accept the will of the other (as in the Röhm purge) or refrain from any use of force and accept a compromise.[47]

Whatever will be our findings in regard to power and ideologies, there can be no doubt that because of the Hitler government the German economy became subject to strong military and fascist influences. Any attempt to assess this influence and trace its impact upon the economy will have to step outside the traditional boundaries of economic analysis. Noneconomic ideologies and power achieved a strategic signifiance in the Third *Reich*. It is in terms of these two variables that our investigation has to proceed.

NAZIFICATION OF THE MIDDLE CLASS

CHAPTER TWO

The annals of the Weimar Republic record three classes: capital, labor, and the middle class. Capital and labor occupied the arena during 1919–30. Both were fully developed social classes that acted as well-organized, self-chosen opponents in the economic, social, and political struggle of the republic. Each class was independent, resourceful, and powerful. Each opponent was able to meet and check the other in almost every field of activity. This produced a typical bilateral power relationship, especially in the fields of social policy and labor affairs, in which major decisions could be reached only through a struggle, ending with some compromise that satisfied hardly anyone.

The middle groups had no uniform economic position. Some were small entrepreneurs who lived on their incomes as managers as well as owners of capital. The property of artisans and peasants served mainly as a means of self-employment. Professionals sold their skill or services on the market and secured thereby some form of economic independence. An increasing number of employees sold their services for salaries and thus became economically dependent upon their employers. In consequence, the middle groups enjoyed different economic positions, performed different economic functions, had different economic, social and political interests—and did not develop a common ideology. Nevertheless, these groups were united by a similar type of life and attitudes. Their predominant feeling during the period of the republic was the sentiment of being different from and averse to capital as well as labor.

PRE-NAZI CLASS STRUCTURE

What was the relative proportion of these three strata in democratic Germany? One excellent statistical study investigated the data of the occupational census of 1925 according to the sociographical mode of analysis.[1] Professor Geiger regrouped the occupational data into socio-economic positions of classes by giving due weight to income and property. For instance, professionals or peasants were not counted as one subgroup of the middle class. Doctors who owned or directed hospitals and/or earned more than 30,000 marks a year were included in the capitalist class because their income was in part a return on invested capital. All independent physicians were recognized as members of the middle class; doctors who handled almost exclusively patients of the official sickness-insurance corporation and/or earned less than 3,000 marks a year were regarded as belonging to the proletarian section of the middle class.[2] The result of this reclassification of the German population data of 1925 can be seen in the table appearing on next page.

These figures measured the population only according to the economic positions of the three classes. The term "class"

	Gainfully Employed Individuals	Per Cent of Population	Gainfully Employed Individuals and Their Families	Per Cent of Population
Capitalist Class	299,630	0.84	574,752	0.92
Middle Class	8,745,252	24.39	16,026,135	25.68
Labor Class	26,808,848	74.77	45,809,732	73.40
	35,853,730	100.00	62,410,619	100.00

was here defined as an economic *stratum*: whoever occupied a certain economic position belonged to his respective class. No other criteria were permitted to enter. The main finding of Professor Geiger's study, which provided a very accurate measurement of the socio-economic composition of the population, was the high proportion of the labor class in relation to other segments of the population. Yet these figures did not measure the socio-ideological composition of the population. Thus one may ask to what extent the economic positions of the three classes were modified by the factors of class awareness and ideology in the actual behavior of those who made up the membership of these classes.

German labor and capital were very conscious of their socio-economic position. They recognized themselves as opponents in a distinct class situation. Each class had its own interpretation of its class interest and class mentality and was guided by different class ideologies. First labor, then capital, formed economic organizations. The clash between collective actions and ideas was instrumental in setting up an intense class struggle that penetrated into most spheres of collective activity.

Awareness of their socio-economic position produced in both classes a peculiarly collective outlook and developed distinct attitudes towards their own class as well as towards the others. The two most conspicuous attitudes among laborers as well as employers were solidarity with one's fellows and antagonism towards the opposite class. Solidarity developed into class pride. German laborers were proud to be members of the "toiling masses." Capitalists insisted upon deference from their workers. The result was increased social distance between the classes that hardened into class hostility and antagonism.

There was, however, a marked variation in the extent and intensity of solidarity and antagonism in both social classes. The conservative-feudal element in the intellectual make-up of the German upper class intensified the contempt felt by employers for organized laborers and unions. The patriarchal idea of the lord's castle as his kingdom was transferred to the industrial scene. Employers regarded themselves as the absolute masters of their business. Unionization was seen as an infringement of well-established property rights. Many industrialists (e.g., the Krupp concern) fought furiously against unionization of their workers. It was due to the rising power of unions during the First World War and the subsequent revolution that many employers were compelled to recognize their unions and modify their antagonism against organized labor. Later events proved conclusively that this change in sentiment was conditioned by the fact that the revolution established labor as a power bloc in industrial relations with which capital was forced to negotiate and cooperate. In the minds of many employers, cooperation was a necessary evil; cooperation did not often generate from a genuine recognition of unions.

Labor, on the other hand, was unable to organize all sections of the working class. Two economic groups of employees rejected the typical ideas of the German labor class. These groups included, first, the salaried employees in industry and government, and second, the marginal independents (quasi-proletarians) who operated shops or stores on their own account, cultivated a few acres of land, or sold their labor as services to customers (e.g., house painters). These groups were economically dependent. Neither income nor standard of living distinguished them very much from German laborers. Yet they retained or acquired some form of middle-class outlook on life. Solidarity within labor was thus confined to the traditional groups of labor. Salaried employees and small independents did not recognize themselves as laborers. Their sentiments, attitudes, and some of their actions, were largely determined by their middle-class ideology. In spite of their economic dependency, these two groups belonged ideologically to the middle class. Identification of the quasi-labor groups with the middle class created a cleavage between their economic position and their ideas of themselves. These ideas of their social-ideological position influenced their actions decisively and required a revision of the merely economic groupings as presented in the preceding table. Salaried employees and small independents had to be shifted from the economic groups of labor to those of the middle class.

How large was the numerical influence of the two quasi-labor groups? The statistical information was again furnished by Professor Geiger. He subdivided the middle class into three distinct sections. Artisans, dealers in goods and services, and most of the peasants appeared in his classification as members of the "old" or traditional middle class. Salaried employees and the lower strata of professionals were designated as the new middle class. The group of small independents was called the quasi-proletarian sections of the middle class. The results of these detailed studies have been condensed in the table on the next page showing proportional relationships between the three classes.[3]

Although some of the methods employed to ascertain middle-class social position may be questioned, Geiger's data clearly show how large a section of the economically dependent groups did not recognize themselves as a part of the labor class. Quantitatively, the economically dependent class of

	Gainfully Employed Individuals (% of Population)	Gainfully Employed Individuals and Their Families (% of Population)
Capitalists	.84	.92
Middle Class		
Old Middle Class	18.33	17.77
New Middle Class	16.04	17.95
Quasi-proletarian	13.76	12.65
Proletarians	51.03	50.71

73.4 per cent of the population (see table on p. 62) was reduced to 50.71 per cent, which constituted the proletarians or the socio-economic labor class. Correspondingly the economic middle class of 25.68 per cent of the people increased to 48.37 per cent by becoming the socio-economic middle class.[4] This increased the relative chances of the middle class in social and political affairs.

The diversity within the middle class, the divergency of economic position and class awareness, carried with it a train of economic and organizational, as well as political and ideological, problems. A brief outline of these problems will show an internal structure of the German middle class that differed significantly from that of the other two prevailing classes—laborers and capitalists.

Economically, the three groups of the middle class experienced significant differences in their interests. Relative to the means of production, each group was placed differently. The "old" group was relatively independent as owners; the "new" group was economically dependent as non-owners; the marginal independents often owned their stores but not their raw materials and were economically dependent upon the banks—who, in turn, "supplied" large industrial buyers. Yet even the marginal owner cherished his freedom to work at his own pace—without supervision—in his own store or shop, even though the working hours were often very long. In consequence of these different economic positions, the three groups developed different economic interests.

Peasants favored high food prices and tariff protection for their products, whereas storekeepers and salaried employees demanded low food prices. Debtors in city and country insisted upon low rates of interest for loans but middle-class savers argued for high rates and for protection of their investments. Salaried employees and civil servants organized themselves into influential unions, fighting for better working conditions and higher salaries, whereas peasants, artisans, and traders hated unions which, when effective, raised their unit costs of operation. Most of the middle groups demanded special services and subsidies from the government but loudly decried high tax rates and demanded tax exemptions for themselves. The diversity of interests was thus so strong that a common class interest did not develop, and preference was given to the interests associated with crafts and trades.

The divergent interests of these smaller economic units prevented organization along class lines. The "old" group in cities was organized along the lines of craft and trade, the "new" groups (Berufsorganization) according to occupation and profession. The most important organizations for artisans were the guilds (Innungen). The mandatory guilds had obtained the rights to regulate apprenticeship, vocational training, the employment and placement of journeymen. That is to say, when the majority of a craft voted for a mandatory organization, all artisans of that craft had to join the guild. The result was a gradual shift from optional to mandatory guilds. The latter comprised 83 per cent of all organized artisans in 1929. Total membership in 1925 comprised 17,543 guilds with 910,388 members.[5] Thus about 70 per cent of the artisans were organized in the various guilds, and all the guilds were united in the Association of German Artisans, which comprised the organizations of sixty-three different crafts.

The other groups of the middle class were similarly organized. Forty-five specialized retailers' organizations accounted for about 50 per cent of the retail trade. Farmers were organized in three different organizations which competed for membership and for recognition of their particular interests but which acted jointly in regard to over-all agricultural policy through their central committee. Finally, salaried employees joined the independent unions, which comprised 1,200,000 of a total of 4,000,000 employees.[6] There were three unions for salaried employees, similar to the three kinds of unions for workers. The Christian organizations comprised 498,000 and the national unions 350,000 members. The remaining group of organized employees belonged to the social-democratic trade unions. That there was a trend towards comprehensive organization of the middle class was thus beyond doubt, but these organizations separately—rather than collectively—promoted the economic interests of the guilds, trade associations, and professional or occupational groups. Each organization pursued a different policy. There was no attempt to arrive at a common goal or to achieve a united economic class.

Ideologically, two diverse trends could be observed. All three groups of the middle class aspired to the same social status. Many studies of the 1920's clearly show that the various groups did have a similar sense of status distinction. Sentiments of belonging—based on an actual or desired style of life—originated a state of mind, created a range of prestige and deference that defined a distinct status group. Actually, just one feature of a fully developed class was present, namely the unity of status. The three groups thus formed only a social class; the economic and political as well as the organizational features of a single comprehensive class were missing. This unity of status was, however, very strongly felt. Within the setting of the class structure of capital and labor the status sentiments of the middle groups amounted to a distinct "class" attitude, as if there were a united middle class. The unity of sentiments and status was especially pronounced in relation to the labor class, from whom all segments of the middle class deliberately tried to distinguish themselves.

In addition to this anti-labor attitude, there was, among many rural and urban enterprises run by the "old" middle class, a pre-capitalist attitude. The pre-capitalist attitude was expressed in the form of opposition to free trade, the open craft, and the capitalist market, which was thought to operate on the principle of unfair competition. This attitude survived among many peasants, but small urban business was slowly penetrated by the capitalist spirit. Procapitalist spirit penetrated slowly into small urban business. Procapitalist ideas led to the adoption of machines and modern methods of production. Purchasing and credit cooperatives adopted modern marketing and banking methods. One acute observer estimated for 1907 that about 700,000 of the 3 million small enterprises acted as if they were capitalistically minded.[7] Even the majority of the salaried employees nurtured procapitalist aspirations. Many felt a sense of belonging to the plant and identified their interests with those of their employers. Some of the unions sought to promote a harmony of interest between employees and employers and to facilitate the promotion of its members to higher managerial positions. It was only among the members of the socialist unions and among some small sections of the marginal independents that anticapitalist sentiments could be observed. Yet pre-capitalist sentiments, especially among the peasants, were much more important than the aspirations of anticapitalism. Diversity of interests and organizations was thus accompanied by a significant differentiation in ideologies held by the different middle groups.

Politically, the middle class did not develop a specific preference for one party. Diversity of interests and ideologies was accompanied by a variety of political beliefs and party affiliations. Those cherishing pre-capitalist sentiments definitely evinced a preference for conservative ideas and parties after the hyperinflation, but anticapitalist sentiments hardly led the marginal independents to support labor. The majority of them belonged to the politically indifferent who scarcely ever voted in elections. Those motivated by procapitalist sentiments voted either for the liberal or Catholic parties. In the second half of the 1920's, there was a definite preference for "interest" parties that tried to enter the political scene for the express purpose of promoting the economic interests of the middle class, but these parties succeeded only in gaining the support of *some* of the economic interest groups and organizations of the middle class. Thus, the three groups of the middle class did not enjoy a united political representation in parliament.

The dependent and marginal sections of the middle class created a special problem for the labor parties. Two different schools of thought prevailed within the Social Democratic party. One group accepted the status preferences and aspirations of this new middle class as unalterable and proposed a change in the party program.[8] The special interests of the new middle class, consisting for the most part of salaried employees, were to be promoted and their political support gained in this way. The other group regarded the status preferences of the dependent and marginal sections of the middle class as a transitory complication. Sooner or later, the class interests would become stronger than the professional interests, and the status distinctions would be replaced by an appropriate class ideology. Yet the efforts to organize the salaried employees into socialist trade unions met with small success. The educational and propagandistic attempts to speed up the "inevitable" process of class awareness were essentially failures.[9] Status preferences thus served to prevent

the labor movement from organizing economically and politically the dependent and marginal groups of the middle
class.

The situation was almost exactly the opposite for the Nazis.
Suffering from their unsatisfactory economic position, the
dependent and marginal groups were predisposed to adopt a
politically drastic program, especially when the depression
started to exert its pressures upon them. This is clearly observable in the election statistics. In 1930, most of the 2.5
million former nonvoters cast their ballots for the Nazi party,
which achieved a gain of 5.5 million votes from 1928 to
1930.[10]

The principal aim of many families in the dependent or
marginal segments of the middle class was to raise themselves
economically so as to become full-fledged members of the
middle class and to increase the social distance between
themselves and labor. The economic development of the
country ran counter to these goals for improvement. Rather
than raising their economic chances, the depression increased
the divergency between economic class position and class self-
awareness. Many of the marginal and some of the dependent
members of the middle class adopted an attitude of protest
against the unfavorable economic pressure. Radicalization
set in first in the lowest layers of the middle class. The first
mass membership as well as the core leaders of the Nazi movement came from these lower strata of the middle class.[11]

Divergence between economic position and social status
magnified the impact of the depression upon the marginal
group of the middle class. Wounded status pride intensified
the sense of revolt. Nazification of the middle class was greatly
facilitated by this status preference, the loss of which was
most keenly felt by the marginal and dependent groups. Why
then did the older segment of the middle class also become
Nazified? Why did the bulk of the middle class become the

social basis of the Nazi party? Which conditions facilitated the transformation of the diversified middle groups between capital and labor into a politically strong, ideologically uniform, counterrevolutionary movement?

UNIFICATION OF THE MIDDLE CLASS

Economists have often explained the rise of the Nazi movement by saying that it sprang primarily from the depth of the Great Depression. In this general form, however, such a thesis cannot be correct, since all countries with a similar decline in economic activity would have had to experience a similar fascist movement. In this connection, a comparison of the major economic indicators in Germany and the United States—which show how great was the fall in production and income in each country—is instructive.

EXTENT OF THE CYCLICAL DOWNSWING, 1929-32*
(Percentage decline since 1929)

	United States	Germany
Total Industrial Production	46	42
Producer-Goods Production	69	50
Consumer-Goods Production	25	21.4
Total National Income	52.3	40
Income from Labor	40	40
Income from Manufacturing	61.4	49.2
Income from Agriculture	70.2	30.9

* *Historical Statistics of the United States 1789–1945* (Washington, D.C.: Government Printing Office, 1945); *Konjunkturstatistiches Handbuch* (Hamburg: Hanseatischer Verlag, 1935).

As can be seen from the preceding table, the shrinkage in the American economy was more severe, especially in agriculture and many branches of urban small business. Thus, if the severity of the depression had been not only a necessary but also a sufficient cause, then the political receptiveness to fascism should have been at least equally great in the United States.

Actually, the relationship between economic and political events is somewhat more involved. It is certainly true that the Nazi movement could have arisen only in such a period of severe depression. But it did not have to occur. In and of itself, the severity of the depression was a necessary but not a sufficient cause for fascism. The depression gave rise only to a political upheaval, as is attested by both the American and German experiences. Given this extreme degree of privation, the particular forces at work in Germany might have been expected to produce a political change (reformist, revolutionary, or counterrevolutionary) of some kind. Economic shrinkage and recovery provided the opportunity for an extraordinary political decision. Hence, since the German middle class occupied a strategic position, we must ask ourselves why all the middle classes expressed their resentment by voting in increasingly large numbers for the Nazi party. Why, in the battery of successive elections, did these groups thereby turn the scales in the direction of a political counterrevolution?

The best available answer hinges on some special economic events that accompanied the depression, on the particular political constellation of the Weimar Republic, and on the ideological preferences that existed and the transformations that took place during the depression years.

The credit crisis, which created an extreme situation of external and internal deflation, was crucial.[12] The flight of capital, foreign and domestic, in the summer of 1931 produced a run on the banks, which was followed by the failure of a few banks, by bank holidays, and by subsequent credit restrictions. Money was, of course, very difficult to obtain, especially after the Central Bank had temporarily raised its rediscount rate from 7 to 15 per cent.

The monetary and banking crisis produced three lasting effects. There was a drying up of short-term credits for small business, since the financial support of the central bank helped big business primarily. The result was an extreme downward pressure upon the level of middle-class employment. At the same time, the credit crisis froze interest rates at a very high level. The usual process of easing financial obligations either by converting loans into lower-rate contracts or by replacing old with new debts that benefited from lower rates of interest was interrupted. Financial stringency rather than increasing liquidity became the peculiar condition of small business. Finally, the subsequent devaluation of the British pound not only hampered severely all efforts to keep up the German export business, but seemed to be a calculated attempt to shift the burden of the depression upon Germany. Indeed, when the German government introduced foreign-exchange control in reply to the British action, most of the German business groups suspected that the credit crisis—and the subsequent devaluation and exchange controls—had been fabricated abroad for the sinister purpose of curbing the recovery in Germany.

A price differential arose during the depression. The prices of farm products and of some consumer goods fell drastically, while the prices of many producer goods remained fairly high because of the concerted efforts of cartels and combines. The response of the farmers, which was to try to help themselves by increasing production, only intensified the decline in net income. Banks responded with attempts to foreclose farms. The auctioning off of farms incensed farmers into acts of violence. Resistance to foreclosure became the slogan and practice of the peasants in many regions of northern Germany. In fact, the sharp increase in the number of foreclosures was one of the main reasons why the peasant vote shifted from the two conservative parties to the Nazi party.[13]

The combined impact of price and income decline plus

the credit crisis was especially felt by the urban middle class. Not many of them were able to rely upon past savings, most of which had been destroyed during the previous hyperinflation, and the owners of stores or shops, whose net income often fell almost to zero, were not able to secure unemployment compensation, since they were not covered by social-insurance. On the other hand, white-collar workers who lost their jobs tried their hands at retailing, if they had some funds. Thus, the number of retail stores increased greatly while the total volume sold and the turnover per store diminished severely. The urban middle class had no cushion whatsoever to soften the shock of depression and deflation.

The democratic governments were quite willing to subsidize the peasants; but inadequate methods were adopted. High tariffs ceased to afford adequate protection when home production exceeded the domestic demand for farm produce. A heavy duty on grain merely increased the costs of the livestock industry, which had to pay higher prices for domestically produced animal food. An adequate program of support prices and government storage did not become effective during the period of the Weimar Republic.[14] The greatest share of the subsidies paid went to the owners of the large estates in East Prussia upon the personal insistence of President von Hindenburg, who dismissed Heinrich Brüning and Kurt von Schleicher as chancellors in the depth of the depression when they became reluctant to continue paying subsidies to the landed estates. The preference given to the *Junkers* thus stood in the way of an effective program of agricultural price or income support, as did the opposition of big business and some liberal economists who rejected the principle of government price support. The funds spent for agriculture thus did little to soften the impact of depression and deflation upon the peasants.

The misery created by the depression and the deflation inevitably caused a shift in the attitudes and outlook of the middle class. A deeply felt protest arose against private capitalism and democracy, which were held responsible for the depression and the deflation. The middle class also insisted that capitalists and liberals as well as trade unions were to be blamed for the misdeeds that had been inflicted upon small business.

Economic suffering and protest against misery, reinforced by unchanged status preferences, produced the effect of a change in the ideology of the middle class. Procapitalist sentiments rapidly disappeared, especially among the members of the dependent group. Studies made by nonsocialist unions of the economic conditions of salaried employees from 1928 to 1930 reveal widespread discrimination against white-collar workers; salaries paid were below the ones fixed by collective agreements. Promotion to the higher managerial positions had almost ceased.[15] As the economic situation for salaried personnel got worse, procapitalist sentiments declined rapidly.

Anticapitalist ideas spread first among the white-collar workers and marginal independents, then among the peasants, and finally among the traders and artisans. An intense hatred pervaded all these groups. They were looking for an enemy, and they found it in some features of private capitalism. The peasants hated, especially, the bankers' and wholesalers' buying of or speculating in farm products. Artisans and traders were incensed by the competition of chain stores, department houses, and consumer cooperatives, as well as by the low prices of industrially manufactured consumer goods which replaced handmade products. Many white-collar workers hated industrial capitalists and their personnel policies, especially the policy of dropping older workers on principle or of replacing members of the office staff with machines. All these policies not only threatened the economic position of salaried employees but deeply offended their feelings of status distinction.

In all, four features of private capitalism came under increasing attack. They were the prevailing credit and banking system; the methods and organizations of monopolistic pricing and buying; the capitalist markets that created such great fluctuations in the demand for and the prices of the products of small urban and rural business; and the large-scale methods of production and distribution of goods by modern combines. Although these institutions were hardly ever attacked by any two groups simultaneously, they incurred the wrath of the various segments of the middle class. Anticapitalist sentiments made all sections of the middle class receptive to radical ideas.

These sentiments were transformed into a distinct middle-class ideology in response to three distinct historical conditions. There were, first, the intense animosity that many peasants or artisans felt towards the labor movement; second, the lack of democratic ideals and the indifference of many middle groups (between capital and labor) to the Weimar Republic; and, finally, the widely felt preference for a preindustrial way of life. These three factors gave the growing radicalism of the middle class a counterrevolutionary direction that was beneficial to the Nazis.

The middle classes had three complaints against organized labor during the 1920's. The increasing power of the trade unions had led to a rise of real wages after the hyperinflation. The power of the unions penetrated into small shops; higher wages raised the cost of production for their owners and frequently reduced their net profits. Organized labor was able to get the whole social-insurance program upon the statute books. These laws demanded contributions from small-scale employers, who were not able to protect themselves and their families against the risks most laborers had secured protection against. Increase in income, protection against the risk of unemployment and occupational hazards, and greater political influence gradually raised the standard of living for workers and gave the skilled worker an economic position that was higher than that of most white-collar workers, marginal independents, and many poor peasants.

The middle and upper groups of the middle class also experienced a decline in their economic positions in relation to the economic positions of many workers. The resultant animosity and envy were transformed into outright hatred when the trade unions succeeded in slowing down the wage decline during the depression and secured insurance payments for jobless workers. There was, thus, a conflict of economic interests affecting both wages and prices, a conflict which became increasingly bitter during the depression. There was also an ideological aversion to working-class socialism of whatever shade, which many small owners had come to fear as a threat to their businesses and their way of life. Hence, all efforts of the trade unions and the Social Democrats to make their own policies accommodate some of the economic interests of the small business groups and to effect a political alliance between labor and the middle class bore no fruit whatsoever.[16]

For the majority of the German upper and middle classes, democracy was merely one political credo, one mode of government among many, to be chosen according to its practical usefulness in a specific situation. As a result of the breakdown of the monarchy and the defeat of Germany in the First World War, the majority of the urban and rural middle class voted for democratic parties. When the hyperinflation of the early 1920's had largely destroyed the savings of the urban middle class and undermined the economic and political order, the middle-class vote went mainly to the two conservative parties, one of which was antagonistic to the Weimar Republic. The disintegrating effect of the inflation thus destroyed the mild beginnings of democratic sentiments and ideals among those groups. The middle class merely tolerated the Weimar Republic. The "small-interest" parties, which increased in number prior to the depression, tried merely to represent and to protect the special interests of segments of the middle class. The rise of many splinter parties attests to the fact that a significant portion of the middle class had become ideologically detached from democracy even before the rise of the Nazi movement. The experiences of the Great Depression, some eight or ten years after the inflation, destroyed middle-class confidence in conservative parties and further undermined middle-class tolerance of the Weimar Republic.

Finally, there was a definite estrangement between big and small business. Alienation between the two groups arose because of a conflict of economic interests as well as because of a divergence of ideologies. The lower unit costs of many large concerns were exploited during the depression for capturing the markets of small firms, either by promoting department stores and chain stores or by supplying small retailers with goods on credit. This economic conflict was transformed into anticapitalism when the leaders of small business became convinced that the combination of bigness and irresponsibility had undermined the foundation of the capitalist system. Formerly, freedom of contract and private property had been pillars of capitalism. Disposal of private property provided the opportunity to realize profits and entailed the risk of losses. The element of risk in turn acted as a brake upon the unrestrained drive for an expansion of property, but this barrier to unlimited acquisition had been removed within and by large corporations. Although shareholders provided the capital and had to assume the risks, control over the corporations rested with the top managers, who were not personally responsible for the risks they imposed upon corporations. In fact, the responsibility for the failures and scandals of some large corporations in 1931 was placed upon the shoulders of non-propertied managers who were suspected of speculative investments for personal gain.

Equally repellent was the large banks' practice of offering

the opportunity to deposit shares in return for being allowed to exercise corporate voting rights. Bank managers thus accumulated directorships in manufacturing companies. Yet neither these directors, nor the banks behind them, were responsible for the consequences of their influence upon the controlled companies. The result of bureaucratic management and the influence of the banks was a degeneration of private capitalism. Business profits went first and foremost to the controllers whereas the losses had to be assumed directly by shareholders and workers, and indirectly by the government.

Two alternative inferences were drawn from this interpretation of capitalism. Some believed that the lack of responsibility would be removed (a) by making the managers personally and financially responsible for the losses of the enterprises, (b) by keeping the banks responsible for the obligations of those manufacturing enterprises in which bank directors exercised voting rights.[17] As the depression increasingly threatened the existence of more and more small firms, many of their owners became convinced that large-scale capitalism had to be abolished so that small business could live.

The feelings against labor and capitalism and the rejection of democracy produced a twofold effect on the lower middle class. All its segments discovered their common class interests in a negative way: the depression threatened the existence of all the middle groups. Relief from this danger could not be expected from the policies of big business, trade unions, or democratic government. These negative beliefs induced the leaders of the middle groups to concentrate upon their future common interests. Emphasis upon the future gave rise to a new economic and political ideology that outlined the main features of a guild-oriented form of corporatism (*berufsständische Wirtschaftsordnung*).

The first proposal for a guild-controlled economy had been worked out by Dr. Heinrich Meusch, general secretary of the German Handicraft and Small Business Organization. The principal ideas of a subsequently proposed bill had to do with the special quality of the artisan product, the occupational honor of the artisan master, compulsory membership in guilds, and the rights and responsibilities of the guilds to engage in economic self-government. Under the pressure of the depression the handicraft organizations, in the resolutions adopted at their conferences and in the bills proposed to governmental agencies, evolved a fairly comprehensive program of guild-oriented corporatism.[18] Briefly, this program included:

a) Appointment of a *Reich* commissioner to look after all the interests of, and examine all proposed policies for their effects upon, the middle class.

b) Acceptance of a large-scale public-works program which would aim especially at providing funds for renovating old houses and thus bring orders to handicraft firms.

c) Elimination of all public enterprises and repair shops and an extensive revision of the bidding system as it pertained to governmental contracts.

d) An effective fight against all forms of substandard work (*Schwarzarbeit*) as well as against cutthroat competition within the field of small business.

e) Placing special taxes upon chain stores and department stores, as well as upon anyone who peddled goods from house to house, so as to raise their unit costs relative to those of small retail stores.

f) Restoring the discipline of workers in shops and stores and freeing small business from any reduction of the working week during the depression.

g) Introducing a special comprehensive and compulsory system of examinations for all owners of stores and shops so as to exclude all incompetents and all other intruders into artisan professions.

h) Reducing substantially the wage rates of skilled workers

by government action but abolishing all forms of compulsory arbitration in wage disputes.

i) Increasing the training period of apprentices from three to four years and lengthening the minimum apprenticeship of journeymen to five years.

j) Granting authority to guilds to adopt a system of self-government which would allow them to regulate their markets, and imposing the conditions upon shops and stores through compulsory membership in guilds.[19]

This radicalization of the middle class went beyond a negative opposition to big business, the unions, and democracy. The traditional handicraft organizations developed a positive program for substantial economic reform which was directed against private capitalism. Beginning with proposals to increase the demand for and reduce the supply of artisan products, the suggested ten points aimed at eliminating large-scale enterprises and at excluding trade unions from the sphere of small business. It was especially the last point, on self-government, that later developed into an extensive program for a new type of economy in which all major economic decisions would be made by the guilds. The Great Depression had thus not only unified the various segments of the middle groups into one social class and created a unified class consciousness but had provided the essentials of a new program for economic reform.[20] This program could not be disregarded by any political party that tried to obtain the support of the middle class.

NAZI POLICIES FOR THE MIDDLE CLASS

How did the Nazis exploit the situation of a middle class that had become united through anticapitalist, antilabor, and antidemocratic sentiments, and through its newly found class ideology? The Nazis seized the unique chance to lead and represent the middle class, to rise to power on the wave of resentment and energy proceeding from a radicalized middle class. Nazi policies with respect to these groups can be summarized readily under four headings: (*a*) glorification of the romantic ideals of the middle class, (*b*) political redirection of its antidemocratic sentiments, (*c*) identification with its new economic program, (*d*) efforts to obtain a Nazified leadership of the middle-class organizations.

The Nazis captured the minds and hearts of the majority of peasants and small businessmen through a glorification of the pre-capitalist ideology of the middle class. The peasants' desire for security of land tenure, for protection against creditors, for the stability and continuity of the family farm were glorified by the Nazis into two ideals. The peasantry was to be the wealth-giving and value-creating class of the "new Germany." In the words of a leading Nazi agricultural leader, "The Third *Reich* will be a peasant *Reich* or it will be nothing at all."[21] Peasants were to live the best possible lives on model farms, cultivate the land in the most effective manner, produce the healthiest children, and own and utilize their land perpetually. The vision of a society, built upon blood and soil, in which the peasants were to be honored as the most important social class, produced a great enthusiasm for the Nazis in all segments of the rural population.

Similar versions were presented to small businessmen and to the uprooted and unemployed laborers in cities. The slogan of "a house for every family," to be built in the countryside or in small communities, satisfied the longing for independence of many workers who would not have known how to pay the next rent if the welfare office had withdrawn its monthly subsidy. Storekeepers and shopkeepers were heartened by the picture of an artisan economy in which all small owners would have to be thoroughly trained before practicing a trade, where all would produce first-rate products with their own hands, in which everyone would deal honestly with the other masters of his trade or guild, and in which all trade organizations were to be governed by an ethical code that would be enforceable by special courts of honor. Glorification of craftsmanship, recognition of the guild system, and the establishment of autonomous "courts of honor" appeared to many members of the urban middle class as heralding the beginning of a new epoch in which industrialism and ruthless competition would be forever banned.

The interpenetration of corporative and Nazi economic ideas can best be seen in the proposal suggested by Gottfried Feder for an extensive work-creation program.[22] There should be (*a*) a sensible autarchic foreign-trade policy that would exclude imports of goods which could be produced at home, (*b*) a compulsory labor service for all young men engaged in building canals and draining hitherto unarable land, (*c*) an extensive program for the repair of residential houses—to be financed through rebates from the house ownership tax, (*d*) an extensive program for the building of electrical power stations that would provide the basis for an extensive program of industrial decentralization, (*e*) a long-range resettlement program and a population policy which would resettle workers in the east of Germany and thereby conform to the decentralization program of industry. Feder expected that the program would cost the federal government about 5 billion marks, which would be spent over a period of ten years. The first three points of his program were regarded as self-financing in that existing subsidies would bring in larger tax revenues at a later date. The deindustrialization and resettlement programs, however, would require new credit. This was to be provided for by the issue of new money, the control of which would call for the nationalization of all private banks and the creation of new cooperative financial institutions. The first part of Feder's program incorporated many of the proposals of peasants and artisans, whereas the second part provided the main economic ideas for the intransigent Nazis in the first period of the regime.

The Nazis became masters in exploiting the wounded pride of the middle class and its hatred of other groups. These aversions were transformed into active antagonism towards labor, capital, and foreign powers. Labor was identified with communism, the arch enemy of Germany. Liberals, democrats, and socialists were all called "communists." A fear of an immediate communist revolution was created that became an obsession with many of the new followers of the Nazis. A few of them became zealots in the cause of saving the fatherland from the "red menace." Identification of the whole labor movement with communism enabled the Nazis to present labor leaders as subhuman beings who should be eliminated at the first opportunity. Marxism was to be eradicated from the minds of every man and woman in the nation; the designation of communism as the arch enemy, the debasement of its ideology, and the vilification of its leaders were very powerful devices for moulding the middle class into a counterrevolutionary mass movement.

The aversion of the German middle class to the Treaty of Versailles was transformed into intense hatred of the powers that had been victorious in the First World War. The treaty was represented by the Nazis as the main cause of German economic and political misery. Territorial losses and the payment of reparations, it was asserted, had reduced Germany to a proletarian nation. Although the payment of reparations was greatly mitigated by the extensive foreign loans, reparations were said to be the major cause of the severe depression. Then came the master trick: the Weimar Republic was pictured as the tool of the victorious powers. Democracy was said to be alien to the German national character. Democratic government was claimed to be instigated and imposed by the victors in order to suppress Germany. Hence, democracy had to be destroyed so that Germany could live again; national freedom had to be regained so as to put an end to the depression.

The stage was set for a unilateral destruction of the Treaty of Versailles; nationalism became chauvinism. In placing responsibility for the economic crises upon foreign powers, and in accusing the German republic of being their tool, the Nazis created a link between depression and democracy, between economic misery and the Treaty of Versailles. The fight against democracy was thus effectively disguised. There was no frank discussion, no careful weighing of the advantages or disadvantages of either democracy or dictatorship. The democratic form of government was simply declared to be responsible for the depression, and this accusation was linked with the promise that a new *Reich* (its dictatorial character not specified) would remove democracy and thereby create national freedom and full employment for all.[23] The preference of the middle class for dictatorship was thus created through the illegitimate identification of democracy with internal depression and external oppression, of dictatorship with full employment and "national freedom." No fascist party or regime has ever been able to win middle-class support solely on the merits of dictatorship as a form of government. Dictatorship was therefore presented and accepted as the great saviour of the country from internal and external enemies that threatened its very existence.

The Nazis identified themselves with the specific economic interests of the various middle-class groups. They fought against the forced sale of land or farms by private bankers. They opposed the industrial monopolies or cartels that charged high prices for machines, tools, and other supplies bought by the small businessman or the peasant. They attacked ferociously the chain and department stores as well as consumer cooperatives because they were competing with the small merchants. They accused the large concerns of paying too-low salaries to white-collar workers and demanded continued employment of older salaried employees. Almost all the economic complaints of the various segments of the middle class were thus accepted by the Nazis and incorporated into their program for immediate action upon their coming to power.

In interpreting this economic policy, however, the Nazis modified the anticapitalist sentiment of the middle class. A distinction was made between German and Jewish capital. The latter had to be destroyed or driven from German soil. German capital was declared desirable and necessary. Only two branches of German capital that had misused their power were attacked. Banking capital had exploited the peasants and small businessmen through excessive interest charges and through foreclosure on encumbered farms. Hence, the banking system had to be reorganized in order to protect the small borrowers from exploitation by financial capital.[24] Equally, trusts and combines were accused of successfully maintaining their prices almost at the predepression level, whereas the prices paid by these concerns for the products of peasants or suppliers had been drastically reduced. Hence, the Nazi newspapers in one phase called for the abolition of trusts and for the control of cartels. The misuse of power by large banks and cartels was to be eliminated, but these same organizations should be granted protection from Jewish competitors.

This interpretation of the role played by large banks and combines had two consequences. Violent anti-Semitism became accepted by various segments of the middle class as a policy of economic reform. Not capitalism itself, but only the association of some capitalists with Jewry, should be terminated; Jewish property should be expropriated by the State. In supporting "German capitalism," the party had to revise its "eternally valid" program. "German socialism," they said, was not against the system of private property. Hence, they deleted from their program the demand for expropriating land without compensation. The proposal to nationalize trusts was also struck from the program. The demand that workers should share the profits of the firms at which they were employed was to be limited to giant enterprises. Private savers should receive the full, prevailing market rate of interest on their invested capital; the fight against the "thraldom of interest" was to apply exclusively to large-scale banks.[25] This revision practically eliminated the economic demands of the original party program.

At the same time, those factions of the party which favored public ownership of the means of production were excluded from leading positions. Nazi representatives had presented a bill in the Prussian parliament demanding the abolition of all public enterprises,[26] but the revised program incorporated only those demands of the middle class which facilitated the interpenetration of the party and the middle class. Finally, recognition of "German capital" allayed the suspicions felt by some industrial leaders who were now willing to finance the party more freely. As the middle class became more Nazified, the party leaders became more property-minded and friendlier towards a "German" capitalism. This foreshadowed the resistance of the party leaders to "middle-class socialism." Even in the formative period, however, property-mindedness made the Nazi party more acceptable to capitalists as well as to peasants and artisans.

A similar process of interpenetration can be observed on the level of organizational activities. On the one hand, the Nazis built up their own organizations for the middle class. Many of the younger members of these groups became active Nazis. Mass meetings, parades, and organized violence against members of opposite political organizations increased the self-esteem of these young men and transformed them into experienced workers for the party. On the other hand, these same party members were given the assignment of penetrating into the existing middle-class organizations—to become their leaders and to spread Nazi ideas. The Nazified leaders familiarized themselves with the economic problems of the members of those groups and organized campaigns against the foreclosure of farms, "unfair" competition from department stores or consumer cooperatives, and the like. They even engaged in tax strikes and organized a collective refusal by the farmers to pay interest on their bank loans. Such actions established the Nazis as the genuine and effective leaders of many economic organizations of the middle class. In other organizations where the old leaders remained at the helm, the rank and file were induced to adopt resolutions supporting the Nazis. In this manner, the membership of these organizations entered politics on the Nazis side and steadily increased the influence of this party within the middle class.

Ideological penetration, political direction, economic "actions," and organizational infiltration exerted a profound effect on the middle class. For the first time in many decades, there existed one genuinely accepted ideology that united all sections of the middle groups—namely, "middle-class socialism." There was now uniformity in political beliefs and action. The traditional middle-class parties were almost swept from the scene. The Nazis had become the main party of the middle class.[27] Organizational multiplicity and economic conflicts among the various organizations had come to an end. The economic identification of the party with these organizations gave their interests a rapidly rising significance that could no longer be overlooked by governments.

In consequence, the middle class became the social basis of the Nazis, who had established themselves as the recognized leaders of a counterrevolutionary mass movement.[28] As the social basis of the party, the various groups of the middle class saw in the Nazi party a political instrument for realizing their economic interests as well as their middle-class ideology. The general expectation of the organizations of small business was that the Nazis would champion their program for economic reform. These groups expected the party to destroy the power of capital as well as of labor and thereby establish a dictatorship of the middle class.[29] It was because of this support and enthusiasm of the middle class that the power of the party and its para-military organizations became so irresistible and effective in destroying or dissolving all other political parties.

THE UPPER CLASS AND COUNTERREVOLUTION

Clearly the Nazified middle class played a large role in Hitler's rise to power, but one may ask what part the upper class had in establishing the Nazi regime. Did big business and the *Junkers* join the Nazi movement, oppose it, or merely support it financially while refusing to grant it open political support? Within limits, each one of these three alternatives of action was selected by some members of the upper class, but the great majority neither joined nor opposed the Nazi movement. In 1931–32 the choice facing them, as most of them saw it, was either disguised support or an open alliance. Which specific events were responsible for the fact that the upper class did not utilize its power to oppose the rise of the Nazi movement? The answer lies in the relationship between big business and the trade unions or democracy, and between the *Junkers* and democracy.

It was only a few years after the hyperinflation in the 1920's that big business accepted the Weimar Republic and the trade unions. Big business' fight against independent trade unions, collective bargaining, so-called political wages, and comprehensive social insurance had already begun in 1928, when the corporate rulers of the Ruhr steel industry imposed a lockout upon 250,000 workers. Unable to defeat the unions, the employer organizations in the steel industry succeeded in largely destroying the right of the government to make collective bargaining agreements mandatory for all firms in an industry. Governmental participation in collective bargaining was resisted in the years 1928–30 under the slogan of "free" collective negotiations, but in 1931–32 the employer associations dropped their fight against compulsory governmental awards in wage negotiations because the governments of these two years were willing to reduce wages by compulsion.

The Brüning government was successfully pressured into imposing a wage reduction of 10 to 15 per cent as an emergency measure. This governmental violation of valid collective bargaining agreements was first demanded by the largest steel concern in 1930 and then generally accepted by the employer associations. In 1932, the von Papen government undermined collective bargaining with another emergency decree granting employers the right to reduce wage rates unilaterally up to 20 per cent if they found it difficult to continue their productive operations. This emergency law, too, generated from a proposal made by the employer associations.[30]

The success of the employers in their dealings with labor was more than a function of the depression and served to increase the power of the employer associations relative to the trade unions. Also, as we should expect, the animosity of the employers toward trade unions and social legislation intensified itself into a fundamental opposition to the Weimar Republic.

When asked in his trial in Nürnberg about the political affiliation of big businessmen, the industrialist Flick correctly answered that the German People's party expressed the political attitude of the businessmen. "I should say that Stresemann's party, that is the *Volkspartei,* would in general be considered the industrial party."[31] It is significant that this party turned against the Weimar Republic at the same time that the United Steel Works A.G. demanded that the government should violate the collective agreements negotiated between employers and unions. In April of 1931, the People's party demanded a revision of the constitution. Parliamentary government should be terminated. President von Hindenburg should be granted the power to appoint a federal government of his choice. He should also be the head of the largest state, Prussia, and appoint the government of this state. This increased power of the President was justified by the argument that the authority of the state had to be strengthened.[32] Hence, the party of big business was in effect demanding an end to democracy and the establishment of a presidential dictatorship—even before the rise of the Nazis, who would later use the presidential dictatorship as a means of achieving their own dictatorship.

The presidential dictatorship derived its political power from the armed forces and its economic power from big business. In 1931, the leaders of big business publicly proposed a new economic program. This "common declaration" was signed by the over-all economic associations of manufacturing and handicraft, trade and banking, as well as the agricultural organizations.[33] In demanding a reduction of wages, a retrenchment of all forms of social insurance, as well as a series of economic favors for big business, the united power bloc of the upper class indicated clearly that it desired a private capitalism in which there would be neither trade unions nor collective bargaining, in which social insurance would be replaced by relief for the poor, and in which the government would be fully submissive to the economic interests of big business. The policy proposed was not to be implemented by the government in office but by a new Economic Council (*Wirtschaftsbeirat*). The decisions of the council were to be implemented by a group of new undersecretaries in the economic ministries, who would be independent of political parties as well as of ministers. Since the council was to comprise primarily industrial leaders, big business was actually trying to take over the function of determining the economic policy of the government.[34] The military dictatorship of the President was thus to be accompanied by the economic dictatorship of big business.

The economic crisis had a somewhat different effect on the political position of the *Junkers*. The decline of agricultural prices reduced the incomes of landowners as well as peasants. Many members of both groups were unable to pay their debts and were threatened by compulsory foreclosure of the mortgages on their properties. Using their political influence upon the aging President von Hindenburg and the German National party, the landowners were able to obtain a shift to a highly protective agricultural policy in 1930. A year later a special subsidy program for the agriculture of eastern Germany was adopted, and in 1932 a broad program for the salvaging of this area was proposed by the Brüning government. One part of this program aimed to provide comprehensive relief from indebtedness. Large creditors were to receive new debt certificates from the government, and small creditors were to be compensated in cash for their loans, if the creditors were willing to accept lower rates of interest; but this opportunity to substitute new loans for old was not to be offered to those enterprises that no longer had any chance of repaying their debts. The property of such insolvent estates was to be sold at compulsory auctions.

The second part of the agricultural program provided for the extensive resettlement of farmers. The intention was to set aside the land of the insolvent and auctioned estates for settlement by small farmers. The two parts of the program thus supplemented each other, and both were accepted by von Hindenburg.[35]

Representatives of the large estates, on the other hand, violently attacked the program as a form of land expropriation. The over-all agricultural organization demanded that any decision as to which estate could not be salvaged and had to be taken over by the state should be made exclusively by the chambers of agriculture. The state would have to pay a price that was also determined by these chambers. The purchase of such estates should be permitted only if all attempts to reduce the loans and interest rates, through negotiations with creditors, had definitely failed.[36] The agricultural interest groups were thus determined to prevent any transformation of large estates into resettled farms.

In the spring of 1932 von Hindenburg went for a rest to his estate (which had been given to him by a group of industrialists some years earlier) in East Prussia. In "the midst of his neighbors, friends and old comrades," von Hindenburg became an opponent of the agricultural reform program of his own government. He accepted the argument of the landowners that the proposed reform was a form of "agrarian bolshevism" because it aimed at the expropriation of their estates.[37]

The compulsory sale provision, which was regarded as a last resort for a very few estates, had become of increasing significance since the rapidly falling agricultural prices had imposed insolvency upon an increasing number of estates. It is likely that the reform, if implemented, would have led to a reduction of the possessions of the *Junkers* in subsequent years.[38] Against this possible threat, the political friends of von Hindenburg achieved the dismissal of the Brüning government. The *Junkers* thus bore the responsibility for having eliminated the last cabinet that was still supported by a reluctant majority of parliament.

We have here a clear case in which the power bloc of the upper class not only terminated a government but also constituted one of the driving forces in the destruction of German political democracy. Yet there was a peculiar form of interaction between economic and political power. Big business increased its economic power because of the depression, first in relation to the trade unions and second in relation to the government. The various organizations of big business imposed a policy of wage reduction upon the Brüning government and finally withdrew their representative in that government when further demands were not accepted.

In contrast, the *Junkers* experienced a decline in their economic power during and because of the depression which brought many estates to the brink of bankruptcy. As we have seen, however, some of the landowners had mingled friendship with economic interests to obtain control over the aging President von Hindenburg and to demand of him that the federal treasury should protect their properties and assure them of a sufficient income during the depression. Whatever the specific source of their power, the two segments of the upper class arrived at the same goal. Not only did the life of the Brüning government have to be terminated, but the economic requirements of democracy—collective bargaining between big business and the unions and equity in the subsidizing of agriculture—had come into conflict with the economic interests of big business and the landowners. Both groups thus came to the conclusion that protection of their economic interests required a political dictatorship.

Why did political dictatorship, in the thinking of the leaders of the upper class, become a precondition for overcoming the depression? Up to the middle of 1931, big business and the landowners were not united. The former thought to overcome the depression by reducing the economic functions of the government, while the latter effectively increased these functions. With the deepening of the depression, however, and the development of the credit and currency crisis, the leaders of big business lost hope in the possibility of overcoming the depression by weakening labor and by acquiring control of the economic policy of a democratic government. A reassessment of the depression took place and resulted in the formation of a common goal for big business, the landowners, and the generals.

The new goal was characterized by three distinct beliefs.

Economically, the deepening of the depression was seen as the result of the "fetters of Versailles," which were said to be responsible for the reparations, the indebtedness to foreign countries, the drain upon the foreign-currency reserves, and thus for the currency crisis. The "political wages" of trade unions were regarded as the main obstacle that prevented employers from reducing their unit cost of production and from holding their sales position in foreign and domestic markets. The increasing severity of the depression convinced most of the leaders of the upper class that the Treaty of Versailles had to be eliminated, that reparations had to be cancelled, and that the power of labor had to be broken before the depression could be overcome.

Politically, the common goal—as expressed in the joint declaration of almost all the economic organizations of business—required a strong government. Big business, for example, abandoned its advocacy of a weak government. At this time, however, a strong government could not be realized through the existing democratic parties, since their majority in parliament had steadily shrunk. Nor could the rising election gains of the Nazis, in the deliberately fabricated series of elections, lead to a majority in parliament. Labor could be dislodged from its position of power only if and when parliamentary government was abolished. Then, within a few weeks after the closing of the banks—in the summer of 1931—the leaders of big business adopted the characterization of the Weimar Republic as a "system of dishonor" and called for a "national dictatorship."[39]

Militarily, the size of the armed forces would remain limited, and the military power of Germany would remain restricted, so long as Germany adhered to the Treaty of Versailles. An aggressive foreign policy was necessary to achieve "military equality" with other powers. This military aspect of the common goal had far-reaching consequences. Many leaders of business and owners of landed estates turned from nationalism to chauvinism and favored a foreign policy that was widely proclaimed by the Nazis. Of even greater importance is the fact that the goal of military equality appealed strongly to the generals of the army. As the chances for rearming Germany became better, an increasing number of high-ranking officers deserted the Weimar Republic and accepted the idea of a national dictatorship.

The worsening of the depression thus had a profound effect upon the position of the upper class. One mutually shared goal united the leaders of big business, the landowners, and the army. In gradually blending their thinking and pooling their resources, the leaders of the upper class became a distinct and highly organized power bloc. In its policies, this bloc ceased to be conservative—no longer trying to maintain the status quo. In favoring a fundamental change of the political system, the leaders of the upper class lost their fear of the Nazi counterrevolution. In fact, they sponsored a kind of reactionary counterrevolution of their own. Coordinating different strands of counterrevolution, the Nazis and the various segments of the upper class became allies in the fight against labor and democracy, and in the struggle for "military equality."

ALLIANCE OF TWO POWER BLOCS[40]

The first proclamation of an alliance occurred at the conference in Harzburg in September of 1931, hardly three months after the banking crash. The Nazis (NSDAP) and the German National party (DNVP), together with the veterans' organization of the *Stahlhelm*, formed an alliance which became known as either the "National Opposition" or the "National Front." In spite of the many differences among the new allies, they agreed on two vital points at the conference. They loudly manifested their opposition to the present government and to the Weimar Republic. In equally certain terms, they claimed the right to form a government of national concentration, a term which became known as a euphemism for political dictatorship. The alliance was thus formed for the express purpose of eliminating democracy and for establishing a dictatorship.

The Harzburg conference was not limited to politicians. In prominent attendance were the leaders of big business and the landowning groups. These economic leaders not only subscribed to the political alliance of the rightist parties but also arranged for a tie-in between their economic organizations and these parties. The alliance between the parties was thus accompanied by an economic-political alliance that eventually benefited all participants. In order to see how this dual interallied grouping coordinated its plans and activities so as to defeat democracy, we must study the understandings reached by the Nazi party and the segments of the upper class, some of which coincided with an estrangement between the political allies.

The political alliance had lapsed during the presidential election, when Hitler had run against von Hindenburg in the spring of 1932. This electoral fight was the last instance of division within the upper class. Responsibility for the elimination of this split rested primarily in the hands of the leading generals, who were the "kingmakers" of the presidential cabinets. While still missing as a partner at Harzburg, General von Schleicher and his friends allied themselves with the arguments of the landowners against the "agrarian bolshevism" of the reform plan proposed by the Brüning government. Mutual opposition to the land reform and to the Brüning government incorporated many generals of the army into the power bloc of the upper class.

Closely connected with this was a new understanding between the generals and the Nazis. As a first step, Generals Kurt von Schleicher and Kurt von Hammerstein restored "the political independence of the *Reichswehr* from all political entanglements." They turned against General Wilhelm Groener, who as Minister of the Interior and Minister of Defense had outlawed the SA, the para-military army of the Nazis. Groener was forced to resign because he no longer enjoyed the confidence of the *Reichswehr*.[41] As the second step, von Schleicher entered into negotiations with the leaders of the Nazi para-military organizations, Röhm, Himmler and Helldorf. The generals had worked out a plan for forming a new militia, called "Organization Stuelpnagel." The supposed function of this prospective militia was to absorb all the private armies of the political parties. Von Schleicher proposed to the Nazi leaders the eventual incorporation of the SA into a militia commanded by generals of the regular army. Röhm accepted this proposal, and von Schleicher succeeded in having it confirmed by Hitler. On this basis, von Schleicher was willing to support a repeal of the outlawing of the SA. In his private diary, however, Goebbels praised Röhm for his "masterpiece" of intrigue.[42]

The government of Franz von Papen (which replaced Brüning's) was the joint product of the unification of the upper class and of the understanding between the generals and the Nazis. In its economic policy, the von Papen government acted as the agent of the upper class. All thought of land reform was banished, and subsidies were freely handed out to estate owners. Collective bargaining was destroyed, and employers were permitted to reduce wages unilaterally. This was celebrated as restoring the principle of "free wage determination." Even in its policy of fostering re-employment, the government preferred subsidies for business concerns. Tax rebates were granted to concerns but denied to consumers. The upper class had taken over the government which promoted an economic policy of dictatorship prior to the Nazis.

Politically, the von Papen government existed only because of the secret support of the Nazis. In return for not attacking the von Papen government, the Nazis demanded and received three invaluable concessions. The von Papen government dissolved parliament and announced another election in which the Nazis achieved their greatest electoral victory. Von Papen also reinstated the SA and SS, which had been outlawed by the Brüning government. The subsequent street fights led in Prussia alone to ninety-nine dead and many wounded in the election campaign.[43] Finally, dispossession of the Prussian government and subjection of the Prussian police by a commissioner of the von Papen government destroyed the only force that could have checked the excesses of the Nazi military groups. These three concessions to the Nazis constituted important stepping stones for Hitler's rise to power. The historical contribution of von Papen and von Schleicher is thus clear. Both circumvented the danger of an open civil war by breaking up the only armed forces willing to defend democracy. They established the conditions of a concealed civil war in which the military units of the Nazis began their rule of the streets. In these fights, the Nazis were freely tolerated by the von Papen government and benefited greatly from the benevolent neutrality of the armed forces of the state.

What was the relationship between big business and the Nazis? Prior to the banking crash, many businessmen, favorably inclined towards the Nazis, had considerable misgivings about the economic ideas of Gottfried Feder and Walther Darré, whom Hitler had put in charge of the economic policy of the party. Examining the various Nazi leaders for their economic soundness, leaders of the big coal concerns of the Ruhr came to the conclusion that Gregor Strasser was more trustworthy than any of the other Nazis. Because it was expected that he would strengthen his position within the party and adopt a reliable economic policy, Strasser was heavily subsidized.[44] Here then was a significant effort on the part of big business to mould the Nazi party after its image.

In the summer of 1931, when he was in Munich, "Hitler suddenly decided . . . to work systematically on the influential personalities of business."[45] In the confidential conversations, which culminated in his speech to the captains of the Ruhr industries in January 27, 1932, Hitler revised the economic program of the NSDAP. He had previously conceded to the small firms that his party supported private property, but he was now extending his policy by largely adopting the ideas of big business. He argued for the elimination of unions and for the managerial freedom of employers within concerns. He outlined his program of public works and rearmament, which would lead to recovery and to many orders for business concerns. These public orders would not have the effect of delegating more economic functions to the government, since the leaders of big business were to be given the task of directing the economy through the economic organizations under their control. Hitler promised also a stable government that would stay in power for a long time.[46] Taken into his confidence, leading businessmen trusted Hitler and convinced themselves that the party, once in power, would provide big business with the opportunity to determine the economic policy of his government.

Clarification of the "real" economic intentions of the party was accompanied by corresponding changes in the organization of the Nazi party. In the fall of 1931 the Nazified businessman Wilhelm Keppler was appointed as Hitler's economic advisor, while the activities of Gottfried Feder were substantially reduced. At the time of his appointment, Hitler told Keppler "that the previous economic program of the party had been mainly theoretical and that it was really necessary to consider the practical needs of the country. He therefore suggested that I should bring together a circle of business leaders who have proved themselves in industry. Hitler suggested that I should form these men into a circle so that they could advise me. He mentioned also that it was in no way necessary that these people be members of the party."[47]

In the "circle" the Nazis had found an organizational device that enabled them to bring leading businessmen close to the party leadership and thereby create the impression that the party had changed its economic policy. Many of these businessmen thought they would be able to determine the actual economic policy of the party and of the future regime. The reactions of businessmen were thus quite favorable to Keppler's efforts: "When I approached these members of industry and told them quite frankly that the Führer had ordered me to reconsider all economic questions and asked them whether they were prepared to give me their advice, there was a definite sense of relief among those industrialists."[48] The Keppler circle was thus a peculiar form of alliance in which the party furnished the organization and businessmen the advice, both aiming at a common economic policy.

In addition, there were all kinds of personal connections between individual businessmen and leaders of the party, on a national as well as on a regional level. Some of these contacts were arranged by agents of big business. Heinrichsbauer made the arrangement in 1931 for several Ruhr industrialists to meet Hitler.[49] Other contacts were established by Walther Funk, who was then simultaneously an agent of some leading businessmen as well as of the party. (Hitler appointed him as head of the *Kommission für Wirtschaftspolitik* in 1931.) Funk's survey of the industrialists who maintained contact with and supported the Nazis includes most of the leaders of big business.[50] In return for these promises, the industrial concerns contributed heavily to the coffers of the Nazi party. Funk reports that the contributions of business concerns lay between 40 million and 60 million marks in the first year of the Hitler regime.

Particular concerns made special deals with top leaders of

the party. In 1931, Flick decided to sell to the federal government the shares of Gelsenkirchen A.G., which gave their holders control over the United Steel Works, A.G. concern. Prior to the sale, Flick had invited Göring to examine the transaction, and Göring gave it his approval in the name of the party. At the same time Flick paid 50,000 marks to the NSDAP.[51] I. G. Farben also contacted the Nazis. Said Dr. Heinrich Gattineau, then head of the press office of the I. G. in Berlin: "At the end of 1932 it was suggested to me by Professor Bosch to arrange a visit to Hitler for Dr. Buetefisch. I did so through Professor Haushofer and Hess and took part in the visit myself. It was intended to clarify the position of the NS party regarding the question of German gasoline production."[52] Hitler assured his visitors that his government would actively support the production of synthetic gasoline. I. G. Farben thus acquired an economic interest in the installation of a Hitler government. In February of 1933 it actively supported the new government by attending the meeting of industrialists with Hitler and Göring, in which the decision was made to finance the Nazis, the German Nationalist party, and the People's party in the election of March, 1933. In paying 400,000 marks for this purpose, I. G. Farben became the largest single contributor to the terror-election.[53]

There was thus a dual alliance between big business and the Nazi party. Leading businessmen joined the Keppler circle as a quasi-party organization and were given the opportunity to advise the party on its economic policy. In return for adjusting its economic policy to the interests of big business, the NSDAP received payments for its political activities. The second form of alliance arose from the understandings between individual businessmen and some party leaders. The latter promised some political service, either in the present or the future, and received in return political contributions from the concerns involved. In neither case did the ideology of the Nazi party constitute a barrier that prevented businessmen from arriving at a deal with the party leaders. The latter quite clearly surrendered objectionable elements of their ideology in return for receiving substantial contributions from private concerns or business organizations. In the formative period, the Nazis confirmed through their actions Max Weber's thesis that in case of conflict private interests would prove stronger than party ideology.

It was in the last month of 1932 that the financial-economic alliance between big business and the party came to be of primary political significance. Members of the Keppler circle entered into negotiations with the various political leaders and (a) restored the broken alliance between the Nazis (NSDAP) and the German National Party (DNVP), and (b) contributed decisively to an understanding between Hitler and von Hindenburg.

After the election of July 31, 1932, von Papen and Hitler negotiated about the formation of a new government but were unable to agree because each one desired to be Chancellor.[54] Schacht sent Hitler "a word of most sincere sympathy" and designated himself as Hitler's "reliable assistant."[55] The leaders of big business were also to have an opportunity to show how much they appreciated their alliance with Hitler. When the von Papen government had fallen, the leaders of the army turned against Hitler. Moreover, von Schleicher, who was forming his own government, had lost confidence in his ability to incorporate the SA into a militia commanded by the *Reichswehr* and was proposing to split the Nazis into two groups and take one of them into his government. It was at this strategic moment that a group of big businessmen intervened. As early as September of 1932, leading Ruhr industrialists had informed Gregor Strasser that they had suggested to the "decisive offices in Berlin that Hitler be appointed Chancellor of the *Reich*."[56] At that time it was expected that the Nazis would drop their opposition to, and reach an agreement with, von Papen. When this expectation did not materialize, business leaders took a more active hand in attaining a Hitler-von Papen government. Led by Baron von Schröder and Albert Vögler, both members of the Keppler circle, the businessmen sent a petition to von Hindenburg in which they requested a government of national concentration under the leadership of Hitler. The petition was presented to the presidential secretary on November 28, 1932.[57]

At the same time, von Hindenburg asked Hitler to form a parliamentary government under two sets of conditions. On the one hand, the ministers of foreign affairs and defense would have to be men agreeable to Hindenburg. On the other hand, the new Hitler government would have to rule under the discretionary power of Article 48 in the constitution, accept the incorporation of Prussia into the *Reich*, and submit a suitable economic program. Hitler was willing to accept the first condition and expressed no opposition to a suitable economic program, but he inquired as to the source of power for such a government. Would it be a presidential or a parliamentary government? When von Hindenburg insisted that it should be both at the same time, Hitler refused to accept the opportunity that was being offered him to form a government.[58] Thus, the second effort of the business leaders to support a coalition government under Hitler and von Papen had also failed.

Turning against the new government of General von Schleicher, the business leaders consulted each other and came to the conclusion that they had to arrange for a direct reconciliation between von Papen and Hitler. Meeting in the home of Baron von Schröder in Cologne, on the 4th of January, 1933, von Papen and Hitler discussed their misunderstandings and agreed that most of them had been deliberately created by von Schleicher. Von Papen then proposed the formation of a new government to be led by both. Hitler presented his

demands saying that von Papen and his supporters could enter Hitler's government if they were willing to support his
policies. There was finally an understanding that the two
parties should form a government of national concentration
led by both Hitler and von Papen.[59]

This secret conversation involved a kind of intrigue on von
Papen's part, since he had not yet received von Hindenburg's
assignment to prepare the ground for a new government.
Furthermore, when von Hindenburg was deciding whether
to retain von Schleicher as Chancellor or to accept Hitler,
the leaders of big business and of the landed estates turned
against von Schleicher and supported the efforts of von Papen.[60] As a result, the Hitler-von Papen government was not
only a coalition between the NSDAP and the DNVP; it was
also the government of big business and the landowners,
because it was their alliance with the Nazis that had persuaded von Hindenburg to appoint Hitler. The third attempt
of big business to obtain a coalition government was thus
successful.

The first Hitler government faced its initial crisis in the
first month of its existence. Hitler proposed, and Hugenberg
rejected, a new election of parliament. In this dispute, the
leaders of big business sided with Hitler. The leaders of the
Reich Association of German Industry, led by Gustav Krupp
as its president, attended a meeting in Berlin at which they
discussed with the Nazis the financing of the election of
March, 1932. "After Hitler had made his speech, the old
Krupp answered Hitler and expressed the unanimous feeling
of the industrialist in support of Hitler."[61] Yet this support
was granted only after Hitler had expressed his belief in the
need for a fundamental cleavage between democracy and
private capitalism. Private ownership of the means of production could be secure only when democracy had been
destroyed. The new government required for its task full control over all means of power; all its enemies would have to be

wiped out. In his reply, Krupp welcomed Hitler's programmatic remarks and looked forward to a politically strong and independent state that would provide the necessary conditions for business prosperity.[62]

Göring appealed to the industrialists for help in financing the new election. It was agreed that a minimum of 3 million marks was required, and Krupp announced that the industrialists of the Ruhr would supply 1 million marks. Schacht, acting as treasurer, received the checks from the private concerns, deposited the funds at a private bank, and allocated the funds among the NSDAP, DNVP and the DVP (German People's Party).[63] In financing the terror election of 1933, the leaders of big business made a substantial investment in the new government and became thereby a full partner in the Third *Reich*.

The Great Depression and the Nazification of the middle class were necessary—but not sufficient—causes for the rise of the Nazi system. There were three supplementary developments that together enabled the Nazis to rise to power without having to fight a civil war. The first was the unification of the upper class into a single power bloc dedicated to overcoming the depression by promoting a political dictatorship. Of equal importance were the alliance which the generals, big business, and the landowners had used their influence to restore between the two parties, the NSDAP and the DNVP and the tie-in between these parties and the upper class. Finally, as parliament lost its power because of a Nazi-Communist majority, the subsequent presidential government came under the effective control of the various segments of the upper class. This power bloc had captured the government prior to the rise of the Nazis.

In permitting a Hitler government to come into power, the upper class formed a coalition with the Nazis in the expectation that the Nazis would be only junior partners in the regime and that the real power of the state would remain in the hands of the upper class. The Nazis were given control only over the police, whereas the presidency, the army, and the economic ministries were all in the hands of members of the upper class. Its leaders were convinced that their instruments of power, namely the army, the government purse, and control of the economy, were superior to the power held by the Nazi party and its para-military organizations.

There seems to have been no written agreement on the goals of the coalition government. All understandings—with one exception—seem to have been oral. Hindenburg named the men for the Ministries of Defense and Foreign Affairs; the Nazis were limited to the chancellorship, the Ministry of the Interior, and the commissionership of Prussia. All other ministers were named by von Papen and Hugenberg and by their friends in business. The economic program of the new government was thus to be formulated and implemented by non-Nazis. Hugenberg seems to have been sincerely convinced that his party would tip the scale of power, since the Nazis had a majority neither in the cabinet nor in parliament. Hugenberg thought that Hitler needed experts who were natural allies of the upper class. He also told his friends that Hitler had given his word for the "eternal" existence of the DNVP, and he believed that Hitler would not forget who had relieved his financial dilemmas in the earlier years.[64] Von Papen equally believed that as the confidant of Hindenburg he would be able to exercise equal power with Hitler and thereby neutralize the chancellorship. The civilian allies thus trusted Hitler's word and displayed an excessive confidence in their own abilities to keep the reins of government tightly in their own hands.

In contrast, the military allies had received a written statement from Hitler on his views of military and foreign policy. General von Reichenau had asked Hitler, through Bishop Müller, to give special attention to the delicate position of East Prussia in his foreign policy statements. In his letter of

December 4, 1932, Hitler used this opportunity to present to von Reichenau, who was then General von Blomberg's chief of staff for the region of East Prussia, a detailed statement of his views on military and foreign policy.[65] Briefly, his main goal was to attain military and political equality with the other powers. Realization of this goal required a foreign policy that aimed at a close collaboration with England and Italy and the separation of France from Soviet Russia, so that Poland would not be in a position to attack and incorporate East Prussia. Realization of the military goal called for a process of regeneration of the German people in which all forms of Marxism would be exterminated and the national German youth would become the spokesman of the country. Once the ideological unity of the nation was achieved, the military goal could be realized through a fourfold program. There had to be (a) a moral rejuvenation of the fighting spirit of the nation, and this was to be accompanied by (b) a technical and organizational rearming of Germany's military forces; (c) rearmament had to be correlated with making all other resources of the nation available for an active military policy. When these three aims had been realized, Germany's policy (d) would have to wrest from the other powers the legal recognition of equality which had already been attained through the appropriate actions at home.

This program of Hitler's seems to have been presented to General von Blomberg and to President von Hindenburg. As their subsequent actions indicate, both accepted the proposition that the goal of militarily rebuilding Germany could be attained only through the alliance of the army and the Nazi party. Hitler's military proposal became the core of the subsequent understanding between Hitler and von Blomberg. Hindenburg's confidence in von Blomberg then led to the Hitler-von Blomberg government, which remained in power from 1933 to 1938.

The duration of this coalition government was dependent

upon two conditions. First, army power had always to be equal to the political and police power of the Nazi party. Each partner had to accept the other as an equal and carefully respect his sphere of interests. Second, the economic interests of the Nazified middle class had always to be compatible with the economic interests of the upper class. The third feature, agreed to by the participants in the preliminary negotiations, that there must always be a political alliance between the Nazi party and the German Nationalist party, became a point of dispute. On the very day that the Hitler government was formed, there began a struggle for superiority between the allies. Why was the coalition stronger than all efforts toward an exclusively fascist or reactionary dictatorship?

FAILURE OF ARTISAN SOCIALISM

CHAPTER THREE

Within six months of Hitler's appointment to the chancellor-ship, the Nazis had changed by threat and violence the most significant political institutions of the country. All other parties were abolished or forced to dissolve themselves. Legally and actually, the Nazi party achieved an all-inclusive political monopoly which initiated, organized, and dominated all political activities in the country through its compulsory mass organizations. All forms of communication, opinion-formation, and entertainment came under the control of the party. The same was true of all the obvious political institutions and functions of the state. A single-party rule had been imposed upon the country.

How was this possible? The secret of the one-party system lies in the interlocking of four different types of organization. The ruling party possesses all political instruments of power and acts as the sole source of political opinion and legislation. The party maintains a private army that operates within all communities as an organized body of the most faithful young members of the party and as an agent of terror and violence. The party captures the police of the state, builds up an extensive secret police that acts through an extensive network of spies and through legal courts and prisons as well as extralegal concentration camps. Finally, there are the compulsory mass organizations that comprise anyone gainfully occupied in any occupation and profession and that function as large-scale instruments of indoctrination and intimidation.

The building up of such a monolithic organizational network was the result of the fascist counterrevolution staged by the Nazis. It began with the outlawing of the Communist party—which was blamed for the burning of the *Reichstag*—and culminated in the terror election of March, 1933. Falling short of a clear majority in spite of extensive violence by the Nazi para-military organizations, Hitler demanded and received extraordinary powers that practically enabled him to rule without approval of his policies by parliament. He unleashed his military cohorts by permitting them to occupy the buildings of the trade unions, arrest their leaders, steal their funds, and herd the workers into the new Labor Front. Finally, all other political parties were dissolved; the Nazis granted themselves the privilege of being the sole political party in the country.

The fascist counterrevolution had an unexpected side effect for the conservative political allies of the Nazis. The "eternal" alliance between the Nazi party and the Nationalist party was dissolved. Hugenberg and his associates were ousted from the government. The Nationalist party was forced to dissolve itself, and the *Stahlhelm* was merged with the SA. The third condition on which the first Hitler government originally rested had disappeared. Political death was thus the penalty visited upon those two conservative parties whose leaders had entertained the illusion of sharing political power with the Nazis.

The second Hitler government was based upon a coalition of the Nazis with the generals and the leaders of big business. Neither one of the two segments of the upper class gave any support to Hugenberg and his party. The generals had no objections to the violent methods used by the secret police and the Nazi private army, provided their extra-legal actions were inflicted upon those not belonging to their own class. In joining Hitler's second government, the generals and the business leaders expressly accepted the Nazi monopoly in the political sphere. In return for this support, the two conservative groups demanded the right to obtain exclusive control over the military as well as the economic spheres of the regime.

There is convincing evidence that the top leaders of the Nazis conceded to these demands of their military and business allies, but neither the para-military forces of the Nazis nor the Nazified groups of small business were willing to limit Nazi power to the political and some segments of the ideological spheres. A threefold struggle arose within the Nazi regime shortly after the success of the fascist counter-revolution. There was first the split within the Nazi party, with the intransigents insisting upon a full and immediate realization of all parts of the Nazi ideology while the temporizers under Hitler sought to achieve their program in installments. There was second the increasing tension between the regular army and the SA because the leaders of the latter insisted upon Nazifying also the military sphere of the regime. Finally, there was the clash between Nazified small business and big business, each of which claimed the right of reorganizing the economy in its own fashion.

Since the top Nazis could not restrain their radicalized followers, the generals and business leaders used the instruments of the state in fighting the intransigent Nazis. While the temporizing Nazis deliberately disinterested themselves—with some few exceptions—in economic issues, big business met the intransigent Nazis on the economic ground, whittled down their power, and prevented the realization of middle-class socialism.

The first fundamental issue between capitalism and middle-class socialism (represented by big and small business, respectively) furnishes the key to the Nazi economy. The struggle between these economic groups raises three questions for detailed analysis: What were the specific features of the so-called middle-class socialism? How did the organizations of the Nazified middle class seek to realize their new economic goal? Why and how was small business defeated?

ARTISAN SOCIALISM

The concept of middle-class socialism comprises three distinct features, as evidenced in the expressions and actions of the Nazified middle class. One dealt with the life of the peasants and was usually called "peasant socialism" *(Bauernsozialismus)*. The other was concerned with the economic and social position of artisans and traders and was thus known as "artisan socialism" *(Handwerkersozialismus)*. The third feature was a peculiar brand of ruralism which formed the link between the "socialism" of the artisans and peasants. The attempt to realize these ideals produced a program for an economic counterrevolution.

The methods of defeating artisan socialism differed in various respects from the one applied to the other two ideals. It therefore seems advisable, in this chapter, to concentrate on artisan socialism, and the rise and fall of the artisan groups, and to consider the fate of the ruralist ideals separately, in Chapter IV.

Artisan socialism had its roots in the German romantic movement of the nineteenth century. Four distinct characteristics of the earlier romanticism were still alive in the sentiments and attitudes of the middle groups. For the sake of brevity they may be called a sentiment of anticapitalism, a yearning for economic independence and attachment to the land, a desire for a predominantly artisan economy, and a quest for economic self-government through the organizations of small firms. These romantic attitudes were accepted by the party but considerably modified as they were moulded into the fascist ideal of artisan socialism.

Anticapitalism. During the years 1930-32 the Nazi attack upon capitalism became increasingly bitter as the Nazis exploited the rising sentiment of the middle groups. Nazi theory seemed to explain the plight of these groups; party theory and the sentiments of the middle groups were said to have merged. The theory of the "thralldom of interest," for instance, provided the basis for violent attacks upon big banks. These attacks had full meaning for artisans and peasants who suffered under a heavy burden of debt and foreclosures. Moreover, the sentiments against capitalism were given an anti-Semitic tinge by the Nazis. Anti-Semitism became especially effective among tradesmen. The small firms engaged in marketing fervently called for the closing of all department houses, chain stores, and the consumer cooperatives of labor organizations. The virulent assaults upon international plutocrats were gradually extended to large-scale German concerns, cartels, and combines. The anticapitalists declared: that plants should not market their products; that cartels should not have the right to fix wholesale and retail prices; that the sales agencies of cartels should be abolished; that independent traders alone should be permitted to market goods; that the workshops attached to large plants, doing the work of artisans, should be closed; and that the orders for products or services should be reserved for small firms. The Nazi contempt for the democratic state had an economic import for the middle groups. These Nazified groups insisted that all publicly owned enterprises should be dissolved and public orders filled exclusively by artisan shops.[1]

In consequence, the anticapitalism of the Nazified middle

groups was primarily a revolt against big business, whether in manufacture, trade, or finance. The demands were of a counterrevolutionary nature; the anticapitalists wanted to replace big business by small and to transform modern, large-scale industries into a primarily handicraft economy. If realized, anticapitalism would have spelled the end of big business, and Germany would have returned to a preindustrial economy.[2]

The Artisan Economy. Prior to their Nazification, the handicraft organizations demanded a reorganization of small business. They thought that reorganization should include a twofold program: entry to the trades should be controlled through special examinations and extensive vocational training; the small producers should be organized into a special kind of artisan economy *(Handwerkswirtschaft)*.

Many German artisans were convinced of the value of a vocation *(Beruf)*. They believed that the individual should learn his vocation through years of training as an apprentice and journeyman and that, when he passed an extensive practical and theoretical examination, he should become a master. The privileges of the master, they felt, should be contingent upon his ability to produce goods of exceptional quality; his vocational achievement should give him a sense of belonging to, and pride in, his artisan group. Training, quality of workmanship, and a sense of belonging were regarded as the typical objectives of artisans in an artisan economy.[3]

The two leading ideas of a separate artisan economy centered around the guilds *(Innungen)* and self-government. It was believed that all artisans should belong to a distinct economic organization, membership in which would be compulsory and would confer many rights and impose many duties on both owners and employers and employees. It was proposed, furthermore, that these new organizations have the right to govern the artisan economy. Competition was regarded as a source of economic evil that should be banned from the artisan sphere. When the depression hit many small shops and stores, the demand for an artisan economy became a political issue. "Artisan economy" became a slogan that was adopted by all conservative parties as well as by the Nazis. The slogan carried the connotation of a stable economic order; of security for all trained artisans; of effective protection against depression and technological progress; of terminating the economic penetration of big concerns into the field of small business. When the Nazis adopted the program of an artisan economy, the small businessmen filled the ranks of that party. It became the representative of the urban middle class.

Economic Corporativism. How were the various artisan organizations to govern their economic affairs? The widely accepted answer was either to form estates, as in German feudalism, or to establish corporatives as in Fascist Italy. The more commonly accepted term among small businessmen was the guild (*Innung*). Significantly, the first step towards economic corporativism was not undertaken by the Nazis. This dubious honor belonged to Hugenberg, the leader of the German Nationalists, who initiated the program as Minister of Economics in the first Hitler government. Hugenberg appointed Dr. Wienbeck, a member of the Nationalist party and an influential leader of the artisan organizations, as general commissioner for the middle class.[4] His main function was to retain control over the policies of the artisan organizations and synthesize the various demands for a corporative organization of small business. Hugenberg also asked Dr. Meusch, the general secretary of the German Handicraft Chambers (*Deutscher Handwerks-und Gewerbekammertag*) to prepare a bill for new organizations of handicraft.

Dr. Meusch suggested the following distinct organizations: compulsory guilds for masters and compulsory organizations for journeymen, supervised by the old semiofficial chambers of handicraft (but with enlarged functions). These organizations were to be affiliated with the new handicraft estate, and each organization was to operate according to the following principles: leaders were to be appointed from above, not elected by members; guilds were to govern the artisan economy, and the government was to be limited to a general supervision of their activities; problems of labor relations were to be handled by the new estate; and adjudication of legal disputes of handicraft firms was to be transferred from the civil courts to a new system of estate courts.[5]

This particular bill was never acted upon, and Dr. Meusch had to leave office after twenty-six years of service. Yet the program indicated that both partners of the first Hitler government, Nazis and Nationalists, had accepted the principles of an artisan economy and economic corporativism. Dissension was restricted to disagreements about certain details of organization and to competition between the partners for exclusive control over handicraft affairs.

Thus, the ideology of middle-class socialism had taken a definite form in the minds of the Nazified middle groups. Here was an ideology that originated from, and was promoted by, the middle groups in the Nazi movement. It was primarily because of their activities that (*a*) anticapitalism, (*b*) artisan economy, and (*c*) economic corporativism became the features of artisan socialism. The question arises as to how far the Nazis went toward realizing this ideology. Through which actions did they attempt to implement artisan socialism? Who were the opponents to such a program; why and how did they prevent its realization?

ANTICAPITALISM

The anticapitalist sentiments of the Nazified middle groups were concentrated upon three major enemies. These middle groups wished to destroy the consumer cooperatives, chain stores, and department stores; to eliminate monopolies in big business and especially the sales agencies of cartels; and to reform fundamentally the banks and industrial corporations. The anonymity of the corporations and their secret concentration of power were considered to be particularly objectionable.

Significantly, the Nazified middle groups and the oligarchic clique of the party could not agree as to the means of destroying or reforming the various features of private capitalism. Three different devices were employed or preferred during the first eighteen months of the regime. Local leaders and their followers engaged in sporadic activities. They closed consumer-cooperative stores, put Jewish merchants out of business, compelled some companies to sell some of their "chains," or induced department stores to dispense with certain lines of merchandise which were regarded as the exclusive reserve of smaller competitors. Moreover, local and regional leaders appointed special commissioners for certain plants or firms and thus followed the pattern, established by the Labor Front in dealing with the trade unions, of moving in and taking over the organization and property of the enemy. The commissioners of enterprises either dismissed managers or gave instructions for their operations. In doing this the smaller leaders translated their newly acquired political power into prerogatives of management, but they neither destroyed capitalism nor established the economic basis of middle-class socialism. Their actions were mostly sporadic and unplanned, affected a relatively small number of firms, and had, primarily, the effect of disrupting business routine. This was, however, a matter of great concern to the leaders of big business and the party, who saw that the implications for political and managerial authority were dangerous and who feared for their power and privileges. Their concerted efforts stopped the sporadic attacks on capitalists and resulted in the dismissal of the commissioners. Then, having been stalled in their efforts to put their anticapitalist sentiments into action, the Nazified middle groups called for a "second revolution." This third line of action never materialized because the leaders of the party, supported by leaders of business and the regular army, carried through the purge of June, 1934. The sporadic actions of the masses and the interference of the commissioners led to the Schmitt-Hitler deal of July, 1933, and the danger of a second revolution precipitated the purge.

STRUGGLE FOR THE CONTROL OF RETAIL BUSINESS

The middle groups fought against chain and department stores and against the consumer cooperatives. Three measures against chain and department stores were proposed: (*a*) to introduce discriminatory taxes, (*b*) to close certain lines of business, such as restaurants, that were operated as units in a larger organization, and (*c*) to liquidate all department and chain stores of any description. The first two of these demands were met, but the third was not.

Two discriminatory taxes became law on March 18, 1933. States with special tax laws for department and chain stores were authorized by the federal government to increase the tax rates by 100 per cent. The Prussian government, for instance, used the opportunity to raise the tax rate by 20 per cent. Moreover, municipal governments were permitted to introduce a special tax upon chain stores.[6] In most cases, the new taxes were prohibitive. The business of the two kinds of stores declined because of various boycotts, waged by the Nazified retail organizations. The various commissioners gave instructions to the stores. For instance, the general commissioner, Dr. Otto Wagener, a Nazi whose appointment was accepted by Hugenberg, ordered all department stores to close their handicraft shops. He also instructed producers of goods not to grant rebates to the department or chain stores.[7]

In consequence, their volume of business, which had already declined from 1.6 billion marks in 1930 to 1.1 billion in 1932, fell still further because of Nazi discrimination.

Yet when the Nazis who were in control of the retail and wholesale organizations insisted upon an outright liquidation of department and chain stores, Hugenberg protested loudly. Liquidation was out of the question, he said,[8] because of the losses it would impose on creditors. It was estimated that the total debt of department-store owners amounted to 600 million marks. This money had been provided primarily by the big banks, which would have had to write off their loans if the intransigent Nazis had had their way. As it was, however, the bankers exerted their influence and achieved a change in policy.

Three actions were taken in July, 1933,[9] in connection with the agreement between Schmitt and Hitler. The deputy leader of the Nazi party instructed all party organizations to abstain from any "independent" action against department and chain stores. All appropriate actions would come solely from the government. This was soon followed by a special law on department stores. All chain stores and department stores were subjected to a uniform and discriminatory tax; the municipal and state taxes were repealed. The concerns were forbidden to operate any handicraft shop or restaurant on their premises; nor could any chain or department store be established in the future. Finally, the law was accompanied by a change in ownership and management of the surviving stores. Jewish directors were dismissed; Jewish owners had to sell out. The banks, as former creditors, became the legal owners of the stores. New lines of credit were extended to the new managers on the condition that the government provide police protection to the stores. The top Nazis kept this part of the bargain, and the aryanized chain stores and department stores stayed in business. Thus, the intransigent Nazis were unable to liquidate their larger competitors, and the NS Hago, the over-all Nazi organization of the middle groups, lost out in this phase of its anticapitalist program.

The consumers' cooperatives were equally hated competitors of the Nazified retailers. The total sales volume of the cooperatives had risen from 481 million marks in 1924 to 1.44 billion in 1930; the number of "co-op stores" had increased from 10,000 in 1924 to 13,000 in 1932. Hence, economic competition as well as ideological opposition to this kind of business fed the determination of the Nazified groups to eliminate the cooperatives.

As with the trade unions, the private army of the Nazis forcibly occupied the extensive properties of the cooperatives. The old managers were dismissed; and the leaders of the cooperatives were herded into concentration camps. Stores, savings banks, and wholesale establishments were taken over by Nazis. Ley of the Labor Front instructed the commissionary manager of the Labor Bank, formerly controlled by the trade unions, to begin the dissolution of the cooperatives "preferably without losses."[10] A month later, however, Göring directed the Prussian police to prevent the Nazified Fighting Organization of the Industrial Middle Class (*Kampfbund des gewerblichen Mittelstandes*) from interfering with the cooperatives.[11] The *Reich* government announced that it alone would deal with the future of the cooperatives. Ley sought a compromise solution: The wholesale establishments would be continued, but the stores would be leased to private retailers. Actually, however, the cooperatives became the property of the ruling party. In July, 1934, a few days after the purge, the deputy leader of the party declared:

1) No party organization or other agency has any right to meddle with the business or policies of the Nazified cooperatives.
2) The reorganized cooperatives have the same opportunity as any other business to advertise their goods and solicit new members.

Hence, although subjected to the changes imposed by the party, the cooperatives as a form of business enterprise survived the onslaught of the Nazified middle groups. What followed in 1935 was a reorganization of the cooperatives that was intended to eliminate losses and fit them into the growing number of party enterprises. The law on the consumer cooperatives, issued on May 21, 1935,[12] specified the conditions for reorganization and partial liquidation. All unprofitable cooperatives would be liquidated, and the Minister of Finance would spend up to 60 million marks to compensate any members who lost their savings. It was estimated that those cooperatives which prior to 1930 controlled 50 per cent of the total turnover of the cooperatives would be dissolved. Moreover, all cooperatives had to liquidate their savings departments and return the deposits before the end of 1946.

In consequence, the Nazified middle groups failed in their attempt to eliminate the consumer cooperatives and to destroy the department and chain stores. Nazi opposition reduced the volume of business and the efficiency of operation of the concerns, but the stores and cooperatives that came under attack remained as a distinct form of retail business throughout the Nazi regime. In this field, as in others, anticapitalism fell short of success. What was the reason for this failure after the Nazis had established their political dictatorship?

THE SCHMITT-HITLER COMPROMISE

Responsibility for the defeat must be attributed to the opposition of big business and of the oligarchic clique of the party to anticapitalism. Both opposed the Nazified middle groups for different reasons, and expressed their opposition in different ways, yet both agreed on a common policy. The new policy was a definite compromise between big business and party leaders, embodied in the Schmitt-Hitler agreement. What were its contents? How did it influence the fight for or against capitalism?

The new policy was evolved in July, 1933. It was preceded by the resignation of Dr. Hugenberg both as Minister of Agriculture and as Minister of Economics. Dr. Kurt Schmitt, the general director of the largest insurance concern in Germany, became Minister of Economics. The Nazi leader Walther Darré was appointed Minister of Agriculture for Prussia and the *Reich*. On the face of it, this looked like a mere reshuffling of positions in a coalition government, but actually, Schmitt, as spokesman for light industries and chemicals, Fritz Thyssen, for the heavy industries,[13] and Oskar von Hindenburg, for the regular army leaders and the *Junkers*, had negotiated a comprehensive compromise with the oligarchic clique of the Nazi party. It covered all the controversial issues that existed between the party and the traditional upper class. Hence, the agreement of July, 1933, had political and economic as well as social implications which can be merely summarized here.

Politically, the Nazi party achieved a major gain. The law of July 14, 1933, declared the NSDAP the sole political party of the land. Political activity became the privilege of party members. New parties of any kind were forbidden. The property of the old dissolved parties was confiscated by the Nazis. The result was that the upper class, not only labor, was deprived of political representation. The leaders of the upper class, however, were relying upon two other sources of power when they made their deal with the Nazis. They derived power from their possession of the means of production as well as from their alliance with the leaders of the regular army. On this basis, big business became a partner of the second Hitler government. It secured control over the ministries of economics, finance, and labor, and determined the policies of the Central Bank (*Reichsbank*). Big business

therefore enjoyed a preferential position in regard to economic policies, with the exception of those pertaining to
agriculture. Equal influence in government administration
was thus the rule accepted in the compromise.

The two partners shared in the formulation of economic
policies. The Nazis determined the policies in the agricultural ministry, the leaders of big business the policies of the
economic, labor, and finance ministries. Dr. Schmitt secured
a number of concessions from the Nazis. He issued a decree,
jointly with the party headquarters, which ordered all party
members to resign their jobs in the management or on the
boards of private enterprises if their positions were obtained
through political influence.[14] At the same time, Hitler
appointed Wilhelm Keppler as his counselor in economic
affairs. He was the intermediary between the economic ministries and the party offices. Dr. Otto Wagener, of the party's
office for economic policy, was deprived of his office and sent
to a concentration camp for six weeks. Dr. Schmitt secured
the power to determine the wage policies of the Ministry of
Labor. All wage decisions required his consent. The wage
division of the Ministry of Labor, formerly under the exclusive influence of the trade unions, was now headed by Dr.
Werner Mansfeld, who had been the legal advisor of the
employer association of the steel concerns on the Ruhr.[15]
Mansfeld remained at the head of the wage division until
1942 and was quite influential in formulating the "stable
wage policy" of 1933 and in integrating the policies of the
two ministries.

The new Minister of Economics soon announced a new
economic policy for the government. Schmitt wanted neither
revolution nor reform, but economic recovery. The Minister
outlined his program before a group of leading businessmen
on July 13, 1933, at which occasion Krupp expressed thanks
for the "German economy." Public and private information
reveals the content of the Schmitt-Hitler bargain.[16]

1. Businessmen will be given full police and legal protection against Nazi interference with their property or managerial rights.
2. The main economic policy of the government will be to achieve economic recovery. The various public-works projects will be curtailed, and recovery will be achieved primarily by offering tax, and other, incentives to enterprises engaging in new lines of business.
3. Wages and general business conditions will be stabilized, and trustees of labor will be instructed to keep wages down. Government price control will be dropped, except for a check on essential items in the cost-of-living index.
4. Business will be given a voice in the formulation of the economic policies of the government, through a proposed economic advisory council. [Of the eighteen appointed members of this council, almost all came from banks and heavy industries.]
5. The government will help all business organizations, such as cartels, that aim at stabilizing markets. [This promise produced the two decrees on compulsory cartels issued in July, 1933.]
6. The special problems of business, such as deciding the fate of department stores, will be handled speedily by the government, and activities of "irresponsible elements" will not be tolerated. The various "fighting organizations" of the middle class must be eliminated.
7. The attempt to build up a new system superseding the cooperatives has been stopped because of the danger that a "whole series of non-authorized persons would engage in experiments and seek to build up a sphere of influence so as to realize all kinds of plans." It is the will of the Führer to establish here a clear line of policy and to follow the road of healthy and slow development.

Dr. Schmitt's economic program concentrated exclusively upon the interests of big business and produced loud protests in the meetings of the Nazified middle groups. The answer of big business to the anticapitalist demands of the middle groups was to reactivate private capitalism through a vigorous policy. Hitler supported this policy in various speeches. Schmitt spoke of economic recovery; Hitler pronounced the new program of the party: to fight against unemployment. Thus Hitler merely tried to make the "deal" acceptable to his followers.

The fight against the "irresponsible elements" became the first task of the new economic leaders. Typical of this development was the fate of three organizations representing small-scale iron-product firms. United by the new commissioner, Dr. Rudolf Scheer-Hennings, these organizations sent to the Minister of Economics a radical program directed against the huge concerns. They demanded (a) that all the divisions of the integrated concerns should pay a turnover tax on their intra-concern shipments, (b) that the sale agencies of the cartels should be subjected to price-supervision by the state so as to assure equal treatment between the integrated and non-integrated members of the cartels, (c) that the large concerns should be compelled to give up the unprofitable fabrication of finished steel products (the intention being eventually to limit the large concerns to the production of pig iron and ingots), (d) that a just price should be secured for all finished steel products by authorizing the chambers of commerce to fix prices and punish those selling goods below their unit costs, (e) that strong support should be granted to the independent dealers in steel materials by reducing the business of those dealers who were under the control of the huge steel concerns.

As the new commissioner, Dr. Scheer undertook to implement this program by negotiating with the steel cartels and the large concerns, gaining various concessions from them under the prevailing pressure of the Nazified small-business organizations. On July 14, 1933, however, Schmitt terminated the chances of putting the counterrevolutionary program into effect. He recalled the commissioner and made him his advisor on matters concerning fabricated steel products but refrained from assigning him any functions in this capacity. The three small-business organizations were merged into their respective economic groups and thus deprived of their independence.[17]

Big business was determined to prevent the development of the "new social order" of the Nazified middle groups. The question was whether the economy should be organized along the lines of regular business organizations or fascist corporatives. Schmitt was able to stop temporarily the trend towards corporativism. First, M. Frauendorfer, the Nazi leader of the office for corporativism, instructed all party organizations to delay their plans for a corporative organization of big and small business. The postponement seemed necessary, he said, because of the "complexity of industry." Second, the Labor Front and the new Estates for Handicraft and Trade claimed to be the sole economic organizations in their fields of activity. The Labor Front had announced its intention to organize all employers and employees. Thus there was the danger that big business would be deprived of all organizational instruments of power. Ley, however, instructed his subordinates to go slowly in organizing employers.[18] Third, one minor agreement could be reached: The corporative order was first to be introduced in the plants and built from the bottom upwards. This agreement was the basis for the Labor Act of January, 1934, which called employers the leaders of and workers the followers in the plant community. In consequence, the opposition of business to the Labor Front was successful. Ley conceded in August, 1933, that the business organizations should be the economic agency and the Labor Front the social agency of the new regime. In this indirect fashion the Nazis recognized that the business organizations were not to be dominated by the party.

The compromise reached by the Nazi party and the businessmen had two consequences for the proponents of anticapitalism. Apparently, the intransigent Nazis had failed in the fields of handicraft and trade. The Hitler government accepted the proposal for compulsory cartels, as it was presented by the cartel committee of the *Reichsverband der Deutschen Industrie*.[19] The middle groups accepted the argument of the oligarchic clique that all economic changes had to come gradually; but where was the line to be drawn between economic reform and counterrevolution? The leaders of the intransigent wing tried to achieve their goal of middle-class socialism through less violent methods than those originally contemplated. The Schmitt-Hitler agreement ended the period of violent economic change and introduced the phase of gradual economic modifications through the collective pressure that was being put upon the party by the small-business organizations.

SHOULD THE BANKS BE NATIONALIZED?

The anticapitalist sentiment of the Nazified masses was especially pronounced in regard to the big banks. Two factors had produced a widespread demand for actions against the banking system: first, the credit crisis, with its subsequent bank holidays and credit restrictions; and second, the Nazi belief that most of the banks were controlled by Jews. The intransigent Nazis felt called upon to break the "thralldom of interest" and thereby destroy the power of the banks over small and honest businessmen.

In April of 1933 the Nazis ordered an investigation of the banking business. It was the purpose of the investigation to bare the misuse of funds by banks and to propose a basic reform of the banking system. Yet the selection of personnel to serve on the investigating commission did not bode well for the purpose of the intransigent Nazis. The members were almost exclusively taken from banks and universities. Dr. Schacht was appointed as its chairman. The "revolutionary youth," as one economist complained, was not represented in the commission.[20]

The investigation lasted seven months, during which all party agencies were forbidden by Hitler to interfere with the banking system. The commission concentrated upon two problems: Shall the big banks be nationalized? What is the proper relationship between private and public banks? The battle was fought in public as well as behind closed doors.[21]

Gottfried Feder, the new undersecretary of the economic ministry under Schmitt, became the leader of the intransigent wing of the Nazis who were fighting for the nationalization of the banks. Feder had presented his point of view in the party program of 1920, and he restated it in the debate of 1933. He felt that private property should prevail in the manufacture, distribution, and transportation of goods, but that in the financial sphere, private interests had to give way to the common interests of the people. According to Feder, the creation and circulation of money should be the exclusive function of the government; the mortgage business, too, should be nationalized. Hence, Feder called for the nationalization of the commercial and mortgage banks. He wanted the small banks and savings banks, however, to be left undisturbed because their private interests would hardly conflict with the common interest of the people.[22]

Some younger economists, like Hermann Bente of Kiel University, favored nationalization of big banks as an antidote to the prevailing trend toward monopolies. These young economists held that bank trusts went far beyond the sphere of private business—that they did in fact accumulate political power—and believed that this concentration of private power compelled the state to nationalize the big banks. Nationalization would be advantageous for two reasons: Credit could be distributed more equitably, and more funds would become available to finance public-works programs. Moreover, nationalization would not reduce the efficiency of the banking system; and since management is an art in any economic order, it should be equally easy or difficult to practice this art in private or nationalized banks.[23]

Feder and his followers were opposed by Keppler, Hitler's economic counselor. Keppler, who represented the conservative wing of the party in economic questions, preferred the decentralization of the banking business and the breaking up of big banks, but he strongly opposed any extension of governmental activities into banking[24] and fought against the nationalization of banks. In this, he was fully supported by Schacht, who used all his influence in wielding public opinion against the nationalization of banks.

In the first meeting of the investigating commission, Schacht made nationalization the order of business. After a brief discussion, the commission rejected unanimously the nationalization of any section of the banking business.[25] Although many attempts were made during the following year to modify the proposals of the commission, its rejection of nationalization proved to be final.

The fight for and against the public banks was extremely intense. Strangely enough, Schacht, as the head of the central government bank, was the leader of the movement against the public banks, most of which were owned by municipal or provincial governments. Public banks, according to him, had expanded beyond their proper scope, and their number as well as their functions should be drastically reduced, with commercial banking reserved for private banks.[26]

Commercial banking was generally accepted by the Nazis as a private business, prior to their seizure of power. In the early years of the regime, however, some Nazis had usurped the management of governmental savings banks. These banking officials joined the intransigent wing of the party, in the issue of bank ownership, and used their new power to strengthen the position of public banks in party circles. The central organization of German savings banks was reorganized into a compulsory party organization. Hence, the opponents were well defined. Big banks, industrialists, and the conservative wing of the party took the side of the private banks, while the intransigent Nazis and the Nazified savings banks and public banks fought for a greater range of opportunities for governmental and savings banks.

The Nazified savings banks presented their demands at their annual conference in October, 1933. Feder, the leading speaker, fully supported their proposals: They should be fully represented on the banking commission, they should be legally authorized to extend their business into the field of commercial loans, and they should receive equal opportunities in dealing in securities and foreign exchange.[27] Feder's support increased the influence of the public banks and saved them from outright dissolution of their business. Furthermore, as undersecretary in the economics ministry, he used his position to increase the influence of the intransigent Nazis. But he was unable to achieve his goal. His enemies insisted that the savings banks should be limited to financing the real estate business, and this position prevailed in the banking commission, whose report was completed in December of 1933. Yet no action was taken. The two factions in the party were about equally strong, and the oligarchic clique could not arrive at a decision. Hence, the conflict had to be fought out between the public and private banks and their respective political supporters.

The governmental savings banks recovered quickly from the credit crisis in 1931. During the emergency, they had received a government loan of 1.1 billion marks. At the end of 1933 this loan had been reduced to 97 million marks. Repayment of the loan was primarily a result of rising savings deposits, for the credit crisis had shaken the confidence of the public in the private banks, and funds were shifted from private to public banks. Hence, these banks were able to restore their liquidity. The new controllers of the savings banks proposed to utilize these funds for new loans on two conditions. First, the savings banks were to be relieved from the special liquidity requirements imposed during the credit crisis. Such relief was granted partly in two decrees of March, 1934.[28] Second, all rates of interest were to be reduced by governmental action. Savings banks reduced their rates voluntarily. In order to increase the weight of these demands, the leaders of the savings banks offered to the party and the government a credit of 1.5 million marks for financing public-works projects.[29] Hence, pressure and favoritism were well mingled to influence party leaders for the public banks.

In contrast, the big private banks continued to suffer under the credit crisis. The "Big Three" in Berlin, for instance, had to write off a loss of 1.3 billion marks from 1931 to the end of 1933.[30] Many private banks could stay in business only because of continued governmental loans. Hence, the private banks had to make concessions to the investigators in return for a curbing of the increased competition from public banks. First, the big banks declared themselves ready to accept governmental supervision of the banking business. Second, they accepted compulsory organization of all banks, provided the leadership would not fall to the Nazified savings banks. This condition was accepted by Schacht. The new compulsory organization of banks was headed by C. Fischer, a party member and also one of the leading men of the *Reichskreditanstalt,* the largest governmental bank.[31] In consequence, the big bank trusts accepted the leadership of the largest public bank in order to find some allies against the Nazified savings banks.

The savings banks, however, refused to compromise. They wanted interest rates reduced for all forms of credit, they wanted to expand, and they insisted upon their right to lead organized banking. Everything seemed to favor their victory over the private banks. Schmitt was slipping, and many expected Feder to be his successor. Yet the intransigent Nazis overplayed their cards. They had underestimated the resilience of big business and overlooked the alliance between big business and the regular army. In May of 1934, Schacht, as head of the Central Bank, rejected the demand for reduced interests. At the same time, the negotiations between Hitler and von Blomberg about the SA were under way. Then, on June 30, 1934, the power situation was changed by the purge. The intransigent Nazis lost much of their power and submitted to the oligarchic clique. The relative increase in the power of big business gave Schacht the opportunity (*a*) to subdue the public banks and reduce the scope of their activities, (*b*) to install extensive governmental supervision of all banks, and (*c*) to impose compulsory organization upon all banks by giving the private banks positions of leadership.

Schacht insisted upon removing the intransigent Nazis from their positions in the savings banks. The president and vice-president of the central organization, Dr. Kleiner and Dr. Wein, respectively, took a vacation "on account of illness" in December, 1934. Schacht then appointed two commissionary managers whose function was to reorganize the headquarters and credit organizations of the savings banks.[32] The executive committee of the association was limited to two members, and its board of directors was cut from twenty-nine to eleven members. The budget was to be prepared and executed by three directors who were not responsible to the board for their actions. The association of savings banks was transformed into a compulsory membership branch of savings and small banks.[33] When the commissioners had done their work, Schacht appointed Dr. Heintze, a high official of his ministry, as president of the reorganized association. Member banks lost control over the association; its credit policy was now determined by Schacht himself. Big business, by using its regained political power, thus destroyed the stronghold of the intransigent Nazis in banking.

The policy of transforming the banking system into an instrument of government finance was first applied to the savings banks. The association of these banks had to grant a loan of 500 million marks to the federal government. No strings could be attached to the loan. The rate of interest was 4.65 per cent, which was below the prevailing long-term rate. Schacht reduced even the rates of interest by government order—a policy he had rejected prior to the purge. Reduction of the rates on current loans was accompanied by a statement that the government would soon seek lower interests for outstanding loans through a policy of conversion.[34]

In consequence, the intransigent Nazis and the savings banks were defeated by big business. By December, 1934, all opposition to the original report of the investigating banking commission had been eliminated. Its proposals, with minor changes, became the Banking Act of 1934.[35] The act rejected nationalization, withdrew the privileges of public banks, imposed extensive regulation upon all banks, and gave the Central Bank full authority to determine the policies of all banks. The banking act also laid the foundation for the regulation of money and capital markets. The banking reform was thus a crushing defeat of the anticapitalism of the intransigent Nazis.

The defeat of anticapitalism assured the survival of capitalist institutions, but the result was that big business had to accept the principle of governmental regulation of money and capital markets. Indeed, a few years later, market regulation was to become one of the most significant features of a state-directed capitalism.

CORPORATIVE ORGANIZATION

The Nazi party, in its program of 1920, generally demanded the corporative organization of the economy. This kind of organization was one of the twenty-five points in the

Nazi program. Yet the party itself had no definite ideas as to the nature of such an organization. Within the party three different concepts of a corporative order prevailed: (*a*) the corporative state; (*b*) the corporative economy; and (*c*) compulsory party associations.

The concept of a corporative economy *and* state was presented by Othmar Spann and his school. The state was regarded as an "estate" (*Stand*), the economic organizations as corporatives (*Berufsstand*). The state had peculiar functions of its own, the formation of foreign policy, for example; it also had the power to supervise the economic corporatives. Did that mean a dictatorship of the state over the corporatives? The universalist school, led by Spann, admitted that a state in a corporative order might be dictatorial. Yet such a dictatorship could have existed in a decentralized state,[36] not only in the highly centralized state desired by the Nazis. In the subsequent fight within the party, the group that favored a corporative state was defeated. The other group, fighting for a one-party state, won a decisive victory.[37]

The purely economic corporatives were to include agriculture, industry, handicrafts, and professions. These corporatives were to direct economic and social activities within those spheres and exercise executive, legislative, and judicial functions. Furthermore, each corporative was to participate in economic legislation concerning all sections of the economy. This version of a corporative order, compatible with a one-party state, was widely accepted in the Nazified middle groups. It was a part of the ideology of middle-class socialism.

The system of compulsory party associations comprising everyone in the nation was actually in opposition to any kind of corporativism, although many Nazis within such associations gave lip service to it. The leaders of the party associations insisted upon three points: (*a*) that leadership positions should go to Nazis only; (*b*) that membership in at least one of the compulsory party organizations should be all-inclusive;

(c) that all relevant activities should be completely dominated by the party. Consequently, there was a severe struggle
within the party on three issues: Who would lead the corporatives? What should be the relationship between compulsory
associations of the party and the new economic organizations?
How far could the dictatorial party-state tolerate economic
organizations, apart from, and independent of, compulsory
associations of the party? Thus, the corporative issue was
essentially the problem of how the power structure of the
party should be adjusted to the prevailing or new economic
order.

The conflict was solved in three ways: (1) Labor was subjected to the compulsory party associations; (2) from 1934 to
1937, big business was able to maintain economic organizations that were independent of any compulsory party association; (3) small business combined two different types of
associations, economic and political, within the same organizational network.

Various lines of action within small business can be distinguished during the years 1933–36. They included (a) synchronization of the artisans' and dealers' organizations with
the party, (b) a temporary delay of middle-class corporativism
owing to the Schmitt-Hitler compromise, and (c) a resultant
drive on the part of the artisan groups to establish the handicraft corporatives.

As the first step toward corporativism, the Nazis assumed
control of the small-business organizations. At first, the artisan organizations were either taken over by members of the
"fighting organizations of the middle class," who simply had
themselves elected to office, or were placed in office by a government appointed commissioner. Later, Dr. Heinrich Schild,
a Nazi who succeeded Dr. Meusch, attended the conferences
of the organizations as the new commissioner of handicraft.
At these conferences Schild either appointed the new leaders

or presented a list of candidates who had been sanctioned by the representatives.[38] Finally, the government dissolved a number of the organizations, such as the journeymen committees associated with the various guilds and Handicraft Chambers. New committees were then formed whose officials were selected from among leaders of the Labor Front.

A reorganization followed after the Nazis assumed leadership of the artisan and trade organizations. On May 3, 1933, the Fighting Organization of the Industrial Middle Class announced the formation of the Estates for Handicraft and Trade. Adrian von Renteln, the leader of the "fighting organization," became president of the new estate, which, however, remained temporarily a paper organization for the existing artisan organizations under Nazi leadership. The attempt to eliminate or reorganize the traditional organizations was interrupted by the Schmitt-Hitler compromise. This agreement hindered the evolving corporativism in handicraft and trade in three ways. First, Schmitt, as Minister of Economics, rejected the proposal of Dr. Meusch which Hugenberg had solicited in May of 1933. Second, the building up of the handicraft estate had to be postponed for a while. This resulted in a confused situation in which old and new organizations existed side by side. Last, and most important, was the dissolution, in August, 1933, of the Fighting Organization of the Industrial Middle Class. Two new Nazi organizations took its place, the NS Hago and the NS GHG,[39] which became the new instruments of party control.

What were the purpose and effect of these organizational changes? The NS Hago became the integral organization of the Party; it was the instrument through which the oligarchic clique tried to control and lead the middle groups. The NS GHG was the compulsory association that comprised all employers in trade and small business. It was incorporated into the Labor Front and governed by the leaders of the NS Hago.

In addition to these party organizations, the old guilds continued to exist. The result was a triple organizational network for artisans and merchants.[40]

The new organizational setup provided the framework for the conflict between big business and the Nazified groups over the issue of corporativism. In the fall of 1933, Minister Schmitt agreed to the reorganization of the traditional artisan and merchant organizations under two conditions. These groups could be unified if (a) the economic organizations of artisans and traders were kept separate from the two political organizations of the party, and (b) if these economic organizations were under the control of artisans who were independent of the party. These conditions were formally accepted by the oligarchic clique, but the Nazi leaders of the artisans and merchants used the agreement as a lever to unify the artisan organizations under Nazi domination.

The reorganization of the economic organizations proceeded rapidly. The National Organization of German Handicraft (*Reichsverband des deutschen Handwerks*) was dissolved on October 1, 1933 and was replaced by the previously announced Estate of German Handicraft, which was based upon the previously existing organizations of guilds and committees for journeymen and apprentices. The guilds were transformed into occupational corporatives (*Fachverbaende*), and the committees became a branch of the Labor Front. Everyone employed in handicraft had to become a member of the NS GHG, employers as well as employees. Hence, the Nazis in handicraft and labor achieved an agreement on their respective organizational functions. Moreover, a personal union was established between the Estate of Handicraft and the old Handicraft Chambers: The Nazi Schmidt-Wiesbaden became the official leader of both.[41]

Unification of the head organizations initiated a fight over the future role of handicraft. Big business insisted that the economic organizations of artisans should become a part of the economic organizations of industry. This was opposed by the new leaders of the Estate of Handicraft. Its new general secretary, Dr. Heinrich Schild, the former Nazi commissioner who had been given responsibility for reassigning the leadership of the artisan organizations, resisted this demand publicly. He said in a speech given on October 18, 1933, that the main question was whether the new corporatives should be organized along the lines of production and services or according to the social position of each producing group. Schild rejected the first alternative. He held that the social differences between artisan shop and factory were too great and important to be overlooked in the formation of estates and that industrial construction firms and artisans should not be pressed into the same corporative. The new estate supported its general secretary. It officially demanded the formation of five different estates which were to include industry, handicraft, trade, transportation, and agriculture.[42]

The leaders of the new Estate of Handicraft were successful at first. An act of November 29, 1933, authorized the Minister of Economics and the Minister of Labor to prepare a preliminary constitution for an Estate of Handicraft, based on the principles of appointed leadership and compulsory membership. The two ministers were also instructed to define the term "handicraft," simplify the prevailing artisan organizations, and determine their future functions; and the Minister of Economics was to consult with the Minister of Agriculture in regard to the line dividing agriculture from handicraft.[43]

The subsequent first decree on handicraft organizations was issued fourteen days prior to the Röhm purge. It dealt with the compulsory organization of the guilds. Four principles were to be applied to the new guilds. All leaders were to be appointed, not elected by members. Although guild assemblies could be held, the power to appoint local leaders rested with the Handicraft Chambers, and the guild assemblies had no power to hold the leaders responsible for their actions. Compulsory membership was the second principle of the new guilds. Every artisan had to become a member of his guild and the Labor Front. The same requirements were applied to the firms of the so-called "related artisan industries" which could be organized in supplementary guilds (special *Fachgruppen*). Of course, all members had to pay the fees set by their leaders; and the guilds and their leaders were the sole representatives of their respective crafts. All the remaining traditional organizations were dissolved. The guilds and the Estate of Handicraft alone could deal with artisan affairs, whatever their nature. Finally, each guild had certain legislative and executive functions which were not defined in the decree, but a special court of honor was established whose jurisdiction was at first very broadly conceived. For instance, the court of each guild could punish acts of unfair competition. Presumably, the court could also deal with most questions relating to the artisan economy.[44]

Obviously, these features stamped the new guilds as compulsory economic organizations. But who controlled them— the party or some business groups? An intense fight took place behind the scenes. Party leaders in the handicraft estate were determined to merge the features of a compulsory economic organization with those of a compulsory party organization. The actions through which the Nazis tried to achieve this goal were (*a*) to build an integral party organization into the handicraft estate; (*b*) to coordinate closely the handicraft estate with the Labor Front, the largest compulsory party association in the land.

The "historical day" of German handicraft came on January 26, 1934.[45] Dr. Schmitt, the Minister of Economics and representative of big business, officially appointed a Nazi, Schmidt-Wiesbaden, as the leader of German handicraft (*Reichshandwerksführer*). Schmidt was also appointed as president of the Handicraft Chambers. Heinrich Schild was appointed general secretary of the Estate of Handicraft. On the same day, the leader of handicraft appointed his thirteen regional deputies. All were party members, responsible to Schmidt-Wiesbaden for all artisan questions in their region. Actually, they had mainly political and promotional functions. The regional leaders organized all the meetings and conferences of artisan organizations, watched over relations with the press and public, and maintained contact with governmental agencies. Incidentally, the regions of the estate coincided with those of the trustees of labor. Most important were the party functions of these deputies, who had to establish a personnel department with files of all actual or potential leaders in handicraft. This enabled them to place Nazis in every office of the Estate of Handicraft.[46]

The Nazis were eager to obtain the right to appoint the 20,000 local officials and 800 district leaders of the guilds. Said Schild, the general secretary of the estate: "The experience of the agricultural estate has shown that the self-government of estates must be limited by the right of the party to determine the personnel policies of the Estate of Handicraft. The appointments," he announced, "will be made in agreement with the political organization of the party." The instructions of July 3, 1934, accompanying the first handicraft decree, contained a provision that all local-organization leaders of the estate had to be party members. Similarly, all local leaders of journeymen had to be representatives of the Labor Front.[47] The instructions, which were issued by the Ministry of Economics, gave the Nazis the desired opportunity to build an integral organization in the Estate of Handicraft. The local leaders of the guilds were taken from the NS Hago, the party organization of artisans. Integral party organizations thus monopolized the leadership positions and thereby tried to transform the guilds into affiliated organizations of the party. What started as a fight for corporative middle-class socialism eventually resulted in domination of the middle groups by the party.

Domination of the NS Hago over the Estate of Handicraft took care of the masters in artisan shops. But who should lead the journeymen and apprentices? Leadership was equally claimed by the Labor Front and the NS Hago. The intra-party fight was settled through an agreement between the two organizations. Schmidt-Wiesbaden was made head of the division of handicraft in the Labor Front, and, in the party, he was appointed division chief of the NS Hago in charge of artisan affairs. At the same time, all journeymen and appren-tices in handicraft, individually organized within the Labor Front, became corporate members of the handicraft estate.[48] Personal union of leadership—effected by the handicraft lead-ers becoming officials of the Labor Front—and corporate membership in party organizations were the means by which Nazi leaders divided political domination between them-selves.

Consequently, the Nazis were able to establish within the handicrafts a corporative order which contained all the fea-tures of a compulsory business organization and of a com-pulsory party organization. It has to be emphasized, however, that neither the formation of an integral organization, nor the agreement with the Labor Front, nor the first decree on the corporative organization of handicraft received the ap-proval of big business. The decree of June 15, 1934, was pub-lished after Minister Schmitt had become a member of the Keppler circle and was under effective pressure from the SS. The first administrative instruction under this decree, mak-ing party membership a requirement for officeholders, was issued on July 3, 1934, and signed by Dr. Erich Wienbeck, the commissioner on affairs of the middle class in the eco-nomic ministry. This was at a time when Schacht had not yet taken control of the ministry. The Nazis in handicraft thus used the uncertainties preceding the purge and accompanying the change in the leadership of the ministry to lay the cornerstone of their corporative order. Schacht was thus faced with the accomplished fact of a party-organized handicraft estate when he became Minister of Economics in August, 1934.

When, in July of 1934, big business again took over full command of economic policy as a result of the von Blomberg-Hitler arrangements, it tried to achieve two goals relative to artisan corporativism. The aims were (*a*) the destruction of the integral organization within the handicraft estate and (*b*) the reduction of the estate to a compulsory business organization, fully under the control of big business. The actions which followed gave full evidence of the intentions of big business.

The intransigent Nazis in the estate became Schacht's first victims. Dr. Heinrich Schild, general secretary, and N. Zelany, deputy leader of the estate, were both dismissed by Schacht. Schild's place was taken over by Dr. Schüler, who until that time had been the general secretary of the Handicraft Chamber in Berlin.[49] These actions against the top leaders were followed by several others. Schacht instructed the new handicraft honor courts to establish disciplinary departments; all new officials of guilds and chambers had to sign a statement in which they recognized the higher authority of these departments. It was the function of the departments to judge any official who acted contrary to his duties. Such officials could either be dismissed or sent on "vacation" for an indefinite time.[50] Officially, intransigent Nazis were eliminated not because they were party members but because they had "misused" the authority of their offices.

Similarly, the power to appoint the personnel of guilds and chambers came under the general supervision of Schacht. A decree of November 9, 1934, modified the preceding decree of July 3, 1934. It gave the leader of the estate three rights: (a) to determine the budget of the chambers and guilds, (b) to set fees for the members, and (c) to instruct the guilds and chambers that any additional expenditures required prior official approval. All these actions could be taken only with the consent of the Minister of Economics.

Equally important was the provision that all officials of the chambers, but not the guilds, would be subject to the regulations of the civil service. That is to say, Nazis in the chambers had to pass examinations and satisfy the rigid requirements of the civil-service code. This removed many of them from their positions. In cases of doubt, the decree specified, the final decision would rest with the Minister of Economics. Moreover, all leaders of guilds had to be appointed in the future by the Handicraft Chambers, the secretaries of which were government officials. Hence, the regional deputies of the leader of handicraft lost their power to appoint party members as officials of guilds and chambers.

With these measures Schacht reduced the power of the NS Hago as an integral party organization in the Handicraft Estate. But only the most intransigent Nazis were ousted from their positions as guild officials. The thirteen regional deputies under the national leader of handicrafts, for instance, remained at their posts. Schacht merely limited their functions and controlled their finances. Thus, an instruction of March 23, 1935, overhauled the organizational setup of the guilds, authorizing the Minister of Economic Affairs to reduce the number of national guilds and to dissolve the regional offices of the guilds. Within a few months the number of the national guilds was reduced to fifty. The others were either dissolved or merged. All the regional offices of the guilds were dissolved if they acted as agents of national guilds.[51] This eliminated some of the over-organization which the Nazis had imposed upon artisans.

Extortionate membership fees and the expenditures of artisan organizations created much bitter feeling among shopowners. Their complaints were fully utilized by Schacht and the economic press against the party officeholders. Criticism centered upon the personnel expenditures of Nazi officials. Many instances of wasted funds were published. In one central organization of the retail trade, for instance, total expenditures rose from 280,000 marks in 1932–33 to 1.7 million in 1934–35. One of its sub-organizations with 20,000 members had a personnel budget of 40,000 marks in 1932–33. Two years later its membership had increased to 54,600 and its personnel budget to 219,000. The chairman alone, occupying an honorary position, had a salary of 36,000 marks.[52]

The use of funds for paying exorbitantly high salaries to Nazis gave Schacht the opportunity for two coordinated actions. He instituted a strict budget control over the chambers and guilds and also specified a scale for membership fees in two decrees. A preliminary measure established two principles: Every member had to pay a minimum fee; members with larger establishments had to pay a supplementary fee according to their business turnover.[53] On July 7, 1936, came the final regulation of fees for all business organizations in handicraft as well as in industry. Three different memberships were established, and the fees were graduated according to the kind of membership and business turnover.

Although Schacht was unable to reduce expenditures of the artisan organizations appreciably, he certainly equalized the burden on individual members and imposed financial restrictions upon the new Nazi officials. Hence, party domination became less effective. The intransigent Nazis quite freely expressed their disappointment, and the oligarchic clique reinterpreted its stand on corporativism. Point twenty-five of the party program, it was said officially,[54] had to be understood in the light of the prevailing situation of 1920. In the Third *Reich*, the leader had decided that the corporative order could come only after an extensive education of the German people.

Gradually, Schacht introduced the policy of reducing the Estate of Handicraft to the status of a mere organization under the control of big business. In his first decree of November, 1934, following the law of the preceding February, Schacht reversed Schmitt's concession to the Nazis. Handicraft was eliminated as a separate estate. It was no longer on the same basis as agriculture or the professions. Instead, handicraft was one of twelve groups of the industrial economy (*gewerbliche Wirtschaft*); it was now a part of that sector of the economy which was under the control of Schacht. Subsequent actions were all aimed at transforming the handicraft estate into a business organization that would be beyond the control of the Nazi party.[55]

The second decree on handicraft, of January 18, 1935, reorganized the Handicraft Chambers. The chambers were organized upon the three principles of leadership, compulsory membership, and responsibility to the government. Presidents and personnel of the chambers would have to be governmental officials and appointed by the Minister of Economics. Board members of each chamber had to be full-fledged artisans. They had to have their master title and were required to have been registered in the list of artisan establishments for more than one year. These requirements gave preference to experienced artisans and discriminated against many younger Nazis. The decree assigned a long list of functions to the governmentally controlled chambers. Two functions overshadowed all others: (1) The chambers alone could supervise firms within any given area of handicrafts activity, especially in vocational training and the production of artisan goods; (2) the chambers had the right to appoint guild leaders, change guild bylaws, and veto any undesirable decisions reached by the guild.

In fact, Schacht tried to make the guilds subsidiaries of

the chambers. He definitely prevented the Nazis from incorporating the chambers into the handicraft estate, and the term itself was never accepted by Schacht. The official name used was "Economic Organization of Handicraft." Schmidt-Wiesbaden, the leader of the estate, was not even mentioned in the second decree on handicraft. In fact, the chambers became the instrument through which Schacht supervised and subdued the guilds, even when they were still under Nazi influence.

ORGANIZATIONAL TOTALITY

The non-Nazi political parties, the trade unions, and a large number of social organizations had been wiped out in 1933 through the process of *Gleichschaltung*. The organizations were dissolved, and their property was taken over by Nazi organizations. The same tactics were not applied to business organizations, since the Nazi commissioners had been withdrawn from the offices of private concerns or trade associations; but in 1935–36 the Labor Front sought to reverse this course of events. Its new claim of "organizational totality" involved a plan for the Labor Front to incorporate all groups and guilds, determine their policies, and thereby establish party control over the organizations of big and small business.

The first attempt to establish "organizational totality" came in a special decree of June 13, 1935, when Dr. Ley formed the National Chamber of Labor and eighteen regional chambers, which were intended to give the Labor Front a counterpart of the Chambers of Industry. This was to be achieved by ordering employers to become individual members, and the Minister of War was invited to delegate officers to the meetings of the regional chambers. While the business groups boycotted the Chambers of Labor, the Minister of War authorized civilian officials to represent his ministry as a large employer.[56] But the boycott was effective; as

an attempt by the party to seize control over business organizations, the Chambers of Labor were a failure.

As a next step, the Labor Front concentrated its efforts
upon the handicraft organizations. One of the subdivisions of
the Labor Front that had organized the artisans and journeymen was given the new name of "German Handicraft." At
the national conference of the handicraft organizations in
Frankfurt in 1936, the Labor Front dominated the meetings.
Dr. von Renteln delivered a speech in which he instructed all
artisan organizations to clear all public meetings with his
NS Hago at the headquarters of the Nazi party. Shortly after
the conference, Schmidt-Wiesbaden was instructed by Ley
to present to him proposals for the transfer of the guilds to
the Labor Front, and when Schmidt-Wiesbaden refused, he
was threatened with removal from his position in the Labor
Front. Eventually, Schmidt-Wiesbaden resigned from his offices in the guilds, chambers, and Labor Front, rather than
obey Ley's instructions.[57]

In reply to these attacks, Schacht wrote a confidential letter
to Ley in which were recorded all the efforts of the Labor
Front to obtain control over the handicraft organizations.
Schacht declared that the economic groups and guilds were
not only essential for implementing the policies of his ministry but "were independent organizations of private concerns that were also indispensable for military reasons."[58]
Very emphatically, Schacht stated that the Leipzig agreement
(between the Ministers of Economics and Labor, on the one
hand, and the Labor Front on the other) of March, 1935, had
completed the economic and social self-organization of the
economy. Ley was also informed that von Renteln had no
authority to give directives to organizations that were responsible to the Minister of Economics.

In a twenty-two-page memorandum of July 20, 1936, Ley
surveyed the whole history of the Labor Front in its relations
with the economic groups of handicraft and industry, ex-

pressing his conviction that the agreement of Leipzig was a step towards the eventual incorporation of the economic groups into the Labor Front. Accordingly, Ley proposed to Schacht a new scheme of organization in which (*a*) the Chambers of Industry, Trade, and Handicraft would remain unchanged; (*b*) the economic office (*Wirtschaftsamt*) in the Labor Front, in accordance with the Leipzig agreement, would be headed by a man of Schacht's choice who would also issue the economic and vocational instructions for the operation of the office; (*c*) some private concerns—such as exporters, armament-producers, or members of cartels—would be allowed to form organizations for performing specified tasks, but these organizations would have to be dissolved as soon as their assignments had been performed. Ley left no place in his proposed plan for the economic groups of business. He presented evidence that many executive secretaries of these groups had formerly been in charge of employer associations and concluded that this duplication of leadership indicated the economic groups' acceptance of the exploitative policies of the employer associations, for the revival of which there was no place in the Nazi regime.[59]

Rather than seeking an agreement with Ley, Schacht in subsequent weeks informed Hitler "of the proven participation of local agents of the Labor Front in the strikes of the last week" (5.1260, frame 10817114). In negotiations with Hess's office, Schacht received a letter from Martin Bormann which contained this sentence: "The Führer does not approve that the Labor Front characterize itself as the organization comprising all gainfully employed Germans."[60] The oligarchic clique of the party decided to dissolve the NS Hago at party headquarters, thereby indicating that the top Nazis regarded the coalition with the generals and big business as being of more importance than party domination over the handicraft organizations.

This step had been ordered by Rudolf Hess, who was

deputy leader of the party at the time and acting under instructions from Hitler; but the decision was not final. The Labor Front, supported by one or another of the *Gauleiter,* continued its attacks upon the handicraft organizations—under the slogan that "the party gives orders to the state." Furthermore, Ley published a secret decree signed by Hitler on October 24, 1934. In presenting this abortive decree (which did not become law because Schacht had refused to countersign it) to the public,[61] Ley gave the functions of the Labor Front a new interpretation. In addition to indoctrinating workers in Nazi ideology, providing facilities for physical training, and organizing sport events, the Labor Front now claimed the right to direct or supervise all vocational training in plants and schools. Ley also insisted upon the principle of organizational totality. All economic organizations, especially those of industry, trade, handicraft, and transportation, should become members of the Labor Front and thereby become subject to its jurisdiction. The implication was that these economic organizations would now also become mass organizations dominated by the Nazi party.

One day after Ley's publication of Hitler's decree Schacht sent a circular letter to the offices of the business groups in which he rejected Ley's interpretation. The published decrees of the Labor Front, he said, had no binding validity for the economic groups and chambers of business. He told the members and officers of these organizations that any intervention of the Labor Front should be immediately reported to him.[62]

In this explosive situation, General Georg Thomas, chief of the economic section in the Ministry of War, seemed to side with the Labor Front. In the last week of November, 1936, he delivered a speech on the tasks of the Labor Front in regard to economic preparedness. The news agency of the Nazi party distributed a report of Thomas' speech. The report contained the statement that "insuring the stability of

prices and wages and providing for the vocational training of
skilled workers and apprentices were functions of the Labor
Front."[63] As a matter of fact, this particular sentence did not
occur in Thomas' original speech. The Nazis had deliberately falsified the meaning of the speech in order to break
the resistance of business organizations. But this trickery did
not work. In addition to many letters of protest, Thomas
received a detailed statement from the *Reichsgruppe* for Industry and also a letter from Dr. Mansfeld, head of the wage
section in the Ministry of Labor. To correct the falsification,
Thomas had the original of his speech distributed to the officials of the business organizations and officials of the economic agencies of the government. The leading newspapers
published a guarded but clearly understandable correction—
written by Thomas himself—of the published version of the
speech.[64] Thus the trick had the effect of uniting the generals and business organizations more effectively in their opposition to the aggressive tendencies of the Labor Front.

Of equal importance was the question of whether officials
of business organizations had to have the explicit approval of
the *Gauleiter* in the various party districts. A dispute arose
on this issue in 1935. *Gauleiter* Schwede-Coburg of Pom-
erania ordered Dr. Lange, the president of the chamber of
commerce in Stettin, to resign his office. Dr. Lange referred
the case to Schacht, who asked for evidence, interrogated Dr.
Lange in Berlin, decided that the charge of insufficient initiative was unproven, and rejected Lange's request for release from his office. Schacht also wrote Hess, who agreed
with Schacht's decision and promised to inform the *Gauleiter*
accordingly. Dr. Lange, wanting to re-establish his contact
with Schwede-Coburg, asked for an interview with him.
When Lange's request was refused, steps were taken to arrange a meeting in which Schacht would appear as the main
speaker. Infuriated, Schwede-Coburg ordered the members
of the directorate and the board of the chamber of commerce

to resign from their positions, refused Schacht's invitation to
drive with him to the meeting place in Stettin, and ostentatiously declined to hear Schacht's speech. In punishment for
this deliberate "affront to the Ministry of Economics and thus
to the authority of the state," Schacht removed all those members of the chamber of commerce who had refused to hear his
speech from their positions in the economic groups.[65] When
Schwede-Coburg asked that the dismissals be rescinded and
Dr. Lange be dismissed because as a party member he had
been disobedient to his *Gauleiter,* Schacht refused the request, underlined that his decision was covered by his original
understanding with Hess, and suggested that the *Gauleiter*
should accommodate himself to Schacht's policy. Not the approval of the *Gauleiter* but the authoritative decision of the
minister was the means by which positions of leadership were
filled in economic organizations.

In order to protect the handicraft organizations more effectively against future encroachments of *Gauleiter* and the
Labor Front, Schacht utilized the decree of July 7, 1936,
which had authorized him to reorganize the business groups.
A law was passed that established new economic chambers
(*Wirtschaftskammern*) for the purpose of bringing them under the control of the business organizations and giving the
handicraft groups support in their resistance to the Labor
Front.[66] Creating the new chambers also forestalled the attempts of many *Gauleiter* to impose the party's *Gau* structure
upon the economic organizations. In an instruction issued on
July 27, 1936, Schacht ordered the divisions of the Ministry
of Economics to transfer some of the daily administrative
tasks to the business groups in order to free the officials from
details and to promote the principle of economic self-government within the business organizations.

Another conflict with the party and the Labor Front arose
in the state of Mecklenburg. The Labor Front, in the fall of

1936, demanded that there be a personal union of leadership, on the district level, between the handicraft organization and the handicraft department of the Labor Front.[67] When this demand was rejected, several of the existing district leaders were dismissed and replaced by officials of the Labor Front. The resulting conflict was reported to Schacht, who found that the regional handicraft leader of the Nordmark had not approved of these changes in personnel. Schacht ordered the dismissal of the new officials and asked for the appointment of practicing artisans; but these new appointees did not receive the prior approval of the district leaders of the Nazi party. The result was that the conflict between the Labor Front and the handicraft organization was extended into a struggle between the Minister of Economics and the *Gauleiter* in the state of Mecklenburg. How was this dispute resolved when Schacht ceased to function as Minister of Economics in September of 1937?

Gauleiter Hildebrandt permitted the Labor Front to organize a rival handicraft organization. All handicraftsmen who were either party members or local political leaders were instructed in closed meetings to vote openly either for the existing handicraft organization or the substitute provided by the Labor Front. In the western part of the state not less than three fourths voted for the Labor Front, while in the eastern part the opposite result was reported. Those who resigned from the old organization were threatened with a fine of 500 marks, while those who revealed that they acted under pressure from the district leader were dismissed from the party. Dismissal was justified with the remark that "such information was immediately reported to Schacht,"[68] and that such action was damaging to the prestige of the Nazi party.

The rival organizations coexisted for several months during which the dispute was fought in the newspapers, in meetings, and even through the distribution of leaflets. The officials at the headquarters in Berlin could not act because there was no national leader of the handicraft organization, since agreement on who should replace Schmidt-Wiesbaden could not be reached. The party in Mecklenburg was determined to fight for the principle that any official appointed in the state would have to receive the prior approval of the party leaders. In the absence of Schacht, officials of the Ministry of Economics asked for the intervention of Rudolf Hess, while deputy leader Lehmann of the handicraft organization gave a detailed report to Göring. The dispute had thus become a quarrel between party and state, both represented by leading Nazis.

The agencies of the state remained victorious. The regional leader of handicraft in Nordmark, Ferdinand Schramm, was a former district official of the Nazi party. He had—contrary to Schacht's instructions—permitted the political officials to participate in the selection of leaders for the handicraft organizations. This practice, Schramm wrote to district leader Sievert, was not adhered to when the conflict arose in Mecklenburg. Schramm then asked, in December of 1937, for the retroactive consent of the party to the appointments of the controversial handicraft officials.[69] When this effort at compromise failed, Göring as temporary Minister of Economics signed a decree which reappointed the same rejected handicraft officials. The *Gauleiter* and his district leaders in Mecklenburg accepted Göring's decision as final and withdrew their support from the rival organization of the Labor Front.[70]

At the suggestion of *Gauleiter* Karl D. Kaufmann of Hamburg, Göring appointed Ferdinand Schramm as leader of the handicraft organization in January of 1938. Two months later, Minister Funk had already signed the letter that tried to dismiss Schramm. Göring successfully intervened.[71] He not only kept Schramm in office but also prevented the Labor

Front from realizing its goal of "organizational totality."
Business organizations thus survived the onslaught of the
Labor Front in the second phase of the regime because, in
their efforts to remain outside the party's jurisdiction, they
were able to secure the support of Hitler and Göring.

DEFEAT OF THE ARTISAN ECONOMY

CHAPTER FOUR

Big business won its fight against anticapitalism and the guilds. This raises the question of what happened to the plan for an artisan economy, the third part of the small-business reform program. This program originated from an aversion to the capitalist market system and the cutthroat competition created by large factories that produced cheap goods at prices below the unit costs of skilled masters. To fight such competition, the annual conference of the old artisan organization adopted a demand for closed markets which were to be extensively regulated by governmentally authorized organizations of small sellers.[1] The central feature of the artisan economy was thus expected to be a system of self-regulated markets of artisans and dealers acting collectively.

The Great Depression, which severely hit all branches of small business, gave rise to persistent demands for emergency measures to save the economic life of small firms. Just as the big concerns clamored for armament orders, so the Nazified small firms called for a public-works program that would provide orders for handicraft and trade. Elimination of special taxes on houseowners, tax relief for shopowners and storekeepers, and a moratorium on the loans of small debtors were urged upon the government to keep the financial ship of small business afloat. The Nazi movement fully accepted these emergency demands of small business in their political campaigns, and the first Hitler government accepted an emergency public-works program.

There was, however, a difference of opinion between small and big business about the significance and duration of the economic-recovery program for small firms. Leaders of big business and of the military regarded the recovery program as a short-lived emergency measure to be terminated at the first opportunity. Leaders of the Nazified artisan organizations, however, accepted the notion that economic recovery should provide the opportunity for introducing the main features of their ideal of an artisan economy. As a result, an organizational conflict arose between big and small business. What were the specific issues of this conflict? By which actions did big business succeed in limiting the recovery program and finally defeat the attempt to build up a distinct artisan economy in Germany?

RECOVERY OF SMALL FIRMS

There is no reason to describe in detail the public-works program of the Nazi government in the first phase of the regime.[2] Of particular interest to us, rather, are those recovery measures which became steppingstones for the attempt to build up an artisan economy. Such measures include (*a*) the embargo upon the establishment of new retail stores, (*b*) the public subsidies for repair and improvement of residential houses, (*c*) the fight against unfair competition by eliminating the new sweatshops created by the depression (*Schwarzarbeit*).

An act of May 12, 1933, imposed an embargo upon all new retail stores for six months.[3] Originally, this law was regarded as an exception to the legally guaranteed principles of free trade and free competition. Subsequently, the act was repeatedly extended and gradually provided the framework for governmental regulation of the retail and wholesale trade. Permits were required for the establishment of a new retail store or the modification of an existing one. A permit also became necessary when a store was sold or transferred to a new manager.

Since the government's goal was to reduce the number of retail stores, permits were granted only in exceptional cases, namely, when there was a special demand for a new store in a given locality. The issue of a permit was also dependent upon the personal reliability of a businessman and his vocational training and knowledge as a retailer. Candidates who could not satisfy these requirements were rejected.

What began as an exception became the rule. The government decided who was and who was not to be in the retail business and in addition passed on all transfers of retail property. Gradually, the professed willingness to return to free trade disappeared. Even Schacht concurred with this point of view when he agreed in December, 1935, that the law pertaining to retailers should be made permanent. This was his concession to the intransigent Nazis in the retail business who clamored for a "new order" in trade. Moreover, entry into the business was made dependent upon personal and financial qualifications which were examined by government agencies. The intransigent Nazis concluded that an elaborate system of vocational training for everyone engaged in trade or handicraft was an indispensable feature of an artisan economy.

The so-called irregular work (*Schwarzarbeit*), or production of goods in sweatshops, became widespread during the depression. Laborers on relief were employed at very low pay by firms who had no charters and paid no social-insurance premiums or business-turnover taxes; they sold their products much below regular prices. These uncharted firms. were said to constitute cutthroat competition that had to be eliminated if the regular firms were to survive. Three lines of action were adopted. The Nazis utilized their private armies as well as the regular police to raid the premises of suspected firms. These agents of violence checked the books for wages and taxes paid, or prices charged. Moreover, employment compensation or welfare offices eliminated "illegal" laborers from their lists and refused to pay them any relief.

How were "illegal" laborers to be identified? Employment offices began to issue labor passes to bona fide laborers. Labor passes were first made compulsory in the restaurant business of Berlin. All laborers in this line of business had to have passes dated earlier than December 1, 1933; if they did not, they were regarded as illegal workers.[4] Guilds issued identification cards for regular firms. The common experience was that only a fraction of the turnover tax was paid to the government. As a result of these actions, the irregularity in business was eliminated within a period of two years. This experience suggested several lessons to the Nazis. First, the worker's pass, originating in the fight against the illegal employment of laborers, became the "labor book" which was imposed upon all laborers in 1936 and incorporated into the war economy. Second, artisan guilds found that the registration of artisan shops, introduced in 1930, was incomplete. Hence, the artisan guilds demanded a compulsory registration of all small firms. Finally, the finance offices relied upon the experiments in some cities where a double-entry bookkeeping system was introduced for the collection of the turnover tax.[5] In 1935, all firms were compelled to keep books on all ingoing and outgoing transactions for the calculation of the turnover tax. The result was a great increase of revenue from this tax.

The public-works program of 1933 and 1934 was devised primarily for the benefit of small business. The government mainly subsidized construction of semimilitary projects (national highways) and the repair or improvement of residential houses. An applicant for a subsidy had to present a contract with an artisan firm, a statement of the expected cost, and an estimate of time necessary for completion. Up to September 7, 1933, as a condition for receiving a subsidy, the artisan firm had to be registered with the Handicraft Chambers. This provision was dropped upon the insistence of Minister Schmitt. Guilds and Handicraft Chambers participated significantly in the execution of the program. They formed various "fronts" for the construction, electric, and gas industries, and by means of these fronts directed the placing of orders and the delivery of materials, and thus tried to raise the prices of materials and services to the predepression levels.

This program of repair and rebuilding supplied remodeled homes as follows:*

1933	1934	1935	1936
69,240	129,180	50,500	35,100

* Hans Kruschwitz, "Die Deutsche Wohnungswirtschaft seit 1933," *Jahrbücher für Nationalökonomie und Statistik*, CXL (1937), 30 ff.

It was officially estimated that the public subsidies for the repair and rebuilding of existing houses gave rise to a total expenditure of 2.8 billion marks. Of this total, government subsidies were said to be around 500 million marks.[6] These figures were questioned, however, and a more conservative estimate, which appeared in *Deutscher Volkswirt* in 1934, suggested that a total expenditure of 2 billion marks had created employment for about 800,000 laborers. The writer of the article came to the conclusion that most of these private and public funds "financed the public-works program of the middle class."[7] The funds benefited primarily two groups. Orders for the repair and improvement of houses—new residential houses were not included in the program—went primarily to artisans in the construction industry. These artisans comprised, in terms of volume, about 50 per cent of the whole handicraft business. Improvements of houses appreciably increased the value of real estate. Houseowners who had suffered greatly during the depression were able to change business offices into apartments, and remodel large into small apartments and thus lease their properties to renters with lower incomes. It is not surprising that the beneficiaries of the program were greatly disappointed when the government refused to grant new subsidies for this program in April, 1934. Tax relief and guaranteed loans for investment in new houses took the place of the subsidy program for old houses in 1933–34.

Two inferences can be drawn from the various recovery measures of the Nazi government for the middle groups. On the one hand, the recovery of small business was merely a transitional phase of a government program that lasted about eighteen months in all. It was increasingly replaced by a rearmament program that involved extensive orders and subsidies for big business, especially in the heavy industries. On the other hand, the experience of fighting the depression convinced the artisan leaders that recovery was not enough. The ideal of an artisan economy took the form of a definite program of action. Control of the retail business had taught the Nazified dealers the need for a comprehensive system of vocational training in trade as well as in handicraft. The fight against the so-called irregular firms convinced many artisans that compulsory organization and registration of small firms were highly desirable. The governmentally subsidized construction boom had given the guilds and chambers an opportunity to experiment with practical economic planning. These organizations had used the occasion to eliminate "inefficient firms" through registration: they supervised the placing of orders, the delivery of materials, and the hiring of laborers; and they increased prices and regulated the markets for the services of craftsmen.[8] Mere recovery did not satisfy small business. As big business increasingly insisted upon free-market prices for handicraft products, the artisans made stronger attempts to fix their prices through concerted action and clamored more loudly for a reorganization of the economy.

FEATURES OF AN ARTISAN ECONOMY

An examination of the insistent praise for the artisan ideal suggests that the artisan economy would have four distinct features. First, guilds and chambers would determine who should enter and practice an artisan business. Every firm would be registered and receive a handicraft license (*Handwerkerkarte*) as a permit for doing business. The aim was thereby to transform each handicraft into a closed business.

Second, everyone in an artisan shop would receive or would have already received an extensive vocational training. This demand included extensive training of apprentices and journeymen followed by detailed examinations. Graduation certificates were regarded as prerequisites to taking a master's examination after "extensive" experience. Only a master could receive a certificate of competence, which in turn would be the indispensable requirement for the issue of a handicraft license, constituting a permit to open shop.

Third, guilds and chambers would be given the authority to regulate the markets and fix prices for all products and services of artisans. This would involve four steps: the setting up of quality standards and the granting of appropriate labels for all artisan products; the clearing of markets by prescribing procedures for the marketing of artisan products; the fixing of prices for the various kinds of goods; the fixing of wages for employees and settling of wage disputes. Hence, these organizations would control all interactions between artisan firms, their suppliers, and customers.

The fourth feature of the artisan economy would be a code of honor introduced for all artisans. It would contain all essential principles for the economic behavior of everyone engaged in handicraft. Special estate courts would be set up to punish those who violated the code of honor.

These were the four principles of the artisan economy for which the Nazified guilds and chambers fought in 1934. How far did they succeed in establishing such an artisan economy against the opposition of big business?

In June of 1934 and January of 1935, three decrees were issued supplementing the handicraft law. The first decree established a system of honor courts. The second decree imposed a system of vocational training, and the third decree embodied the principles of a closed craft. None of the decrees, however, authorized the handicraft organizations to regulate markets and fix prices. Hence, a fight ensued between small and big business about the specific meaning of the decrees and about the regulation of artisan markets.[9]

Let us begin with the three decrees and see how they were applied to the artisan economy. Closing the artisan economy was accomplished by the three devices of defining an artisan shop, registering artisans, and listing handicraft branches. The artisan shops were classified into two kinds of firms. They were either "regular handicraft establishments" supplying goods to buyers, or they were "related handicraft establishments" performing artisan services for customers. Owners and managers of these two kinds of artisan establishments had to have handicraft licenses in order to operate such a shop. The names of such owners or managers were included in the register of artisans.

In addition, a classification of industries was required which involved a decision as to whether a branch of business belonged to (a) handicraft, (b) agriculture, (c) industry, or (d) trade. This was accomplished through a list mentioning the various branches of handicraft. The original agreement between the Minister of Economics and the Minister of Agriculture covered seventy-two industries, including two hundred branches which were regarded as belonging to handicraft. Two guiding rules were laid down: Every artisan shop in handicraft had to belong to a guild and Handicraft Chamber; any firm not included in the list of handicraft establishments could not become a member, even if it produced artisan products.[10] This simple arrangement, however, was soon discarded, and a bitter struggle over the question of which firms and industries belonged to handicraft began. The details of this fight will concern us presently.

The vocational training of artisans was divided into three phases, for apprentices, journeymen, and masters and ending with an examination at each stage. Apprentices and journeymen had to be registered and had to pass examinations, and a master's examination was made the basis for issuing a certificate of competence. Control over the administration of these examinations was granted to the Handicraft Chambers—guilds were not even mentioned in the decree. Nor did the training of apprentices become a monopoly of the artisan shops. Section 22 of the law specified that apprenticeships and journeyships were not required as prerequisites for a master's examination. A skilled laborer who had received his training in an industrial plant could become a candidate for a master's examination. The guilds, however, were fully prepared to demand a clear sequence of training and examination from apprentice to master. All control over training should be vested in the handicraft organizations, provided these were actually dominated by the guilds. Hence, there ensued a fight for the control of handicraft training.

The first decree established estate courts at the seat of each chamber. Their most important function was to settle cases of unfair competition. In this capacity, however, the courts were shortly to be checked by the fact that Schacht was soon in a position to nullify their economic functions. He instructed all economic organizations to get his permission prior to the indictment of a firm by the honor courts. Thus it was declared that the courts would be granted permission to act only if the indictments were not aimed at limiting competition.[11] In addition, the power to pardon defendants or modify the decisions of honor courts was transferred from Hitler to Schacht. Schacht thus got control over the existing courts of honor, which played a very insignificant role indeed, and thus need not be dealt with at any length here.[12]

A CLOSED ARTISAN SECTOR

The closing of crafts (usually called a protection of handicrafts—*Berufsschutz*) to undesired members created two problems: How could the incompetents in handicraft be eliminated; and what line would effectively separate handicraft from industry, agriculture, and trade?

The fight against incompetents in handicraft remained in the preliminary stage up to 1935. It concentrated upon the issue of who had taken, or should be permitted to take, a master's examination to receive a certificate of competence. The relevant decree distinguished three cases. First, shopowners who were registered in a handicraft roll prior to January 1, 1932, were exempted from the required master's examination. Equally exempted were the old artisans who had been born prior to 1900, even if they had not been previously registered. Second, all younger owners not registered before December 31, 1931, were given a period of grace. They had to take the master's examination prior to December 31, 1939. Third, every newcomer had to take his master's examination prior to receiving a license and establishing a business. In consequence of these examinations, the guilds and chambers could apply their rules of admission to the artisan economy only to young applicants for a master's title whose applications preceded 1937. Thus the fight against incompetents in handicraft was postponed. This fight was not a part of the attempt to establish an artisan economy but was a feature of the squeeze on small business, which began in 1938 and became a part of the war economy.

The organizational network for the giving of master's examinations was set up speedily. A list was published of all crafts in which master's examinations had to be taken. The old boards of examination were abolished and new ones established. A total of 7,000 such boards were set up, one for each district. Uniform requirements for examination were issued to all applicants. The requirements specified that a candidate had to pass tests on (1) his vocational ability, the main requirement of which was that he be able to make a special product (*Meisterstück*); (2) his theoretical knowledge of his materials and the products derived from them; (3) his knowledge of cost accounting, bookkeeping, and managerial problems that would arise in a shop; (4) his knowledge of laws affecting an artisan enterprise; and (5) his knowledge of the essentials of citizenship (i.e., Nazi ideology).[13] Many complaints were published that the candidates were insufficiently prepared. In 1937–38 not less than 16.8 per cent of the candidates failed to pass the examination. It is certain, however, that the boards were more interested in keeping the number of masters low than in testing the ability of candidates.

Attempts to set up the handicraft sector as a distinct artisan economy produced three jurisdictional disputes with industry, trade, and agriculture. Each of these quarrels found a different solution. The conflict between the Estate of Agriculture and the handicraft estate, about who should control the food trade and processing industries, came up for a decision in 1934. The third decree on the preliminary organization of the Estate of Agriculture laid down two rules: (*a*) The whole retail trade in food and drink was to be under the jurisdiction of the Estate of Agriculture (this affected more than half a million stores); (*b*) all the food-processing industries were to be under the jurisdiction of the Estate of Agriculture. This affected 293,000 industrial enterprises.[14] Hence, a total of almost 800,000 trading or industrial firms were incorporated into the agricultural sector of the economy.

Schacht was able to secure a minor modification of this provision. It related to the membership of firms in compulsory organizations. Three different groups of retail stores were distinguished for the purpose of organizational classification. Stores that sold mainly goods controlled by agricultural marketing organizations had to become members of the Estate of Agriculture if the food they sold comprised 80 per cent of their turnover. Firms that handled only a small fraction of such products, up to 20 per cent of turnover, were to be organized exclusively by the compulsory organization of retail trade. All foodstores and restaurants falling between these two groups were called mixed enterprises. These firms had to be members of both organizations. That is to say, in all questions of prices and market regulations, mixed enterprises were subject to the rules of the Estate of Agriculture. In organizational questions, however, these firms were under the jurisdiction of the organization of retail trade.[15] Hence, through a classification of firms into full members, dual members, and nonmembers, Schacht was able to limit slightly the power of the Estate of Agriculture. In the main, this agreement was a victory for Walther Darré, who had been appointed Nazi Minister of Agriculture in July, 1933. It indicated that as far as the von Blomberg-Hitler deal was concerned, agriculture was a dominion of the Nazis in which big business had no right to a share in power.

Disputes between handicraft and retail trade as well as between wholesale and retail trade were settled by similar agreements. The conflict between handicraft and retail trade concerned primarily those many artisans who sold products they themselves had made or considerably improved (*Zubehörhandel*). The trade organization demanded that the artisans either desist from selling these products and close their stores or that they be subjected to the law on entry restrictions for the retail trade. The handicraft estate opposed these demands. The clash between these Nazified groups became so violent that Schacht, on November 14, 1935, issued an order that brought all organizational activities to a standstill. He also ordered the organizations to negotiate an agreement. After a year of bickering, the Ministry of Economics approved a settlement of the dispute. The agreement laid down three rules as to the classification of firms. Artisan shops with a retail turnover of 50 per cent in their total business volume, or a retail turnover of 3,000 marks a year, had to be members of the retail organization. Artisan shops having an insignificant volume of sales were released from any regulation of the retail organization. Artisan shops with retail sales between 3,000 marks and a minimal amount below which sales were regarded as insignificant had to become members of both organizations, to each of which they had to pay half their membership fees.[16] The amount of retail business which was regarded as insignificant had to be agreed upon between individual guilds and retail groups. The negotiations, it was estimated, would affect between 60,000 and 70,000 artisan shops. They would seem, however, to have produced no permanently satisfactory result, for in 1938 Walther Funk, as the new Minister of Economics, decided that artisans who sold products they had produced or improved should not belong to a retail organization.

The dispute between industrial and handicraft organizations was even more intense. It had already begun prior to the issue of the third decree on handicraft. The national economic chamber (*Reichswirtschaftskammer*) proposed that the decree should provide for coordinating offices which would define the line of division between industry and handicraft. This proposal was rejected by the handicraft leaders. The third decree subjected all related handicraft enterprises to the same provisions as were imposed upon the shops of artisans. When the decree became effective, however, Schacht as Minister of Economics directed that two of its provisions be set aside temporarily. One of the provisions pertained to the "related" artisan shops, the other to the master's examinations in handicraft. In time, the Minister received the power to issue a new definition of the term "related handicraft enterprises." Owners of related handicraft enterprises would be relieved from the retail requirement if their shops were actually operated by managers who were in possession of certificates of competence.

Schacht announced in February, 1936, which persons had to take a master's examination. The exemption of owners of related handicraft shops from examination was preceded by negotiations between the rivals. No agreement could be reached. At this turn of events, Schacht appointed the Nazi Albert Pietzsch, economic advisor of Hess, to arbitrate the case.[17] A standstill in organizational activities was decreed in March, 1936, so that no rival could enlarge his organization. Out of the negotiations grew a temporary procedure for the settlement of the most urgent individual conflicts and a final decision on the position of related enterprises in handicraft.

The Ministry of Economics established an office which pre-examined all serious disputes and presented suggestions to the Minister, whose decision was final. The ministry took into consideration the kind of machines used, the degree of specialization exercised, the skill of the laborers employed, the nature of their vocational training, and the form of taxation levied upon disputants. These findings were utilized as criteria for reaching a decision.[18] Moreover, a final distinction was made between auxiliary industrial plants and related handicraft enterprises. Auxiliaries to an industrial enterprise were excluded from the jurisdiction of the handicraft organization if they:

a) produced goods or provided services exclusively for the concern by which they were owned;
b) provided services or goods that constituted merely an insignificant modification of manufactured goods (e.g., adjustments of men's suits for individual buyers);
c) provided unpaid services that were added to the sale of manufactured goods (e.g., installation);
d) repaired products for which a quality guarantee was granted to the buyer.

The retail sales of these auxiliary shops fell below the minimal amount that defined a significant volume of business and were thus outside the artisan economy.

Conversely, related artisan shops, usually owned by industrial enterprises, came under the jurisdiction of the handicraft estate if they were akin to artisan shops (a) in their volume of business and (b) in the length of their working week. Both criteria had to be met before the shops could be included in the handicraft organization. Hence, small repair shops associated with manufacturing concerns that worked the usual forty-eight hours or less belonged to the industrial section of the economy.[19] The chambers of both industry and handicraft had to agree that these two conditions existed in a given industry.

What then was the final result of the master's examinations and the jurisdictional disputes between the industrial and handicraft organizations? Undoubtedly, both measures divided the economy into a few airtight compartments: industry, handicraft, trade, and agriculture. Moreover, closed crafts within handicraft gradually became an established fact. To be sure, Schacht denied this furiously. In a speech delivered in May, 1935, he warned against the compartmentalization of business: "We did not destroy the class state in order to build up a new guild state." Yet he suffered from a misconception as to the significance of compulsory organizations coupled with extensive vocational training. He believed that compartmentalization of the economy could come about only when the monopolistic organizations were in a position to tell each firm what products it could produce, as in the old Austro-Hungarian Empire under the handicraft law. Actually, compulsory organization, exclusive jurisdiction over firms, and vocational training achieved an extensive degree of economic compartmentalization—in spite of the professed intentions of the government.

Judging from his actions, one would say that Schacht had a twofold goal in these jurisdictional disputes. First, he wanted to prevent the Nazis from capturing the guilds and chambers and employing them as instruments of power against big business; in this he was fairly successful, as long as the von Blomberg-Hitler deal lasted. Second, he insisted that all sections of the economy should be governed by different economic principles and that the relationships between firms and corresponding sectors of the economy should be determined by the rules of "reasonable competition." In effect, he stopped the encroachment of small upon big business. But he could not prevent both small and big business from building up economic compulsory organizations,[20] nor did he realize that such organizations were constitutionally unable to engage in reasonable competition, whatever its definition.

MONOPOLIZED VOCATIONAL TRAINING

The guilds busily introduced an extensive system of vocational training after the Nazis' rise to power. They set up a vocational roll for apprentices, made examinations compulsory, established boards of examiners, and began to extend the period of training from three to four years. The second and third decrees of the law on handicraft—those imposing a system of vocational training and embodying the principles of a closed craft—provided the legal authority for these actions, although Schacht was later able to shift the right to supervise vocational training from Nazified guilds to officials in the Handicraft Chambers. The decrees also enabled the artisan organizations to make the examinations more uniform and to set up national standards for boards of examiners. Through all these activities, the guilds and chambers undoubtedly acquired a monopoly over vocational training in handicraft. They determined who should become an apprentice, what he should be taught, how long he should be taught, when and in what fields he should be examined, and whether he would find a job as a journeyman after receiving his certificate.

The trend towards monopolistic control of vocational training was even more striking in the retail business, where the initiative for compulsory training and examination came from the Labor Front. The sales-personnel branch of the Labor Front agreed with the organization of retail dealers on the main outlines of training apprentices.[21] Both insisted that masters must have had either five years' experience or a successfully completed apprenticeship, that the master himself had to instruct the apprentice, that large enterprises should have no part in the training of young people, that training had to follow the rules laid down by the two organizations, that the contract of training should be good for three years—with an examination at the end of that period—and that any violations of the rules should deprive a master of his right to employ apprentices. Naturally, all apprentices were expected to "be ready to believe and act in the spirit of the Nazi party." The Hitler Youth was given the right to check up on this provision of the agreement.

The result of this and similar efforts was an increase in the number of apprentices who took examinations. The figure rose from 10,300 in 1934 to 51,000 in 1936.[22] The increase was primarily a result of the fact that examinations had been made quasi-compulsory. Evidently many of the applicants were poorly prepared since, according to the Chamber of Industry and Trade of Saxony, about one fifth of the candidates failed the examinations.

What was the interest of the Labor Front in extensive vocational training of sales personnel? Leaders of this section of the Labor Front harbored the idea that trained salesmen should become independent store owners. The organization demanded that only trained men should be granted permission to open retail stores. This demand was strenuously opposed by the owners of the stores and by the Chambers of Trade. The Berlin chamber, for instance, reported that of 8000 requests for a permit to open a store, just 20 per cent of the applicants had received a proper apprenticeship. Yet there was no statement from the chamber that such an apprenticeship had been made a requirement for granting a permit.

The different interests of retailers and the Labor Front led to an open conflict in 1936. The Labor Front accused the organization of retail trade of not wanting trained salesmen to become independent store owners.[23] Available evidence supports the charge of the Labor Front. Retail organizations were mainly interested in preventing the opening of new stores regardless of who might be the future owners. They also tried to circumvent the demand of the Labor Front that many apprentices should be trained. A chamber of trade in a western district reported in 1937 that it had registered 565 male and 3,496 female apprentices for retail trade in 1936. Girls were given preference because they received less compensation. High-school certificates were asked of boys when they applied for apprenticeships. The result was a drastic decline in the number of male apprentices in retail trade. But the attempts of the Labor Front to remedy the situation failed. The Ministry of Economics refused to declare that the retail organization was biased in pre-examining requests for opening new stores. Thus the Labor Front failed to move the salesmen upward into the middle group of independent store owners, while the retail organization retained its right to keep the retail business closed even to Nazified salesmen.

A triangular conflict about vocational training developed in the artisan sector. The guilds were determined to keep the number of apprentices down, yet opposed any training of young people by industrial establishments and fought political domination by the Labor Front. The result was a dispute between the organization of industry and the Labor Front about the training of industrial workers. Furthermore, an important group of industries was seeking to increase their training facilities in order to take care of the rising demand for trained workers. Their interest lay in a substantial increase of the number of apprentices. Finally, the Labor Front prepared an extensive campaign for an increase in the number of apprentices and for political domination of vocational training as well as education by the Nazis.

At the same time, the Handicraft Chambers and guilds were demanding a monopoly over all vocational training because (according to their view) they had the necessary number of masters and shops and supplied a substantial number of the trained workers for industrial production. The last part of this claim was correct. As of October, 1936, an extensive statistical investigation revealed that a significant number of industrial workers were hired by industrial concerns after reaching the age of eighteen. Of the 412,000 male youngsters employed in industry only about 214,000 were apprentices. In contrast, the handicraft sector employed in 1936 not less than 516,000 apprentices of whom about 200,000 could find employment as journeymen in artisan shops. The remaining 316,000 were expected to find employment as trained workers in manufacturing enterprises.[24] It was this artisan contribution to the supply of skilled workers in manufacture that provided the basis for vocational training in the handicraft shops and organizations.

While acknowledging the contribution of the artisan shops, the industrial leaders forcefully rejected the claim advanced by the guilds. The same statistical study disclosed also an important inter-industry migration of trained workers. Of the 214,000 industrial apprentices in 1936 not less than 167,-000 were trained in the workshops of the iron, metal, and sheet producers or users. The machine-tool industry alone trained over one third of the industrial apprentices, whereas it provided adult employment for only one sixth of these apprentices. The excess of those trained in building or handling machines or other steel and metal products usually found employment as craftsmen in other industries.[25] The significance of the large number of industrially trained workers was enhanced by the fact that the rearmament boom had created a scarcity of adult trained workers, especially for the producer-goods industries. Rather than handing over the training to the artisan shops, many of the manufacturing concerns involved embarked upon an extensive program of recruiting young men for training in industry.

The number of industrial workshops increased steadily from 1934 onwards. A model contract for industrial apprentices, which received the approval of the Minister of Economics, was worked out by the business groups. The principle adopted was that the "leader of the enterprise" was responsible for the training of the industrial apprentices. He was officially advised to appoint an instructor, who preferably should have a master's certificate himself, as the man actually responsible for setting up the program and putting it into effect. Advisory and supervisory agents were then appointed to assist in the training of apprentices in the plants, and a Committee for Vocational Schooling (known as the *Datsch* and recognized by the Minister of Economics) worked out a classification of the various occupations. For the most important of them the *Datsch* defined the training goals, indicated the best teaching devices to be used, and described the practical tasks that each apprentice should have completed at the end of each year's training. The proposals submitted by the *Datsch* were then examined by the economic groups concerned and, if approved, were attached to the apprentice's training contract.[26]

In negotiations among the economic groups of manufacturers it was decided that the total number of industrial vocations in which active training would take place should be relatively small. The aim of this decision was to prevent premature specialization of trainees. In order to establish minimum standards and insure some degree of uniformity of procedure the *Datsch* formulated a number of rules for testing the ability of trainees and for training them. In these and similar arrangements, industrial training became subject to some of the rules that had been developed in the handicraft organizations.

The economic groups signed an agreement with the Chambers of Industry in the summer of 1935 which specified that the industrially trained apprentices would have to pass a formal examination. A set of rules and boards of examiners were accepted for thirteen metal occupations. The firms would have to enroll their apprentices in a special list, kept by the Chambers of Industry, as a condition for admission to the examinations.[27] In consequence, the large steel concerns imitated the handicraft estate by accepting the idea of a vocational roll for apprentices and a uniform system of examinations. These devices were necessary if big business were to keep its control over vocational training in industry.

Not very surprisingly, however, a dispute arose between the groups and guilds as to who should have the right to arrange for and supervise the examinations to be taken by the industrial apprentices. Separate and rival boards of examiners were not acceptable to the government agencies involved, whose policy it was that there should be no dual examination boards for industrial and artisan trained apprentices. The Minister of Economics insisted that industrial apprentices must be admitted to the artisan examinations even when they were not registered in the artisan roll of apprentices. His aim, he said, was to have the same boards—with different membership—examine the candidates of industry as well as handicraft. The Minister of Labor moved in the same direction when he informed the boards that industrially trained apprentices must be given the opportunity to take the examinations for journeymen. Finally, both ministers announced that industrially trained skilled workers had a right to take the artisan master examinations a few years after they passed their examinations as journeymen.[28] The handicraft organizations thus failed to establish their monopoly of vocational training. Both industry and handicraft were given the same rights and responsibilities in training young workers for their vocations in the economy.

In July of 1936, the estate of handicraft signed an agreement with the economic groups of industry in which the former promised to admit industrial apprentices and journeymen to the system of examinations originally built up for the handicraft sector only. The dispute thus ended with a compromise. Guilds and groups each engaged in vocational training, and the examinations in each case carried the same significance and prestige. The guild leaders no longer had the distinction of being the only ones who trained qualified workers and produced quality products, but at least the training and examination of industrial apprentices and journeymen followed the pattern that had been established by and for the handicraft organizations.

VOCATION AND IDEOLOGY

The Nazis had three reasons for seeing a connection between vocation and Nazi ideology. Middle-class socialism gave rise to two divergent policies of vocational training.

Nazified artisans developed the related ideas of a closed craft
and careful selection and training of future masters. Nazified
white-collar workers saw in vocational training an opportunity for salaried employees or their children to move upward into what had been the domain of the urban middle
class. Finally, all Nazis were very fond of the idea that vocational education should be utilized for the extensive indoctrination of young people in Nazi ideology.

The idea of a vocation as a way of making a living and also
as a way of serving the community had originated with the
former right-wing unions of white-collar workers. When they
became Nazified, they carried the idea of a calling into the
Labor Front. The leaders in the Labor Front who pushed
the program for vocational training and education were the
former leaders of the nonsocialist unions of white-collar
workers. Under their influence, the Labor Front developed
a manifold program: every boy should receive his vocational
training; apprentices should not be treated by employers as
cheap laborers but as masters of the future; every youngster
should have a right to a comprehensive vocational education
regardless of whether he expected adult employment in industry, commerce, or handicraft; all trained apprentices
should pass their compulsory examination and should have
a reasonable chance of becoming masters and owners of their
own business.[29] Of course, all phases of training and education should be fused with Nazi ideology.

The Nazi influence over vocational education was quite
successful. The Hitler Youth and the Ministry of Education
saw to it that Nazi ideas were taught in vocational classes.
Vocational knowledge had to be modified and combined with
the teaching of Nazi political ideas, on both of which students had to pass examinations. The Labor Front established
a division of vocational training that comprised sixteen departments. Each of these was responsible for vocational education in specific groups of vocations. These departments pro-

duced many plans for Nazifying vocational education as well as training. In regard to training, the Labor Front promoted especially two ideas. One was the formulation of a model training contract for apprentices which was urged upon single employers as well as upon guilds and groups. The resistance of the latter organizations to the idea of a model training contract became one bone of contention with the Labor Front towards the end of the first period of the regime.

The other idea was that of giving every boy vocational training. The Labor Front and Hitler Youth urged upon teachers and employment offices an extensive program of registration and placement for the apprenticing of young workers. Registration was fairly successful. The number of young people who sought vocational advice from the counselors of the employment offices rose from 250,000 in 1933–34 to 848,000 in 1934–35. Yet the actual number of those who were placed in apprenticeships increased only from 184,000 to 260,000. This discrepancy between the supply of, and demand for, apprentices induced the Labor Front to urge and pressure each artisan to hire one additional apprentice and thereby provide jobs for German youth. In doing so, however, the Labor Front was running contrary to the unspoken but clear intention of the guilds to keep down the number of apprentices and weed out those owners of shops who could not get a master's certificate.

The opposition of guilds and groups as well as the rising demand for industrially trained apprentices induced the Labor Front to shift its emphasis in vocational training. In October of 1935 the sixteen departments of vocational education were dissolved, and the former union leaders of the white-collar workers were dismissed from their positions. A new office of vocational training was established. The man placed at its head was an engineer named Karl Arnhold, who had formerly directed the vocational training in some steel mills in the Ruhr Valley and who had made a name for him-

self through his *Institut Dinta*. Arnhold was strongly in favor
of vocational training in specially organized industrial workshops. Under his influence the Labor Front dropped its demand of an apprenticeship for every boy. It now accepted
industrial training shops as preferable to training in artisan
shops.[30]

Arnhold established pilot training shops, which were financed by the extensive funds of the Labor Front, and
trained "social engineers" who in turn developed special
techniques for training young workers. In order to induce
industrial enterprises to accept Arnhold's methods and teaching devices, the Labor Front instituted a competition among
industrial workshops to determine which was the most effective training center. The tokens of achievement bestowed
upon the winning firms not only established good relations
with the Labor Front but also functioned as an effective
method of promoting the training of apprentices by industrial concerns.[31] A shift in policy by the Labor Front and a
rising demand for skilled laborers in industry had the effect
of increasing the number of apprentices in industrial concerns. From October, 1936, to the summer of 1938, the number of apprentices in the eight industries that traditionally
trained young workers rose from 122,940 to 169,208.[32]

By recognizing the value of industrially trained workers the
Labor Front had put itself in a position to challenge the
methods and controls of vocational training by groups, guilds,
and chambers. In November of 1935 Schacht wrote a letter to
Ley protesting against the policies of Arnhold's office, which
tried to lay down binding rules for the training of apprentices. Schacht also objected to the vocational competitions
among firms and demanded that the business groups and
chambers should participate in determining the standards
and in judging the performance of the participating enterprises. Not until the fall of 1937 were the economic groups
permitted to play a role in the vocational competitions. At

the same time Arnhold's office was continuing to promote its policies.[33]

In fact, an intense rivalry developed in 1936 between Arnhold's office and the *Datsch*. The Labor Front established its own vocational rolls for apprentices, promoted a model training contract, and advertised new training methods that were to be adopted by private concerns. At the same time, the *Datsch* presented its own teaching materials to firms and suggested to chambers that they keep a special book for each apprentice and record his vocational achievements in it. It was to be only a matter of months until this rivalry over methods of training would turn into a jurisdictional dispute between the Labor Front and the Ministry of Economics.

Ley created the occasion for the dispute when he reinterpreted Hitler's decree on the functions of the Labor Front, as described in the previous chapter. Ley asserted that the Labor Front alone should have the responsibility for vocational training and education. On September 5, 1936, two days after Ley's proclamation, Schacht sent a circular to the *Reichsgruppe Industrie* in which he emphasized that Ley's interpretation did not have the force of law and should be disregarded by groups and guilds. Schacht asked for immediate reports on any interference by the Labor Front. Information soon accumulated that the Labor Front had put some employers under pressure to drop the plans and teaching devices of the *Datsch* and replace them with those of Arnhold's office. Schacht hit back. In an ordinance of October 31, 1936, he instructed the training shops to use only materials provided by the *Datsch,* and made the use of the performance-book binding on all chambers.[34]

The dispute was temporarily halted when Schacht and Pietzsch put the case before Göring in a joint meeting. Schacht insisted that the matters of "wages, prices, and vocational training could not be permitted to become the tasks of the Labor Front."[35] Göring tried to reach a compromise.

Schacht asked Pietzsch to negotiate with the Labor Front. After many meetings the *Reich* Chamber of Industry agreed to the proposal of the Labor Front that there should be only one training contract for all apprentices.[36] Business leaders were hopeful that this minor concession would settle the dispute with the Labor Front.

At the same time, the Labor Front was seeking to abolish the Handicraft Chambers and guilds, and the leaders of industry utilized the resulting weakness of the handicraft organization for their purpose. On April 16, 1937, the Handicraft Chambers and industry groups signed an agreement in which they professed to accept the model training contract suggested by the Labor Front—but the agreement also included three other provisions:

a) Industrial apprentices should be employed according to the model contract and registered in the roll of apprentices under the administration of the Chambers of Industry.
b) The training of industrial apprentices should follow the rules worked out by the *Datsch*.
c) The Chambers of Industry were authorized to establish their own boards of examiners, who were to be in charge of administering the examinations to industrial apprentices and skilled workers, and issue the respective certificates.[37]

This agreement freed vocational training in industry from the handicraft examination system. The new examination boards for industrial apprentices proved to be quite successful, since the number of accepted candidates increased from 2,801 in 1935 to 17,500 in 1937. This success also indicates that the guilds lost out in their fight to acquire a monopoly over all vocational training in the country.

The Labor Front, however, regarded the new model contract only as the opening wedge in the struggle for final control over industrial and artisan training. Arnhold's office promoted its own vocational registration system. In some industries, the Labor Front even organized its own boards of examiners for apprentices who had been trained according to Arnhold's method. These attempts were loudly condemned by Schacht. He decided to take a dramatic step in order to defeat the Labor Front. The handicraft organization for Berlin arranged a large meeting at which a group of selected apprentices were to receive their diplomas as journeymen. Schacht was to give the major address at the largest auditorium (*Sportpalast*) in Berlin. Then, seeing what Schacht was up to, Ley obtained from Hitler an instruction declaring that the meeting was illegal and could not be held.

Schacht visited Hitler early on the morning of May 11, 1937, and was told that the meeting could not be held because there would be disturbances. Said Schacht, "If there are any noisy demonstrations, then [it will be] only because Ley has organized them. I will have to reject forcefully this affront to my authority as Minister."[38] It was only when Schacht threatened to resign from the Ministry of Economics that Hitler gave Schacht permission to hold the meeting. It was not disturbed by the Nazis.

Exploiting the occasion, Schacht proceeded to explain his policies. He emphasized in his speech that only those young men who were registered in the official roll of apprentices could be admitted to the regular examinations. He also underlined that only the official examinations assured future employers of competent training and of an officially recognized diploma. Strongly condemning the intervention of the Labor Front, Schacht pointed out "that the Minister of Economics was alone responsible for the vocational training of workers . . . and that I will not tolerate any interference with my power to give commands."[39]

This forceful declaration hindered the Labor Front in taking over control of vocational training during Schacht's tenure as Minister of Economics, although Göring did not accept Schacht's demand that Arnhold's office be dissolved. Apart from party politics, Arnhold claimed that his methods would speed up the training of apprentices, and Göring welcomed any effort that would mitigate the prevailing scarcity of skilled workers in 1937. Thus the Labor Front had had a partial success in the dispute over vocational training; but this was not a gain for middle-class socialism, since its main vocational ideas had already been discarded in 1935. The top leaders of the party gave partial support to the Labor Front only because of its claim that it had at its disposal a method of training that would more effectively implement the goals of the Four Year Plan than could the plans of guilds, groups, and chambers.

A CORPORATE PRICE SYSTEM?

The artisans' demand for "fair prices" and "ordered markets," regulated by the guilds, was the most important part of the economic order visualized by the middle groups. This demand was accepted by the Nazi handicraft leaders. The fight for the regulation of markets and prices within the artisan economy began in the fall of 1933. The agricultural and cultural estates, established in the summer of 1933, were given the power to regulate markets and fix prices. Leaders of the artisan organizations demanded the same rights for handicrafts,[40] but this right was not included in the act of November, 1933, which authorized compulsory organization of artisans. Nor did the three subsequent decrees on handicrafts confer upon artisan organizations the right to fix prices or regulate markets. A severe struggle for the power to set prices developed between small and big business.

Four ordinances indicated the opposition of the leaders of big business to a price system controlled by the guilds. In February of 1934 the Minister of Labor prohibited further increases in prices in the construction industry. Public subsidies for the improvement of houses, he said, would not be granted if the cost figures proposed for public orders implied a rise in the prices of the services and products of firms. The Minister asked all governmental agencies concerned to give him reports on the prices of subsidized projects. A month later a decree of the Minister of Economics appeared which prohibited prior understandings among applicants for public orders, or any other rigging of bids, in the construction industry. In May of 1934 the Ministers of Economics and Labor issued an instruction against the rise of prices for essential consumer goods. It specifically forbade guilds and chambers to set minimum prices on goods without prior permission from the ministers. Existing agreements on prices were not to be changed to the disadvantage of consumers.[41]

Finally, a decree issued by Schacht on August 7, 1934, extended price control to all goods and services in handicrafts and industry. The immediate goal was to combat price rises for imported goods and for prices of goods bought by the government, especially for construction projects. In addition, the prices of all goods in short supply were subjected to control. The decree was legally based upon the special authority of the Minister of Economics to determine economic policy, which had been granted to Schacht's predecessor. Schacht emphasized that his decree was intended to stabilize wages as well as prices.[42]

These government decrees defined the price issue. Small business organizations were accused of raising prices, and price indices supported this charge. The index for industrial consumer goods had risen from 109 in April, 1933, to 118 in September, 1934, including the products of artisans as well as those of industrial firms. It was said that higher prices, if extended to other fields, would produce a demand for higher wages. Hence, the price-wage stability policy was in danger. This set the stage for a reformulation of the price policy of

guilds. In principle, Schacht was not against price-fixing by
business organizations. He merely fought against higher
prices for artisan products. Schacht called for the support of
the oligarchic clique of the party to assist him in keeping
prices stable.

Usually, the oligarchic clique secured information through
party offices before making any decision. In October of 1934,
local leaders of the Labor Front and the NS Hago—the party's
integral organization for artisans and traders—were instructed
to undertake an investigation of prices in artisan shops. They
were to ask what prices were charged by party members who
owned shops and were to report the prices to headquarters.
The party wanted to determine how far complaints against
higher prices were justified. The problem of prices was also
considered at the conference of the provincial governors
(Reichsstatthalter) on November 8, 1934. No report on its
decisions became known; but an order from Göring to the
city and county officials of Prussia revealed the sentiment
that had been expressed at the conference. Officials were instructed to take the most effective actions against any owner
who raised his prices without prior government consent.[43]
Some butcher shops were closed in Prussian cities, and their
owners were removed to concentration camps.

A federal act of November 5, 1934, concentrated authority
over prices into one hand. The two offices of price supervision, one each in the Ministries of Agriculture and Economics, were abolished. Their functions were transferred to
the office of the new price commissioner, Dr. Carl Goerdeler,
the mayor of Leipzig, who was made directly responsible to
Hitler. This appointment highlighted three facts. First, the
power to check the rise of prices was not given to Schacht but
to a man who was definitely against a price system based on
the guilds; Goerdeler favored effective price competition and
a modified laissez-faire economy. Second, although Goerdeler's authority was at first limited to the prices of goods and

services regarded as necessities, his jurisdiction was soon extended to other prices, including those controlled by business organizations and public corporations—but not to those set by the Estate of Agriculture and the so-called estate for the "cultural professions." Third, the immediate task of the price commissioner was to check the hoarding of goods, a practice that had arisen in the fall of 1934, partly in response to the import restrictions imposed under the "New Plan." Hoarding was stopped through persuasion and through a more effective allocation of imported goods.[44]

What were the functions of price supervision in general? The commissioner clarified, in many speeches, the distinction between control and supervision of prices. Price control works through commands and penalties that seek to impose maximum prices and divide goods by rationing. Such actions the commissioner rejected as undesirable and unworkable. The purpose of price supervision, he said, was to strengthen price competition, to prevent cutthroat competition, and to abolish prices fixed by agreements among producers. Such fixed prices usually involve the danger that the price will be fixed according to the average costs of the high-cost producer, and this procedure deprives the economy of the beneficial effect of the more efficient firms that could through their low prices set the tone for whole industries. "I have thus decided," Goerdeler announced, "that all new price agreements can become valid only after my consent. All agreements concluded since June, 1933, will have to be reported to me. . . . If they cannot stand careful scrutiny, then the fixed prices will have to disappear. It would be best if those involved would cancel these agreements voluntarily."[45] Any increase not reported would become illegal on December 15, 1934.

The immediate difficulty, he said in the same speech, lay in the extensive increase in prices that had occurred during the last months. Wage rates were too low in some industries, he continued, and many laborers had only part-time employment; thus, price increases were socially undesirable. He further declared that there were not sufficient reasons for raising some prices since the costs of production had not risen, that a general increase was not necessary because of the substantial portion of unused capacity, and that a rise in output would enable firms to reduce prices because of the decline in unit costs. The price commissioner thus sought to induce sellers not to look at the rising demand but to base their price decisions primarily upon their falling average costs. He felt that his basic functions were to encourage businessmen to estimate their costs realistically and to provide an acceptable procedure for estimating costs. Expecting a decline in prices, the commissioner was very much incensed by rising prices. "I will without mercy abolish all unjustified increases in prices, while at the same time protecting all those prices that are economically correct and socially justified."[46]

It so happened that the areas in which prices had increased most significantly were agriculture and the food trade, and the construction and textile industries. The beneficiaries of these increases were thus the Nazified farmers, traders, and artisans. Apparently, price supervision was meant especially for small business. This raises the interesting question of whether Goerdeler could have succeeded only by fighting against the "ordered markets" of the Nazified Estate of Agriculture and the "corporate price system" of the guilds.

One of Goerdeler's first actions was to clarify the functions of the Nazi party in price supervision. The issue came up shortly after Goerdeler's appointment as commissioner, when he was paid an official visit by Dr. Ley as organizational leader of the party. Ley suggested that the commissioner should transfer his authority to the Nazi party, pointing out that a few demonstrations would eliminate the whole problem of hoarding. Goerdeler refused and decided that his authority would have to be implemented through the regular offices of the state administration. A day later Hitler officially presented the same request, but when he learned that the issue had already been decided in favor of the state agencies and that the party would become very unpopular if it burdened itself with a task in which neither the buyer nor the seller could be fully satisfied, Hitler acceded to Goerdeler's wishes.[47]

In subsequent negotiations with party officials, Goerdeler not only sought to obtain their cooperation but also to stop price regulation by local Nazi officials and to concentrate in his hands all power to formulate price policy. Insistence upon this authority was accepted by the Nazi party without any fight. In return for this concession, Goerdeler agreed that the party, the Labor Front, and the NS Hago each would have a liaison official at his headquarters; he also agreed to inform the *Gauleiter* of each party district about all current price issues. In each *Gau* there would be one party official dealing with price problems who would receive the price complaints of the party locals and the Labor Front and report them to the commissioner.[48] Goerdeler thus succeeded in keeping the party from making price decisions but utilized its agencies as informers on the price actions of businessmen.

Goerdeler's attitude towards the guilds was absolutely negative. Publicly and privately, Goerdeler refused to allow the Estate of Handicraft to deal in any way with matters of prices. The guilds were instructed to refrain from setting prices, from suggesting cost figures, or from issuing instructions for calculations that could be utilized as guides for setting prices. The sixty minimum prices fixed by guilds during 1933 and 1934 were declared illegal by the price commissioner. The courts of honor in handicraft were not permitted to examine the price behavior of guild members, except when the offices supervising the guilds gave their prior consent. At the same time, the economic groups of big and small business were officially invited by the commissioner to present their price proposals to him. Special meetings were arranged for the iron and steel groups as well as for representatives of industrial construction and the paper-manufacturing industry to discuss price policy.[49]

Speaking at the conference of the Estate of Handicraft in June of 1935, the commissioner tried to sell his idea of a competitive price to the artisans: "The ideal is not a maximum or minimum price or any other fixed price but a just price. Such a price has to contain all justifiable elements of costs that arise in the shop of a sufficiently trained master."[50] This definition identified the just price with the competitive cost price. Thus Goerdeler was able to accept two demands of the guilds. On the one hand, he condemned the cutthroat price, at which goods were sold below justified unit costs. On the other hand, he emphasized the importance of proper cost accounting and permitted the guilds to educate their members in this art.

The price commissioner approved a decree against unfair competition that was published by the Ministry of Economics. Cutthroat prices were said to arise when a seller sold his goods below his unit cost and compensated himself for the loss by reneging on his obligations to his creditors, to the government, or to his workers. Whenever such prices were charged, the guilds and groups were authorized to check with the tax office and the Labor Front to discover whether the cut prices were a result of unpaid taxes or wage rates below the legal level. A neutral office then had to undertake a cost calculation and report the result to the price commissioner. In cases of financial delinquency, the joint actions of the tax collector and the trustee of labor would force the delinquent firm to meet its obligation. At the same time, the law on bankruptcy was changed in such a way that the firm involved had to go out of business rather than arrive at a partial liquidation of its debts by agreement.[51] In this way, the guilds were enabled to fight successfully against cutthroat competition.

A dispute arose in regard to the calculation of justifiable unit costs. The commissioner suggested that only the average costs of individual firms could become the basis of an acceptable cost price, whereas the groups and guilds insisted that the average cost for the whole industry should be used as the basis for calculating the cost price. In practice, however, the pricing of goods on the basis of averaged individual unit costs proved to be administratively cumbersome, if not unworkable. On the one hand, the commissioner permitted economic groups—but not the guilds—to settle controversial cases within their industry and present only intractable cases to him for decision.[52] On the other hand, a number of groups secured the right to agree upon so-called "calculation prices." The resulting price was based upon the unit costs not of particular industries but upon the cost figures suggested by the headquarters of the economic group.

The calculation price (*Richtpreis*) was particularly important in the construction industry. After much resistance, the commissioner agreed that the business organizations in this industry could have the right to introduce uniform cost accounting. The cost tables of these organizations, which allowed a reasonable percentage for profit, became in fact the basis for determining minimum prices for the industry, because the agents of the organizations involved received the authority to check the books of firms that accepted orders at prices below those set by the organizations. In addition, lists of honest firms were compiled which alone could receive public orders.[53] Since most of the orders in construction came directly or indirectly from governmental agencies, the individual firms had either to charge the organizational prices or go out of business.

The right to set calculation prices was not granted to the

guilds, however, and was later also withheld from the economic groups. Price-fixing became a right that could be exercised only by cartels. While the calculation price in construction was accepted in return for the promise to cancel most of the price increases of the fall of 1934, recognition of cartel prices—for small as well as big business—by the price commissioner came only reluctantly and conditionally. When in March of 1935 the decree against rigged biddings expired, Goerdeler extended this decree from construction to all other industries. Yet he did not outlaw understandings among bidders. They were permitted to select one of their members as the only serious bidder provided the contract involved called for exceptional products and extensive calculations. The commissioner also insisted that the selected bidder could not be told what price to charge or be forced to compensate other firms that refrained from bidding.[54] Selection of a particular bidder by the potential bidders was to be dependent upon the permission of the public agency placing the order. For all practical purposes, however, the enforcement of this provision was placed in the hands of military procurement agencies at a time when price supervision within the Ministry of War was still very ineffective.

The supervision of prices determined by bids was further complicated by the fact that distressed areas asked that they be given special consideration in the placing of public contracts. A letter of October, 1935, written by Dr. Posse of the Ministry of Economics, reveals that the special efforts that were made in response to regional and local influences had destroyed all uniformity in the placing and pricing of public projects. A special office (Reichsausgleichsstelle) was established which had to give its consent before contracts could be finalized. A new decree of April 9, 1936, legalized the increases in the expenditures for projects in distressed areas. Special charges for freight, for regionally higher wage rates, or for costs arising from special locations could be paid as additions to the price offers of other bidders.[55] Rather than preventing a rise in prices, the government merely regularized the extent and scope of the regional price increases. What happened to the requirement that cartel prices be reported? From the reports submitted, it can be seen that in 1933–34, 1,500 privately fixed prices, covering about 100 major lines of produce, were established.

The price commissioner did not subsequently follow up his original intention of eliminating such fixed prices. In March of 1935 he explicitly decreed that cartel prices would be recognized if the goods were either sold abroad or if the abolition of such prices threatened to drive firms with higher unit costs out of business. A general elimination of all privately fixed prices would have been possible only if the conditions for effective competition had been established. The commissioner limited his task to examining only those cartel prices that were especially objectionable. Since this shift in regard to cartel prices was announced at meetings of the steel and coal producers or stated to representatives of the agricultural interests,[56] one can infer that their united opposition prevented the price commissioner from attacking cartel prices.

Thus, as a result of price supervision, the guilds were prevented from introducing their system of regulated prices, and the prices fixed by cartels both in big and small business were recognized. The commissioner's goal of a competitive price could not be achieved in any sector of industry. This raises the question of whether the commissioner was able to stop the deliberate policy of the Ministry of Agriculture to raise farm prices.

From the beginning of his activities Goerdeler's position toward the pricing activities of the Minister of Agriculture had been diplomatic. Goerdeler publicly explained that he had decided to refrain from exercising any price-reducing influence upon agricultural producer prices. Some farm prices had risen substantially, while other prices, especially those for potatoes and sugar beets, could have been reduced. Yet the price commissioner did not touch them. "The aim," Goerdeler explained, "is to give the German peasant a system of prices that will induce him to increase production and efficiency. This important goal shall not be modified. It is the special accomplishment of the Estate of Agriculture to have secured a stable bread price for consumers. Yet in the distribution of food there are certain overhead costs that are in need of special examination in order to obtain a price reduction of the distributive share of food prices."[57] Higher prices were thus acceptable to Goerdeler only when they promised to increase production.

Accordingly, the commissioner investigated the prices of processors, wholesalers, and retailers of many food items. He found that the profit margins of bakers and butchers could not be further reduced, but the prices fixed by the canners of fish and vegetables, which had been increased in 1934, were reduced by order of the commissioner in 1935. In some cases the number of middlemen between farmers and consumers was reduced, and the fixed prices of some of their organizations were declared illegal.[58] Here, too, the commissioner gave up his original intention of eliminating all fixed prices of processors. The question of what to do with the cartel prices of processors and dealers in food, he said, "has to be decided from case to case."[59] In fact, he never attempted to make the pricing of farm products and food competitive. He not only recognized the price-fixing actions of the Estate of Agriculture but even asserted on one occasion that without the actions of the estate the actual prices for important food items would have been substantially higher.

We do know that the commissioner's attitude towards the Nazified Estate of Agriculture was in part a reflection of his desire to remain on good terms with the Nazi party. We also know that it was primarily because of the pricing policy of the Estate of Agriculture that the official cost of living index rose by 10 per cent during the tenure of the price commissioner. The prices of many food items rose even more; cattle prices, for example, increased by 14 per cent during the year 1934–35. Indeed, during the first three years of the regime, according to an unofficial estimate, the cost of living rose by 30 per cent.[60] Price supervision was thus a failure.

The price commissioner was fully aware of this fact. In many speeches he surveyed the whole range of problems that were connected with successful price stabilization. In a special memorandum which he sent to Hitler at a later date, Goerdeler declared that price supervision could be only partially successful.[61] Decisive actions were necessary, he said, to increase exports and reduce the scarcity of imported raw materials. The policy of the Ministry of Agriculture would have to be revised to eliminate all restrictions imposed upon peasants; some of the farm prices would have to be raised to induce food producers to increase efficiency and production; and public investments should be concentrated upon subsidizing residential construction and the building of small settlements for part-time workers.

With the expiration, on July 1, 1935, of the law that had established his office, Goerdeler presented Hitler with a request for extraordinary authority. At the end of this conversation, in which Schacht also participated, Hitler accepted Goerdeler's proposal. Said Hitler, "You can have all the authority which you desire. Please present to me a bill for my signature."[62] Goerdeler submitted his bill on the same day and enclosed with it, as an alternative proposal, his resignation. The subsequent negotiations among the Ministers did not lead to the granting of the additional authority requested by Goerdeler. Especially the Nazis in the Ministry of Agriculture refused to submit to the authority of a man whose real desire (as it seemed to them) was to destroy their control over agricultural markets. Hitler invited Goerdeler, who had ceased to exercise his official functions, to return to Berlin, but Goerdeler refused because his demand had not been granted. The office of price commissioner was then abolished, and the Ministers of Economics and Agriculture again became responsible for the price policy of the regime.

As we have seen, the end result of the episode in price supervision was to prevent the guilds from establishing a regulated system of prices for small business. Furthermore, when price supervision came into conflict with the policy of raising farm prices, as promoted by the Nazified peasant organizations, it turned out that the Nazis had entrenched themselves so well in the private and governmental organizations of agriculture that they could no longer be driven from their positions. The weakness of the Nazis in urban small business was thus accompanied by Nazi domination over agriculture.

END OF MIDDLE-CLASS SOCIALISM

CHAPTER FIVE

The economic counterrevolution of the intransigent Nazis failed in the cities; the goals of anticapitalism, corporativism, and artisan-economy were frustrated by big business, effectively assisted by the oligarchic clique of the ruling party. What happened to peasant socialism and Nazi ruralism? Did these aspirations of the rural Nazified middle class also fall short of realization? If so, why did these rural goals fail and which group became the successful opponent of rural middle-class socialism?

In the first Hitler government in office for the first half of 1933, Hugenberg was Minister of Economics as well as Minister of Agriculture. Joint control of the two ministries by the leader of the Nationalist party, who was a former manager of the Krupp concern, was widely regarded as a maneuver to keep the Nazis out of any position that would enable them to determine governmental economic policy. When the Nazis destroyed the political alliance with the Nationalist party, Hugenberg lost his position in the government. The subsequent re-alliance between the party and big business offered the Nazis a chance to extend their control over agriculture. The Schmitt-Hitler compromise applied only to urban business. The Nazi leader Darré, who had ousted the leaders of the old farm organizations and transformed them into a Nazified peasant movement, became Minister of Agriculture.

The enabling act of July 15, 1933, transferred all authority in the field of agriculture to the *Reich* and abolished the jurisdiction of the individual states. This act thus conferred upon Darré the power to determine agricultural policies for the regime. The new Minister's program was introduced within a period of three months. The main features of this program can be briefly summarized:

a) The debt moratorium of 1932 was preferred over Hugenberg's law of May, 1933. Hugenberg's law was rejected by the Nazis because it was said to grant favors to the agricultural credit institutions. While the Hugenberg law reduced the interest rate for indebted farms to 2 per cent, creditors could still claim 4.5 per cent for their loans. The difference was to be paid by the government. The Nazis refused to subsidize the creditors of agriculture in this way.

b) The Act of September 13, 1933, enabled the Nazis to introduce the principle of corporative organization into agriculture. The Estate of Agriculture was established under the floodlight of Nazi propaganda. Everyone engaged in farming, and in the processing and distribution of agricultural produce, had to become a member of this compulsory farm organization. The leadership of the estate rested exclusively in the integral NS farm organization of the ruling party.

c) The same act established an extensive marketing organization in agriculture. New agencies regulated all the

various prices and manipulated the supply of and demand for all agricultural produce.

d) The hereditary law of September 29, 1933, established
three new principles for landed property and its inheritance. An estate or farm became a legal entity that could
be neither sold nor encumbered. A definite line of property inheritance was imposed upon the owner, who could
pass on his farm only to one of his sons. Also, a farm
could not be mortgaged or sold, and foreclosure proceedings could be taken only against the products of the
farm, not against the farm itself.[1]

e) The Nazis agreed not to touch the estates of the large landowners. It was because of this deal with the *Junkers* that
the Nazis reduced the scope of their plans for resettling
farmhands. In the following years resettlement was confined to land that was either bought on the market or
reclaimed through the activities of the Labor Service.

In consequence, agriculture was dominated by the Nazis almost from the beginning of the regime. Having an opportunity to "take agriculture out of the capitalist nexus,"[2] they
introduced (a) a new property system, (b) a new market and
pricing system, (c) and a new form of compulsory economic
organization. These changes were basic; they established a
new sector in the economy that was different from all others
and, from the beginning of 1934, was governed by the principles of rural middle-class socialism.

Many attempts were made to wrest control over agriculture
from the Nazis. Schacht attacked the temporary decline of
agricultural production and deplored the rising imports of
foreign foodstuffs, both of which he attributed to the inefficient management and "utopian" ideas of the Nazis. Schacht
insisted that the supervisory boards controlling imports of
agricultural goods be transferred to his ministry; and Goerdeler criticized the pricing policy of the Estate of Agriculture
after he had ceased to act as price commissioner. None of

these efforts to reduce the power of the Nazis over agriculture were in any way successful. Anticapitalism in agricultural production and marketing was the price big business paid for the exclusive right to dominate the economic sphere of urban business.

The *Junkers* and the generals were more successful. The military insisted that great emphasis be placed upon the production of grain. Large landowners in eastern Germany had best adapted themselves to grain production, and the generals and the *Junkers* succeeded in preventing the intransigent Nazis from dividing the large estates into many small farms. There was thus a decisive check upon the Nazi program for land resettlement and ruralism. This part of the Nazi ideal for the countryside failed as much as did artisan socialism in the cities.

In contrast, peasant socialism experienced a different fate from that of its urban counterpart for small business. The peasant program had the full backing of the oligarchic clique of the party. A significant portion of this program was put into operation up to the end of 1936. Prior to the Four Year Plan it seemed that peasant socialism was—slowly but surely—on the road to success, but the shift from the rearmament boom to the war economy in time of peace gave a new direction to agricultural policy. The goal of peasant socialism was gradually discarded over a period of years. The new corporative organization was given the task of regulating agricultural production and markets for the purposes of the war economy. Peasant socialism also failed, because the Nazis had ceased to believe in "socialism" and were giving priority to the ideal of fascist imperialism.[3] Preparation for war seemed to the oligarchic clique a necessary step for the building up of a fascist empire. Preference for an empire over internal reform was thus the cause for the failure of peasant socialism.

The rise and fall of peasant socialism is an interesting case study for the evolution of state capitalist institutions in agriculture; but in this study, with its emphasis upon the industrial sphere of the economy, Nazi ruralism is of greater interest because its fate shows how the intransigent Nazis tried to reduce the size and importance of industry and big business. Nazi ruralism also exemplifies the struggle between big and small business, between counterrevolutionary and imperialist Nazis, this time in regard to the settlement of labor, the location of industries, and the use of land. Most important, the ruralist program brings into the foreground the conflict between internal reform and external aggression, between economic cooperation among countries and the building up of a war economy in time of peace, and between those who were for and those who were against the economic preparation for war.

THE PROGRAM OF RURALISM

Nazi ruralism aimed at a new type of "rurban" community. The extensive literature on the subject contained strong criticism of modern city life. City people, no longer rooted in the soil, had lost their place in, and feeling for, the community. Children were regarded as a burden; intensive family life was considered a nuisance. In fact, cities, with their large apartment buildings and impersonal relations, tended to destroy the personalities of the people. This trend towards degeneration, the Nazis declared, had to be stopped. They said that the large apartment buildings had to be levelled, that the slums had to be transformed into parks, that laborers had to be given the opportunity to build their own homes in small towns, that factories had to be relocated and dispersed all over the country, and that families should be able to combine the advantages of rural life with the necessities of modern industry—workers should raise large families, produce food on their few acres of land, and lead the lives of semi-peasants. It was hoped that the resettled laborer would gain all the biological advantages which were attributed by the Nazis to the mystic qualities of the soil. Socially, it was expected that the semi-peasant would exert a stabilizing influence in society and gradually move upwards into the rural middle class. The "rurban" community was thus regarded as an effective way of eliminating proletarian living conditions and thereby solving the problem of the proletariat in modern society.[4]

The subsequent program included provisions for increasing the number of peasants (here regarded as small, but independent, property holders), for the settlement of laborers in "rurban" communities, for the dispersal of industries over all parts of the country, for a shift from rail to canal transportation, and for general planning in the use of land. The most counterrevolutionary features of this program related to industrial location and transportation.[5] If realized, these goals would have dispensed with the prevailing industrial setup, which was organized around railroads and coal deposits. The new canal program would have shifted the center of industry from western to central and southern Germany.[6] Hence, these two features of the rural program faced the adamant opposition of the regular army and big business. At this time, however (early in the regime), few industries were actually relocated. Our discussion here will therefore be limited to the attempts to transform farmhands into independent peasants, to establish laborers in "rurban" settlements, and to arrive at a general plan for the use of land.

SETTLEMENT OF PEASANTS

When the Nazis came to power, 70 per cent of the people lived in cities, 30 per cent in rural communities. The intransigent Nazis declared it as their aim to reverse the ratio between urban and rural populations. This called for an extensive increase in the number of farmers. The commissioner for settlement in the Ministry of Agriculture set the goal at 15,000 new farms each year. Did the Nazis realize this goal?

A new law of July 14, 1933, separated "rurban" from farm settlement and gave full authority for the settling of farmers to the Nazified Ministry of Agriculture. The Minister announced the two principles of his settlement policy. First, farm settlement was to be limited to land that could be made available through purchase or reclamation. Hence, no major change in the property structure of land was intended; the estates of the *Junkers* remained untouched. Second, candidates for resettlement were to consist only of young peasants who had been disinherited by the Nazi law on estates or of farmhands with extensive experience.[7] Correspondingly, preference was given to prospective applicants in the following order:

a) disinherited sons of the farm
b) farmhands on estates
c) fully or partly unemployed farmhands.

The priority list excluded all city dwellers. The law thus dispensed with the goal of a general increase in the farm population. Farm settlement became a means of helping young farmers whom the law on entailed estates deprived of their inheritance.

The most difficult problem was that of securing land for settlement. During the depression many large indebted estates were willing to sell land to special purchasing agencies of the government. This supply gradually disappeared when higher food prices raised land prices; therefore, the new settlement act of January, 1935, was intended to keep land prices down and facilitate the transfer of indebted land to the government. The act emphasized the pre-emption rights of the governmental purchasing agencies. These agencies were authorized to reduce "unreasonable" land prices prior to purchase. A ceiling was thus established for the prices of land for prospective settlers. Moreover, the act laid down three rules for the creditors of indebted larger estates:

a) A mortgagor was forbidden to give notice on his loan when the indebted estate passed from a private owner to a government purchasing agency.
b) A mortgagor could not object to the division of the indebted land among many settlers as long as they jointly assumed the obligations of the original debtor.
c) When the transfer was completed, the mortgagor could ask for a new collateral on his loan. If so, he would receive new papers from a government bank in place of his old mortgage deed.

These provisions were advantageous for government and debtors but not for creditors. Indebtedness ceased to be a bar to the settlement of farmers on unprofitable estates. The government could secure indebted land merely through an exchange of private for public mortgage papers. The continued pressure on creditors prevented them from attempting to do anything about the new settlement act.

Nevertheless, the act of 1935 fell short of its desired goal and proved to be singularly unsatisfactory. The price ceiling on the sale of settlement land was made ineffective by the fact that the price paid by governmental purchasing agencies per acre of land rose from 643 marks in 1932 to 1,457 in 1938.[8] Fewer applicants were interested in resettlement after 1935 because they were finding better-paying jobs in the cities. Profits in farming enabled many estate-holders to settle their debts. Higher prices reduced the available land for settlement.

In fact, the much-despised Weimar Republic had a much

better record in farm settlements than did the Nazis. This
can be seen from the following table:

WEIMAR REPUBLIC			THIRD REICH*		
Years	*New Settlements*	*Acreage (hectares)*	*Years*	*New Settlements*	*Acreage (hectares)*
1927	3,372	36,704	1933	4,914	60,297
1928	4,253	50,616	1934	4,827	72,969
1929	5,545	61,213	1935	3,905	68,338
1930	7,441	79,833	1936	3,308	60,358
1931	9,283	99,642	1937	1,900	37,000
1932	8,877	101,926	1938	1,894	26,649
Total	38,771	429,934		20,748	325,611

* *Wirtschaft und Statistik*, 1929, 1932, 1937, 1940. The decline in new farms
continued throughout the Nazi regime (see ibid., 1942, pp. 375–78).

There were three reasons for this dismal failure of the Nazis'
program in farm settlement. Politically, the two deals with
Schmitt and von Blomberg set definite limits to the amount
of land available for settlement. These agreements prevented
the Nazis from using violence against the *Junkers*. Nor could
the Nazis buy out the holders of indebted estates. The German Settlement Bank had very limited funds. It could not
sell bonds and bills because of the ban imposed on such
issues by the Central Bank. In effect, Schacht refused to give
the Nazis the cash with which to finance their extensive resettlement program.

Economically, the rapid increase in resettlement under the
Weimar Republic and the poor showing under the Nazis
were due to the same cause: the relationship between migration and business cycles. When city life afforded less opportunity and unemployment rose, migration to cities slowed
down and was even reversed. People who had been farmers
were ready to return to the country. But in periods of prosperity more jobs at better wages were available, and young

farmers moved to the city. During the years 1936–39, this correlation between prosperity and migration became effective again in spite of all Nazi propaganda for the healthy rural life.

Militarily, more laborers had to be employed in war plants; and when skilled laborers got scarce, the earlier restrictions upon migration to the cities were removed. For three years, agriculture became the reservoir for industrial manpower. Ideologically, the Nazis in agriculture found it increasingly difficult to reconcile the requirements of the war economy with their ideal of ruralism. Many lost interest in their original "peasant socialism"; others followed the "necessities of the day," as dictated by the oligarchic clique of the party. For all these reasons (political, economic, ideological, and military), the resettlement of workers on farms was a failure.

OVER-ALL LAND-USE PLANNING

The core of Nazi ruralism was the ambitious idea of general planning for the use of all land. This planning was expected to be based upon definite principles, which were stated by Gottfried Feder in a speech made in Berlin.[9] First, the right to build homes or factories or to use land according to the personal interests of owners or builders was to be abolished. Instead, land must be utilized according to a comprehensive plan of land use formulated by the government. Feder promised to provide such a plan (*Reichsplanungsgesetz*) in the near future. Second, the whole pattern of city codes for houses and the construction of buildings was to be basically revised. A new uniform building code was, he said, necessary in order that a uniform housing policy might be followed in all parts of Germany. The principles of such a policy would be stated in the forthcoming law on construction (*Reichsbaugesetz*). Third, though the principles of industrial relocation and of urban housing policy could not yet be stated, two preliminary principles relative to the location of industries were emphasized by Feder. (1) A few basic industries only should be located near sources of raw materials. All other industries should be dispersed over the *Reich*. This would do away with the concentration of industries in a few overdeveloped areas. (2) The federal government should assume the authority to issue directives to industrial and municipal landholders and initiate the relocation of industries. For this purpose, the office of the commissioner for resettlements would prepare a law on expropriation (*Reichsenteignunggesetz*) which would enable the government to take possession of any property required for land-use. Furthermore, the various local and regional plans for the use of land and the building of villages and cities had to be integrated. The new office of the commissioner for resettlement would establish a department for formulating land-use plans. The department would study the local and regional plans and integrate them into a general plan for the *Reich*. Moreover, the commissioner would revise the present local and regional planning offices and appoint the local and regional officials as representatives of the central office.

This was Feder's program for the use of land. Shortly before he delivered his speech (in March, 1934) he had been appointed general commissioner of "rurban" settlement policy. Feder and his friends regarded his appointment as a victory over the conservative elements in the party. *Gauleiter* Koch welcomed the new commissioner and saw in the appointment an endorsement of his own attempt to relocate or settle industries in East Prussia.[10] The leaders of the Food Estate, however, emphasized the scarcity of land and opposed its use for non-agricultural purposes.[11] Big business disapproved of the ideas, based upon race and population, that were implicit in Feder's resettlement program and held that settlement should be regarded as primarily an economic problem: projects were to be adopted only if they were self-supporting. Above all, governmental subsidies would have to be avoided.[12]

Feder began to build up elaborate administrative machinery for his office. Department IV in the Ministry of Labor, dealing with the settlement of laborers and the granting of rent subsidies to the unemployed, was transferred to Feder's office. Also, the two divisions on housing and settlement policy in the Prussian Ministries of Economics and Labor were made accountable to Feder. Feder thus got control over all governmental agencies dealing with settlement policies outside of agriculture. As usual, party organizations were closely connected with governmental agencies. Johann Ludowici became Feder's deputy. He was appointed to a civil-service position although he remained a party official, and, having been put in charge of all settlement policies of the party and made head of the office of labor homes (*Heimstaettenamt*) in the Labor Front, he could assure his superiors that a specialized party agency would keep track of all the governmental agencies administering settlement policies. Feder's first, and almost only, official act was the preliminary settlement law of July 3, 1934. The purpose of the act was to give his office full information about all residential construction of significance. Builders and governmental agencies were ordered to report (*a*) on all building projects that created more than fifty homes, (*b*) on the relocation of non-agricultural plants creating more than twenty-five homes for workers, and (*c*) on the extension or repair of plants if this led to the employment of fifty additional laborers or the resettlement of twenty-five families. Obviously, Feder meant business; he was in the process of imposing upon the country a Nazi housing and industrial location policy.

The belief among leaders in the construction industry—a belief which was shared by the generals—that Feder's land policy would affect their business detrimentally created a welcome opportunity for Schacht. After his appointment as Minister of Economics, Schacht threw Feder out of his ministry; Feder was also removed from his offices in the party. The deputy leader of the party announced on November 26, 1934, that Feder was on vacation. In his place, Fritz Todt was appointed as the new leader of the party organization of technicians. Two weeks later the news came through that Undersecretary Feder had been pensioned off from his positions and relieved from his duties as commissioner of settlement policies.[13]

In short order, Feder's new administration was destroyed. Jurisdiction over settlement and housing policies was transferred back to the Ministry of Labor. A new board was created whose function was to advise the Minister of Labor on settlement policy. The head of this board was Ludowici, who had survived the purge and retained his offices in the party and the Labor Front. He was willing to accept as a condition of his new appointment that party officers could only advise. All administrative functions were to be handled exclusively by the local and regional offices of the ministry.[14] Similarly, Feder's ruralist policies were gradually replaced by a policy of using land primarily for military purposes and in preparation for war. In addition to the office in the Ministry of Labor, offices in two other ministries were authorized to deal with land policy. Most important was the land office in the war ministry. The director of this office was appointed with the consent of the Minister of Agriculture. The military office had two functions: to determine principles for the use of land by the armed forces and to select the kind of land that should be made available for urban and rural settlements. In effect, the land policies of the Minister of Agriculture and the Minister of Labor were formulated and approved by the war ministry.[15]

To be sure, Hitler did create an academy for research in

land-planning, but this academy came under the control of the Minister of Education, who used it to predetermine the research carried on by professors and students at universities. An office of space-planning (*Raumordnung*) was also established, and the Minister of Church Affairs, Hanns Kerrl, was appointed as its head. He revealed that the initiative for the formation of this office had come from the Ministry of Agriculture, which was opposed to the army's tendency to use agricultural land for military purposes;[16] but Kerrl's office was actually of little help to the Nazis in agriculture. The office itself was soon reduced to serving as headquarters for the compulsory planning organizations that were formed in most cities, whereas the army succeeded in securing the land that it needed for military purposes. The land available for agricultural cultivation fell from 20.5 million acres in 1933 to 19.2 million in 1938.[17] The activities of army and party—with their highways and stadiums—reduced the land available for farmers, and this reduction corresponded to the declining number of people living on the land.

Thus there were interesting causal connections between the purge of the SA leaders in June, 1934, the re-establishing of big-business control over the Ministry of Economics, the elimination of Feder and other intransigent Nazis from their positions of influence, and the failure of the counterrevolutionary programs for land-use and industry dispersal. If Feder and his cohorts could have relied upon the quasi-military power of the counterrevolutionary SA leaders for a longer period of time, the defeat of these programs would have been much more difficult for the leaders of big business.

HOUSES FOR EVERYONE

One of the original demands of the intransigent Nazis was that everyone should own his home. Such a goal was coupled with ruralism in two ways. In cities, the geographical distribution of housing was determined by income: each income group lived in a different residential section. This "class distinction in housing" was to be eliminated through a program providing every family with its own home. The new houses were to be located in rural areas, in small communities, or in the outskirts of cities. Therefore, three kinds of houses were given preference: (*a*) the house with a small farm attached where a worker derived his income from a job in a factory as well as from his crops (*Landwirtschaftliche Nebensiedlung*), (*b*) the self-owned home with a few acres of land to be cultivated by the family (*Kleinsiedlung*), (*c*) the self-owned home with a garden in a small community or on the fringe of a city (*Heimstaette*). These were the kinds of homes which the intransigent Nazis wanted to build for laborers.[18] It was hoped that such a housing policy would establish social harmony among groups and move laborers upwards into the middle class.

In the first year of the regime, the Nazis gradually abandoned the practice, which had been developed in the depression years, of resettling the unemployed. Under the Weimar Republic, rent subsidies were transformed into resettlement subsidies if the worker and his family moved to the fringe of the city, where they could live more cheaply in temporary living quarters (*Stadtrandsiedlung*). These settlements were bitterly attacked by the Nazis. Their main argument was that the unemployed had no chance of making a living. The small plots of 1,000 square meters could bring, at best, some supplementary income. Hence the Nazis refused resettlement subsidies to wholly unemployed workers. Only workers with part-time jobs were granted such subsidies. Moreover, more funds were made available for resettlement in small communities instead of in the outskirts of large cities.[19]

A new over-all housing policy was proposed by Feder when

he was appointed commissioner for settlements. His program
for housing included the following points:

1) Cities of over 100,000 inhabitants had to be reduced. The
   slums and old-town sections in cities had to be eliminated
   or rebuilt. The new settlements at the fringe of cities
   would have to go. The cost for transportation to plants
   was too high; conditions were not favorable for raising
   large families.
2) New cities should be located in the country, be small in
   size, and be built in every province of the land. These
   "rurban" communities should be the backbone of the
   German settlement, racial, and population policies.
3) A program to resettle industries had to be adopted. Most
   of them would have to be removed from the large to the
   small cities. This would put an end to the conglomeration
   of millions in a few large cities, and would prepare the
   ground for healthy and decent living.[20]

In all, Feder's program visualized 20 million new homes in a
period of 50 years, compared to the total of 16.3 million
homes which existed at the end of 1932 in Germany.

Schacht nipped these plans in the bud. The dismissal of
Feder and the dismantling of his office were severe defeats
for the housing program of the intransigent Nazis. This is
obvious from the train of events that led to the formation
of the actual housing policy that was finally adopted.

The authority for housing-resettlement was returned to the
Ministry of Labor. The ministry issued a decree (Ablösungs-
erlass) on February 19, 1935, which revised the whole policy
of small settlements in the country or in small towns (Neben-
erwerb and Kleinsiedlung). The decree was based on the
principle that the federal government should no longer subsidize this form of housing. The necessary funds would have
to come either from settlers or banks or through the repayment of federal loans by previous settlers. Formerly, the loan

from the government had been about 3,000 marks. Now it could not exceed 1,000 marks, except for "old fighters" in the Nazi party, whose loans could be increased by 200 to 400 marks. The contribution of the settlers was raised; it was not to be below 20 per cent of the total value of land and home. The greater part of the funds for settlement was to come from private loans, and interest was not to exceed 4.5 per cent. But the credit institutions opposed this limit and secured a rate of 5 per cent plus a commission for banks. The total value of the settlement was not to exceed 3,000 marks, as compared with 8,000 to 10,000 marks for a worker's home in the "free market." Subsequently, however, the sum was increased to 3,500, then to 4,500 and even 5,000 marks. In order to keep the cost of construction and maintenance down, city governments had to reduce their fees for schools, streets and sidewalks, and so forth. The homebuilding officers of the Labor Front had to keep the prices of land down and make sure that builders would adhere to the government's construction specifications.[21]

The prospective settlers were carefully selected. Applicants had to have reasonably secure jobs and incomes. Unemployed workers were excluded from the whole program. Monthly wage income had to be four times as high as the obligations for the settlement. Among the fully employed laborers, with sufficient income, preference was given to (a) old fighters in the Nazi party, (b) families with more than four children, and (c) families who were racially sound and politically reliable.[22] In short, the Nazis received preference over others in the new regulations pertaining to urban settlements.

The tests of racial soundness and political reliability were administered by the Labor Front. Its home offices (*Heimstaettenaemter*) cooperated with city governments and employment offices in considering the applicants for houses and in examining the land designated for settlement. When the

Labor Front came to a negative decision, the governmental
agencies concerned had to drop the case. But when the Labor
Front approved, all subsequent administrative functions
were performed by the appropriate government offices. Thus
the usual division of function between party and government
offices was not introduced until after the intransigent Nazis
were defeated.

There were many small changes in the provisions for
"rurban" settlements. Rates of interest were reduced, the
total cost of settlements was increased, the necessary size of
the land was decreased.[23] These modifications were intended
to satisfy the criticism expressed by the settlers: that the actual living space was too small, especially for the third child;
that construction was poor and the general conditions un-
sanitary. In spite of all these modifications, however, the decline of "rurban" settlements continued. Their number fell
from 30,000 in 1934 to 14,000 in 1936.

To be sure, the intransigent Nazis did try to develop a substitute policy. They induced employers to build "rurban"
settlements for their workers; they announced a new program
for a German settlement policy that would become effective
in the future; they gradually made demands for "normal"
houses for laborers. How successfully did the intransigents
carry through these supplementary policies in housing?

Even before it was implemented the program ran into trouble. When candidates for "rurban" settlements heard of a
more favorable program that had been promised for the future, they withdrew their applications. Applicants preferred
to wait for the cheaper houses. The Nazis took steps to destroy this notion. Ley, in one of his speeches, declared that
"cheaper homes" in the future would not be "given" to the
settlers. Workers would have to pay for the full value of their
homes in any case. Savings in construction would provide the
opportunity for the government to reduce its subsidies and
withdraw from the financing of "rurban" settlements altogether.[24]

The Labor Front had argued furiously against "company towns" for workers. In 1935, it tried to induce employers either to build "rurban" houses or to transfer the ownership of houses gradually to laborers. In the spring of 1935, an agreement was reached among the Labor Front, the economic organization of the construction industry, and the credit cooperatives for housing. This agreement was to the effect that industrialists would build houses near the plants but sell them to their laborers. Employers would make use of the federal subsidies for "rurban" settlements, put up a part of the contribution expected of settlers, and take responsibility for the mortgage money provided by banks.[25] In spite of this proposal, 20 per cent of the necessary capital remained uncovered. The headquarters of the construction organization suggested that employers should take over the missing 20 per cent on the condition that workers would repay such loans.

Yet not much came of the agreement. Companies remained owners of the houses for their workers. When employment rose, labor turnover increased. Employers asked laborers who left their jobs to vacate the houses. The agreement with the Labor Front was dropped. Leaders of the construction industry suggested that a program of building "straight" labor houses should be adopted. The Labor Front put up some resistance but gradually gave in.[26] The second part of its housing program, by which workers were to become owners of their houses, was discarded.

It has to be emphasized that repeal of the program for "rurban" settlements and house ownership by laborers was caused by the opposition of big business to the program and by the preparations for war. The former limited the Nazi housing program to small dimensions; the latter killed even the reduced plans for housing.

The table on the next page classifies the new homes built under the Nazis and gives the total built in each of the five years from 1933 to 1937.

The number of "rurban" settlements and houses owned by

	1933	1934	1935	1936	1937*
A. HOMES PREFERRED BY INTRANSIGENT NAZIS					
Home with Some Acres	25,000	30,000	22,000	14,000	19,000
Home with Small Garden	8,400	15,000	10,200	4,200	400
Rural Houses of Farm Hands	100	200	100	0	1,500
Emergency Houses	0	5,000	7,800	700	800
	33,500	50,200	40,100	18,900	21,700
B. HOMES PREFERRED BY IMPERIALIST NAZIS					
"People's Homes"	0	0	0	7,500	35,000
Privately Built and Privately Owned Houses Partly Financed Through Federal Loans	1,000	7,000	28,000	64,000	80,000
Total of New Homes	34,500	57,200	68,100	90,400	136,700

* "Das Wohnungsbaujahr," *Soziale Praxis,* April, 1937, pp. 501–2; June, 1938, p. 693.

laborers declined after 1934. From 1936 onwards, the "people's" houses, that is, dwellings without any land and not owned by workers, increased, as did loans for privately built houses. Increased employment of laborers in war plants induced the Nazis to abandon their "rurban" housing program. At the same time the total outlay of construction rose from 3.2 billion marks in 1933 to 12 billion marks in 1938. The portion spent for residential construction fell from 28 per cent to 18 per cent, whereas the portion for public and military construction increased from 72 to 82 per cent.[27] Residential construction was limited to the building of houses essential for the war economy. The same picture of declining government funds for private housing can be seen from the table on the opposite page.

The total funds for residential construction declined during the depression and then rose slowly. Private funds, organized

FINANCING RESIDENTIAL CONSTRUCTION*
(in million marks)

Years	Mortgages of Credit Institutions	Private Funds not from Banks	Government Funds
1928	1,325	135	1,340
1933	165	600	185
1934	375	825	300
1935	600	775	225
1936	880	960	165

* Kruschwitz, "Die Deutsche Wohnungswirtschaft seit 1933," pp. 26–53.

and unorganized, accounted for the increase in total funds. Governmental expenditures were very small compared to the considerable public expenditures under the Weimar Republic, and even the small expenditure of governmental funds fell after 1934.

The shift to the war economy required a further change in the organization of the Labor Front and a weeding out of intransigent Nazis. When the Four Year Plan was adopted, Ludowici published an article on "total defense."[28] He distinguished between two kinds of defense, one for peace, another for war. Each required an active settlement policy and a general planning of land use. The Labor Front, he said, had prepared in part for the defense of peace. Its future settlement and housing policy would from now on concentrate upon "defense for war." Yet these artificial distinctions did not help him. A new leader was appointed for the *Heimstaettenamt* of the Labor Front, and the Labor Front radically changed its housing policy. Said the new leader in charge of labor homes: "One cannot overlook the fact that large sections of the population do not appreciate the small rural settlements. The majority of laborers prefer apartments in cities."[29] Therefore, the original goal of the intransigent Nazis of a house for everyone was discarded—presumably the workers preferred apartments.

In reality, the Four Year Plan of September, 1936, ended the last features of ruralism. It called for a change in land policy as well as in housing policy. Agricultural land policies were subordinated to military requirements. Housing had to satisfy the needs of laborers in war plants and substitute industries. A decree of the Ministry of Labor on November 17, 1936, announced that financial support of "rurban" settlements would be stopped. Financial support and mortgage guarantees would be given only for houses built for laborers in industrial centers. The monthly maximum rent for homes of this kind was not to exceed forty marks. Similarly, a new estate tax law of December 1, 1936, withdrew all tax exemptions for privately owned houses and "rurban" settlements. The real estate market came under government regulation; rents for apartments and houses were fixed in connection with the general price ceiling of October, 1936. Housing for the purposes of war was the only criterion for governmental and party actions after 1936.[30]

In consequence, the three features of ruralism failed for different reasons. Resettlement of farmhands failed because of the opposition of the *Junkers* and the generals. Planned land-use failed because of the opposition of big business and the generals. "Rurban" housing, however, was opposed primarily by the oligarchic clique of the party, which established a war economy in time of peace through its Four Year Plan.

REARMAMENT VERSUS RURALISM

From 1934 to the end of 1936, rearmament was the main economic policy of the party, the army, and big business. This policy was a first step toward the development of a war economy in time of peace. How and in which way did rearmament and the war economy contribute to the failure of ruralism?

Briefly, rearmament constituted an effective limit to the realization of ruralism. Big business and the army did not fight openly against ruralism, which would have brought them in conflict with Nazi ideology. Instead, ruralism was fought as a detriment to German rearmament. Intransigent Nazis, on the other hand, tried to prove that social harmony via ruralism was a means of increasing the inherent strength of the regime.

When the party leaders introduced the Four Year Plan, they decided to eliminate the remnants of ruralism. Land-use and housing policy were radically changed in order to conform with the requirements of the war economy. This new policy produced also an ideological conflict between two Nazi ideals: middle-class socialism and imperialism. In the field of practical policy, the change was radical and decisive. All believers in ruralism were removed from office and deprived of any influence. In the ideological field, however, a gradual transformation took place. Features of middle-class socialism were incorporated into the predominant ideals of fascist imperialism and racialism.

Conflict between ruralism and rearmament appeared as a competition for funds. Scarcity of capital constituted the major economic difficulty for the realization of both programs. Under Schacht's leadership, the government adopted a program of investment planning which involved the reservation of available capital for financing rearmament and also extensive control of the capital and money markets. The policy of investment planning for rearmament provided big business with a weapon with which to fight against the realization of ruralism.

Normally, funds for rural settlements and houses were obtained through the issue of special mortgage titles (*Pfandbriefe*) by land or real estate banks, public or private. Under the Weimar Republic, the German Settlement Bank was set up to finance the purchase of land for rural settlements. The bank secured funds through the sale of bills and bonds. Under Schacht, however, the Central Bank closed the capital market to private and public mortgage banks. Schacht imposed an embargo upon the issue of new bills and bonds. Restriction of entry to the capital market was also applied to the German Settlement Bank, which was dominated by the Nazified Ministry of Agriculture. In consequence, land and mortgage banks suffered from a dearth of capital. The Nazis in agriculture were unable to buy land for rural settlement.

An embargo was also imposed upon the conversion of outstanding securities. Permits for conversion were issued only if new funds were not required. Permitted conversions usually had to lead to an effective reduction of interest on securities. The policy of deliberately lowering the rate of interest was legalized in July, 1936. Creditors of mortgages not yet converted had to reduce the rate of interest "voluntarily." If no agreement could be reached, the debtor could obtain a reduction by court action.[31] The restrictions upon issue and conversion as well as a lowering of interest rates reduced profit opportunities and caused investors to refrain from investing their funds in agricultural and, especially, ruralist projects.

Refused issues and rejected conversions lowered the effective demand for funds. Employment springing from rearmament, however, increased the supply of funds. Capital accumulated in savings banks, but their traditional investment opportunities were closed by the actions of the Central Bank. The result of manipulating the demand for and the supply of funds was a seeming liquidity in the capital market. This enabled the treasury to place governmental bills and bonds with private banks or the public. Funds obtained were utilized to finance rearmament orders. In consequence, investment planning produced two effects: it deliberately reduced the investment of funds in agriculture and small business; it channelled the available funds to the armament industries via increased orders from the military.

The policy of deliberately limiting investment in residential construction and resettlement was opposed not only by the intransigent Nazis. Opposition was strong also among the leaders of the mortgage and savings banks and the leaders of the construction industry. The numerous complaints of financial institutions were based on two arguments. Increasing bond prices and direct investments were regarded as evidence that funds were available for investment in new issues. Bankers asserted that government investment planning could not reach these funds and that financial institutions should be permitted to absorb idle funds or that government agencies should prevent direct investment in less desirable projects. Moreover, a causal connection was asserted to exist between governmental subsidies for housing and the Central Bank's embargo on new bonds. The smaller the funds absorbed by the credit institutions, it was said, the greater the demand for governmental subsidies. Thus, if the private credit institutions were permitted to issue new bonds, the government would be enabled to reduce its subsidies.

As our preceding table on the financing of residential construction has shown, however, governmental subsidies consistently declined, while direct investment as well as institutional investment rose. The argument of the financial institutions therefore amounted to a complaint that the embargo fostered direct investment and thereby reduced their business opportunities. Leading Nazis emphatically rejected the complaint. The interests of the state and of national defense, they insisted, were more important than the private interests of the banks.[32]

The construction industry, in contrast to the credit institutions, did not suffer from a limit on its volume of business. Firms in this field experienced a marked shift from residential to public and military or industrial construction. The close relationship between nonresidential construction and the armament boom, however, made it difficult to attack directly the increasing governmental expenditures. The camouflaged criticism of the leader of the residential-construction group proceeded along two lines. He accepted the official justification of rearmament: a temporary redirection of business until Germany had reached military equality with her neighbors. Looking into the future, he asked himself how the prevailing level of employment could be maintained when public orders for construction ceased. His answer was that residential construction would provide an important reserve. He calculated a backlog of 1.2 million homes. To this he added the net demand for each year in the future. He concluded with the plea that everything should be done to keep residential construction firms going so that they would be ready to fulfill their function of taking up the future slack in employment.[33]

The discussion of the future demand for houses was quite extensive. The various estimates did not differ greatly. Goerdeler, during his tenure as price commissioner, had initiated a study of the demand for homes. His staff estimated a probable need for 1.5 million homes and a minimal need for 1 million. The latter alone he regarded as effective demand, since the former was based on an estimate of what kind of minimum shelter people ought to have, while the latter was based on their capacity to pay. To this backlog of 1 million homes had to be added the yearly requirement of 200,000 homes. Hence, Goerdeler anticipated a need for 1.8 million homes for the coming four years. This was a conservative estimate. The expert of the official Research Institute on Business Cycles estimated a need for 4 million homes for the years 1938–48.[34]

The estimates of the future need for houses were closely related to the general economic policy of the regime. The estimates were based upon the assumption that there would be a definite limit to the rearmament boom. Economists, in estimating demand, tried to prove that a decline in armament orders would not have to lead to a depression. Instead, the armament boom could be transformed into a residential construction boom. Such a change, from armaments to housing, would guarantee a level of high employment in the future. Thus without saying so, the economists established an even more vital point. The backlog demand for homes proved conclusively that the rearmament boom was not an economic necessity. Full employment could have been secured by concentrating upon residential construction and increased exportation of goods. The argument that Germany in the thirties either had to produce military equipment or suffer severe unemployment was incorrect. Not the nature of the German economy, as is frequently asserted, but the militarist policy of the Nazi regime made the rearmament boom inevitable.

An alternative to rearmament was proposed by the intransigent Nazis as well as by the leaders of the construction and export industries. The latter demanded that economic policy be shifted to create a boom either in residential construction or exports while the intransigent Nazis fought for the realization of their program of "rurban" settlements. Thus it gradually became clear that the policy of increasing residential construction and exports was the real alternative to an armament boom as well as to a war economy.

The man who stated this alternative comprehensively and fought for it publicly was Dr. Carl Goerdeler. During his tenure as price commissioner, Goerdeler came into conflict with the rearmament policy; the price level could not be stabilized under conditions of the rearmament boom. In his search for opportunities to reduce unit costs Goerdeler surveyed all aspects of the rearmament policy. His conclusion was that a drastic change in economic policy was called for.

He proposed his economic program in many articles published in the general and economic press.

His basic suggestion was that Germany should return to a full participation in the world economy. As he pointed out, such a policy would have entailed (a) a return to an international currency and elimination of exchange control, (b) balancing the budget and calling a halt to the rise in the national debt, (c) a reduction in armament orders and increased emphasis upon exports, and (d) a concentrated program of home-building. The boom in home-building was regarded as a necessary complement to the expected boom in exports, for it was expected that residential construction would help to shorten the transition from the production of war to civilian materials and sustain the export boom.[35]

How large a capital investment would be necessary for extensive residential construction? Goerdeler estimated that to build 360,000 homes each year, each house costing 6,000 marks, would call for an investment of about 2.2 billion marks. Such a large investment program, covering many years, would require a basic change in the financial policy of the government. The government would have to reduce drastically its subsidies to builders. It would also have to refrain from placing governmental bonds, balance its budget, and open the capital market to private banks and firms. The financing of construction projects was again to become the function of mortgage and savings banks. Moreover, every effort was to be made to reduce building costs. Goerdeler recognized, however, that a substantial decline in capital outlay for standard houses could not be expected and that a new type of inexpensive house would have to be built. He therefore supported a program of small settlements (*Kleinsiedlung*) in rural areas. The houses could be built cheaply, and the settler could realize about 200 marks in real income from his plot of land. Goerdeler believed that a total of 1.5 to 1.8 million families would be willing to return to the land, live as settlers, and work part-time in factories.[36] Thus, the settlement program would satisfy the elementary needs of families without homes; and the investment program would provide the capital for extensive building of "regular" (relatively more expensive) houses. High-level employment could thus be insured without resort to the stimulus of war-materials production.

In spite of his inability to see the value of deficit financing under conditions of unemployment, Goerdeler's economic program was no small achievement. He recognized that the existing needs for more residential construction and more exports could be used to stimulate business in general, and he initiated a plan similar to the intransigent Nazis' settlement program. His adoption of a plan of this kind was a shrewd move, based on the established fact that, in 1936, an economic program could be adopted only if it were supported by the party. Implicitly, Goerdeler's program tried to mobilize the adherents of middle-class socialism against the ruling group of the party. The same policy was pursued relative to business. The construction and export industries were played against the leaders of heavy industries whose rising profits depended upon continued armament orders. In a democracy this unification of otherwise diverse interests would have had a definite political effect. What happened to this economic program in the Nazi regime?

The crisis in raw materials and foreign exchange, which limited the armament boom, reached its peak in the summer of 1936. Hitler appointed Göring as head of a commission which was to examine all aspects of economic policy. This commission also accepted outside proposals for alleviating the crisis. Two such memoranda had been prepared for the fateful cabinet meeting of September 4, 1936. One came from Minister of War von Blomberg, the other from Dr. Goerdeler. The former proposed a substantial increase in the production of military materials. Dr. Goerdeler's memorandum summarized his economic program, which Göring condemned as "absolutely useless," because it proposed "a considerable limitation of armaments."[37]

The opposition of the party leaders killed the chances for the projected boom in construction and exports. Goerdeler and his allies were powerless. They did not command the military forces and economic organizations with which to fight successfully against the imperialist Nazis and the generals, nor could Goerdeler present his program to the public after the party leaders had condemned it. Hitler's decision against internal reform and increased civilian employment turned the scales in favor of war and also settled Goerdeler's future.

The War Minister's proposal of an extensive military-economic expansion became the central feature of the Four Year plan, through which a war economy was to be established in time of peace. All fields of economic activity soon felt the impact of the new plan. Some areas were greatly expanded, others were drastically reduced. Rising residential construction was one of the fields on which the government imposed severe restrictions. The new housing policy of the regime was laid down in a decree of November 17, 1936. "Rurban" settlements ceased to be the goal of the public-housing authorities. The new aim was to build inexpensive homes for "essential" workers. Governmental subsidies were limited to projects providing homes for such workers.[38] The aversion to huge apartment buildings for workers, to crowding them into cities, was completely discarded. Housing had to satisfy the requirements of the war economy. The rural settlement program became the victim of the Four Year Plan.

The construction of small or makeshift homes was extensive from 1935 to 1939 in middle Germany, which became the second industrial center of Germany. The population of this region increased by almost a million. Some cities experienced an increase of over 100 per cent in their population.

From 1933 to 1938, the population of Magdeburg rose from 102,000 to 233,000, that of Halle from 98,000 to 202,000, that of Bitterfeld from 38,000 to 80,000. These cities became the centers of the various industries, fostered by the Four Year Plan,[39] that were producing substitutes. In this region, the new housing policy found its most vivid expression; but the new homes that were built did not satisfy the rising demand for shelter. The result was a widespread scarcity of homes, general overcrowding of families, and rising rents, which led to extensive rent control by the government, beginning in 1937.

In all regions, residential construction came under extensive regulation by the government. Göring issued a decree on November 7, 1936, which gave employment offices full control over the supply of skilled laborers. Construction firms had to report every project which involved a payment of over 5,000 marks in wages. At a later date, all projects requiring hired workers had to be reported. They could no longer be hired by employers directly but had to be secured through employment offices. This requirement enabled the offices to channel workers to the desired construction projects and to withhold them from nonessential projects. The result was a substantial decline in residential construction. Total expenditures for residential construction fell from 2.2 billion marks in 1936 to 1.5 billion in 1939.

At the end of 1938, Göring appointed the Nazi leader Fritz Todt as a plenipotentiary for the construction industry. Todt already had full charge of the construction of military roads and fortifications, and the extension of his authority to include civilian construction gave him the opportunity to utilize firms and laborers for war construction. A priority system for building projects, public as well as private, was introduced which established governmental allocation for scarce building materials. The working period was extended to the winter months. Methods of construction were simplified and "rationalized" by governmental decree. Firms were instructed to form cooperatives so as to assume jointly the responsibility for large public projects.[40] The resulting allocation of labor and materials to public projects incorporated the construction industry into the war sector of the economy. Over-all regulation of the industry for war preparation destroyed any opportunity for a socially desirable and privately financed residential construction boom.

VICTORY OF PARTY RULERS AND BIG BUSINESS

In the decisive and fateful year of 1936, middle-class socialism in all its aspects had been defeated. Artisan socialism was effectively stifled by the joint efforts of the top Nazi leaders, the organizations of big business, and the generals. Peasant socialism alone recorded some degree of success but fell short of the Nazi goals, either because of the Nazis' alliance with the generals or because of the Four Year Plan, which incorporated agriculture into the developing war economy in time of peace. Rather than concentrating upon the victorious and defeated groups themselves, let us attempt to determine the significance of the defeat of the economic counterrevolution for the ideology and policy of the party, for the program of economic rearmament, and for the policy of invigorating German capitalism in the first phase of the regime.

The defeat of middle-class socialism spelled the end of the ideological and political counterrevolution of the original mass movement started by the Nazis. Ideologically, a basic change developed in the relative significance of the six genuine ideals. In 1933 all these ideals seemed to be of the same relative importance. At the end of 1936 the ideological situation had changed drastically. Fascist imperialism, racialism, and the rule of the elite were the only ideals in which the oligarchic clique genuinely believed and which continued to guide their actions throughout the regime. Middle-class socialism, Nordic religion, and social harmony between laborers and employers had been discarded as ideals influencing the major economic or political goals of the rulers. Nazi ideals were effectively divided into active and passive ideologies. Fascist imperialism and racialism functioned as the supreme ideals for the second phase of the regime, the realization of which had to be sought at any price.[41]

The passive ideologies ceased to be active goals of governmental policy, and the organizations of the Nazi party were no longer permitted to push for their realization. Individual party members, however, continued to accept the beliefs originally advocated by the Nazis. The ideal of a Nordic religion remained alive among the SS troops, many of whom quit the regular churches and tried to live up to their "Nordic" beliefs individually. Nordic religion led to auxiliary policies either for the air force or for the new province of the Warthegau, carved out of western Poland. Catholic pilots in the air force suffered from discrimination in the earlier aggressive phase of World War II, and an extensive campaign was waged by the Nazi authorities in the Warthegau to eradicate the Catholic church.[42]

Politically, the defeat of middle-class socialism led to changes in personnel in the second-string leadership of the party and prepared the ground for a new policy to be adopted by the oligarchic clique. In the years 1937–39, the remaining representatives of middle-class socialism lost their positions of influence in party and state. The Labor Front rallied in a last-ditch effort to realize its goal of organizational totality. At the end of 1936 it was announced that all retail organizations would be dissolved and their functions performed by the Labor Front. When Göring reorganized the Ministry of Economics after Schacht's resignation, Rudolf Schmeer, the deputy leader of the Labor Front, took over the department for economic organization. In this new capacity, Schmeer

tried to incorporate the handicraft guilds into the Labor
Front. This attack failed when it was shown to Göring that
the handicraft organization could become a useful agent for
promoting the tasks of the Four Year Plan. Ferdinand
Schramm was appointed as the new leader of the handicraft
estate on January 17, 1938. As an opponent of organizational
totality, Schramm was able to secure Schmeer's downfall and
achieved a reconciliation with Minister Funk, the successor of
Hjalmar Schacht.[43] While the small business groups were
thus able to retain their organizational identity, they lost any
form of self-initiated policy or self-chosen implementation in
the second phase of the regime.

The defeat of middle-class socialism had thus a twofold
significance for the oligarchic clique of the Nazi party. The
split in ideology was not an accidental occurrence but seems
to confirm a rule generally valid for one-party regimes. Those
ideas that have a mass appeal and seek to realize popular
aspirations must be utterly defeated and its spokesmen eliminated before the rulers of the party can proceed to concentrate upon the ideals that are closest to their hearts.[44] The
discovery that ideals appealing to the masses "do not work"
was a necessary condition that had to be satisfied before the
dictatorial rulers of the party could begin to implement fascist imperialism and extreme racialism.

Elimination of all major parts of the economic counterrevolution was followed, in 1936, by the adoption of the
Four Year Plan, which became the new economic program of
the Nazi party. The authority granted to the office formulating the new policy was so comprehensive that Göring was
able to take over ultimate economic leadership also of the
urban small-business groups. All officials of guilds and chambers for handicraft and trade had to become members of the
party and be responsible for their actions to the department
of handicraft and trade (headed by Adrian von Renteln) at
party headquarters.[45] Schacht's famous ruling that only active

artisans and traders could hold offices in these organizations and that they were not to take orders from the party was thereby repealed.

In accepting planning as a means of preparing for fascist imperialism, the oligarchic clique imposed three requirements upon small business. Rather than being respected as a self-contained sector of the economy, small business had to accommodate itself to a limited and prescribed role under the new policy of a war economy in time of peace. On the one hand, the party's principle of organizational domination was applied to small business, the leaders forming an integral organization and the members a mass organization that were incorporated into the apparatus of the party. On the other hand, the whole organizational network of guilds and chambers was simplified. For instance the number of compulsory guilds was reduced from 16,000 in 1935 to 14,024 at the beginning of 1939.[46]

A decree of February 22, 1939, defined the new tasks of small business under the Four Year Plan. The previous exclusion of insufficiently trained masters or merchants now became an open fight against the "incompetents." The crafts of bakers, butchers, barbers, tailors, and shoemakers were declared to be overcrowded, and the criteria of incompetence in these crafts were increased so that more small business firms could be weeded out. In addition to vocational qualifications, any shop or store could now be closed if the master-owners were inefficiently financed, or did not perform an economically justified task, as judged by the government. The new decree not only took away from the guilds the power to decide which firms should be closed but speeded up the tempo at which small businesses were eliminated.

During the years of the depression the total number of handicraft firms had risen from 1.38 million to 1.65 million. The actions of the handicraft organizations produced a reversal of this trend, and the number of stores actually declined with the increased employment opportunities in industry. The extent of the decline can be seen from the following official data.

ENTRY AND EXIT OF HANDICRAFT FIRMS*

Years	New Entrants	Exit of Firms	Net Decrease
1936	104,234	132,109	27,875
1937	75,153	137,726	62,573
1938	59,700	122,642	62,942
	239,087	392,477	153,390

* *Der Vierjahresplan* (Berlin), 1939, p. 1029.

This decline continued, with two interruptions and some exceptions, during the war period, mainly because of the policies sanctioned by the Office of the Four Year Plan. Rather than bringing the originally promised economic stability and security to the handicraft firms, the new economic policy of the Nazi party reinterpreted the handicraft decrees to such an extent that a systematic squeeze was imposed upon small business, in the process of which an increasing number of property-owning masters were transformed into armament-producing workers.

The squeeze was accompanied by a reversal or reorientation of policy for handicraft and trade. This change in policy affected especially the power to set prices for goods and services. The not yet fully achieved authority of the cartels to fix prices and determine the output of small firms was eliminated through the appointment of a price commissioner who froze all prices to the level of October 18, 1936. The Nazi leaders of the compulsory trade associations, Carl Luer and Franz Hayler, not only defended government control of prices but pointed out that for the store-owners, the new price control entailed effective reduction of unit costs and the elimination of incompetents.[47]

The reversal of policy was most pronounced in the field of

vocational training. Faced with a scarcity of skilled workers, the Office of the Four Year Plan attempted to solve the problem by requiring that young workers be trained for specific tasks. Industrial as well as handicraft concerns in steel, other metals, and construction were ordered to report the age composition of their workers, on the basis of which each firm was assigned an apprentice-training quota. If a firm failed to train enough apprentices, without giving acceptable reasons for the failure, the employment office could collect a fine of fifty marks per month for each untrained apprentice below the quota.[48] As a result of this action the number of apprentices in the three industries increased by 49,000—10 per cent of all apprentices for the year 1936–37. By January 1, 1938, a total of 700,000 firms had accepted their obligation to train apprentices.

The increase in the number was accompanied by a reduction in the required period of training. It was decreed by the commissioner of the Four Year Plan that for 103 occupations the training period had to be reduced from four to three years, while partly trained young people had to be released, upon their request, from their contracts after eighteen months of instruction. Apprentices were given the right to request an examination prior to the three-year period, and the chances of passing such examinations were increased because examiners were under pressure to simplify the requirements. Emphasis was increasingly placed upon the training of young men for semiskilled jobs, especially in the coal-mining industry. At the same time, the three rest periods for young people working eight and a half hours a day could be abolished and extensive overtime and night work were specifically permitted. Rather than enjoying a vocational monopoly in which emphasis was placed upon a declining number of increasingly qualified trainees, the guilds and industrial training centers were forced to turn out the largest number of apprentices in the shortest possible period of time.

All these new policies in support of the war economy were implemented by the compulsory craft and merchant guilds. Instead of building up a self-governed artisan economy, the guilds and chambers had become instruments for (*a*) supporting the price-freeze imposed by the state, (*b*) reducing the unit costs of small firms, (*c*) training more apprentices for industry, and (*d*) supplying masters as skilled workers in industry. The new compulsory organizations of small business were thus readily converted by the oligarchic clique of the party into a form of statist control over small business. Thus the middle class joined labor as the oppressed underlying population of the regime.

What was the relationship between economic rearmament and middle-class socialism? In principle, there was no doubt that rearmament was the superior goal. In a memorandum to Hitler, Schacht said, ". . . the accomplishment of the armament program with speed and in quantity is *the* problem of German politics, that everything else therefore should be subordinated to this purpose, as long as the main purpose is not imperiled by neglecting all other questions."[49]

On the levels of specific goals, however, there prevailed a kind of mutual indifference. The generals were so involved in their own military and other tasks that their extensive files reveal no interest in the various aims of middle-class socialism. Nor did the intransigent Nazis in their many writings express themselves on either military or economic rearmament, apart from showing a desire for a stronger Germany. It is likely that in a democracy the two sets of ideals would have clashed at some point, but in a system of partial fascism there was silence on both sides of this particular ideological question.

On the organizational level, however, there was one significant instance of limited mutual support. In 1935 Schacht tried very hard to convince the generals that the principles of compulsory membership and closed crafts or industries should not be applied to economic organizations. At this crucial moment—in September of 1935—General Georg Thomas received a visit from Carl Luer, head of the Nazified trade organization, who attempted to show that the guilds and chambers of small business were of great significance for a future war economy. Luer pointed out three functions that were regularly performed by his *Reichsgruppe Handel*: giving technical and economic advice to individual members; playing down or eliminating conflicts of economic interest among the various branches of trade; and directing suborganizations in fulfilling the economic policy of the state. It was emphasized that each leader of a trade group possessed the authority to give binding directives to the members in regard to the purchase and storage of raw materials, the financing of projects, and the size and composition of inventories.[50] On the basis of the evidence submitted, the economic division of the Ministry of War decided that the compulsory organizations of small business were of military significance. It was thus the potential allocational capacity of these organizations in a future war economy that induced the generals to lend their support to the craft and merchant guilds in small business.

On the level of financial resources, however, there was an increasing antipathy between economic rearmament and middle-class socialism. Under the rule that all militarily significant programs had first call upon the financial resources of the state, a number of decisions were made that directly or indirectly limited or withheld funds for the financing of projects favored by small-business groups. First, in April of 1934, the public-works program was terminated; then the subsidies granted to "rurban" homes were reduced; and finally restrictions were imposed which denied the mortgage banks entry to the capital market and thus deprived them of funds with which to finance resettlement and special housing projects.

Although the specific goals and organizations did not clash, there was a good deal of incompatibility between rearmament and middle-class socialism on the level of financial resources. The priority of economic rearmament was so strong, however, that middle-class socialism could hardly have achieved a significant success even if the organizations of big business had not opposed the goals and programs of the intransigent Nazi groups. As it was, the opposition of big business made the defeat of middle-class socialism inevitable.

The response of small business to the Great Depression was middle-class socialism, and the response of big business was its policy of invigorating capitalist institutions. The two ideals developed independently prior to the Hitler government, but there was a short interlude, during Hugenberg's tenure as Minister of Economics, in which they entered into a positive affinity. In fact, it was Hugenberg's intention to reconcile and realize these ideals simultaneously, but in this, Hugenberg was attempting the impossible. He succeeded only in depriving himself of the support of big as well as small business. The conflict of interests was too great to be compromised, and the antagonism that existed between the two groups of advocates became open as they attempted to implement their ideals.

For many leaders of big business, middle-class socialism stood for a vicious form of economic counterrevolution. In promoting the nationalization of large banks and the breaking up of the landed estates, and by seeking to replace corporate with personal property the intransigent Nazis—as we shall see in the next chapter—had mounted a deliberate attack upon concentrated private property, the central institution of modern industrial capitalism. In trying to substitute guilds for cartels, in promoting closed markets and "socialist" rather than capitalist principles of price-fixing, the Nazified business leaders presented a form of guild-dominated market structure that implicitly denied any justification for the special privileges enjoyed by large concerns in cartelized markets. In coupling entry restrictions with vocational excellence, in demanding a monopoly of vocational training, in making management dependent upon solidity of performance and the right to sell conditional upon the quality of the product, small business claimed a superiority for its own conduct that was overtly or covertly denied to big business. At least in these three respects there existed in the first phase of the Nazi regime such a mutual antagonism between the economic goals and policies proposed by these two major economic groups that the conflict could be resolved only by the defeat of one or the other.

There were four specific reasons that assured victory for big business. The economic power of the large concerns (whether expressed in the ability to create employment, to supply a large and varied output of industrial goods, or to control many of the instruments of forming economic opinions) far exceeded the economic power of small business. The split within the Nazi party and the subsequent purge of the intransigent leaders of the SA not only deprived the Nazified small business organizations of the support of the oligarchic clique of the party but also permitted the economic power of big business to exert its full weight. Perhaps most significant was the similarity of the interests of the leaders of the heavy industries to those of the generals. The former group was fully able and ready to supply the military equipment and weapons that the rearmament program of the generals called for, while the economic demand for military goods was an essential condition for restoring profits to big business. Extending their influence from business concerns and organizations to the economic agencies of the state, the leaders of big business secured the opportunity to realize their economic interests and promote their ideology by initiating and implementing the economic policy of the state.

Rather than insisting upon the *status quo* in each struggle with the intransigent Nazis, the leaders of big business developed their positive program for invigorating capitalist institutions. Many of its features have already been discussed in connection with the plans and policies of the intransigent Nazis, but some proposals for invigoration faced special problems that demand further consideration. The most important of them was the problem of governmental coercion which arose in regard to the incorporation of concerns, the membership of business organizations, and the formation of compulsory cartels. Did the state impose its will upon big business or did the leaders of big business use the power of the state to invigorate certain institutions of private capitalism?

ORGANIZED CAPITALISM AND PARTY DICTATORSHIP

CHAPTER SIX

The purge of 1934 terminated the hopes of the intransigent Nazis that the masses could compel the leaders to conform to, and translate into active policy, the political will of the Nazified masses. The defeat of middle-class socialism facilitated the transformation of a mass-supported dictatorship into a monolithic party dominated by a small oligarchic clique imposing the will of the leaders upon the masses.

This change in the nature of the dictatorship affected also the alliance between the Nazis and the generals and the relations between big business and the Nazi party. The related events contributed to a peculiar form of interaction among the three power groups—the Nazis, the generals, and big business—and gave rise to two questions about the nature of the regime, specifically: whether the party dictatorship provided the power to determine, formulate, and also execute the economic policies of the government, and how the party dictatorship and private capitalism managed to coexist with each other.

As the party became more hierarchic in its internal organization, more dictatorial in the relations between leaders and members, more dominating in its control over the instruments of governmental administration, the party leaders tended to exert a check upon the power of big business and the regular army. If these two groups wanted to retain their power, they had to reorganize themselves in such a way as to become organized power blocs that would be able to defend their respective spheres of power effectively. The result was a bilateral structure of power that prevailed up to the end of 1936.

In this structure of power, the party and its network of interlocking organizations formed one power bloc, and the upper class, with its military and economic groups, formed the other. Officially, one bloc was the ally of the other, and joint participation of both in the government most clearly symbolized this alliance. Operationally, however, the partners had arrived only at loose understandings so that the respective spheres of influence were not clearly defined and significant decisions often involved a struggle for power. In such situations, the allies became opponents, as pairs of two against two with each side seeking to increase its power at the expense of the other. Our analysis has thus to begin with the nature and content of the understandings and then proceed to the various disputes that arose within the general framework of the coalition.

The two-sidedness of the power structure was complicated by the peculiar relationship that existed within each power bloc. Big business represented the economic and the generals the military interests of the upper class. These two partners thus alternated as leaders and defenders of their class. In economic matters, leadership was in the hands of the spokesmen of big business, while in military matters the generals occupied the leading position. The organizational subdivision of the upper class thus modified the bilateral power structure, in the sense that big business confronted the party in economic matters, and the generals faced the Nazis in military matters. Accordingly, we shall from time to time speak of the economic or military aspect of the bilateral power structure.

On the party's side, complications arose from the ideological differences between intransigent and temporizing Nazis. The former usually opposed the military and economic policies of the upper class, while the temporizers were willing to accept compromises for the sake of the coalition. The conflict between the SA and the army caused a split in the party which was overcome when Hitler temporarily crossed the power line and stamped out the threat of counterrevolution created by the intransigent leaders of the SA. In economic matters, however, the temporizers were often indifferent to, or hesitant to commit themselves on, disputed issues. The economic policy proposed by big business did often give rise to conflicts with the intransigent Nazis, who, in the ensuing struggle, had to be prevented from receiving the support of the top party leadership. We shall thus have to investigate the proposed policies and attitudes of the intransigent and temporizing Nazis towards such capitalist institutions as the corporation, the cartel, and the independent but compulsory business organizations. It is the task of this chapter to study especially the economic aspect of the bilateral power structure by examining those disputes between big business and the party that could or should have produced a change in the nature of private capitalism in this first period of the Nazi regime.

THE VON BLOMBERG-HITLER DEAL

General von Blomberg contributed significantly to the formation of the first Hitler government and was in a large measure responsible for his own appointment as Minister of the *Reichswehr*. As a German delegate to the disarmament conference in Geneva, von Blomberg sent reports to President von Hindenburg that created a distrust in his mind as to the reliability of Chancellor Brüning. When von Papen and von Ribbentrop and, later, Hugenberg, von Schröder, Oskar von Hindenburg, and Meissner combined their efforts to convince the President that a Hitler government was the only way out of the crisis, von Blomberg assured von Hindenburg that a "national concentration of all groups under Hitler was the best solution and one that would be welcomed by the *Reichswehr*."[1] Enjoying excellent connections with the Nazis through his deputy, General von Reichenau, von Blomberg became a candidate for the position of Minister of the *Reichswehr* and was supported both by the Nazis and the conservatives around von Papen and Hugenberg. Von Blomberg not only became a minister of the armed forces in the Hitler cabinet but was sworn in two hours before the other members because von Papen and the other kingmakers were apparently frightened by a rumor that General von Schleicher was starting a military revolt.

The original Hitler government was changed twice: once when the other parties were eliminated and the Nazis became the sole political party; and again in June, 1934, when the purge led to another change in the membership of the cabinet. Each of these shifts produced a new understanding between the Nazi party and big business. In the first instance, the power of big business was excluded from the political field and limited to economic and commercial affairs. In the second instance, big business was able to stop the attack of Nazified small business and recover control of economic affairs. Each change in the membership of the cabinet in the first two years was thus accompanied by changes in the power sphere of big business.

The same was not true in the military sphere. Hitler very

carefully adhered to the new division of power which had developed between the party and the army. The subsequent actions and the available documents indicate clearly on which basis an effective collaboration developed between the heads of the Ministry of War and the top leaders of the party. The essential features of this mutual understanding on the common goals, on the division of functions and power between the participants, can be summarized as follows:[2]

1) Both partners agreed that securing military equality with other powers should be the main objective of the military and foreign policy of the regime.
2) A policy of secret military rearmament should be adopted —this policy to be legalized as soon as the necessary conditions had been established.
3) A mass army should again be built up and universal conscription decreed at the first opportune moment.
4) The traditions of the "Prussian soldier" should be respected and continued in the new army, and the old flag of Imperial Germany should be the official banner of the expanding armed forces.
5) A program of extensive economic rearmament should replace the program of public works and subsidized construction by private firms.
6) The military establishment of the state (including the new Air Force) should constitute the sole armed forces of the nation.
7) The Nazi party and its SA should be the sole political force of the nation and have sole responsibility for the political will and education of the nation.

The last two points indicate the division of power in the new regime. The generals were to have exclusive control over military affairs and were to be given full economic and political support in building up a modern mass army. The

Nazi party was to have exclusive control over all the political, ideological, and educational affairs of the nation. There was thus a bilateral power structure.

The old imperial flag was restored at a meeting in celebration of the new Nazified *Reichstag* at Potsdam. The principle of the division of power was stated by Hitler in the summer of 1933 at a meeting in Godesberg which was supposed to establish personal relations between army officers and SA leaders: "The *Wehrmacht* is the sole bearer of arms of the nation; the SA is responsible for the political education of the people."[3]

The preliminary law forming a Council of Defense was passed secretly in April of 1933; this law gave the Ministry of War the right to embark upon a policy of military rearmament.[4] The subsidies for the repair and rebuilding of private housing were terminated in April of 1934 so as to reserve the available funds for financing economic rearmament. The adoption of a militant foreign policy which sought to realize the goal of military equality through unilateral action was announced in connection with Germany's withdrawal from the League of Nations. In spite of all resistance within the party, Hitler defended his policy of collaboration explicitly on various occasions. He said in March of 1934: "I am determined to adhere to the agreements with and obligations to von Hindenburg and the Army."[5]

An attack upon the von Blomberg-Hitler agreement by the intransigent Nazis led to the major internal crisis of the early regime. The SA assaulted the dominant position of the army; its leaders sought to build up a new army, in which the SA would constitute the core of the troops as well as the leaders. The Nazi leaders of small business pushed hard for their guild system. All sections of the intransigent Nazis clamored for the "second revolution," whereas Hitler and most of the top leaders worked for implementation of the deal with the established powers—army and big business. After long negotiations, an agreement was signed on February 28, 1934, between von Blomberg and Röhm, leader of the SA, in which the SA was granted just two quasi-military functions. Some of its units were recognized and given small numbers of weapons with which to operate as a police force along the German borders. The SA was also permitted to engage in the physical training of men outside the armed forces—as an agency for pre-military training. A special office under SA leader Krueger was set up for the physical training of SA members. This office had to operate under the directives of the Minister of War, who was also to make the final decision about the amount of money to be supplied by the federal treasury for this purpose.[6]

Röhm and his consorts, however, had no intention of adhering to this agreement. Many subsequent negotiations took place between Hitler and Röhm that had only the effect of clarifying the divergent opinions between the two Nazis in regard to the army. Reconciliation of the conflicting intentions was impossible. One had to give way. When von Hindenburg demanded that Hitler take effective action, Hitler decreed a furlough of one month for the SA. In accepting this order, Röhm said that he expected all SA men to return to their posts with new vigor for the great task which the fatherland had a right to expect of them. Several SA units were alerted. Meanwhile, General von Fritsch concentrated troops in the neighborhood of Berlin, put a heavy guard around the buildings of the Ministry of War, and ordered the army commanders to be prepared for an uprising by the SA. Weapons and other equipment were made available by the army to the SS. Each side was thus preparing for the beginning—or the suppression—of a revolt.[7] As is well known, the revolt was suppressed even before it had begun. Hitler thus demonstrated that murder was an acceptable political device whenever that seemed necessary for reaching desired political goals.

The immediate aim of the bloody suppression was to restore the bilateral power structure, as it had developed out of the original deal between von Blomberg and Hitler. The military refrained from exploiting this moment of weakness within the Nazi party. General von Blomberg approved the act by which the cabinet declared the wholesale murder that had taken place in the purge to be an instance of emergency law. The officer corps' demand that the murder of Generals von Schleicher and von Bredow be condemned and their names rehabilitated was rejected by von Blomberg.[8] He said explicitly that Hitler had acted primarily in the interests of the *Reichswehr*. General von Blomberg agreed that the functions of the President should be merged with those of the Chancellor, after the death of von Hindenburg. In return for this full support by the Ministry of War, Hitler pledged again, in his speech justifying the murders to the *Reichstag*, and in a personal letter to von Blomberg, that "the army is the sole bearer of arms of the nation."[9] The army was to be responsible for the external strength of the nation; the party was to assure the political unity and ideological fortitude of the nation. This theory, by which the regime rested upon "two pillars," explicitly recognized the bilateral power structure which had now been cemented through the blood of the murdered victims.

AN ECONOMIC DICTATOR

The purge of June, 1934, was not only a result of the conflict between the intransigent and imperialist wings of the party and between the SA leaders and the generals of the regular army. The purge was also an expression of the crisis between the party and big business in regard to economic affairs. Both the generals and business leaders turned against Director Kurt Schmitt, who had been put in charge of the Ministry of Economics on the insistence of both these groups.

Why did the economic crisis arise and why did Schmitt fall into disfavor?

The economic dispute among the allies centered on three issues. The first was created by the struggle for reorganization of the business organizations; the second, by the crisis in foreign exchange (to be discussed in Chapter IX of this study); and the third, by Schmitt's resistance to the ideas of the generals on the domestic production of natural and synthetic oil. How did these disputes give rise to the demand for an economic dictator?

The controversy over the form and principles of business organization can best be seen in the evolution of the *Reich* Association of German Industry. As we have seen, the leaders of the *Reich* Association participated actively in the formation of the first Hitler government. After the election of March, 1933, the *Reich* Association sent a letter of thanks to Hitler, emphasizing its determination to do everything in its power to support the Hitler government.[10]

At the same time, the *Reich* Association presented its demands to the Ministry of Defense on the international regulation of the production of and trade in war weapons. The association demanded military equality with other powers and rejected any international control of weapons, and its leaders publicly welcomed Hitler's unilateral withdrawal from the League of Nations. There was thus full agreement on military and foreign policy between the first Hitler government and the business association.

The translation of this alliance between the new government and the *Reich* Association into practical arrangements occurred at a meeting on March 27, 1933, to which Göring had invited the heads of the large concerns. The Nazis suggested a reorganization and simplification of the prevailing business organizations. After a lengthy discussion, in which Fritz Thyssen and Albert Vögler, especially, participated, an understanding was reached. The Hitler government promised that it would refrain from issuing any decree on industrial organization during a period of six months. A commission would be appointed in which the whole question of organization would be investigated. Thyssen and the others left the meeting with the conviction that there would be no attack upon the principle of organizational self-government by business.

Nevertheless, there was a short period in which the principle of Nazi corporatives prevailed in business organizations. The intransigent Nazi Otto Wagener had been put in charge of business-organization at the headquarters of the Nazi party. He installed one commissioner, Hans von Luke (whose counterpart, Alfred Moellers, was appointed by Hugenberg), at the head of the *Reich* Association. Both von Luke and Moellers demanded the dismissal of the association's business manager, Ludwig Kastl, and the latter, acting under threat, gave up his position temporarily. Krupp received the commissioners and accepted Kastl's resignation—and then went a step further. On April 25, 1933, Krupp informed Hitler that he had been entrusted by the *Reich* Association with the handling of all negotiations involving industrial organizations and emphasized that, as for himself, he accepted the leadership principle for the new business organizations. The executive committee, however (in a resolution enclosed with Krupp's letter), stated that "the valuable privileges of free industrial self-government must be preserved."[11]

Noticing this difference of opinion, Hitler negotiated with Krupp von Bohlen separately and succeeded in getting two ideas accepted. The dual organization of the *Reich* Association and the Employer Associations was to be terminated, and the idea of a corporative form of organization for industry was accepted. Krupp von Bohlen asked the members of the executive committee to resign from their positions and appointed others who were either Nazis, such as Albert Pietzsch, or collaborators. In a letter of June 19, 1933, Krupp informed

Hitler that the two business organizations had united them-selves into an Estate of German Industry.[12] The association had accepted its dissolution without a fight primarily because Krupp von Bohlen had accepted the Nazi's ideas. In letters to Hitler and von Hindenburg, Krupp expressed his satisfac-tion over Germany's unilateral withdrawal from the League of Nations. All the economic organizations of big and small business met on November 7, 1933, in Berlin, where they adopted a resolution promising to stand united behind the Hitler government in its fight for "military equality" with other nations.[13]

The shift to the Estate of Industry was only a temporary setback. In July, 1933, the Nazi leaders changed their eco-nomic course. Under pressure from big business, Hitler ap-pointed Schmitt as Minister of Economics. Acting in accord-ance with his deal with Hitler, Schmitt tried to put an end to all efforts to set up guild organizations. Rudolf Hess re-called all party commissioners in private firms or organiza-tions. Otto Wagener was dismissed from his position in the party. Thus, directly or indirectly, the efforts of the intran-sigent Nazis to establish one "classless and harmonious" or-ganization that would comprise all laborers and employers had been stopped by big business. During a meeting on July 13, 1933, at which a general economic council was es-tablished, Hitler underlined in different words the main points of his deal with Schmitt.[14]

The Nazis, however, made still another attempt to secure indirect control over the industrial business organizations. Schmitt announced the preliminary law for the business or-ganizations on February 27, 1934. This law introduced the principles of compulsory membership, of unity of repre-sentation, and of appointed leadership. Subsequently, all forms of economic activity were put into separate organiza-tions that broke down the formerly united industry into seven craft-like units. Krupp von Bohlen was demoted to the leadership of just one of these organizations, and Philipp Kessler, from the electrical-equipment industry, was appointed as leader of all the economic organizations. Schmitt and Hitler thus built up an organization that was very close to the Nazi idea of corporatives. Even Krupp protested against this form of organization. His own proposal opposed the division of the industrial organization into seven different units and sought to modify the leadership principle. The leader of the industrial organization, he thought, should be advised by a council of sub-leaders who in turn should meet and discuss common issues.[15]

Ruhr industrialists other than Krupp, however, were not satisfied with a mere reorganization; they demanded that Schmitt and Philipp Kessler be dismissed. Both had lost the confidence of the majority wing of big business because they had joined the Keppler circle, had hobnobbed with SS leaders, and had accepted some of their ideas. The Keppler circle thus turned out to be a device for splitting big business and for transforming it into an organization under the command of the party. In a speech given in March, 1934, Schmitt explained why, in the Nazi system, business cartels had become undesirable. Two days later the steel industrialists registered their protest in a special memorandum outlining the reasons why they regarded cartels as indispensable.[16] There was thus an insurmountable conflict between Schmitt and the large Ruhr concerns about the nature and functions of the market and the industrial organizations of business.

In a letter of May 20, 1934, General von Blomberg complained to Hitler that Schmitt's measures were falling short of what was needed for economic mobilization. The Ministry of War opposed Schmitt's intention of minimizing the program for the production of synthetic and natural oil. The three military forces—army, navy, and air force—demanded that all economic programs preparing for war should be administered by a high official directly responsible to Schmitt.[17]

A month later the Minister of War, supported effectively

by the navy and the air force, as well as by big business, was preparing to remove Schmitt from office. Von Blomberg acted on the basis of a memorandum of June 20 presented to him by General George Thomas. Thomas asked for the appointment of an economic dictator who would have full control over all economic agencies of state and party, including the Labor Front and the Nazified Ministry of Agriculture. The economic dictator was to act in the name of the Chancellor but surround himself with a group of six men representing industry, commerce, banking, and agriculture as well as the army and the party. The main task of the dictator would be to engage in a systematic policy of economic rearmament.[18] This demand was presented to Hitler on June 23, 1934.

Two days before, a business group had presented a statement to the Ministry of War arguing against guild organization for business and proposing a reorganization of the compulsory organizations in which the industrial sector would have its own leaders and be given a chance to represent its own interests. At the same time, the *Reichsbank* under Schacht took drastic actions by imposing a moratorium upon all foreign debts and severely reducing the foreign exchange available for the purchase of foreign goods. Through stringent exchange control, Schacht in effect transferred some of the authority of the Minister of Economics to himself.

Faced with these demands, Schmitt sought to accept the proposal for an economic dictatorship. He prepared a short bill in which he suggested that the Minister of Economics be authorized to take, on his own responsibility, all measures necessary to meet the crisis in foreign exchange. This discretionary power was to be limited to three months; Schmitt justified it by pointing out the dangers to the economy that he alone had to meet during the summer months, when there were no cabinet meetings. Surprisingly enough, this bill was accepted and published as a law by Hitler.[19] Instead of being made an economic dictator, however, Schmitt was removed from office because he was opposed by the military and big business.[20]

Hitler accepted almost all the demands of his allies during the days of the suppression of the "second revolution." All party agencies were ordered to refrain from economic actions. The move to impose a guild organization upon big business was effectively halted, although Hitler hesitated for one month to appoint a new Minister of Economics who would have been able to exercise the discretionary power granted him by law. Another letter (dated July 19) from General Georg Thomas to Hitler's economic advisor was required before Schacht was appointed as acting Minister of Economics.[21] It is fairly clear that Feder's opposition to Schacht, as well as Keppler's, was behind the decision to give Schacht only a provisional title. Nevertheless, he managed to get full control of most of the ministries and agencies that handled economic and financial matters. Feder was driven from his position as undersecretary in the Ministry of Economics and disappeared from public life. Keppler, as Hitler's economic advisor, was excluded from the ministry buildings.[22] Not only the "wage division" over which Schmitt had had jurisdiction, but the whole Ministry of Labor came under Schacht's direction. The same was true of the Ministry of Finance, the agencies controlling foreign trade and raw materials, and the organization for forestry. Schacht originally had even the right to give directives to the Nazified Ministry of Agriculture in matters of economic rearmament and foreign trade.

When the law providing for an economic dictatorship expired, Schacht continued to be in full control of economic affairs, and his dictatorial authority was soon formally confirmed. The new law for the defense of the *Reich* became effective on May 21, 1935. Its major provision was the delegation of power, in case of war, to the Minister of War and to the "plenipotentiary-general for the war economy." Schacht was appointed to the second position.[23] In this unpublished law Schacht was given the authority to direct all economic preparations for actual war. This authority did not, however, give him complete power in the determination of current economic policies. Hitler had succeeded in retaining for the Nazis control over the Ministry of Agriculture. This Nazi foothold in the economy contributed later to Schacht's downfall and permitted the Nazis to participate in the process of economic decision-making in the next foreign-currency crisis. But for the time being Schacht was a dictator of economic affairs except in the sphere of agriculture.

BIG BUSINESS FIGHTS THE GUILDS

As economic dictator, Schacht adopted a comprehensive economic program. In its leading features, the program tried (*a*) to realize the goal of economic rearmament, (*b*) to reorganize the foreign exchange and trade controls, (*c*) to increase business opportunities and profits, (*d*) to maintain wage control and achieve price control, and (*e*) to strengthen the economic institutions of private capitalism.

One capitalist institution was under severe attack. The Nazis, taking advantage of the weakness of the economic ministry under Schmitt, had tried to establish compulsory business organizations and temporarily destroyed the organizational freedom of big business. Soon after his appointment as minister, however, Schacht stopped the attempts to establish a guild organization for big and small business. Director Kessler, of the electric industry, was dismissed from his office as "leader of the economy"; and Albert Pietzsch, who in addition to being a leading Nazi was Hess' economic advisor, had to resign as chairman of the organization of chemical industries. The scheduled conferences of industries, aiming at a guild organization for big business, were "postponed" by Schacht.[24] These actions eliminated the Nazi influence in the organizations of big business.

Schacht issued his first decree on the organization of the

economy on November 27, 1934. This decree called a halt to all attempts to organize guilds in industry and trade. The guilds were to be replaced by the so-called self-government of industry. The new industrial groups were still compulsory organizations (all businessmen were required to belong, and the monopolistic position of each "group" within its industry was confirmed), but the decree retained the provision requiring leaders to be elected and thereby rejected the practice of appointing leaders for the business organizations. The functions of the former leader of the economy were taken over by the *Reich* Economic Chamber (which was, however, ultimately subject to Schacht's control), and the Minister of Economics, in addition to fixing the dues and approving the budgets of each industrial group, had the authority, which he occasionally made use of, to remove elected leaders from office if they were found to be unsatisfactory in the performance of their duties.

In consequence, voluntary business organizations disappeared for good; and Schacht did not succeed in reviving them. Responsibility for the abolition of these voluntary business organizations rests exclusively with the military leaders. Compulsory business organizations were demanded by Minister of the *Reichswehr* von Blomberg in a letter of October 20, 1933, to the Minister of Economics.[25] Von Blomberg argued that compulsory business organizations were necessary as a part of the economic organization for war. Compulsion was required to bring all firms of an industry into an organization. Such organizations, in addition to having the right to represent the interests of their industries, were to be responsible for carrying through governmental functions in the preparation of the economy for war.[26] These proposals were put into effect by Schacht when he became Minister of Economics.

Thus, in the first phase of the regime, compulsory business organizations were not subject to the control of the party. The organizations were jointly controlled by the most influential businessmen in each industry and by the Minister of Economics. As we should expect, Schacht favored the leaders of big business over those of small business. For instance, when all the banks were pressed into one compulsory organization, Schacht was able to get the director of one of the big banks elected as leader of the new "group" for all banks. Non-incorporated banks and savings banks, on the other hand, had to submit to the leadership of the big banks.[27] In addition, Schacht became the recognized leader and spokesman for big business and its organizations. He established a special department in his ministry which determined the policies of the compulsory business organizations. Finally, he built up a comprehensive network of organizations that dealt with foreign exchange as well as imports and exports. Since the actions and decisions of these organizations affected most of the large business concerns, Schacht secured control over private and public organizational instruments of power that could compete with and were pitted effectively against the various organizations of the party.[28] In fact, big business became comprehensively organized and had to tolerate its own leader, Schacht, in order to function effectively as a partner, and opponent, of the ruling party.

Thus, when the generals insisted upon certain specific elements of statism, big business was usually not able to defend capitalist institutions effectively, but the results were quite different when the interest groups of the upper class—industrialists, landowners, and big merchants—were united in the defense of capitalist institutions. This became evident in the attempt of Nazified small business to modify important features of big business. The program for the reorganization of modern industry was the counterpart of middle-class socialism. Large concerns were to be reduced in size and diminished in function so as to fit into the picture of an artisan economy. The attempt to penetrate into the sphere of big business led to a series of fights.

Three issues were involved in the conflict between big and

small business: (*a*) the intransigent Nazis wanted a law on corporations that would reform the institution of capitalist enterprise; (*b*) in the struggle for the control of markets, small business sought to abolish the private monopolies of big business and subject the exchange of goods to the control of the guilds; (*c*) in those capitalist markets in which large concerns were dealing with small firms, there arose the question of who was to have the superior position, the cartels or the guilds reorganized into "groups." To what extent was big business victorious in the struggle over the reform of the basic institutions of private capitalism?

PERSONAL OR CORPORATE CAPITALISM?

Three ideas were gradually adopted by the intransigent Nazis in their fight for a reorganization of industry. First, there was widespread agreement among them that Jews would have to be eliminated from business. This opposition to Jews was closely related to the intransigent Nazis' animosity against financial or "grabbing capital" (*raffendes Kapital*), a feeling which culminated in the struggle for an extensive reorganization (see Chapter III) of the banking system. Finally, a distinction was made between personal and corporate capitalism, with the intransigent Nazis demanding that corporations be eliminated from the industrial scene.

Small-scale enterprise, it was contended, fostered personal relations among businessmen and between laborers and employers, whereas large-scale enterprise gave rise to impersonal relations within and between business concerns. The worst feature of the latter was the "anonymity of capital." The modern corporation, seeking to accumulate capital, abolished the principle of property as a tool used by owners. The corporation also severed the connection between ownership and management and thereby destroyed the owners' control over corporations. This attitude toward modern corporations induced the intransigent Nazis to give preference to the more personal forms of business. They also demanded, as has been noted, a new law on corporations.

Two laws, passed in 1933 and 1934, respectively, sought to facilitate the shift from corporations to individual proprietorships and partnerships. Corporations with a capital of less than 20,000 marks were required to adopt a legal form of personal ownership prior to 1941. Official statistics report that between 1933 and December, 1940, 1,860 joint-stock corporations and 18,883 limited-liability corporations became either individual proprietorships or partnerships.[29] In consequence, one demand made by the intransigent Nazis was accepted in the early years of the regime and even carried through under Schacht. Its effect was to exclude the corporate form of enterprise from the field of small business. Dwarf enterprises, employing a few laborers, had to organize themselves as personal owners. Big business had no interest in seeing small firms organized as corporations and thus did not oppose this Nazi policy.

The story of the demand for a new—and more drastic—law on corporations is quite different. The Nazi organization for jurists, the Academy of German Law, presented a draft for such a law. Its outstanding features were:

a) Only large corporations with a capital of more than 500,-000 marks were to be granted the charter of incorporation. This provision would have eliminated 58 per cent of the existing corporations.

b) The value of a share was not to be below 1,000 marks. The proposal made by some Nazis that only personal shares should be permitted was rejected.

c) The main responsibility for the corporation was to rest with the board of directors. The assembly of stockholders was to retain a few rights only, such as the power to decide on the distribution, but not the total, of profits.

d) The chairman of the managing board was to become the
leader of the corporation and make all significant managerial decisions.[30]

This proposed corporation law was criticized by the leaders
of big business and was not recognized as the basis for a compromise. A new committee formed by the academy contained
more Nazis than the earlier committee had, a few business
leaders, and even fewer university teachers. The second proposal was published in May of 1935. It again suggested a
minimum capital of half a million marks and minimum
shares of 1,000 marks. The two new suggestions aimed at
finding a concrete form for the leadership principle and at
further extending the right of incorporation to amalgamated
concerns and trusts. Here obviously the business leaders and
the party were attempting to compromise their differences.

"The board of managers (*Vorstand*) is the leader of the
corporation."[31] Managers were to be given the power to make
all major decisions, and four means were suggested to achieve
this end. Managers were to decide on the total amount and
distribution of profits; 20 per cent of all the voting rights
were to be transferred to the board of managers, who would
own no shares; permanent shareholders were to deposit their
shares with the board and receive a higher dividend and dual
voting rights in return; managers were to be given substantial
bonuses, the exact size depending upon the profits realized,
without sharing in the losses of the business. Simultaneously,
the committee rejected all proposals to compel the parent
companies to publicize their financial connections with their
subsidiaries or with other firms because this would lead to
"confusion." Thus an attempt was being made to legalize the
privileged positions attained by the top managers in large
modern corporations.

The criticism expressed by the Labor Front and other
party organizations was concentrated upon the question of

salaries and bonuses for managers. The following discussion produced two arguments: The rise of profits was a result of the government's policy of recovery; profits did not derive from the special inventiveness or business acumen of managers. Higher profits should not be used to raise the salaries of directors, for the employees were not allowed to receive higher wages, either. Instead, profits should be utilized for further investments.[32]

The second proposal, which vested leadership of the corporation in a board of managers, was severely criticized by the economists, who rejected the idea of giving the managers sole responsibility for profits and of having the permanent shareholders deposit their shares with the board of managers. A number of economists feared that these two provisions would enable any given board to control a majority of votes and would in effect deprive all other stockholders of any participation in the affairs of the corporation, especially since minorities could not claim representation on the board of managers.[33]

Criticism of the second proposal reached its climax in December, 1935, when Schacht delivered a speech on the role of corporations in capitalism. He pointed out that in spite of the praiseworthy revival of folk dances and spinning wheels, Germany could not live without capitalism. "Guns, aeroplanes, submarines, and anything else that might be needed for defense in modern times are unthinkable in the absence of the highest development of capitalist industry," he said. Hence, capitalism was primarily defended for military reasons. Corporations were also held to be essential to modern industry. State officials could not become manufacturers, farmers, or traders. Corporations were the most effective means of combining the savings of the many with the managerial abilities of the few. Finally, it was the function of corporation law to facilitate the operation of business. The leader principle and the permanent-shareholders plan were impediments to corporations. It was unnecessary to legalize the leadership principle because the real leader of a corporation would always have sufficient influence with his shareholders. Limiting shares to an individual, reducing their transferability, would destroy the share market and suggest to savers that they should not invest their capital in private corporations.[34] Such obstacles could not be tolerated in the present fight for "national freedom."

The discussion subsided after this speech. The Ministry of Justice worked out its own version of the corporation law, which was accepted by the government in January, 1937. In the main, the law recognized Schacht's objections and those of the Labor Front. The idea of permanent shareholders was dropped, as was the proposal to transfer shares and votes to the board of managers; most of the shares that carried plural voting rights were eliminated, but voteless shares were legalized. Furthermore, the shares retained their traditional form, which meant that a functioning share market would be maintained after the act was adopted. Thus the new law undoubtedly represented a success for Schacht.

A very modified principle of leadership was incorporated into the act. The assembly of stockholders was deprived of the opportunity to pass on the balance sheet of the board of managers or to decide on questions of corporation policy. Although stockholders were permitted to discuss the distribution of profits, they could not question the balance sheet presented. Managers continued to serve on the boards, but the suggested one-man corporation leader was rejected. The board could, however, appoint a chairman to settle differences of opinion through his decision. The managers were also permitted to receive bonuses, on two conditions: the size of the bonus had to be in proportion with profits, and bonuses could be granted only if the board also provided for "voluntary social contributions" for the benefit of the employees. Hence, managers could receive bonuses only if the corporations contributed to the various activities, such as "Strength through Joy," of the Labor Front. In all, the modified leadership principle enhanced the power of management at the expense of shareholders.[35]

What did this compromise mean for capitalism? "In Germany," said the correspondent of the *Economist,* "it is indeed necessary to be pro-capitalistic and socialistic at the same time; and no wise man neglects to assert that he is both."[36] That is to say, one had to recognize both holders of power simultaneously. Big business was able to obtain full recognition of the corporation. But the function of corporations changed. To realize maximum profits for shareholders was no longer their prime goal. The interests of managers supplanted those of shareholders in many respects, as, for instance, in the rapid increase of undistributed profits. Moreover, corporations had to pay increasing attention to the policy of the government. The act allowed specifically for governmental penetration into business.

In consequence, the corporation survived the onslaught of the intransigent Nazis. The most capitalistic form of business organization existed throughout the regime, but big business had to pay a price for its victory. The government secured the right to give directives to private corporations. This concession was harmless as long as big business had control of all the significant economic governmental agencies and determined the over-all economic policy of the government. There is no indication that the leaders of business considered the eventuality of what they could do if they lost their strategic position in the state.

COMPETITION OR MONOPOLY?

Free competition also came under increasing attack. The manifold forms of monopoly, as well as the cutthroat competition of the Great Depression, had induced the courts to distinguish between various kinds of competition. The German Supreme Court differentiated between competition resulting from superior performance and competition that destroyed the very existence of its rivals. This distinction gave rise to a new theory of competition.[37] Thus it was insisted that efficient competition (*Leistungswettbewerb*) indicates superior performance which either reduces the cost of production and prices or increases the quality of products. In a different category was competition (*Behinderungswettbewerb*), which threatens or actually destroys the economic existence of non-monopolistic competitors. Such destructive competition had to be outlawed by the courts. It destroyed the essential preconditions of a free market by reducing the number of competitors, bringing less goods to the markets and tending to raise their prices.

Another school of thought distinguished between individual and collective, unorganized and organized competition. The former alone was to be subject to the law of fair competition, whereas organized and collective competition was to be judged according to the cartel law of 1923.[38] Each school thus gave a different definition of competition and proposed different legal actions. The official school was opposed to most forms of monopolistic activities, whereas the minority school aimed at legalizing but regulating the actions of cartels and other monopolies.

The Nazis, as well as big business, professed to accept the competition of superior performance and to reject destructive competition. Specifically, what was meant by the competition of superior performance? Was the organized competition of cartels destructive or a sign of superior performance? It is necessary to study the record in order to ascertain the actual roles of competition and monopoly in the earlier period of the regime.

Up to December of 1934 big business resisted the efforts of Nazified small business to dispense with the principle of free trade and the basic law of fair competition (*Wettbewerbs-recht*). The various groups of small business—fearing to be destroyed by the big concerns—could merely secure some exceptions to the law of fair competition, which were limited to a given period.[39] In three areas these exceptions became permanent. The final law (December, 1935) for the protection of the retail trade actually abolished the principle of freedom of trade in this field. Government and retail organizations determined entry to the trade and clearly regulated business. Similarly, the law on the regulation of all kinds of advertising prohibited a long list of objectionable sales methods and appeals. The enforcement of the law was turned over to the Chambers of Culture, which were under the domination of the Ministry of Propaganda. Finally, a similar law was passed that regulated all "cultural vocations," such as the press, theater, radio, etc. An involved system of permission to do business and regulations pertaining to the operations of the "permitted" establishments were put in force by the Ministry of Propaganda. Detailed regulation by compulsory business and governmental organizations, acting along lines laid down by the party, replaced the traditional principles of free entry and free competition in these industries.

The lower the prices during the depression, the more strongly did small business insist upon doing away with unfair competition. This fight against "chiselers" scored its first main success with the issue of a decree in December, 1934, which prohibited "unfair" price-cutting. The decree declared price-cutting to be an act of unfair competition. Its professed aim was to establish the essential conditions for effective competition based on superior performance. Price-cutting became a punishable act when goods were sold below the cost of production, and when—through losses—the seller was unable to cover his obligations to creditors, tax collectors, and his employees; but the courts could impose punishment only if a firm had declared its inability to meet obligations. Of much greater significance was the right of business organizations to secure an injunction against price-cutting which was beneficial primarily to small-business groups. Prior to the decree, such injunctions, although granted by the lower courts, had been rejected by the higher courts.[40]

Why did Price Commissioner Goerdeler, whose professed function was to lower prices, issue the decree of December, 1934, against price-cutting which, in effect, set a minimum price for products? The answer is that the decree was a compromise between big business and Nazified small business. The latter tried to fix prices through its guilds and groups, whereas Schacht and Goerdeler used their power to nullify such prices. The result was a compromise; unfair competition and price-cutting were outlawed by Goerdeler on the condition that the groups and guilds abstain from fixing prices for their industries. Although it satisfied neither big business nor Nazified small business, the compromise had two unexpected results. On the one hand, in the process of determining what prices were below cost, governmental agencies and courts became involved in fixing minimum prices. This activity required cost data, and the groups and guilds saw their opportunity. They began to introduce uniform systems of bookkeeping and cost accounting in their industries—ostensibly for the purpose of preventing cutthroat prices. The result of the combined actions of courts and business organizations—a result which was of the greatest importance for small firms—was to put a floor under many prices. Although the groups and guilds of small business were forbidden by law to fix prices for their industries, the cartels could fix prices if they had the permission of the price commissioner to do so. Hence, as we shall see presently, cartels were formed in many industries comprising a large number of small firms that wanted prices fixed.[41] In all, the attempt to eliminate cutthroat competition obligated the government to fix minimum prices and furnished a stimulus to the formation of cartels in hitherto non-cartelized industries.

MONOPOLY PRICES VERSUS PRICE CONTROL

The next step in the fight between big and small business was to impose price-supervision on all cartels and to require the new cartels of small business to use the so-called "calculation price." The question no longer was whether competition or monopoly should prevail. That issue had actually been settled with the appointment of the price commissioner and with the decree against price-cutting. The latter, in effect, gave preference to monopoly over competition, fair or unfair. The former action established the rule that the government should supervise monopolies by checking on their prices.

The supervision of cartel prices was introduced by Schacht in the summer of 1934. Actual supervision of such prices became a function of the price commissioner, to which position Goerdeler was appointed in November of 1934.[42] He instructed all cartels to report to him any price agreements reached since June, 1933. He expected to cancel all agreements that fixed unreasonably high prices, but since the cartel leaders were mostly successful in resisting price reductions, the number of price agreements actually cancelled was very small. In December of 1934, for instance, the leader of the iron and steel cartels informed Goerdeler that any lowering of prices would destroy their profits and that reduced prices would diminish sales, since the buyers would wait for further price reductions.[43] Goerdeler expected the opposite effect; lower prices would increase the volume of sales, permit a subsequent reduction of unit costs, and then provide the profits for further investment. Since an agreement could not be reached, the price commissioner examined the cost and price figures of the various iron and steel cartels and arrived at the decision that many of them would have to reduce their prices by 6 per cent. This order was later intercepted by Schacht, however (who alone had the administrative power to implement the decisions of the price commissioner), and was never enforced.[44] Thus, instead of being able to use price supervision to restore the conditions for effective competition, as was his professed aim, the price commissioner was obliged to accept a system of governmentally sanctioned prices.

Although the index of cartel prices compiled by the institute of business-cycle research remained unchanged in the first four years of the regime, this index was based on the list prices issued by cartels in 1929.[45] In practice, many firms that had sold goods below these list prices during the depression returned to the same list prices during the rearmament boom. These actual changes in cartel prices were not reflected in the index, nor were the fixed prices determined by the new cartels. The rise itself was especially pronounced in 1936, when the prices of many steel products were so systematically increased that—according to a government official—nearly all the members of one finished-steel cartel asked prices above the price set by their own cartel, and the *Ruhrstahl* firm actually insisted upon prices 50 per cent higher than the cartel prices. Even under these conditions, Schacht rejected the proposal that the state should declare the prevailing cartel prices as legally fixed maximum prices. In a circular letter to the offices of the cartels and economic groups, he merely suggested that the firms should adhere to the cartel prices.[46] In relying only upon appeals, Schacht implicitly admitted that price-supervision by the state was not binding upon the cartel members of the heavy industries.

This leads us to the "calculation prices" arrived at by the groups or new cartels in the field of small business. Prices in the construction industry had risen considerably. In this industry, however, the largest orders came from the government; hence, since rising prices reduced the purchasing power of public funds, the price commissioner was determined to prevent cartel prices in construction. The organizations of the handicraft and construction industries resisted. The result was a compromise between the commissioner and the industries. The commissioner forbade the practice of "cornering" bidders for public contracts unless the government agency involved consented to such an agreement. If consent were given, the agreement was not to be reported to the commissioner. The construction industry and handicraft groups were then authorized to introduce a system of uniform cost accounting. The resultant cost tables were utilized for the fixing of "guiding prices." Whenever a contractor accepted orders at lower prices, the agents of the groups were given the power to check his books. Moreover, each group compiled a list of "honest" construction firms which was handed over to the public agencies placing orders.[47]

What was the general effect of the calculation price—the price which presupposed a uniform system of cost accounting and which was introduced with or without the permission of the commissioner? It was suggested that the "calculation" cartel—the cartel which charged calculated-cost prices—would replace cartels which restricted production and fixed prices.[48] The uniform accounting system of some cartels and groups was expected to produce a more "competitive" price, for cartel prices would now be based on the actual cost of production. But this expectation did not materialize. "Calculation cartels" did not replace but supplemented price and production cartels. The new kind of cartel was limited mostly to branches of industry that—because of changes in fashions— had to alter their designs frequently and contend with many small firms in the same cartel. These industries found it difficult to fix a minimum price for the cartel.[49] Instead of basing a price on the cost of the least efficient producer, the "new" cartels adopted a price derived from the average total cost to the producers. Thus there was merely a change in the method of calculating the cartel price. Possibly, this method of calculation produced a price lower than the average cost of the least efficient producer, but the difference between the lower price and the average cost depended on the actual spread of unit costs among firms. Comparative cost studies in later years revealed a wide spread of unit costs and indicated that the monopoly profit of the few large-scale producers was considerable even in the "calculation cartel." Also, the "average cost" of production in these cartels was high because of the large number of small, less efficient firms in such industries.

What lessons can be drawn from the fight for new principles in the formation of prices? In the three-cornered struggle between competitive, monopolistic, and governmentally supervised prices, competition lost out completely. The decree against price-cutting destroyed all effective competition through the lowering of prices, fair or unfair. The increased monopolistic activities of cartels and groups reduced the opportunities to start a business, to bid effectively, and to compete product-wise. In consequence, free competition was either destroyed or remained significant only in a very few markets.[50]

All prices became subject to governmental price supervision, but although the price commissioner did indeed make a genuine effort to prevent a rise in prices, price supervision failed, and the price level rose for the following reasons: (1) The demand for war materials in armament industries increased. (2) The prices of imported goods went up. (3) The deliberate raising of the farmers' income led to higher food prices. (4) The shift from competitive to monopolistic pricing by big and small business resulted in higher prices for consumer goods. These factors were an outgrowth either of the armament boom or of the struggle between big and small business for power.

To be sure, the causes for the rise in prices could have been controlled by price regulation, that is, by governmental price fixing, but this was still opposed by the party as well as by big and small business. Neither the party nor business was as yet able to secure exclusive and dictatorial control over prices. In consequence, the rearmament boom was accompanied by a substantial rise in prices. The regime failed to live up to its slogan: to stabilize wage rates and price levels and enjoy a prosperity based upon increased production of goods (*Mengenkonjunktur*).

Monopolistic price fixing became the rule in most industries, and cartels were no longer confined to the heavy or large-scale industries. Monopolistic practices replaced free competition in many previous noncartelized industries. Cartels and quasi-cartels (whether of big business or small) set prices, engaged in limiting production, and agreed to divide markets and classify consumers in order to realize a monopoly profit. In resisting the corporative order that the Nazis wanted to impose on small business, the guilds or groups of small business were either forced to adopt or willingly embraced the monopolistic market organization that was formerly confined to big business.

VOLUNTARY AND COMPULSORY CARTELS

The increased significance of monopolistic pricing in most industries raises a question: What was the fate of the cartels in the earlier phase of the regime? Briefly, two complementary trends could be observed. On the one hand, cartels increased in number and influence and were formed in industries that hitherto had been outside the cartel sector of the economy. On the other hand, there was a noticeable shift from voluntary to compulsory cartels. Either new cartels were formed by governmental decree or outsiders were forced to join cartels that were otherwise voluntary. In consequence, the element of compulsion became increasingly important in the cartel economy. Partially or fully compulsory cartels gradually replaced the formerly voluntary cartels.

Two cartel laws were issued on July 15, 1933. One law authorized the government to form compulsory cartels and control real investment in plants. The other law gave the Minister of Economics the authority to deal with outsiders (nonmember firms) and supervise cartel prices.

Both laws originated in connection with the Schmitt-Hitler compromise and were strongly advocated by business. Prior to 1930, big and small business had opposed compulsory cartels, but the cutthroat competition of the depression period had produced a change in business sentiment. Many cartels were threatened either by new competitors or by internal squabbles. A shift to compulsory membership was thus deemed necessary to protect existing cartels. In the new cartel committee of the *Reichsverband,* appointed by Krupp von Bohlen, sentiment was predominantly in favor of compulsion. The subsequent inquiry conducted by the cartels of the various industries rejected compulsion for sales agencies but insisted upon compulsory-membership cartels for all industries whose interests called for a monopolistic organization of markets and whose members were unable to arrive at satisfactory understandings voluntarily. Conflicts between cartels, voluntary or compulsory, were to be aired by the cartel committee of the then-existing Estate of Industry. The principle of business self-government was thus to be combined with the principle of compulsory cartels, and the state was to be limited to a general supervision of cartels. Compulsion was also to be extended to investment made by cartel members, who would have the right to build new plants or enlarge existing ones only after receiving the permission of the state. The proposals of the various industrial cartels were integrated and sharpened into specific rules that were to guide the government.[51] The government accepted these rules of the private cartel committee by issuing them as the two cartel laws of July, 1933. Both laws were presented as emergency measures, but they existed almost to the end of the regime.

The two laws created a dilemma for the Nazi party. They involved not only the recognition but the active support of cartels by the government. Point 13 of the original party program, which demanded nationalization of cartels, trusts, and other large-scale organizations, had to be discarded, and the party program revised. The office of economic policy at party headquarters announced a new cartel policy. It explicitly recognized cartels (*a*) in industries producing raw materials and (*b*) in industries suffering from overproduction. Cartels in all other industries were to be permitted only for a period of transition. In return for this conditional blessing of cartels, the party demanded the supervision of cartel prices by the government.[52] The "eternally" valid program was thus changed to satisfy big business.

After 1933, many Nazis clamored for a new cartel law, and the Academy for German Law appointed a committee for drafting such a law. According to its preliminary report, the committee gave up the idea of abolishing cartels at any time. It favored extensive private regulation of markets on the condition that cartels submit to supervision by the government.[53] Consequently, big business and the oligarchic clique saw the role of cartels in the same light. Party leaders favored a more effective supervision of cartel policies, whereas big business desired governmental support primarily for the benefit of influential cartel members. In any case, the committee of the academy failed in its task; no new cartel law was enacted between 1933 and 1943.

What was the experience with the two cartel laws of 1933? What kind of policies did they initiate, and what were their results? Let us begin with the law on the formation of compulsory cartels and then proceed to the relationship between a cartel and its outsiders after 1933.

The Minister of Economics was authorized to form compulsory cartels (*a*) if the special conditions of enterprises made such action desirable, (*b*) if negotiations for forming a voluntary cartel had failed, (*c*) if compulsion were necessary for economic welfare. Given these conditions, the Minister could select one of two different courses of action. He could either instruct the enterprises in an industry to form a new cartel or compel outsiders to join an existing voluntary cartel. In the former case he had to issue the bylaws of the new cartel; in the latter, he could revise or modify the existing bylaws. Once established, a compulsory cartel could be terminated only by governmental action. Members could neither leave the cartel nor dissolve it. The law authorized the government to supervise the activities of a compulsory cartel, but it did not specify the aims or means of such supervision.[54]

How was the law enforced? Two different actions have to be distinguished: governmental mediation in the negotiations of cartel agreements and the formation of compulsory cartels. From July, 1933, to December, 1936, not less than 1,600 new cartel agreements were signed that benefited from governmental mediation. Cartel prices and new bylaws were approved either by the Minister of Economics or the Minister of Agriculture. Similarly, during the first four years of the regime about 120 compulsory cartels were formed by the government.[55] The net effect was an enlargement of the cartelized sector of the economy.

The expansion of cartels occurred primarily in industries producing finished products and/or in small business. How the law operated can easily be seen from the events that took place in the printing industry. Fourteen thousand printing shops—among which were 5,000 one-man shops and only 133 with more than 300 employees each—became members of a compulsory cartel. The new cartel issued a price schedule based upon the average cost of production prevailing in the industry. Simultaneously, the government prohibited new capital investments in printing shops. An agreement between the cartels of machine producers, dealers, and printers initiated a program for the scrapping of old printing machines. The funds provided by these cartels were used in buying up the machinery of small printers. These owners could hardly buy new machines and went out of business.[56] Another method was employed when small shops could not be driven out of business. In the glass industry members of the compulsory cartel were forced to join a "cooperative," which alone could belong to the cartel.[57] Hence, the law on compulsory cartels became a means of stabilizing existing cartels and of establishing new ones in industries hitherto beyond the reach of cartels. This law also became an instrument for reducing the number of existing firms and preventing new firms from entering an industry.

The second cartel law, of July, 1933, discontinued the practice of giving outsiders and consumers protection against the actions of cartels. The cartel court previously had the authority to protect consumers against high cartel prices and support outsiders in their struggle against an overpowering cartel. The new law reversed this cartel policy; not consumers and outsiders but cartels were to receive the support of the government and the cartel court. Involved here was a twofold change in the original cartel decree of 1923. The government was authorized to modify cartel agreements directly without obtaining the prior consent of the cartel court. The court was forced to withdraw its previous support of outsiders and to enable or actually help cartels to eliminate their outside competitors.

The German Supreme Court, in its ruling on the famous Duesseldorf gasoline case, had changed the role of outsiders in 1932. Clause No. 8 of the original cartel decree had granted the protection of the court to outsiders if they sold their goods below cartel price. The new decision of the Supreme Court, however, regarded such lower prices as an instance of unfair competition. The result was a discrepancy between the law on unfair competition and the original cartel decree as well as between the respective decisions of the Supreme Court and the cartel court. This discrepancy disappeared with the cartel law of July, 1933, which legalized the decision of the Supreme Court and modified the original cartel decree in favor of cartels.

The new law instructed the cartel court to give the cartels a delivery embargo against outsiders or to reject their requests for injunctions if they were not considered sufficiently reliable to be in business. How was reliability determined? The main criterion was the question of price. When the outsiders attempted to sell their goods below cartel prices, the court had to ascertain whether the prices of the outsiders were below their costs of production and detrimental to the welfare of the nation.

At first the law did not have the desired effect. By making "unfair prices" the criterion for the approval of embargoes, the government saddled the cartel court with the obligation to examine the prices of the cartel as well as of the outsiders. The result was a lengthening of the period required for the court to reach a decision. Schacht had to overcome this unexpected delay. He issued a decree which declared that any cartel that had received an approval for an embargo could carry it through regardless of an appeal by outsiders. All the chairman of the cartel court had to do was to require the cartel to deposit a bond until the court had reached its final decision on an appeal.[58] This new procedure in the approval of embargoes deprived outsiders of the court's protection. Schacht obviously took the side of the cartels in their fight against outsiders. A digest of seventy decisions of the cartel court in 1935 revealed that in fifty-nine cases the court granted the cartels the use of the embargo.[59]

When the court judged that an outsider was unreliable or insufficiently trained or that he lacked storage space or other facilities, the firm had to go out of business. The cartel court acted here as an administrative agency that examined the business conduct of outsiders. Undesirable firms were destroyed; competition was eliminated. An entrance-restriction clause was introduced which applied retroactively to all firms that did not submit to a cartel. The description of the outsiders in court decisions indicated that exclusion from business was practiced for the most part against small firms. When the court decided, however, that an outsider had to submit to the cartel agreement or come to an understanding with the cartel, or if the court modified the cartel agreement, another action took place: The outsider had to join the cartel. The court, in effect, became the police officer of the law on compulsory cartels, either forcing the outsiders out of business or requiring them to become members of originally voluntary cartels.

In consequence, the law against outsiders supplemented the law on compulsory cartels. The former was a lever through the use of which voluntary cartels were transformed into compulsory cartels. This was accomplished not through compulsion by the government but through discrimination against outsiders by the cartel court.[60] Gradually, voluntary cartels became the exception; compulsory cartels—"children of the emergency"—the rule in most industries. Schacht, through his cartel decree of 1934, became the father of the system of comprehensive cartelization.

The trend towards comprehensive cartelization took three different forms. All producers in an industry were compelled to join the cartel for that industry. Compulsion was exerted through court approval of an embargo, through court orders requiring outsiders to join cartels, or through orders issued by the Minister of Economics. The result was an all-inclusive membership of producers in the cartel. The agreement between two or more cartels, each comprising all the producers in a field, exerted another form of control. Such inter-cartel agreements were called exclusion contracts. A cartel of dealers, for instance, agreed to buy products exclusively from members of a producer cartel. These agreements were usually accompanied by understandings on the purchase prices as well as on the quantities to be bought. Such understandings covered an increasing sector of the economy. Finally, when a cartel was not available or effective, groups or guilds engaged in similar activities. Often the groups supplemented the activities of the cartels. The over-all result of these controls—compulsory membership, exclusion contracts between cartels, and cartel-like actions by groups—was a monopolistic manipulation of most markets.

Comprehensive cartelization had its effect upon the formation of prices. The law on fair competition, recognized by the Supreme Court as late as October 5, 1935, laid down one important rule: A businessman is master of his costs and prices. This rule was considerably modified by the decree on price cutting and by the cartel court's practice of examining the prices charged by outsiders. Any producer who sold his goods below the prices enforced by the cartels or suggested by the groups or guilds had to expect unfavorable action on the part of his competitors. Recourse to the courts usually had a definite effect. Non-conforming producers were deprived of their right to calculate costs and prices. If they desired to stay in business, they were compelled to charge the minimum prices fixed by cartels or groups. In consequence, the right to calculate prices was widely shifted from individual firms to cartels or groups. Indeed, the fixing of prices by these organizations became one of the typical features of the monopolistic manipulation of markets in the earlier phase of the regime.

On the other hand, the protection of consumers against exorbitant cartel prices was almost entirely discontinued. The cartel court deliberately refrained from examining the effect of cartel prices upon consumers. In fact, the power to determine maximum prices for cartels and groups of small business was actually transferred to the government. The cartel court merely required of cartels that they secure governmental approval of their prices.[61] Such approval could be easily obtained after the price commissioner's unsuccessful attempt to supervise cartel prices.

Extensive cartelization also modified or reduced rivalry within or between cartels. Deviant behavior was no longer permitted to dissolve cartels. Members could not leave a cartel without first obtaining the consent of the cartel court. Outsiders could no longer profitably exist outside a cartel. Conflicts within a cartel of small firms were usually solved through governmental mediation. The threat of imposing a compulsory cartel upon an industry gave the mediators great influence. In effect, governmental mediation stabilized the cartels and did much to reduce the disruptive effect of rivalry upon existing cartels.

Nevertheless the operations of many cartels were still affected by intra-cartel competition. Overcapacity was the major source of conflict. The burning question in cartel circles was: Whose plants shall be shut down? Excess capacity was closely related to the fight for a greater share of total production in industries. Some large corporations built new plants or purchased others with the expressed intent of securing a larger production quota in the cartel. The result was an intense struggle to eliminate small members and shift their quotas to the larger corporations in the cartel. The law on compulsory cartels did not mitigate this struggle significantly, for the purchase of plants or the transfer of quotas was permissible if the Minister of Economics gave his consent. Approval was given freely as long as purchase or transfer did not increase the total capacity of an industry.[62] When the members of a compulsory cartel refused to sell their plants, the Minister could dissolve the cartel temporarily. The larger corporations then bought up the properties of the recalcitrant minority, and the Minister again imposed the bylaws of the original compulsory cartel. The purchases of plants reduced the membership of many cartels and intensified the trend towards amalgamated large-scale corporations in an industry. Horizontal amalgamation was preferred, but vertical or diagonal amalgamation also took place.[63] Monopolistic activities reduced the number of enterprises and shifted a greater share of the prevailing volume of business to the large-scale concerns.

Competition between cartels and quasi-cartels had no uniform effect. In traditionally cartelized industries, inter-cartel agreements fixed prices of many goods, ranging from raw materials to final products. Here was a definite trend towards a comprehensive network of cartels, comprising all stages of production and trade in a given sector of the economy. In newly cartelized industries, inter-cartel competition produced serious conflicts. The old cartels refused to grant a fair profit margin to concerns organized in new cartels. Producer-goods industries fought against consumer-goods industries for their relative shares of profit. Big business was pitted against Nazified small business. The struggle between these groups remained undecided. Each opponent sought to increase his control over the instruments of organization and thereby accumulate power for the coming showdown. The cartels of big business and the groups or guilds of small business were the two most important opponents. How was the struggle between these opponents finally resolved?

CARTELS VERSUS SMALL-BUSINESS GROUPS

The process of cartelization produced three kinds of inter-relationship between cartels and groups in different fields:

a) The cartels fulfilled the functions of groups which did not exist or existed only on paper. The cartels did, however, adopt some of the corporative ideas of the groups or guilds—as in coal-mining and the manufacturing of radios and some iron products (e.g., iron plates).

b) The opposite relationship prevailed when a group established one or several cartels. The latter acted effectively because a group or guild lent aid in enforcing the cartel agreement. Leading cases were the printing and glass industries.

c) A coexistence of groups and cartels prevailed in many industries. Both had different leaders, organizations, and bylaws.

These manifold interrelationships resulted from the overlapping of functions. It was obviously difficult for the groups to find their proper place in the economy. The result was a conflict between big business and Nazified small business about the role of the groups. On the one hand, the law on the formation of industrial groups specified that they should not engage in price-fixing or market control. Schacht, who wanted to keep the cartels apart from the groups, repeatedly reminded the groups of these restrictions. On the other hand, the intransigent Nazis and the leaders of many of the groups either tried to incorporate cartels into groups or sought to absorb the functions of cartels. For instance, the secretary of the over-all organization of industry recommended that the groups be given the right to regulate the markets.[64] Others went even a step further, trying to absorb the cartels into an over-all estate of industry. The model was the Estate of Agriculture, in which cartel-like and political organizations were merged into one organizational structure.

The struggle between the cartels and the groups was particularly intense in the development of the so-called total cartel. A cartel of this kind was established in the coal-mining industry when the coal dealers attempted to free themselves from the domination of the producer cartel. This attempt led to the cartelization of the whole industry and trade.

Some of the Nazified coal-dealer organizations were determined to reorganize their business along the lines of middle-class socialism. Specifically, they demanded the severing of relationships between coal producers and dealers (the so-called captive dealers); a revision of the sales and delivery contracts (which were imposed by producer cartels); a fair profit margin and equal treatment for independent dealers; and the appointment of a commissioner who would reorganize the coal industry.[65]

The large coal concerns, organized into powerful cartels for decades, were sensitive to these demands for four reasons. They were eager to have the government repeal the law of 1919, which had imposed limited government control upon the coal industry, and at the same time they were engaged in an inter-cartel fight in preparation for a new over-all cartel agreement. One solution to the problem of marketing their coal was to work out an agreement with the Nazified dealers, which would have been preferable to the alternative of being assigned a Nazified commissioner, who might be as bad as some of the commissioners in other industries. Finally, the chances for a compromise with the Nazified dealers were favorable because the captive dealers (those depending upon producer cartels) were in a strategic position.

The negotiations produced a compromise, a "general agreement," which was published in July, 1933, shortly before Schmitt became Minister of Economics. Legally it was an exclusion contract between various producers and one dealer cartel. The partners reached an agreement on sales volume as well as on the prices to be charged by producers, wholesalers, and retailers. The net effect of this agreement was that coal prices went up by 40 per cent. The partners also reached an understanding as to who should be permitted to trade in coal. The accepted dealer cartel compiled a list of honest wholesalers and retailers. This list was supplemented by firms acceptable to the producer cartels. Dealers named in this final list received a card that enabled them to receive coal. Whoever had no card could not expect delivery of coal. Outsiders, dealers without a card, were eliminated through two devices. Unofficially, a boycott was employed to coerce undesirable dealers out of business. Officially, the dealers were required to prove their occupational training and financial reliability, to possess all the necessary facilities for carrying on a coal business, and to show that their service was really needed by the community. Firms that could not live up to these requirements faced a delivery embargo if they did not prefer to leave the business voluntarily.[66]

The elimination of firms that were not acceptable to the cartels was temporarily delayed because the cartel court had to give its consent to the issue of a delivery embargo. Schacht's cartel decree, however, removed this obstacle; embargoes could become effective immediately after the chairman of the court had given his consent. Court action and unofficial embargoes drove 2,000 of a total of 54,000 dealers out of business during 1933–35. Parenthetically, the number of eliminated outsiders was even greater in the radio industry, where a similar inter-cartel agreement had been signed. The 60,000 radio retailers were reduced to 37,000, and the wholesalers from 1,500 to 750 within a year.[67] The principle of exclusion here produced cartels without outsiders.

Agricultural purchasing cooperatives constituted a problem for the coal cartels. The cooperatives protested against the rise in the cost of coal and refused at first to accept the exclusive cartel agreement. The new Nazified leaders of the cooperative protested even against the decision of the Minister of Economics, who nevertheless finally approved higher prices required by the coal cartels. Subsequent negotiations, however, brought an understanding with the cooperatives. They did not have to become members of the coal-dealer cartel, and the individual cooperatives were not compelled to accept cartel prices. They could negotiate with the locals of the cartel. If no agreement could be reached, the head-quarters of the cooperative could fix the price, based upon a cost formula agreed upon with the cartel.[68] The effect of this agreement was that members of the cooperatives received their coal somewhat below the cartel price. Yet the cartel still had indirect control over these prices and thus incorporated the cooperatives into its marketing system. Similar agreements were later signed with importers of coal and dealers in coal from the Saar when that district was returned to Germany.

Significantly, events in the coal industry led to a fusion of the features of the cartel with those of a guild of Nazified dealers. On the one hand, there was a comprehensive price cartel, setting the sale prices for producers, wholesalers, and retailers, and on the other, membership requirements based upon the corporative idea of the vocational ability and business reliability of dealers.[69] These two features were linked together through two traditional cartel devices: the exclusion contract and the delivery embargo. "Incompetents" were thus eliminated through cartel weapons. The dealers did not attain the status of a guild; instead, they actually achieved control over their markets as a cartel. The Nazis called such a fusion of cartel and guild features a "total" cartel.[70]

When Schacht took over the direction of economic policy, he objected to the "total" cartel. He instructed the cartel of coal dealers to sever the cartel from the group functions. In consequence, the dealers had to form a new organization that became the "group" of the coal trade. It was this group that now secured the right to impose compulsory membership upon all coal dealers. Yet the organizational separation was merely a formality. Cartel and group functions remained interconnected, and the total cartel operated effectively even after Schacht's directive. This was confirmed by an agreement which stated that the special situation of the coal trade required the closest cooperation between both the cartel and the group.[71]

Actually, although its functions were not uniform throughout the economy, the "total" cartel was generally used by big business or Nazified small business as a means of dominating an industry. In the coal and radio industries, for instance, the producers held a position superior to that of the dealer cartels, mainly because the accepted dealers were actually captive agents of the large concerns. In other industries, such as printing, the groups dominated the newly formed cartels through which the "incompetents" were eliminated. In consequence, a total cartel indicated merely the fusion of cartel and group functions. As has been said, however, the total cartel was used as an instrument of power both by big and small business.

The intransigent Nazis tried to use the total cartel as a wedge against big business and thereby overcome the dualism between cartels and groups. They presented a theory which purported to prove the superiority of the "total" cartel over both the old-fashioned cartel and the group.[72] There were three reasons, they insisted, why the total cartel proved successful in regulating markets. The decisive fact was that the "leadership principle" was introduced into the cartel organization. The leaders secured full authority to formulate policies and keep their members in line. Also, the registration of members in a roll and the issuing of a permit to do business provided the basis for eliminating incompetents. Finally, the exclusion contracts had the twofold advantage of enforcing cartel prices by withholding goods and of bringing "order" into whole sequences of industries, from the processing of raw materials to the manufacture of finished products for the consumer.

The intransigent Nazis demanded that, for the future, the total cartel should function as a model for the regulation of all markets and be given the legal identity of a compulsory cartel. In this way, the registration requirement and the issuing of permits to do business could be dispensed with, and membership would be compulsory for every firm in any given industry. It was also felt that the existence of both cartels and groups involved a wasteful duplication of effort and created undesirable rivalries and that this dual organization should be replaced by a single, unified organization.

The intransigent Nazis were strongly opposed by the traditionalist proponents of cartels, who argued for a continued separation of cartels and groups. The traditionalist position was that cartels and groups were differently organized and had different goals and functions.[73] The cartels attempted to increase the profits of the member firms, who gave up the right to compete freely in return for a share of total production; whereas the groups had no specific goals that directly benefited their members and were primarily educational organizations attempting to improve the ethical standards of their members. Also, the cartels were voluntary organizations whose membership consisted only of direct competitors within a given market, whereas the groups were compulsory organizations to which all the firms in any given industry belonged, regardless of market connections. Hence the two organizations did not include the same membership.

The traditionalists further contended that the groups were constitutionally unable to regulate markets because their membership was organized along production lines, not in terms of markets. Finally, the cartels set their prices on the basis of the costs of marginal producers (since the more efficient members would be compensating the less efficient if prices were based upon average cost), whereas if the groups controlled prices, they would try to arrive at some sort of "just" price. Consequently, the coexistence of groups and cartels was declared to be inevitable as long as private property and private initiative were recognized features of the economy.

These theories reflected the conflict of interest between the heavy industries and the traders in or producers of finished products. The former wanted only cartels; the latter, only groups. After a long fight behind the scenes, a compromise was reached. It was declared that in principle, cartels and groups were fundamentally different organizations. The groups were regarded as superior to the cartels because they carried compulsory membership and were said to be governed by the leadership principle. The cartels, on the other hand, were asserted to be "voluntary" associations that ordered their affairs by means of decisions of the majority. Since compulsion was seen as preferable to freedom, the groups were given the right to supervise the activities of the cartels. It was hoped by the Nazis that the cartels would exist only for a transitional period and would be superseded by the groups.[74]

Actually, Schacht's decree of November 12, 1936, regularized the dual organization of groups and cartels. Both existed simultaneously throughout most of the Nazi regime. The groups, formerly only "educational" organizations, were now assigned two additional functions: to promote uniform bookkeeping and cost accounting and to supervise the cartels.

In 1935 the German Supreme Court had still adhered to the notion that each enterprise was its own master in matters of bookkeeping and cost accounting; but Schacht's new decree authorized the groups to formulate principles—which, however, had to be approved by the Ministry of Economics— for uniform bookkeeping and cost accounting. If any firm rejected these principles, they could be imposed by the group leaders upon all the firms in an industry. The expectation was that uniform cost accounting would increase the efficiency of plants, which would enable them to reduce unit costs or to prevent a rise in prices. The groups were expressly forbidden to utilize uniform cost accounting for the fixing of prices.

The supervision of cartels was legally a function of the government and the cartel court. The new decree, however, authorized the groups to participate in the supervising of cartels. A cartel had to register with a group and provide full information about its bylaws and activities, but only national leaders or executive secretaries of the groups had the right to participate in the meetings of cartels and be fully informed about their plans and policies. Prospective agreements had to be presented to the cartel office of a group, which had the right to veto an agreement but was required to present the case to the Minister of Economics for his final decision. Finally, the groups received the right to pre-examine all requests from compulsory cartels for charters and present reports to the Ministry.[75]

The cartels were thus given the explicit right to regulate markets and fix prices within the rules of the cartel court and under the general supervision of the groups. Also, the cartels were instructed to sever any organizational connections with the groups. Uniting in one official the leadership of both a cartel and a group was forbidden, except in unusual cases which required the express permission of the ministry.

Although the new decree tried to divide economic functions between the cartels and groups, it did not eliminate exclusion contracts between cartels. Inter-cartel agreements among producers, wholesalers, and retailers were still setting prices on three levels of sale, and the Ministry of Economics approved several such agreements during 1935 and 1936.[76]

Surprisingly, the "superiority" of the groups did not in any way reduce the effectiveness of the cartels; for only high-ranking group leaders could secure information from the cartels, and the leaders were obliged to regard the information as confidential. In fact, only the administrative procedure of cartel supervision changed: the groups became the link between cartels and the Ministry of Economics. The final decision as to when and how the plans or policies of the cartels should be changed still remained with the Minister of Economics. Thus, the right of the groups to supervise the cartels did not modify the trend towards comprehensive cartelization. On the contrary, new cartels were formed in industries where the groups had to give up their former cartel-like activities, so the result of the new decree was a further penetration by the cartels into non-cartelized industries.

In consequence, the decree of November, 1936, represented a victory for big business and Schacht. He won the main battle of securing for the cartels the sole right to fix prices and regulate markets. The groups were no longer permitted to participate in price and output decisions, but they had been assigned the new function of instituting uniform bookkeeping and cost accounting. In many industries, this ruling transferred the responsibility for cost accounting from small firms to the groups. Large-scale concerns were usually seen as models of modern cost accounting and were thus not affected by this provision of the decree. For the small firms, on the other hand, the loss of the right to keep their books and count their costs as they pleased was one of the prices paid for the victory of big business.

ORGANIZED CAPITALISM AND BILATERAL POWER

What lessons can be learned from the changes observed in corporations, competition, cartels, and groups? Briefly, two lessons emerge from our discussion. One relates to modifications in the nature of the economy; the other pertains to the relationship between the structure of power and the economy. The fact that the economy could not be completely insulated against the party's monopoly of power was decisive. Instead of keeping the party outside the economic sphere, as originally intended, big business itself gradually developed into an organized power bloc. Hence, two blocs of power were pitted against each other. The penetration of organized power into the economy intensified the otherwise prevailing trend towards increasing compulsory organization. This, in turn, produced a significant modification of several important institutions of private capitalism.

In particular, four principles of economic activity were either changed or abolished. The principle that all businesses should enjoy equal economic rights was greatly changed. Freedom of business enterprise as a commonly accepted condition for economic activity and free competition as a basic institution of the economy were both abolished. The fourth principle, that businessmen should be free to form voluntary associations and pursue their interests collectively, was either dropped or greatly modified. These four changes eliminated the last elements of liberalism from the economy. The monopoly capitalism of the Weimar Republic was transformed into a comprehensively organized capitalism. To the economic causes of this organizational transformation must be added an important political cause. The new organizational institutions greatly facilitated the capacity of big business to determine the economic policy of the regime and to cooperate with the generals in defining and implementing the policy of economic rearmament.

Even when comprehensively organized, however, the power of big business could not be readily extended to non-economic spheres of activity. Business rule was effectively limited by the Nazi party to the private economy and to matters involving the economic policy of the state. The political and ideological spheres were dominated by the party. The result was a new division of power between the party and big business. Coexistence between the two produced a bilateral power structure in which organized capitalism and the party dictatorship acted as equals, each enjoying an almost exclusive sphere of domination.

Under the Weimar Republic the upper class had been subdivided into different interest groups. Not only the wealthy industrialists and the owners of large estates but also the officers corps of the army and the higher echelon of the bureaucracy were organized in groups that promoted their common interests. But each group also fought for its special interests. The less any one group had to defend itself against the others, the greater was the emphasis upon the special interests. The organized power of the party changed this situation. The various groups of the upper class had to give greater weight to their common interests because it was only by marshalling all their resources that they could limit the power of the party to the political field.[77]

In order to realize their common interests, the leaders of big business went one step further and formed a union with the generals. This understanding followed closely the von Blomberg-Hitler deal. As a result, the alliance between big business and the party was such that in economic questions big business and the generals enjoyed a prerogative. The leader of the economic division of the Ministry of War, General Thomas, promoted Schacht's appointment as Minister of Economics and obtained his appointment as general plenipotentiary of the war economy. The principles of economic policy were agreed upon between the Ministries of War and Economics. In his testimony before the allied interrogators in 1945 Schacht said that he was always in agreement with General Thomas.[78] Full agreement on aims and policy as well as coordination of respective organizations led to a pooling of power that produced one united power bloc of the upper class.

The trend towards centralization of power and comprehensive organization of all powerful groups influenced the mean-

ing of the bilateral power structure.[79] The simple version of
this structure sees only a confrontation of two distinct but
single holders of power. Yet such singleness did not exist
during the first period of the regime. Comprehensive organization developed differentiation on each side of the power
structure. For the Nazis, there were the party and its subsidiary organizations, together with, but distinct from the SS,
with its concentration camps and secret police. For the old
upper class, there were the comprehensive business organizations that stood side by side with the growing organization
of the regular army. As a result of this development into two
exclusive party organizations and two compulsory non-party
organizations, the bilateral power arrangement rested upon
four pillars of authority.

In issues concerning one particular sphere of action, each
of the four organized units acted as an organized power bloc
that possessed a prerogative in decision-making. The SS dominated the whole sphere of the police, public and secret, and
enjoyed a monopoly of the instruments of extralegal organized violence. The generals of the regular army determined
the strictly military policies and possessed a veto power in all
other matters that influenced military and economic rearmament. The oligarchic clique of the party dominated the
strictly political—the educational and political-ideological—
activities which were governed by the deliberately formulated party line. Big business was able to invigorate major
capitalist institutions and extend or reimpose them upon
small urban business. Each holder of power occupied a predominant position in a fairly well defined domain, in which
a small clique enjoyed the privilege of laying down the lines
of policy and of making the final decisions.

The connections among the four holders of power were
governed by the principles of mutual opposition, cooperation, coordination, and ultimate veto privileges. It was the
operation of these principles that governed the arrangement

of the four power blocs into a bilateral power structure in which the party-SS faced the organized combinations of big business and the generals.

The principle of mutual opposition became visible when any one of the blocs tried to increase its power at the expense of the others. The whole network of Nazified small business organizations failed to impose their ideas of self-governing guilds because of the effective resistance of big business. The Labor Front made many attempts either to influence economic policy in regard to workers or to establish the principle of organizational totality, but neither goal could be achieved because of the joint opposition of big business and the generals. Similarly, many attempts were made to change the "cultural" policies of the Nazis, e.g., to modify their anti-Jewish policy for the sake of increasing exports. The Ministry of Finance as well as Schacht tried repeatedly—and failed—to secure control over the financial affairs of party organizations.[80] The united opposition of the party organizations defeated all these efforts. Interestingly enough, mutual opposition created lateral power relations among the organized blocs that led to a reciprocal limitation of power to fairly specific spheres of action.

The principle of cooperation operated whenever a particular task involved the organizations of two or more power blocs. Pre-military training was officially a function of the reorganized SA, but the aims and plans of such training had to find the approval of the Ministry of War. Some of its officers were delegated to the SA in order to supervise actual instruction in the barracks and the field. Building up the air force was a joint task of delegated officers of the regular army and of a group of Nazis led by Göring. Cooperation was necessary to the extent that the available funds and trained manpower had to be shared and the procurement plans adjusted among the three branches of the armed forces. Although the Labor Front agents in factories were very conscious of their political power and financial independence from employers, most employers cooperated with the agents of the Nazi party in preventing the rise of any underground movement of trade unions, and assisted the Nazis in their political indoctrination of workers. The Nazified Ministry of Agriculture imposed its system of interlocking organizations upon all farmers and processors but cooperated carefully with the large landowners in their attempts to increase the output of their estates and to become again profitable capitalists. Although there were disputes, compromises, and partial postponement or modification of goals, the division of functions was usually beneficial for both parties because policies could be implemented in a way that exceeded the capacity of any particular power bloc.

Coordination took place when policies which called for the synchronization of the actions of agencies controlled by several holders of power had to be implemented. The defense laws of 1933 and 1935 laid down the agreed rule in all relevant spheres of action. Every holder of power was obliged to live up to and defend his own policies in terms of this long-term goal of the coalition government. In fact, priority of rearmament became the dominant principle for coordinating the activities of the various power blocs. Price and wage stability, for instance, were said to be necessary conditions for successful economic rearmament. Indeed, price supervision well illustrates the success as well as the limitations of coordination. When the prices of imports and farm products rose in 1934, the subsequent negotiations among the ministries led to the acceptance of general price supervision. Although the party leaders accepted this principle, they tried to obtain control over the enforcement of price policies. The Minister of Agriculture, Walther Darré, achieved an agreement with the price commissioner that some increase in farm prices would be justified, but he obtained the commissioner's promise not to interfere with Darré's price policy. Similarly, the numerous cartels provided information about their price agreements to the commissioner but successfully prevented him from changing most of the prices fixed by cartels. It was only in the field of urban small business that the price commissioner was able to register a small degree of success. As a result of the various exemptions from, and modifications of, the commissioner's rulings, economic rearmament was accompanied by increases in prices. For a time there was a certain amount of effective coordination in connection with rearmament, but in the end the coordination of economic rearmament and price policies failed.

The ultimate veto privilege was employed sparingly. It required that one powerholder be appointed to arbitrate policy conflicts among the power blocs. Such an appointment could be made only in the event of an impasse which necessitated the acceptance of a new policy and a new leader. Particularly severe was the conflict between the regular army and the counterrevolutionary SA. General von Blomberg's ultimatum, that unless the threat to the position of the army were removed by Hitler, the generals would act, forced the hand of the oligarchic clique. It was the presence of two para-military organizations that enabled Hitler to eliminate the leaders of one organization by employing against them the leaders of the other. The ultimatum and the subsequent purge of the SA thus had the effect of destroying one of the two quasi-military organizations of the party.

None of the other ultimate vetoes touched upon the foundations of the power structure. Their impact was limited to either accepting or rejecting a certain policy proposal. In April, 1934, the generals successfully laid down the rule that new public-works projects that had no specific military significance should be rejected and that those in operation should be gradually abandoned. In October of 1934, the Labor Front tried to pass a law that would have given it the right to organizational totality over all economic organizations of business. The joint veto issued by the generals and Schacht foiled this and subsequent attempts of the Labor Front to partake in economic policy-making. Through these and similar vetoes the generals and big business were able to determine the economic policy of the regime.

In some cases, however, the ultimate veto power turned out to be an insufficient instrument for adjusting the domestic economy to the economic requirements of the military. A poor crop in 1935 called for an import of foreign grain which endangered the import of militarily significant raw materials. In trying to keep grain imports to a minimum, the economic division of the war ministry as well as Goerdeler proposed a general rationing of all fats for human and industrial consumption. This proposal was vetoed by Hitler in October, 1935. When, in July of 1935, Goerdeler asked for additional discretionary power in his attempt to stop the rise in prices, Hitler agreed to the request, yet the Nazified Ministry of Agriculture and other party organizations later vetoed the transfer of power to Goerdeler, who failed in this case to obtain the support of the generals. Perhaps most crucial was the struggle for the appointment of a commissioner over the production and consumption of oil. In June of 1934 the war ministry nominated a general for this position, but Hitler did not act because Keppler, as well as Schacht, was against the appointment. In June of 1935, von Blomberg officially proposed that an industrialist should be given authority over the whole oil industry. Schacht refused and persuaded von Blomberg that the head of his mining department should be granted dictatorial power. When this common proposal reached Hitler, he refused to act because Keppler—and, through him, I. G. Farben—was unwilling to accept an official of the Ministry of Economics as his boss.[81]

There is little doubt that these vetoes, especially the first and the last, contributed significantly to the restlessness of the generals as well as to the exchange crisis of 1936, which together constituted important causes for a change in economic policy from simple rearmament to the Four Year Plan. The inability to reach decisions vital for rearmament, whether through coordination or ultimate vetoes, constituted a major weakness of the bilateral structure of power.

Nevertheless, the system prevailed because each power bloc had established for itself an unassailable power base. Big business derived its power both from concentrated ownership of property and from its comprehensive organization. The property base alone was not enough. Voluntary associations had to be transformed into compulsory associations in order for business to hold its own in the struggle among the power blocs.[82] The power of the party was also organizational in nature, but this organizational strength was based upon the principle of exclusion and singleness. The closed party elite dominated compulsory mass organizations. As long as there was this interlocking of property and compulsory organization, on the one hand, and of exclusionary and compulsory organization, on the other, the bilateral power structure did not exhibit any tendency to develop into a system of total power.[83]

As for the armed forces of the generals and the police forces of the SS, there existed a fusion of organizational and military power. The military possessed the instruments of legalized external force and the police organizations, of internal law enforcement, or extralegal violence. Neither organization was following the principle of political neutrality. In any conflict between party and business organizations, the power of the generals supported the interests and policies of big business. Equally, the Nazi party could always rely upon the ability of the SS to reinforce the will of the party leaders by means of potential or actual violence. Both the military and police forces, however, recognized that each had a privileged sphere of action. Each respected the armed strength of the other, and there was mutual opposition to an extension of one sphere of influence at the expense of the other. This mutuality of interest and respect was largely responsible for the staying power and durability of the bilateral power structure.

The increase in the extent and the shift in the nature of economic organization gave rise to organized capitalism. The interlocking organization of the party made the dictatorial rule of the Nazis unassailable. With each partner to the coalition government effectively organized, capitalism and one-party dictatorship were fully compatible with each other. In terms of power and profits, there was no inherent tendency for the bilateral power structure to be of short duration.

The partnership among the holders of power disintegrated only because the policy of rearmament ran into great difficulties that could not be resolved except through the adoption of a new economic policy. It was in the formation of this new line of policy that a split arose within big business, and within the regular army, producing an estrangement between strategically placed business leaders and leading generals. The dual power structure disintegrated only when the split within the formerly united upper class enabled the Nazis to establish themselves as the major holders of power in the regime.

THE REARMAMENT BOOM

CHAPTER SEVEN

Shortly after the Nazis usurped power in Germany, they announced their new economic policy of overcoming the depression through the "battle for employment." The battle for employment comprised two distinct programs. Officially, the Nazis announced their public-works program in the spring of 1933. Secretly, the new government engaged in a program of rearmament.

The whole public-works program involved a total expenditure of 5.4 billion reichsmarks, which was divided among eight major projects. Obviously, this estimate inflates the outlay for genuine public-works projects. On the one hand, it includes quasi-military programs, such as most of the 2 billion for superhighways and most of the expenditures for railroads. On the other hand, it includes the public-works programs of 1932 and thereby also gives the Nazis credit for the actions of previous governments. Deducting previous expenditures—including semimilitary—from this total leaves an

EXPENDITURES FOR PUBLIC-WORKS*
(in thousand marks)

Repair of Private Houses	900
New Houses and Improvements	170
Agricultural Resettlements	300
Regulation of Rivers, etc.	160
Construction of Streets	210
Construction on Underground Projects	216
Modernizing the Railroads	1,055
Construction of the Superhighways	2,000
Miscellaneous	439
	5,450

* Calculated from "Arbeitsbeschaffung und oeffentliche Finan-zen," *Vierteljahrsberichte für Konjunkturforschung*, Vol. IX, Part A, pp. 70 ff.

outlay for civilian projects of all kinds of between 2.5 and 3 billion marks for the first two years of the regime.

In April of 1934, the government terminated the subsidy program for repair and improvement of houses. Instead, tax rebates were granted on the cost of repairing old houses or building new ones. The builders of small homes and rural settlements could obtain a government guarantee on their private loans; and in some cases, small government loans were granted to preferred builders. Whether guaranteeing loans or extending them, the governmental agencies specified in detail the sizes of plots and houses, the number of rooms, the size of bank loans, and the amount of minimum funds to be provided by the builder. Direct controls increased as the volume of governmental funds available for such projects declined, indicating that public works were of diminishing significance to the government.

FEATURES OF REARMAMENT

Governmental subsidies for home improvement and con-struction projects were subject to a second new policy. In the

summer of 1934 the government intensified its deliberate
policy of rearmament. A law was passed in November of 1934
which gave priority to rearmament and directed that all other
policies had either to be coordinated with or subordinated
to rearmament. What were the specific features of rearmament?

Rearmament was divided into two parts. Military rearmament became the function of the armed forces. Economic
rearmament was directed by Schacht and the governmental
agencies under his control. Each form of rearmament entailed some partial planning. In 1933 the Ministry of Defense
adopted the military plan of creating an army of sixty-three
divisions by the end of 1938,[1] but no binding financial estimate for the five-year period was agreed on. Schwerin von
Krosigk, the Minister of Finance, said in 1945: "I had the
opinion that we should try to fix a certain sum for rearmament, if possible for some years. Schacht as well as von Blomberg had the opinion that that was not possible, and Schacht
always thought that the natural limit for rearmament was the
capacity of labor and industry to produce. I always thought
that the fixing of a certain sum would lead the Minister of
War to more careful thrift." Failing to fix a financial plan for
rearmament, the three participants came "to the arrangement to fix a sum not for several years but always for one
year."[2]

These yearly plans were formulated by the three armed
forces. They developed two types of budgets each year. The
military plan indicated the number of men to be recruited,
the supplies to be ordered for the troops and the weapons and
equipment to be produced within a fiscal year. The financial
budget contained the estimates of funds necessary to finance
the items in the military plan. After months of negotiations,
the budget officers of the army, navy and air force arrived at
a uniform financial plan. This was usually accompanied by
much jealousy, intrigue, and friction among the three

branches of the armed forces, and occasionally, when the navy did not recognize von Blomberg's final decision, Admiral Raeder would present his own claims to Hitler for recognition. For instance, the budget of the navy, drawn up in May of 1934, called for a substantial increase in funds for the building of U-boats and of warships. Hitler had authorized the construction of warships of the 25,000-ton class under the condition that this program would be camouflaged as an improvement of 10,000-ton ships, which were permitted under the Treaty of Versailles. Similarly, when the navy ran out of funds, Hitler repeatedly instructed the Labor Front to transfer a portion of its funds to the navy.[3] In this fashion Hitler helped to reduce the frictions between branches of the armed forces, and probably discovered how easily the generals and admirals could be played against each other and utilized for the furthering of Nazi goals.

The unified financial plans of the armed forces were presented to Schacht and Schwerin von Krosigk by von Blomberg. According to Schwerin von Krosigk, negotiations between these officials led to some reduction of the amounts requested by the armed forces.[4] The treasury evolved its tax programs according to this final financial rearmament plan. Similarly, the *Reichsbank* developed its programs of short-term and long-term borrowing in accordance with the financial plan. In consequence, military plans, the placing of orders, and the stockpiling of war materials became the exclusive function of the military forces. The formulation of financial plans was the result of agreement, first by the respective officers of the armed forces, then by the highest leaders of the army and economic ministries.

The authority to formulate the economic plans for rearmament and to supervise their execution was granted primarily to Schacht. Until 1936, Schacht initiated the economic policy decisions of the regime. Neither the military nor the party participated decisively in formulating economic policy. In this period, Schacht accepted only one condition proposed by the military: that the principles of the economic plans would have to be discussed with Minister of Defense (since May, 1935) General von Blomberg. The purpose of these discussions was not to tell Schacht what he should do. Rather they were aimed at coordination of military and economic rearmament. What lines of policy did Schacht introduce in order to implement the program of economic rearmament?

Briefly, the policy of rearmament gave rise to selective economic planning and partial regulation of some markets in the economy. Regulation aimed at or led to: (a) stable wages, (b) extensive control of foreign trade and exchange, (c) selective depreciation of the German mark when it was used to repay foreign creditors, (d) a series of restrictions in the money and capital markets, (e) deliberate reduction of employment in some consumer-goods industries, (f) supervision of prices, and (g) a high level of taxation. Let us briefly indicate the main features and results of these seven lines of a coordinated policy of economic rearmament.

STABLE WAGE RATES

The destruction of free trade unions had enabled the Nazi government to impose a policy of stable wages upon laborers. Hourly wage rates were fixed by the trustees of labor, who usually froze wages to the level of the previous depression. These trustees were responsible to the Minister of Labor. Through his extended control over other ministries, Schacht was able to give instructions to the trustees through his liaison in the wage department of the Ministry of Labor. The result of this policy was stability of wage rates.

The following data show the hourly wage rates in Germany for the periods of the Great Depression and rearmament. During the depression, money rates declined by over 20 per cent, and real rates rose by 5 per cent. From 1933 on, fixed-

HOURLY MONEY AND REAL WAGE RATES*
(1929 equals 100)

Years	In Pfennigs	Index of Money Rates	Index of Real Rates
1930	86.8	102	106
1931	82.3	96	109
1932	69.7	82	104
1933	67.6	79	104
1934	67.5	79	101
1935	67.5	79	99
1936	67.5	79	98
1937	67.6	79	98

* *Yearbook of Labor Statistics* (published by the International Labor Office [Geneva, 1943–44]), Section XIII, A.

money rates in Germany remained at the depression level, and real rates fell 5 per cent below this level. In keeping down wage rates, the state deliberately depressed the income of, and consumption by, workers while at the same time providing low unit-wage costs for employers. Both effects of low wage rates constituted an effective support of economic rearmament.

Officially, the fixing of wage rates at the depression level was justified by a cyclical argument. According to a letter of August 30, 1933, from Schmitt (Minister of Economics from July, 1933, to June, 1934) to the leading business organizations, an increase in the purchasing power of workers should be achieved only through an increase in the number of gainfully employed and an extension of the working hours. The aim of the government was a *Mengenkonjunktur,* in which an increase in consumption was to be the result of more work, not of rising wage rates.[5]

Although he accepted wage-fixing as a function of the state, Schacht (who had succeeded Schmitt as Minister of Economics) was not in favor of comprehensive regulation of the labor market. He rejected the proposal of the intransigent Nazis that labor turnover should be directed by the state. A conflict arose on this issue. On May 15, 1934, the intransigents had induced the government to pass a law which had two goals: A considerable portion of the working population should be shifted from the city to rural communities and unemployed workers in cities channeled into farm employment. The law thus authorized the Employment Offices of the state to prevent workers with previous experience in agriculture from accepting jobs in industry. In cities with many unemployed, workers could be hired only with the consent of the Employment Offices. Finally, these offices were authorized to direct firms to dismiss their workers who were under twenty-five years of age. These were to be shifted to agriculture and replaced by older men who had been unemployed for a substantial period of time.[6]

Compulsory allocation of young people from factories to farms aroused the resentment of employers, who saw therein a threat to their supply of young and strong workers. This apprehension against governmental allocation was shared by Schacht. A new decree was issued in August of 1934, at the time that Schacht obtained discretionary authority to determine governmental economic policy. This decree enjoined all agencies of the party from directing the movement of laborers.

The Employment Offices were also instructed to refrain from asking firms to dismiss their young workers. Employers could be asked to give preference to older workers, but the respective hiring decisions rested exclusively with the employers, and the Employment Offices abstained from suggesting to employers the desired age composition of their labor force.[7] In consequence, the Nazis in agriculture and the Labor Front were prevented from imposing labor allocations upon business and government. Labor turnover, Schacht insisted, should not be directed by the state. The occupational movement of laborers should be influenced exclusively by the demand for and supply of labor. Since unemployment was widespread and since there were no independent unions, the turnover of labor was primarily influenced by the num-

ber of jobs offered by employers. This gave employers
practically free choice among the large numbers of workers
looking for jobs. In this way, employers obtained the full
benefit of governmentally frozen low wage rates and extensive freedom in the hiring and firing of laborers.

SCHACHT'S "NEW PLAN"

A second exchange crisis developed in the spring of 1934.
The crisis resulted from the "battle for employment" in
Germany, from the retaliation of other countries against
the Nazi regime, and from the extension of clearing agreements to most of German trade. Imports exceeded exports by
316 million marks in the first half of 1934. The import restrictions of the summer of 1934 threatened to cause widespread unemployment, and this led to two proposals for reorganizing the control of imports and exports. One came
from the intransigent Nazis in agriculture, the other from
Schacht and his economic ministry.

The intransigent Nazis called for a change in foreign trade
policy along "estate" lines. The new policy was (a) to reduce
foreign trade to a mere supplement of the internal economy
and (b) to replace the prevailing quota system by extensive
barter agreements which would be negotiated by trading
monopolies of corporatives. In order to make foreign trade
secure against the vicissitudes of depression and foreign exchange, goods were to be bought in the most reliable instead
of in the cheapest markets. This proposed policy was an
application of the principle of autarchy to external trade.[8]
The Nazis in agriculture proposed to solve the exchange
crisis through reduced imports and increased subsidies for
agricultural production at home. In proposing this policy the
Nazified leaders of agriculture tried to secure control over
foreign trade and attach the governmental agencies for trade
to the Ministry of Agriculture.

Schacht rejected the corporative trade policy. He preferred regulation of markets and introduced his "New Plan" in September of 1934. The plan adopted contained four distinct features.[9] There was first the estimated balance sheet of receipts and expenditures of foreign exchange. This "estimate" plan enabled the Central Bank to decide a program of action six months in advance. A strategy was devised by means of which the volume of foreign exchange could be increased and the expected funds most effectively allotted to meet the various needs of the economy. Secondly, an "allocation" plan was adopted. Foreign exchange was to be distributed according to a priority list. The six priority groups included (a) essential military goods, (b) essential civilian commodities, (c) goods essential to foreign-trade negotiations, (d) goods necessary to fulfill short-term foreign credit agreements, (e) goods obtainable under the clearing agreements, and finally (f) commodities negotiated in barter agreements. In addition, a subdivision was adopted for each of these groups so that a portion of the expected foreign currency could also be made available occasionally for items of lower priority. It was decided at the same time that future imports would have to be restricted to goods that were essential from the German point of view and, as general conditions pertaining to imports, that the volume of uncommitted foreign exchange would have to be increased and that the extent of German discretion to dispose of these funds would have to be widened. A strategy was thus developed for the future realization of the foreign exchange and allocation plans.

Thirdly, a new procedure was adopted for implementing the plans and facilitating the accepted strategies. The foreign exchange offices retained exclusive authority over the final receipts and payments of foreign exchange. The granting of rights to use foreign exchange was the joint function of these offices and the newly established supervisory boards of the state. The code numbers of these permits had to be attached to the freight papers of all foreign goods entering Germany, and customs officers were instructed to prevent the import of any other goods. Finally, a new principle was adopted for selecting permissible imports. Formerly, general monthly permits had been issued which enabled an importer to buy the allotted amount when and where he pleased. The new specific permits, however, were limited to a single transaction and expired within a month. The transaction itself was examined carefully, and the place of origin, price, and quality of goods involved were noted. Also, the respective users of imports in Germany were checked.[10] The result was a qualitative regulation of imports, coupled with price control, and a selective allocation within Germany of the quantities imported.

The new form of trade regulation resulted in the economic insulation of Germany. Price connections with other countries were severed or greatly modified.[11] Foreign exchange was governed by an extensive clearing system. At the end of 1938, about forty clearing agreements existed which covered about 80 per cent of German imports.

The regulation of foreign trade constituted an essential condition for the rearmament boom. The composition of imports and exports changed greatly. The volume of imports of manufactured goods—from 1934 to 1937—declined by 63 per cent. In the same period, imports of iron ore rose by 132 per cent and those of oil by 116 per cent. Extensive restrictions on the use of export proceeds reduced the purchase of food or other items not essential for rearmament. The main economic function of the "New Plan" was thus to provide the supply of essential imports either by cutting down nonessential imports or by fostering exports.

SELECTIVE DEPRECIATION OF CURRENCY

As has been noted, the extensive exchange control under Schacht insulated the monetary system. The domestic value of the mark was separated from its external value, and a policy of selective depreciation of the German mark was introduced in connection with the foreign debt. On July 1, 1934, Schacht announced a complete transfer moratorium for the foreign debt. That is, Germany refused to fulfill her obligations to foreign long-term creditors in foreign money. The creditors were offered the alternative of either accepting payment in German scrips or of reinvesting their interest and amortization funds in Germany. But a scarcity of foreign exchange was no longer the inevitable consequence of the original credit and exchange crisis of 1931–32. Scarcity of exchange became a chronic state of affairs because an increasing amount of export proceeds was spent on foreign raw materials needed for rearmament. (Very little military equipment as such was available for export.) The transfer moratorium— originally transitional—became permanent. Under the conditions of rearmament, Schacht could never expect to obtain enough foreign exchange to repay even a part of the foreign loans, in spite of his many promises to do so.

Instead of working out a plan for gradual repayment of the debt, Schacht adopted a policy of depreciating the assets of foreign creditors. German debtors had to pay their interest and amortization, not to the foreign creditor, but to a special government bank. These funds were deposited in the name of the foreign creditor, who, if he decided to withdraw them, was paid in special scrips. Yet the scrips had to be spent in Germany or used in paying for exports of specific German goods. The limited uses of the scrips led to their depreciation. The depreciated scrips in turn were used by foreign buyers who either purchased German goods or who spent their vacations in Germany. In consequence, the foreign loans were utilized to "subsidize" either German exports or the tourist business. The additional export proceeds contributed to the supply of foreign raw materials for rearmament.

When the volume of scrips fell off, German exports tended

to decline, and exporters clamored for relief. Many demanded a general devaluation of the reichsmark in order that they might again compete effectively with British exporters. The campaign for devaluation was very intense behind the scenes. On this issue, big business was divided into devaluers, "autarchists" for the duration of the rearmament and "autarchists" in principle.[12] The military autarchists, led by Schacht, dominated the situation. Schacht rejected devaluation, whether outright or *de facto*, and imposed a compulsory export levy upon domestic business in 1935. Firms producing for the internal market had to pay a special turnover tax. Only the German farmers did not have to pay the tax. The returns, which amounted to 1.2 billion marks in 1938, were used to reduce German export prices. The subsidies helped to maintain German exports and thus increased the supply of foreign raw materials for the production of armaments. The compulsory export levy was thus the price imposed upon business for rearmament and economic insulation.[13]

PLANNING AND DIRECTION OF INVESTMENT

Economic rearmament called for the collection and investment of funds primarily for the purchase of war materials from private producers. In spite of his conservative leanings, Schacht engaged in a policy of deficit financing for the realization of these goals. In the process he introduced two new devices that were not present in American deficit financing as practiced under the New Deal. First, he employed a new method of borrowing funds. Procurement offices paid private producers in special notes. These notes, or "mefo-bills," were accepted by a dummy organization of four large private concerns and two ministries, disguised as the Metall-Forschungs GmbH, whose debt was guaranteed by the government. The mefo-bills ran for six months and could be renewed for a period of five years. Thus they could be used as commercial bills or for the payment of goods delivered. Unlike promissory notes, special bills were not paid at their date of maturity but continued to function as money for further payments.

Accepted mefo-bills came to private banks and either led to the issue of new currency—a currency increase of 33 per cent from February, 1933, to February, 1938—or to the creation of demand deposits by private banks. Savings banks were obligated to invest 30 per cent of their deposits in mefo or special bills, and commercial banks were soon subjected to similar requirements.[14] Having been induced to lend funds to the government through the purchase of such bills, the private—commercial and investment—banks gradually invested an increasing amount of their assets in this way. On the one hand, as private borrowers repaid their loans, many private accounts became liquid. On the other hand, armament producers were no longer in need of bank loans, for many new investments were financed out of undistributed profits. The volume of commercial papers thus fell, while the volume of mefo and special bills rose. Private banks became, in their own self-interest, filled with special government bills; but since the special bills could be rediscounted by the Central Bank, it was the Central Bank, in the last analysis, that provided the funds for financing rearmament. From 1934 to 1938, when this policy was discontinued, a total of 12 billion mefo-bills were issued.[15] The Central Bank reasoned that as long as there were unemployed workers and unused plants, the financing of governmental orders by special bills was a calculated risk that would endanger neither the monetary system nor the banking system of the country.[16]

But one concession had to be made by business to the state. The financing of rearmament through government bills intensified government regulation of the money and capital markets. Schacht had four reasons for continuing to regulate those two markets by means of the system which he had inherited from the previous banking crisis. First, the process of hoarding, which began during the credit crisis of 1931–32, had not yet come to an end. In order to avoid the possibility that some of the newly supplied money might be hoarded, the Central Bank insisted that the restrictions upon the disposal of deposits and the embargo upon the new issue or conversion of securities be continued. These and related devices restricted private demand for loanable funds, which were thus reserved for the financing of rearmament. Second, the private banking system was full of frozen accounts or unsalable securities. The Central Bank felt it necessary to supervise closely the "unfreezing" of the accounts and the conversion of bonds outstanding[17] and was also anxious to avoid an excess liquidity of assets among the private banks. Consequently, they were required to invest their accumulated funds in special bills or government bonds. Third, public investment was given preference over private investment on the capital market, and a ban on private investments in many consumer-goods industries was imposed. These embargoes on investment prevented an increase of existing excess capacity in plants and kept down the demand for new funds that would have financed civilian industries. The specific bans were accompanied by a general embargo against the issue of new securities, including mortgages. Only when new issues of securities definitely financed armament projects was permission for the floating of an issue granted.[18]

Finally, the Central Bank was determined to reduce drastically the very high rates of interest. This could not be expected to happen quickly under the prevailing conditions of scarce money. The Central Bank employed three devices to bring the rates of interest down. Private demand for funds was reduced through embargoes and bans in the capital markets and through restrictions on the disposal of deposits in the money markets. The government either negotiated with the banks to reduce their rates of interest or instructed them to do so. In the case of mortgages outstanding, the government imposed an outright reduction of interest rates, either by "agreement" among the partners or by court action.[19] The interest policy was successful. The yield of long-term government bonds declined from 7 per cent in 1933 to 4.5 per cent in 1937. The private discount rate was reduced from 3.88 in 1933 to 2.91 per cent in 1937. In consequence, rates of interest fell while the public investments that were being used to finance rearmament were increasing. The only exception was the rediscount rate of the Central Bank, which was deliberately kept at 4 per cent from 1933 to 1940.

The result of these governmental policies was a comprehensive regulation of money and capital markets. Private banks and other financial institutions had to submit to extensive governmental control of their business. Apart from some uncontrolled direct investment of funds in residential construction, the regulation of the two kinds of markets (money and capital) was a success. The volume of savings as well as of public and private investment rose. The savings of individuals rose from 900 million marks in 1933 to 7.11 billion in 1938. The total of individual and institutional savings amounted to 19.35 billion marks for the first six years of the regime. The flotation of securities on the capital market totalled 22.4 billion marks. Of these, 16.6 billion marks comprised the securities of governmental agencies.[20] This increase in the supply of funds and their investment in governmentally desired projects was accompanied by a consistent decline in interest rates. The government thus excluded private demand for funds, fostered the increase in the supply of funds, and determined the price it was willing to pay for the funds it borrowed. In this way Schacht maximized the volume of public investment, excluded competitors from the market (at the same time reserving available funds for rearmament), and reduced the price of these funds to the minimum attainable.[21]

Government regulation was not unlimited, however. Saving was voluntary, not controlled by the government. Under Schacht's guidance, two lines of policy were pursued to foster an increase in savings. Thrift was glorified and savers were praised. Schacht, in his well-known speech at Koenigsberg in August of 1935, said "It would really be suicide . . . for the government to violate the interests of thrifty persons. In the final analysis, re-employment must be financed by the saved surpluses of business and labor."[22] Moreover, the government supported the policy of private concerns of accumulating undistributed profits. A dividend ceiling was imposed in 1934, indicating that the government favored the accumulation and reinvestment of profits by corporations. The retained profits for the first four years of the regime amounted to 6.4 billion marks, and taxation of these funds was reduced by tax abatements. This constituted an incentive to build up open and hidden reserves.[23] In consequence, the government fostered the formation of capital by business concerns. The only obligation of the business concerns was to invest these undistributed profits in projects considered desirable by the government.

The regulation of the banking business by no means curbed the profit opportunities of the private banks. To be sure, investment opportunities for banks in the private sector declined, in part because of governmental policies; but the Central Bank opened new opportunities for investment. Since the private banks had become excessively liquid and were complaining of a decline in earnings, the Gold Discount Bank, a subsidiary of the Central Bank, issued *Solawechsel* to private banks. These three-month bills carried an interest rate of 3¾ or 3⅞ per cent and were eagerly bought by private banks, since the discount rate of the private banks was only 2⅞ per cent. Thus the private banks benefited from the high rate of return (in effect, extended to them as a privilege by the Central Bank) that was realized on the purchase of the *sola* bills.[24] These bills in turn could be rediscounted with the Central Bank, whose rediscount rate was stabilized at 4 per cent. This granting of special profit opportunities to private banks led to strong protests from the treasury, for the treasury was required to pay an interest of 4 per cent on mefo and *sola* bills which were in the possession of the Central Bank. Schacht put the interests of private banks—in this case—above those of the treasury. This certainly was one of the reasons why private bankers accepted regulation of their business willingly and praised Schacht in public.[25] Other reasons were that the private bankers were attaining liquidity and, by paying their debts to the *Reich,* were able to repurchase their shares from the state and thus reduce public ownership in commercial banking. Moreover, the private bankers accepted the prediction implicit in the theory of compensatory finance. They believed that public investment through special bills would come to an end when full employment was reached. In this expectation, however, the bankers were as mistaken as Schacht himself.

DECLINING QUALITY OF CONSUMER GOODS

The scarcity of foreign exchange and the redirection of imports to essential raw materials caused a scarcity of imported foodstuffs and raw materials for consumer-goods industries. Three related policies were introduced to alleviate these scarcities. Imported foodstuff was limited to essential goods for a consumer's diet. Dispensable food items, such as citrus fruit and related goods, were no longer imported. This restriction reduced the choice of goods available to families. Another policy was compulsory substitution of domestic for imported raw materials or the compulsory admixture of such materials. The result was a reduction in the quality of many consumer goods. Finally, a few industries were instructed to reduce production in order to diminish their demand for foreign raw materials. The most conspicuous example was the limitation of employment in the textile industry. What was the result of reducing consumption through a governmental limitation upon employment?

In the second quarter of 1934, imports of cotton and wool were drastically reduced and then prohibited. When these materials could be imported again, they were subjected to a stringent permit system. This was followed by a decree instructing firms in the fiber industry to limit their working week to thirty-six hours (a 30 per cent reduction of previous working time). Second and third shifts of employment had to be dropped (but, without wholesale dismissals), and part-time employment was to become the rule in the industry.[26] Only when workers were employed for less than twenty-four hours a week could they draw on unemployment insurance. In addition, firms were forbidden to expand their production. New plants could not be established, and the capacity of existing plants could not be increased. Any attempt to shift to other products or to improve existing methods of production was also forbidden. These limitations on working time and output were accompanied by a price ceiling for the products of the industry. Prices were frozen to the level of March, 1934, and exceptions were granted only for those products that had experienced a rise in the cost of their foreign raw materials.

On the whole, the attempt to regulate the fiber industry proved to be a failure, for various reasons. Limiting the working time proved to be an inadequate method of restriction. Total employment in the textile industry fell by only 7 per cent from November, 1934, to November, 1935. Better utilization of machines and improved organization of plants took place because no effective check was imposed upon the managerial policies of enterprises. Restriction was not extensive enough; weaving enterprises alone were subject to the decree. The expectation that the spinning mills would be controlled indirectly proved to be false. The mills began to import half-finished cotton and wool goods from France which were routed through Switzerland. These goods entered Germany under the Swiss clearing agreement, which limited only the total quantities of goods to be bought in Switzerland. The spinneries thus obtained raw materials by misusing the clearing agreement with Switzerland. In consequence, the imports of materials for the textile industry did not decline from 1934 to 1935.[27]

Failure to regulate the textile industry through employment restrictions led to the extension and adoption of other forms of regulation. The whole spinning industry, and, later, other parts of the textile industry, became subject to restrictions. The new law of December, 1935, repealed the limitations upon working time. Instead, production was reduced through controlled allocation of foreign raw materials. The supervisory board of textile products controlled imports by granting monthly quotas which were based upon the quantity of material imported by the industry in the previous year. Import quotas were supplemented by inventory controls of raw materials and half-finished products. Ultimately, however, the attempt to regulate the capacity of the mills, as well as their organization and methods of production, was given up. Only the provision for price control and the prohibition against the establishment of new plants were retained.[28] Furthermore, the restrictions on investments were liberalized, in 1936, for mills that produced or utilized artificial fiber. Compulsory allocation did not apply to domestic raw materials. The mills could even obtain a permit to return to two production shifts, if an increased use of domestic fibers made this desirable. These measures led to an increase in the use of artificial fibers, from 6.6 per cent of the total supply of textiles in 1933 to 11 per cent of the total in 1935.[29]

There was thus a deliberate shift from foreign to domestic raw materials for civilian clothing. This shift enabled the government to restrict the imports of raw materials for textiles and save foreign money for the purchase of essential imports.

IMPORTS OF TEXTILE MATERIALS*
(in million marks)

Years	Import of Textiles	Total Imports	Textiles as a Percentage of Total Imports
1935	909.5	4,159	21.9
1936	808.1	5,468	14.8
1937	953.6	6,052	15.7
1938	840.9	5,207	16.1

* The Textile and Clothing Situation in Germany During the War (Special Paper No. 7, U. S. Strategic Bombing Survey [Washington, D. C., 1945]).

Textile imports thus fell by 7 percentage points of total imports from 1935 to 1936. The slight increase in the two subsequent years was possible only because of a shift in the areas supplying foreign cotton. Egyptian and Brazilian cotton replaced American cotton because the former could be obtained through barter or clearing agreements.

Restriction of imports was accompanied by a policy of admixing domestic synthetics with foreign raw materials. This policy was first applied to orders placed by public agencies in August of 1934. Compulsory admixture was gradually extended to private orders until it became an established policy under the Four Year Plan.[30] Domestic production of textiles was pushed vigorously. In 1938, domestic production of textiles had increased 16 per cent above the rate of production in 1929, which was a per capita increase of about 8 per cent. How much of this higher production went into civilian consumption, how much was stored for future consumption, and how much was stored for use by soldiers is still unknown. Consequently, the actual increase in civilian consumption from 1932 to 1939 cannot be ascertained, but it is certain that the quality of clothing deteriorated since even the best substitute, *Zellwolle,* did not fully replace the protective quality of wool in winter.

RELATIVE RESTRICTION OF INDUSTRIAL CONSUMER GOODS

The net national product of German industry, excluding handicraft and agriculture, was 32.7 billion marks in 1928 and 31.7 billion in 1936. The share of the manufactured consumer-goods industries fell from 44 to 33 per cent of total production. A secret census on the net product of the consumer-goods industries showed the following result (in billion marks):

INDUSTRIES*	1928	1936
Textile Industry	2.6	2.8
Paper Industry	2.0	1.5
Leather Industry	0.6	0.6
Foodstuff Industries	5.0	3.5
Lumber Industry	1.9	1.0
Clothing Industry	2.0	0.8
Others	0.3	0.5
	14.4	10.7

* Rolf Wagenfuehr, *Aufstieg und Niedergang der deutschen Rüstung,* (Berlin: Ducker und Humblot, 1954).

There was thus a significant deficiency in the supply of clothing and foodstuffs in 1936 relative to the supply in 1928, even if the supply in the former year is calculated according to 1928 prices. Actual consumption and production of these consumer goods lagged substantially behind the output of the producer-goods industries.

Yet the picture changes for the period of the Four Year Plan in peace time. Production of consumer goods, while definitely declining for the year 1934–35, rose steadily from the end of 1936 until the invasion of Poland. If we add the production of agriculture and handicraft to the output of industrial consumer-goods and adjust the figures for growth in population, then the per capita volume of production of total consumer goods rose by 3.5 per cent from 1929 to 1938. Official calculations further increase this figure by discounting from the output of 1929 about 2.2 million marks as the excess of exports over imports of industrial consumer goods, an excess which had almost completely disappeared in 1938.[31] If this discount is accepted, the total domestic supply of consumer goods in 1938 was about 8 to 10 per cent above that in 1929.

The crucial question is, of course, whether this *supply* of consumer goods was actually transformed into effective purchases by civilian consumers. Available data do not permit a direct measurement of total consumption by the civilian population. An approximation is afforded, however, by a comparison of the quantities of food consumed by industrial workers, as stated in family budgets. In his careful study of family budgets for groups of varying incomes in 1927–28, Joseph Rosen found that a decline in income led to a shift in consumption from high-quality to low-quality food items.[32] If one applies his list to the years 1929 and 1938, then we obtain for these years the following shift in food items consumed:

PER CAPITA CONSUMPTION OF IMPORTANT FOODSTUFFS*
(in kilograms)

	Commodity	1929 Consumption	1938 Consumption	Percentage change
Group I	Rye flour	51.8	53.0	+2
	Potatoes	172.0	183.0	+6
	Margarine	7.0	5.4	—23
Group II	Seafood	9.2	11.9	+29
	Sugar	23.4	24.3	+4
	Cigarettes	520.0	676.0	+30

Group III	Wheat flour	55.7	51.9	—7
	Milk (liters)	117.0	112.0	—4
	Eggs (numbers)	141.0	124.0	—12
	Beer (liters)	88.6	68.6	—23
	Butter	8.0	8.8	+10
	Meat (without fat)	44.9	47.8	+6
	Coffee	1.9	2.3	+21

* Hilde Oppenheimer-Bluhm, "The Standard of Living of German Labor under Nazi Rule," *Social Research,* Supplement V, 1943, p. 48.

Group I contains commodities the increased consumption of which is believed to be indicative of a decline in income. The representative items show a relative rise in consumption, save for margarine, the availability of which was reduced by governmental policies. Group II includes goods the increased consumption of which seems to be independent of changes in income. The high increase in the use of cigarettes was partly a result of the clearing agreements with Turkey and Greece. The increase in fish consumption resulted from the deliberate substitution of fish (much of which was stored) for meat. The last group includes commodities the decreased consumption of which indicates a decline in real purchasing power. The decline in consumption between 1929 and 1938 is remarkable for most of the significant items. Increases are due to special causes. Butter consumption was temporarily fostered by the government; more coffee became available because of favorable compensation agreements with Brazil. (The figures for lean meat are uncertain because official statistics included fat with meat.) In all, the changes in the relative quantities consumed suggests that the per capita consumption of high-quality products was lower, and that of low-quality products higher, in 1938 than in 1929. This suggests that the over-all level of civilian consumption had not, in 1938, reached its previous level of 1929.

There is thus a discrepancy between actual consumption as shown in the table on page 320 and the rise in the supply of consumer goods by 8 per cent for the first phase of the regime. The discrepancy resolves itself if we examine the stocks of goods on hand. This can be done for rye, wheat, and potatoes.

STOCKS AND CONSUMPTION OF GRAINS AND POTATOES*
(in thousands of tons)

Product	Crop Year	Inventories	Changes in Inventories	Quantities Consumed in Germany
Rye	1932/3	611	+411	7,185
	1935/6	487	−871	7,437
	1936/7	637	+150	6,485
	1937/8	1,084	+446	5,689
	1938/9	2,763	+1,679	6,163
Wheat	1932/3	645	+346	4,332
	1935/6	693	−679	4,942
	1936/7	494	−199	5,068
	1937/8	780	+286	4,839
	1938/9	2,048	+1,269	4,868
Potatoes	1932/3	840	+387	34,513
	1935/6	874	+204	30,378
	1936/7	505	−366	34,978
	1937/8	899	+391	44,434
	1938/9	695	−204	40,989

* *Statistisches Handbuch von Deutschland 1928–1944* (München: Franz Ehrenwirth, 1949), pp. 489–90. The definition of inventories was changed in 1936–37; stocks of industrial users were added to the figures given in the table.

Both inventories and annual excesses above consumption for grains, with a few interruptions, rose during the period under consideration. The quantities of grains and potatoes stored were substantial in the two years prior to the invasion of Poland. These stocks explain why supply exceeded actual consumption for grains during these two years. In all, a "grain reserve of 6.5 million tons was amassed in 1938 and in the beginning of 1939 which was financed by German banks whose grain credits were guaranteed by the Ministry of

Finance."[33] The result of the storage policy was a relative decline of consumption per capita.

The stability of prices and wage rates was an important part of the Schmitt-Hitler bargain. Prices rose in 1934 because of the price policy of the Estate of Agriculture, and also because of the import restrictions that grew out of the foreign exchange crisis of 1934. Schacht demanded a decree on price supervision, and the decree was issued on August 7, 1934. A three months' struggle was waged behind the scenes as to who should be appointed as price commissioner. The details explaining why Goerdeler was chosen and appointed on November 5, 1934, have not become known. The attempt of the Nazi party to usurp the power of the price commissioner one day after his appointment is an indication that the Nazis were against him, but Goerdeler must have had the support of the leaders of the army and big business.

Price supervision not only had the function of keeping prices close to their respective average costs, but also contributed directly to the success of the "battle for employment." According to Goerdeler, stable wage rates and prices were indispensable conditions for effective deficit financing. A rise in prices or wages would reduce the employment-creating effect of public investments. "The government must thus lay special stress," Goerdeler said, "upon the fact that prices and wages have to remain as they were in 1933. In line with sound economic principles, the government can expect the private concerns to overcome the profitless situation through an increased sales volume, the rising revenue of which has become possible through the increased volume of employment."[34] Prosperity was thus to be attained not through raising prices or wage rates but through increased output, sales, and productivity. Price stability would give rise to a *Mengenkonjunktur*. This policy was mostly ignored by the leaders of Nazified small business. In a letter of complaint to Keppler on September 15, 1933, Minister Schmitt said: "I have made the observation that considerable pressure has been exerted by business organizations and various national socialist offices to force producers into new organizations and that the price agreements of the latter were followed by higher prices."[35] All indications are that the top party leaders could not or did not stop the upward movement of prices.

In 1934, import restrictions also caused price increases. Foreign sellers insisted upon additional payments to cover the uncertainties springing from exchange control. The supervisory boards were instructed to discover and prevent such price increases. On December 4, 1934, the boards were charged with the function of controlling prices for all imported goods. In particular, the prices resulting from compensation agreements had to be examined, and permission was refused when foreign sellers tried to realize special gains.[36] Importers were urged to buy in the cheapest market and were warned that if they did not, the requested permits would be refused. As soon as the general rise in prices abroad set in, however, importers were allowed to add the increase to their costs—but not to raise their profit margins. The prices of some imported goods rose, and so did the prices of domestic manufacturers.

The experience of the textile industry, depending heavily upon imported raw materials, shows us what the impact of higher import prices was. The first decree had imposed a price ceiling on textile products, with a view to reducing textile production. Prices were frozen to the level prevailing in March of 1934. The mills could ask for higher prices only under two conditions. When raw material prices in foreign countries rose above the level of March, 1934, the absolute unit amount of this expense could be added to the prices charged by the mills; or when domestic costs which were beyond the control of the producers rose, the supervisory board of the textile industry could grant a price increase. But the increase in costs resulting from the reduced working week and/or part-time employment of machines furnished no acceptable reason for an increase in prices. Governmental agencies tried to keep the exceptional cases to a minimum. The supervisory board set prices for raw materials and for half-finished and finished textile products. Producers, at least in the district of Arnsberg, were prosecuted by the courts when they violated the governmentally fixed prices.[37]

In spite of governmental price-fixing, however, prices rose. The wholesale index of textile goods showed a 12 per cent increase in 1934. The rise was especially noticeable during the last six months of the year even though a price ceiling had been introduced. Domestic textile prices rose percentage-wise above the rise in the cost of foreign raw materials. The financial statements of the larger textile concerns in 1934–35 showed an increase in net profits and a high rate of depreciation on invested capital. In consequence, price-supervision was not successful. Neither prices nor profits could be stabilized through the original decree for the regulation of the textile industry.[38]

When, on November 5, 1934, Goerdeler became responsible for the official price policy, he gave two instructions to the producers of textile products. A few days after his appointment he reminded producers that the replacement price had been outlawed for this industry. His argument was that such a price was not based upon actual average costs but upon the anticipated increase in the price of raw materials to be purchased in the future. In addition, the commissioner tried to minimize the impact of the acceptable increase in cost prices upon the standard of living of the low-income groups. In negotiations with producers, the commissioner's office worked out a plan for distributing unavoidable costs among products. The textile-industry economic groups were authorized to introduce uniform cost accounting for standardized products made of cheap materials, to be sold primarily to the recipients of small incomes. The prices of such products were to be uniform in all localities and were to be reduced as far as possible to the level of March, 1934. If the lowered price resulted in a loss, the commissioner was to approve a price increase for luxury products after an appropriate investigation.[39] This plan was largely abandoned when Goerdeler resigned from his position on July 1, 1935.

A new method of price supervision was introduced with the second decree, issued on December, 1935. All firms were directed to adopt a uniform method of cost calculation. Each firm had to evaluate its costs, including overhead, according to definite rules promulgated by the supervisory boards. Whenever the prices of foreign raw materials rose, producers were permitted to increase their costs and prices—but not profit margins—correspondingly. Evidently, the goal of the new price ordinance was no longer price stability. The aim seems to have been merely to slow down the rate of increase in prices, in correspondence with the actual rise in unit costs. When Goerdeler resigned from his office, the producers were able to attain their goal of a "minimum" price. The only restraint upon minimum prices set by business organizations was that they had to be approved by the Ministry of Economics.[40]

The program of price stability failed in most industries, not only in those depending on imported raw materials. From 1933 to 1936 world prices rose by 1.6 per cent, but the picture was quite different in Germany. The official cost-of-living index rose by about 7 per cent, and wholesale prices advanced by 13.7 per cent. The prices of finished and half-finished industrial goods whose raw-material prices were determined in world markets—and were, in consequence, sensitive—rose by 23.5 per cent. Moreover, the minimum prices charged by cartels—or economic groups, if they functioned as quasi-cartels—were recognized by Schacht. The replacement of price-supervision by permitted price increases was accepted by most business firms and was thus fairly successful during the years 1935 and 1936.

In the fall of 1935, however, a crisis did arise in the pricing and supply of food products. The crisis was partly the result of a poor crop and partly of the pricing policy of the Estate of Agriculture. Goerdeler, in a memorandum sent to Hitler on October 25, 1935, analysed the agricultural situation and proposed some important remedies.

In Goerdeler's view, expressed only after he had resigned as commissioner, the main cause of the food crisis lay in the policies of the Estate of Agriculture. Rather than limiting itself to minimizing seasonal fluctuations in prices, the estate adopted policies that significantly reduced the peasants' incentive to produce goods. This was especially true for the compulsory delivery of milk to creameries and the prohibition against the production of butter on the farm. The fixing of milk and butter prices, which were equal for all producers regardless of location and unit costs, reduced the supply of milk and butter in cities. The dealers' practice of storing goods when they were cheap and selling them when they were dear was eliminated, and the price-equalizing tendency between seasons disappeared. The consequence of these policies was an extreme scarcity of butter and other animal fat. People began to hoard butter. Goerdeler reported in his memorandum to Hitler: "I decided to urge retailers in Leipzig to introduce lists of their regular customers and sell fat only to them. My reason was that I regarded hoarding as the greater danger. . . . In Leipzig not less than four fifths of all fat stores possessed no butter at all as of October 18, 1935."[41]

Goerdeler suggested that the government should temporarily ration all fats and that, in addition, all restrictions upon the peasants' production of milk and butter, and upon their raising and selling of pigs, hogs, and other livestock, should be removed so that the higher prices would induce producers to increase their output and thereby eliminate the need for rationing. It so happened that the "fat issue" had been brought to Hitler's attention prior to his receiving Goerdeler's memorandum. The Minister of Agriculture asked for more foreign exchange to pay for a substantial increase in imported fats; whereas the Minister of War suggested that fat be rationed, and the Minister of Economics, that control over food imports be transferred to him. Hitler rejected rationing, but accepted the two other proposals.[42]

An integrated program of price control and rationing was not a part of the rearmament boom. Fat-rationing was rejected by Hitler. Price supervision failed to maintain the stability of prices. Nor did the rise in prices lead to a subsequent increase in wage rates, since jobs were still scarce and unions were nonexistent. The price increases reduced the real income of consumers, because—although many families suffered from a meat famine for significant periods of time—[43] foreign currency was made available only for the importing of fats. Much of the increase in income, derived from more jobs or longer working hours, was thus absorbed in higher prices and profits for those farmers who sold a substantial part of their produce in markets.

HIGH LEVEL OF TAXATION

In the first period of the regime, the Hitler government made one basic decision in regard to taxation: There was to be no general tax reduction or reform; the increase in tax rates or the additional taxes resulting from the deflationary policy of the Brüning government was continued. Two exceptions to this basic policy were introduced in the subsequent years. Tax reductions were granted to farmers, to house-owners, to employers of servants, and to concerns purchasing machines with a life span of ten years or less. There were also some loans to newly married couples and builders of residential houses, most of which were repaid in later years. The total of these tax reductions was estimated to have resulted in a tax loss of 1.59 billion marks for the government.

At the same time, there were some increases in tax rates or an increasing efficiency in the collection of taxes because of an improved tax administration. The poll tax, imposed in 1930 as a depression measure, was made permanent but was graduated according to income. The unemployment-aid tax, reduced for couples with children, was made a part of the wage tax and the assessed income tax. A number of exemptions in the personal income tax were cancelled so that many farmers became subject to this tax. The turnover tax was rigidly enforced and extended to vertically integrated enter-prises, to department stores, to consumer cooperatives, to professional men, and even to charitable institutions. The result was an increase in the returns from the turnover tax of 1 billion marks from 1932–33 to 1936–37. The wage tax became more severe because the tax rate was raised from 10 to 15 per cent in 1936. The share of indirect taxes rose from 30 per cent in 1928 to 41 per cent of the total tax revenue in 1936. In contrast, an increase in the rate of the corporation tax by 5 per cent did not come until the fall of 1936, when the rearmament boom had reached its peak. The high social-insurance tax of the depression years was transformed into a source of revenue for the treasury because the claims of the insured were successively reduced.[44]

The result of tax abatements and tax increases was two-fold. Abatements and subsidies functioned as business incentives. Tax increases were levied primarily upon non-business

taxpayers in the population. The tax burden was thus enlarged for wage earners and consumer groups in general. The
second result was an increase in total tax returns that exceeded the rate of increase in national income. The government's share of the national income can be seen from the
following data.

GOVERNMENT FINANCE AND NATIONAL INCOME*
(in billion marks)

Years	National Income	Taxes	Non-Tax Receipts	Borrowings	Total Gov't. Receipts
1933	46.5	10.6	3.5	3.1	17.2
1934	52.7	11.9	3.6	1.6	17.1
1935	59.1	13.5	3.8	4.4	21.7
1936	65.8	15.6	3.9	4.7	24.2
1937	73.7	18.6	4.8	6.2	29.6
1938	82.0	22.7	5.3	10.7	38.7
1939 (Aug. 31)	74.6	11.5	2.6	5.4	19.5
	454.4	104.4	27.5	36.1	168.0

* *Statistisches Handbuch von Deutschland 1928–1944*, p. 600; Paul Hermberg,
"German Government Finance," May, 1945. I am indebted to Dr. Hermberg for
making available to me his valuable unpublished studies and for his permission
to use them here.

Total national income, measured in calendar years, and
the receipts of all governmental bodies, measured in fiscal
years, experienced a very substantial rise. Government receipts up to August of 1939 constituted not less than 37 per
cent of national income. Equally remarkable is the fact that
borrowings comprised only 21 per cent of the total of governmental receipts—but the data on borrowing seem to be incomplete. In his extensive study of the indebtedness of the
Reich, Dr. F. A. Freundt adds to the official debt of 37.3
billion marks the full amount of the 12 billion marks in
mefo-bills, arriving at a total debt of 49 billion marks as of

August, 1939.[45] The mefo-bills were not officially regarded as a debt of the *Reich* because the first installments had to be amortized no earlier than 1939; but if the mefo-bills are included in the calculation, the total receipts increased to 180 billion marks, amounting to 40 per cent of national income. The amended total debt then raised deficit financing from one-fifth to one-fourth of the government receipts.

Whichever of the two percentages one chooses, each indicates the major difference between the New Deal experiment and the rearmament boom. While one-half of the United States' government expenditures were deficit-financed in the years 1932–36, the prewar period produced a deficit of only one-fifth or one-fourth of the governmental receipts in Germany. The large amount of revenue collected supports the previous finding that a significant portion of the government's military efforts had the effect of reducing civilian consumption relative to the civilian effort in production.

The policy of economic rearmament led to a boom in which the volume of production and employment rose much faster than the volume of consumption. This leads us to the questions of how much precisely was spent for military purposes and who contributed the greatest share of these military outlays?

MONETARY FUNDS FOR REARMAMENT

Materials for rearmament and war are not reproductive, as are goods produced for the working population. Products destined for civilian use provide labor energies which can be utilized as new resources for future production. This reproductive capacity does not exist for materials destined for the military purposes of armed forces. Either the weapons are used for destructive purposes, or they deteriorate and become obsolete over the course of years. In a sense, the production of war materials constitutes an economic loss for a country. Special resources are required to produce war materials, the consumption of which does not lead to a corresponding increase in economic welfare.

It has become customary to distinguish between two sources of rearmament for war, namely, real funds and monetary funds.[46] What kinds of resources were utilized to finance rearmament in the first phase of the regime, and what was their magnitude? Under the Weimar Republic, the Ministry of Finance occupied a strategic position in determining the annual budget of the government. Other ministries presented their budget requests to the Ministry of Finance, where the individual items proposed were carefully examined for their feasibility and acceptability. Invariably, some of the expenditures requested were sliced off. This applied also to the armed forces—with some notable exceptions, such as the building of destroyers. When the ministry affected contested the reduction, a conference between ministers took place. Different points of view entered into the common decision, but the Minister of Finance often exerted a decisive influence. Under the Nazi regime, "financial control" was discarded. In a cabinet meeting of April 4, 1934, the armed forces were authorized to draw up their own final budgets. The Minister of Finance no longer had the power to examine and accept proposed military expenditures but was to confine himself to the sole task of obtaining the revenue and loans required to finance the rearmament plans of the military. What were the total funds spent both for rearmament and for the war economy in peacetime?

The leading officials of Nazi Germany presented different estimates of the expenditures for these periods in the trials at Nürnberg. A careful examination of the relevant available documents enables us to give a comprehensive statistical statement of the minimum actual expenditures for military purposes.

Military Expenditures in Time of Peace*
(in million marks)

Rearmament

	1934	1935	1936
Army	1,083	1,793	3,449
Navy	559	385	491
Air Force	642	1,036	2,224
War Ministry	3.5	5	127
Mefo-Bills	2,145	2,715	4,452
Four Year Plan		(Planned figures only)	
Total	4,432.5	5,934	10,743
Grand total: 21,109.5			

War Economy in Time of Peace

	1937	1938	1939	(to August 31, 1939)
Army	4,611	9,148	5,614	"
Navy	747	1,633	2,095	"
Air Force	3,257	6,025	3,941	"
War Ministry	346	452	278	
Mefo-Bills	2,688			
Four Year Plan	2,866	3,067	1,979	
Total	14,515	20,325	13,907	
Grand total: 48,747				

* Documents NG-4062, NG-4984, NG-5548, NI-5549, and EC-281. See also Schwerin-Krosigk, "Wie wurde der zweite Weltkrieg finanziert?" *Bilanz der Zweiten Weltkrieges* (Oldenburg: Gerhard Stalling Verlag, 1953). In his 1945 study on "German Government Finance," Paul Hermberg arrived at an expenditure of only 54.9 billion marks, based primarily upon residual data. This figure is incomplete because it did not take into account (*a*) the mefo-bills, (*b*) the planned investments of the Four Year Plan Office, and (*c*) the secret fund for building up a national reserve of raw materials. (For details on this last item see the three volumes of "Haushaltungsangelegenheiten des OKW," available in the microfilms Wi/IF 5.326, 5.327, and 5.328, in the National Archives.) None of these sums was included in the public budget of the federal government during the time when these funds were actually utilized for rearmament. The only element of doubt in the above table lies in a possible discrepancy between the projected figures of the Four Year Plan and the actual figures, which have not been discovered.

All these data present actual outlays of the various armed forces in the regular budgets plus the loans used for military payments. In addition to the military expenditures listed, there are the estimates ("Planned figures only"; see table preceding) for investments that were to finance the Four Year Plan. A large portion of the funds for the construction of plants was provided first by private concerns but was eventually recovered from the government during the war years. Since the actual resources were utilized in the prewar period, they have thus to be included as planned payments for the war economy in peacetime.

The expenditures in the table constitute minimum outlays because two kinds of quasi-military expenditures are not included. We are referring to the expenditures of civilian agencies of the government for military purposes as well as to the quasi-military outlays of some party organizations. No precise information is available, for instance, as to how great were the military expenditures of the SS, SA, NS Air Corps, NS Automobile Corps, and the Todt Organization prior to the invasion of Poland. One financial official estimated the military expenditures of the civilian governmental agencies as being in the neighborhood of 4 billion marks before the invasion.[47]

The approximate minimum figures thus show an expenditure of about 21 billion marks for the financing of rearmament up to the end of 1936. The expenditures for the war economy in peacetime amounted to almost 49 billion marks. If the estimated outlays of civilian agencies are included, then the total is raised from 70 to 74 billion marks. Thus, Hitler's assertion that a total outlay of 90 billion marks was spent for military purposes prior to the invasion of Poland seems—on the basis of presently available information—untenable.

How large a share of national income was spent for military

purposes? National income for the years 1934 to 1936 amounted to 198 billion marks. The minimum military expenditures for the rearmament period constituted an outlay of 11.1 per cent of national income. Germany during the time of Schacht's economic dictatorship was thus engaged in pursuing a policy of limited rearmament. A relatively small rearmament boom was grafted upon a depression-afflicted economy.

A different picture emerges when we look at the next three years, from 1937 to August of 1939. Total national income during these years amounted to about 230.3 billion marks. The minimum expenditures for the war preparation constituted 22.4 per cent of national income. There was thus a distinct increase in the proportion of national income spent for military purposes. The total outlays as well as the percentage shares of national income clearly support our distinction between the rearmament boom and the war economy in peacetime. These expenditures for the respective periods enable us to reject the thesis, presented in Nürnberg by the Nazi Minister of Finance, Schwerin von Krosigk, as well as by the financial expert of the War Ministry who testified at the trials, that "there was no financial indicator for the shift from defensive to aggressive rearmament."[48] On the contrary, even the less costly strategy of "lightning" warfare called for a financial military outlay of one fifth of the national income for the last three years prior to the invasion of Poland.

THE REAL RESOURCES FOR REARMAMENT

There are two ways of measuring the magnitude of the real funds of rearmament. Either one can ascertain the total of goods and services spent for rearmament, or one can concentrate upon the materials and man-hours utilized in the production of military equipment and in the maintenance of the armed services. Unfortunately, neither method of calculation can be employed here because the precise information required has not yet become available; but as can be seen from the following table, the increase in total production and employment from 1933 to 1938 is impressive.

INDUSTRIAL PRODUCTION AND EMPLOYMENT*

Years	Gross National Product (in billion marks)	Index of Industrial Production (1928 = 100)	Employment of Civilian Laborers (in millions)
1928	90	100	18.4
1929	90	101	18.4
1932	58	59	12.9
1933	59	66	13.4
1934	67	83	15.5
1935	74	96	16.4
1936	83	107	17.6
1937	93	117	18.9
1938	105	122	20.1
1939			20.8

* Hermberg, "The German National Income and National Product Between the Two World Wars," unpublished manuscript, used with the permission of the author.

Thus, industrial production more than doubled from the beginning of the Nazi regime in January, 1933, to the invasion of Poland. The gross national product in current prices rose somewhat less than industrial production in 1928 prices. The total of employed workers rose by 8 million. The number of unemployed fell from about 6 million in January of 1933 to about 70,000 in May of 1939.

This substantial increase indicates that additional production, and employment, was the first and most important resource for military preparations. Widespread unemployment among laborers and under-utilization of industrial facilities provided the most favorable preconditions for the rearmament boom. In utilizing these resources, the Nazi government was in a position to generate employment and thus do something which was desired by people in all walks of life. Immediate privations were not called for, beyond those already inflicted by the depression. The main line of policy adopted by the government was simple: to channel the increase of production primarily into those industries that were important for the realization of military goals. Whereas production in producer-goods industries had fallen in 1932 to 45 per cent, it rose to 136 per cent by 1938. The index of the consumer-goods industries rose from 78 per cent to 107 in the same period. Thus, production in the former industries increased by about 200 per cent, and in the latter by about 38 per cent.

Relative under-consumption was the second resource that contributed to the real fund for rearmament. The drastic change in the composition of imports cut the supply of consumer goods and increased the quantities of raw materials supplied for producer-goods industries. How much the supply of essential industrial raw materials from foreign countries increased is depicted graphically in the imports of iron ore.

IMPORTS OF IRON ORE PRIOR TO WORLD WAR II*
(in thousand metric tons)

1934	1935	1936	1937	1938	1939
8,264	14,060	18,468	20,621	21,928	18,526

* *The Effects of Strategic Bombing on the War Economy* (Washington, D. C.: Government Printing Office, 1945), p. 247.

In 1938, imports of iron ore were about 170 per cent larger than in 1934. Such increases were necessary to achieve a substantial rise in the production of producer goods.

How large was the volume of consumer goods and how much could the supply of consumer goods have been increased if instead of military programs the German government had really fostered a civilian employment program? A comparison of private consumption in Germany and the United States provides an approximate answer to this question.

Goods and Services Available for Domestic Use*

In Germany

Years	Total National Product (in billions of dollars)	Private Consumption	Per Cent
1929	25.3	18.5	73
1930	24.2	18.1	75
1931	19.7	15.7	79
1932	16.9	13.2	79
1933	16.0	12.2	76
1934	18.1	12.9	71
1935	20.3	13.0	64
1936	22.1	13.4	60
1937	25.6	14.7	58
1938	27.6	14.4	52

In the United States

Years	Total National Product (in billions of dollars)	Private Consumption	Per Cent
1929	99.0	70.8	72
1930	87.4	64.9	74
1931	71.7	54.2	76
1932	55.1	43.0	78
1933	54.2	42.4	78
1934	63.1	47.7	76
1935	70.4	52.2	74
1936	82.0	59.1	72
1937	87.2	62.5	72
1938	79.4	58.5	74

* Hermberg, "National Income and Private Consumption in Germany and the United States," prepared for Board of Governors of the Federal Reserve System. National product includes gross national product less export surplus of goods and services. Marks were converted into dollars at a rate of 1 mark to 28.1 cents.

Comparison of the shares of private consumption in the gross national products of the two countries indicates clearly how great was the change the Nazis imposed upon German consumers. In the first period, from 1929 to 1933, the percentage shares of private consumption behaved in pretty much the same way in the United States and Germany. The share of private consumption increased from 72–73 to 78–79 index points in both countries. Then came the developments of 1933 to 1938. Whereas in the United States the share of consumption never fell below that of 1929, military efforts in Germany claimed an increasing portion of the national product. In 1938, German private consumption had declined to a little more than half of all goods and services available for domestic use. The decline of consumer-goods production by one-fifth of the national product indicates the relative loss in consumption which the German consumers suffered under the Nazi dictatorship, primarily because of rearmament.

Every boom, of course, increases the share of the producer-goods industries relative to the consumer-goods industries. The boom in the United States was insufficient for full employment and did not fully reflect the "normal" increase in producer-goods industries. It is nevertheless clear from the data in the table that the relative decline of the German consumer-goods industries was extraordinary. The extent of this decline was possible only because the government deliberately and systematically retarded the production of consumer products and thus was responsible for relative underconsumption in Germany.

The exploitation of foreign creditors also contributed to the real fund for military programs. The nominal value of the foreign debt declined steadily, as can be seen from the following table.

This decline in the foreign debt brought two advantages to Nazi Germany. One was the advantage springing from the currency devaluations in the creditor countries. Since most

VALUE OF GERMAN FOREIGN INDEBTEDNESS*
(in billion marks)

July 31 1931	Feb. 28 1933	Feb. 28 1934	Feb. 28 1935	Feb. 29 1936	Feb. 28 1939
23.8	19.0	13.9	13.1	12.4	9.5

* Howard S. Ellis, *Exchange Control in Central Europe* (Cambridge, Mass.: Harvard University Press, 1941), p. 231. *Statistisches Handbuch von Deutschland 1928-1944*, p. 604.

of the foreign loans were contracted for in foreign currencies, the practice of sustaining the fixed exchange rate of the reichsmark through the use of exchange control brought a significant gain to the debtor country. This gain was estimated as being about 4,000,000,000 reichsmark by 1936.[49] The Central Bank decided that the advantage created by currency devaluation in other countries should not accrue to private debtors in Germany. As a result of exchange control, the Central Bank became the only seller of foreign money to permitted domestic buyers. The unchanged parity of the mark enabled the Central Bank to charge a pre-devaluation price for foreign money. The German debtor paid the full amount of his loan in marks, whereas the creditor received his payment in the depreciated currency of his own country. The difference between the two rates accrued to the German government as a gain resulting from exchange control. Exchange control permitted Germany to transform the advantage of devaluation into a gain for the Nazi government. Although no official data have become available, the best private estimate is that the German foreign debt declined by 13.8 billion marks from July 1, 1931 to February 28, 1938, and that of this decline not less than 43 per cent (amounting to about 6 billion marks) was attributable to foreign devaluations.[50] Since the greatest portion of this decline occurred during the Hitler regime, the "windfall" was transformed into an exploitation gain which became a significant contribution to the real fund for German rearmament.

The second advantage derived from the exploitation of foreign creditors originated with the refusal of the German government to pay interest and amortization quotas in foreign money. The so-called moratorium of July, 1934, laid down the principle of paying interest and amortization through the issue of new bonds or by offering certain reinvestment opportunities in Germany. German debtors were directed to pay their obligations to the Conversion Office, a subsidiary of the Central Bank. German debtors benefited from this shift in payment only if and when the rates of interest were reduced, primarily through unilateral action on the part of the German government. Foreign creditors were the losers. They began to sell their original bonds in markets outside of Germany at a substantial loss. Some of the bonds were then purchased at bargain prices by the *Reichsbank,* and the difference between the nominal value of the bond and its purchase price abroad constituted the gain that the German government derived from the moratorium.

Creditors who were hanging on to their securities received interest payments or amortization in scrips which could be taken out of Germany and sold in foreign markets at a substantial reduction to other foreigners who would then use the scrips to purchase additional German goods or to pay for tourist expenses in Germany. Scrips thus functioned for Germany as a form of export subsidy paid for by foreign creditors. These gains were the result of the moratorium coupled with the very limited use of scrips for purchases in Germany. The total gains from these forms of selective depreciation have been estimated at 1.0 billion reichsmark,[51] but a final calculation will be possible only if and when the official data become available.

The final source of rearmament funds was made possible by exploitation of the partner in foreign trade. The gains involved also took two different forms. One was the accumulation of involuntary credits in clearing agreements. They hovered around 500 million marks during the years 1934–37 and fell to 250 million marks in 1938.[52] These credits that were imposed upon foreign firms doing business with Germany contributed to the real fund for rearmament.

The advantage that Germany enjoyed in trading with foreign countries is further illustrated by the terms of trade. From 1929 to 1938 the index of German export prices remained substantially and steadily above her index of import prices. In part, especially in the depression years, the price differential was a result of the fact that the prices of agricultural products had fallen more than the prices of industrial products. Since the exports of Great Britain and Germany were preponderantly industrial, both countries benefited equally from the lower agricultural prices, so that the export prices of both countries, if measured in gold, should have found a similar level.

INDEXES OF GERMAN AND BRITISH EXPORT PRICES*
(1927 = 100)

	1929	1930	1931	1932	1933	1934	1935	1936	1937	1938
British Gold Export Prices	111.1	104.3	84.1	60.4	56.8	52.7	50.3	52.4	57.0	56.1
German Export Prices	100.0	94.1	82.5	76.1	64.7	62.0	59.0	60.0	64.0	67.1
2 as percent of 1	90.0	90.2	98.1	118.5	113.9	117.6	117.2	114.5	112.3	119.6

* Ellis, op. cit., p. 239.

At one point in the depression period, English export prices exceeded German export prices, but from an almost equal level in 1931, German export prices fell but remained consistently above the British, the excesses varying from 12 to 20 per cent. This relative gain was the combined result of two events. Overvaluation of the German mark enabled German exporters to secure better prices. As an increasing share of German trade came under clearing and other agreements, German export prices could also be kept at a higher level because of the greater bargaining power enjoyed by the German side in clearing negotiations. Since both overvaluation and clearing policies were a result of deliberately chosen German policies of exploitation, at least after 1934, the gains in higher export prices were the product of German exchange and trade control in the 1930's.

Thus, in summary, it will be seen that the real funds for rearmament were derived from (1) unused production facilities, (2) unemployment among laborers, (3) depressed consumption of consumer goods, and (4) exploitation of foreign creditors and traders. Although no precise measurement of the total funds obtained from these sources is possible, the rough approximations presented indicate that underemployment and under-utilization contributed most to rearmament, followed by relative underconsumption. The real resources resulting from the exploitation of foreign creditors and traders were smaller in absolute size but were still significant because of the prevailing scarcity of foreign exchange in Germany.

THE TYPICAL FACTS OF REARMAMENT

There is no agreement among economists as to the specific significance of the rearmament boom. Some investigators make a careful distinction between "The Nazi Way and the New Deal Way" of economic activity on the part of the governments.[53] Others see in the German rearmament policy a simple case of pump-priming which did not differ from a genuine recovery in spite of the military intentions of the rulers.[54] The difference of opinion arises in part because of a disagreement about the typical facts that constituted the rearmament boom. Thus, our task is to distill from the record the pattern of facts that characterized the rearmament boom, employing the typological method that Spiethoff used in presenting the *Tatsachenbild* of the business cycle. Different interpretations also sprang up because of the methods of investigation employed. Those who seek to verify the Keynesian theory usually find in the Nazi experience certain facts that confirm this theory. The question is whether, in leaving out other equally important facts, their interpretation does not become invalid through the sin of omission.

The first feature of the boom consists in the dual goal that motivated the government in initiating and directing a policy of increased employment. The so-called "battle for employment" provided the first goal: the economic welfare of the people was to be increased by providing jobs for the unemployed, by supplying new orders for idle firms, and thus creating a rise in national income for all.[55] This goal was to be implemented through two distinct lines of action. A fund of 5.4 billion marks, of which 5.1 billion were to be derived from work-creation bills, financed the public-works program. Various subsidies were paid to private individuals for the repair of private homes, or for the remodelling of other private buildings. Governmental investments in housing amounted to 855 million marks from 1933 to 1936. This subsidy program provided employment for a fairly large section of the handicraft industry. Yet early in 1934 the government decided not to initiate further projects of public works and to terminate those in process at an early date. The subsidy program, too, was tapered off gradually. The welfare goal thus performed the dual function of stimulating employment and serving as an introduction to the rearmament boom, thereby providing an ideological smoke screen for concealing the governmental policy of rearmament.

In 1934, economic rearmament became the main governmentally selected goal. The implied effect of this goal was to require the economy to provide the supplies for a new mass army. The military decision to rearm gave rise to a military and economic power goal: available idle resources should be utilized for increasing the military and subsequently the economic power of Germany relative to other states and economies. The responsibility for the selection of this economic power goal falls equally upon the generals, the Nazi party, and the leaders of big business.[56] Their freedom of action in so proceeding in the first phase of the regime followed quite "naturally" from the elimination of labor as a power group, and from the von Blomberg-Hitler agreement, which led not only to the Röhm purge but also to the decision to defeat the economic demands of the Nazified middle classes.

In the first period, which was governed by the terms of this agreement, there was full unanimity of opinion between the generals and the leading Nazis on the question of military goals. The Nazis limited themselves to the task of providing the political preconditions for a mass army. Apart from the air force, all military tasks were in the hands of the generals. In bringing in Schacht as a partner to the deal, the generals established an association with big business, in the process of which private concerns adopted economic rearmament as a preferred economic goal that was fully in their own interests. In consequence, the goal of economic rearmament was neither immaterial nor accidental. The economic power goal adopted grew necessarily and inevitably out of the bilateral power structure that had developed between the Nazis and the generals in the first phase of the regime.

Deficit financing was the second feature of the rearmament boom. In terms of total governmental expenditures, deficit spending provided the funds for one fifth or one fourth of all government outlays. In terms of income-creating expenditures, however, the share of funds derived from deficit financing was much greater. In the short-lived "battle for

employment," almost the total costs of the federal government were paid for out of newly created money. As for rearmament, the relationship between money transferred from
private sources to the government and money newly created
can be seen from the following data:

SOURCES OF MILITARY EXPENDITURES*
(in million marks)

	1934	1935	1936
Budgetary Expenditures	2,287	3,199	6,291
Mefo-Bills	2,145	2,715	4,452
Totals	4,432	5,914	10,743
Share of Deficit Spending	48%	47%	41%

* Derived from the following documents: NG-4062, NG-4984,
NG-5548, NI-5549, and EC-281.

The proportion of deficit-financed projects thus declined
with each additional year as rearmament increased. The share
of expenditures derived from taxation increased from 52 to
almost 60 per cent of the military outlay during the rearmament boom.

A substantial shift in the tax structure was the third characteristic of the rearmament boom. The increase in tax revenues was not merely a result of the rise in income in which
the various social groups made the same relative contributions to total revenues. The tax receipts from income and
profit taxes (*Personalsteuern*) rose much more rapidly than
did business taxes (*Kostensteuern*). "In 1932–33, business
taxes exceeded income and profit taxes by 3.5 times whereas
they were twice as large in 1936–37 . . ."[57] This was largely
the result of a deliberate change in fiscal policy. On the one
hand, all efforts were made to maintain or increase the tax
burden falling upon consumption. The poll tax, a product
of the depression, was continued. Average deduction from

gross wages for taxation was 3 per cent in 1932 and 4.5 per cent in 1937. Deductions from gross wages for social insurance were 9.5 per cent in 1932 and 9 per cent in 1934. Yet this slight decline was more than offset by the fact that a declining percentage of the contributions collected was repaid to the insured, the rising surplus in the insurance funds accruing as revenue to the state. The government thus deliberately refrained from employing a compensatory tax policy favorable to consumption.

In contrast, a series of fiscal privileges were granted to private concerns. These concessions either acted as incentives for desired forms of investments to be undertaken by specific industries, or they provided a more general opportunity to reduce the base for the corporation tax. The value of capital items replaced by equipment made in Germany could be written off taxwise in the year of acquisition. This concession was extended to all "short-lived goods" with a depreciation period of up to five years. The deductions reduced by 10 to 45 per cent—depending upon the industry involved—the effective purchasing price of some kinds of equipment and thereby exempted about 500 million marks of corporate profits from the corporation tax.[58] Such inducements manifested a compensatory tax policy that fostered the growth of corporate profits and their reinvestment in private corporations.

A fourth characteristic of the rearmament boom was a significant increase in the volume of public investments. Private investment no longer called the tune. The following data show the rise in public and private investment.

For the period as a whole, public investment amounted to 40 billion, and private investment to 33 billion marks. The increasing rate of public investment—except in 1936—created a twofold change in the nature of the economy. The government became the predominant borrower of newly saved

TYPES OF GROSS INVESTMENT*
(in billion marks)

	1933	1934	1935	1936	1937	1938
Public Investment	2.5	4.5	6.3	7.2	8.9	10.6
Private Investment	2.6	3.7	4.8	6.6	7.1	7.9
Total Investment	5.1	8.2	11.1	13.8	16.0	18.5
Share of Public Investment	49%	54%	56%	52%	55%	57%

* Hermberg, "The German National Income and National Product Between the Two World Wars," Part B, p. 10.

funds. Access to these funds could be obtained only by changing the existing financial organization and by transforming the banks into large-scale holders of governmental debt certificates. The government became the largest investor and buyer in the country during the rearmament boom, and there was a corresponding increase in the government sector of the economy. The expectation of the pump-priming theory, that the volume of public investment would become smaller in relation to private investment during the course of the boom, never materialized in the Nazi regime.

The fifth characteristic of the rearmament boom and the peacetime war economy was the substantial difference in the rate of growth between the producer-goods and consumer-goods industries. The discrepancy in the rates of growth has been shown above in our comparison between the United States and Nazi Germany in regard to the share of national income devoted to consumption. The same unequal rates of growth can be observed for the division of gross investment between two sectors of German industry prior to the invasion of Poland.

It is interesting to note that the shift in emphasis from public works to rearmament was accompanied by a reallocation of investable funds between the producer-goods and con-

SECTORAL GROSS INVESTMENT IN MANUFACTURING INDUSTRIES*
(in million marks)

	Rearmament			War Economy in Peace			
	1933	1934	1935	1936	1937	1938	1939
Producer-Goods Industries	309	700	1,221	1,637	2,208	2,952	3,596
Consumer-Goods Industries	248	360	415	522	635	739	836
Total Investment	557	1,060	1,636	2,159	2,843	3,691	4,432
Share of Consumer-Goods Industries	45%	33%	24%	24%	22%	20%	18%

* *Statistisches Handbuch von Deutschland 1928-1944*, p. 605.

sumer-goods industries. The share of the consumer-goods industries in total investment fell from about one half to one fourth. The percentage of investment in the consumer-goods industries remained at that level during the period of rearmament. A further relative decline set in with the adoption of the Four Year Plan. The share of consumer-goods industries became less than one fourth of the total manufacturing investment. Again, there is no indication that the backflow of the injected money enabled the consumer-goods industries to experience, in relation to the producer-goods industries, a similar—though belated—rate of growth. The rate of investment by consumer-goods industries definitely declined as the Nazi economy moved from rearmament to the war economy in peacetime.

Last but not least, partial governmental regulation of certain markets became an integral part of the rearmament boom. First came the governmental fixing of wage rates at the depression level, which had the dual effect of keeping down unit wage costs and mitigating the workers' increased demand for consumer goods. Then came the rearrangement of foreign exchange and import controls, with the government giving priority to those imports that were essential for the rearmament boom. Finally there were the investment bans (especially in consumer-goods industries), the reservation of private investable funds for governmental purposes, and the indirect fixing of interest rates. All these actions led to a regulation of the capital and money markets, wage rates, import quantities, and exchange rates.

In all, the rearmament boom had six distinguishing characteristics. First, the goal was not economic welfare but military power. Second, public investment was deliberately given priority over private investment, with the former increasing steadily prior to World War II. Third, investment of capital in consumer goods was kept down by various actions so that its share in total investment remained unchanged during the period of rearmament. Fourth, wage rates were fixed by the government at the depression level, and an increase in money income per family could be achieved only through greater effort on the part of the workers. Fifth, priority of foreign raw materials over foodstuffs in imports reduced the share of consumption in total imports. Sixth, the relative scarcity of many food items increased the prices of these goods and thereby led to a decline of real-money wage rates.

In consequence of these policies, there can be no doubt that factually the rearmament boom was neither identical with, nor similar to, a governmentally primed recovery. Nor is there any justification for applying the same Keynesian welfare theory to both, since the theoretical issue is not the same. The central problem in explaining the operation of a pump-primed recovery is to show how the volume of employment can be generally increased by the manifold forms of deficit financing. This is radically different from the problem of explaining the governmentally promoted rearmament boom in Germany under the Nazis. Here we must show how the power goals were realized by simultaneously increasing militarily essential production and retarding the growth of consumer-goods industries—by coupling deficit financing of government orders with increased taxation of consumers. Thus, any future theory of a deliberately promoted rearmament boom must explain the causes and effects of a policy that simultaneously combines rising and falling rates of growth (or investment) for different sectors of the economy.

LABOR IN ORGANIZED CAPITALISM

CHAPTER EIGHT

During the rearmament period in Germany the government and the economy were divided into three spheres of influence that were dominated, respectively, by big business, the party, and the military. Each of these organized groups, whose power assured the realization of policies, whether singly or jointly selected, functioned simultaneously in government and business. The state itself did not appear as something alien or superior to the groups but was instead controlled by them.

Each organized group formulated a set of multiple goals. The goals of these power blocs were realized in various ways: those of big business, through managerial directives within individual concerns; those of the cartels, within specific markets; those of the economic groups, within industries; and those of the governmental agencies, within the economy. The managerial goals remained largely the affair of private enterprise, whereas the goals of the cartels and the economic groups became increasingly matters of public concern. The policies adopted had to be argued in public and were implemented under the supervision of state economic agencies which were dominated, in turn, by big business. Thus, when originating a state economic policy, the economic groups had to present their private aims as goals that reflected the public interest.

The unique feature of such goals was that they made political demands on the state that went far beyond the usual requests for governmental assistance to private enterprise. It was indeed to become the function of the government to suppress all attempts to reform or replace private capitalism and to invigorate capitalist institutions that had suffered during the Great Depression. Furthermore, in helping to form the coalition with the generals and the Nazis, big business adopted a plan for capturing the economic agencies of the state and utilizing them deliberately as instruments for realizing the interests of the upper class.

A similar process of arriving at multiple goals and policies took place in the military and political fields. The three ruling groups formulated the political goal of achieving military and political equality with other nations, decided upon the military goal of building up a modern mass army, and determined the policy of economic rearmament. The last of these—the determination of a rearmament policy—gave rise to a series of military-economic goals that were formulated and implemented either by the procurement agencies of the three armed forces or by the economic-preparedness division of the war ministry. In seeking to realize these economic goals, the military agencies, supported by their Nazi and business allies, pushed for (a) attaining the desired military imports, (b) building up stocks of food and fodder, (c) securing the necessary manpower and labor skills, (d) maintaining industrial peace, (e) keeping wage rates low and thereby assuring high profits for business. At the same time, the military and po-

litical leaders were behaving as if their recommended policies were actually superior public goals that deserved priority
in implementation, and the result of their military policies
was the formation of a rearmament sector in both economy
and state.

Eliminating the distinction between public and private
goals and between public and private agencies caused a significant modification of the organizational institutions of
economy and state. The sphere of strictly private institutions
declined in importance. Quasi-private institutions (e.g., cartels) fulfilled their private functions by relying partly upon
governmental power. Some public agencies were required to
act as if they were private agencies, whereas others were given
military functions that had to be implemented authorita-
tively. In either case, public institutions ceased to be agencies
of public welfare and became instruments for realizing either
the interest goals of big business or the power goals of the
generals and the party.

The institutional change in economic organizations led to
an extension of the economic functions performed by government, which can be outlined in the following fashion.

TYPES OF GOVERNMENT ECONOMIC CONTROLS

1. Direct Controls
    a) Pricing Decisions (e.g., Price Control)
    b) Quantity Decisions (e.g., Quotas)
2. Indirect Controls
    a) Fiscal Policies
    b) Monetary Policies
3. Strengthening of Capitalist Institutions
    a) Direct Price and Quantity Inducements
    b) Direct Price and Quantity Deterrents

4. Promotion of Business
    a) Dispensation of Public Rights
    b) Avoidance of Full Social Costs
    c) Gifts of Public Tangible Property
    d) Tax Abates, Tariffs, and Other Subsidies
5. Supervision of Business
    a) Controlling Specified Market Actions (e.g.,
        Antitrust Policy)
    b) Prohibiting or Supervising Cartels
    c) Regulation of Natural Monopolies
    d) Supervision of Private Banks and Insurance
        Companies
6. Conciliation of Conflicting Private Interests
    a) Mediation
    b) Mandatory Mediation
    c) Arbitration
7. Social Policy
    a) Social Insurance
    b) Minimum Wage Laws
    c) Extensive Labor Legislation
8. Modification of the Property Structure
    a) Anti-merger Policy (e.g., Dissolution and
        Deconcentration)
    b) Public Ownership of Enterprises
    c) Mixed (Public-Private) Enterprises
    d) Public Ownership of Property Rights
        (e.g., Shares, Bonds, Land)

In order to show how the economic policies of the state
shifted as a result of the dictatorship, we shall have to examine the change in the government's economic functions in
terms of this typology of controls.

There also remains to be discussed the crucial question of

how these economic policies of the state affected the system of private capitalism. Direct controls are usually expected to arise either in situations of extreme emergency or in cases of one-party dictatorship. Whatever their origin, direct controls are widely believed to alter detrimentally the basic institutions of private capitalism.[1] Direct controls are seen as elements of statism, in which the government (a) seeks to realize noneconomic or emergency goals, (b) makes price and quantity decisions that apply to specific markets, (c) eliminates individual free choice in trading, (d) restricts detrimentally the income attainable for private units, and (e) destroys thereby the capitalist institution of the free market. In consequence, direct controls are considered to be the instruments by which capitalism is replaced by statism.

Indirect controls as a systematic form of government action became very popular during the Great Depression. Monetary or fiscal controls are widely used today to implement a genuine public policy, to achieve and maintain full employment. Although affecting the income chances of some persons or groups detrimentally, indirect controls are expected to act in the same way as market forces in a competitive market. Indirect government action may reduce some opportunities for private enterprise, but it often creates new chances for profit and employment. The indirect actions of government are not believed to affect the capitalist market detrimentally. In fact, indirect controls remove one major deficiency of private capitalism, a deficiency which has been described either as the insufficiency of aggregate demand or as the absence of a self-directing steering device that would assure full employment. Indirect controls are thus generally accepted as new government institutions that improve and strengthen private capitalism.

Our discussion of the rearmament has shown, however, that this generalization is in need of qualification. When public investment finances rearmament rather than ordinary public works, the output in producer-goods industries is expanded, and the imports of raw materials for these industries are increased. The minimized leakage keeps down the employment-stimulating effect in consumer-goods industries and produces an effect of disproportionality in the structure of production. How this one-sided investment, coupled with the fixing of wage rates, led to a modification of private capitalism will be shown in Chapter X. For the moment, we shall say only that not every form of indirect control is neutral in its impact upon capitalist markets, or necessarily beneficial for *all* major groups of income receivers.

The three subsequent policies of supervision of business, improvement of working conditions, and the achievement of industrial peace by means of mediation or arbitration presupposes a specific defect in private capitalism. The policy of business supervision originally sought to prevent the rise of cartels, tried to limit the number and the extent of mergers, and introduced the regulation of natural monopolies. The aim of these actions was to prevent or minimize the monopolistic tendencies in private markets and thereby retain or re-establish a competitive capitalism. In the period of the Weimar Republic, however, Germany had not adopted this type of supervisory policy, so the coalition-state under the Nazis did not have to discard already established supervisory measures.

Under the social amelioration policy of the Weimar Republic attempts were made to improve the position of laborers, including women and children, through minimum-wage laws and related actions. The various forms of social insurance were based on the proposition that, since laborers were not usually property-owners, they could not be expected to assume the full risks of unemployment and were necessarily handicapped in their attempts to get better working conditions. Further attempts were made, by means of labor legislation, to eliminate cutthroat competition in labor markets and, eventually, to establish some form of social capitalism. After the establishment of a coalition state under the Nazis, the three ruling groups were, of course, in full agreement that these social policies would have to be terminated.

Conciliation aimed at industrial peace, which the government sought to promote by establishing agencies for mediation or arbitration. Voluntary mediation became compulsory mediation during the Weimar period, and the government agencies responsible for it were exposed to the intense animosity of employer associations. The conciliating agencies of the state were therefore dissolved as soon as the first Hitler government came to power.[2] All tendencies toward the reform of private capitalism were thus suppressed during the first phase of the Nazi regime.

The promotion of business and the invigoration of capitalist institutions in a capitalist society originate as private goals that have either fanciful or actual relevance to the public interest. In each case it is the power of private interest groups that provides the will and determines the direction, if not also the particular content, of government actions. As we shall see from the following analysis, however, these two kinds of governmental support are not implemented or used in the same way and have differing effects upon the scope of governmental economic activities.

Business "promotionalism" usually arises whenever business groups succeed in determining particular government policies. Their effect is to increase the assets, improve the profit opportunities and extend the scope of the private sector of the economy. In helping to implement private policies government agencies act only indirectly upon prices and quantities in markets, thereby enlarging the profits realized by the concerns affected. In its effect upon the government, promotionalism produces a relative or absolute shrinkage of tangible and intangible public properties and requires a very small number of government employees for the dispensation of privileges and subsidies. Promotionalism thus does not violate the ideological tenet of limited government traditionally espoused by most business organizations.[3]

Measures of invigoration, on the other hand, usually presuppose the existence of a threat—such as a major depression—to the particular institutions of private capitalism. The immediate purpose of such measures is to help businessmen to avoid or reduce losses, to mitigate the depreciation of their assets, and to remain solvent. Their ultimate goal is to reduce, and eventually remove, the threat to capitalist institutions, especially to private corporations. Government policy thus goes beyond the dispensation of favors to particular concerns and seeks, through a policy of over-all assistance to business, to remedy the damages suffered by private capitalism.

When a policy of direct governmental intervention for the purpose of helping industrialists is chosen, the government's action takes the form either of inducements or deterrents. In both cases the government or its agents act directly upon prices and quantities in markets. Inducements may take the form of minimum prices, compulsory cartels, or investment bans, or they may provide for the compensation of certain specific business groups for the restrictive effects of direct controls that are introduced for the realization of public goals other than the restoration of capitalist institutions. Deterrents, on the other hand, reduce the prices of particular goods or of interest rates and thus redistribute the burden of the depression among business groups. In either case, whether by means of inducements or deterrents, business is encouraged to act in such a way as to speed up the process of restoration.

In Nazi Germany the effect of these direct controls and inducements was to multiply the functions and enlarge the personnel of government. At the same time, through its support of the two goals of rearmament and restoration, big business effectively contributed to the rise of the public sector of the economy.

In trying to ascertain the significance of the change in the economic functions of government and to evaluate the modifications of capitalist institutions introduced by the actions of the party and the state, we have to analyse two central issues. How were the economic position, the income, and the degree of participation of labor affected by the decision of the ruling groups to destroy trade unions and systematically reorganize the labor sector of the economy? What happened to the profit opportunities, the economic organizations, and the economic power of business groups when the coalition-state modified business promotionalism and introduced "invigorations" as well as direct and indirect controls? In analysing the labor issue in this chapter we will be able to show precisely what happened when a government energetically eliminated "creeping socialism."

DOMINATION OF WORKERS

On May 2, 1933, uniformed and well-equipped units of the Brownshirts and Blackshirts arrested the trade union leaders, seized their funds, occupied their buildings, and later acquired title to all the property of the trade unions. This seizure was followed by two declarations. One outlawed all independent trade unions; the other outlawed strikes. Both actions were presented as steps leading to industrial peace and social harmony between employers and employees, whose organizations dissolved themselves a few months later. The destruction of independent trade unions, the elimination of free collective bargaining, the abandoning of mediation and arbitration, the bans on labor participation in industrial affairs, and the suspension of collective actions on the part of labor organizations established the principle that indepen-

dent organized labor had no place in a state politically dominated by the Nazi party.

Who decided that the trade unions should be abolished?
Wilhelm Keppler has revealed the antecedents to this decision. "In May 1932, after I had met with the gentlemen of the
Circle of Friends several times, I asked the Führer whether
he could not meet with them. The Führer received the business leaders in the small hall of the *Kaiserhof* on May 18,
1932. As far as I can recall, all the gentlemen who were at
that time members of the Circle of Friends were present. The
Führer made a short speech, and in it he disclosed, among
other things, the following points in his program: abolition
of trade unions and abolition of all parties other than the
NSDAP. No one raised any objection. On the contrary, these
points of the Führer's program met with the fullest approval
of the members of the Circle of Friends. They only expressed their apprehension that he would not be able to carry
out these excellent ideas."[4] This shows clearly the role of
the Keppler circle as an agency of policy formation. Hitler
presented his ideas to the selected businessmen, and these
either approved or rejected his ideas. In proposing the abolition of the trade unions, Hitler bears the main responsibility for this infamous act, but in approving the abolition,
the business allies of the Nazis participated in the decision
and thus were accessories to it. As allies these business leaders were fully willing to let the Nazis be the only political
party, if only Hitler would destroy the trade unions for them.

Each group of rulers had a different motive for depriving
labor of its power, and each actually obtained a different kind
of advantage from a powerless labor class. The Nazis sought
unlimited political power for themselves, and the elimination
of independent trade unions was an indispensable condition
for the achievement of this objective. There was and is a
mutually exclusive relationship between the monopolistic
organization and power of a single party and the organization

of independent unions. Their goals have to be diluted, their power destroyed, their organization suppressed, if the dictatorial party is to enjoy an all-inclusive political monopoly.

Destruction was not and is not enough. The masses were dominated by party leaders who controlled the Labor Front. Compulsory membership herded everyone into this association, and the leadership principle assured the Nazis of the exclusive right to occupy all leadership positions. The small-sized party thus extended its power of indoctrination and organizational manipulation to the masses of gainfully employed workers. There is thus a positive relationship between the single party and the dominated mass organization. A single political monopoly is complete and effective only if the party is controlling all political thinking and activity through a network of dominated mass organizations.

The Ministry of War called for an extensive study of the "preparedness economy" (*Wehrwirtschaftsordnung*). Subsequent blueprints proposed that wage scales be fixed by the state and suggested that second and third shifts be adopted for workers in essential factories. The generals insisted upon a comprehensive registration of all employees through the issue of labor books. Implementation was in the hands of the Ministry of Labor, which spent a total of 10 million marks (obtained from its secret funds) for this purpose.[5] Fixed wage rates, double or triple shifts, and universal registration of workers would certainly have been rejected by free trade unions. The generals' plans for economic rearmament were thus built upon the presupposition that the independent trade unions would have to be effectively suppressed. At the same time, the suggestion advanced by some of the procurement agencies that the government build its own armament plants was rejected by the ministry.[6] In this way there developed a positive correlation between armament factories and private property and a negative correlation between economic rearmament and independent trade unions. Private ownership of the productive facilities remained typical for the first phase of the Nazi regime.

Keppler's "Circle of Friends" comprised only a small number of business leaders. Yet none of the others protested when the Nazis destroyed the trade unions.[7] There was, however, some apprehension among leading industrialists about wage-fixing by the state. This is indicated in Fritz Thyssen's memorandum, which was presented to the government at the end of 1933. He proposed that a "council of leaders" should be formed at each plant, comprising the employer, one white-collar employee and one factory worker, who would decide upon all questions of industrial relations. The decisions of the leaders could be appealed to a council of the industry concerned. If deliberations still did not lead to an understanding, the issue was to be presented to the labor trustee, whose decisions would be final. Thyssen's proposal was welcomed by the Ministry of Economics as "a meaningful relief of the trustees of labor from a crowded schedule."[8]

It was not the Thyssen plan, however, but the Schmitt-Hitler compromise that was actually adopted. A joint declaration was published by Ministers Schmitt and Seldte, which was also signed by Keppler and Ley. It was clearly stated that the Labor Front would not be the instrument for settling labor grievances or for adjusting the conflicting economic interests of employers and workers. Nor would the Labor Front comprise national unions that would be engaged in interest representation.[9] This mutual declaration, in which Keppler again played the role of liaison between big business and the Nazi party, provided the basis for the national labor law of January, 1934. The Labor Front was not mentioned in this law at all. Wage setting became a function of the trustees of labor, who were state officials, receiving their instructions from the wage division in the Ministry of Labor,

which in turn was responsible to Minister Schmitt. All functions of collective bargaining were transferred to the state
and were definitely beyond the influence of the Nazi party.

The party did, however, claim the privilege of organizing
laborers. A compulsory mass organization was formed that
eventually comprised all gainfully employed persons outside
the civil service of the state. The principle of compulsory
association was thus first applied by the party to blue- and
white-collar workers. The purpose of the Labor Front was to
secure political control over all laborers. This was achieved
by selecting a type of organization that was heterocephalous
as well as heteronomous.[10] The leaders and the whole administrative staff of the Labor Front were selected from among
party officials, and appointment to an office in the Labor
Front was made dependent upon party membership. Equally,
the bylaws, rules, and policies were all imposed upon the
membership by party leaders. In fact, the Labor Front was
not financially independent, for its income and expenditures
were extensively controlled by the party treasury. The Labor
Front was thus a dependent political organization of the
party which dominated labor and prevented all workers from
engaging in independent organizational activity.

There was no agreement in the party as to whether the
Labor Front, which had originally been organized along occupational lines, should also engage in economic activity.
The intransigent Nazis, however, pushed hard for the adoption of a program of partial unionization by the Labor
Front. In this effort they were supported by other Nazis, including Ley, who worshipped the principle of "organizational
totality." They also hoped to get control over all economic
organizations in the country by means of this principle. Before and after the purge of 1934, the leaders of the Labor
Front claimed that their organization should include all
forms of economic organizations, and a bill was worked out
detailing the rights and functions of the Labor Front. It was

clearly stated that the Labor Front was to include all gainfully employed persons and to occupy a position of supremacy
in relation to all other economic organizations. The Labor
Front was also to be given the function of insuring industrial
peace by reconciling the interests of employers and workers
and was to be responsible for the whole task of vocational
training. Other features of the bill provided that the Labor
Front was to prescribe the use of leisure time by the workers,
improve their physical health and well-being, and beautify
the industrial plants and other places of business where they
worked. This bill was signed by Hitler on October 24, 1934,[11]
but it never became a law because all the organized groups
of big and small business stood united against the Labor
Front's claim of organizational totality.

In fact, all vocational functions were turned over to the
economic groups of industry and the handicraft guilds and all
youth activities were transferred to the Hitler Youth, while
the Labor Front was limited to the political supervision of
schools and of vocational examinations for handicraft apprentices.

In November of 1934, Schacht transformed the business
organizations from "estates" into organs of self-government.
The new relationship between the Labor Front and the business organizations was legalized in the agreement of Leipzig,
signed by Schacht, Seldte, and Ley, and was confirmed by
Hitler in March of 1935. Although Schacht and Ley interpreted the agreement differently, Schacht and Hitler agreed
that in the new "social self-government" the business organizations and the Labor Front were equal partners. The purpose of the Leipzig agreement was to provide for mutual
cooperation and for a division of functions between the two
organizations, and a new system of chambers of labor was
devised in which both organizations were to discuss mutual
problems. Yet the business organizations never participated
in these chambers, which became a mere appendage of the

Labor Front. Much more significant was the division of functions hinted at in the agreement. The Labor Front promoted
a "social" policy but refrained from engaging in the formulation of "economic" policy.[12] This division of responsibility
was strictly enforced in the first phase of the regime.

The social policy of the Labor Front evolved as an extensive program for the supervision of workers and the improvement of working conditions, including the beautification of
factories, provision of factory lunches, construction of sports
fields, vacations with pay, and certain limited pension plans.
In implementing this program, the Labor Front built up a
huge organization for the control of the workers' use of
leisure time.[13] Thus, the direct action of party and state was
not limited to the prohibition of certain specified private
actions but abolished all independent organizations of workers and imposed upon labor an extensive form of political
domination. We shall now see how this political domination
was translated into economic injustice.

UNFETTERED MANAGERIAL PREROGATIVE?

The influence of trade unions exerts itself in three ways,
most obviously in the relationship between employers and
employees in labor markets, but also in the type of "work
order" that grows up in unionized plants and, finally, in the
political influence that trade unions bring to bear upon the
economic and social policies of the various governmental
bodies and of other organized groups. In each of these spheres
of action, German trade unions created a new form of social
capitalism during the period of the Weimar Republic.[14]

In order to appreciate fully the significance of the suppression of trade unions for the character of private capitalism,
we shall have to examine two problems: (a) What was the role
of the trade unions within plants prior to their rise to a
position of strength, during their period of influence in the

1920's, and after their suppression by the Nazis? (*b*) How did trade unions change the character of labor markets through collective bargaining, and what did their suppression do to labor markets?

Prior to the rise of the trade union movement, the capitalist enterprise in its internal structure was organized along the lines of a patriarchical order. The employer acted as the absolute master in his factory, as if it were a part of his own household. His managerial prerogative was a part of his absolute power over the internal order of the plant. Having largely unlimited powers, the employer formulated and executed the rules prevailing in the factory and expected of every laborer unrestricted subordination and obedience. As we should expect, most employers adopted a paternalistic attitude toward their laborers, with the result that a patriarchical order of work generally obtained in German industry.

A twofold subordination developed in this kind of work order. The laborer had not only to submit to the technical and efficiency requirements of capitalist production but to subordinate himself personally to the employer and his agents. This combination of submission to the technical and impersonal requirements of the plant and subordination and obedience to the personal commands of the employer established an economic and political managerial prerogative.[15]

The development of trade unions, especially as they operated in the Weimar Republic, modified each kind of managerial prerogative. There was considerable pressure to eliminate the personal paternalism of employers. This pressure arose, on the one hand, from the increased self-confidence of the unionists, who insisted that they be treated as personalities in their own right and, on the other, from the election of work councils representing the workers of each department. These representatives not only established a regular grievance procedure but also broke the full force of the employer patriarchy by serving as a second center of authority in matters having to do with the welfare of the employees. Although the effectiveness of the work councils was reduced by many difficulties, the plant stewards and the councils did succeed in limiting the personal power of employers over workers.

The trade unions, aided by the government's labor policy, succeeded in limiting the employer's previously unrestricted freedom to make decisions in regard to the work done by his employees. The length of the work day and the work week and the amount of time to be allowed for rest periods were to be fixed by law or contractual agreements reached by the unions and employers, and these legal and contractual requirements were reinforced by the further requirement that employees be paid for overtime work. Accidents on the job were reduced in number by preventive measures, and the risk of accidents was covered by accident insurance. The emphasis on speed and discipline was kept within limits by standards which the stewards helped to set up, and the traditional strictness of German factories was mitigated by giving the worker a chance to obtain a hearing before the manager and the steward and to protest against punitive measures on the part of the foreman. In addition to these provisions, the union contracts specified many forms of minimum working conditions which eliminated the worst dangers to the health and morality of the workers.

The power of the employer to dismiss workers was reduced by requiring him to give sufficient cause and notice in advance. On the one hand the opportunity to discriminate on the basis of sex or creed was largely eliminated, and, on the other, membership in a union was not a prerequisite for employment. The impact of trade unions upon the managerial prerogative was thus threefold. The personal power of the employer was somewhat restricted; minimum working conditions were established; and many managerial decisions in industrial relations were made by employers and work councils jointly. The goal of such decisions was to satisfy both the profit interests of the employer and the special work, health, and employment interests of labor.

The suppression of trade unions changed this situation radically. Not only did the personal power of the employer over his workers increase, but the employer's superior authority was expressly legalized in the new labor law. The basic ideas of this law were derived from the ideology of leadership and community voiced by Karl Arnhold, who was the head of an institute for the vocational training of so-called "social engineers." Albert Vögler, board chairman of the largest steel concern in Germany, came to the conclusion that business concerns "had maneuvered themselves into a blind alley in the labor question,"[16] and Arnhold was given an opportunity to apply his ideas in some of the plants of the steel concern. The national labor law maintained, just as Arnhold did, that the plant was a "social community" in which the employer or the production engineer was the leader and the laborers were his followers. As in a feudal order the "leader" was given the authority to demand of his workers loyalty and the greatest possible performance. The relationship between "leader" and "followers" was said to be akin to the one between an officer and a soldier in the army. As soldiers of work, as comrades in a common task, the leader and his followers were to enjoy mutual confidence and respect. The leader was thus to be advised by a "confidence council." Violations of the workers' honor by employers were to be punished by the social honor courts. In this way, the plant was seen as a kind of community; a mutual confidence was expected to arise which would transform the antagonistic relationships between employer and workers into the "social harmony" prevailing between the leader and his followers.

In practice, the two institutions that were supposed to integrate the worker into the "plant community" were of minor significance from the start and eventually fell into oblivion. Officially, the abolition of the independently elected work councils was declared to be a measure *not* directed against workers, and the law that replaced work councils with the new councils of confidence was asserted to be a better expression of the increased responsibility placed upon employers, who, as true leaders, would necessarily have the well-being of their workers at heart. Actually, however, the election of representatives to the councils of confidence in 1935 revealed a significant opposition of workers to the leader-follower arrangement of the Nazi regime. As Bormann reported to Hitler in April of 1935, "not even 50 per cent of the labor force in many plants gave an affirmative vote" for those nominated by the party for membership in the councils.[17] In response to this unfavorable result the Nazis abolished the practice of electing council representatives. The authority of the existing councils was administratively extended from year to year, and vacancies were filled by appointment of the trustees of labor. The confidence councils thus became instruments of the Nazi party. The functions of the councils later declined, and most of them became mere ornaments when the Nazis concentrated their energies upon fulfilling the Four Year Plan.

The courts of social honor suffered a similar fate. Officially, these special courts were assigned the function of protecting the honor of both worker and employer. Cases were brought to these special courts by the trustees of labor. Out of a labor force of over 20 million, only 516 cases were presented in the courts in the years 1934–36 (61 in 1934, 204 in 1935, and 251 in 1936). Of these cases, only 13, 128, and 156 (for the years 1934, 1935, and 1936) ended with a definite penalty. Of the cases adjudicated, about three fourths involved small business firms whose owners had violated some of the rules set by the trustees of labor.[18] Thus, neither big business nor the overwhelming majority of workers was in any way affected by the social honor courts.

What was the significance of the new labor law for the managerial prerogative of private concerns? The new law granted the "leader," in his position as employer, the right to determine the rules of work in his plant. In all the crucial functions of scheduling the work, determining how many hours were to be spent on the job, defining penalties for damages caused by carelessness, paying for overtime, assigning rank and responsibility, and maintaining proper working conditions, employers again enjoyed the full managerial prerogative. The suppression of trade unions thus abolished the rights of independent labor representatives to participate in determining plant rules and also dispensed with the grievance procedure and the work councils. Hence, in economic matters, the old rule of centralized authority was restored.

Officially, the authority of the plant leader was supposed to depend upon an intensely felt sense of honor and other personal qualifications. Actually, authority was arbitrarily vested in the employer, exclusively, because he was the owner or manager of the firm. In large corporations, one of the executive directors—usually someone in charge of personnel relations—was appointed to the position of plant leader. In general, therefore, authority over the workers was held by those who either spoke for the substantive property rights of the concerns or who held the top managerial positions in large corporations. This so-called leader-follower principle may seem feudalistic to us, but it was at work in modern capitalist enterprises.

In some respects, however, the authority of management was no longer unlimited. For example, responsibility for the political reliability and indoctrination of the workers had to be shared by employers with the agents of the Labor Front. Most employers cooperated with the party by giving prefer-

ence to "old fighters" when hiring additional workers, by
paying extra wages to workers who participated in indoctrination meetings or camps, and by dismissing workers who refused to respect the Nazi flag or declined to become members
of the Labor Front. Workers were dismissed without notice
if they failed to raise their right arms in a "Heil Hitler"
greeting on the appropriate occasions.[19] Employers thus respected the political prerogative of the party in return for the
party's restoring their economic prerogative in plants. There
was not only a coalition on the national level between the
party and big business, but a modified form of cooperation
between the employer and the party representative in the
plant. Employers did not possess sole authority as they had
in the earlier, patriarchic order; rather, they recognized a
distinction between economic and political prerogatives and
found it advisable to limit themselves to the enjoyment of
their economic authority. The two types of authority, one
based on the possession of the means of production in plants
and the other on possession of the monopolized instrumen-
talities of political action, thus existed side by side in practically every enterprise.

ORGANIZED JOB MARKETS

What was the nature of labor markets before and after the
suppression of trade unions? In the Weimar Republic, the
impact of trade unions and employer associations resulted in
a structural change within labor markets. The job market
became distinct from the wage market.[20] Wage and job decisions became institutionally separated from each other because wage decisions were arrived at by collective bargaining
between the organizations, whereas the job decisions were
made by individual workers and employers.

The institutional severance between wage and job markets
was intensified by the fact that different criteria entered into

the process of decision-making in each market. Most wage-markets were national in scope, and the negotiated wage rate was only to a very minor extent influenced by the expected quantities of jobs and labor services in the related job markets. Neither seasonal nor cyclical variations in the number of available jobs could be taken into account, since the wage contracts were usually valid for several years. Nor could the expected entry or exit of workers into job markets influence the wage decisions, since the rates agreed to usually remained stable during the contract period. Finally, local variations in jobs and labor services could hardly ever be utilized by the majority of employers because the industry-wide wage rates entered unchanged into the employment contracts between the individual worker and employer. Both the different locations and persons involved in decision-making and the particular nature of the collectively arrived at wage contracts thus produced the separation between wage and job markets.

A similar set of new conditions arose in the job markets. Most of them were local in size, limited to workers in specific occupations, and concerned only with matching available jobs with available workers. Lack of mobility between locations and occupations effectively minimized the links between local job markets. While the local job decision was usually made by the individual employer, most employers offered working conditions that were fixed in agreement with the work councils in their plants, and when the work requirements were predetermined by the policy of the local trade union leader, who usually advised the members of the work councils, the job offers from different plants became very similar. The single worker had then only to decide whether or not to accept a particular job offer on considerations that lay outside the employer created conditions within the plant.

Before the suppression of trade unions, there were no supply-and-demand schedules in the job markets, nor was there any elasticity in the supply-and-demand relationship between jobs and services, on the one hand, and wage rates, on the other. There was no automatic interaction, as if in obedience to some anonymous forces at work in the markets. Instead, the number of jobs or labor services was directly determined by the respective actions of individual employers and workers and indirectly by the actions of employer associations and unions.

The opponents in job markets possessed two kinds of power, depending on whether control was exercised over the availability of jobs or the availability of labor services. Whoever was able to influence the number of available jobs enjoyed a certain degree of absorption power. This power was positive when the number of available jobs could be increased and negative when the available jobs could be reduced. Correspondingly, ability to influence the number of labor services indicated a certain degree of suction power. Whoever could reduce the number of service units applied negative suction power, whereas a deliberate increase in the service offers pointed to the possession of positive suction power.

Typically, workers and unions sought to acquire and hold negative suction and positive absorption powers, whereas employers and their associations wanted, and usually held, some degree of negative absorption and positive suction powers. The extent to which such power was possessed created particular power constellations that indicated the opportunities available to the opponents for realizing certain job policies in markets.

During the Weimar period, two kinds of job policies were developed. One was local in scope and was arrived at through negotiations between work councils and individual employers; the other policy embraced whole industries or even larger sections of the economy. Industrial and national policies were evolved either through the actions of unions or employers (each group acting collectively) or through specific actions of the government.[21] These national policies not only presented a framework for, but also determined the direction of, local actions. Because of the changes in power constellations among the opponents, however, national policies were by no means inspired by the same goals or consistent in content. Significantly enough, these variations in relative power did not prevent the national policies from creating new institutions in labor markets. The variability in the power structure only interrupted the smooth evolution of these institutions, slowing down the extent of their acceptance by some groups of employers but greatly influencing the specific organizational form chosen for each new institution.

What particular institutions can be attributed to the operation of absorption power? Immediately after the revolution of 1918, the trade unions possessed greater power than management. The subsequent hyperinflation reversed the situation by strongly increasing the relative power of the employer associations. Finally, a fairly even balance of power between the two groups developed and remained in effect from 1924 to 1929. Policies introduced immediately after the revolution of 1918 bore the stamp of trade-union influence; policy decisions made in the last phase of the inflation were predominantly determined by employer associations; and policy decisions in the second half of the 1920's usually involved some compromise between the two powerful groups. How far did these variations in relative power correspond to the rise of different types of institutions in job markets?

Let us look first at the operation of absorption power. Immediately after the revolution of 1918, the trade unions employed their absorption power in three different ways. The new government announced in certain provisional laws that forty-eight hours constituted the maximum working week, that the twelve-hour shift would have to be replaced by the eight-hour shift in plants which operated continuously, and that the liquidation of business enterprises would be possible only under certain stipulations by which workers were to be notified of their dismissal from four to six weeks in advance. When the French army marched into the Ruhr Valley in 1923 and the French government demanded reparations in kind, the large concerns of that district unilaterally returned to the twelve-hour shift and widely disregarded the forty-eight-hour week. The large coal concerns increased the working day from six to eight and a half hours for underground workers, although a surplus of coal led soon afterward to part-time employment. When the French army withdrew, the illegal working time was nullified, but after a series of negotiations, some significant concessions were granted to employers. The triple-shift system (consisting of three eight-hour shifts) was restored, and the six-hour shift for underground workers was increased to seven hours. The forty-eight-hour week became law in 1927, but additional hours up to ten could be added for a specified number of days when such overtime was agreed upon through collective bargaining, when governmental agencies gave their consent, and when the employer was willing to pay an overtime wage amounting to 25 per cent more than the regular rate. Recognition of overtime work was a concession to employers, but the payment of a higher wage rate kept the number of actual overtime hours to a small portion of what it had been between 1923 and 1926. The restrictions on the closing of plants and the dismissal of workers remained in force, without change.[22]

The trade unions' efforts to increase the number of jobs by shortening the working day were quite successful. Positive absorption power established three new institutions: a forty-eight-hour week, three eight-hour shifts, and the conditional and delayed closing of plants. The negative absorption power of employers had only the effect of temporarily interrupting the effectiveness of these institutions or of imposing careful limitations upon them in their daily operation. Superior positive absorption power thus functioned as the originator of three new institutions in job markets. The previously unrestricted negative absorption power, responsible for a long work day and fewer jobs, was substantially reduced through the activities of trade unions.[23]

How important were the variations of suction power in the Weimar regime? Reconversion to a peace economy, hyperinflation, and repeated recessions created situations of underemployment. Employers thus felt no need to enlarge the scope of the job markets, nor did trade unions possess an opportunity for effectively limiting the number of workers looking for jobs. Employer associations thus tried to intensify or keep fully alive the unemployed workers' need to find a job, whereas the unions sought to reduce this urgency by providing adequate compensation for unemployed or handicapped workers. What kinds of institutions did this fight for control over laborers without jobs eventually create?

The re-employment of 6 million soldiers and the finding of new jobs for 3 million armament workers led to a law for the compulsory hiring of a certain number of disabled veterans, which was later extended to cover all heavily disabled persons. In addition, returning soldiers had to be rehired by those firms for which they had been working on August 1, 1914. Workers who were hired during wartime but did not absolutely need a job had to be dismissed. Re-hired soldiers had to be retained in their jobs, even when the volume of orders was insufficient to justify their employment. Part-time employment was ordered in such cases.

Subsequently, under the concerted pressure of employers in the last quarter of 1923, these governmental directives on the hiring and firing of workers were, with the exception of those applying to disabled persons, abolished. Thus, for a few years after World War I, the positive suction power and the negative absorption power of the employers were combined to prevent the provision of job guarantees for former soldiers.

The alternative to compulsory assignment of jobs was a reorganization of the placement facilities and of unemployment compensation. Existing placement offices were either private or municipal in character, large in number but small in scope of operation. The number of workers seeking jobs through these offices had increased from 2 million in 1913 to 5.5 million in 1919. Such a huge task required the reorganization of the placement agencies into a comprehensive network of employment offices that would collect information on vacancies and available workers in all parts of the country and effectively place those in need of employment. In view of the widespread unemployment, employers agreed to discontinue their own employment offices, and in 1922 a national organization of public employment offices was set up. All vacancies were to be reported to these new employment offices, but they were not to fill vacancies in a plant that was on strike. The trade unions succeeded in having adopted the stipulations that all services of the employment offices must be available free of charge, that workers were to be placed only in those jobs that paid union rates, and that the orientation and placement of young workers in occupations and jobs should be the exclusive function of the employment offices. The result of this compromise, based upon comparable strength of negative and positive suction power, was an organized center in job markets that was able to bring together available workers and vacant jobs. This center developed into a new institution, the integrated system of employment offices. Rather than relying upon the principle of self clearance in the market, which is usually expected to spring from automatically operating equilibriating forces, both employers and unions agreed (a) that markets had to be organized through a governmental center, (b) that the necessary information on the availability and the conditions and terms of jobs or services should be systematically collected through appropriate administrative actions, and (c) that such information and other assistance should be made available to workers and employers free of charge.

The new organizational centers systematically investigated each job market, directed young workers into promising occupations, urged the development of facilities for retraining adult workers, or provided these themselves, and thereby laid the foundation for long-range planning of the prospective volume of labor services for the expected job opportunities. In accepting this organizational institution, employer associations and trade unions gave up their previous efforts to engage directly in placement activities. Yet the public employment agencies were not given a monopoly over all placements; private placement was permitted provided the private units gave their services free of charge.[24] Furthermore, the transfer of functions from private to public offices did not involve a decline in power for management and labor, since both effectively participated in the formulation of policies to be implemented by the employment offices.

A similar compromise was achieved in regard to the introduction of unemployment insurance. Agreement was reached only after a long fight lasting nine years, during which time the unemployed depended primarily upon a modified form of public-welfare payments. Employers associations at first rejected the principle that unemployment was an involuntary risk for which the workers affected should not be held solely responsible. During the currency depreciations, however, employers found that unemployment insurance would have been a less costly way of supporting the unemployed. In this reversal of position, the issues under dispute were shifted to the financial and administrative details of unemployment insurance. Trade unions insisted upon (*a*) a short waiting period, (*b*) a long payment period, (*c*) a minimal difference between the amount of weekly compensation and take-home pay, and (*d*) a premium to be paid by employers that would be more than half of the expected cost of the insurance. Compromises on these issues were reached piecemeal and incorporated into the prevailing system of governmental dole. A final agreement became possible only after the government decided to separate the insurance for short-term joblessness from the compensation for long-term unemployment. The latter alone remained subject to a means test. The difficult question of who should bear the cost was solved by the agreement that worker and employer should pay equal shares and that the government should assume the expense of administration. Unemployment-insurance payments were expressed as a percentage of the weekly wage received by the worker in his last job. Percentage calculation insured a minimum income for the worker in addition to giving him an incentive to search for a new job. Finally, unemployment insurance became the law of the land when unions and employers between themselves, and with the cooperation of the leading political parties, agreed that the insurance and placement of workers must be administered by the same agency and that this common agency should be a self-governing organization, the policies of which would be determined jointly by the representatives of employer associations and trade unions.

The positive and negative suction powers of the employer associations and the trade unions were thus of equal strength after the hyperinflation. Employers were able to prevent the adoption of closed shops for union members as well as job guarantees for returned veterans and to avoid the proposed compulsory plan to hire only workers recommended by the employment offices. Furthermore, the temporary prohibition against dismissing certain groups of workers was largely repealed. On the other hand, employers had to accept unemployment insurance and accommodate themselves to the principles that unemployment could not be used to keep down union wage rates, that the placement offices were to remain neutral in industrial disputes, and that employment offices were to supply labor services only on condition that employers paid union wage rates and operated their plants under legal working conditions. The period of employer predominance in job markets had thus come to an end; control was shared with trade unions as well as with the government.

Control over job markets had become institutionalized. From 1919 to 1931 there had existed organized job markets, characterized by institutionalized rules on working time, the eight-hour shift, and the hiring and firing or laying off of workers. As has been said, these rules were supplemented and reinforced through the establishment of placement offices and unemployment insurance. The new organizations were recognized public agencies, but their policies were largely determined by the joint decisions of employer associations and trade unions.

LOPSIDED JOB MARKETS

After the abolition of trade unions and the voluntary dissolution of employer associations, there was no return to a "natural labor market," in which wages and hours are determined by the independent forces of supply and demand. Instead, the party, the coalition of the military and big business, and individual employers—rather than employer associations and trade unions—became the strongest influences in the labor market, with each possessing and using a different kind of power. The political power of the party was used to dominate the workers; the bureaucratic power of the state, acting under the direction either of the generals or of big business, sought to determine standards for hour and wage decisions; and the property power of the employers operated within these standards to set working requirements, conditions, and hours within the plants. The combined impact of these powers in industrial relations created lopsided job markets because labor was not represented.

In establishing the Labor Front, the Nazi party violated an

old ideal of many conservative employers, who usually insisted that trade unions should be independent from any political party. Yet there was no reason for the industrialists' concern. All attempts by the intransigent Nazis to utilize the Labor Front as a "national" labor union movement were ruthlessly suppressed, and all occupational functions undertaken by the intransigent Nazis were excluded in the reorganization of the Labor Front which took place in January, 1934.[25]

The main political function of the Labor Front was the indoctrination of workers in Nazi ideology. Through compulsory meetings, parades, cheering sections, and all sorts of fund collecting drives, workers were forced to identify themselves with the Nazi party and its ideology. Indoctrination was reinforced through intimidation and terror. The shop steward—who in larger corporations was an employee of the Labor Front, not of the private concern—directed indoctrination and checked on the political reliability of the workers and had at his disposal a number of cell and block stewards who acted on his instructions. In addition, shock troops were organized that functioned as listening posts for the party and executed the more violent actions of the Labor Front in factories.[26] The Labor Front in turn provided informers for the Gestapo who reported on the conversations and actions of workers. As a result, most of the workers lived in continuous fear of violence and sought to protect themselves by accepting the Nazi vocabulary and some of the Nazi ideas as well as by refraining from open and direct collective actions.

Apart from its political functions, the central economic purpose of the Labor Front was to prevent laborers from organizing new trade unions that would engage in slowdowns, strikes, and collective representation of specific economic interests. The joint opposition of the Labor Front and employers to independent trade unions provided the basis for their collaboration in the first phase of the regime. It was precisely this mutual support that made the continuous suppression of trade unions so effective and the realization of collective interests impossible.

Preventing laborers from promoting their economic interests could not be done merely through direct state control, since prohibition by state order would have driven the unions underground. In addition to the outlawing of trade unions, there had to be two specific organizations that made secret union activity impossible. One was the Gestapo and its network of spies, which ferreted out all secret organizations, tortured their leaders, and imprisoned their members. The other was the Labor Front, which through its principle of all-inclusive membership herded all workers into a monolithic organization. The Labor Front established two conditions as requirements for obtaining or holding jobs. Every worker had to become a member of the Labor Front and pay weekly dues which were deducted from his wage by the employer. These tributes, which amounted to 360 million marks in 1937,[27] provided the party with one of its major sources of income. Whoever refused to submit to these two stipulations was dismissed by the employer. All-inclusive membership was thus a means by which the party, through the Labor Front and the collaboration of employers, controlled the availability of jobs.

When admitted to the job, the worker could no longer participate in job and wage decisions, whether individually or collectively. Workers became the passive objects of the decisions of the employer and the Labor Front and were, in effect, an atomized supply in the labor market, where they were at the mercy of both powerholders. In its economic aspects, the Labor Front thus performed functions that were exactly opposite to the actions of genuine trade unions. Whereas the latter clarify economic interests and organize the workers in order to obtain economic benefits for them, the Nazis transformed this political into economic power and used it to control jobs. Thus the workers were prevented from realizing their economic interests either individually or collectively.[28] It was this economically applied political power, exercised by the Labor Front and the Gestapo, that undercut secret unions, prevented slow-downs and strikes, and thereby effectively protected employers against the economic demands of their workers. In consequence of these elaborate measures for subduing workers, the Labor Front became the most important institution of the lopsided job market.[29]

In addition, the state implemented three policies that exerted a direct effect upon the availability of workers in job markets. There was first the policy of promoting employment opportunities for the unemployed. In the first year of the regime about 800,000 workers found jobs at various public-work projects. This total was supplemented by pressing about 200,000 men into the Labor Service. A total of about 1 million laborers were thus withdrawn from regular job markets. Yet most of the substitute forms of work were only of temporary significance. In April of 1934, the generals and the big concerns decided to terminate public-work projects when it became clear that such projects were reducing the available funds for financing rearmament, and when the skilled among the substitute workers could be utilized for filling rearmament orders.[30] The "battle for employment" thus exerted no lasting influence upon the structure of job markets.

More significant was the imposition of compulsory military service in 1935. Within a few years, the number of men recruited or employed by the increasing military establishment was close to a million. Although the personnel involved rotated, the military goal of the state had the effect of reducing the number of available laborers in job markets. Yet the actions of the labor trustees or the Labor Front prevented laborers from benefiting from this militarily inspired reduction of the civilian labor force.

Another policy originated from a demand made by the

generals. Beginning in February of 1935, workers in one industry after another were issued books that recorded their training and vocational experience. These work books also contained information on the three skills of flying planes, driving cars, and handling agricultural machines. The work books thus provided the state with a detailed occupational census that was to supply the data necessary for the allocation of laborers to essential jobs in the second phase of the regime. Even in the first period, however, a work book became a precondition for finding a job. Employers had to enter new information and return the books to workers who changed jobs. Later, in the second half of 1936, when some kinds of skilled labor became scarce, employers refused to return the books to men trying to move to better jobs. Legal action was taken by some of the workers affected, but this was nullified by a decree of December 22, 1936, which instructed the labor courts to reject such pleas.[31] Employers thus profited from the work books even before the government used this device to assign or bind workers to particular jobs.

The political power of the party and the military-bureaucratic power of the state joined forces in creating indispensable conditions for the entry of workers into job markets. The party insisted upon political reliability, compulsory membership, and the payment of dues to the Labor Front as requirements for finding or holding a job. The state stipulated that the worker had to submit to military conscription and obtain a work book if he wanted to hold or regain a job. Party and state thus fenced in the civilian labor force by creating a set of political-military conditions that had to be fulfilled before access to jobs was granted. Widespread unemployment in the first years underlined the penalty implicit in these job requirements and assured ready compliance by practically all workers.

The two job-market institutions previously discussed—employment offices and social insurance—were subjected to important revisions. The system of self-government by unions and employer associations was abolished, and the two institutions became subject to a modified form of the leadership principle within the state. Employment offices were given a monopoly position in regard to the placement of workers, and all private placement offices were abolished. New functions were assigned to the public employment offices, which in two significant instances did participate in policy decisions affecting jobs. From 1934 to 1936, it was decreed that no person engaged in agriculture could be permitted to accept a non-agricultural job without having the prior permission of an employment office. A similar function was performed by the offices for the metal industries. When the increased production of aircraft in middle Germany lured metal workers to this area, the non-resident skilled metal worker could be employed only if he had received the permission of the employment office in his home district.

In directing the flow of workers to particular jobs, the state tried to provide sufficient workers for agricultural and armament producers. This was accomplished by making the employment offices the third party to specific job contracts. Finally, the task of keeping a central file of all the relevant information contained in the work books was assigned to the employment offices. These new functions increased the power of the employment offices. Experience in directing the flow of workers in some occupations and in gathering all the information about the occupational distribution of workers prepared these governmental agencies for the detailed allocation of laborers in job markets during the second phase of the regime.

Modification of social insurance took three forms. Most important was the limitation of the right of workers to obtain unemployment insurance. While the contributions of workers and employers to the insurance fund remained at the same level, the compensation paid to the unemployed was either reduced or denied. In this way, by refusing to compensate the unemployed, the state obviously intended to abolish the former principle of protecting existing job and wage markets from the pressure of the unemployed. The state clearly desired that the unemployed should through their pressure enable employers to reduce or keep down wage rates. There was thus a systematic effort to eliminate the separation between job and wage markets and thereby return to the structure of an unorganized labor market.

The impact of this new policy expressed itself in a new division of the funds spent by the unemployment-insurance system. In the fiscal year of 1933–34, a total of 1.5 billion marks was received from workers and employers. Not more than 680 million marks were spent for unemployment compensation. About 120 million marks went to the part-time unemployed or paid the contributions of the unemployed to the sickness and old-age insurance funds. A total of 580 million marks were used to create jobs by granting all kinds of subsidies to private enterprises.[32] All kinds of devices were used to eliminate various categories of idle workers from the list of claimants for compensation, until, in 1939, the whole system of compensation was abolished. The continued payments of workers and employers, amounting to about 6.5 per cent of wage income, became an outright tax, which was spent for financing the war.

In contrast, the depression-depleted funds set aside for old-age insurance were restored, and its coverage was extended to about 4.5 million handicraftsmen. In making the old-age insurance universal for all gainfully employed, the government was able to impose another tax upon artisans and dealers, to employ the funds for purposes of war, to introduce a form of forced saving and thereby keep down the volume of disposable income for consumption.

Emasculation of unemployment insurance provided an opportunity to inaugurate a new policy of "public assistance."

The so-called *Winterhelp* occupied the stage in this theater. Dominated by the party, this organization collected "voluntary" contributions of about 350 to 400 million marks per year during the first phase of the regime. These funds were primarily distributed as relief in kind among low-paid workers who had become dependent upon Nazi charity. Having been deprived by the Nazis of their right to a minimum wage rate or to unemployment compensation, workers suffering from low income were given supplementary rations, the value of which amounted to 30 or 40 marks in all, during the winter months.[33] The economic function of the *Winterhelp* thus was to keep alive the "deserving" families who found themselves at the bottom of the income ladder after the party and the state had succeeded in destroying the worker's right to unemployment compensation.

Another function of "public assistance" was performed by the NS Welfare organization. In the last days of 1936, a wage dispute arose in an arms plant in Wahn, in the Rheinland. Military leaders, in cooperation with the Ministry of Labor, had decided to reduce the hourly wage rates by ten pfennigs. The wage reduction was disguised as an attempt to unify wage rates by reducing the rate in Prussia to the lower level which prevailed in the arms plants elsewhere. The case in Wahn was mishandled by first delaying the reduction and then imposing it retroactively, so that workers in the plant were asked to repay the "excess" for the preceding three months. This aroused considerable opposition and produced threats of strikes. The NS Welfare organization then stepped in to prevent the strike and for a while compensated the laborers for the wage reduction. Subsequently, in a letter to Göring, Martin Bormann suggested that the workers in Wahn be granted a local addition to the reduced pay equal to the previous wage cut. This proposal was accepted by the Minister of War.[34] The reduction itself remained in force in all other military plants in which the workers did not threaten to strike.

Having restored the unorganized job market, the state did not withdraw from industrial relations. There was no return to a competitive job market.

The state issued a decree on hours of work on July 26, 1934, a month after Röhm had been purged. Officially, the eight-hour day was retained, but employers and government officials were granted a wide latitude in making exceptions. On the one hand, the trustees of labor were given the authority to determine the number of work hours by which an employer could exceed the eight-hour day. This resulted in great variations of working time among different firms and industries. On the other hand, employers were authorized to deviate from the regulations of the trustee. Concerns could freely redistribute working hours as long as the total did not exceed ninety-six hours over a two-week period. In such cases, employers were not required to grant premium pay for overtime work. When an employer desired to increase the working day permanently, he could apply for an extension. The request was usually granted whenever the employer could show that such an extension would relieve him of additional capital outlays. As a result, overtime ceased to be expensive from the employer's point of view, and the standard eight-hour work day was gradually eliminated as output came close to full capacity.

A substantial increase in the length of the work day occurred in 1936 as a result of military orders. Either the procurement agencies gave employers (illegally) permission to extend the daily working hours, or the factory inspectors freely issued permits to increase the working day to ten hours. A letter from the Minister of Labor to the Minister of War, written on October 23, 1936, detailed the widespread violations of the law on the eight-hour day. The Minister of Labor spoke of "social retrogression" because the daily working time in chemical and metal industries had risen to twelve hours. "Thousands of women again work eight or ten hours at night, with the special permission of the factory inspectors." In a subsequent meeting between the experts of the two ministries, the "absolutely untenable extension of working time in the plants of the Borsig A.-G." was discussed. The Ministry of Labor announced its intention to limit the working time in this enterprise by a binding decision. This threat to their purchasing programs induced the procurement officers to ask for the intervention of their superiors. A directive was promptly issued. "According to a decision of the Minister of War and General Göring, the present tempo of rearmament and overtime employment shall be continued, in spite of the social consequences for the workers affected."[35]

With the disappearance of collective bargaining and work councils, the function of determining working conditions became a discretionary privilege for employers. In the new labor law, employers were explicitly granted the authority to formulate and execute the rules of the shop. The council of confidence had to be heard, and the labor trustee could issue guiding principles for employers, but the shop rules were decided unilaterally by the employer. Such rules could be set aside by the trustees only when the confidence council could prove that a particular set of rules was "unsocial." Interference by the trustees in such cases happened only in exceptional circumstances. Thus, the unorganized job market again became associated with the employers' managerial privilege of determining working conditions unilaterally. Not until 1938 were the employers required to have their shop rules explicitly approved by the trustee of labor.

At the same time, the previously established law protecting workers against sudden dismissal was substantially diluted, and new causes for dismissal were recognized. One derived from the particular policies of party and state: Women could be dismissed so as to provide jobs for unemployed men, and anyone could be dismissed who was found guilty of expressing dislike of the Nazi regime. Other dismissals, such as layoffs necessitated by the circumstances of the particular concern, were the more readily accepted by workers because of their feeling that they too would be endangered by the failure of their employer's business.

Legally, when the requirement of giving a worker proper advance notice was infringed upon, he had the right to sue for damages; but actually, access to the labor courts was often contingent upon obtaining the consent of the Labor Front, which had an almost exclusive right to represent workers in the labor courts. When admitted to the court, some laborers found that the courts accepted the arguments of employers by refusing claims for damages that were written into collective regulations or shop rules. Thus there was no longer any guarantee that the worker would be notified in advance of his dismissal and given a chance to find a job elsewhere.

The whole grievance procedure became dominated by the Labor Front. Workers were often deprived of the assurance that they could obtain an impartial decision on interpretations of shop rules and collective regulations. In case of complaint, the Labor Front could decide whether to reject a request, negotiate with the employer, or bring the complaint before the labor court. The aim of the Labor Front was to reduce the number of disputes and prevent so-called unnecessary litigation. This policy was quite successful. The number of cases settled by the labor courts fell from 427,604 in 1929 to 174,476 in 1936.[36]

The organized job market differed from the lopsided market in two crucial respects. There was first a significant difference in the economic situation. The prosperity from 1924 to 1929 greatly enhanced the negative suction power of the union and diminished the negative absorption power of the employer. The depression in the first phase of the Nazi regime produced an excess of available laborers over the total of available jobs in the overwhelming number of job markets. In the absence of trade unions and government action, excess of labor services would have created cutthroat competition among workers, and would have enhanced the opportunities of employers. It was because of the actions of the party and the state, however, that there developed not a cutthroat but a lopsided labor market in the first phase of the regime.

A new power structure was the second and major characteristic of lopsided job markets. The type of power enjoyed by employers was still the same but their relative power had increased significantly. Their plutocratic power of property could be readily translated into increased positive suction power. When price and quantity are interacting, an increase in the demand for labor services will reduce the positive suction power of the employer because he can get more services only by offering better terms; but in Germany, after the suppression of the trade unions and the emasculation of unemployment insurance, the labor supply became atomized and negative suction power ceased to have any effect on the labor markets. Laborers had to accept any job, even if the working conditions or earning opportunities were lower than those granted to the workers who were already employed. Even when looking for more laborers, employers were able to benefit fully from the surplus of services and the destruction of independent trade unions.

Of at least equal importance was the new kind of political and bureaucratic power that became effective in job markets. The bureaucratic power of the state acted in such a way as to increase the power of employers. The emasculation of unemployment insurance abolished the partial insulation of the employed from the unemployed. Every part of the job market was now flooded by unemployed workers. Relaxation of the restrictions against summary dismissal increased the degree of replaceability of employed by unemployed workers. Even those still employed stood with one foot in their respective markets because they could lose their jobs at any time. The interconnection between the internal and external structure of job markets[37] was so much intensified that the lopsided market provided a ready channel for translating the weakness of laborers in markets into effective submissiveness on the part of workers in plants. The leader-follower arrangement of the labor law legalized the submissiveness of workers and glorified ideologically the superior power of employers.

Most important in the new power structure was the role of the Nazi Party. Building the Labor Front upon its monopoly of the instruments of domination the Nazis were able to achieve a twofold success in job markets. Compulsory membership in the Labor Front and proof of political reliability as conditions for obtaining work, control by Nazi stewards and shock troops on the job in plants, the restriction of representation in the confidence councils and labor courts to Nazis, and extensive supervision of the emasculated grievance procedure all enabled the party to transform the temporary atomization of laborers into a permanent one. The power of the Labor Front thus was not utilized to organize and strengthen workers but to prevent their self-organization and to impose industrial peace upon an atomized labor class. In addition, the Labor Front succeeded in driving underground the interest orientation of the workers, forced workers to behave as if they had accepted Nazi doctrines, and attempted to make the Nazi rule more palatable by providing either a few new advantages (e.g., more paid vacations, low-cost transportation) or by pretending that laborers were no longer second-class citizens in plants and in the economy. Since the secret police assured acceptance of Nazi pretenses and propaganda, the Labor Front succeeded in preventing most forms of individual or collective interest realization by workers.

THE DICTATED WAGE MARKET

Elimination of collective bargaining enabled the state to decide whether wage rates would be set by the state or negotiated between individual employers and laborers. Although various business organizations had argued for years against the interference of the state in wage markets, a compromise was reached among the ruling groups. In return for accepting the principle of governmentally fixed wage rates, business groups were able to nominate and actually to appoint the majority of the trustees of labor. It became the function of these trustees to set the wage rates for specific industries, while individual employers fixed the wage rates for their plants by either accepting or deviating from the rates set by the trustees. In practice, the wage rates set by the trustees were widely accepted by the larger concerns. The following table shows the wage rates set by the trustees and reported to the Ministry of Labor.

HOURLY MONEY AND REAL WAGE RATES*
(1929 equals 100)

| | GERMANY | | | UNITED STATES | | |
| | *In Pfennigs* | *Index of Money Rates* | *Index of Real Rates* | *In Cents* | *Index of Money Rates* | *Index of Real Rates* |
Years						
1930	86.8	102	106	55.2	98	100
1931	82.3	96	109	51.5	91	103
1932	69.7	82	104	44.6	79	99
1933	67.6	79	104	44.2	78	103
1934	67.5	79	101	53.2	94	120
1935	67.5	79	99	55.0	97	121
1936	67.5	79	98	55.6	98	121
1937	67.6	79	98	62.4	110	132

* International Labor Office, *Yearbook of Labor Statistics,* 1943–44, Section XIII, A, p. 111.

Three inferences can be readily drawn from this comparison between the wage rates of Germany and the United States. First, wage reductions of the previous governments of Brüning and von Papen had been quite effective in eliminating the influence of the trade union upon wage rates. When the Nazis came to power, wage rates had fallen almost to the lowest point of the depression. Second, the extent of the decline in wage rates was almost the same in Germany and in the United States. In both countries money rates had fallen about 20 per cent, while real rates had risen slightly, from 1929 to 1932. Finally, there was a striking divergence between the respective wage rates in the subsequent upswing. Although the rate of re-employment was faster in Germany, money rates remained at the depression level, while real rates fell by six points of the index. In the United States, however, money rates went up by thirty-two points and real rates by twenty-nine points from 1933 to 1937. Increased union activities and New Deal legislation raised money wage rates 10 per cent above the level of 1929, whereas in Nazi Germany money rates were 22 per cent below those of the predepression period.

Actually, the German wage rates in the above table, containing only the officially set wages, are in need of a twofold modification. In the years 1933–35, the actually paid rates were frequently below the ones set by the state. In the two following years, actual money rates exceeded the official ones. A secret census of the money wages paid to workers showed an increase in the new index from 100 in December, 1935, to 104.3 in December, 1937. In the period of full employment, the official influence was such as to limit the rise in money wages to less than 5 per cent. At the same time, the actual increase in prices was not fully reflected in the official cost-of-living index because the food items had been given an insufficient weight in the index. According to the calculations of the statistical office of the city of Königsberg, the real purchasing power of laborers fell by 15 per cent from 1933 to 1936.[38] The slight increase in money rates was thus accompanied by an approximate 10 per cent decline of real wage rates for the years 1933–37.

Cooperation of the Labor Front, the state, and employers produced an extraordinary distributional effect. The actions of the three powerful groups together had achieved a substantial increase in employment which was accompanied by almost fixed money and a significant decline of real wage rates. While the social capitalism of the New Deal was able to raise the real wage rate by one third above the depression level, the organized capitalism of Nazi Germany was able to keep money rates almost stable and—through the agricultural price policy[39]—press real wage rates even below that level. How was labor deprived of its share in the rising national income?

Wage rates were fixed by the labor trustees in accordance with a deliberate decision to prevent any rise in money wage rates. This policy established a dictated wage market. The power of the state was used to prevent almost any increase in money wage rates through the suppression of trade unions as well as through effective collaboration between the state and employers. Legally, employers could have raised the plant rates above the rates set by the trustees. Yet there is no evidence that such a policy was adopted by many employers prior to 1936. Making the most of the suppression of the trade unions, employers fully accepted the state policy of keeping wage rates at the depression level. The first feature of the dictated wage market was thus a dual power structure. The power of the state was reinforced by the power of employers. In regard to wage fixing, the two powerholders did not oppose each other but collaborated in implementing the same policy. It was because of this collaboration that wage-fixing was highly effective up to the beginning of 1936; the interest of the employers was identical with that of the state.

Direct controls in the form of fixed wage rates did not produce any shrinkage in the labor supply. The law of supply was ineffective because there was no decline in the quantities of labor services offered when money rates declined relatively and real rates absolutely. There were two reasons for this ineffectiveness. One lay in the inability of workers to get command of the capital required to establish a business. If they could have employed themselves and benefited from the slowly rising level of employment, many workers would have left their jobs because of the decline in real wages. Unemployment was the second reason why the law of supply was ineffective. If any worker had protested against the decline in real wage rates, he would have invited his own dismissal because many of the unemployed would have been only too willing to accept his job.

Lack of property and widespread unemployment thus had the effect of preventing any interaction between dictated wage rates and the quantities of labor services offered for hire. This severance between the two markets occurred in two different periods and economic systems, proceeded from different causes, and produced distinctly different effects. Under the Weimar Republic, in Germany, and under the New Deal, in the U. S., collective bargaining between national unions and employer associations constituted the main cause for the separation of the markets. During the Great Depression, however, lack of required capital and unemployment kept the two markets apart. In keeping this separation alive even during the rearmament boom, the Nazis produced a remarkable effect: the money wage rates in organized capitalism lay about one fifth below those of the social capitalism of the New Deal. How was such a privation possible?

The stabilization of wage rates was the result of three decisions. The Ministry of Labor instructed the trustees to keep the money rates at the level of 1933. The Labor Front prevented workers from resisting the imposition of the stabilized rates, whether by individual or collective action. Employers supported the actions of state and party by keeping the plant rates very close to the fixed rates set by the trustees. All these decisions were based upon three distinct kinds of power, namely the bureaucratic and police power of the state, the political and secret-police power of the party, and the property power of employers. The impact of these three powers was felt in the demand that employees work for, and be satisfied with, the fixed money rates. Under conditions of increasing employment, productivity per unit of labor had a tendency to rise, but as a result of state policies and controls, the money rate was kept below the productive contributions of the workers, who were inevitably exploited. Such an exploitation of labor was more effective and more advantageous than monopsonistic exploitation, since the former could be achieved at a time when labor services were increasingly needed and used by employers.

A second form of exploitation was related to the decline of real wage rates. If the official policy of stabilized prices had been implemented, real-wage rates and money rates would have been equal; but in fact, while the cost of living was being raised by policies that coordinated agricultural production, foreign-exchange rates, and imports, real wage rates (in the absence of trade unions) inevitably declined and remained steadily below the money rates. As the statistical data above show, this exploitation resulted in a rise of ten points in the index by the end of the first phase of the Nazi regime. Under the New Deal, on the other hand, real wage rates rose by twenty-nine points from 1933 to 1937, a development which clearly indicates what could have happened if Germany had been able to avoid the Nazi dictatorship.

The exploitation of labor by the state was followed by still another form of exploitation which may be described as quasi-compulsory self-exploitation. If the workers had acted according to the principle of marginal productivity, they would have systematically reduced their efforts until their marginal product equalled their reduced real wage rate; but this reduction would have resulted in wholesale dismissals, since other workers were readily obtainable. Unemployment thus prevented the workers from engaging in such a process of equalization. The response of employers and workers to the decline in real wage rates clearly contradicted marginal productivity theory.

An increasing number of factories offered laborers a shift from hourly to piecework wages. Eager to compensate themselves for the decline in real wage rates, many workers intensified the speed of their operations and thus engaged in a form of self-exploitation. For instance, the officially fixed money rates for women in Thuringia were thirty pfennigs in the toy industry, thirty-eight in the metal industry, and forty-five in uniform-producing textile firms. The actual piecework wages, when expressed in hours, raised the earnings of women to forty, forty-four, and sixty pfennigs in the respective industries.[40] For the labor force in general, the real earnings rose slightly. Hourly earnings were three pfennigs in 1933 and seven in 1936 above the fixed hourly money rates. In spite of self-exploitation, the real hourly earnings of these workers in 1937 were still 20 per cent below those in 1929.

The detrimental effect of the direct and indirect controls of the state was thus only to a minor extent offset by the shift to piecework wages. The deterrent effect of these controls could be minimized only when laborers increased their efforts. The impact of wage dictation was quite different for employers. Under conditions of increasing output, the fixed wage rates and the dividend ceiling together resulted in a rise in the volume of undistributed profits, which became the preferred form of capital accumulation. Direct controls of wages and dividends thus functioned (*a*) as special inducements for employers to raise their profits without increasing their efforts per unit of input, and (*b*) as a kind of class legislation directed against laborers and shareholders, who were prevented by the powerholders from obtaining a proportionate share of the increase in national income. The enrichment of private concerns was thus a definite result of dictated wage markets.

Information is lacking for measuring the rise in the rate of profit per unit of capital investment, so we must be satisfied with showing the trend in the percentage increase of total profits realized. The following table gives the principal items in the accounts of 1,420 corporations which together had a nominal capital of 8.5 billion marks.

EARNINGS OF LARGE CORPORATIONS*
(in million marks)

Years	Write-off for Depreciations	Gross Earnings	Wages and Salaries	Total Profits	Total Losses	Net Profits
1932	730	5,800	2,700	250	640	—390
1933	740	6,300	2,900	360	240	120
1934	890	8,000	3,650	450	80	370
1935	970	9,500	4,350	500	40	460
1936	1,160	11,300	5,080	590	70	520

* "Aufwand und Ertrag bei den Industriellen Aktiengesellschaften," *Wirtschaft und Statistik* (Berlin), 1938, pp. 576-77.

Gross earnings rose by almost 100 per cent in these five years, and total wages and salaries, by about 90 per cent. The effect of the rearmament boom, which lasted from 1933 to the end of 1936, on incomes in the same period can best be understood by comparing total profits and losses for the four years of the boom. Accordingly, if we subtract the total losses from the total profits, we see that net profits rose by 433 per cent between the beginning of 1933 and the end of 1936.

It is not possible to say how much of the rise in the rate of profit was attributable to lower unit wage cost and how much resulted from the increased utilization of production facilities. Yet there can be no doubt that the dictated wage markets and the lopsided job markets contributed, directly and effectively, to the restoration of profits. Thus, we may say that the direct controls exercised by party and state, far from being harmful to business, simultaneously exploited labor and enriched business and restored the institution of private profits.

INDUCEMENTS AND UNDEREMPLOYMENT

The use of direct controls in a period of underemployment is not in accord with modern employment theory, which holds that underemployment calls for indirect controls, especially deficit financing, which alone can restore profits for private enterprise. It is further contended that direct controls have economic meaning only in a situation of scarcity. When particular bottlenecks occur in specific markets, direct controls may be the appropriate means for allocating the scarce resources to users who most need them. Modern employment theory thus sees a causal nexus only between scarcity and direct controls.

One observer utilized this scarcity theory for explaining the origin of direct controls in the Nazi economy.[41] Indirect controls were used for increasing the volume of employment, whereas markets suffering from bottlenecks became subject to the principle of compulsory state controls (*Zwangswirtschaft*). The question thus arises as to whether scarcity of the quantities supplied is the universal cause for direct governmental action in the determination of prices and quantities in markets. Why did the ruling groups as well as most of the capitalist enterprises clamor for direct controls in a situation of underemployment?

Fixing wage rates, creating compulsory cartels, and prohibiting investments in certain industries had no connection with any kind of scarcity. Introduced in 1933, these forms of direct control arose in a period of excess labor, insufficient demand for products, and idle plant capacity. Direct action by the government in a period of excess supply suggests a twofold paradox. Why did employers accept minimum wage rates after the unions had been suppressed? Why were direct controls necessary when there were more laborers than jobs?

Minimum wage rates usually seek to establish an acceptable pay above the rate prevailing in at least some markets. Employers thus affected normally have to pay higher wage rates than would otherwise prevail. Yet this detrimental effect was avoided by many employers or whole industries in Germany. The labor law of May, 1933, granted exceptions from the minimum-wage stipulations established by the labor trustees for any firm or industry that claimed to be unable to pay minimum wages and in effect authorized the continuance of substandard working conditions. According to a study made by the Labor Front, one fourth of the establishments in a handicraft industry paid wage rates below those set by the trustees of labor.[42] As a result, the workers did not necessarily receive the benefit of minimum wages since most of those industries normally affected by minimum-wage legislation were exempted from the governmentally fixed minimum wage rates. The familiar observation that independent unions are necessary for the enforcement of minimum wage rates is again seen to have been confirmed by the experience of Germany under the Nazis.

Why then were wage rates fixed at all? The answer lies in the causal connection between unit labor costs and the prices of products. During the depression declining wage rates enabled employers to reduce their prices. Price competition disintegrated cartels, since some of the members became outsiders. In small business, the level of prices shifted downward for whole industries when independent unions were suppressed, and wage rates tended to fall to the level of unemployment compensation. Many employers suddenly discovered that unionized wage rates had put a floor under the prices of their products. They realized to their surprise and dismay that when, in a severe depression, union wage rates are abolished, wage rates do not decline only to a "natural" equilibrium rate. A "black work" practice developed in many industries which enabled laborers to receive unemployment compensation while they were working secretly in factories at rates that were frequently only one fourth of the rates that had been paid before the suppression of the unions. Firms enjoying such low wage rates drastically reduced their prices, thereby undermining the market for those firms that did not violate the law on unemployment compensation. Thus, instead of realizing an advantage from the abolition of unions, producers experienced extreme price competition in product markets. This nexus between wage and price reductions confirms the theory that low wage rates constitute the main cause for cutthroat price competition among small firms.[43] The same experience does not in this respect confirm the Keynesian theory, which assumed that workers were guided by the "money illusion" and would not willingly consent to lower rates.[44]

The organizations of small Nazified businesses engaged in a threefold struggle against cutthroat competition. First, they used their political influence in favor of minimum wage rates fixed by the government. Second, they cooperated with the employment offices and the Nazi party in an attempt to discover and punish those employers who in effect counted on unemployment compensation as a part of the wages paid to their "black" workers. Finally, the business organizations tried hard to fix the prices of their products. They insisted that businesses in setting their prices calculate unit labor costs in terms of the minimum wage rate. As we have seen, the government and the courts in the fall of 1934 gave the business organizations the legal right to enforce prices that were based upon minimum wage rates, even when the wages paid to the employees were below that level. Rather than raising the income of workers, fixed wage rates thus served the purpose of avoiding or eliminating cutthroat price competition in product markets. Thus, it was only with the assistance of direct government controls that employers could capitalize on the abolition of union wage scales.

A similar causal nexus existed between fixed wage rates on the one hand, and compulsory cartels and investment bans on the other. Compulsory membership eliminated outsiders and thereby enabled the cartels to set uniform prices that were adhered to by all the producers of any given commodity. Prohibition of investments prevented any member of the cartel from increasing its plant capacity as long as there was any excess capacity for the industry. In small business, these two measures were supplemented by the policy of reducing the existing business population by eliminating the incompetents. Surviving firms then had to charge prices that were based upon the average total cost of competent producers, and this policy was accepted by the government and tolerated by big business. Not only fixed wage rates but also the reduction of the number of producers, the fixing of the volume of output or the freezing of existing capacity were necessary for eliminating cutthroat competition. These direct actions by the government do not bear out the hypothesis that all forms of direct controls originate in situations of scarcity.

The actions taken to fight cutthroat competition resulted from the cyclical surplus of the Great Depression. In response to this surplus, the prevailing scheme of institutions for specific markets was changed by the government to provide effective support for sellers. On the one hand, compulsory cartels strengthened existing voluntary cartels, whose effectiveness was further assured by the forbidding of additional plant construction. These privately initiated institutions were therefore once again in a position to control prices effectively. On the other hand, fixed minimum wage rates maintained a lower cost level for the calculation of effective cartel prices. Thus, government action made monopolistic control by private organizations possible in a situation of economic surplus.

New government economic organizations reinforced the

actions of the private cartels in their control of markets, since cartel methods alone had proved to be ineffective in fighting the detrimental consequences of the cyclical surplus of the Great Depression. In effect, however, wage-fixing and the bans on investment and the controls exerted by the compulsory cartels, which had all arisen in response to the problems created by the cyclical surplus, were not regarded as direct controls. Instead, they served as inducements whereby private business firms acted in a way that would be favorable to the restoration of cartelized markets and profits for private enterprise.

In terms of Keynesian theory, we observe here the twofold paradox of monopolistic action in situations created by an overabundance of facilities for production and of direct action by the state in the situation of insufficient aggregate demand. The paradox resolves itself as soon as we drop the assumption that competition necessarily exists in commodity markets. In seeking market control, as well as profits, monopolies obtained the help of the state in retaining their market control. Rather than waiting for the unemployment-creating effect of indirect controls, the large firms pressured state agencies into giving them orders. Thus, the use of direct controls for the sake of realizing private profit goals gave rise to inducements as a new form of economic action by the state.

Eventually, as the rearmament boom replaced the depression, the purpose of wage-fixing took a different form. Wage-fixing, compulsory cartels, and investment bans had arisen because of the cyclical surplus. When profits came back the leaders of big business discovered that the same controls, sufficiently modified, were equally useful during the rearmament boom. Compulsory cartels facilitated monopolistic control of markets in the new situation of reactivated business. Not only did the fixing of wage rates at a low level permit a quickly rising volume of profits, but the reinvestment of profits made business concerns independent of shareholders and of the capital markets. Retaining profits became as important as earning profits. A ceiling upon dividends functioned as a prosperity control, the purpose of which was to increase the volume of profits coming to the corporation itself.

Fixed wages and dividend inducements enlarged the significance of the capitalist institution of profits. In addition to the usual income and profit benefits, the government provided the incentive of reinvesting profits in corporations. The original "surplus controls," such as depressed wage rates, set up by the government were used to increase private profits, and the new prosperity controls, such as the ceiling placed on dividends at the end of 1934, became the means of directing the use of profits within corporations themselves. As we might expect, influential businessmen had no quarrel with the surplus controls and accepted gladly the new prosperity controls. In fact, as far as business was concerned, controls *qua* inducements had become an important feature of organized capitalism. What was good for business must be advantageous for the capitalist system.

CREEPING SOCIALISM AND STATISM

The abolition of "social capitalism" in the first phase of the Nazi regime came close to what is now proposed as the elimination of "creeping socialism." In each case, labor is the major enemy, and the total elimination of the labor movement is the central aim. Like their forerunners in Germany, the opponents of labor call for the elimination of "socialism" in the name of free enterprise or self-government for business. In their choice of allies, however, the present advocates of freedom for business differ considerably from their German counterparts in the 1930's. In Germany big business allied itself with the Nazis in attempting to suppress labor, whereas in the United States, the extravagant advertising campaigns in praise of free enterprise usually borrow their arguments from genuine liberals. In spite of these significant differences, however, capitalists in the United States would do well to be mindful of the lessons that can be learned from the suppression of labor in Germany.

For the fighters for business freedom in Germany there was first of all the problem of ending the "labor monopoly." Unable to discover any democratic, peaceful, and effective solution, business organizations increasingly favored, as the depression progressed, a policy of state intervention against trade unions and the social philosophy supported by them. Yet it was not the force of the state but the extralegal violence of the Nazi troopers that alone was able to suppress organized labor. Nor would the wage dictation of the state have been successful if the Gestapo and the Labor Front had not prevented the rise of secret unions and quelled all forms of labor resistance. Whether they liked it or not, German businessmen had to admit that it was only because of the "dirty work" done by the Nazis that capitalism became free of organized labor.

Shortly after the unions had been eliminated and the state had assumed the function of setting wage rates, the business organizations engaged in a campaign to rebuild their cartels. Unable to beat down outsiders by themselves, they successfully enlisted the power of the state. The laws on compulsory cartels and investment bans provided the foundation upon which the control of markets by cartels was re-established. The prospect of stabilized money and declining real wage rates did not in the least induce private business concerns to give up their monopolistic practices and move in the direction of a competitive capitalism. In fact, from their behavior in this respect, we may justifiably discount the charge that "labor monopoly" is the basis of all product monopolies.

Finally, there is the notion that once business firms are

freed from the shackles of the state, they will become self-reliant, shun government support, and strive only for those profits that are compatible with economic freedom. The actions of big business in the first phase of the Nazi regime belied this expectation. The two standards by which they evaluated their own actions as well as those of the government were primarily profit and power. That the wage rates were dictated by the state was immaterial as long as government wage-fixing was favorable to private enterprise. That the economic freedom of laborers was destroyed did not count as long as the power of capitalist enterprise was increased. As a result, the fight for business freedom ended in the denial to labor of its freedom of association and its right to participate in economic affairs. The freedom of organized business groups to control markets was largely realized, and the direct or indirect controls of the state became associated with various forms of inducements, as we shall see presently. Statism was imposed upon labor as early as 1933, while business concerns enjoyed the great advantages of organized capitalism. In fact, it was in the field of labor that the meaning of statism was first developed by the Nazis. For labor, statism included (1) the suppression of self-chosen and self-directed economic, political, and social organizations; (2) the compulsory obligation to join, and pay tribute to, an organization dedicated to mass domination; (3) the extensive indoctrination of laborers in, and submission to, Nazi ideology; (4) the constant threat of being spied upon, arrested, and tortured by the Gestapo and of being thrown into a concentration camp. In addition, the party and the state—supported by employers—exploited and dominated the labor markets, exerted pressure upon workers to increase their output through self-exploitation, and subjected them to the joint managerial prerogative of employers and the Labor Front.

The first four features of statism have been generally regarded as typical and necessary consequences of one-party dictatorships, be they fascist or communist in nature. Our analysis has shown, however, that in the field of labor there were three additional features of statism, namely: imposed exploitation, quasi-compulsory self-exploitation, and a combined economic-political domination of laborers in plants.

Was the relationship between the first and second set of statist features accidental? The answer must be negative. There was and is an inherent necessity that tightly links the noneconomic and economic elements of statism. One-party regimes usually set themselves the goal of promoting massive projects of economic reconstruction which require all the attainable resources of the nation. The new goal is not self-selected but must be imposed upon the people by a one-party dictatorship. The rearmament policy constituted the central goal for the first phase of the Nazi regime. The new project called for large efforts and new sacrifices, at least by the laboring classes. It was this need for new forms of capital formation that induced the Nazi party and the state to utilize their instruments of power for imposing effective exploitation upon German workers.

Imposed as well as self-chosen exploitation could become operative only if the party and the state engaged in a deliberate institutional realignment of the prevailing labor markets. Neither the lopsided job markets nor the dictated wage markets could have been established and maintained solely by the direct actions of the state. In addition to fixing wage rates, prohibiting strikes and collective bargaining, imposing entry stipulations, emasculating unemployment insurance, regulating labor courts, and imposing work books upon laborers, there had to be an effective and complementary policy of coercion that would make direct actions by the state permanently effective. This policy was formulated and enforced by the Nazis and involved the suppressing of independent trade unions, the herding of all gainfully employed workers into the Labor Front, and the use of this organization to prevent

effective forms of resistance, quell incipient strikes, replace
union spokesmen by Nazi stewards, dominate and redirect
the grievance procedure, and divert the attention of workers
from a realization of their economic interests. Behind all
these actions of the Labor Front stood the ever-present organization of the Gestapo—its spy system, its torture chambers
and concentration camps, which were utilized whenever the
actions of the Labor Front fell short of their desired success.
It was not only the direct action of the state, not only the
domination and violence of the Nazi organizations, but the
combination and coordination of the two that constituted
the meaning of statism for labor in the regime.

For employers, the meaning of these statist actions was
quite different. The first four noneconomic features of statism did not at all apply to any segment of big business, and
the economic features created exceptional benefits for employers. The gains springing from imposed and self-chosen
exploitation went largely to the employers, who enjoyed a
veritable paradise of profit-making. The institutional realignment of labor markets enabled business concerns to
make their property and trading powers effective on both
sides of the market, since laborers could not use their absorption or suction powers in any form whatever.

In return for these material gains as well as for the ideological advantages of being in complete control of the plants,
employers had to pay a twofold price. On the one hand, they
could make use of these advantages in labor markets only
because of the armament orders placed with them by the
procurement agencies of the armed forces. Given such orders, which created the necessary markets for producer goods,
employers could see in the low unit cost of labor only an
inducement for increased production and profit-making. On
the other hand, plant leaders had to recognize the political
prerogative of the Labor Front in factories. Yet the economic
outlays involved "cost really relatively little, compared to

the increases in real wages that could have been given, and which were granted in quite a number of other countries."[45] At the time, this twofold price appeared to most employers as an exceptionally good bargain.

Finally, the statism imposed upon labor was not at all incompatible with organized capitalism. On the contrary, statist dictation to laborers gave employers the means of establishing and maintaining direct influence and control over "their" workers. It was precisely in the labor issue that capitalism had been most defective, and it was in this field that many employers were most eager to restore their power and again receive the total obedience of their workers. The prevailing wage rate, the readiness to submit to managerial instructions, the intensity and speed of work, could not have been better for effective production and were all products of statism. Instead of contradicting the principle of extensive organization, the dictation of labor markets turned out to be the most profitable and the least dispensable feature of organized capitalism.

What then was the influence of the state in other markets? If political statism was absent, did intervention of the government give rise to economic statism?

PRIVATE BUSINESS AND STATISM

CHAPTER NINE

The modern state, according to laissez-faire theory, does not give rise to statism when three essential conditions prevail: (1) when the sphere of government is strictly delimited to a narrow range of functions, clearly set off by civil liberties which will not be significantly infringed upon by any one of the five groups—parties, interest groups, bureaucracy, armed forces, and police—controlling and acting through the state; (2) when the specifically assigned governmental functions are administered according to the rule of law by which everyone concerned will receive equal consideration and treatment; and (3) when limited government, rule of law, and an inviolable private sphere of autonomous action are regarded as sufficient safeguards against political dictatorship and economic statism.

The accumulated knowledge of political sociology, however, has taught us to reject the laissez-faire view of the state as idealistic, nondescriptive, and unattainable. Analysis of the actual practices of states has established two lessons. First, modern states will not and cannot restrict themselves to a few functions, such as internal protection and external security, that are implicit in the concept of limited government. The deficiencies of the capitalist economy, as well as the pressures exerted by interest groups, have greatly enlarged the economic functions of the modern state. Second, administrative agencies supposedly serving the state disinterestedly, as well as private groups, have often had ample opportunity to employ the governmental instruments of power for their personal or group benefit. The danger of a misuse of the state's power for the ends of particular groups may thus arise from the actions of bureaucracy, police, or military, as well as from those of political parties and organized interest groups. Any one of these has historically had the chance to appropriate instruments of the state to itself, to elevate its group goals into so-called general interests that deserve priority over all other public and private goals. The modern state is thus continually in danger of being privately appropriated by some group which will use the power of the state for its own ends.

As a result, there is no predetermined line of division between private and public functions in modern society. It is thus incumbent upon us to investigate empirically what has been the particular distribution of private and public functions in a particular economic system. In other words, what kind of relationship exists between private business and the state in a regime such as that which prevailed in Germany in the first phase of Nazi rule?

Three possible types of relationship can be distinguished at the outset. In the first, private business groups use their power to get their policies adopted by the state. If they are successful, we have private economic goals that are politically implemented by the state. Business promotionalism and policies of capitalist invigoration are characterizing features of a "politically implemented capitalism." The interest groups of private business thus stand behind the state, determine its will, and utilize its power by realizing through political means their private economic ends.

In the second type, political groups—parties, armies, or bureaucracies—define political goals for the state which tend towards an expansion of the activities of the government. Realization of the groups' noneconomic goals calls for economic resources. Rather than collecting the required funds compulsorily and producing all needed goods in state-owned and state-operated enterprises, the political groups controlling the state adopt a policy that deliberately creates new profit opportunities for private concerns. The result is a "politically oriented capitalism."[1] Monetary and fiscal policies as well as franchises and other privileges constitute the typical devices for creating such profit opportunities for private concerns. In return for creating these privately utilized opportunities, the state-controlling groups are enabled to realize their noneconomic goals.

Finally, private appropriation of the instruments of the state by military, political or economic groups may give rise to a political dictatorship. The dictatorial group sets new goals for internal or external expansion of the state. These imposed goals are given priority over all other aims in the economy. The resources necessary for realizing these goals are requisitioned, and private economic actions are adjusted to the priority goals through a series of direct controls, most of which are detrimental to the interests of private groups. If no major economic institutions are abolished, imposed goals and direct controls give rise to a "state directed capitalism." The dictatorial state does not itself engage in capitalist activities but enlarges the economic functions of government and realizes its will primarily through a re-structuring of capitalist markets.

It has to be emphasized that none of these types of politically influenced private capitalism existed in all its features in the first phase of the Nazi regime. What we do find is a combination of various elements of all three kinds of political influence. Our task is to identify and analyze the prevailing forms of state action in order to see how invigoration and indirect as well as direct controls interacted with (by modifying or reinforcing) one another. How these variously combined actions of the state affected private capitalism will be investigated in Chapter X.

In economic matters, the three powerful groups placed full emphasis upon two coalition goals. As we have seen, economic rearmament and the suppression of trade unions received priority over all other economic goals. The secondary economic goals of the three powerholders could be realized only in so far as they did not interfere with the paramount goals and only if at least two of the powerholders could agree on what these secondary economic goals were to be. Middle-class socialism, as an original economic goal of the Nazi party, was defeated through the collaboration of the other partners in the coalition. The invigoration of capitalist institutions was the joint goal of all business groups. Its success depended (*a*) upon how strongly the generals supported this common goal of private enterprise and (*b*) upon how far invigoration could be integrated with the policy of economic rearmament. Thus, although the suppression of trade unions gave rise to mass domination and economic statism, there is still the question of what particular methods were selected by the state to implement economic rearmament and the policy of invigorating capitalist institutions.

ORIGIN OF INDUCEMENTS AND DETERRENTS

The view of direct controls as undesirable but inevitable in situations of emergency originated in the Great Depression. The crises in credit and banking induced great amounts of foreign and domestic capital to leave the country and resulted in the reduction of the foreign exchange reserve of the Central Bank by almost 3 billion marks within one year. Foreign loans and an increasingly high rediscount rate—reaching 15 per cent in August of 1931—did not stop or reverse the flow of gold to foreign countries. In spite of a rising surplus of exports, the loss of gold steadily exceeded the excess of export proceeds over import payments—primarily because of a decline in import values. Exchange control, introduced in August, 1931, was the only available weapon of defense in the currency crisis. This particular kind of control was not independently arrived at but arose in response to the circumstances of the Great Depression and the intense credit crisis of 1931.

Germany's financial problems were made worse by the decision of the British to devaluate the pound and by the decision of the Brüning government to protect the banks against runs by restricting credit and initiating a deliberate policy of deflation. Fear of a German devaluation increased the outflow of capital and further diminished the currency reserves of the Central Bank. The result was an extension of the range of exchange control. All foreign money and other claims had to be sold to the Central Bank, if they exceeded the amount of 200 marks. An increasing portion of imports was directly restricted through allotting declining sums of foreign exchange to importers. Thus, the function of exchange control, which had arisen as an emergency measure against the credit crisis of 1931, changed into a means of trade protection because of the British decision (apparently made without regard for the economies of other industrial countries) to devaluate.

The new purpose of exchange control in 1932 was (a) to balance ingoing and outgoing payments at the level of foreign trade prevailing in 1931; (b) to facilitate the liquidation of reparation payments; and (c) to reconstruct the nation economically and reduce in an orderly fashion the excessively high foreign debt. The first goal required bilateral trade agreements with other countries. The third goal produced a series of standstill agreements which reduced rates of interest and established an orderly procedure for the payment of interest and amortization to creditor countries. The annulment of reparations (if we leave out of consideration the obligations under the Dawes and Young plans) could be obtained within one year, whereas the gradual reduction of the foreign debt was necessarily a long-term undertaking. Given this huge foreign indebtedness and the existence of the new sterling bloc, exchange control could not have been dispensed with very soon, even if there had been no Nazi movement.

Subsequent events were increasingly unfavorable. The export surplus fell rapidly. "The depreciation of the pound, the growth of protectionism in Great Britain, and later the operation of the Ottawa agreements severely impaired Germany's competitive ability on international markets. In the Balkan countries, for example, Germany lost 50 per cent of her export demand during the first half of 1932, whereas England actually increased exports to the same region."[2]

Internally, the Central Bank not only kept the rediscount rate exceptionally high but also engaged in credit rationing in order to reorganize and re-establish the private banks. This credit policy of the Central Bank, acting more as the agent of the private banks than of the economy, was accompanied by the deliberate and compulsory reduction of wages, some prices, and interest. One of these policies would have been deplorable enough, but in coupling a high bank rate with imposed wage reductions, the Central Bank all but destroyed the few chances of creating employment by means of compulsory deflation. The high interest rates undermined investment incentives, and credit rationing eliminated employment opportunities that were expected to arise from lower wage rates. In consequence, the German and British central banks as well as the German and British governments in these depression years contributed—unwittingly but significantly—to the existence of a necessary precondition—widespread underemployment in Germany—for the success of the Nazis in capturing leadership of the impoverished middle class in the crucial year of 1932.

Direct deflationary controls were coupled with indirect ones. Government expenditures were drastically reduced, while taxes were increased. From 1929 to 1932, the amount of national income paid in taxes rose from 19.9 to 24.2 per cent.[3] The two deflationary policies reinforced each other, so that governmental policy became one of the major reasons for the continued increase in the number of the unemployed. The simultaneous policy of raising rates of interest and rationing credit increased the debt burden of all producing units in the country, with the result that the agricultural organizations, especially, turned against the "usury rates of interest" and demanded an extensive policy of relieving agricultural enterprises from their debt burden through governmental actions.[4]

Exchange control turned out to be successful in the emergency but failed as an effective promoter of recovery.[5] A gradual reduction of the foreign debt could have been achieved only under three conditions: (1) if the decline in foreign trade had been arrested, (2) if Germany had retained in 1932 the same export surplus as in 1931, and (3) if the volume of employment had behaved in Germany as it did in Great Britain during 1932. Inasmuch as none of these conditions materialized, the depression type of exchange control failed to attain its first and third goals. Exchange control in this period succeeded only as a temporary instrument of currency policy, reducing the flight of capital, diminishing somewhat the run upon the currency reserves, and supporting the old parity of the mark. These gains were nullified by

GERMAN FOREIGN TRADE AND MONETARY RESERVES*
(in million marks)

Years	Total	Exports	Imports	Excess of (+) exports (—) imports	Average Annual Holdings of Gold and Foreign Currency
1928	26,277	12,276	14,001	—1,725	2,405.4
1929	26,930	13,483	13,447	+36	2,506.3
1930	22,429	12,036	10,393	+1,643	2,806.0
1931	16,326	9,599	6,727	+2,872	1,914.4
1932	10,406	5,739	4,667	+1,072	974.6
1933	9,025	4,821	4,204	+667	529.7
1934	8,618	4,167	4,451	—284	164.7
1935	8,429	4,270	4,159	+111	91.0
1936	8,986	4,768	4,218	+550	75
1937	11,379	5,911	5,468	+443	70

* Stand der wirtschaftlichen Lage," February 1, 1938, contained in Wi/IF 5.582, roll 140, T-77.

credit rationing, tax increases, and the official reduction of wages, all of which intensified the decline in aggregate demand to such an extent that the effect of restricted imports on employment could not and did not materialize.

Historically, exchange control created the first three incipient elements of statism. The Central Bank increasingly abolished the market in foreign money. Holders of gold and foreign money were ordered to sell these assets to the Central Bank, which became the sole holder of foreign currency. In effect, the government established the institution of public property in foreign money. The export of German money was increasingly restricted, so as to reduce and eventually prevent the flight of capital from the country. Finally, imports from foreign countries were increasingly restricted as the supply of foreign money in the vaults of the Central Bank fell, and in 1932, import quotas were steadily reduced. Direct controls thus gave rise to (a) the possession of all foreign money by the Central Bank, (b) forced sales of export and security proceeds in foreign money, and (c) sales quotas for

German money, whether used to purchase foreign goods or foreign currency.

These statist controls, inflicted as a result of the depression, were viewed with pronounced dislike by exporters and importers as well as by foreign creditors—all of whom regarded the controls as detrimental to their individual interests and to the continued operation of private capitalism. There were, however, two groups of German capitalists who greatly welcomed these direct controls. The recipients of foreign loans, especially banks holding short-term loans, insisted that sales quotas for the exporting of German money were indispensable to their economic survival. The subsequent standstill agreements with foreign creditors postponed amortizations and reduced interest rates, and some producers then found themselves in the same situation as the bankers. In a request for assistance the owners of German metal-ore mines reported to the Ministry of Economics that they "had financed the reorganization of their enterprises out of a 6 million mark short-term foreign loan . . . and that the danger of a recall of these funds was hanging like the sword of Damocles over their concerns."[6]

Of even greater significance was the insistence of German producers upon a reduction of imports. Fighting the entry of foreign goods through the raising of tariffs had proved futile in all those cases in which a foreign price reduction had more than offset the increase in duties. Firms suffering from foreign competition thus not only welcomed restrictions of imports through exchange control but actively sought to hasten the adoption of import quotas. Especially vocal in their demand for quantity restrictions were the various farm organizations. Dr. Hugenberg as Minister of Industry and Agriculture was their spokesman in the first Hitler government. In a letter to the cabinet he complained that the 1932 import quotas for agricultural products had not become effective because of the existing commercial treaties with other states. As Minister of Agriculture he demanded from the cabinet a decision on the autonomous adoption of import quotas in all those cases in which higher duties did not exclude the import of foreign goods. This decision was to be taken even in regard to countries with whom Germany had definite contractual import obligations; indeed, it was precisely these countries against whom protection was sought.[7] The clamour for quotas attests to the fact that a significant number of business groups welcomed or supported exchange control—provided it were utilized to give them effective protection against foreign competitors or creditors.

An interesting shift in attitudes arose among the protectionist business groups. Those—such as the *Metallhüttenverband*—who had insisted upon higher tariffs in 1932 turned, in 1933, to purchasing quotas as a solution. It was their contention that if the higher duties really did become effective, they would merely put a floor under prices and would not provide a guarantee of sales. The small state of Braunschweig, for instance, proposed to the Minister of Economics that metal users should be ordered to purchase minimum quantities from German mines.[8] The request was accepted in the summer of 1933 by the buyers, who acted under government pressure. A similar proposal had already been implemented in some food-processing industries. The producers of margarine had consented in December of 1932 to purchase specified quantities from the suppliers of animal fats. Three months later the same arrangement was extended to the soap and candle producers. The Minister of Agriculture proposed to the cabinet a law which would enjoin the soap producers to purchase specified quantities of German animal fats. His plan divided the country into definite purchasing districts in which soap producers would have to buy animal fats at a price greater than the import price. In seeking the power to impose such purchasing quotas and to fix the domestic price of fat, the Minister told the cabinet of a voluntary agreement between the participants and indicated that the new law would merely force some outsiders to adhere to the agreement.[9]

Review of these events indicates the twofold origin of deterrents and inducements. The depression and the credit crisis gave rise to the undesired but inevitable statist measures that enforced compulsory sales of export proceeds to the Central Bank, severely restricted the flow of German currency to foreign countries, and placed all foreign money in the possession of the Central Bank. The inducements, on the other hand, were made necessary by the deterrents imposed on German producers and borrowers or resulted from the pressure that was deliberately put on governmental agencies by organized business groups. Thus, direct controls, in the form of deterrents, became coupled with automatic or deliberate inducements. Once this coupling effect had been recognized, it became the new policy of business to make the inducements large enough to offset the impact of unavoidable, or avoidable, deterrents. The question of how these inducements affected the policy of economic rearmament then arises. In other words, was this political implementation of capitalism—in the new form of inducements—compatible with economic rearmament?

SCARCITY CONTROLS IN CAPITAL MARKETS

A depression does not produce universal surpluses; in fact, smaller countries suffer in two areas from scarcities. With a high degree of regularity, a fall in aggregate demand leads to a scarcity in foreign exchange and in readily investable loan capital. Exports tend to fall faster than imports, and a deficit in the balance of payments is created. Many borrowers lose their ability to service their debts, and creditors refuse to invest funds in the face of falling profits. Defaulted or postponed payments indicate a discrepancy between the values of the tangible assets of debtors and of the intangible property rights held by creditors. The result of these uneven movements in the flows of imports and exports, of credits and debts, is a disequilibrium in the balance of payments as well as in the financial ability of debtors and the rights of property holders.

The extent of the deficits was so great in the Germany of 1931 that the losses had to be assumed by the government. The credit crisis was met by declaring bank holidays, restricting withdrawals of deposits, and granting extensive government loans to the banks. The demand for funds was then reduced and the supply of funds increased, with the result that the credit crisis was significantly mitigated. Nevertheless, although the run on banks was stopped, their solvency did not help debtors. Since a large number of the still existing claims were frozen, the situation of illiquidity in short-term loans and the scarcity of loan capital continued to exist. How and why did this scarcity lead to direct controls in the capital market?

Government actions in money and capital markets were necessitated, on the one hand, by the great volume of frozen debts and, on the other, by the financial requirements of rearmament. The frozen debts and the high interest rates moved debtors to ask for governmental inducements; and the requirements of rearmament generated additional direct government controls. Both forms of direct action were undertaken at a time when the government was engaged in the extensive creation of new money.[10]

The scarcity of loan capital was the result of the flight of capital from Germany, the hoarding of funds at home, and the decline in the yield of real capital assets. Diminishing rates of gross profits prevented an increasing number of debtors from servicing their debts, and at the same time amortization schedules and interest rates were fixed by loan contracts. On the one hand, the adjustment of interest rates to the reduced level of profits was possible only with the consent of creditors; and on the other, the funds needed for the payment of premiums to creditors for voluntarily converting old into new loans were usually not accessible to debtors. As a result of the discrepancy between reduced profits and the high contractual rates of interest, many debtors defaulted on their obligations (either postponing payments or going into bankruptcy) while some creditors instituted foreclosure proceedings.

In 1931, the prevailing long-term rate of interest was 8 per cent. This rate became the target of a major attack by big and small business. Indebted farmers were especially infuriated by their debt burden. First the democratic and then the presidential cabinets of the Weimar Republic had been under pressure to adopt a policy of compulsory conversion. In December of 1931 came the first decree of a general compulsory reduction of interest rates for all domestic long-term loans. Private and public debtors were permitted to reduce their payments to 6 per cent, regardless of what was said in their loan contracts. A year later the government ordered a further reduction of interest for agricultural mortgages. The rate had to be reduced to 4 per cent within a period of two years. Subsequent loss of interest income adversely affected agricultural credit institutions, some of which survived only because of governmental subsidies. Compulsion was limited to the reduction in interest rates and was intended to lower the price of loan capital. The depression furnished the occasion for, and the pressure of organized debtors provided the immediate cause of, the rise of inducements in capital markets.

The Hitler government decreed two compulsory conversions in 1933. One reduced the debt burden of local governments, the other brought further relief to indebted farmers. Specific interest rates had now to be reduced. Individual debtors could ask for a lowering of their interest rates if they were actually or potentially insolvent. Creditors of local governments were forced to accept new loan certificates for old.[11] Refusal to accept the reduced rates had the effect of postponing the servicing of debts for five years. In the case of business firms, new contracts were negotiated between individual parties. If they could not come to an understanding, special governmental offices achieved a "compulsory adjustment." Although the rate of interest was reduced in all converted loans, the sum of the loan capital was also lowered in some of these loan contracts. The major portion of the capital lost was covered by a subsidy from the government; but some compulsory property losses were also imposed upon certain groups of creditors by the Nazified Ministry of Agriculture.

Direct control in the form of a reduction of interest rates, however, was not universal. There was a deliberate effort to increase the price of securities with fixed rates of interest in the security markets. Raising the yield of such securities was not accomplished through open-market operations, although the Central Bank had obtained authority to engage in such transactions in 1933. Schacht preferred to raise the prices of securities by ordering savings and commercial banks to reduce the rates of interest to their depositors. This and other related reductions brought the short-term loans into line with the lower level of interest for long-term loans.

In order that deposits might be diverted into the purchase of securities, their decline in value had to be reversed. This was accomplished through an embargo upon all new and converted issues of securities. Special permission to overcome this deterrent was granted only when the new securities did not threaten to cause a further decline in security prices. There was thus a dual price policy that guided the actions of the Central Bank. While the interest rates of short-term and long-term securities were directly and drastically reduced, the market prices of securities were raised by re-

ducing the quantities offered for sale. The aim of the price
inducement and the quantity deterrent was to overcome the
illiquidity of the banking system and to restore the functioning of the capital markets.

The dual price policy was successful. The index of securities with fixed interests rose from 80 at the end of 1933 to 96
in January of 1935, at which time the Central Bank decided
upon a large "compulsory conversion." All long-term domestic loans, except for the "industrials" of the manufacturing corporations, had to be exchanged for new titles if
their rate of interest was 6 per cent or more. The new certificates had to carry a rate of interest of 4.5 per cent. Creditors were not given much of a chance to ask for repayment
of their capital. They received a bonus of 2 per cent of the
nominal value of their loan capital if they consented to the
conversion.[12] By refusing, a creditor drew a penalty upon
himself. He could no longer trade his securities on the stock
exchanges or present them as collateral at the Central Bank.
The penalty was so effective that only one-fourth of 1 per
cent of the creditors refused to accept the conversion.[13] A
total of 8 billion private and municipal loans, and of 2 billion government bonds, were converted under the act of
1935. "Compulsory conversion" was undoubtedly a success.
Strangely enough, the market prices of the converted securities remained at the previous level, and the banks did not
have to keep up these prices by purchasing of securities.

Scarcity of investable funds, illiquidity of the banking system, unsalable securities, and low prices in capital markets
gave rise to governmental reduction of interest rates and an
embargo upon new issues of securities. Why did the Central
Bank adopt direct actions in order to fight these consequences
of the Great Depression? Why did the financial institutions of
private capitalism have to be rescued through a policy of
invigoration? Why were open-market operations not em-

ployed? Why was there no confidence in the liquidity-creating and interest-reducing effects of newly created money?

These questions call for an evaluation of the factors that gave rise to inducements and deterrents in money and capital markets. The objective causes lay in the extent of the liquidity crisis and in the flight of capital from the country. The subjective causes resided in the political power of well-organized debtors and in the determination of the state to reserve the capital market for the financing of rearmament. Objective scarcities required the government to act. The subjective power goal of the generals and the interest goals of debtor groups determined the direction as well as the methods of government policies.

Not the creditors but the debtors were wielding considerable power. Among the debtors, large landholders and Nazified farmers enjoyed direct access to the rulers. Influential landholders were close to the ear of President von Hindenburg and enjoyed the support of influential generals. Manufacturing concerns had close connections with the Central Bank. Nazified farmers employed their positions in the *Reich* Estate of Food to obtain relief from their debt burden, glorifying their purposes by voicing the Nazi ideology of breaking the "thralldom" of interests. The combined influence of the owners of big and medium-sized farms crystallized into an imperative for the government to reduce the rates of interest forthwith. Of even greater significance was the insistence of the generals upon a financial policy that would reserve the largest share of investable funds for rearmament. Illiquidity of the banking system had thus to be overcome without infringing upon the imperative that financing the military policy had first call upon investable funds. In this situation the Central Bank could not wait for the liquidity and unhoarding of the newly created money. Its interest policy was determined by the directive of implementing the military and political power goals of the coalition-state and the economic interest goals of indebted manufacturers, *Junkers* and Nazified farmers.[14]

Both goals called for the same action, namely a substantial reduction of the rates of interest. Lower rates facilitated the financing of rearmament and also minimized the interest burden for private concerns. But why was it necessary to pass three laws in the first month of 1935 which decreed a maximum long-term rate of 4.5 per cent and a short-term rate below 3 per cent?

The answer to this question is seemingly paradoxical. The quantity of money in circulation had actually risen from 5.6 to 10.4 billion marks in seven years (1932–38),[15] and the embargo on private issues was keeping down the demand for funds. Consequently, there was an increased supply of loanable funds which would have automatically led to lower interest rates if the creditors had agreed to accept a voluntary conversion. In this way, the institution of the long-term loan contract could have functioned without interference; but, in fact, the treasury and the private debtors were unwilling to pay creditors the traditional bonus for voluntary conversion. The severity of the two penalties set for those creditors who would not accept a reduction in interest at the time of the great conversion of 1935 and also the legalized refusal of the debtors to pay cash for nonconverted bonds suggest that the Central Bank did not expect creditors to accept a reduction of contractual rates voluntarily.

Two other hindrances to an automatic reduction of interest rates were the weak financial position of the big banks and their eagerness to raise their net incomes. Still suffering from the previous banking crisis, operating close to the margin of illiquidity, and seeing the volume of their commercial bills decline, bankers were very reluctant to reduce voluntarily the interest charged to their customers. The long tradition of fixing interest rates by cartel agreement provided the bankers with an effective means of defending their high interest rates. In the meantime, however, many indebted firms would have disappeared from the scene if corrective measures had not been taken.

Finally, the Central Bank and the generals were eagerly supporting the reinvesting of profits by private concerns.[16] This was accomplished by promoting a rising rate of realized profits and by lowering the current rates of interest. Self-financing became prevalent when the rates of profit exceeded the rates of interest. Ploughing back profits reduced the demand for funds and thereby reserved the loan capital for the financing of rearmament.

Fixing maximum interest rates was detrimental for creditors and bankers; yet these direct actions functioned as effective inducements for producers and debtors. From 1932 to 1936, the index of net interest charges for corporations fell from 100 to 45.[17] Just as wage fixing kept down unit labor costs, so did the ceiling on interest rates bring forth a decline in unit interest charges. Thus, the fixing of wages and interest rates, which had had a deterrent effect on consumption, also acted as an inducement to investment.

EXPROPRIATION AND EXPLOITATION

Much has been said about the "Schachtian devilries," as Mr. Harrod once described them.[18] Not infrequently, the "devil" theory implies that Schacht alone was responsible for the trade and debt policies of the Nazi regime. Actually Schacht's deftness in inventing instruments of expropriation, discrimination, and exploitation was as effective as it was only because the devaluations in foreign currencies diminished the chances for German exports and the rearmament policy substantially increased the import requirements of Germany.

Under the prevailing conditions, the military demand for

imports created a new crisis in foreign exchange and trade. Eighteen months after the appointment of the Hitler government, a break in economic relations with other countries occurred. The favorable trade balance of 667 million marks in 1933 turned into an unfavorable balance of 284 million marks in 1934. The allowance granted to German travellers in foreign countries was reduced from 200 to 50 marks per person. The quota of foreign money granted to importers was drastically reduced from 50 per cent of its level in 1931 to 5 per cent in August of 1934. Germany's currency reserve fell to 2.5 per cent of the notes in circulation. German clearing debts amounted to 450 million marks, so that, in effect, foreigners paid for the unfavorable balance by granting involuntary loans to Nazi Germany.

Two specific conditions were primarily responsible for this particular impasse. Foreign currency devaluations, especially that of the dollar in 1933, were responsible for the continued decline of world market prices, even though the decline in the number of jobs had come to an end, and employment rose slowly. These price movements intensified the disparity between German export prices and the prices for the same goods produced abroad. The higher German price level contributed appreciably to the decline in German exports and, in part, caused the unfavorable balance of trade.

The other condition resulted from the new regime's internal policy, which was dominated by the objective of rearmament. Rearmament had the effect of increasing the total value of imports by 243 million marks from 1933 to 1934, thus accounting for almost the entire total of the unfavorable balance of trade. The trade deficit was not caused by external or uncontrollable forces but was a product of the deliberately selected policy of the ruling groups in the regime. The new scarcity was self-inflicted and clearly endangered realization of the military goal. The dilemma facing the rulers had to be resolved either by keeping down the volume of armament orders or by forcing civilians and foreigners to assume involuntarily a portion of the burden of rearmament. The second alternative was the one adopted, and direct controls were assigned a new function. Rather than being used as equilibrating forces, direct controls were intended to make possible a continuous disequilibrium in the external balance of payments.

The impasse in foreign payments was overcome through two policies. One, initiated through a moratorium upon German obligations to foreign creditors, sought to reduce or cancel the foreign debt. The other went under the name of the New Plan and included a new technique of exchange control as well as of foreign trade control. What were the significance and effect of the new policy of defaulting deliberately on the foreign debt?

In its unilateral declaration of, first, a partial moratorium, in the summer of 1933, and, second, an absolute moratorium, in June of 1934, the German government produced a negative result which we may call the "debt effect." Default on the foreign debt arose when the German government refused to pay interest and amortization quotas to foreign creditors in their own currency. This transfer moratorium reduced the need for foreign exchange for "unproductive" purposes. If no compensation had been paid to creditors, the debt effect would have led to an expropriation of foreign capital by the German government.

Yet there was sufficient foreign pressure to obtain a partial servicing of some foreign loans. In addition, the Central Bank under Schacht sought to find, as a countermeasure to the foreign devaluations, some means of offsetting the decline of German exports caused by the pegging of the mark at the gold-parity level. "Selective depreciation" of securities held by foreigners was the method chosen for this purpose.[19] How and why did this method lead to an exploitation of foreign creditors?

The individual German debtors, whether private concerns or local governments, were not permitted to default on their foreign loans. Debtors were ordered by the German government to pay interest and amortization quotas to the *Konversionskasse,* a subsidiary of the Central Bank. These funds created accounts in the name of the foreign creditors. Consequently, when the accounts were frozen, responsibility for the action of defaulting was automatically assumed by the German state.

Frozen accounts furnished the basis for the issue of scrips, originally by agreement with foreign banks representing the foreign creditors, and as partial compensation for the interest paid by the German debtor. Later, subsidiary moneys were derived from other frozen accounts. These so-called blocked marks had two features in common. The subsidiary marks were transferable to other countries and salable in foreign markets. Yet they could be used in Germany only for the purchase of specifically designated German goods, or as payment for tourist or travel expenditures in Germany. Restricting and specifying the ultimate use of the blocked accounts produced the "barter effect": "additional exports" from Germany became the condition required of foreign creditors who wanted to realize a portion of the interest payments of their loans. By tying the subsidiary moneys to specific uses in Germany, the German government was availing itself of the opportunity to force foreign countries to buy additional exports, the volume of which rose from 2 per cent in 1932 to 14 per cent of total German exports in 1934.

The issuing of blocked marks created a special market for these subsidiary moneys abroad. Seemingly, the price at which the blocked marks were exchanged abroad was a result of the privately demanded and supplied quantities appearing in the new market. Actually, however, the ultimate quantities of blocked marks and of additional exports were determined by the German authorities. In manipulating these quantities on both sides of the same market, governmental agencies created the "involuntary subsidy effect." The prices of subsidiary moneys were deliberately kept down by issuing blocked marks in excess of existing opportunities for sale; in this way, foreigners were given an incentive to buy German goods and pay for them partly in blocked marks. The price of the registered mark in London (for use by tourists only) fell from 81 to 49 per cent of the official gold parity from the beginning of 1934 to the end of 1936. The declining price at which these subsidiary marks were sold to foreigners thus functioned as a "subsidy" for additional German sales and had to be shouldered by the foreign creditor.

The exploitation gain was divided among the foreign buyer, the German exporter, and the German government. Reduction in German export prices was usually less than the difference in value between the official and subsidiary foreign moneys, and a part of the price difference was collected as a devaluation gain by the state. The German exporter, when presenting blocked marks for cash at the Central Bank, had to forego a portion of his gain by making a stipulated payment to the Central Bank.[20] Since additional exports had to be paid for partly in foreign money, the additional exports still contributed to the Central Bank's supply of foreign exchange.

Although no reliable information is available on the total of the exploitation gain realized, there is little doubt that selected depreciation functioned as an effective countermeasure to the foreign currency devaluations and reduced their negative impact upon German export proceeds. In translating the political power of the state into effective economic power, Schacht was able to create the debt, barter, and "involuntary subsidy" effects.[21] Thus, the resultant exploitation of foreign capitalists helped to support the rearmament boom and became, under Schacht's leadership, an important forerunner of state-directed capitalism.

Another form of exploitation, this time of foreign traders or governments, arose in connection with the clearing and payment agreements. The clearing agreements were negotiated in response to the credit crisis of 1932–33; the payment agreements became very important after Schacht had imposed the absolute transfer moratorium in June of 1934.

Bilateral clearing agreements specified the total of goods that could be exchanged with other countries within a specified period of time. It was the task of the supervisory boards to enforce those provisions of the bilateral treaties which applied to Germany and which fixed the total attainable imports from, and the total of permissible exports to, the country concerned. Under any given treaty each board received a quota of import rights which it then had to divide among the various applicants under its jurisdiction. In spite of this extensive apparatus of regulation, Germany accumulated debts on current trade with treaty countries which hovered around 500 million marks a year.

The existence of clearing debts is attributable to three causes. Not all transactions were originally included in clearing agreements. Payment of these uncovered items appeared as a clearing debt. Similarly, the import rights of the various boards were not synchronized at the beginning, so that too many permits were issued for imports from a particular country. Both these deficiencies were removed in 1934. Yet the involuntary credits did not disappear in spite of these administrative improvements. If Schacht had so desired, he could have used the clearing offices and the supervisory boards as a means of keeping the clearing debts to an insignificant sum. Hence, the existence of clearing debts after 1934 must mean that Schacht deliberately made no provision for paying for German imports within a reasonable period of time. Thus, in the process of being exploited, the foreign country that traded with Germany involuntarily produced interest-free capital which covered the German deficit in the balance of payments.

Other countries fought the absolute moratorium and tried to check the rise of the clearing debts. Countries with which Germany had a favorable balance of trade insisted that a portion of the German export proceeds be reserved for debt service. Most of the West European countries fell into this group. These nations did obtain an exemption from the transfer moratorium because of their active trade balance. They withheld a portion of the payments for German goods in order to have funds with which to compensate their own nationals for the debt service refused by Germany. This withholding of funds was legalized by the payment agreements.

Success in undercutting the transfer moratorium produced the effect of reducing the volume of frozen accounts out of which German exports could be subsidized. At the same time, however, foreign governments became interested in maintaining the German export surplus so as to obtain funds for the compensation of creditors. Payment agreements could only reduce, not eliminate, involuntary credits made available by foreigners to Germany. Exploitation via such credits continued, but there was a shift to the weaker countries, whose share of the involuntary credits obtained by Germany increased in the subsequent years. Bilateral trade also reduced the range of choices and involved the purchase of substandard goods in excessive quantities, with the result that bilateralism diminished the benefits of trade and thus produced a "negative trade effect."

The exploitation of foreign creditors and traders was opposed by some German exporters. One of their spokesmen in the rearmament period was Geheimrat Buecher, head of the second largest electrical equipment concern in the country. In two memoranda written, respectively, in 1934 and

1935, Buecher proposed a fundamental change in Germany's economic policy, particularly in relation to the United States and France. He urged the government to adopt a policy of collaboration with the Western powers (*a*) by seeking to consolidate the old foreign debt, (*b*) by trying to obtain substantial gold loans from America and France in return for a devaluation of the German mark, (*c*) by negotiating new trade agreements with both countries in return for abolishing German exchange control, (*d*) by reducing the sale of government bills and bonds and dropping regulation of the money and capital markets, and (*e*) by working hard for a final understanding on the relative military strength of the respective powers. The last suggestion was specified as the indispensable condition for all other actions toward peaceful economic relations with other countries.[22]

It is very unlikely that the generals and the Nazis were impressed by these ideas, since their acceptance would have entailed a shift from a unilateral to a multilateral policy in foreign affairs. Schacht toyed with the idea of devaluating the currency in return for a gold loan in 1936, but the opportunity for reaching such an agreement was muffed. A year earlier, however, having rejected all of Buecher's proposals, Schacht had adopted the subsidy scheme for German exports and pointed proudly to his success in "settling accounts" with the foreign debtors.

The German foreign debt declined rapidly for several reasons: clearing agreements successfully counteracted the effect of currency devaluations in foreign countries; additional exports were financed out of frozen accounts; and German banks and industrial concerns were permitted to purchase securities in foreign markets. It was this last kind of debt reduction that involved a peculiar form of price discrimination.

The decline in the market price of the German foreign debt, as represented by securities in the possession of foreign countries, fell substantially owing to the depression. A further decline was caused by the exchange controls and the transfer moratorium, which eliminated or reduced the chances of ever getting a repayment of principal from the German state. Finally, when the market prices had reached an exceptionally low level, Schacht made foreign currency available to banks or exporters so that they could purchase a substantial portion of these foreign-held securities at the depressed price and resell them to the German debtor.[23] In permitting this differential between foreign and domestic prices, Schacht was, of course, allowing the German banks or exporters to realize an exceptional profit. According to the calculations of the Central Bank, these governmentally created discriminatory profits of the private banks had reached 90 million marks by March of 1935.[24]

In permitting the realization of such profits, Schacht coupled inducements with direct controls. The edict against amortization and interest payments on foreign loans would have enabled the Central Bank to fix the commission of the banks and to transfer the discriminatory gains to the treasury of the state. In allowing the banks or exporters to pocket a major portion of these profits and to use scarce foreign currency for this purpose, Schacht was, as we have seen, dispensing favors to private concerns. He utilized direct controls to create discriminatory profits and in this way strengthened the opposition of bankers and debtors to devaluation of the mark while at the same time weakening the position of the exporters, who wanted to devalue. It was not until September of 1935 that the economic group of the big banks agreed to pay half of the future discriminatory profits to the government; whereas payments by other groups had been made as early as July 1, 1935. This payment was the banking group's contribution to the fund for export subsidies.

Discrimination by means of state controls was thus at least as profitable as discrimination by means of private monopoly.

In fact, direct controls were able to overcome two limitations encountered by monopolies. First, the inherently weak position of the debtor was strengthened by direct controls; and, second, by depriving foreign creditors of a portion of their capital and also of their interest income, the state could deliberately depreciate the market values of the non-serviced securities in foreign countries. In this way, direct controls enabled the state to operate in foreign markets and to share the discriminatory profits with private banks and exporters at home, rather than with foreign cartels.

Of course, the gain would have been even greater if there had been no repurchase of the foreign securities at all. There were, however, three obstacles to total default: (1) the west European governments threatened to impose reprisals, in particular, to wipe out the German export surplus and thereby eliminate the chance for Germany to obtain any uncommitted foreign currency; (2) total default would have made it impossible to issue scrips and utilize the frozen accounts for subsidizing additional German exports; (3) refusal to repurchase the securities in foreign possession would have defeated Schacht's policy of coupling inducements to the banks with direct foreign-debt controls. Although the first two reasons carried greater weight in turning the scale towards a policy of partial default, the inducements were so effectively married with direct controls that the governmentally created profits satisfactorily compensated the bankers and some of the exporters for direct governmental intervention in their markets.

FOREIGN TRADE SUBSERVIENT
TO REARMAMENT

The external crisis of 1934 taught the German rulers that the type of foreign-trade control inherited from the depression was not serving the needs of their economic policy. During the Great Depression, direct control of foreign trade was primarily a device for protecting the currency. The volume of imports was restricted in proportion to the declining level of currency reserves. There was no specific reason to change the commodity composition of imports. In fact, governments under the Weimar Republic had limited themselves to imposing an equal percentage reduction from the level of 1931 upon all importers of comparable goods. Clearing agreements served for the most part to permit an exchange of goods between two countries in such a way that the respective payments did not involve a transfer of money between the countries. Regulation of foreign trade had thus been mainly a means of alleviating the depression-born scarcity of foreign currency.

Economic rearmament changed this situation. While most public works could be realized through the use of domestic resources, armament orders called for specific industrial raw materials that could be obtained only from foreign countries. That these armament orders generated a demand for specific imports is readily indicated by the volumes of particular raw materials imported. The figures in the following table definitely reveal a steady rise of imports. As the volume of investment and national income increased and the volume of imports rose, a continuing supply of so-called essential imports became indispensable for successful investments in producer-goods industries. How and why did the German economy become import-oriented under the Hitler regime?

Keynesian economics postulates an inverse relationship between imports and investments below the level of full employment; an increase in imports will have a depressing effect upon investments and the level of employment. The smaller the volume of imports, the greater the volume of investments. If this thesis were universally correct, then the imports in the preceding table should have either fallen or remained stable until the level of full employment was reached in 1936. The steady rise of the armament-oriented imports shows that the

IMPORTS OF PRINCIPAL ALLOY METALS*
(in metric tons)

Years	Chrome Ore	Manganese Ore	Nickel Ore	Tungsten Concentrates
1934	76,979	224,745	4,400	4,385
1935	95,435	394,255	5,200	7,881
1936	123,369	229,634	5,500	8,726
1937	132,156	554,170	8,000	11,373
1938	176,398	425,785	9,000	14,200

* *Effects of Strategic Bombing on the German War Economy,*
Washington, 1945, p. 247.

Keynesian theory is not applicable to the rearmament boom. Why then was there a necessary and positive relationship between imports and investments in Germany at this time?

Speaking of the recovery after World War II, Hirschman has observed that the causal relationship between imports and investments is positive "when the net imports, because of their 'bottleneck' nature, permit use of large quantities of hitherto unused domestic labor and raw materials in reconstruction and investment activities while individual savings are at very low levels."[25] This positive relationship was previously overlooked because Keynes failed to subdivide total imports into certain groups according to their uses (e.g., "recovery imports"). Equally important is the fact that he had no theory of the physical structure of production, which alone can enable us to see the mutual dependency between domestic and foreign items in industrial countries whenever they do not have the natural endowment and productive facilities necessary to supply the required raw materials, whether for rearmament or recovery, and must therefore import the needed real capital as a condition for domestic investment.

The positive import-investment relationship was also in evidence in the situation of import cuts, generated by the foreign-exchange crisis of 1934. A decline of imports reduced the level of employment in the textile industry and eliminated many of the stocks of foreign raw materials essential for rearmament. This decline of essential imports "directly endangered the rearmament of the armed forces," and led to a series of significant decisions.[26] There was no willingness to tolerate any modification of military plans for the economy. These plans were regarded as categorical requirements that had to be fulfilled, regardless of cost. Any threat to rearmament plans galvanized the strategically placed generals into action. Their opposition to Dr. Schmitt, Minister of Economics, because of his reluctance to promote the production of synthetics at home, culminated in the determination to remove him from his position. As we have seen previously, this political intervention on the part of the Minister of War was successful.[27] In his demand for an economic dictator, General Thomas outlined an economic program that centered on the supply of militarily indispensable raw materials. Thomas called for (*a*) a central agency for the planning and direction of all foreign trade, (*b*) state trade monopolies of all militarily important raw materials, (*c*) an extensive quota system for importing, stocking and using essential raw materials, (*d*) a detailed program for the production of essential domestic raw materials, (*e*) a precautionary program for meeting the grain deficit expected to arise from the poor crop of 1934, and (*f*) an intensive propaganda program to prepare the public for the inevitable restrictions of domestic consumption.[28]

These demands of the military leaders became the frame of reference for Schacht's subsequent foreign trade policy. The "New Plan" of September, 1934, provided the central agency for the over-all planning of foreign trade. The greatly enlarged network of supervisory boards imposed the quota system for most imported goods. A new program for the development of natural and synthetic oil from domestic sources was adopted, the administration of which was put in the hands of military officers.[29] Schacht rejected the idea of state trade monopolies, yet it was readily accepted by the Nazified Ministry of Agriculture, whose trade monopolies engaged in bulk purchases of certain agricultural goods.[30]

How did the New Plan and the system of import quotas try to satisfy the import requirements of economic rearmament after the impasse of 1934? The first step was a reorganization of government agencies and a modification of the principles of direct import controls. Each main industrial network came under the direction of a supervisory board, and the total number of these boards was increased to twenty-seven, with each administratively responsible to the Minister of Economics. Formerly, import quotas had been granted by the boards up to the amount of foreign exchange available, but now they were given additional instructions to engage in a policy of selective quantity discrimination by imposing nonproportional import restrictions. Rather than evaluating the requests of importers on the basis of their former trading positions, the boards allotted available foreign currency according to the principle of priority. First preference was given to raw materials required by the armament industries: second, to raw materials imported for heavy industries; third, to raw materials for the export industries; and fourth, to essential food items that had to be imported from other countries.

In addition to implementing priority, the supervisory boards were ordered to examine most of the requests individually. Not only the quantity of goods to be imported, but also the price to be paid, the quality to be selected, the country of origin, and the method of payment to be chosen were checked upon whenever there seemed to be any advantage in doing so. In this way, the boards acted as a brake against avoidable price increases, changed the commodity composition of imports, facilitated the desired geographical redirection of trade, and enforced many of the clearing and payment agreements with other countries. The boards were especially successful in changing the composition of goods, as can be seen from the relative position of raw materials and foodstuffs in imports.

CHANGES IN THE COMPOSITION OF GERMAN IMPORTS*
(in million marks)

Years	Total Imports	TOTAL FOOD		RAW MATERIALS	
		Value	Per Cent	Value	Per Cent
1929	13,446.8	5,380.6	40.0	3,927.4	29.2
1930	10,393.1	4,229.7	40.7	2,904.4	27.9
1931	6,727.1	2,783.2	41.4	1,832.2	27.2
1932	4,666.5	2,132.7	45.7	1,271.7	27.3
1933	4,203.6	1,629.7	38.8	1,367.6	32.5
1934	4,451.0	1,543.2	34.7	1,540.7	34.6
1935	4,158.7	1,435.2	34.5	1,567.9	37.7
1936	4,158.4	1,499.4	35.5	1,571.1	37.2

* *Statistisches Jahrbuch für das Deutsche Reich* (Berlin, 1938).

From 1929 to 1933, the total value of imports fell faster than that of exports. In 1934, the decline in total exports continued but total imports rose because of an increased import of raw materials. The percentage of raw-material imports in total imports rose from 27.3 in 1932 to 37.3 in 1936, while that of foodstuffs fell from 45.7 to 35.5 in the same period. Quantity discrimination by the supervisory boards was largely responsible for the reduction of food imports and for the increase of raw-materials import during the rearmament boom.

Of course, any cycle brings forth a change in the composition of foreign trade. The percentage of raw materials falls faster in the downswing and rises faster in the upswing of a cycle than does the percentage of foodstuffs in total imports. Yet this cyclical discrepancy between the two components of imports was greatly magnified by discriminatory direct controls. In terms of value, total imports during the rearmament period remained fairly close to the level of the depression, whereas the quantities of raw materials rose far beyond the usual rate of increase of the upswing. Yet this increase did not benefit all producers simultaneously, or uniformly. Imports of raw materials for the textile industry were cut down, whereas those for the heavy industries rose substantially, in some cases extraordinarily. Direct controls thus became associated with deterrents. Because of nonproportional quotas, producers and consumers in some of the consumer-goods' industries experienced a considerable restriction of their output and employment opportunities. This was not true, however, of the producer-goods industries, since most of the import demands of these producers were satisfied through the discriminatory direct controls of the government, which therefore served, in effect, as inducements. Since big business predominated in the producer-goods industries and small business in the consumer-goods industries, these discriminatory direct controls amounted to a class administration by the government.

The second task of the reorganized trade controls was to impose a geographical redistribution of trade. Under Schacht, Germany shifted an increasing portion of its trade to the Balkan and the South American countries. From 1933 to 1937, Germany raised her imports from 288.6 million marks to 732.2 million and her exports from 241.2 million to 518.1 million in her trade with South America. Unhappily, this increase meant a rise in Germany's unfavorable annual balance of trade from 47.4 to 214.1 million marks. Germany had thus found new markets for her imported raw materials, many of which had formerly come from the United States; yet she had lost most of her European export surplus, out of which the unfavorable balance in the overseas trade had been covered.

This imbalance resulted in an increase in involuntary clearing debts, which led, in turn, to temporary interruptions of trade that lasted until the debt was at any given time reduced. Trade with South America was therefore carried on for the most part by means of special deals and, since there was never a sufficient surplus of foreign exchange, was at no time during the Nazi regime put on a sound basis.

The drive into the Balkans produced a similar effect. Both imports and exports rose. From 1933 to 1936, German imports increased from 236.4 to 505.4 million marks and her exports from 190.6 to 454.3 million marks in her trade with southeastern Europe. At the same time, Germany's unfavorable balance of trade rose from 45.8 to 51.1 million marks. In the years 1934 and 1935, the German trade deficit was almost 100 million marks. This deficit, too, was covered by the trade partners in the form of involuntary loans. Consequently, a surplus of German imports was created even though there had formerly been an export surplus.

In German trade with Western Europe there was an overall shrinkage rather than an increase. From 1933 to 1936, German imports fell from 875.7 to 775.9 million marks whereas her exports declined from 2,274.5 to 1,492.8 million marks—and the export surplus for those four years from 1,398.9 to 716.9 million marks.[31] Even this reduced surplus did not accrue to Germany as freely spendable foreign currency because a portion was reserved for the payment of interest and amortization to creditors. This decline in the amount of spendable currency prevented Germany from paying for the rising import surpluses, and elements of statism were introduced to make up the deficit funds in foreign currency.

The clearing-trade system was modified so as to provide a continuous import surplus. Under the Weimar Republic the main functions of clearing agreements had been to finance trade without any transfer of funds to other countries and to balance the values of goods being exchanged. Under Schacht, however, the balancing function of the agreements was de-

liberately replaced by systematically creating import surpluses. The technique of the supervisory boards was to overissue import permits beyond the targets set in the agreements. Instead of being restrictive, the Germans usually favored a greater volume in the next negotiations and then
issued permits in excess of the trade figures agreed to. Other
countries either had to restrict their exports or were forced
to grant involuntary loans, thereby covering the German
import surplus. If neither alternative was acceptable, the
other countries had to buy more German goods.

The rise of German exports in bilateral trade resulted
primarily from the state-imposed requirement of centralized
payments. Importers from clearing countries did not pay
directly to the foreign seller but to a German clearing agency
which used these funds to compensate the respective native
exporters. The use of a central payment device in such
clearing arrangements was translated into an opening wedge
for German exports. This was made possible by the incon-
vertibility of clearing rights. Accumulated clearing rights,
arising from a German import surplus, could be used for one
purpose only—for the purchase of additional goods from Germany. The combination of overissued permits and inconvertible excess clearing rights functioned as an effective promoter of German exports.[32] These statist elements, which
served to establish preferential markets, thus operated as
inducements for German firms to export additional goods.

The countries of Western Europe could not be subjected
to a similar pressure because the German export surplus could
not be maintained or increased unless foreigners were willing to purchase German goods. This willingness declined
significantly when British and American export prices were
reduced after the respective currency devaluations in the
two countries. At first, "additional" exports were subsidized
out of the gains derived from the discounts on scrips or
bonds, but as the volume of salable scrips declined, the lower

prices of the "additional" exports tended to reduce also the prices of the "regular" exports. In 1935 a different source for the payment of subsidies had to be found that would not intensify price competition among German exporters.

Export business groups demanded either an open or a concealed devaluation, and all kinds of plans were presented to the authorities. The proposal to allow exporters to sell their foreign currency either on an open market or at a premium to the Central Bank was widely favored. Higher prices for foreign currency were justified as a profit incentive to increase the volume of exports and thus raise the supply of foreign currency. Private speculation in the price of foreign currency was thus said to be identical with the public interest of the country.[33] These plans were rejected, however, because they would have been the first step toward devaluation; they would have raised import prices but would still have provided no assurance for higher export proceeds.

In May of 1935 a peculiar levy was imposed upon German firms active in domestic markets. This levy, amounting to a 2 or 3 per cent tax on the sales volume, was collected not by the government but by the economic groups of business. Each group had to pay a lump sum to the state and divided the amount payable among its members by allowing each an exemption for 15,000 marks of sales per year. None of the firms was permitted to raise prices to compensate for the levy.[34]

The payment of subsidies was coupled with an examination of export prices. Each business group had to establish an office for price examination which was responsible only to the Ministry of Economics. A price office engaged in sample studies of unit costs and prices to ascertain the extent of the loss suffered in a typical export transaction involving a specific product. Firms could receive the subsidy only if (*a*) the export proceeds had been sold to the Central Bank and (*b*) if the price office had certified that the export price

charged was satisfactory. The threat of the Ministry to refuse
a subsidy if goods were offered at cutthroat prices had the
effect of either enabling existing export cartels to enforce
their prices or of forming new export cartels that set prices
for their members.[35]

There was thus a striking similarity between import and
export controls, in that both tended to increase the volume
of goods traded. Direct controls or supplementary action by
the state mitigated or removed the deterrent effect involved
in import permits or in an overvalued currency. In raising
the quantities of essential imports as well as of exports involved in the clearing-trade system, the government transformed losses into profits for most concerns. Having no control over the quantities of goods sold in areas readily accessible to Anglo-American exporters, Schacht used the subsidies
and the strengthened export cartels to sustain or raise the
prices of German exports. This combination of promotional
and monopolistic devices had the effect of removing the hur-
dle of an overvalued currency and still permitted exporters
to realize a sufficient rate of profit. Direct control of foreign
trade was thus not incompatible with the profit principle.[36]

In the spring of 1936, about 60 per cent of the exports received a governmental subsidy, the extent of which varied
from 10 to 35 per cent of the profitable export price, as determined on the basis of the revenue from sale and the subsidy.[37]
The payment of subsidies, of course, constituted a loss for Germany. Equally unprofitable during the period of rearmament
were many of the projects for the building up of synthetics
industries. These subsidies to exporters and developers of
new industries, whether paid by non-exporting firms or the
government, reduced the real funds for rearmament. The
net gain derived from the favorable terms of trade (discussed in Chapter VII) were thus reduced by the amount of
subsidies paid by non-exporting producers. There seems little
doubt that even for the rearmament period, the "Schachtian

deviltries" were distinctly profitable for private business as well as beneficial for Nazi Germany.

Several conclusions may be drawn from the foregoing discussion. First, the impact of direct controls and capitalist invigoration on the German economy seemed at first to be limited in effect to the implementation of this particular policy. The number of markets affected, and the number of direct controls imposed, was small, and, in form and extent, the controls themselves appeared to many businessmen to be temporary in nature. Furthermore, state economic rearmament proved to be profitable to the largest concerns and seemed to most of them to be simply a program for economic recovery. Finally, direct controls were so effectively compensated for by inducements and monopolistic advantages that big business felt no infringement of its economic interests and thus failed to recognize the first signs of state-directed capitalism. Thus, the combined effect of rearmament in rebuilding markets, in restoring profits, and in finding induce-ments to compensate for direct controls produced the strange but significant result that the original elements of statism in the Nazi economy were simply not opposed by organized big business.

DIRECT CONTROLS FOR PRIVATE AND PUBLIC GOALS

Analysis of direct controls and inducements in the first phase of the Nazi regime clearly reveals the validity of our distinction between direct actions for public and private goals. For each kind of direct action we can locate the specific causes or goals, indicate the methods of operation or organization, and assess the effects or benefits, for the private as well as for the public sector of the economy. But why did many businessmen fail to understand the distinction between inducements and direct controls and underestimate their duration? At which particular point did the one shade into the other? Did direct controls constitute a necessary condition for the granting of inducements?

During the Great Depression, the currency and credit crises not only imposed undesired direct controls but also gave rise to three new economic institutions, all of which were implemented by means of direct actions on the part of the state. Foreign-exchange control—the first institution—required unauthorized holders of foreign money or gold to surrender it to the Central Bank and imposed a quota system on all purchases of foreign money. Trade and capital controls—the second institution—necessitated the use of specific permits for the purchase of goods and put increasingly numerous restrictions on the export of capital located in Germany. Both of these new institutions effectively protected the currency but failed to halt the decline in German exports. The third institution arose in the clearing (and barter) trade. This institution involved the use of global quotas that were intended to balance the trade between any two participants (i.e., Germany and one other country) and, by means of centralized payments, eliminated any flow of money from one country to the other.

The three new institutions became significant features of statism because they created deterrents to private actions. Importers and exporters as well as creditors and bankers were suffering from restrictions in two specific ways: Certain specified actions were entirely prohibited, while many of the permitted actions became less profitable. These deterrents were a necessary, although undesired, consequence of governmental actions which were successful only to the extent that the corresponding negative effects actually took place. In fact, these two deterrents became the essential determinants of statism in the external economy. Thus, the three new institutions—all created by the depression—were regarded as statist because they imposed prohibitions and profit restrictions on certain forms of private enterprise.

At the same time, however, these same institutions created, as a side effect, important benefits for other business groups. Restrictions upon imports granted an effective protection for industries that would otherwise have suffered from foreign competition. The statist institutions acted here as a substitute for a high tariff wall. Equally, restrictions upon capital exports and the related standstill agreements with foreign creditors protected German debtors against the withdrawal of foreign loans from Germany. Indeed, when such protection was not forthcoming or was insufficient, business organizations asked for additional protection. In granting such requests the government employed other direct controls which were accepted by the business groups concerned as new devices for business promotionalism—instead of being condemned as manifestations of statism.

Thus there arose a new criterion for the definition of economic statism. Direct controls appeared to the economists as being destructive of capitalism because through price and quantity decisions the state destroyed private markets (see p. 354 above). For businessmen, however, the central point was not the right to determine prices and quantities but the effect of governmental action on their profit and investment opportunities. In using the profit criterion as their standard of judgment, direct actions by the state restricting their profit chances appeared to them as statism, whereas direct controls providing protection or new opportunities were seen as invigorations of capitalist institutions and as benefits for private enterprise.

This intellectual experience of the Great Depression exerted a re-educating effect upon many businessmen in their attitude to the economic functions of the state. They saw no reason for objecting to economic rearmament provided that any direct controls were coupled with inducements or compensations for themselves.

Creation of the rearmament boom called for a significant modification of the depression-created institutions. Rather than minimizing the impact of the credit crisis, the function of the new institutions was to insulate the German economy from the world and thereby provide the conditions for an independent rearmament boom. Punishment for violation of the intensified restrictions on handling foreign money became so severe that even the black markets for German money abroad disappeared. The principle of equal treatment was replaced by nonproportional import quotas which turned out to be an appropriate device for discriminating against the import of industrial consumer goods and for speeding up imports of military significance. The institution of the clearing trade was transformed into a method of exploiting foreign traders or creditors. Default on the foreign debt became the new institution for systematically exploiting foreign creditors. An excessively contrived issue of scrips became the means by which the exploitation gains had the effect of subsidizing German exports. In being cut off from their defensive origin, the formerly restrictive institutions now became a means of economic aggression by which trade was deliberately expanded through the devices of discrimination and exploitation.

There arose thus a difference between the restrictive statist institutions of the depression and the refurbished discriminatory institutions of the rearmament boom. In the latter period, restriction was still applied to German concerns, whereas discrimination and exploitation were practiced primarily against foreigners. Yet neither of these institutions was as extreme as the statism applied by the Nazi party to German workers, who were subjected to domination and exploitation as well as to the constant threat of physical torture. Economic statism was limited to the three fields of industrial relations, capital markets, and foreign exchange and trade. In each of these spheres, economic statism was not of the same intensity nor did it entail the same degree of privation or the same kind of detrimental effects. It was this limited and differentiated type of statism that prevailed as a minor feature of the economy in the first period of the Nazi regime.

Economic statism transformed especially the nature of the public sector of the economy. At its center were the economic establishments of the armed forces, which not only increased their stocks of military equipment and weapons but also obtained property rights in the facilities for procuring goods and services of military significance. The military establishment was surrounded by the statist economic institutions that operated in the market areas of foreign exchange, foreign trade, and international finance. The military establishment was also effectively assisted in the financing of its activities by the other ministries of the state. Most important here were the Central Bank and the Ministry of Finance, both of which were responsible for new statist institutions that became of increasing significance in the money and securities markets. Thus, in militarizing the public sector of the economy, the state widened the public economy by creating new statist institutions that functioned as instruments for controlling the six markets. While private units still did most of the business in these controlled markets, they constituted an area of government influence that lay between the public and the private sectors of the economy.

It was the development of this governmentally controlled area that was the source of much misunderstanding by business leaders and other observers at the time. The numerous efforts to identify this controlled area either with the sector of private cartels or with the public sector of the state were unsatisfactory then and today must be regarded as untenable. It was the mingling of the capitalist institutions of export cartels and profitability, via inducements and compensations, and the statist institutions of restriction, discrimination, exploitation, and domination that prevents us from assigning this controlled area to either the private or the public sector of the economy. The question thus arises as to why and how this peculiar mixture of elements of two distinctly different economic systems did occur. Once established, did the controlled area remain neutral relative to the private and public sectors of the economy? Or did the application of direct controls modify the nature of organized capitalism and also change the character of the state?

REARMAMENT MODIFIES CAPITALISM

CHAPTER TEN

Broadly speaking, the economic policies of the Nazi regime in the first phase fell under four headings: economic rearmament, the invigoration of capitalist institutions, the fight for or against middle-class socialism, and the suppression of trade unions. Our analysis of the first three policies revealed a two-fold relationship between big business and the Nazi party. There was simultaneously a relationship of collaboration as well as of opposition between the two power blocs. How was such a paradoxical situation possible?

The opposition of big business to the Nazis was both fundamental and incidental. Fundamental opposition was primarily economic and was directed almost exclusively against the middle-class socialism of Nazified small business. The counterrevolutionary program of economic reform tried to realize a pre-capitalist type of economic organization, in which the craftwork of the artisan would hold a position of central importance and quality products would be exchanged

453

according to the rule of a guild-regulated market. Middle-class socialism thus aimed at the elimination of capitalist enterprise as well as the capitalist market. It is in terms of this fundamental conflict that we can speak of big business *versus* the Nazis. The fundamental conflict was thus not directed against the Nazi party as such but only against the Nazified guilds and their ideology of middle-class socialism.

In spite of its fervor and great political significance, the counterrevolutionary reform program produced no striking change in any of the basic capitalist institutions. On the contrary, in defeating the Nazified small-business organizations, big business succeeded in getting two capitalist institutions well established in the field of small business. One was the cartel. Compulsory cartels as well as exclusive delivery contracts between the cartels of big and small business functioned as additional devices to overcome the large number of small producers and to counteract the lack of organization, which had hitherto prevented the rise of effective cartels in small business. The other capitalist institution was book-keeping and capital accounting. The compulsory groups of small business were the means by which this device was generally introduced and enforced in small business.[1] Fundamental opposition was thus successful. Rather than limiting capitalist institutions to the sphere of big business, the latter succeeded in extending capitalist institutions to the field of small business. Middle-class socialism did not modify private capitalism.

Strange as it may seem, it was the collaboration of big business with its two allies, the generals and the Nazi party, that was productive of a significant modification of private capitalism. The coalition goals of rearmament and political dictatorship produced a sixfold alteration of capitalist institutions during the first phase of the Nazi regime. We are referring to:

1) Suppression of trade unions and the restoring of the employers' managerial prerogative in industrial relations.
2) Acceptance of the principle of compulsion in private organizations for market control, whether for the purpose of eliminating all outsiders or of imposing cartels upon small business and making them submissive to the cartels of big business.
3) The use of inducements by which governmental agencies, using direct controls, could channel favors to particular business groups with a view to invigorating particular institutions of capitalism.
4) The replacement of voluntary trade associations with compulsory economic groups.
5) Expansion of the noncapitalistic institution of public investment with a view to facilitating rearmament.
6) Acceptance and intensification of specific direct controls in a few markets, through the use of which funds and essential raw materials for rearmament were allocated by governmental decisions.

The first three alterations were demanded by big business itself. The desire of corporate controllers to modify the existing capitalism grew out of two experiences. The Great Depression created a twofold threat to the existing capital structure of private enterprise and to the prevailing system of voluntary cartels. This threat gave rise to the demand for compulsory cartels as well as to a governmental policy that modified the rules of indebtedness and thereby prevented bankruptcy. Governmental inducements and compulsory cartels thus became two business-sponsored goals of governmental policies that originated in response to the Great Depression.

The goal of restoring the managerial prerogative was nurtured by the determination to return to a pre-union situation in which laborers were hired on individual contracts and were economically dependent upon the directives of the employer and subject to his control. At the time of the Great Depression, when trade unions were strong enough to prevent many employers from reducing their wage costs and thereby passing on the losses of the depression to the workers, this determination to suppress trade unionism was merely intensified. The suppression of the unions was in fact a long-range goal of big business which could be realized only through political dictatorship and, specifically, with the political and police assistance of the Nazi party.

The last three changes resulted from the military goals of the regime. Although favored by all three allies, the generals were the most precise formulators, and the Nazis the loudest promotors, of the military goals. The economic proposals inferred from these military aims were investigated and directed primarily by the War Ministry. The effect of public investment, compulsory trade associations, and the use of direct controls in a few markets was to impose military demands upon the economy. Big business accepted these demands, even though each of them involved a significant modification of private capitalism. The reason for the acceptance or toleration lay in the fact that these three noncapitalist institutions were essential for implementing the rearmament boom. The orders and profits created by this boom were so urgently desired by big business that the three alterations were accepted—enthusiastically or grudgingly—as a price necessary to restore profits to private enterprise.

The cost of prosperity was regarded as reasonable because the changes were widely believed to be temporary deviations from private capitalism. Direct controls in foreign trade and exchange were expected to disappear soon after Germany had again become a great power, in full command of its own sphere of foreign trade. Public investment was expected to diminish as soon as the rearmament program had been completed. The use of compulsion in trade associations was seen to be compatible with the ability of businessmen to represent their economic interests collectively in the political sphere. Owing to these expectations, some businessmen felt that many of the alterations would either disappear after a period of rearmament or that the rearmament would liquidate itself. Others believed that private capitalism could readily adjust itself to the military goals of the regime without entailing any structural changes of the economy itself. How accurate were these assessments of the impact of rearmament and political dictatorship upon private capitalism?

As we have seen, the alterations divided the economy into a private sector of organized capitalism and a public sector of state-directed capitalism. Did these sectors exist separately or did there develop a pattern of mutual interaction? Was the state sector necessarily and always superior to the private sector? Did the requirements of the public sector weaken the principles and undermine the operation of organized capitalism? The purpose of this chapter is to answer these questions by examining the relationship between privately organized capitalism and publicly directed state capitalism.[2]

PRIVATE OR PUBLIC PROPERTY?

The financing of rearmament gave rise to the militarized institution of public property. Since private ownership in the means of production is one of the most essential features of any form of capitalism, one may ask whether this new kind of public property constituted a threat or was fully compatible with capitalist ownership of productive facilities.

Government financing of rearmament called for loan capital which was obtained either from the money or the capital market. The volume of credits required was determined by the financial plans of the armed forces, minus the tax receipts devoted to rearmament.[3] The net volume of short-term credits constituted the target plan for the volume of long-term credits to be obtained through the sale of government bonds. These financial plans represented the time schedules for the Central Bank according to which the bank had to issue the bills and bonds and sell them in the markets.

The relative magnitudes for borrowing can be seen from the financial plan of December 31, 1935.

FINANCIAL PLAN FOR REARMAMENT, 1933-36*
(in billion marks)

Bills for Work Creation and Armament Orders to December, 1935	4.87
Bills for the Autobahn, to the end of 1935	0.78
Estimated Funds for Armament and Autobahn, 1936	3.25
Total of Bonds to be Sold in Capital Market	8.90

* See Wi/IF 5.1504, roll 289, T-77.

The amount of capital saved annually was estimated to vary between 1.75 and 1.9 billion marks. Hence, the bond sales needed for a total bond issue of 8.9 billion marks in the capital markets would have absorbed all of whatever capital was saved in the following years, from 1936 to 1940. In addition, it was anticipated that the budgets of 1935–36 and 1936–37 would lead to a deficit of 4.71 billion marks. The total of loan capital to be obtained for the rearmament phase thus rose to 13.61 billion marks. The financial plan of 1936 called for a staggered bond issue, the total amount of which equalled the anticipated savings of seven subsequent years. Was it possible to realize this plan?

The short-term financing was primarily a function of money creation. The idea was that the government would "pre-finance" the armament orders and "repay" through a subsequent sale of bonds which would return the additional money to the government. Rather than compensate producers with newly printed banknotes for their products, the Central

Bank relied upon the device of mefo-bills.[4] A special company was formed, known as the *Gesellschaft für Metallforschung,* whose founders were the Central Bank, the Ministry
of Defense, and the four armament producers—Krupp, Sie-
mens, Rheinmetall, and Deutsche Werke. Capital in the
amount of one million marks was supplied in equal shares by
the four armament concerns. The method of payment was
quite simple. Armament producers received mefo-bills in
payment for their goods. When accepted and endorsed by the
Metallforschung, the bills went to commercial banks as if
they were ordinary bills. The Central Bank supported these
bills by accepting them as collateral for short-term loans. Endorsement and collateral by government agencies were thus
the means by which the armament bills became similar to
commercial bills.

This direct increase in the supply of new money was partly
offset by additional bill transactions in the opposite direction.
The Central Bank sold blocked bills, and its subsidiary, the
Golddiskontbank, sold sola-bills. Purchase of these bills by
commercial banks brought money back to the Central Bank,
thereby reducing the volume of additionally supplied money.
These backflowing funds were used to transfer mefo-bills to
the *Golddiskontbank* bank, or the blocked bills, when sold,
served to offset the purchased mefo-bills in the balance sheet
of the Central Bank. The banks, in turn, counted these special bills as substitutes for commercial bills, which helped to
satisfy the liquidity requirements of the banking law.
Through this manipulation of bills not less than a total of
6 million marks, or 50 per cent of the mefo-bills issued by
1938, were sold by the private banks.[5] The secondary impact
of deficit financing via mefo-bills was thus substantially reduced. These efforts to reduce the multiplier effect of new
money were deliberate. Neither Schacht nor the generals
were interested in seeing the flow of new money used to
finance an increased production of consumer goods.

In addition, Schacht coupled money creation via bills with the practice of extending inducements to private banks. The sale of sola and blocked bills to private banks was accompanied by a significant subsidy. This was accomplished through an adroit fixing of the relevant interest rates. The discount rate of the private banks gradually fell to 2⅞ per cent, which had to be paid by those selling commercial bills to the banks. The sola and blocked bills, on the other hand, carried an interest rate of 3¾ or 3⅞ per cent. By creating a significant price differential between the bills of private banks and government bills, the Central Bank in effect granted a subsidy to private banks. This subsidy had to be covered by the treasury, which paid 4 per cent for the mefo-bills held by the Central Bank. Inducements to buy special bills were thus created by direct controls which fixed the price of mefo-bills as well as of blocked and sola bills. Government-created bills filled the vaults of the commercial banks, which were thereby compensated for the decline of their business with private concerns. By March of 1938, a total of 12 billion marks in mefo-bills had been used to finance rearmament.

The sale of government bonds was promoted by two forms of direct control. The first related to the embargo upon newly issued securities; the second, to the imposition of purchasing quotas for government bonds.

The embargo in the security markets made its appearance in 1931. In August of 1931, municipal governments were forbidden to place new bonds upon the market. In December of the same year, the same restriction was placed upon the sale of mortgage securities by financial institutions. The primary motive for these embargoes, however, was to preserve the financial solvency of creditors. A further decline in the market prices of securities would have had a detrimental impact upon financial institutions and would have intensified the banking crisis.

Quite different was the purpose of the new embargo announced in May of 1933 by the Hitler government. In October of 1933, the listing committees of the stock exchanges were directed to present all applications for the introduction of new securities to a committee of the Central Bank for review. Non-listed securities of corporations were brought under control in May of 1934. Supervisory bodies checked on the purchases of new securities by insurance companies and other financial institutions. In December of 1934, requirements for admission to trading in the stock exchanges were tightened. The minimum nominal value for the trading of an issued was raised from 500,000 to 1,500,000 marks by the stock exchange of Berlin; and the number of exchanges was reduced from twenty-one to nine so that government control over trading on the exchange might be increased and speculative dealings prevented.[6]

Why an embargo upon issues and restrictions upon trading in new securities? Interest in a genuine recovery would have welcomed such sales and facilitated their introduction through appropriate open-market operations. The government's intention is revealed by the imposition of a ceiling on dividends. Corporate requirements for new capital were to be financed out of the undistributed profits of private business. Investable funds in the capital markets had to be reserved first for the compulsory conversion of 1935—when many outstanding bonds had to be exchanged against new ones—and second for the purchase of government bonds, the purpose of which was to finance rearmament.

Yet the exclusion of private demand for investable funds was not enough, because the financial requirements of rearmament exceeded the prevailing amount of newly formed capital. As a result, new issues of government bonds could not be fully placed with private institutions, especially since the interest was set at the prevailing rate of 4.5 per cent. Unsold portions of the first issue were then allotted to private institutions, thereby giving rise to the second form of direct control, the use of purchasing quotas for government bonds. Naturally, the quota increased the amount of salable bonds beyond the quantity that would have been voluntarily acquired. At first the allotted portions were placed by agreement between the Central Bank and the groups of different kinds of banks. Later on the quotas were set by unilateral government order.

Beginning in January, 1935, one particular issue, the so-called liquidity bond, was placed with savings banks and insurance companies only. The liquidity requirements were changed, and savings banks were required to regard government bonds as a part of their liquid assets, up to 50 per cent of the legal requirement. Private insurance companies were authorized to purchase government bonds for permanent investment, whereas before 1933 only mortgage bonds could be purchased for such a purpose. Social insurance companies prior to 1933 could purchase bonds of the *Reich* only up to 25 per cent of their invested funds. By 1938 not less than 75 per cent of the annual accrual to the reserves had to be invested in government bonds, the volume of which could go up to 50 per cent of total investments. City governments were ordered to invest 90 per cent of their annual reserves in government bonds until 75 per cent of their total reserves had been so placed. A comparison of the relevant statistical data for the years 1932–38 shows that "Reich loans accounted for some 72 per cent of the additions to the investment portfolios of savings banks, 56 per cent of those of life-insurance institutions, and 68 per cent of those of social-insurance agencies."[7]

The second type of government bond was saleable over the counter. Commercial and investment banks had to accept designated quotas of each issue. It was the task of the banks to place as many bonds as they could with their customers. Sales to private investors were facilitated through a requirement of the banking act of 1934. Private banks had to present monthly reports on the larger amounts of deposits and debts to the commissioner for credit control. These reports enabled the banks to locate the potential buyers for government bonds. Sales to private parties included an element of coercion, mingled with persuasion, with the result that the purchasing quotas for larger private investors were semi-compulsory.

Embargoes and purchasing quotas were successful in greatly facilitating the financing of rearmament. This can be seen from the following figures:

NEW ISSUES OF PUBLIC AND PRIVATE SECURITIES*
(in million marks)

	PUBLIC ISSUES			PRIVATE CORPORATE ISSUES		
Years	*Government Bonds*	*Public Corporation Bonds*	*Total*	*Shares*	*Bonds*	*Total*
1933	66	11	77	91	2	93
1934	74	1	75	143	4	147
1935	1,642	1	1,643	156	3	159
1936	2,129	542	2,671	395	47	442
1937	3,110	40	3,150	333	258	591
1938	7,718	26	7,744	822	107	929
	14,739	621	15,360	1,940	421	2,361

* *Deutschlands wirtschaftliche Lage in der Jahresmitte 1939* (publication of Reichs-Kredit-Gesellschaft [Berlin, 1940]), pp. 52–53.

From these data on the placing of securities, we may draw two conclusions. (1) There was a remarkable shift from private to public issues during these six years. The private papers constituted only 13 per cent of all new issues floated in the capital markets, and these private funds were granted only because they were of military significance. (2) The seven-year financial plan of 1936 could be fully realized. Indeed, almost 13.7 billion of public securities were placed in the capital markets within three years.

This was possible for several reasons. Foremost was the embargo upon new capital loans. The supplementary measures in regulating banks and stock exchanges fenced in the capital markets to such an extent that unauthorized loans were negligible. Next was the use of the purchasing quota as an instrument of direct control. Both institutional and private savers had little choice in buying securities. From 1935 onward all funds flowing into capital markets were directed into the purchase of public securities. At the same time, the process of money creation continued. Rather than experiencing a decline from these purchases, the relevant deposits of the commercial, savings, and cooperative banks increased by 1.5 billion marks from June, 1935 to March, 1938. The rise in the volume of deposits during a period of extensive bond purchases points to a further creation of money by the banking system.[8] Finally, under Schacht's leadership, the state started to promote savings. Individual savers were praised for their patriotic deeds, and the opportunities for institutional savings were expanded. At the same time private and social insurance funds had to be invested in government bonds. Thus, the improvement of direct controls and the coupling of direct with indirect controls effectively implemented the purposes of the government in its attempts to create new money and increase investment in government bonds. As a result the state was enabled to realize its seven-year financial program of 1936 by the end of 1938.

What was the significance of the rapidly rising public debt for the capitalist property structure? When the state appears in the capital market as one bidder for funds among others, the subsequent increase in demand for funds produces a twofold effect. Loan capitalists and banks experience an increase in their volume of business and enjoy a rise in the total volume of profits. This quantity effect may be coupled with a price effect. If only demand—but not supply—increases, the lenders and banks will be able to raise the rate of interest on loans. The price effect will then bring forth an increase in the unit rate of profit as well. The public debt thus generates two kinds of politically created profit opportunities which can be realized by private loan capitalists.

In the Nazi situation, however, the two effects were separated. The loan capitalists' volume of sold bonds increased because there was a greater demand for, as well as a larger supply of, loanable funds. The remarkable increase in trade volume was exceptionally beneficial for bankers as well as lenders because the usually deflationary effect of such bond purchases was largely missing. Yet the banks were arguing that the rate of interest on government bonds should also be raised. Their argument was based upon the expectation of a given or severely limited supply of funds. Such an expectation is typical of loan capitalists. Since the sale of government bonds precedes in time the creation of new money bankers consider only the previous supply and raise their interest rates.[9] The bankers' argument was rejected by Schacht. The government bonds carried an interest rate of 4.5 per cent, which was in 1935 slightly under the going rate in the market. The increase in the unit rate of profit was denied to loan capitalists because the state continued its program of interest reduction, discussed previously. This policy was now motivated by two goals. Not only were private debtors to benefit from lower rates but the state was to be able to place rearmament bonds at an unchanging rate of interest. In contrast to the usual form of politically oriented capitalism, state borrowing granted only the quantity effect to loan capitalists but denied them the benefit of the price effect.

Another modification of the capitalist property structure resulted from the embargo upon private issues. As is indicated by the table on p. 463, in which 1933 is taken as the base year, the share of new corporate securities fell from 52.8 per cent in 1933 to 13.3 per cent in 1938. Thus the net addition to intangible property rights in the country reflected a shift from private to public ownership. The direct control imposed by the embargo became a property control that diminished the private share capital financed through the capital markets. The result was a restructuring of share markets. The insufficient supply of private shares led to a price level that far exceeded the anticipated dividend earnings of shareholders. Keeping down these prices proved to be difficult in later years and led to the price fixing of shares in 1942.[10]

A third change related to the portfolios of banks and other financial institutions. As illiquidity disappeared, the income of the banks from private loans became smaller. Recuperating producers repaid their debts. Orders created by rearmament called for diminishing requests of loan capital per unit of output, since procurement offices made substantial payments in advance of delivery. Government financial transactions took the place of short-term loans by banks, and undistributed profits were substituted for long-term loans. Actual short-term credits via commercial bills fell from 4.11 in 1932 to 3.01 billion marks in 1937. At the same time, the private deposits of all banks rose from 3.79 to 4.6 billion marks.[11] An increased supply of funds was thus accompanied by a decline in the opportunities for doing private business, but actual or potential loss was avoided through the purchase of government bills and bonds. The increasing public business compensated the financial institutions for their diminishing private business; hence, the willingness of the controllers of large private banks to live peacefully with purchasing quotas, which merely intensified and finalized the process of substituting public for private assets in the holdings of financial institutions. At the same time, however, the increase in the volume of business and profits was accompanied by a decline in the economic freedom of private enterprise and in its power to control the financial markets. Thus, from the fact that the financial capitalists did not protest against their decline of power in the markets, one must conclude that in ranking the various capitalist institutions they preferred profit and newly formed capital within concerns to economic freedom and private market control.

Finally, there was a significant alteration within the property structure of corporations. The orthodox theory assumes that shareholders, through a social contract, form the corporation and supply its capital, which in turn becomes a charge against the corporation. In the first phase of the Nazi regime, there was another kind of capital that did not belong to the shareholders. This other kind of capital consisted of undistributed profits that became corporate capital (*Eigenkapital*). The dividend ceiling intensified and justified the preference of corporate controllers for keeping a significant portion of their realized profits within the concern. By not imposing an income tax upon undistributed profits, the state enhanced the value of this corporate capital.[12] When this capital was reinvested, refinancing or expansion became possible without access to capital markets. Productive enterprises could enlarge their operations in spite of the fact that the embargo had closed the capital market to private concerns.

From a critical assessment of the effects of financing rearmament two inferences may be drawn. One pertains to the changes in the money and capital markets; the other, to the modifications of the capitalist property structure. In regard to the financial markets, we arrive at two apparently contradictory conclusions:

a) The money as well as the capital markets were flooded with government papers. Yet through an adroit combination of direct and indirect actions the state was able to place its bills and bonds at either declining or governmentally fixed prices. These state actions were responsible for the fact that the financial capitalists lost their previous control of these markets.

b) Strangely enough, this loss of control was not accompanied by a decline in the volume of business and profits. The rising traffic in government debt certificates was so profitable that most of the private banks were able to repurchase the strategic bundles of shares that had slipped into government possession during the credit crisis.

Changes in the capitalist property structure were also, in some respects, contradictory:

c) Owners of share capital experienced a period of discrimination. The widespread retention of a portion of profits deprived shareholders of a significant part of the distributable corporate income, and the reinvested profits became an interest-free corporate capital that was beyond the control, and withheld from the income, of most shareholders.

d) Once the capital markets had been reserved for the use of the state, the newly formed capital or created money went into government bonds. Most German bondholders operated on the assumption that the ultimate debt burden would eventually fall on non-property-owning taxpayers or upon foreign nationals. Public ownership of borrowed assets was thus seen as a temporary and self-liquidating phenomenon.[13] Public ownership operated here as a form of politically oriented capitalism.

e) The property structure of most capitalist enterprises was fully restored during the rearmament period. Not only were the debts of previous periods repaid but new capital was obtained free of charge either because of the advance payments of procurement agencies or because of reinvested profits. In fact, many nonfinancial corporations (e.g., corporations primarily involved in some form of manufacturing activity and only secondarily concerned with matters of investment and finance) were able to acquire control over other companies and thus achieve new concentrations of power.[14]

In consequence of these divergent effects, statism and organized capitalism became compatible with each other. The specific goals of each could be realized simultaneously. The financial capitalists lost control over their respective markets but regained profits and recaptured possession of their strategic share capital. The state, in the process of financing rearmament, excluded private concerns from capital markets; but, because of the increasing opportunities for self-financing, the non-financial corporations did not seriously suffer from this exclusion. Therefore, the so-often-asserted conflict between the principles of statism and capitalism cannot be observed in the financial sphere during the first phase of the Nazi regime.

DOMINATED SCRIP MARKETS

Was statization also compatible with organized capitalism in other areas of the economy? In order to ascertain the significance of the other statist actions, we shall have to analyze those direct and indirect controls which caused a detrimental income effect for private concerns. The handling of foreign capital and German exports furnish the most important examples. The markets involved were subject to the bureaucratic power of the state. How did its actions affect the income opportunities of German exporters and foreign creditors? What kind of institutional shifts were created by the state in these markets?

As we have seen previously, German export prices lay from 12 to 20 per cent above British gold export prices. The result of the price differential was a decline of German sales to the countries of Western Europe.[15] The sale of German goods to non-clearing countries was thus possible only if

German export prices were reduced. Such a reduction tended to wipe out the profits of German exporters, and also to diminish further the German receipts of foreign exchange. Since the latter were indispensable for rearmament, the state felt the need for keeping up the export proceeds of German sellers that accrued in the form of foreign currency. The result was an identity of interest between the state and most German exporters.

There was no opportunity for the party to herd these foreigners into a mass organization and force them to buy from Germany, so it became the task of the German state either to limit the choices available to foreign buyers or to grant them special incentives for acquiring German goods. It was because of the clearing agreements that the method of restricting the available choices called forth actions that were quite different from those elicited by the granting of inducements to foreign buyers in the non-clearing trade.

Clearing agreements usually outlawed the conversion of money between the two countries involved. Money did not go over the border. In each country, importers paid the price of foreign goods to their respective government-clearing banks. The funds received were utilized to pay exporters in domestic money for the goods that they sent abroad. Given this system of centralized payments within each country, Nazi Germany employed the technique of quantity manipulation in order (a) to obtain more foreign goods than were specified in the official clearing agreements, and (b) to secure these additional goods without having to pay higher import prices or grant lower export prices. Overissue of import rights was the means by which more goods were obtained. The money used to pay for these excess commodities went to the German clearing bank. Yet the foreign sellers could not be compensated so long as no more German goods were sold abroad. The foreign government had either to advance the funds for the excess imports received by Germany, or it had to force some of its firms to buy more goods from Germany. This was usually done by imposing import restrictions upon the purchase of goods from third countries (i.e., countries other than those participating in the contract) so as to increase the purchase of German goods. The foreign government as clearing partner had thus to increase the demand for German goods by coercing its own nationals. The increase in the quantity of demand made it possible for Germany to raise her exports without having to lower her prices.[16] The resulting insulation of price markets in the clearing trade was achieved through the three new institutions of centralized payments, unconvertible clearing rights, and foreign export quotas.

In the case of sales to non-clearing countries, however, the German state had to act mainly in open price markets. Incentives had to be offered to foreign buyers that would increase their willingness to purchase German goods. Apart from individualized barter deals, the German state offered foreign buyers inducements at the expense of foreign creditors. A foreign capitalist could recover his assets, impounded by the conversion bank, only if he accepted scrips. These negotiable certificates could be sold abroad but could ultimately be used only in Germany, either in payment for German goods or tourist expenses.

The export and scrips markets became linked when German exporters were permitted to accept scrips as payment for their goods. This coupling of the two markets was, however, only the first step. There had to be a built-in price differential in the scrip market so that the foreign buyer of German goods could pay with low-priced scrips and the German exporters resell the scrips to the German Central Bank at their face value. The differential between the two prices of scrips constituted the source for a subsidy of German exports.

The state-created scrip markets were beneficial for German exporters because of two simultaneous income effects. The foreign creditors lost a portion of their capital and interest

income, whereas the German exporters were assured of a
continuous profit from the sale of their formerly over-priced
goods. Just as in the case of the labor markets, a detested
group suffered from a governmentally created negative income effect, while a preferred group benefited from a positive
income effect.

How was this redistribution of income achieved? In terms
of methods, the state utilized indirect controls by creating
scrips as a new kind of money, the price variations of which
had the effect of offsetting the high prices of German exports.
If we accept the teaching of orthodox economic theory, such
monetary controls should not have exerted a modifying influence upon the institution of capitalist markets. In reality,
however, such a modification did occur. The state did not
limit itself to the single isolated action of issuing a string of
subsidiary kinds of money but adopted a policy of deliberately manipulating capitalist institutions.

Institutional manipulation began with the direct action of
forbidding German debtors to fulfill their obligations to foreign creditors and by requiring them instead to pay the
amounts due to a German conversion bank. Direct controls
here discarded two capitalist institutions—the inviolability of
the private contract and the protection of private property.
In issuing scrips on the basis of the frozen accounts, the German state acted as if it were the owner of the foreign capital.
Possession of the capital permitted the state to decide who
should be "paid" in scrips and for which purchases scrips
could be eventually used. The transformation of frozen accounts into scrips involved a violation of the principle of free
choice: foreign creditors either had to forego a return of their
capital or, by order of Hjalmar Schacht, accept the scrips and
submit to a partial expropriation. Most of these expropriated
funds belonged to Americans, who were especially willing to
sell their frozen claims substantially below their nominal
values.[17]

The moratorium on the transfer of German money abroad was accompanied by the abolition of two kinds of market. Foreign securities in Germany could no longer be sold except by permission—which was rarely granted—of the Central Bank. The purchase of such securities had lost its meaning because these certificates had to be registered and their transfer to other countries was forbidden. The moratorium thus abolished the market for securities issued by foreign underwriters and traded in Germany. The place of this abolished market was taken by the frozen accounts held by the conversion bank, a subsidiary of the German Central Bank.

Exchange control and the moratorium were supplemented in the spring of 1935 by the government's attempt to dry up the market for German money in foreign countries. An import embargo on German bank notes prevented travellers from buying such money cheaply abroad and using it at the official rate in Germany. Leading foreign banks refused to deal in German money. A legitimate money market was destroyed, and the limited volume of transactions that still took place was driven into the black market. Keeping the foreign loans in Germany thus led to the statist action of destroying well-established capitalist markets.

The abolition of these capitalist institutions was followed by the creation of a new kind of market. Various markets were created by the German government as it issued scrips and, while allowing them to be sold abroad, required that they be cashed only in Germany. Although used for the most part by foreign buyers and sellers only, the scrip markets were dominated by the German state. Without appearing in the market, the state was the sole supplier of scrips and determined the ultimate demand for scrips by designating the goods or services that could be paid for in scrips. The state also determined, indirectly, the extent of the price differential between scrips abroad and in Germany. Thus, in the issuing and pricing of scrips, the government exercised an indirect control and, in fixing the quantities of goods that could be bought with them, a direct control.

The synchronized use of direct and indirect controls enabled the government to adopt the policy of deliberately realigning institutions. As a result of the moratorium on the transfer of German money and of the statist principle of exchange control—the foreign money market in Germany, the market for foreign debt certificates, and the German money market abroad were abolished. The issue of scrips gave rise to the creation of a new market abroad, and the state had thus obtained the power of engaging in a policy of institutional manipulation: Prices and quantities could be dictated or dominated, and the markets themselves could either be created or abolished. But why were both these extreme forms of institutional manipulation employed against the foreign creditor?

There is little doubt that if the power of the state had been unhindered by other governments, Schacht would have liked to impose full expropriation upon foreign capitalists. Direct action alone would then have been employed. The moratorium would have kept all the borrowed foreign capital in Germany. After receiving the interest and amortization payments from the debtor, the state would have become the *de facto* owner of the foreign capital and would then have reinvested all these funds in rearmament projects. Said Schacht in a confidential letter of June 6, 1936 to General von Blomberg: "The Central Bank has the German mark funds of foreigners under its control almost exclusively reinvested in rearmament bills. Our armaments are thus partly financed from the deposits of our political enemies."[18] Given a chance, Schacht did use a portion of the foreign capital borrowed for financing German rearmament.

Yet the threats of foreign countries having an active trade balance and also the dwindling of German export markets induced Schacht to couple full with partial expropriation.

The security market was destroyed, accounts were frozen, and one portion of these funds was reinvested for rearmament by direct action of the Central Bank. The other portion was used to subsidize German exports. Partial expropriation had to be accomplished through indirect controls and by the creation of various scrip markets. The issue of scrips formally recognized but actually violated the principle of private property. The substitution of a state-imposed market for a privately created market was the institutional realignment inflicted upon foreigners. Direct and indirect controls were coordinated so as to accomplish a partial expropriation of foreign capital.

In the scrip markets, quantity decisions were divided between private traders and the state. The foreign creditor sold scrips, and the foreign importer bought them, each deciding how much and when to buy or sell. The German state did not participate in these private quantity decisions, and the individual transaction price was beyond the control of the German state; but in issuing scrips the state did determine the total supply and, by designating the export items that could be paid for in scrips, also determined the ultimate demand for them. This direct action, in turn, permitted the state to control indirectly the difference between the price of scrips at home and abroad.

The action of the state created a definite nexus between the issuing of scrips and the subsidizing of exports: The greater the total quantity of scrips issued and the smaller the resale opportunities permitted, the greater were the price differential and the funds available for the subsidizing of exports.

In its decisions to manipulate markets, the Central Bank acted as the monetary agent of the state, as well as the *de facto* owner of frozen accounts, and thus occupied a property position in the economy. Consequently, in deciding how many scrips it would issue the Central Bank created subsidiary money; and in permitting the scrips to be traded abroad and in setting the amount it would cash within a given period of time, the bank was making property decisions. These property decisions transformed the frozen accounts into negotiable intangible property rights, the repurchase of which would terminate the property contracts with foreign capitalists.

Two conclusions are suggested by this coupling of monetary and property decisions. First, when the state is the sole owner of subsidiary money or certificates which private traders are willing to accept, the supposedly monetary actions of issuing and cashing certificates become property decisions that can—through appropriate stipulations—determine the total quantity of funds in a market. The intention to engage in expropriation motivated the state to capitalize upon its property position, stipulate conditions for the use of scrips, and thereby transform monetary actions into direct total quantity decisions.[19] Second, as *de facto* owner of foreign capital and as a representative of the German state, the Central Bank abolished some markets and created others, with the result that foreign capital was partially expropriated and a special subsidy made available to German exporters. It was because of these redistributional actions that the state succeeded in shifting to foreign creditors a portion of the burden that rearmament and exchange control had imposed upon German exporters. As a result, statization and organized capitalism became compatible also in the field of international finance.

CARTELS IN SUBSIDIZED EXPORT MARKETS

In spite of its great advantages, the institution of the scrips market turned out to be a transitional phenomenon. Two of its inherent limitations caused trouble for the policy of rearmament. At the beginning of the regime, the extensive use of scrips tended to diminish the percentage of foreign currency received per transaction. State agencies not only had to limit the total quantity of scrips on the markets but also found it necessary to decide how large a percentage of the export price could be paid in scrips. In depending upon the receipt of foreign currency, the rearmament policy could tolerate the profit interests of exporters only within fairly narrow limits.

By the middle of 1935, the second limitation of the scrips market had also become evident. Whether because the volume of frozen American accounts declined at this time or because the European creditors either preferred or, upon the insistence of the German government, were required to reinvest their capital in Germany, the opportunities to issue scrips diminished. At the same time that the volume of scrips declined, the pressure for either open or concealed devaluation of the mark increased. This pressure was resisted by the state, which preferred to adopt a new subsidy program for exports.

A subsidized export market differs in two ways from an ordinary capitalist market. There usually occurs a peculiar dual price for the same commodity. The partner receiving the subsidy experiences two prices in each transaction, the market price and the subsidized price. The seller's final price, including the subsidy, will lie above the market price; the reverse is true when the subsidy is paid to the buyers.

In addition, a subsidized market usually involves a third party that facilitates the exchange of goods between buyers and sellers. If private firms have to provide the subsidy—whether in scrips or as premium payments for foreign currency—a special market (supplementary to the export market) must be created; or, if the subsidy is paid out of tax receipts, a fiscal agent must be attached to the export market. Neither of these methods was acceptable to the state. Premium payments for foreign currency would have raised import prices and thereby created difficulties for the rearmament program.[20] The same would have been true of the fiscal method because the tax receipts used to pay for subsidies could not have been invested in rearmament projects. It was therefore Schacht's task to find a method that would support the profit interests of private exporters without reducing the opportunities for effectively executing the rearmament policy of the state.

These dual private and public goals could be achieved only by coupling direct controls with inducements. The New Plan of 1934 contained the two features of import restriction and a new program for promoting exports. The previous arrangement of subsidizing only "additional" exports was dropped in 1935. In the new export program, every producer suffering from too high prices when selling abroad was granted an opportunity to receive compensation for his prospective losses. Whereas previously the compensation had depended upon an examination of unit costs, the new subsidy was uniform and amounted to 25 per cent of the price in the foreign markets. This uniform rate, set in advance, enabled exporters to deduct the subsidy from their asking price and thereby to conclude promptly their contracts with foreign buyers. The subsidy itself was paid when the exporter delivered his foreign exchange to the Central Bank. In August of 1934 it was estimated that from 60 to 70 per cent of the exports would have to be subsidized. At a rate of 25 per cent, the expected payments were estimated at 60 million marks per month or 720 million marks per year.[21]

The shift from an individualized to a generalized export subsidy produced three defects. Being relieved from a specific scrutiny of their costs, even those exporters who did not suffer from a decline in profits received subsidies. Other exporters utilized the subsidy to request lower prices and thereby engaged in price competition with other German firms. Finally, the subsidy payments, which not only compensated exporters for losses but also assured them of an adequate rate of profit, were originally paid for by the Treasury. These three defects gave rise to a revision of the export program, as it was originally adopted in August of 1934.

First, the fiscal burden of the subsidy was shifted. The state issued a secret law of June 28, 1935, which imposed a levy upon producers selling in domestic markets.[22] The justification for this levy was that domestic producers had gained from the policy of rearmament whereas exporters had suffered from the same policy. Domestic producers were thus to share their profits with exporters. The allotting and collecting of the levy were declared to be functions of self-government. The economic group of each industry was ordered to obtain funds from domestic sellers in order to pay a subsidy for sales abroad. The total payments amounted in 1935 to not less than 700 million marks and rose gradually to 1 billion annually in subsequent years.[23] In shifting the financial burden to private firms, the state supplemented the principle of self-government with the one of co-responsibility. Domestic producers had to forego a portion of their profits so as to assure a sufficient rate of profits for exporting enterprises.

The principles of a uniform subsidy rate and freedom from cost control for subsidized exports were abolished in June of 1935. If domestic sellers had to provide the funds for the subsidy, then they should be assured that exporters would not receive excess profits or engage in price reductions abroad. The state decided that it was the task of the economic groups of business to prevent both excess profits and cutthroat prices. Each industrial group engaged in exporting had to establish a price-examination office. The duties of these offices were twofold. On the one hand, they had to collect information about the movement of actual prices in foreign markets and report to the Ministry of Economics; and on the other, to see whether the subsidies promised actually enabled German firms to meet the prices of foreign competitors. The offices aimed (*a*) at translating the subsidy into an effective part of

the final price received by the exporter and (b) at insuring
the German exporter of a sufficient rate of profit. In applying
the principle of self-government to price examination, the
state laid down the rule that whoever paid for the subsidy
received the right to participate in its administration. Thus,
although the price-examination offices were agents of the
Ministry of Economics, they worked together closely with the
economic groups of business.

Business participation in the control of export markets led
to two modifications of the subsidy procedure in subsequent
months. Foreign price competition was of unequal intensity
in different parts of the world. Prices declined especially in
the export markets of South Africa, whereas prices in European markets rose slightly. Acting upon the information
supplied by the offices of price examination, the Ministry of
Economics raised the subsidy rate from 25 to 33 per cent for
African markets and lowered them from 25 to 23 per cent for
European markets. This action of September 29, 1935, replaced the principle of a uniform subsidy rate with the other
principle of increasing the subsidy for goods suffering from a
decline in foreign prices. Also, when the subsidy did not
cover the price differential, individual exporters could obtain
additional grants if their cost and price data showed to the
price offices an actual or threatened loss.[24]

In comparing prices, some price-examination offices discovered violations of the subsidy rules. In the electrical
equipment industry, for instance, exporters delivered to foreign buyers additional goods (in excess of what was specified
in the original contract) free of charge. Assertedly, the unpaid commodities were given in compensation for defective
goods or goods that had been damaged during transport.
Available evidence supported the suspicion, however, that
the firms involved had indirectly granted a price reduction.
To assure an adequate checkup, exporters were instructed to
supply the examination offices with the necessary information

for all transactions involving price reductions or supplementary deliveries that were not called for in the original contract with the foreign buyer. The responsibility for enforcement was assigned to the foreign-currency offices of the state, not to the price-examination offices, which were so closely allied with the business organizations. The Minister of Economics ruled in February of 1936 that whenever a firm delivered less in foreign exchange than was indicated in the original permission, the currency offices had to deduct the difference from the subsidy payment. Punishment was thus handed out only by the state.

The examination offices did, however, become instruments for initiating or implementing cartel prices for exporters. In his February ruling the Minister had directed exporters to report monthly to the offices their originally negotiated prices as well as any subsequent price reductions. On the basis of this information, in the case of any given product and country, the offices could arrive at an "adequate" offer price. The foreign-currency agencies were to insist upon such a price as a condition for promising or granting subsidy payments. At the beginning of 1936, the price situation in exports had thus reached the point at which price control was regarded as necessary. Who, then, should control prices—the cartel or the state?

The examination offices tended quite naturally towards a cartel solution because they were frequently associated with or came from the administrative staffs of the business organizations. There was some disagreement, however, as to whether the cartels should be voluntary or compulsory. The examination office of the machine-tool industry called a meeting of the exporting firms, and a price cartel was arranged. Any firm quoting a lower-than-agreed-upon price did not receive a subsidy. This procedure—amounting to an indirect compulsory cartel—was rejected by the national chamber of industry and commerce in its memorandum of April 3, 1936.

Long negotiations produced a new ruling by the Minister of Economics, issued on October 20, 1936. The power of the price-examination offices to set minimum prices and recommend these to the currency agencies was reaffirmed; but the various business concerns involved were to agree on voluntary price cartels and avail themselves of the information provided by the examination offices for enforcing these prices and preventing deviation from them.

How did the principles of self-government and co-responsibility affect the charactcer of export markets? The situation of a price differential could have been handled either by the competitive, the statist, or the organized-capitalist solution. Which principles were involved in each solution and why was the last one preferred by businessmen and the state?

In an economic system of competitive capitalism, the state should have followed four distinct principles. In the first place, the funds for the subsidy should have been furnished by the state, because the price differential was caused by the state's rearmament and foreign-exchange policy. In the second place, the subsidy payment should have been expressed and paid for as a uniform percentage of the export price, in which case every firm would have received equal treatment from the state. In the third place, the uniform subsidy should have served only one purpose, namely to shift the losses from the exporters to the state. Finally, the state should have refrained from engaging in price fixing and should have rejected any attempt to equalize the rates of profits among firms. This competitive solution was unacceptable to business as well as to the state because the former desired an assured rate of profit, and the latter the greatest possible amount of foreign exchange.

A quite different set of principles would have been introduced if the state had dictated all actions. In that case, the state would have collected the funds for the subsidy and allotted them among exporters. The rate of subsidy would have been discretional for the state agency, which would have varied the payment according to the difference between actual unit costs and the market price abroad. The offer price of German exporters would have been set by the state so as to eliminate any price competition among Germans or with foreign sellers. Finally, the state would have engaged in a policy of equalizing rates of profit among exporters so as to stimulate exports as well as to minimize subsidy payments. These statist principles were not adopted by the state because of the opposition of big business and also because there was no opportunity to secure control over the actions of foreign sellers.

In adopting the principles of self-government and co-responsibility, the state and the business groups preferred the solution most in accord with organized capitalism. The collection of funds was exclusively a function of business organizations. In most cases, the available funds were distributed according to the principle that the subsidy should vary inversely to changes in export prices. State and business were agreed that price fixing was a necessary precondition for an effective allocation of subsidies. Price fixing was handed over to existing or newly created export cartels. These cartel prices became effective even though foreign sellers were not members of the cartel. The price information collected by the price-examination offices, and the threat of the state to refuse or reduce the subsidy to price-cutters, had the effect of making a partial cartel, comprising only German sellers, quite effective in foreign markets.

The solution of organized capitalism exerted a twofold influence upon export markets. The subsidy scheme and the use of a supplementary fiscal institution put a prop under markets that were depressed because of the over-priced currency. As a result the income effect of the over-priced currency was shifted from exporters to domestic producers. The subsidy scheme thus served to compensate for direct controls and the excessively high exchange rates imposed by the state. In addition to working as a prop, the subsidy also provided exporters with an inducement to increase their business by assuring them of an adequate rate of profit. This profit opportunity was not generated by the market but was deliberately created by the joint actions of the state and the cartels. The fiscal measures thus strengthened the organizational features of capitalist export markets.

Subsidies could be obtained, however, only under two stipulations. The exporter had to submit to price-fixing and had to deliver his foreign currency to the state. In this way, price-fixing prevented subsidies from being used as a means of reducing prices as well as from depressing the volume of foreign currency. Furthermore, although the individual producer could no longer set his own offer price, price-fixing was a function of private cartels rather than of the state. The governmental stipulation of minimum prices thus gave rise to a market that was extensively organized by cartels and business organizations. The state could readily shift the function of controlling export markets to private organizations because the interests of the state and the exporters were the same. High prices *plus* a rising volume of exports raised the profits of private concerns as well as the proceeds of foreign currency to the state. Consequently, the actions of the state in propping up export markets and stipulating minimum prices gave rise to export markets that were in effect privately organized.

This whole system of trade regulation introduced by Schacht's New Plan was successful. From 1934 to 1937, the quantities of German imports of finished goods for civilian consumption were reduced by 63 per cent, whereas the total value of German exports rose by 25 per cent or from 4.17 to 5.90 billion marks.[25] Success was achieved through the interaction of statist and capitalist principles. The impact of the export levy upon domestic producers was mollified by granting business organizations the right of participating in the formulation of rules for collecting and distributing the subsidy. When the German rulers felt the need for minimum export prices, they left the actual fixing of prices to private cartels. Rather than imposing a set of quantity rulings upon exporters, similar to the extensive import controls, the government handed over to business organizations the task of promoting exports, providing information on price offers, and preapproving applications for subsidies. In this way, business co-responsibility became a feature of economic administration by the state. Thus, from what has been said about exports, we may conclude that when rearmament called for unavoidable detrimental income effects, private business organizations (e.g., of domestic producers) were given the rights of self-government and co-responsibility in the administration of new functions. These two principles reconciled the requirements of statism with organized capitalism.

THE REGULATED MARKET

In implementing economic rearmament, the state exerted a fourfold influence upon capitalist markets. A very few, such as the market for the sale of German money by Germans abroad, were abolished. Others were newly created when negotiable scrips were issued. The armament manufacturers, on the other hand, sold their final products directly to the state, and operated independently of any market nexus. Finally, there were the six markets mentioned, in which government regulation combined elements of statism and capitalism. What, then, were the common characteristics of these regulated markets?

The first and most important feature was the central position of a government agency in the regulated market. This agency regulated all private activities under its jurisdiction. Thus, when the moratorium on foreign loans had established

a "defaulted" market for foreign securities, it became the
task of the new conversion bank (*Konversionskasse*) to receive
the payments of domestic debtors, reduce the interests specified in loan contracts, and issue scrips or reinvest the repaid
capital in projects favoring rearmament. In the internal
money markets, the credit commissioner (*Kreditkommissar*)
received reports on the affairs of banking institutions,
checked on their liquidity, and examined their loan and deposit policies. In undertaking these functions, the commissioner prepared the ground for the sale of mefo-bills as well
as for the issue of special bills by the *Golddiskontbank*. In
the internal capital markets, the issue commission (*Emissionskommittee*) received and decided upon requests for the
issue of new (or the conversion of old) domestic shares and
bonds; watched the prices of securities outstanding, supervised the reduction of interest rates decreed by the state, and
otherwise increased the receptiveness of the capital markets
for the placement of new government bonds. In the foreign-
exchange markets the exchange commissioner (*Devisenkom-
missar*) held the power of acting as the sole buyer of all foreign money and drafts, of issuing rules for the granting of
foreign-exchange permits, and of collaborating with the
Devisenzuteilungskommission in allotting the clearing rights
or the uncommitted foreign exchange to domestic users. In
the import markets, the supervisory boards (*Ueberwachungs-
stellen*) admitted acceptable traders and issued import permits after examining the expected prices, qualities and
origins of the goods to be imported. Subsequent payment for
the imported goods were received by the *Verrechungskasse*
for the clearing trade, while payments in uncommitted foreign exchange were checked upon by the *Reichsstelle für
Devisenbewirtschaftung*. Finally, in the export markets, the
price-examination offices (*Preisprüfungsstellen*) checked on
the price offers of German exporters in foreign markets, compared the offers with the prevailing prices in these markets,

and assisted German export cartels in fixing and enforcing the highest attainable prices. Acting upon the price information received, the *Devisenstellen* passed on the price offers and paid the stipulated subsidies to the exporters.

In each of the six regulated markets, private buyers and sellers coexisted with one or several agencies of the state. If there had been no private traders, the agencies could not have functioned; private parties, on the other hand, could not have completed any transactions without the permission of the agency concerned. The collaboration of government and private units was thus a typical feature of the regulated market.

A similar coexistence prevailed in regard to the private and governmental goals that each participant tried to implement in the regulated markets. Private buyers and sellers usually operated on the profit principle. Although the state agencies accepted the validity of this principle, each one of them was charged with the task of realizing a specific government goal. The two sets of goals were frequently in conflict and became compatible only by introducing a distinction between permissible and prohibited profit opportunities.

In the foreign exchange markets, a "free" pricing of currencies was forbidden. Exporters could receive only the official acceptance price, and importers had to pay the official release price, both of which were set by the Central Bank on the basis of the official gold-mark parity. Exporters could not make special profits by selling their drafts in foreign currency at a premium, and the supervisory boards eagerly sought to discover and exclude imports that could be purchased by paying the foreign seller a price in excess of the official rate of exchange. Similar restrictions were imposed upon those exporters who delivered goods of low quality but who pretended that they had received high-quality goods. In prosecuting those who tried to earn profits by depreciating the value of the German currency, the foreign-currency offices outlawed any form of currency gains. In general, any profit opportunities that could have been realized if there had been no import quotas, no embargo upon share issues, and no prohibition on the reimporting of German money purchased below the official exchange rate abroad were forbidden. It was thus typical of the regulated markets that the distinction between permissible and prohibited transactions inevitably specified an area of profit opportunities that was closed to private firms.

Rather than promoting rearmament in general, the various government agencies were in search of specific goals that could be implemented in their particular markets and that were compatible with the recognized profit goals of private enterprise. The office of foreign-exchange control sought to increase the total of foreign-exchange and clearing rights, to enlarge the share of uncommitted foreign money, and to maintain the official rate of exchange. Also, by way of inducing private concerns to take an interest in the realization of these goals, some large exporters were granted the privilege of keeping a portion of their export proceeds in foreign countries and were thus given a chance to buy foreign raw materials advantageously and import them to Germany. Some of the large concerns were even permitted to report only every half a year on their export and import transactions.[26] Private banks, on the other hand, were compensated for the loss of their foreign-exchange business when the Central Bank granted them foreign exchange for the purchase of foreign securities that entailed property rights in German concerns.

The issuing committee (*Emissionskommittee*) sought to attain the two state goals of systematically reducing the long-term interest rates and of increasing the supply of funds for the purchase of new government bonds. The placing of these bonds automatically compensated the investment banks for the embargo upon the issue of shares, whereas the manufacturing concerns were assisted in retaining their profits and financing new projects out of their own resources. Only exceptionally high profits from stock-market speculation were frowned upon by the government.

The credit commissioner also tried to reduce the short-term interest rates and to limit the liquidity requirements of commercial banks so as to make more funds available for the purchase of government bills. The pressure of the state was utilized not to restrict but to increase the private purchase of desired bills and notes. Inducements were combined with persuasion when the *Golddiskontbank* offered special profit opportunities by selling sola bills to the private banks.

By granting import quotas, the supervisory offices hoped to increase the percentage share of essential raw materials and foodstuff in total imports, to impose an effective control upon the prices of imported goods, and to provide raw materials for the purpose of increasing exports. The realization of these aims involved discrimination against the importers and consumers of excluded consumer goods. The supervisory offices were quite careful, however, to respect the profit opportunities of the recognized importers. These offices even promoted the business of the private shipping companies, and the Ministry of Economics turned down the proposal of some of the generals to import essential industrial raw materials through government trading monopolies.

The linking of private and state goals was most pronounced in the export markets. The larger the volume of private export business and the higher the German export prices, the greater was the government's chance to realize the highest attainable volume of export proceeds. Price-examination offices thus became an extension of the private export cartels, since both tried to obtain the highest profit per unit of export. The government went so far in support of the profit principle as to accept the responsibility for shifting unavoidable losses from the exporters to foreign creditors or to domestic producers. The institution of profits in the regulated export markets was thus coupled with the violation of the property rights of foreign capitalists and the imposition—via the export levy—of a kind of profit ceiling upon domestic producers and financial organizations. This uniting of state goals with the profit principle was the second typical feature of the regulated markets.

In each of the six regulated markets there existed a duality of private and government instruments of trade. The usual sales and purchasing departments, whether operating singly or through cartels and economic groups, were supplemented by the new trading facilities acquired by the government. It was only through the simultaneous or subsequent use of both kinds of instruments that exchange transactions could be undertaken or completed.

Interestingly enough, the monetary feature of the exchange was not handled in the same way as the regulation of goods and services. In all matters dealing with foreign currency or clearing rights, the government agency in any given market interrupted the flow of money payments, severed the usual nexus between payee and recipient or between creditor and debtor, and established itself as a participant in the monetary aspect of the transactions. The state agency claimed the right to function as an intermediary in a three-party exchange. This was accomplished by requiring that foreign currency be sold to and purchased from the foreign-exchange office and that payers, when meeting obligations to foreigners, make their payments to the clearing agency or the conversion bank. As a result, the government agencies could decide when, where, how, and in what amount monetary transactions could be completed.

These agencies did not, however, participate in the actual flow of goods and services exchanged. Instead, regulation was enforced by giving the agencies the right to grant permits, approve prices, and check on the entry or exit of goods into or from domestic markets. The permits were attached to the order and delivery papers of the private traders and enabled the customs officials to compare the details of the permit with the quantity and quality of the goods in transit. Permission and check-up were thus the devices by which government agencies determined the volume and kind of goods or services for specified periods of time.

Monetary participation and commodity regulation changed the nature of the quantities demanded and supplied in regulated markets. The quantities demanded and supplied should be determined by the utility motives of final buyers and the profit motives of intermediate buyers and sellers; but in fact the agencies of the state interrupted this process by deciding what traders were acceptable and determining how much of their expectational demand or supply could be translated into actual market demand or supply at any given moment or within any period of time. It was not by a process of automatic interaction but through governmental decisions that the transition from expected to actual quantities in the regulated market was determined. As a rule, government action tended to keep up the actual quantities in the export markets, whereas the opposite was true in the import markets. Hence, inducements were required in the former and restrictions in the latter. This splitting of quantity decisions is the third typical characteristic of the regulated market.

Government action gave rise to a new technique for the balancing of trade. Rather than equalizing market demand and supply directly, the supervisory boards engaged in two distinct balancing decisions. One related to the synchronization of the monetary and commodity parts of transactions. Doubting the ability of the German importers to pay for foreign goods, firms in other countries delayed delivery until payment was received. The supervisory boards rejected these demands for "payment in advance" and insisted that the issue of a foreign-currency permit (*Devisenbescheinigung*) entailed a guarantee for the payment of approved imports. Outside the clearing trade, the two parts of approved transactions were thus synchronized only within the customary payment limits.

The supervisory boards also wanted to equalize planned and actual imports, but the importers, fearful of not being able to obtain their full quota rights, often asked for more currency permits than they could use in a planning period. The result was that while some importers were "hoarding permits," other importers were being denied them. Hence, actual imports sometimes fell short of planned imports. In an attempt to remedy this situation, the supervisory boards stamped their permits with an expiration date and then refused to promise the renewal of an expired permit, in the hope of forcing importers to time their requests for permits realistically and honestly. These actions met with some degree of success, but the problem of balancing planned and actual imports remained difficult because of the inability of the supervisory boards to control fully the actions of the foreign traders.[27]

The balancing of total imports *and* exports over specified periods was not typical of the regulated market and actually occurred only if the foreign countries with whom Germany was trading were strong enough to impose such a balance. Germany, for instance, was able to eliminate the maximum figures of goods to be imported from Belgium and Spain, set by those governments, and ordered the supervisory boards to use all kinds of excuses for limiting imports from Great Britain before and after the payments agreement was signed. Instead of being instructed to equalize approved imports and expected exports, the boards were required to issue permits in such a number as to increase the volume of German exports. In other words, imports from countries with a favorable balance of trade were restricted, so that a surplus of uncommitted foreign exchange might be obtained; whereas in the clearing trade an excess of imports over exports was encouraged because it led to involuntary credits for Germany. Thus, instead of favoring a strict balance of trade between countries, Nazi Germany found a deliberate imbalance in foreign trade much more advantageous for the purposes of rearmament.

Private and state goals penetrated into the process of price determination. Non-market criteria usually governed the various price decisions. The traditional gold parity guided the Central Bank in setting its acceptance and release prices for foreign currency. The buying prices of German importers were kept as close as possible to the prices prevailing in March of 1934, and any increase above that level was accepted only if the imports were essential and could not be purchased at a lower price elsewhere. Imports for subsequent export, after improvement, were acceptable only if the export prices were 30 per cent above the import prices. The prices in the scrip markets were pegged to provide a sufficient subsidy for additional German exports. In the clearing trade, the levels of German export and import prices were at first kept close to the prices prevailing in 1932–33; but Germany subsequently attempted to raise her export prices above the import prices charged by the foreign countries with whom she was trading. Also, in the domestic money and capital markets, interest rates were systematically lowered so that the cost of loanable funds would not hinder a high level of borrowing by private and government debtors.

Government price-fixing was thus guided by the goals of defending the gold currency, keeping import prices at the domestic price level, obtaining maximally favorable terms of trade, securing an exploitation gain from foreign capitalists and traders, and reducing interest rates to a cost level acceptable to debtors. With the exception of the first goal, all other aims were fully compatible with the condition that the prices fixed or manipulated by the government had to provide a reasonable profit for private business concerns. In three cases this condition became a point of dispute between state agencies and business organizations. Some firms opposed the use of exports for the purpose of obtaining military equipment; some economic groups objected to the examinations required by the pricing offices; and many business organizations resisted the export levy.[28] In response to the first two criticisms, the government defined the amount of the subsidy to be granted in such a way that the recipients secured a reasonable rate of profit. The response to the criticism of the export levy was to compensate business groups for the reduction of domestic profits by giving them permission to administer the levy. In general, the practice of making government price-fixing compatible with the earning of reasonable profits was also a typical feature of the regulated market.

Finally, government participation and regulation had beneficial as well as detrimental results for private enterprise. The detriments were of four different kinds. Restrictive effects were exemplified by the experience of the importers of consumer goods who, when refused quotas, suffered a reduction in their volume of business. An exclusionary effect prevailed for new firms wishing to enter the import business and for manufacturers wanting to expand their equity capital. Other destructive effects sprang from some of the governmental price-fixing practices, which occasionally prevented an entrepreneur from taking advantage of a rising demand that would otherwise have permitted the realization of special profits. Finally, there were the oppressive effects felt especially by foreign creditors and to a lesser extent by those domestic creditors who had to forego a portion of their contractually secured interest income.

Typically enough, direct state controls had certain compensating effects (five in all) that were beneficial to private enterprise. A protective effect ensued from the import and exchange controls, which kept many goods of foreign com-

petitors out of domestic markets; and the moratorium prevented the withdrawal of foreign capital from German
debtors. A restorative effect resulted from those state actions
that renewed the financial liquidity of many private firms
which were, in turn, relieved from the threat to their corporate property and which benefited from the renewed vendi-
bility of their securities. An opportunity for expansion was
experienced by various financial institutions when the new
bills and bonds issued by the government opened up another
line of business for them that more than compensated the
banks for the relative decline in commercial bills and bonds.
A collusive effect—which was also beneficial—arose from the
cooperative activities of the export cartels and the price-examination offices, while import controls tended to strengthen
the domestic cartels. Finally, exporters benefited from a sub-
ventive effect when the state introduced the subsidy scheme
and thereby absorbed any losses in this line of business.

The coexistence of beneficial and detrimental effects goes
far to explain the relatively small amount of business opposition to the regulation of the six markets. Because of the consequences of the Great Depression, the beneficial effects were
greatly desired even if they involved direct controls by the
state.[29] The sting of the detrimental effects was minimized
through the various compensations that enabled private business to retain some of their profits or that created alternative
opportunities. Of at least equal significance was the fact that
businesses were not excluded from the regulated markets.
Government regulation and business promotionalism were
not mutually exclusive since single firms and business groups
were fully able to defend their economic interests even in
these regulated markets. It was the opportunity for profit
realization and interest representation that made regulated
markets compatible with organized capitalism. Given this
compatibility, it is hardly surprising that the great majority
of business leaders did not see in the regulated markets a

forerunner of state-directed capitalism. Interest orientation functioned here as an effective but mistaken guide to the events that were to follow under the second economic system of the Nazi regime.

REARMAMENT AND CAPITALISM

What was the significance of economic rearmament for private capitalism as it existed prior to the Nazi regime? Instead of one uniform multiplier effect, we find that there was a fourfold impact upon the structure of private capitalism. The changes were caused a) by the demand created by the military program, (b) by the militarization of the public sector of the economy, (c) by the introduction of six regulated markets, and (d) by the abolition of a few private markets.[30]

The first deviation from private capitalism was a result of the new demand created by rearmament. The effort to rearm called for an increasing volume of heavy-industry products which would serve as raw materials for military weapons and equipment. The clothing, housing, and feeding of the rising mass army caused a new demand for militarily important consumer goods. Of the total military outlay of 21 billion marks in the first period of the regime, more than half was spent for the purchase of goods of this kind. The newly created military demand did not call for large investments nor for the innovation of distinctly new products but drew upon the widespread idle industrial capacity. Much of this military demand was heavily concentrated, since 78 per cent of the 4 billion marks spent for such purposes in 1937 was allotted to six industries.[31] The immediate employment-creating effect of the military purchases was thus not spread over many segments of the economy.

The purchase of these semi-military products had two effects on the economy. The first was an extension of the size of the affected commodity and labor markets. Since the state acted in these markets as if it were a private customer, respecting cartel rules and paying cartel prices, military action did not call for a change in the structure of markets but only increased their size. Demand creation acted here as a stimulus to private capitalism. At the same time, the extension of military activities and the financing of military orders by deficits or new taxes led to an extension of the volume of government activities.

Secondly, rearmament gave rise to a militarization of the public sector of the economy. Not only the economic segments of the armed forces but also the Ministries of Economics, Finance, Labor and Agriculture became to a great extent agencies of economic rearmament. The effect of procurement facilities and military stockpiles was to establish new forms of public property the size of which was systematically increased by state action. Corresponding to these physical properties, there was an increasing volume of intangible government obligations that called for systematic debt management. Properties already owned by the state were examined for their possible military significance. A decree issued in 1934 instructed all property-owning or property-controlling agencies of the state to obtain military consent for their future investment policies. Especially affected by this requirement were the agencies of public transportation, communication, agrarian settlement, and electric power.[32] In the same year, a law authorized the Minister of War to extend the military possessions in two ways. On the one hand, the Minister could declare certain areas as military reserves and either encourage or not allow private operations to move into these territories. On the other hand, the Minister could requisition any private properties or impose certain stipulations upon private concerns whose activities were of military significance.

The incorporation of private armament producers into the public sector of the economy gave rise to a dispute within

the military establishment. When two aircraft producers refused to drop the production of civilian planes the Minister
of the Air Force presented to the cabinet a bill giving the
state control over private armament producers. If the bill
had been accepted, no producers of aircraft or aircraft parts
could have operated without permission of the Ministry. The
granting of such permission would have been dependent
upon all kinds of stipulations, including the removal of a
non-cooperating board of managers. Refusal to meet such
stipulations could have entailed the expropriation of the aircraft concern involved. The Air Force also requested authority to build plants for the production of essential raw
materials.[33] The Minister of War rejected these plans for
introducing the principle of public property into the field of
armament production. Navy experience with public enterprises had been deplorable, it was insisted, and the expropriation of private concerns would have an unfavorable
effect upon entrepreneurial initiative. Since rearmament
would be hampered without the cooperation of private concerns, the Air Force bill was shelved, and the Ministry permitted only to issue binding production orders to its armament producers.

The production of military equipment and weapons thus
became the exclusive function of private enterprise. To meet
military specifications, producers had to establish new plants,
build new machines, train laborers in special skills, and supply products that could be sold only to the state. Since the
unit costs of these products could not be anticipated with
any degree of accuracy, armament producers received cost-
plus-profit contracts, which usually gave rise to exceptionally
large profits. The office of price control in the Ministry of
War was still in its infancy and did not as yet re-examine
costs and prices charged by producers. Selling only to procurement agencies, which signed secret contracts unknown
to other sellers, most of the armament producers operated

outside of any market nexus, since neither the terms of trade nor the quality and quantities delivered were influenced by the intentions or actions of other sellers or buyers. Military security conditions were imposed upon employers as well as workers, and trade secrets, by extension, became military secrets. Also, in order that they might be insulated from other industries, the armament producers were not permitted to become members of the economic groups and instead had to join special organizations under the control of the procurement agencies.[34]

Armament producers thus became an appendage of the militarized public sector of the economy. Two principles, usually in conflict with each other, governed their operations. Producing only for state agencies and being organizationally linked with the military procurement and security offices, armament concerns took on the form of quasi-public enterprises. But there were many indications that the managers of such concerns saw themselves as political capitalists who owned their own properties, realized exceptionally high profits, and otherwise benefited directly from the manifold actions of their government supporters. The characteristics attributed by Max Weber to political capitalism (governmentally created profit opportunities and sales outside of markets) were present but not the economic weakness of the state. It was because of this third feature—overlooked by Weber—that rearmament did not give rise to political capitalism. Instead of confirming our hypothesis (stated in Chapter I), rearmament by the powerful German state in this period of history created a state-directed sector of the economy in which the armament producers also found their place.

The third impact of rearmament expressed itself in the institutional innovation of the regulated market. Such situations do not inevitably arise out of every rearmament boom. The regulated markets in Germany resulted from the scarcity of domestic capital and an illiquid banking system, from the scarcity of foreign exchange and an overvalued currency, from a huge foreign debt and the subsequent moratorium on the export of capital, foreign or domestic. Given these conditions, a rearmament boom could be implemented only through the use of regulation in the affected markets.

The six regulated markets not only linked the private with the public sectors of the economy but also provided an opportunity for coupling statist with capitalist principles in the same market. The capitalist principles of profits, a pattern of trading between private firms, and effective interest representation for business organizations coexisted with the statist principles of centralizing monetary transactions, controlling the terms of trade in approved private transactions, adjusting the quantities traded to the requirements of rearmament, and increasing the volume of foreign exchange and exports as well as that of government bills and bonds. Both sets of principles were indispensable for the effective operation of the regulated markets.

In examining statist actions we may adhere to the well-established definition that statism prevails when "the major decisions about what is to be produced, imported, lent abroad, borrowed abroad, etc., are exercised by the state or its agencies";[35] but the coexistence of capitalist with statist principles clearly disproves two corollaries of this theory: namely, the cumulative growth of statist actions and their incompatibility with capitalism. In the first phase of the Nazi period, statist actions were limited to the six regulated markets, and the principles of statism were coupled with those of capitalism.[36]

As long as business groups operate as effective power blocs one can expect that some forms of private compensation will be combined with governmental rules in regulated markets. At the same time, statist agencies effectively operating to realize definite public goals will prevent the deterioration of government rules into business promotionalism, as has happened too frequently in the regulation of public utilities in the U. S.

In the Nazi regime, regulation also produced discrimination against or exploitation of foreign traders as well as some expropriation of borrowed foreign capital. Regulation here became a means of implementing a peculiar form of economic aggression. It was unusual because the involuntary credits, the excess of imports in the clearing trade, and the expropriated foreign capital constituted unearned gains that flowed into Germany and stayed there. These gains, which resulted from actions taken by the state, are to be distinguished from the politically oriented imperialisms of the past, which usually derived their profits from the exporting of goods and capital to dependent countries. Statist actions in the form of market regulation became a substitute for capital investment and the deployment of troops in foreign countries. In reversing the flow of resources to other countries, or in keeping foreign capital within Germany, the statist element in the regulated market produced as its typical effect upon foreigners a new kind of inverted imperialism. It is in this modified form only that politically oriented imperialism became a part of the regulated sector of the Nazi economy.

The compatibility of statist actions with capitalism was greatly enhanced by the new forms of business organizations. Each supervisory board appointed a group of business leaders as its advisory committee, and the economic groups represented the economic interests of their members up to the time that decisions were taken by the government agencies. Chambers of industry or commerce made themselves the speakers for the private interests of their members and gave all kinds of advice to state agencies.[37] Although business pressure was not able to modify substantially the main goals of the state agencies, the concentrated and organized form that this pressure took increased the consideration given to private profit interests. Organized capitalism thus scored a greater success in getting private interests built into government regulation than could have been expected under a private but unorganized form of capitalism.

The fourth and last impact of rearmament existed in the destruction of a few private markets in Germany. Foreign-exchange control and managed currency, functioning as important financial instruments of rearmament, entailed the abolition of the open market in gold and foreign exchange. The prohibition of capital exports induced some capitalists to smuggle German money into foreign countries. As a part of the exchange control, state agencies also tried to prevent the reimport of German money, the result of which was the shrinkage and eventual abolition of German-money markets in foreign countries. In these relatively few instances statist policy destroyed not only the markets but any form of capitalist activity.

Thus, in terms of economic systems, rearmament was responsible for a fourfold modification of private capitalism. The employment-creating demand of the military agencies operated as an invigoration of private capitalism, but the industrial capitalists, who had to give up any preference for peace, became increasingly associated with a militarily oriented state, while the direct armament producers were organizationally and financially incorporated into the militarized sector of the public economy. The regulated markets coupled economic statism with organized capitalism, thereby acting as a forerunner for the economic system of the immediate future in Nazi Germany. Regulation produced a small but important area of effective price and quantity controls by the government. The detrimental effects of these controls were frequently compensated for, so that regulation did not undermine the system of organized capitalism in the private sector of the economy. The same can be said for the abolition of some markets, the functions of which were taken over by administrative agencies of the state, with the result that the volume of economic transactions performed by the government was further increased. The first modification, however, surpassed all others in relative significance because it contributed so mightily to the invigoration of capitalist institutions and to the development of organized capitalism.

FUTURE OF PARTIAL FASCISM

CHAPTER ELEVEN

Reviewing the first phase of the Nazi regime, we arrive at the conclusion that the coalition of the Nazis, generals, and big business was clearly successful. The main goals of the coalition, which included military equality with other powers, political and economic self-determination, military and economic rearmament, the suppression of trade unions, and the invigoration of capitalist institutions, had been largely or fully achieved by the end of 1936.

The dual structure of power had given rise to four distinct groups. In terms of organization and administration, there had developed a quadripartite society. Each holder of power possessed a specific sphere of influence over which he exercised almost full control, but these four spheres of influence were mutually interpenetrating. Big business was largely in control of urban business but had very little to say about agriculture; big business had also to accept the strong influence of the generals over the armament producers. The generals, in turn, dominated the administrative and commanding military agencies but exercised only limited supervision over the air force and the few police regiments of the SS.

The party dominated the political and ideological—the main informational and educational—lines of action but was forced to stay out of the military and most of the economic ministries of the state and had to tolerate the military and economic ideals and policies of its allies. The SS controlled the regular and secret police and the instruments of terror but had to abstain from military intelligence and refrain from acting within the spheres of power belonging to the military and to big business. Whereas in fundamental conflicts there prevailed a close partnership between the party and the SS, or between the generals and big business, in daily policy decisions and administrative matters the lines of authority and influence were clearly drawn.

Each holder of power ruled by fear as well as by obedience, by legitimate authority as well as by illegitimate force. Rather than being neatly separated, legitimate and illegitimate power existed side by side in each sphere of power, the former voluntarily accepted and the latter ruling by means of terror and punishment.

Although kept within the bounds of legality, the formation of the coalition generated a "constitutional dictatorship"; in other words, the presidential authority of the Weimar Republic was illegitimately used to extend the emergency powers of the constitution beyond reasonable limits. The subsequent political counterrevolution of the Nazis constituted a series of violent acts which set in after the burning of the *Reichstag,* proceeded to the destruction of all other political parties, and ended with the "coordination" of most other social organizations with the mass associations of the Nazis. Although these acts of open and direct usurpation were legalized through the law of February 28, 1933, the Nazi usurpers were not bound by that law since their violence was unlimited and illegitimate. Anyone who either opposed or was expected to disapprove of the usurpation of power was subjected to the horror of Nazi terror. In its origin, the quadripartite society of the Third *Reich* arose because of an illegitimate grabbing of power by its allied founders.

The effect of usurpation was the division of the people into the powerful and the powerless.[1] At the beginning only organized labor was powerless, but as middle-class socialism was disowned by the party and defeated as a policy by big business, most of the middle groups were pushed into the category of the politically powerless. The continued impact of usurpation established an underlying population that existed only as an object of decision-making on the part of the rulers.

The principle of legitimacy divided the powerless into two groups, the believers and the disbelievers. The disbelievers, comprising especially anti-Nazis and non-Nazis, saw and experienced only illegitimate power. They accommodated themselves to that power primarily through the motive of fear. In every sphere there was a different reason for submission, a different kind of penalty to fear. In exercising illegitimate power, the party tried to eliminate many forms of nonconformity to party policy and ideology on the part of those who belonged to the mass organizations; the SS sought to prevent all kinds of subversion in thought and action among the powerless; the generals expected unquestioned submission to military regulations from the soldiers; and the employers insisted upon complete acceptance of their plant rules and instructions. Throughout the first phase of the regime there was thus a four-way exercise of illegitimate power, the burden of which fell primarily upon those people outside the power circles who did not accept the party ideology.[2]

Most decisive for those who were in power was the fact that the Nazis were not supremely or solely powerful. Our finding of a dual power structure, in which four distinct organizations divided among themselves the functions of the state, points towards the existence of partial fascism in the first phase of the regime. Whether in terms of power or functions, the top Nazi leaders were only occasionally able to influence, and could not lay down, the economic and military policies of the regime.

The existence of fairly definite limits to the power of the single party is a condition that does not confirm the widely held theory of totalitarianism which equates single-party dictatorship with unlimited rule over all spheres of life. It is certainly correct to say, however, that such a dictatorship is characterized by (1) a monolithic political party possessing all instruments of political power, (2) by a uniform ideology that claims to be the sole valid view of the world, (3) by a terroristic police system that seeks to penetrate into all spheres of private life, and (4) by comprehensive indoctrination through the control of many means of communication and opinion formation. But although the first feature was speedily achieved, the Nazis were unable to penetrate, with their ideology, secret police, and communications controls, into the spheres of life that were dominated by the military and big business.

The theory of totalitarianism is also inapplicable because it includes the hypotheses (5) of party control over military affairs, and (6) of a comprehensively planned and state-controlled economy.[3] Both these features were clearly missing in the early periods of the Nazi regime. The continued existence of the two traditional holders of power raises the intricate question of whether these limitations changed the nature of Nazi ideology and power.

IDEOLOGICAL LEGITIMACY

The nature of a political system influences the meaning of legitimate power. In a democracy, the leaders are responsible for their policies to the voters, who not only obey the laws but also approve or periodically reject the authority of a particular leader or party. Whatever may be the underlying principle of legitimacy, voluntary obedience is thus complemented by the principles of political responsibility and periodic elections. In a one-party dictatorship, however, the responsibility of the leader to the voters is replaced by his devotion to the ideology of the party. The leader personifies a certain view of the world that is shared by the subleaders, the followers, and the sympathizers. The leadership of the party is responsible to no one and faithful only to its ideology. It is this devotion of the leaders to the ideology that justifies the voluntary obedience of the followers, that unites leaders and followers in one belief. Disbelievers are, of course, not covered by the principle of ideological legitimacy, and their acceptance of party rule must be obtained by means of physical and mental violence. The effective application of violence, in turn, requires a particular form of political organization, in which the actions of the monolithic party and the paramilitary organizations secure ideological legitimacy as well as obedience through fear.[4]

The rulers of one-party regimes assert that they do not seek and employ power for themselves—that they utilize it exclusively for the realization of their ideology. The leaders regard themselves as the enunciators of the ideology and assert that it not only transforms their own lives but also excites the enthusiasm and devotion of their followers. In communism, the ideology is said to reveal the "laws of society"; in fascism, the insight and wisdom of the leader is assertedly derived from "the iron laws of nature." As early as 1928 Hitler said that "There will never be a solution of the German problem until we return to the three fundamental principles which control the existence of every nation: the concept of struggle, the purity of blood, and the ingenuity of the individual."[5] It was because of these principles that the Nazis claimed to possess a superior ideology, that they felt endowed with the mission of imposing a counterrevolution upon Germany.

This ideology performed three distinct functions. It acted as the fountainhead for all ideals, as the source of and guide for all policies that the party sought to implement; provided a substitute for religion by supplying a world view and a set of ultimate values acceptable to all subleaders, followers and sympathizers; and finally, served to justify the use of mental and physical violence against all those of the powerless who did not voluntarily acknowledge the right of the party to rule the state.

As we have seen, the party leaders divided their ideology into two distinct parts. The expendable tenets were given up step by step in the daily collaboration of the party with the generals and big business. At the end of the first phase, none of these ideals could be used as a source of policy. The split in the ideology thus introduced a process of shrinkage in the number of components comprising the ideology and resulted in the elimination of the Nazi intransigents from their positions of power in party and state. This move was accomplished peacefully in the economic sphere, where the intransigents were simply removed from office and their particular ideology condemned by the party leaders.

The process of shrinkage called for the use of illegitimate power in the quasi-military sphere. In terms of Nazi ideology, Röhm was on the right track. He supported his demand for a military counterrevolution with the argument "that all successful revolutions based upon ideological claims must have their own revolutionary armies which should be the vital expression of their new Weltanschauung. . . ."[6] In terms of politics, however, Hitler had to choose between the coalition and the military counterrevolution. Since persuasion had failed to change Röhm's proposals, Hitler applied violence against one of his para-military organizations. The practice of purging recalcitrant subleaders became the recognized means of physical violence used within the party itself. This form of power was illegal within the legal order of the state, and illegitimate in relation to the ideology of the party. The recalcitrants were beheaded precisely because they had tried to implement the original ideology and had insisted that no part of this ideology was expendable.

The successful purge produced an organizational as well as an ideological effect. Not only was one of the para-military organizations removed as a power-holder but the supremacy of the party over its integral and affiliated organizations was fully established. The power of the oligarchic clique of the party became unquestioned. No subleader could possibly dare to maintain a line of policy entirely his own. The "party line," as defined by the top leaders, had to be accepted by all Nazis in any line of activity. After the purge and because of it, the party leaders were no longer beholden to the "machine" but could use it for implementing the essential parts of their ideology as well as for realizing the goals of the coalition.

The essential parts of the ideology were then dogmatized by the leaders. The supremacy of the oligarchic clique within the party and the policies of extreme racialism and fascist imperialism had to be accepted as absolute values by all members and sympathizers. The components of the dogma were condensed into a "primer" for instructional use in the party and the public schools. All goals discussed within the party or presented to the nation over the public means of communication had at least to appear to be oriented to the ultimate aims of the party. It was only after the use of illegitimate power within the Nazi movement that dogmatization became successful, which, in turn, supported the claim that only the Nazi ideology could be professed in Germany.

Ideological legitimacy called for the glorification of the Nazi dogma. In their speeches and actions, the Nazis behaved as if their ideology (a) contained a revelation of the highest human insights, (*b*) presented an eternally valid truth, and (*c*) were capable of purifying the blood as well as the thoughts of the believers. Glorification transformed the Nazi world view into the best attainable faith. Acceptance of this belief constituted the most exalted experience that anyone could attain, and desecration was the worst crime that anyone could commit. The party court became the legitimate instrument for investigtaing and punishing violators of the ideological faith, while the SS or the Gestapo took violent measures against the dissenters and vilifiers.

Ideological "persuasion" thus inevitably turned into indoctrination. In genuine ideological legitimacy, obedience to the ruling party is a voluntary act, initiated and justified by a commonly held belief. Indoctrination, in contrast, imposes the dogmatized components of the ideology upon the non-believers (i.e., "Laodiceans") and disbelievers. In the less severe cases, mental violence was used to obtain overt acceptance of the dogma and full respect for the symbols of the Nazi movement. Open defiance was met by administering physical violence in all its sadistic forms. Both forms of violence created a fear in the minds of the indifferent as well as disbelievers, and it was this fear of punishment that compelled involuntary obedience to the commands of the rulers. Thus, by coupling ideologically legitimate with illegitimate power, the party—once established—exerted a force that claimed to be all-persuasive, irresistible, and irreversible.[7]

The use of coercion with persuasion was by no means accidental. On the one hand, all other ideologies were seen as base and evil. The ideology of the rulers alone was supreme. Rival ideologies had thus to be forbidden, and their proponents destroyed or driven underground. The claim of being in possession of the best of all ideologies called for the application of violence against anyone holding to a rival ideology. On the other hand, belief in the Party's dogmas was regarded not only as a privilege but also as a duty. Indifference was thus seen as a sign of shirking one's political duties, and nonbelievers were suspected as potential enemies of the official dogma. In either case, the ruling party inferred from the purity and superiority of its ideology the right to use all legitimate and illegitimate means of indoctrination.

Given this interpenetration of legitimate and illegitimate power, ideological legitimacy is a superior device for getting and holding the obedience of the ruled. Charismatic leadership is handicapped by three conditions: the prophet's inner calling is strictly a personal affair of the leader; the belief of the disciples is based on their faith in the extraordinary qualities of the leader; and the political machine supports the leader only because of these qualities.[8] In consequence, when the inner calling of the leader suddenly ceases or is no longer believed in by his disciples, the spiritual power of the charisma disappears, the power constellation becomes depersonalized, and the elements of the belief become subject to a routine explanation. Why then is ideologically oriented and legitimized power free of these defects?

The answer is that the ideology must be durable—its teachings more or less specific, transferable among persons, teachable to disciples, acceptable and retainable by the larger number of followers. The personal, and extraordinary, qualities of the leader are derived from the ideology. If the character of the leader changes or if he falls by the wayside, one particularly qualified enunciator is succeeded by another more or less qualified. In spite of the difficulties of succession, the ideology does remain as the basic belief of the subleaders and followers. How long the ideology is attractive and acceptable depends upon its value and usefulness to the movement involved. If the ideology demands basic social changes—and succeeds in making them—it tends to last for several generations. Its implicit tasks and moral appeal are often so great that it provides the source for continuous anxiety and repeated excitement. Through their well-planned parades and recurrent propaganda stunts, through their new riots against one political opponent after the other, through their intellectual and quasi-military attacks on others, the Nazis were fully able to exhibit the undiminished vitalism of their ideology—in spite of the limitations upon their power in the military and economic spheres of action.

The exclusive position of the ideology in the realm of ideals intensified the need for dogmatization of the ideology. The more clearly the party line in ideological matters was pursued by the rulers, the greater was the need to state the accepted ideals in fairly clear images for adherents as well as enemies. Deviation could then be more readily recognized and punished. Such dogmatization could turn into routine professions and mere lip service, but this was not true of many of the top leaders in the Nazi regime.

Although the dogma was supplemented by the party edict and enunciated by the "command of the leader," these authoritative proclamations (*Führerbefehl*) were not only an indication of the personal power of Hitler but were widely regarded as an expression of the superior wisdom of the party's ideology. The commands of the leader in non-ideological matters did not make their entry as such in the first phase of the regime,[9] for the order to kill Röhm and his consorts was issued by Hitler in his capacity as "the supreme judge of the German people," so as to avoid imminent treason against the *Reich*.[10] Hitler thus invoked legality but not ideological legitimacy for this openly tyrannical act of power.

Nor was there any evidence of a separation of the political machine of the party from its ideology. The monopolistic position of the party with its principle of centralized leadership and organizational interaction assured that the subleaders would depend for their position on the good will and approval of the top leaders of the party. Subleaders were appointed and promoted by headquarters. *Gauleiter* received instructions from the deputy leader, and the finances of regional offices were controlled by the treasury of the party. Violations of the party's code of honor were investigated and punished by the party judge. Hitler kept—through the party treasurer—supervision over the party funds and the funds of its auxiliary organizations, and contributions received from business organizations were paid to the Hitler Donation, which meant that the office of the deputy leader divided the funds among the party organizations. The same was true of government funds that went from the treasury of the state to the party. Although the extensive party machinery was used to some extent by most of the subleaders to satisfy their own personal interests and desires for power, the top leaders could and did use the machine for implementing the policies of the party; and after the purge the subleaders were forced to obey the commands of the top leaders. This obedience prevailed also in ideological matters. The best known example of disobedience was the "Streicher affair" of 1938. The order to burn the synagogues was followed by the injunction that the seizure of Jewish property must not lead to the personal enrichment of any leader or member of the party. Streicher and his consorts violated this command, and they were investigated by a special commission, headed by Göring. Its recommendation that Streicher should be dismissed as *Gauleiter* was implemented by the deputy leader.[11]

Thus, although corruption was not infrequent, an attempt was made, for the benefit of the public, to keep the image of the ideology untainted either by personal enrichment on the part of the leaders or by excessive use of tyrannical power. In instances of open violence, such as the Röhm murder or the terror in concentration camps, tyrannical power was deliberately kept separate from ideological legitimacy or hidden from public view. Opponents of the oligarchic clique within the party were punished not for vilifying the ideology but for personal reasons (homosexuality) or because of actions against the state—disobedience to the leaders or treason. Ideological opponents, on the other hand, were subjected to "legitimate" violence; they had to be eliminated in order that the purity of the ideology might be preserved. In fact, however, the two kinds of power, and violence, were coexistent, although symbolically separated.

This phenomenon of actual coexistence and symbolic separation does not support the widely held opinion that ideological legitimacy alone existed in the first phase of the regime and was then completely superseded by tyrannical power. Indeed, it was precisely because of the Nazis' ability to maintain the fiction of symbolic separation of the two powers that ideological legitimacy was so extraordinarily effective with the masses in the first phase of the regime.

There were three reasons for the successful coexistence of ideological legitimacy and partial fascism. First, the violence of the Röhm purge broke the power of the intransigent wing in the party and the movement. Thus, a shrinkage of the ideology was possible without any corresponding split within the party or an open fight between the SA and the SS. The second reason resided in the peculiar nature of Nazi ideology, the core elements of which were noneconomic in substance. Social harmony and middle-class socialism could be given up without impairing the core of the ideology; by eliminating democracy and securing a monopoly over the police and the instruments of communication, the party could refrain from making an appeal to the economic interests of the workers and small businessmen—without suffering a decline in its power. The third reason pertained to the peculiar elective affinity that existed between the inverted imperialism of Schacht and economic as well as military rearmament. These three—inverted imperialism and the two forms of rearmament—could and did effectively supplement one another but the first came into conflict with Nazi imperialism. While rearmament was a task that could be accomplished only through the combined actions of the generals and the leaders of heavy industry, the resultant increase in military and economic strength constituted a necessary condition for the realization of Nazi imperialism. Consequently, the ideological concessions that were made to the upper class—by not specifying the nature of Nazi imperialism—did not weaken the party but instead permitted the party leaders to move toward the realization of the core elements of their ideology in the second phase of the regime.

IDEOLOGICAL INNOVATION

While the shrunken scope of the ideology was an obvious fact, the Nazi leaders carefully refrained from acknowledging this shrinkage. The splitting off of the expendable components was misrepresented as a form of ideological innovation. The concessions to the allies were construed as a step-by-step realization of the original ideology. In speaking of a change in emphasis, the top leaders tried to minimize the impact of the modified ideology on the existing principle of interlocking organization. What kind of organizational rearrangement grew out of the shrunken image of the original ideology?

The NSBO (*Nationalsozialistische Betriebszellen-Organisation*) had become the integral organization of leaders in charge of labor. Setting themselves the task of participating in the formulation of economic policy, most of its leaders had been in favor of a second revolution, this time with a view to establishing Nazi control over the economy. The purge took care of the near-revolt of the NSBO. A very few of the outspoken critics of Hitler were killed, and the NSBO was first demoted and then dissolved. Open violence against and final dissolution of the NSBO were thus the means by which the resistance to the splitting-off of one ideological component was removed.

The Labor Front was prevented from realizing its goal of

social harmony in 1933–34, when the function of wage setting was allocated to the employers and the state, and when the Labor Front was forced to give up its occupational for a merely territorial form of organization. Rather than announcing the surrender of this major goal of the Labor Front, the leaders swapped certain elements of their ideology. This "trading" was accomplished by virtue of the distinction between the economic prerogative of the employer and the political authority of the Labor Front in plants. As a kind of compensation for giving up its own strand of ideology, the Labor Front was authorized to engage in the ideological indoctrination of workers at their places of work.

The process of ideological adjustment was greatly facilitated by the introduction of a sham ideology into industrial relations. The labor law asserted that the plant had been transformed into a social community of laborers and the employer. In fact, the employer was elevated to the position of leader, and his workers were spoken of as followers. The employer could claim obedience for his instructions in the name of the plant community, but the restored managerial prerogative of employers could not be exercised in the name of property ownership. Property legitimacy was transformed into a community ideology the function of which was to disguise the practically unlimited power of employers over economic matters in plants. Organized capitalism had to accept this sham ideology in order to live peacefully with the party and its Labor Front, but the concession did not in any significant way hinder the exercise of the economic managerial prerogative in plants.

Outside the field of industrial relations, however, the capitalist ideal of property legitimacy was fully acceptable to the Nazis. Three facets of this ideal could be, and were, fully publicized at the time. Business concerns had to be free to use their property as they wanted to in order that they might function effectively. Entrepreneurial initiative was essential to the successful operation of the German economy and could never be replaced by governmental regulation; hence business organizations had to be permitted a measure of self-government in the management of their own affairs. These three ideals of private capitalism were in full evidence, could be freely expressed, and were even accepted by the Nazis, with the sole exception of the intransigents.

Defeat of the Nazified middle class was associated only indirectly with the second form of ideological innovation. The surrender of middle-class socialism caused only a rearrangement of the integral organization of handicrafts and trade, whereby the NS Hago (*Nationalsozialistische Handwerk, Handel-und Gewerbeorganisation*) came under the full domination of the party leaders, and the handicraft organizations came under the control of the Minister of Economics. Ideological surrender here expressed itself in a shift of organizational control from one ally to another.

The lack of party control was especially resented by the Labor Front. Banking upon the claim of an all-comprehensive ideology, the leaders of the Labor Front demanded that all gainfully employed workers must become members and that all other economic organizations must be incorporated into the Labor Front. In October of 1934, Ley presented to Hitler a bill that contained such a claim of organizational totality. Hitler signed the bill when he was assured by Ley that Hess had participated in the formulation of the bill and had given it his explicit approval. This law, which, in effect, assumed that party control had been established over the economy, demanded the incorporation of all economic organizations into the Labor Front.

The opposition to the Hitler-Ley law was prompt and decisive. One minister after another rejected the law, which they declared to be null and void because none of them had given it his countersignature, and Hess declared the law to be unenforceable, since it violated the rule that all legislative proposals must have received the approval of the deputy leader before they could be presented to Hitler.[12] Thus there arose in the supposedly fully totalitarian regime a situation in which the signature of the dictator could create a law only if a bill was countersigned by a minister of the government and approved by the deputy leader of the party.

When, in 1936, Schacht and his business organizations systematically opposed the attempt of the Labor Front to establish a network of chambers of labor, Ley republished the obsolete law and claimed the right to absorb the handicraft organizations. In two provinces of the East, the old handicraft leaders were replaced by appointees of the Labor Front, but the protest of the two handicraft leaders and Schacht's forceful intervention stopped this move. Driven to a choice between Schacht and the regional leaders of the party and the Labor Front, Hess as deputy leader fully supported Schacht's intervention.

The leaders of the Labor Front did not, however, accept this decision as final. The regional leader of Mecklenburg put the blame entirely on Schacht and in a circular letter of November 11, 1937, predicted Schacht's downfall: "Laws and the men who make them come and go . . . but the ideology of Adolf Hitler is of eternal validity."[13] Ley and his consorts also implied that they had to function in this case as the enunciators of the ideology and in 1938 worked out a new bill that would have granted the Labor Front the right (a) to include all gainfully employed persons and incorporate all economic organizations in the country, (b) to become an independent organization that would be responsible only to Hitler.[14]

The attempt to achieve organizational independence and ideological equality with the party was decisively quashed. Ley had presented his bill to the ministers without having received the prior consent of the deputy leader. In a long memorandum, sent to the *Gauleiter* as well as to the members of the cabinet, Hess rejected both the organizational and ideological claims of the Labor Front. The right to issue ideological proclamations was said to be vested only in Hitler. As his deputy, Hess insisted upon the organizational superiority of the party.[15] A long debate followed because Walter Funk (the Minister of Economics) and a few party leaders sided with the Labor Front. Eventually, Deputy Leader Schmeer was expelled from the Labor Front, and the proposed bill was rejected by Hitler.

As temporary Minister of Economics at the end of 1937, Göring ordered two *Gauleiter* to respect the officially appointed economic organizations of small business, dismissed the leaders of the Labor Front from the positions which they had usurped in the handicraft organizations, and appointed a new national leader of the handicraft organizations. Both the legitimate and the illegitimate attempts of the Labor Front to use the claim of organizational totality as a basis for establishing an independent position in party and state (similar only to that of the SS) failed because of the opposition of the party leadership as well as of the Ministries of War and Economics.

Our survey of these ideological splits and subsequent innovations suggests three conclusions: First, ideological legitimacy could and did become fully compatible with ideological innovation. The legitimized dogma furnished a standard for determining which strands of the ideology could be discarded and which called for an innovation. Being an implementation of the dogma, innovation was seen as a way of strengthening the legitimacy of the ideology. Moreover, the split in the ideology did not significantly weaken the party's domination of its integral and affiliated organizations because the innovations were either deliberately or coincidentally coupled with the discarding of an expendable element of the ideology. The new tasks thus compensated the adherents of whatever was discarded and diverted their attention to new challenges. The use of sham ideologies further facilitated this process of ideological diversion. Finally, both practices—ideological innovation and diversion—were beneficial to organized capitalism. The discarding of certain strategic components eliminated the conflicts of interest with the original ideology of the party, and the sham ideology permitted private enterprise to regain its managerial prerogative without incurring the active and persistent animosity of any influential group in the society. In the first phase, organized capitalism became fully compatible with ideological legitimacy as proclaimed by the political rulers.

VIOLENCE AND CAPITALISM

In many historical situations, private capitalism has had to face the violence of armed noncapitalist groups. If such groups could not be suppressed by the physical force of the state, private concerns usually sought protection against such violence by their own action. Either capitalist enterprises financed armed units under their control or they paid protection money to the leaders of violent groups. It was the latter method that was employed by the German business organizations in 1933.

During the months of the political counterrevolution, from March to July of 1933, the headquarters of some business organizations were occupied by Nazi commissioners, and the large number of integral and affiliated organizations started a campaign to collect funds from all families as well as concerns. In response to these actions, Gustav Krupp as the leader of the central organization of all trade associations arranged with Hitler for the payment of funds by all enterprises to the Nazi party. These funds were collected voluntarily by business organizations (the amounts depending on the number of persons employed) and delivered monthly to Hitler's deputy. The professed aim of the business leaders was

to enable the party leaders to regain control over the para-
military SA. The additional hidden purpose of these payments was to obtain immunity for the upper class from the
violence of the Gestapo. In both respects, the "Hitler Donation" was a success. In only a few cases did rich, but non-
Jewish, people suffer from Nazi violence. Since the payments
were regarded as a business expense, German consumers
eventually paid for the contributions that immunized business against Nazi violence.[16]

Both the SA and the SS received their share of money from
the Hitler Donation. While the SA gave support to the ideal
of an economic counterrevolution, the SS displayed a decided
disinterest in economic affairs. Business concerns, in this
earlier period, had little to fear from the SS because the
secret police were primarily concerned with political matters
and because in the SS the racial ideology was divested of any
economic content.

In building up his organization, Himmler tried to form a
group that would be distinguished by racial superiority and
special status. Desirable behavior was prescribed in a fashion
similar to the caste system. Only Aryans who possessed the
physical characteristics of the Nordic race were eligible for
membership. Applicants had to pass tests of health and physical strength. Members could receive permission to marry only
if the woman chosen exhibited the same superior biological
qualities, and SS couples had to produce at least four children
or adopt an equal number from biologically superior families. As in other status groups each member occupied a definite position and held various honors and privileges. Of
strategic significance was the fact that few of these privileges
aimed at economic gains. Honor ensued from the alleged
biological superiority of the SS and from their collective
responsibility for monopolizing the functions of the secret
and public police. In combining the features of a biologically
oriented caste and a privileged status group, the leaders of

the SS sought to create an aristocracy of blood that was to rule Nazi-dominated Europe. Said Himmler in 1934: "We have fought in vain if political victory is not to be followed by a victory of birth and good blood."[17]

As we should expect, this caste-like status group operated not in a traditional but in a charismatic setting. The group as a whole, as well as each member, was said to be endowed with extraordinary qualities. Given women of good blood and a sense of high obligation, members of the SS were urged to have children out of wedlock, "not promiscuously but out of the deepest sense of ethics."[18] The ordinary rules of sexual morality did not apply to the SS. In addition, they were expected to have an extraordinary sense of obedience and to be willing to accept a granite-like discipline. Said Himmler of the purge: "We did not hesitate on June 30th, 1934 to do the duty we were bidden, and stand up against the wall and shoot comrades who had lapsed. . . . It appalled everyone, and yet everyone was certain that he would do it the next time if such orders were issued and if it were necessary."[19] The SS as an organization thus claimed to possess in an extraordinary degree the qualities of character of a "political soldier" who as a representative of Nazi ideology would accept any duty if in so doing he could serve the cause of a greater and more powerful Germany.

There is little doubt that the racial and ideological charisma claimed by the SS was widely acknowledged and that their authority was built upon the voluntary obedience of a significant portion of the Nazified population.[20] The SS leaders used this authority in ordering their men to take part in specific acts of violence. The executors of such illegitimate power were told that in committing these acts of violence they did not and could not possibly debase themselves. During the war Himmler said that the shooting of ten Poles was a mere nothing and pointed out that "we might later have to shoot tens of thousands in their place . . . [which] would then be carried out at the cost of German blood."[21] However despicable this attitude may seem to us, the use of legitimate authority to justify illegitimate power and thereby institutionalize violence is one feature of the political strength that is typical of one-party regimes.[22]

Although as much appalled by the violence as by the alleged ethics of racial ideology, business leaders benefited in three ways from the racial orientation of Nazi violence. The actions against the Jews at first handicapped and later eliminated competitors in markets and made available many desirable properties for purchase at bargain prices. The ethics of racial ideology eliminated the risks that usually spring from the rivalry of different gangster groups. Business concerns suffered certainly less from the personal demands of Nazi subleaders wanting a share of the profits than they would have from the rival claims of competing gangsters. Furthermore, as another feature of the Hitler Donation, deputy leader Hess issued certificates that served to protect businessmen from claims for additional payments to auxiliary Nazi organizations. In consequence, the centralized payments to the Hitler Donation effectively immunized business against the violence of the Nazis. At the same time, as we have seen, big business was directly indebted to Nazi violence for the destruction of trade unions and the elimination of collective bargaining and, indirectly, for the restoration of the managerial prerogative and the renewal of employer influence in the labor markets.

SELF-GOVERNMENT OF BUSINESS

With the advent of the second Hitler government, the political position of big business changed significantly. Prior to July of 1933, business organizations had extensively implemented the policy of business promotionalism. Subsidies were paid to friendly political parties, and trade associations negotiated with government agencies for promotional favors. In 1931, business support induced the Nazis to modify their party program by dropping the demand for nationalization and by promising active support to German businesses. Hitler also appointed two additional economic advisors, Funk and Keppler, who enjoyed the confidence of business groups. The financial support given to the Nazi and Nationalist parties in 1932 and 1933 was intended to make possible the establishment of a rightist government in which business groups would determine the economic policies indirectly. When the Nationalist party was removed from office by the political counterrevolution of the Nazis, big business lost its chance to control economic policies via a political party; but with the appointment of Director Schmitt as Minister of Economics, and as a result of Schmitt's dealings with Hitler, a new policy of direct business participation was set up. It was this new policy of direct participation that constituted the decisive political step in the formation of organized capitalism.

Command over the economic agencies of the government was used to implement four distinct economic policies. Under Schacht's leadership big business (a) regained control over the organizations of Nazified small business, (b) restored corporate control over markets by strengthening cartels, (c) introduced a uniform network of compulsory business organizations led mainly by the heads of large concerns, and (d) utilized the power of the state to invigorate a string of other capitalist institutions. Now we shall attempt to see how and why big business was able to realize these four goals within the political setting of a fascist regime.

As a result of the ingenious strategy adopted by business leaders, the attack of the intransigent Nazis on private capitalism was successfully counteracted and turned to the advantage of big business. It was understood by the members of the coalition that the economic policies of the regime would be determined exclusively by the economic agencies of the state which were—with the exception of agriculture— answerable to Schacht. The same principle was also applied to the business organizations, control of which was vested in the Minister of Economics. His new division for business organization worked out a plan for breaking Nazi influence in the guilds and chambers of handicraft and trade, and for supervising their policies. Implementation of this plan produced the following sequence of actions:

a) Feder and Keppler, who represented the Nazi influence in the Ministries of Economics and Labor, were removed from office, and the Minister of Economics was given a free hand in all non-agricultural economic policies that had no outright military or political significance.

b) Party membership as a condition for occupying positions of leadership and the requirement that appointments in the business groups or guilds and chambers be approved by the *Gauleiter* were dropped when the Minister of Economics made the business organizations responsible to himself.

c) Artisan master certificates as well as business experience and business competence became the sole requirements for appointments to positions of leadership in small business organizations.

d) The requirement that all firms join their respective groups or guilds prevented the rise of rival organizations and made all concerns subject to the policies of their leaders.

e) A new form of interlocking organization was built up when the chambers of industry, commerce, and handicraft were declared agents of the state whose executive officers had to pass civil-service examinations.

f) The chambers were given the right to veto the decisions of groups and guilds and to supervise them in several respects: (1) check on the contents of their bylaws, (2) confirm appointments to positions of leadership, and (3) pass on rules for training apprentices and journey-men and other matters involving the collection of fees and dues and the levying of fines or the imposition of penalties.

The pattern of these developments shows that Schacht and his associates were adroit builders and controllers of organizations. In integrating the groups or guilds with the chambers and the Ministry of Economics, in supervising the former by means of the latter, Schacht developed his own principle of interlocking organization. Adopting methods similar to those of the Nazis, he was able to break the Nazi domination over the organizations of small business, re-establish capitalist principles in this sector of the economy, and incorporate small business into organized capitalism.

It should be emphasized that this success of big business was achieved only because it did not involve an open conflict with the Nazi party, nor infringe in any way upon its political monopoly. The top Nazis adhered strictly to the goals of the alliance. Whenever a conflict arose between Schacht and a regional party leader on economic issues, Schacht eventually received the support of the deputy leader of the party.

In the first phase of Nazi rule, private concerns did not wait for a rise in prices springing from an increase in aggregate demand. There were many concerted actions that sought to obtain higher prices by eliminating competition in most markets. Business organizations succeeded in getting court injunctions against price-cutting, which was condemned as an act of unfair competition. The prices approved by the courts were usually based upon a unit cost acceptable to guilds or groups. The compulsory cartel law enabled cartels to eliminate the rebates of the depression and raise actual prices to the list prices of the preceding prosperity. Finally, the so-called calculation cartel was established in industries with many small producers. The prices arrived at by this new type of cartel were calculated on the basis of the average costs of the small producers. Whether by restoring the list prices of the existing cartels, by establishing new cartels, or by imposing court injunctions, competition in almost any form was eliminated from most markets. Business domination of markets became the central feature of self-government and thus of organized capitalism.

The direct participation of business in government effectively facilitated the trend towards organized markets. Old cartels were declared compulsory, or new cartels were formed by decree whenever outsiders began to reduce prices. The previous supervision of cartel activities by the cartel court was practically abolished. Not consumers or outsiders but the cartels themselves received the support of the cartel court and the government. "Incompetents" were eliminated from many markets, and business control over prices was reinforced by government action. In consequence, many of the economic agencies of the state became parts of the institutional arrangements of organized capitalism.

The reorganized trade associations applied coercion to their members. Two principles were accepted by these organizations. There could be only one membership organization for each industry. Everyone operating in an industry had to become a member of his "economic group." Oddly enough, these principles of compulsion were said to be necessary in order that business might achieve effective self-government. Hence, we must ask ourselves how coercion became compatible with a policy of economic self-determination in regard to the functioning of business.

The detrimental impact of the Great Depression had created a will to engage deliberately in organized business actions. The formation of organizations and the execution of selected policies had been hampered by the existence of dual organizations, by the indifference of non-participants, or by resistance on the part of outsiders. Unified organizations and compulsory membership were thus desired and eventually achieved by business leaders whose purpose was to obtain a more effective representation of specific industrial interests as well as of business as a whole.[23] The individual freedom of single concerns was sacrificed in order that the economic interests of the majority or of the biggest business concerns might be more efficiently realized; compulsion, far from being incompatible with private enterprise, became the means for a more uniform representation and a more effective realization of business interests in organized capitalism.

This peculiar form of self-government, coercive only for minorities, was not thwarted by the new tasks assigned to business organizations by the state. Governmentally allocated functions were usually performed by the chambers, whose executive secretaries became subject to the bureaucratic code for government officials. In exceptional cases the economic groups cooperated with auxiliary offices that performed certain state functions, such as estimating the extent of subsidies to be granted to exporting firms. Whoever performed governmental functions operated within a business-oriented environment and required for his effectiveness the confidence of the business leaders and executive committees of groups and chambers. Tasks assigned by the state were thus implemented in such a way as to become harmonious with the economic interests of the majority of the private concerns involved.[24]

Self-government by business in organized capitalism required the coordination of the economic interests of business groups and the economic functions of the state. The coordinators, whether in government or business, were either businessmen or their friends in office.

Given this coordination of economic policies, and the state's respect for the interests of big business, why was it necessary for the government to support private interests by imposing direct controls in the form of inducements and deterrents? Why was self-government by business insufficient in the six markets regulated by the state?

The reason was that even the compulsory business organizations were not always able to reconcile conflicts of interests among different firms or business groups. Three such conflicts were of the greatest significance. They arose because of the fight between debtors and creditors about the rates of interest, because of the price competition among German exporters in foreign markets, and because of forced purchasing quotas that reduced non-essential imports and opened opportunities for domestic producers. In these and similar cases, the government sided with one or the other of the disputing groups and imposed its solution upon those whose private power would hardly have prevailed in the markets.

The Great Depression reduced the rates of profits substantially below the rates of interest contracted for during the preceding period of prosperity. Indebtedness threatened the very existence of enterprises, or brought bankruptcy to many small, and also to a few well-known banks, large manufacturers, and insurance companies. Since most creditors refused to reduce their rates of interest voluntarily, tremendous pressure was put upon the government to reduce the contractual rates by force of law. Thus in the money and capital markets the government adopted a policy of deliberately reducing the price of borrowed capital. The result of this pricing policy was a reversal of the trend toward bankruptcy and the beginning of an invigoration of the capital structure of many private concerns.

When the crisis in the export business induced the government to provide subsidies for privately unprofitable but foreign-exchange-producing transactions, an unexpected dispute arose among German exporters. The subsidy induced private firms to reduce German prices in foreign markets, thereby diminishing the proceeds of foreign exchange per transaction. This price competition was suppressed by making the receipt of the subsidy conditional upon the exporter's willingness to charge foreigners the highest possible prices. The new price offices of the economic groups checked prices and unit costs and approved applications for subsidies only if losses were unavoidable. Thus, the charging of cartel prices became a necessary precondition for the granting of subsidies to exporters. Here, too, government compulsion was used to strengthen capitalist monopolies in foreign markets, in which the power of individual businesses was usually ineffectual.

Occasionally, however, inducements did not give rise to capitalist invigoration. When an increase in duties failed to raise domestic sales sufficiently, the producers in some industries obtained a law that set purchasing quotas for buyers in home markets. German soap producers, for instance, had to buy animal fat in specified quantities from certain domestic producers. The regulation of inter-industry transactions became an increasingly important policy in agricultural markets, in which the Nazi-controlled organizations not only set prices but also insisted upon minimum purchasing quotas within a specified period of time. This trend towards a regulated market and inter-industry organization, which flourished in agriculture, was rejected for most other sectors both by big business and by the Minister of Economics.[25] The former insisted that the inter-industry cartels were fully able to perform these functions, including the setting of prices and quotas for the sequence of industries affected. The Ministry of Economics asserted that entrepreneurial initiative and efficiency were an indispensable part of the industrial economy. The implication was that both these attributes were achieved through self-government by business in organized capitalism.

Nevertheless, there were conflicting interests among the various business groups that prevented them from eliminat-

ing regulation in those markets in which self-government
would not work.

STATE AND CAPITALISM

If the specific positions of all business groups are considered, then we have to differentiate among them and consider
four kinds of capitalism. The majority of business firms,
extensively cartelized and incorporated into compulsory, but
self-governing, groups, did effectively operate in a system of
organized capitalism. In contrast, there were three minor
groups that functioned under somewhat different conditions.
The direct producers of military equipment and munitions
acted under the conditions of a state-directed capitalism.
Concerns engaged in foreign trade or international finance
were sometimes given the opportunity to realize exploitation
gains, most of which, however, were created by, and reserved for, the state. Since most of these profit opportunities
grew out of the controlled flow of resources to—rather than
from—Nazi Germany, the private firms involved partook of
the gains available in a system of inverted imperialist capitalism. Finally, in enjoying the benefits of suppressed trade
unions and low wage rates, and of a renewed managerial
prerogative in plants, employers acted as status-ordained
capitalists whose special privileges were said to spring from
their positions of leadership in the "plant community."

Within the setting of the Nazi regime, all four types of
capitalism fell within the broad category of an authoritarian
capitalism, since the power enjoyed had been transformed
into diverse forms of authority.[26] In organized capitalism,
authority was usually derived from the owning or holding of
concentrated property. Leadership in cartels and business
groups was usually reserved for the top managers in the
largest concerns. The major exception, in the chemicals-indus-
try group, underlines the rule, since I. G. Farben exerted its

influence by providing the chairmen for the working committees of the compulsory organization. In most instances, the leaders were not held specifically accountable for their actions, nor did the renewal of their terms of office necessarily depend upon periodic elections. Authoritarian leadership tended to destroy the individual rights of member firms since they could leave neither the cartel nor the economic group. Cartels set the prices, determined the methods of cost calculation, decided upon the conditions of purchase and sale, and thereby synchronized the relationship between firms and markets. The influence of the leaders was paramount in the making of these decisions since there was no procedure for appealing them. The sole exception related to oligopolistic situations in which the other large members could force the leader to respect their interests. Thus, in the economic group of iron and steel producers, the leaders were held accountable for their actions and were periodically elected or re-elected until 1939. In all other situations, however, authority derived from the ownership of concentrated property could hardly be challenged successfully, since the leader and his advising committee usually received the support of the Ministry of Economics. Authority thus tended to eliminate the protection of individual rights and freedom from the sphere of organized capitalism.

In 1935 and 1936, most of the direct armament producers were elevated to the position of *Wehrwirtschaftsführer*. The authority implicit in this title was derived from the power of the Ministry of War, which enabled the producer to act in a semimilitary capacity. He could receive and be trusted with military secrets and could enjoin his employees from revealing military information to anyone else. The orders received from procurement agencies not only involved contractual obligations but were in effect military commands that had to be obeyed. The titled producer, in turn, could claim preferential treatment from his suppliers in regard to special quality and speedy delivery of the materials ordered and received. The authority of the state thus penetrated into the exchange relations among the businesses concerned, thereby attaching the elevated armament producers and their suppliers effectively to the militarized public sector of the economy.

The employer or his personnel chief received the title of plant leader. Although not so meaningful at the beginning of the regime, this title later entailed some specific privileges and duties. As the leader of the plant community, he was authorized to lay down the factory rules for the workers, hear and settle grievances, and determine the penalties for damage to materials or infringement of factory rules. At the same time, the plant leader had to cooperate with the *Betriebsobmann* of the Labor Front in securing the political reliability of the workers; facilitate the indoctrination efforts of the party, and meet the members of the council of confidence and thereby couple effectively the economic and political aspects of authority in the plants. Although the leadership title was created by the state and the rights and duties specified by the Ministry of Labor, the exercise of this authority was equally dependent upon the property power of business ownership.

Businesses dealing in foreign trade and international finance had to obtain specific permissions or exemptions for their transactions. Issued only to highly approved concerns, the permits authorized them to engage in a business that was not open to nonapproved concerns. The permits thus could become privileges and enable the approved firms to partake of the imperialist gains (or subsidies) that were opened up by the actions of the state. Being limited to a relatively few concerns, the exploitation gains could be channelled to specific groups, limited in amount, and terminated at the will of the government. The price for obtaining a share of these imperialist profits was thus a fairly strict adherence to the market regulation imposed by the state. The authority of the imperialist capitalists was thus derived from the regulatory power of the state.

In surveying these elements of authority that were conferred upon the leaders of private firms, we arrive at two conclusions. Whether the special rights and duties were derived from the power of the state or built upon concentrated property, the subsequent capitalism became incompatible with any kind of liberalism and democracy, and with equality and individual freedom. By the same token, the infusion of authority greatly facilitated the cooperation with militarism as well as with partial fascism. In fact, the granting of authority was the specific device chosen for attaining the compatibility of capitalism with militarism and partial fascism.

Why did business leaders accept such titles and privileges? Far from being mere decorations without economic meanings, the particular authority conferred could be and was extensively utilized for gaining the assistance of the state in realizing business interests. Each kind of authority became associated with a particular economic interest so that we can distinguish different types of state policies according to which business interests they supported.

There was first the state policy of business promotionalism. Outstanding examples of such a promotional policy were the compulsory cartel, the acceptance of business groups as agents of interest representation, the return of share capital—owned by the state—to private concerns, the strengthening of the positions of top managers in corporations, and the state-supported financing of expansion out of retained profits. The common effect of these and other promotional policies—whether implemented by indirect or direct controls—was an effective invigoration of capitalist institutions, including especially the restoring of profits to private concerns.

The jointly held military goal of powerful and modernized armed forces gave rise to the rearmament state. In satisfying the requirements of the three branches represented by the

Ministry of War, the public sector of the economy was militarized, and the armament producers were taken out of their market nexus and put under the supervision of the procurement agencies and armament inspectors. In return, the authorized producers not only experienced a significant increase in their volume of business but also benefited from the cost-plus-profit principle. Since for many of the new products it was impossible to estimate the unit costs with any degree of accuracy, producers were not only relieved from the element of risk but were even able to raise their profits by increasing their unit costs. Producers were thus handsomely compensated for the specific instructions and research required by the military agencies.

The financing of rearmament and the regulation of the six markets were based upon the notion of priority for the urgent tasks of the state (*staatspolitische Notwendigkeit*), but our analysis of the regulated market has shown that a second goal was closely linked with the first one. Whenever the urgent tasks called for intervention by the state, the private groups affected could claim compensation for lost income or for a diminished volume of business. With the exception of most creditors and some importers or exporters, the majority of firms in the regulated markets could obtain such compensation. Either a publicly created business (e.g., orders financed by means of mefo-bills) replaced a private one, or new private opportunities which would not have existed otherwise were opened up by government action. If compensation could not be made available in the regulated markets, subsidies were granted to those that incurred a loss by realizing an urgent task of military significance. The result of rearmament and market regulation was the creation of the compensation state.

Last but not least, there was the relative economic insignificance of the fascist state. Business groups were able to thwart almost all efforts to set up an "estate" organization for the economy or to create a middle-class socialism and reversed all preliminary steps toward a counterrevolution in industry while keeping the Labor Front out of the field of wage and employment policies. Although the suppression of trade unions and the maintaining of low wage rates constituted the worst economic effect for labor, the same actions on the part of the fascist state operated as invigorations for capitalist enterprises.

All four kinds of statist activity (promotion, rearmament, compensation, and suppression of trade unions) thus contributed decisively to the fact that private enterprise could enjoy the advantages of the rearmament boom without having to accept any significant increase in wage rates. Since the economic policies of the state were largely compatible with their interests, the leaders of big business found both organized capitalism and partial fascism not only compatible but also acceptable.

EXCHANGE CRISIS AND DISUNITY

If the coalition realized most of its goals and if organized capitalism was largely strengthened by rearmament, why did the successful coalition disintegrate in 1936? The answer is that an external limitation imposed itself upon the policy of rearmament, with the result that each of the partners deliberately tried to modify the dual power structure in his favor. The interaction of these causes produced a split within big business, an estrangement between generals and business leaders, and a re-alliance among the party leaders, the generals and a new group of business collaborators.

Foreign exchange was in short supply throughout the entire period of rearmament, but the scarcity became critical only when the generals doubled their demand for foreign exchange in December of 1935, and when the Minister of Agriculture reported two months later that the poor crop of

1935 called for a substantial increase in the volume of imported grains and fats. The crisis of foreign exchange arose thus from the coincidence of a poor crop with the increased tempo of rearmament.[27] Since the reported demand exceeded the expected supply of foreign exchange by a substantial margin, the rulers faced the necessity of formulating a new economic policy. Four alternatives were discussed as possible solutions: (a) reduce consumption by rationing fats and lowering the quality of bread, (b) stretch the armament-production program over a longer period, (c) substitute domestic synthetics for foreign raw materials, and (d) increase exports by means of a crash program. The alliance broke up because neither the rival business groups nor the generals and the party leaders were able to arrive at an agreement that would solve the crisis within the old coalition.

Let us look first at the split within big business. The air force and I. G. Farben had pushed unsuccessfully for the production of synthetics for several years. The Ministry of Economics had delayed the signing of contracts for the erecting of plants to produce synthetic oil and rubber. Not only were the unit costs substantially above those of the respective natural products but the quality of the synthetic products was still found unsatisfactory by the army testing office. Irritated by these delays, leading directors of I. G. Farben improved their connections with the Nazis, and both tried to exclude the Ministry of Economics from the field of synthetic products. This attempt almost succeeded when in March of 1936 Göring promoted the idea that he be appointed as commissioner for the domestic oil industry. When, a month later, he was appointed chairman of the commission on raw materials and foreign exchange, the jurisdiction over synthetics was immediately claimed by Göring for his staff office. Director Carl Krauch, second in command at I. G. Farben, joined Göring's staff. In his official capacity, Krauch negotiated the decisive contracts for the production

of synthetics with his colleagues from I. G. Farben. Krauch
had also had a leading part in formulating the original Four
Year Plan. There thus developed a close collaboration between the Nazi party and those industries (chemical, alumi-
num, aircraft, and synthetic textiles) that expected considerable gains from an extended military program.

The leaders of the heavy industries in the Ruhr valley,
however, thought the time had come for a substantial increase in steel exports. Many of them favored a crash program for increasing exports. Intensified extraction of low-
grade domestic iron ore was less appealing to them. After
an extensive discussion it was agreed that domestic ore should
be mined if the government would pay the difference between the prices of domestic and foreign ore. A proposal
made by Schacht was accepted by the steel magnates; he suggested that the extracting be done by one company and that
this company be financially supported by all the other steel
concerns. But when the steel industrialists also demanded a
substantial increase in steel prices, Göring balked and started
the Hermann-Göring-Works as a competitor of the private
concerns. In a subsequent meeting, the majority of the steel
producers proposed that none of the private firms should
lend any assistance to the public enterprise. The minority,
led by Krupp and Röchling, rejected this idea. Both of these
private concerns put their pilot plants, trained personnel,
and know-how at the disposal of the Göring Works.[28]

The dispute about the solution of the foreign-currency
crisis thus revealed a basic conflict of interest within big
business. The collaborators with the Nazis preferred a huge
program for the building up of new industries at home that
would bring them exceptional profits and a substantial increase in their assets. The opponents of such a program not
only feared for their immediate profits but desired a substantial expansion of their export business. The split within
business thus centered in the issue of whether expansion

should be used to create new markets at home or abroad—of whether a policy of economic imperialism should be set up immediately or only after the building up of synthetic industries at home. In addition to its economic implications, the split had an immediate political effect. Being divided within itself, big business could not act as a united power bloc but could only support solutions that were offered and pushed by others.

How did the exchange crisis provide the occasion for an estrangement between big business and the army generals? The reasons lay in a series of miscalculations by Schacht as well as in the acceptance of new goals for military policy by the generals. When these developments were followed by the split in business, the previous understanding between business and the military leaders evaporated. Was this estrangement inevitable?

As Minister of Economics and President of the *Reichsbank,* Schacht was primarily responsible for handling the exchange crisis. The initiative was in his hands to reshape the alliance between big business and the generals; but from the available (formerly secret) evidence, one must conclude that Schacht misinterpreted the situation and devised an utterly inappropriate policy for the solution of the foreign-exchange crisis. Why did this otherwise shrewd politician become his own enemy?

One of Schacht's mistakes was that he acted too much as Minister of Economics and not enough as leader of the big-business power bloc. As Minister he strenuously insisted upon his right to decide how the funds of the secret military budget should be divided among, and used by, the various civilian ministries.[29] This irritated the generals and created doubt in their minds as to whether Schacht was seriously interested in collaborating with the generals in their military goals. As Minister he also defended his "New Plan" and emphasized that the chances of increasing exports had been virtually exhausted.

In contrast, General Georg Thomas had formulated the slogan that "without export there can be no foreign exchange, without foreign exchange there can be no armament production."[30] This emphasis upon exports harmonized closely with the interests of many business concerns. Rather than representing these business interests, Schacht relied upon the incorrect forecasts of his bureaucrats, who saw little opportunity for an increase in German exports.[31]

Schacht also failed to appreciate the significance of the split in business and, especially, underestimated the potential political influence of I. G. Farben as a partner of the Nazis. His warnings against the expansionist tendencies of I. G. Farben came too late and merely indicate his failure to see that he himself had to come to an agreement with the largest manufacturing concern in the country. Although the responsibility for the collaboration falls upon I. G. Farben, one has to record the fact that Schacht's unsuccessful opposition to this large concern unwittingly contributed to the subsequent partnership between I. G. Farben and the Nazis.

Schacht made some other mistakes, of a tactical nature, in connection with the establishment of the Göring Works A.G. The long dispute between the Göring office and the steel industrialists about who should have the right to determine the plan for steel production had created considerable animosity against the Nazis. The agreement on the steel plan was hardly signed in June of 1937, when Göring revealed his intention to appoint a government commissioner for controling the iron-ore industry. This information was passed on by Göring to Dr. Schlattmann in a meeting of June 30, 1937 so "that it would not come as a surprise to him."[32] Since Schlattmann was head of the mining department of the Ministry of Economics, it seems clear that Göring was trying to

test Schacht's reaction. Rather than protesting and insisting
upon the implementation of the Schlattmann Plan for domestic ore, which Göring had previously recognized, Schacht
missed this decisive opportunity to kill the Göring Works
A. G. when it was still in the planning stage.

It was only after the Göring Works had been founded that
Schacht sent his protest to Göring and asked Ernst Poensgen,
leader of the iron and steel industry, for a written statement
on the reactions of the steel industrialists to this government
concern. Together with five other producers, Poensgen wrote
a memorandum that protested against confiscation of the
private ore deposits by the government and insisted that only
the private enterprises should have the right to build the
additional steel capacity for fulfilling the steel plan.[33] In their
efforts to resist this new policy of the Nazi leaders, both
Schacht and Poensgen committed the tactical blunder of
permitting the Nazis to observe their activities. According to
Poensgen, his conversation with Schacht had been recorded
and reported to Göring. The meetings of the steel industrialists in Berlin on August 20 and 21, 1937, could not have
escaped the attention of the Nazis, for on the morning of the
24th, shortly before the last meeting of the industrialists in
Düsseldorf to discuss Poensgen's memorandum, some of them
received a telegram from Göring in which they were urged
not to sign the document, since "these maneuvers had taken
on the form of sabotage" against the Göring Works.[34] The
implied threat was sufficient to prevent the united action of
the steel industrialists. Realizing that the defense of their
interests could be interpreted as a challenge to the power of
the party, the majority of the steel industrialists gave up
their united support of the principle of private property,
thereby undercutting Schacht's opposition to Göring's economic leadership.

Finally, Schacht misinterpreted the foreign-exchange crisis
as opening up an opportunity to separate the top Nazis from

the Nazis in the Ministries of Agriculture and Propaganda. In a letter of February 3, 1936, to General von Blomberg, Schacht described the extent of the anticipated foreign-exchange deficit and said, "We must decide whether the size of rearmament shall be changed or whether the agricultural sector shall be reorganized."[35]

Schacht knew, of course, that the generals in the Ministry of War were not willing to reduce their armament plans substantially. His intention was revealed by subsequent letters in which he accused the Nazis in agriculture not only of mismanagement but of having chosen an entirely wrong policy. In his program for economic reform Schacht proposed to abolish the whole system of regulated markets and return to private pricing in agriculture;[36] but he was supported by none of the generals in his frontal attack on the Nazis in agriculture. Rather than getting their support for his economic reform program, Schacht's tactics only brought into the open the well-known facts that in food matters General Karmann of the provisioning office was fully on the side of the Nazis[37] and that General Thomas was only for a partial reform of agricultural policy. The Ministry of War was thus also split in agricultural matters.

Schacht's attack upon the agrarian Nazis resembled his earlier struggle with the Nazified small business groups, but his chances of scoring another victory, in the name of big business, were slight. First, a re-establishment of the capitalist market in agriculture would not have directly reconciled the interests of the divided groups of big business; second, the generals were vitally interested, but the two rival military groups both regarded a frontal attack upon the Nazis as inopportune; and, third, the Nazis, after their experience of the purge, had fully restored their power by building up the SS. Given these conditions, there was no reasonable chance of driving the Nazis from their commanding positions in agriculture. Schacht's campaign against the agrarian Nazis was thus not only ill-timed but poorly advised. He had committed the unforgivable mistake—for a politician—of tackling an issue that was not only unattainable but that aroused his enemies to such an extent that his own defeat was unavoidable.

To make matters worse, Schacht also aimed at the Nazis who were engaged in propaganda and even in the treasury department of the party itself. The former had openly violated the laws of foreign exchange and could have been prosecuted. The latter had spent huge funds for political purposes that should have been devoted, Schacht pointed out, to the financing of rearmament. In conversations with von Blomberg, Schacht sought to convince the general that the party also had to make sacrifices for the attainment of rearmament. Both men convinced themselves that if only they could devise a scheme by which they could prove to Hitler that a shrinkage in the activities of the party was in the interest of rearmament, the top Nazis would be on their side. As a second approach, not an attack but an intrigue was proposed by Schacht to achieve his reform policy against the Nazis.

Schacht and von Blomberg, accompanied by Kerrl, went to Göring on April 4, 1936, and suggested that the four of them should form a commission for settling the foreign-exchange crisis. The visitors made it plain to Göring that neither economic competence nor economic decision-making was required of him. He was told about the sacrifice that would have to be made by the party in matters of foreign exchange, and he agreed to "function as a shield for these measures of a financial nature,"[38] that were to be imposed upon the party. The meeting appeared to be a full success for Schacht. Counting on Göring's ignorance of economics and his devotion to a speeded-up armament program, Schacht tried to use Göring as his tool in subduing the party to the financial requirements of rearmament, as defined by Schacht.

It was precisely this assessment of the situation and of Göring that turned out to be a fatal miscalculation. As one of the most power-hungry Nazis, Göring could not be expected to accept and implement the schemes of others. Being dependent for the continuity of his personal power on the party, he could not possibly agree to reducing the power of the party for the sake of rearmament. While pretending to be at Schacht's service, Göring planned a double-cross of his own. Being greatly dissatisfied with the oil policy of the Ministry of Economics, Göring had tried to get himself appointed as commissioner of the domestic oil industry. This intention should have been a clear warning to Schacht that Göring did not regard himself as disqualified to accumulate and exercise economic power. Rather than utilizing all his power to keep Göring out of the sphere of economic decision-making, Schacht offered him the opportunity to move into the highest economic position in the government.[39]

As soon as Göring had been appointed chairman of the commission on raw materials and foreign exchange, he usurped the power of making final decisions pertaining to the distribution of the available foreign exchange. He formed an office that took control over the production of synthetics and other domestic substitutes. A subdivision of this office worked out the original draft of the first Four Year Plan. In both respects, Göring received the full support of I. G. Farben and later also of Krupp and Röchling. The new alliance between the Nazi leaders and their collaborators in business prepared energetically to take over the leadership of the economy even while the main official task of the commission was still limited to the alternatives for solving the foreign-exchange crisis. There can be hardly any doubt that Göring made the most of the opportunity that Schacht had offered him. Rather than being weakened and then governed by the requirements of rearmament, the party was given the privilege of taking an active role in selecting the policies of economic mobilization for war. In recommending

Göring's appointment without being able to control his policies, Schacht had contributed, unwittingly but decisively, towards the breakup of the original alliance.

The second gravedigger was General von Blomberg. He was thrice given the opportunity to limit or even undercut Göring's growing power. When Göring asserted his authority over the allocation of foreign exchange, Blomberg supported him. Both signed an agreement that specified a division of labor. The economic division of the Ministry of War would integrate the military demands for foreign exchange, and Göring's staff would give first priority to the claims of the armed forces.[40] In return for this support Göring promised that the air force would recognize the authority of the Minister of War in the allocation of foreign raw materials.

When, in June, 1936, the leaders of the party rejected Schacht's proposal that the finances of the party be supervised and the activities of the party organizations be reduced, there was a chance that the generals might turn against Göring. His state of mind when he discovered that they had not turned against him was expressed in his telephone message to von Blomberg on June 25, 1936: "I am extremely happy to receive Bodenschatz's message. Thousand thanks. In everlasting loyalty, your Hermann Göring."[41] Von Blomberg wrote on the same page that Göring was mistaken in assuming that his authority as chairman of the commission was in jeopardy and had informed him accordingly. Von Blomberg was therefore responsible for the failure of Schacht's attempt to make the party submissive to the financial requirements of rearmament. The principle of "rearmament first" was thus given up by the leading generals in the Ministry of War without a fight.

While von Blomberg was accommodating himself to Göring's policies, Schacht, throughout the summer months of 1936, was fighting an intricate battle against party leadership of the economy. For some reason, he must have believed that the extensive discussions in the commission on raw materials and foreign exchange had turned the trend of events in his favor. In his letter of August 20, 1936, Schacht pressured Göring for an immediate decision on the future course of exchange control. In his reply two days later, Göring insisted that a final decision could not be reached before the end of September, since the final memoranda of the Ministers of War and Agriculture had not been received, and the statements of the independent experts could not be expected prior to that date.[42] Actually Schacht's letter produced a magic effect. Within a few days, Göring received the draft of the Four Year Plan, which had been put together by his Bureau of Raw Materials and Synthetics with the active assistance of I. G. Farben and the economic division of the War Ministry.[43] Hitler's memorandum on the Four Year Plan was completed by August 26, 1936, and incorporated the economic proposals of the Bureau of Raw Materials and Synthetics.

Even at this point von Blomberg would still have had an opportunity to torpedo the Four Year Plan, but he did not choose to do so. In a letter to Göring, written on August 31, 1936, von Blomberg presented the new financial demands of the armed forces. A few days prior to the announcement of the Four Year Plan to the cabinet, von Blomberg asked for an increase of military outlays by 42 per cent over 1936.[44] The plan itself was the joint project of the Nazis, the leading generals in the Ministry of War, and I. G. Farben, who together formed a new alliance in economic matters.

THE BREAKUP OF THE MILITARY ALLIANCE

The new alliance, which excluded Schacht as well as most bankers and the majority of the Ruhr industrialists, lasted about fifteen months. At the turn of the year, from 1937 to 1938, a dispute between the generals and the Nazis developed in the process of which a great number of generals were removed from office, the Ministry of War was eliminated as a separate agency, and Hitler himself became the head of the reorganized military establishment. Was the power of the army pitted against that of the party? If so, why was the political power stronger than the military?

The death of von Hindenburg, the transfer of presidential functions to Hitler, and the modification of the Defense Law in 1935 had established a new relationship between the Nazis and the generals. Legally, the armed forces became subordinated to Hitler, who succeeded von Hindenburg as Supreme Commander of the Armed Forces. Actually, the Minister of War was the Commander-in-Chief of the armed forces. Although it was provided that in case of war all executive power would be transferred to Hitler, this authority was to be exercised by the Minister of War, who would give instructions to the other ministers.[45] The Defense Law thus legalized the superior position of the generals in all direct and indirect military matters. But the law left one decisive question unanswered: If the Minister of War were to resign, who would appoint his successor? It was precisely this question of unsettled authority that was utilized by Hitler to limit the formerly unrestricted power of the generals over military affairs.

When Hitler, in a secret meeting in November, 1937, presented his military strategy of lightning warfare, General von Blomberg and General von Fritsch both opposed the proposed shift in military strategy. A fundamental difference in military thinking thus arose between Hitler and the military leaders. There was at this point a united military front, since the leaders of the collaborators as well as the traditionalists in the army argued against the strategy of lightning warfare. Subsequent discussion only intensified the conflict between von Fritsch and Hitler. In the absence of internal disunity, Hitler could not possibly exploit the gap in the Defense Law.

It was von Blomberg himself who shortsightedly provided the cause for a split among the generals as well as for his own dismissal. He married a secretary in his office (with Hitler and Göring acting as witnesses at the wedding) without having adequately informed himself about the moral background of his prospective wife. Soon after the wedding the regular police identified her as a lady "with a past." When the incriminating files were placed before Count Helldorf, head of the Berlin police and also an officer of the SA, he decided to keep this evidence from Himmler and handed the material to General Keitel. Helldorf's suggestion was that the material should be destroyed, but instead Keitel gave the papers to Göring, who passed them on to Hitler.

It was therefore Fräulein Gruhn, and not any Nazi, who precipitated the incident. Her immorality was regarded as an insult to the honor and tradition of the officer corps of the army; but it was also the code of the Prussian officer that turned out to be the greatest enemy of the army as a power bloc. Rather than submitting the incriminating evidence to a meeting of the top generals (with a view to obtaining von Blomberg's resignation) and drawing up a short list of possible candidates for his position, General Beck, as the army's chief of staff, implored General von Fritsch to ask Hitler to dismiss von Blomberg.[46] In taking this course, von Fritsch and Beck not only recognized Hitler as the adjudicator of disputes of honor within the officer corps but gave him a chance to determine unilaterally who should be the new Minister of War. Fate added irony to injury. The course of action followed by Hitler did not originate in his own mind. It was von Blomberg who took revenge on his own officer corps by suggesting to Hitler that he should abolish the office of Minister of War, attach the administration of the Ministry to himself, and appoint Keitel as his own deputy.

Instead of pitting the army against the party, Hitler used the honor code of the traditionalists in the army as a means of changing the Defense Law and becoming the leader in military affairs. Those among the generals who were willing to collaborate with the party were induced either by a desire to injure von Blomberg (because of his violation of the code) or by admiration for Hitler to show the latter how the generals could be made leaderless. Thus, either wittingly or unwittingly, they gave him an opportunity to make the generals responsible to himself. In view of all this, it is difficult to imagine how a status group could have defended its honor more clumsily or contributed more effectively to the undermining of its own position as an independent power bloc than did the German generals in 1938.

In a sense, the "von Fritsch affair" was a sequel to the "von Blomberg affair." Having been shown how easily one can remove a general from his position by attacking his honor, the top Nazis proceeded to use their tactics of calumny and character assassination against von Fritsch. In accusing him of homosexuality, Hitler deliberately tried to destroy von Fritsch as a political leader of the generals, although von Fritsch and many of the other generals saw in Hitler's actions only an attack upon his personal honor as an aristocrat and a gentleman.[47]

Normally, there were two ways of defending one's personal honor as an officer. The accused would offer his word of honor and, if rejected, would challenge the accuser to a duel. Since the "Supreme Commander" could not be challenged, von Fritsch signed the resignation demanded of him and requested a court-martial by his equals. Presumably, von Fritsch expected that when the court had restored his honor he would be reinstated as chief of the army. One can only marvel at how the status blinders prevented von Fritsch—after four years of experience with Nazi leadership—from realizing that the Nazis neither respected nor acted in accordance with the honor code of a Prussian officer.

There is little doubt that if von Fritsch had possessed the political insight and moral courage required of a leader, he would have been able to defeat the Nazis in their attempted character assassination.[48] In command of well-equipped and trusted divisions, von Fritsch needed only to translate his military power into political striking power. The action to be taken at the time was obvious, at least to General Beck. General von Fritsch should have ordered his best regiments to occupy all the SS barracks and offices, disarm the troops and arrest their top leaders, including Himmler. From the documents thus captured and with the assistance of the military intelligence, von Fritsch could have obtained evidence proving that the charge of homosexuality had been fabricated. The disarming of the SS should have been accompanied by a presentation of conditions to Hitler, the aim of which would have been to restore the original alliance of January, 1933. These conditions should have specified (a) that the position of the Supreme Commander would not and could not convey any administrative power, (b) that the generals by themselves should have the authority to select the Minister of War and the Commander of the Army, (c) that the veto power of the Minister of War in all matters of military importance should be restored, (d) that all militarized units of the SS should be permanently dissolved, (e) that the Gestapo should exercise no jurisdiction whatever over any member of the armed forces or his family. A program of this sort would have cancelled the impact of the two "affairs," restored the generals to a position of equality with the party, and halted the SS in its attempt to become supremely powerful.

If the SS had resisted, or if Hitler had refused to accept these conditions, the superior military force of the generals could have terminated the Nazi regime. Knowing their military weakness, the Nazis would have been willing to negotiate for a compromise, but the generals (including, in addition to von Fritsch, most of the other senior officers) apparently did not have enough courage or intelligence to make use of their instruments of power. Accordingly, on the fourth of February, 1938, when Hitler presented the two "affairs" to a group of leading generals, they all received his words in silence. If they had used their technical competence in warfare as a political weapon, Hitler, knowing that he could not win a war without them, would have been forced to make concessions. In fact, as Goebbels later admitted, the party leaders had feared "a collective resignation of all high-ranking officers."[49] In the absence of this—or any other effective resistance—Hitler won his gamble.

The actual sequence of events leading up to the collapse of the original alliance may be described as follows: (a) the split within big business prevented business organizations from bringing their power to bear on politics; (b) the estrangement of the generals from the leaders of big business made it impossible for the two groups to continue to agree on a common policy in military and economic affairs; and (c) the division of the military into two factions—the collaborationist and the traditionalist—helped to prevent the generals from effectively meeting the challenge of the "von Fritsch affair." The ultimate effect of these events was undoubtedly to prepare the way for the Nazi's seizure first of the economic and then of the military leadership of the country.

Was the disintegration of the alliance unavoidable? The available (formerly secret) evidence does not support this thesis. One cannot say that the military was politically weak in relation to the party, nor can one say that big business was weaker politically, than the party. In fact, there never was a real test of strength between big business and the generals, on the one hand, and the party and the SS, on the other. When the time for a test came, neither big business nor the military acted as an effective power bloc. The Nazis did not have to fight either one. What they actually did was to make these groups leaderless, by changing their organizations, by destroying the reputations of these leaders, and by transferring the leadership rights to themselves. It was thus not because of any inherent weakness of military or business power but because of ineffective leadership and the absence of rules of succession that each group became rudderless and was unable to make use of its political strength.

Apart from the personal limitations of some of the leaders, the failure of German upper-class leadership is attributable to two causes. One was ideological, the other organizational. The collaborators within big business were guided by two distinct motives. The expected expansion under the Four Year Plan undoubtedly offered them greater profit opportunities than they had actually experienced during the rearmament boom. In addition, the collaborators were developing into military as well as economic imperialists because they had become convinced that their economic superiority on the continent could be established only after a German military victory.[50] The majority of the generals experienced a similar ideological development that induced them to shift their goal from military equality to military superiority. It was this fervent belief in the ideals of economic and military imperialism that created ideological blinders. In their eagerness to reach the goal of economic and military superiority, the leaders of big business and the military neglected to examine the actual intentions of the Nazis and were thus not able to counter their political designs.

As convinced capitalists, Schacht and his co-workeers suffered from another sort of blindness. They were not only imbued with a notion of their superior managerial ability but had developed a distinct sense of class pride in relation to the Nazis in agriculture and the professions. This class pride induced them to advocate an outright attack upon the Nazis in agriculture at a time when they could not possibly have obtained the support of the generals. In somewhat the same way, the army traditionalists were so infatuated with status and honor that they unwittingly became the victims of the Nazis. Their concept of the Prussian officer prevented them from suspecting the Nazis of deliberately using methods of character assassination. The officers' deep-rooted sense of loyalty to the state, as expressed in their oath to Hitler, made it difficult for them to translate their technical competence or their command over military divisions into political striking power. This enthusiasm for military superiority and the involvement in status and honor produced an astonishing degree of political ineptitude. The collaborators could not even see the dangers of Nazism, and the traditionalists certainly did not prepare themselves in time to cope with the plans of the Nazis to undermine the alliance.

The second cause of ineffective leadership was organizational disunity. The split in big business prevented the appointment of a recognized leader as head of the *Reichsgruppe Industrie*. When Schacht was attacked by the Nazis, the business organizations could not employ their economic power for want of unified leadership. When the "von Blomberg affair" broke, the generals of the army did not have an agreed plan of action because the traditionalists had been trying to regain their full autonomy from the Ministry of War. Some of them even ventilated the idea of abolishing the Ministry of War, thereby playing with ideas that were later implemented by Hitler. The defense of the alliance against the Nazis required not only a unified organization but also definite rules providing for succession in leadership.[51] Given such rules, the Nazis could not—without changing the law— have appointed Göring as Schacht's superior, and Hitler could not have abolished the Ministry of War.

Ideological diversity and organizational disunity constituted the two specific causes for the breakup of the alliance. Together they created the opportunities that had to exist before the Nazis could seize economic and military leadership. It is for their ideological blindness and political ineptitude that the generals and the leaders of big business inescapably bear their share of the responsibility for the shift from partial to full fascism. If they had seen the danger and prepared for it, the Nazis' sneak attack either would not have occurred or would have been defeated. In other words, the defeat of the upper class by the Nazis was not unavoidable.

The significance of these findings on the causes of the defeat of the generals and big business far transcends the Nazi period. It has been the practice of communist rulers, especially in the countries of East Europe, to place their agents in military and economic organizations, undermine the position of established leaders, capture these organizations and translate them into instruments of communist power. If the success of these Trojan-horse methods did not depend upon specific conditions, and if such conditions could not be prevented, the ultimate victory of communism would indeed be inevitable.

The widely held opinion that every partial fascism must necessarily turn into a full fascism is not supported by our findings. Such a development arises only when the military and economic groups that are still allied with the fascists do not bring forth leaders of wisdom and fortitude, when these groups fall into ideological disputes and organizational disunity. These three defects undoubtedly turned out to be the fatal characteristics of the German upper class, and also of some segments of the upper class in other European countries. Our evidence does not prove, however, that every capitalist upper class must have such fatal defects. There are some indications that the new military and capitalist classes in some of the dictatorially governed but less developed countries operated as more vigorous partners of fascist ruling groups than one could observe in Germany. When Peron in Argentina attacked the Catholic church, units of the formerly allied army revolted and eliminated the fascist regime.

There is little doubt that partial fascism and organized capitalism in Germany could have continued to operate for a considerable period of time if the German upper class had

developed leaders with the necessary will and organizational
ability to defend their positions of power effectively against
the Nazis. The major lesson of the earlier Nazi experience is
that partial fascism and organized capitalism do not necessarily constitute a transitional phase to full fascism, which in
turn need not necessarily become the victim of a war of its
own making.

THE REVIVAL OF FASCISM?

There is no reason to suppose that any future manifesta-
tion of fascism will exactly duplicate the German pattern.
The range of objective possibilities is greater than is often
surmised, and in assessing the chances of a revival, we have to
take into account both the lessons of partial (and total) fascism in Germany and the contingencies that may occur in the
foreseeable future.

The rise of a new fascism in any given nation is to be expected only if, in the event of some national cataclysm, a new
government is unable or unwilling to rely on democratic
methods of government in its attempt to survive. It was the
severity of the Great Depression that in the 1930's induced the
upper and middle classes in Germany to accept fascism as the
only means of coping with the economic upheaval. It is not to
be assumed, however, that the cause of any subsequent revival
of fascism would have to be economic in nature; any other
kind of cataclysm might produce a similar response.

In the long view, there are four gigantic tasks that can
hardly be avoided in the future. There is first the challenge
of communism and its attempt by all available means to
overthrow capitalism and suppress any form of democratic
socialism. There is second the tremendous drive for industrialization on the part of underdeveloped countries. In
order to press the untrained masses into industrial patterns
of work and speed up the tempo of industrialization, mili-

tary dictatorships could very well transform themselves into systems of partial fascism, as did happen for a time in the United Arab Republic. There is third the refractory problem of German unification. If all attempts on the part of the democratic governments to solve the German problem fail, there may well be a neo-Nazi movement that will seek unification by force. Finally, we have to resolve the civil-rights issue in the United States and at the same time alert ourselves to the danger that the racial fervor of the segregationists may well work to the advantage of the American Nazi Party.

There is no intention here of saying that failure to perform these exceptionally large tasks must, or will probably, lead to a revival of fascism. Our thesis is that each one of these four assignments for our generation contains a fascist potential that may erupt if we have not the wisdom to grasp the full significance of each of these problems or if we are not capable of developing policies that will provide adequate solutions by democratic methods. A short-sighted imagination or a crippled policy may very well produce a frustration calling for movements of desperation and giving rise to a policy, and an ethic, of violence. The Nazi experience thus provides us with a timely warning. If we cannot or will not tackle the four assignments of our generation effectively, we may lose democracy not by succumbing to communism but by preparing the ground for a revival of fascism in capitalist countries.

Within the scope of this study we can do no more than evaluate the chances of a resurgence of Nazism in West Germany by seeing whether there are any actual or potential causes that might inspire the growth of a neo-Nazi youth movement and any economic interests that might induce a sizable segment of the population to support a revival of fascism.

The Nazis first came to power for three reasons. There was

first an extremely favorable institutional setting, nationally and internationally, that removed all external obstacles to the seizure of power. This was accompanied by the development of a fascist mass movement which also penetrated into many nonpolitical spheres of life. These two—the favorable institutions and the fascist mass movement—were integrated by the formation of a coalition government which permitted the Nazis to come to power without having to gain a majority of the votes or destroy the instruments of power held by their opponents. Can neo-Nazism count on similarly favorable opportunities?

It seems clear enough that the institutional setting is unlikely to be favorable for a revival of Nazism. We have certainly little reason to expect a severe depression. Governments have developed the capacity for creating additional jobs, and the substantial demand created by military needs functions as a built-in prop that sustains the level of employment. The disorganization of the middle class, which was so significant for the original Nazi movement, can hardly be expected to result from the type of recession which we have experienced since World War II. Additionally, in West Germany the quasi-guild organizations for small urban business and the price supports for agriculture will function as barriers to disintegration if a severe depression should reoccur.

The earlier tendency to multiply political parties has been replaced by a tendency in West Germany to work within a three-party system. Hence, in all probability, a new party would face exceptional difficulties in becoming again the largest party in the country. Lastly, the international situation has changed remarkably. Whereas the politics of the Allied Powers had been restrictive in relation to the Weimar Republic, the Hitler regime in its dealings with other governments could count increasingly upon the acceptance of its policies, culminating in the appeasement of 1938. In the foreseeable future, however, the rise of a neo-Nazism would endanger the very existence and external security of the state itself. Soviet policy aims at the complete elimination of West Germany, while the support of the Western nations would certainly be lukewarm or nonexistent if neo-Nazism became a significant force in West Germany. Thus, since the previous institutional setting has disappeared and is unlikely to reoccur, it will hardly provide any opportunities for the rise of a new fascist movement.

In spite of these circumstances, there is bound to be a certain amount of pro-Nazi feeling in West Germany. Two kinds of emotions are likely to keep it alive. There is the sentimental and ideological attachment of convinced Nazis and some of their offspring who would certainly like to revive the mass movement of the early Nazi regime. Not less important is the present territorial split of Germany into several parts and the dependence of West Germany upon American military support. Both constitute new grievances for nationalist Germans. If peaceful unification turns out to be utterly impossible, and if, as a result of its military dependence, West Germany begins to look like an American protectorate, these grievances may well provide the stimulus for a powerful new fascist movement.

Three possible events could very well give rise to anticapitalist sentiments among the intermediate groups between capital and labor. Peasants especially are very fearful of an unrestricted importation of foreign agricultural products and resent unlimited price gyrations. Reconsolidation of large concerns and the new influence of re-established cartels are bound to undermine some of the market chances of small firms. Finally, high rates of interest on loans for small projects or the refusal of loans to little known firms have already given rise to resentment against the remerged large banks. As long as there seems to be a chance of minimizing the monopolistic influences of large concerns and cartels by means of appropriate governmental measures or any other appropriate measures that may be proposed by the opposition, these anti-capitalist sentiments will not necessarily benefit the political efforts of former Nazi officials. Nevertheless, such sentiments constitute a fascist potential in any situation of crisis and will bring some adherents to fascist movements even in ordinary times.[52]

Beyond the anticapitalist sentiments, there is a fairly high degree of receptiveness among some segments of the lower-middle class in West Germany to certain elements of fascist ideology. Most conspicuous is the revival of anti-Semitism, in 1960–61 which resembles the sporadic activities of the Nazis in the 1920's. Equally strong are sentiments for a German imperialism whether of a nationalist or fascist variety.[53] At present these racial and imperialist ideologies are held by very small minorities and do not seem to be causally connected with anticapitalist sentiments. Thus at present the neo-Nazi groups do not seem to be benefiting from the definite support of any economic group. Here again it is possible that improper handling of these ideological remnants will give unwitting assistance to neo-Nazism whereas an effective utilization of the basic dilemma of counterrevolutionary movements of not being able to realize their original goals can supply the weapons for fighting effectively a new fascist movement.

In fact, there is a need as well as an opportunity for devising a strategy directed against a fascist revival. Its central goal would be to hit and destroy the link that is likely to connect the anticapitalist sentiments with a neo-Nazi ideology. In the earlier Nazi movement, this link was the concept of honor. The threatened honor of the peasants and artisans became associated with the racial honor of the Aryan and the national honor of the German imperialist. It was the common fear of a conspiracy against their honor and status position that united the impoverished middle class with the radicalized conservatives and Nazified intellectuals. In seeking to undermine this fear of a conspiracy, German political parties will have to develop a policy of status politics. Economically, it will have to be shown that insufficient aggregate demand and bigness in business are not the results of a conspiracy but spring from identifiable policies that can be replaced by others amenable to the survival of small business.[54] Ideologically, it can and should be shown how a guild-like development of small business can only diminish the chances of survival for the middle class. Politically, it can and should be shown that the defeat of middle-class socialism under the Hitler government would inevitably be repeated under a neo-Nazi regime.

The success of such a policy in counteracting the fear of a threat to middle-class status and honor requires that Hitler's suppression of the attempted counterrevolution of the SA be clearly understood. A future para-military organization would have to fail in its attempt to stage a military counterrevolution because of the resistance of the regular armed forces. In the event of a civil war, the regular army could be expected to defeat the fascist military organizations. If, on the other hand, leadership were attained through a coalition, then the power groups in the state would permit only a political counterrevolution and would obstruct the counterrevolutionary aims of the para-military organizations. Hence, barring the voluntary surrender of the military leaders,[55] it is unlikely that counterrevolutionists would be able to dominate the military establishment in another fascist society, whether they waged civil war or formed an alliance.

The fate of small business in a neo-Nazi movement would also be problematical. An economic counterrevolution could not succeed politically except in the event of civil war. In a coalition, the economic and military interests of the coalition powers would conflict with any basic economic reforms that favored the middle class. Hence, there is no place in a society of partial fascism for a successful economic counterrevolution. The role of an aroused middle class is only to assist a neo-Nazi party in coming to power and then to be gradually pushed downwards into the large group of the politically and economically powerless.

In view of the need for a policy that would effectively counteract the fascist potential in West Germany, one had to register a complaint against the Adenauer government. Dr. Adenauer seems to be utterly unaware of the anti-fascist requirements. While calling recently for the punishment of a small group of young anti-Semites, he actively protected a former leading Nazi. The recent outbreak of anti-Semitism was misinterpreted in two ways by the Adenauer government. The assertion that the whole campaign was a deliberate maneuver of the communists could not be substantiated by later investigations. The fact that more than half of the apprehended "daubers" were still apprentices and had no discoverable connection with political organizations induced the government and many of the courts to regard the whole campaign as a sign of youthful political confusion. Yet the inference that such "confusion" is politically harmless is not convincing. Like the earlier followers of Hitler, these hotheads may turn out to be another set of counterrevolutionaries. Thus, there was a failure of the government and the courts to identify and appreciate the nature of the ideology held by the majority of the troublemakers.

This sin of omission springs from the fact that the counterrevolutionary nature of the Nazis is still not understood by the German government and a large part of the people. If the federal and state governments had had a clear conception of the earlier political, economic and military counterrevolutions, they could have instructed their prosecutors to concentrate on the content of the ideology held by the accused anti-Semites. The political parties could then have devised counter-ideological policies. The notion that only anti-state organizations can or need to be fought is a dangerous illusion. The task is to attack the ideology of neo-Nazism before it hardens into specific organizations. Such counter-ideological policies have a chance of success only if they take full account of the counterrevolutionary ideals of the earlier Nazi movement.[56]

If the institutional setting is not favorable and if the rise of a powerful fascist mass movement can be avoided, is there a chance for the revival of a coalition between neo-Nazis, generals, and big business? Of the various incentives for a coalition, only the Treaty of Potsdam could perform a unifying function similar to that of the Treaty of Versailles in the early days of the first Hitler movement; but the comparison suggested is, in fact, misleading. The Treaty of Versailles provided only the unifying grievances, and it was only the bad conscience of the former victors and their unwillingness to fight for the continued existence of the treaty that created the subsequent international power vacuum necessary for the success of the coalition led by Hitler. In the face of aggressive Soviet pressure, the formation of a new coalition as in 1933 would be pointless. If established in an act of desperation, it would undermine the confidence of the Western Allies in West Germany and supply the Russians with a very effective argument for the official incorporation of the Soviet zone into the Soviet empire, as well as for a possible invasion of West Germany. Therefore, the continued determination of the Soviets to impose the Treaty of Potsdam—by force if necessary—has convinced most Germans that reunification cannot be achieved by a revival of Nazism.

A coalition led by new generals or neo-Nazis would have a chance of success only if the Soviet troops permanently left German territory and if the German communists persistently obstructed any peaceful reunification. The purpose of such a military-fascist coalition would be to prepare for and execute the forceful occupation of the Soviet zone. Military action would thus stand as the immediate task of such a coalition.

If the occupation were successful, there would be little reason to expect a return to democracy. But reunification by force, which appears as the only possible reason for a revival of fascism in Germany, could be maintained only by an alliance with Soviet Russia. Neo-Nazism thus could not assure independence—even after unification.

A viable Germany democracy thus seems to depend upon three distinct lines of action. There should be a shift from the recent "chancellor-democracy" to an effective parliamentary democracy in which the opposition would be an effective part of a healthy political life. Both the government and the opposition should arrive at active anti-fascist policies that seek to undermine or minimize the growth of neo-Nazism. Finally, unification by means of an all-German election is not merely an anti-communist slogan but appears as the only means of carrying democracy over into a unified Germany.

APPENDIX A

Sources and Documents

As we have seen, at least implicitly, in this study, one of the characteristics of organized capitalism in Germany was that a significant amount of economic information continued to be made available in the daily and periodical press. Except in three important areas, this information remained fairly accurate.

Most obvious was the change in the field of labor and industrial relations. Neither the self-chosen interests and ideologies nor the personal or organizational intentions and actions of laborers could be ascertained since the trade unions were suppressed and the whole labor press came under Nazi control. The available information (coming from pronouncements that accompained the actions of the Labor Ministry, the Labor Front, and the labor courts) told us only what the rulers did to the laboring groups. Lack of information made it impossible to present the feelings, ideas, and actions of the workers themselves. In utilizing the information on actions directed at and imposed upon workers, we could in Chapter VIII merely ascertain the impact of the regime upon the economic condition of workers and present their changed position in labor markets.

Somewhat different was the effect of the Nazi dictatorship upon information pertaining to the actions of big and small business. With the exception of the Jews and the relatively few capitalists who were open political enemies of the Nazis, all business groups found it possible to engage in a straightforward pursuit as well as representation of their economic interests. The resulting statements and defenses of these economic interests, and the published accounts of conflicts over them, made it possible for us to use the existing economic press as one major source of information for the earlier period of the regime.

The only qualification to be noted in this connection is that certain ideas or ideals, such as the supremacy of the employer in his own plant, and the profit and property interests of private concerns could not be proclaimed openly or frankly and clearly stated. While the dominant position of employers was retained in fact, the leadership ideology of the labor law was commonly used to conceal the retained power of employers. Business leaders preferred to present their special interests in terms of generally acceptable goals, such as the job-creating capacity of private industry or the private initiative of entrepreneurs, both of which were extolled by Hitler in his speeches. Finally, there were relatively few occasions on which any attempt was made to justify business interests and capitalist institutions in terms of the goals of military power. In all these cases it became necessary to separate genuine intentions from spurious justifications and ideological camouflage.

The same problem arose in a different form in regard to small business. Was the acceptance of middle-class socialism merely an ideological disguise or did the specific goals derived from this ideology express the genuine intentions of the guilds and chambers? For the first period of our research, material was collected on the assumption that the disguise thesis was correct. Yet the cumulative evidence made it quite clear that the conflict between big and small business not only hinged upon the divergency of economic interests but also involved a struggle over ideals between two distinctly different economic systems. In four respects the available evidence does seem to prove conclusively that the guilds and chambers acted largely according to, and accepted as valid guides, the goals implicit in middle-class socialism. First, many components of this ideology were formulated by the middle-class organizations during the Great Depression, even before the Hitler regime. Second, there was a widespread change in the leadership of these organizations during the year 1933 so that the Nazified leaders could and did become fully fused with the tenets of middle-class socialism. Third, the whole range of programs and actions promoted by the guilds and chambers constituted an attack upon the existing institutions of private capitalism, aiming at a counterrevolutionary guild system. Finally, Schacht, along with his military supporters and economic followers, saw this guild system in exactly the same light and fought it in exactly the same way. There was no choice: the relationships between big and small business could be understood only in terms of interests and ideals that stood for two distinctly different economic systems.

Troubled by the possible divergence between genuine intentions and professed justifications, we made two attempts to obtain reliable guides for distinguishing the one from the other, the first in the summer of 1951, when we tried to interview a small but carefully selected group of former leaders of small and big business as well as administrators at district or regional levels in West Germany. The attempt failed either because of the lack of cooperation or because of the blacked-out memories of the respondents. The horrors of war bombardments and the subsequent years of starvation had crowded everything else out of the minds of those who were willing to talk, and many others who might have remembered did not talk for fear of endangering their positions in the new Federal Republic.

The second attempt arose in response to the secret documents that became available at first only as court evidence. While the documents presented by the prosecution were usually informative, many of the exhibits presented by the defense lawyers were usually irrelevant. The complaints of these lawyers that they had not been given sufficient time for preparation and were handicapped by the unfamiliar Anglo-American court procedures, induced us to spend the summer of 1955 in Germany so as to obtain information from the German de-Nazification trials. Visiting one state government after the other, we were given the same information: either the courts or the state legislators had decided that the exhibits and transcripts of these trials had to be locked up for a period of twenty years in order that the defendants might be protected against harassment. Materials already collected by some research institutes that had documented these trials had either to be returned or kept under lock and key—in the words of one director—"on orders of our FBI." The implication was that domestic politics required such a policy of secrecy. This attempt to get the German side of the story had therefore failed. In reading the newspaper reports of many of the de-Nazification trials, however, we came to the conclusion that not much was lost for our study since the courts were either not able or not willing to obtain verified information on the actions of the accused.

One further note needs to be added on the reliability of the information obtained about the intentions and actions of the government. Although the bulk of this information was creditable, some statistical data of an economic nature were withheld. In addition, there were some policies the intention of which was shrouded in doubt or secrecy. Yet, when the secret office files became accessible, almost all of these difficulties were overcome. Most of the formerly secret data could be obtained and the creditability of certain intentions could either be established or disproven. Thus, a fairly complete and adequate account of the role of business groups in the first phase of the Nazi regime could be given only because the relevant secret files were finally made available.

Military intelligence officers captured the files of a very large number of private and governmental offices. The material discovered was utilized as evidence first in the international and then in the American military trials. The documents and transcripts of the *Trial of the Major War Criminals before the International Military Tribunal* were published at Nürnberg in 1947–49. These so-called blue volumes include the following: Vol.

I—Official Court Documents; Vols. II–XXII—Proceedings; Vol. XXIII—Chronological and Subject Index; Vol. XXIV—Document and Name Index; Vols. XXV–XLII—Documents and other Material in Evidence.

The last set of these volumes, which contained the most valuable information, was published in a shortened version by the Chief Counsel for the Prosecution of Axis Criminality under the title *Nazi Conspiracy and Aggression* (Washington, D. C.: U. S. Government Printing Office, 1946-48), 10 vols. Since these "red volumes" are more widely distributed throughout the United States, we decided to use especially this more available set of documents.

Equally valuable information was contained in the *Trials of War Criminals before the Nürnberg Military Tribunals* (Washington, D. C.: Government Printing Office, 1950-51), 15 vols; but these "green volumes" did not give a complete collection of all the relevant evidence. As it was said in the preface of Vol. I, p. 3:

The 12 cases required over 1,200 days of court proceedings and the transcript of these proceedings exceeds 330,000 pages, exclusive of hundreds of document boxes, briefs, etc. Publication of all this material, accordingly, was quite unfeasible. This series, however, contains the indictments, judgments, and other important portions of the record of the 12 cases, and it is believed that these materials give a fair picture of the trials. . . .

Although we used some of the documents reprinted in the green books, our emphasis upon economic actions called for access to the "document boxes." This was especially true for the trials of the Nürnberg industrialists, including I. G. Farben, Krupp, and Flick, as well as the so-called "Ministries Case."

The documents for the prosecution and defense of the last case were studied in great detail at the Institut für Völkerrecht of the University of Göttingen. Three fortunate events made available all the records and documents pertaining to the trials of the Nürnberg industrialists. The presiding judge of the I. G. Farben trials, Judge Curtis Grover Shake of Vincennes, Indiana, and the associate judge of the Flick trial, Judge Frank N. Richman of

Indianapolis, turned the complete sets of their files over to the Law Library of Indiana University, giving us the opportunity of unlimited and convenient use. The prosecution documents of the Krupp trial were received from the Midwest Library Center of Chicago, and the documents of the defense were studied at the Westfälische Wirtschafts-Archiv in Dortmund. Since these were available only in unprinted form, the documents could be cited only by their NI number, standing for Nürnberg industrialists. Now, however, the documents are being made available in the form of microfilm, so that any interested student will be able to verify our references by obtaining the appropriate films from the National Archives in Washington (under microcopy 301).

Although they were invaluable as a source of information, there was a certain selectivity about these documents because they were chosen for their evidential value in courts. We were therefore anxious to get "behind the lawyers" and see the original documents in their folders. According, we spent most of our vacations and leaves with these documents for a period of almost ten years. Piecing together the "story" from an endless number of letters, notes, and memoranda proved to be very time consuming. Happily enough, under the auspices of the American Historical Association, a diligent group of historians established a microfilm team in Alexandria, Virginia, which put the dispersed materials together in their original sequence and supervised the process of microfilming. The bulk as well as the quality of their work is most impressive. From the fall of 1958 to September of 1962, not less than thirty-seven "Guides to German Records Microfilmed at Alexandria, Virginia" have been issued by the National Archives from whom the films can be ordered by the use of these guides.

Covering the whole range of the Nazi regime, three sets of office files from these microfilms were of central significance for our research. Reference is here made to the *Wehrwirtschaft-und Rüstungsstab* of the War Ministry (cited as Wi/IF . . . T-77), to the files of the Ministry of Economics (cited as RWM . . . T-71), and to the National Socialist German Labor Party (cited as EAP . . . T-81). Since all film frames were given consecutive numbers running into seven digits, it seemed more economical to limit references to folder, roll, and microcopy. Any interested scholar can find a particular frame number by consulting the folder in question. One set of the original documents remained at the Berlin Document Center in Germany, an administrative agency of the U.S. Department of State. In consulting the documents of the *Reichswirtschaftsministerium,* the *Reichsorganisationsleiter der NSDAP,* in Berlin and those of the *Reichskanzlei* in Koblenz, we were able to fill some of the gaps in our information. One can safely expect that during the time this book is in print the originals of these documents will have been turned over to the *Bundesarchiv* in Koblenz, and the corresponding microfilms should be available in the National Archives.

The wealth of microfilmed documents presents us with the only case in history in which the inner working of a one-party dictatorship as well as its associated economy is revealed. Once the original files were accessible, the authenticity of documents could be established, intentions and actions could be placed in their historical context, and the genuine goals could be usually separated from self-serving justifications as well as ideological camouflage. By making intelligent use of the documents, we should be increasingly able to recognize the economic policies initiated or supported by dictatorial parties and, in our dealings with other totalitarian regimes, to see the real intentions behind the disguises. A study of the Nazi economy constitutes a necessary step for its comparison with the Soviet economy.

APPENDIX B

Economic Theory and
Economic Systems

There is no agreement among economists as to how dictatorial economies should be studied. Pure theorists either maintain that economics does not deal with man but is a science of commodities which are produced and allocated according to the mathematical principle of maximum,[1] or assert that all economies have the same basic economic goals. Whatever may be the actual differences among the economic systems, they are all allegedly trying to realize maximum output, substantial economic growth, and minimum inequality of income. The implication of this identity of economic goals is that "our basic goals are the same as the basic goals of the Russians."[2] Since the ends are the same, it is only in their means and policies that economic systems are said to differ from one another.

Unhappily, the basic goals mentioned are not inferred from the actual goals held by Americans or Russians in any specified period of time. The 116 days of the steel strike in 1959 indicate clearly that many Americans do not actually hold, or live up to, the goal of "maximum" output. They desire an 'increase" in output only if thereby some specific other goals are not sacrificed. The same holds true for some groups of Russian workers. When 140,000 workers left their machines standing in the grain fields of Western Siberia during the harvest in 1959,[3] they effectively demonstrated that an "increase" in grain output is important to them only if the rulers provide adequate shelter and food for them. Similar modifications apply to the goals of economic growth and minimal inequality of income. The impressive growth rates of the Soviet economy seem to become part of the goals of many individual workers only if their share of consumable goods is potentially or actually enhanced. There are many historical reasons for believing that the pressure for an increase in output and economic growth has resulted (in so far as these goals have been realized) in an increasing inequality of money and real income in the Soviet Union. Thus the thesis of identical goals in both the communist and capitalist economies can not be substantiated by any emperical study.

Any attempt to ascertain the goals actually motivating actions in an economic system must therefore meet some specific requirements. These include (a) the choice of a period of time that is typical for the particular system; (b) the presentation of observable documents as evidence for the goals that motivate action; (c) a clear indication as to whose goals—party rulers', corporation managers', or workers'—are investigated; and (d) evidence for the degree of difference that usually does exist between the intended and the realized goals. Comparisons between economic systems in terms of goals can be successful only if and when they are built upon relevant factual studies.

Pure theory is inherently unable to meet these methodological requirements for the study of economic systems. On the one hand, pure theory aims at *one* general theory that is universally valid and uniformly applicable in time and space. There is no intention of ascertaining the criteria that distinguish economic systems from one another. On the other hand, a universal theory requires identical economic goals. Rather than distilling them from the great variety of historically observable economic goals, the pure theorist obtains his identical goals only by postulating them. The postulated identity of the goals has only analytical relevance for

the construction of a pure economy. The identical goals, relevant
only for the theoretical model, cannot claim descriptive accuracy
for any actual system.[4] The purpose of the pure theory as well
as the postulated nature of its goals prevents us from utilizing
such a universal theory for interpreting actually existing economic
systems.

Since World War II, pure welfare theory has been transformed
into an axiomatic approach to the study of economic systems and
has been significantly modified in two ways. On the one hand,
the theoretical principles are not used for interpreting the actual
economic behavior of men but are regarded as guides for the economic actions that ought to be undertaken. The welfare principle
thus became a means of selecting the "correct" goals, while the
efficiency principle functions as a standard for evaluating the
actual costing and pricing of commodities. On the other hand,
from observation of actual economic systems, it was concluded—
at least implicitly—that some economies do not aim at attaining
optimum efficiency in production and pricing. The process of
normative evaluation was then given a negative twist. Rather
than showing how much must be done to achieve optimum efficiency, it became the purpose of the investigation—at least in the
case of the Soviet economy—to measure the degree of discrepancy
that existed between the theoretic norm and the actual performance. In the work of Professor Abram Bergson and his school, the
pure theory of welfare economics not only permits the study of
the operation of the actual systems but attempts to provide the
scholar with the means of determining approximately the degree
of inefficiency and irrationality prevailing in such systems.

For a study of irrationalities, the theoretical norm of optimum
efficiency had to be put into operational form. The rule that
prices should equal marginal costs could not be followed, since
both magnitudes depended upon the scarcity conditions of perfect
competition. The theoretical standard was therefore defined in
terms of average production costs for all industries, but even
these normative cost factors could not be given quantitative expression, since they too depended upon the existence of nonob-
servable competitive conditions. The subsequent "adjusted cost-

factor standard" merely provides a list of those factor components that must enter into average costs in any economic system. Since the "adjusted standard" could be stated only in qualitative terms, the scientific aim of measuring the difference between "rational" and "irrational" costs or prices was not attainable. The normative list of cost components did, however, provide a criterion for saying which of the cost items would be acceptable and which would have to be excluded from the prices in an actual economic system. By deducting the turnover tax and adding the subsidies to the actual costs, a difference between "established" and "adjusted" ruble prices could be determined, and the degree of inefficiency in the Soviet economy very roughly approximated.

This interesting attempt to ascertain the degree of distortion in the actual cost and price structures of dominated economies suffers from three fatal defects. The process of deduction and addition is necessarily unsatisfactory, since the relevant information on the interest charges for capital, on rent for land, and on the depreciation charges for capital consumed can never be complete. Hence, in the case of a dominated economy, the difference between established and adjusted prices cannot be regarded as a full and reliable indicator of the degree of efficiency achieved or not achieved.

It is implicitly assumed that all the sacrifices and institutional manipulations resulting from the actions of the rulers express themselves fully in the established prices and that a separate and independent study of the institutional setting is unnecessary. The economically relevant sacrifices of slave laborers, for instance, would thus be fully expressed and included in the wage differentials between "correctional" and regular labor inputs having the same efficiency. Since this is hardly ever the case, it follows that the actual list of cost components is either incomplete or inadequate, and that the notion of a universally valid list of normative cost components is questionable as an axiom for the evaluation of empirical action in an actual system.

Finally, the axiomatic approach sets up a standard of evaluation and comparison that is not derived from the goals of the rulers but is taken from welfare economics. Since welfare is not the preeminent goal in dominated economies, the efficiency standard must be postulated by the researcher, who implicitly assumes that the rulers ought to seek efficiency first. A value judgment of this kind requires that the rulers give up their prerogative of selecting goals of their own choice and accept the supposedly universal axioms of pure economics.

Even if these two defects could be overcome—even if comprehensive and otherwise adequate figures on the so calculated degree of inefficiency could be obtained—such information would be useless for the purposes of practical policy-making. The discrepancy data would be uninteresting to the rulers of dominated economies, since the attainment of the adjusted prices would require the rulers to give up a significant portion of their controls. In fact, they would be interested only in that kind of efficiency which could be achieved within the prevailing structure of power and institutional arrangements. Information on the adjusted prices, especially if incomplete, would also be of no use to actual or potential revolutionaries, since it would not measure or approximate the degree of exploitation suffered by the people on account of the dictatorship.

As for the governments and economic groups outside the dominated economies, it would seem that a set of discrepancy figures would be equally inapplicable as a guide in the formulation of policy, since the governments in this area have to act on the basis of alternative policy goals that are attainable within specific situations. Indeed, it was precisely because of the need to limit investigation to the accessible alternatives that the axiomatic approach seemed inapplicable to the Nazi economy. We therefore concluded that the extent of wage and consumption loss for German workers could be approximated only by making a comparison, as we did in Chapter VII of this study, between the relevant economic data for Germany and the United States.

More suggestive is the recently developed theory of economic dualism. Its originators were Hans Ritschl and Alvin H. Hansen.[5] The central issue analyzed was the role of the state in the modern economy. In Ritschl's view, the impact of the state can be fully understood only if we distinguish between a market economy and a state economy. Both economies accept the principle of efficiency, since they try to achieve the greatest utility with given means. Yet there is a significant difference between them in regard to economic goals, types of economic organization, and principles of allocation. In trying to realize social rather than individual wants, those acting for the state are motivated by a communal spirit. Coercion is imposed only with the intention of making a few recalcitrant individuals act as if they were inspired by the communal spirit. When disposing of its funds, the state acts as a public household that is engaged primarily in consumption. Most revenues are the result of compulsory contributions. There is no necessary correlation between the financial sacrifices made by an individual who pays taxes and his gain from public expenditures. Funds are allocated according to the principles of maintenance and social insurance, not according to the principle of compensation. The salaries of government officials are not determined by the market but rather are intended to provide a certain social standing for the official and his family; and the various forms of social insurance seek to provide a minimum standard of living for the insured. Finally, although the state economy and the market economy are held to be equally efficient, the former operates according to principles that differ from (although they necessarily coexist with) the principles of the market economy.[6] In other words, it is implicitly assumed that the state acts only to satisfy the social needs of the community. The other possibilities—of using the state either as a means of realizing the interest goals of particular groups or of militarizing the public sector of the economy for the purposes of waging war or achieving international pre-eminence—are not included in the theory of economic dualism.

Trying to analyze the Nazi economy, Walter Eucken formulated another version of the dual economy. He distinguished between an exchange economy and a centrally administered economy. In both systems, economic action consists in formulating and realizing economic plans. There is thus no difference in goals. In one economy there is a multitude of individual plans; in the other, a master plan is formulated by the central authority. In the exchange economy the individual plans lead to particular scarci-

ties which are expressed by prices in markets, whereas in the
centrally administered economy there is no adequate method of
pricing goods because the master plan is implemented by compulsory allocation. Laborers are put into occupations and places
of work through the orders of the central authority. Prices and
incomes are fixed by decree. The market system is thus partially
or completely replaced by the centralized economic power which
is held by the agents of the State. The inevitable effect of such
centralized power is to impose upon the economy a more or less
extensive system of planning and compulsory allocation.[7]

A comparison of the main features of the Nazi economy with
the principles of the centrally administered economy reveals that
the theory is not applicable to the Nazi economy. First, there is
the implication that political and economic power can be regarded as identical. In fact, however, the political power of the
Nazis (established in 1933) was not followed by centralized economic authority until 1936, when the Four Year Plan was adopted.
Why then was political power not translated into economic power
from the start?

Second, the theory identifies economic goals with economic
plans. In the first phase of the Nazi regime, however, economic
rearmament—the main economic goal—did not lead to extensive
planning. Procurement agencies purchased equipment and weapons from private concerns. The state agencies acted largely as if
they were individual buyers exchanging goods in private (as distinguished from regulated) markets.

Third, the theory reduces all economic organizations either to
private markets or systems of compulsory allocation. This extreme
oversimplification, had we accepted it, would have prevented us
from making any analysis of the intense efforts to transform voluntary into compulsory cartels and to force private trade associations
into the mold of compulsory economic groups.

Fourth, the division of all economies into only two types, elements of which are said to exist at all times in varying degrees,
forces us to interpret all actual economic systems as mixtures of
market freedom and government compulsion. Although much
effort went into the classification of market forms, there is neither

a typology of actually observed economic systems nor a pattern of change within any given system by means of which we could discover its origin, trace its development, understand its decline, and analyze its effects.

Finally, the confrontation of an exchange economy with a centrally administered economy contains a hidden value judgment. The exchange economy not only permits economic freedom but also institutionalizes an adequate method of economic calculation through its pricing system; whereas the model of the centrally administered economy is constructed in such a way as to make it seem that compulsion is equatable with inefficiency. Yet the advances in military and economic technology, first by the Nazis and then by the communists, have taught us that it is very dangerous to underestimate the enemy's economic capacity for functioning efficiently.

There is one feature of Eucken's theory, however, that was clearly in evidence in the Nazi economy. The element of compulsion definitely affected the choice of goals, the principles of allocation and the types of economic organization as well as the setting of prices and wage rates. As we have tried to show, the various forms of compulsion gave rise to political as well as economic statism; and Eucken's thesis that compulsion modifies the pricing process is confirmed by our findings. We could not, however, verify his generalization that compulsion must necessarily destroy all markets or that it must always be analyzed within the framework of a full-fledged command economy. Our problem was, in fact, to show how the elements of compulsion became compatible with organized capitalism.

Much more suggestive for our purpose has been the achievement of Max Weber. The superiority of his work over the so-called "command economy" lies, on the one hand, in his comprehensive view of social economics and, on the other, in his detailed classification of economic systems, especially of the subtypes of capitalism. Being derived from a detailed historical investigation, his conclusions about social economics as well as economic systems can be modified and extended to economies that did not exist in his time.

Basic for his social economics is the novel view of motivation by economic actors. Self-interest is only one motive that leads to economic goals and gives rise to economic incentives. In addition to self-interest, there are motives derived from traditions, religious or ideological beliefs, and emotions, each one of which can give rise to a multiplicity of economic or quasi-economic goals. In accepting this broad view of motives and goals, we came to grips with the economic intentions of the intransigent and temporizing or imperialist Nazis, the non-Nazis, the pro-Nazi or Nazified business groups, and finally with the various military-economic ideas of the different groups among the generals.

In Weber's view, individual motivations are embedded in a series of "institutional regularities." These consist of rules that take the form of usages, customs, conventions, and laws and reflect group and individual attitudes toward these rules. Since the Nazi counterrevolution produced a transformation in these rules and attitudes, we can trace the differential effect of the institutional change. While new laws in the field of big business reinvigorated old capitalist institutions (e.g., cartel rules), the new laws for small business—as associated with the guilds—were largely frustrated, and the laws dealing with labor markets caused a series of genuine institutional innovations.

¯ Weber's social economics gives full play to the role of economic and social as well as political and military power in economic affairs. While the property power of the large concerns was successfully employed to suppress all efforts at the nationalization of banks or the breaking up of trusts, the market power of monopolists declined during the depression, so that cartel control over markets could be restored only by enlisting the political power of the state. Similarly, in the field of small business, the economic counterrevolution of the Nazified small business groups was backed up temporarily by the political power of the party whereas the resistance of the big business groups received effective support from the political as well as from the military power of the state. Eventually, as we have seen, the economic counterrevolution was defeated, but we should not have been able to determine the reasons for its defeat if we had limited our investigation to economic power and, in that area, considered only the roles of firms and markets.

Rather than assuming that allocational problems can be studied "without reference to the economic organization of the social economy,"[8] Weber saw in economic associations a very important means of influencing the creation and distribution of market opportunities as well as of jobs and income. Thus, having accepted his criteria on the different kinds of associations, we found, first, that the tendency toward a compulsory form of economic organization was comprehensive and widespread in the first phase of the Nazi regime and, second, that compulsory membership did *not* mean the same thing for different economic groups. The theory of the "command economy" would not have led us to this conclusion, nor would it have satisfactorily explained the different economic effects of compulsion. Indeed, it is only when the link between compulsory associations and the related power groups is put in bold relief that one can understand why the Labor Front created a situation of economic helplessness for workers whereas the compulsory economic groups provided the opportunity for fairly effective self-government by big business.

In his interpretation of economic systems, Max Weber reasoned on the basis of three assumptions. One can find in any economic system some fundamental economic characteristics that tend to remain largely unchanged over a period of time, whereas the variable features depend for their existence upon less stable conditions. Given this distinction, we can readily understand that the variable features are entirely compatible with the fundamental characteristics, whereas the others act as modifiers of an existing system. Indeed, at any given time, their influence may be so great as to require us to subdivide the phases of an economic system according to its particular modifiers (e.g., the shift from voluntary to compulsory associations in the first period of the Nazi economy). Finally, there is no separation of the economic from the political and military spheres of action (one cannot be expected to function independently of the other); but although there is always some form of interaction, the pattern of intermingling changes over a period of time. In extreme situations there may be a military or political preponderence over the economic or vice versa, so that some of the noneconomic factors may also modify the characteristics of an economic system.

These assumptions enabled Weber to develop his center-pieced concept of a capitalist economy. At the center stands private enterprise, whose major characteristics tend to remain unchanged for significant periods of time. Private enterprise engages in profit-making (a) by seeking to realize a surplus of net income during an accounting period, (b) by supplying goods or services that are salable in markets, (c) by operating with, and steadily improving, modern machinery as a part of its daily activity, (d) by hiring workers who own neither the means of production nor the products they produce, and (e) by steadily seeking an increase in the volume of its assets, either by reinvesting profits or by borrowing capital from others. In examining the operations of big business in Germany, we discovered that all of these five characteristics were in full evidence at the end of the first phase of the Nazi regime. It was primarily the policies of rearmament and invigoration that had succeeded in overcoming the losses of the depression and that re-established profits.

Capitalist enterprises possess the capacity, according to Weber, of operating within a great variety of economic and political or military environments. Of the economic features that are fully compatible with profit-making by private concerns, the following may be described as variable: (1) the modes of capitalist ideals, (2) the forms of capitalist or non-capitalist markets, (3) the sub-types of capitalist or quasi-capitalist property structures, (4) the kinds of business associations, and (5) the working procedures and the assigning of rank and responsibility in places of business. These variable features of the capitalist economy were derived from wide-ranging historical studies that induced Weber to distinguish a great variety of sub-types within capitalism in ancient as well as in modern times.

With the advent of the Hitler government, the intransigent Nazis in small business challenged almost all these variable features of German capitalism. As we have seen, the attacks upon the capitalist ideals, upon the concentrated property structure, upon the cartelized markets were all decisively defeated by the groups of big business and their allies. Elements of statism penetrated into the field of industrial relations, but the labor markets were obviously rigged in favor of capitalist enterprises. The compulsory business associations as well as the compulsory cartels were certainly detrimental to minority groups or outsiders, but they permitted business a form of self-government that was clearly more advantageous than the voluntary trade associations had been. It was only in the few markets under direct controls that the state curbed some of the profit opportunities open to private concerns.

Although the first phase of the Nazi economy did not exhibit the characteristics of Weber's political or imperialist capitalism, it was primarily his emphasis on social economics and his centerpieced definition of capitalism that enabled us to understand the evolution of organized capitalism in Germany. It is reasonable to expect that such a theory will also be most fruitful in the interpretation of other economic systems.

APPENDIX C

Biographical Notes*

Arnhold, Carl R. (1884——). Founder and director of Dinta Institut, which sponsored training program for development of "social engineers" in industrial plants. Appointed head of vocational-training division in Labor Front in 1936. Established pilot training schools for industrial apprentices; strongly influenced apprenticeship policy of Göring's office for the Four Year Plan.

Beck, Colonel-General Ludwig (1880–1944). Appointed army chief of general staff in 1935; proposed defensive strategy for Germany in 1938. Rejected by Hitler as commander-in-chief of the army in January, 1938; resigned his commission in protest against Hitler's preparations for invasion of Czechoslovakia. Organized first military revolt against Hitler in October, 1938. Killed

---

* The following notes are mostly restricted to biographical details having some relation to the text of this book. An attempt was made to include dates of birth and (if the individual were deceased) of death, but this information was not always available. Also, for some entries, it was impossible to determine whether the individuals in question were still living.

himself in 1944 after Hitler's survival of assassination attempt in July of that year.

Blomberg, Field-Marshal Werner von (1878–1943). Commander of First Division in East Prussia. Chief military delegate at Disarmament Conference in 1932. Reported against Brüning to von Hindenburg; appointed Minister of Defense on the latter's insistence. Became Minister of War in 1935. Supported Hitler in Röhm purge and also in his successful attempt to merge the positions of Chancellor and President; but subsequently, as Minister of War, opposed Hitler's strategy of lightning warfare. Marriage to Fräulein Gruhn provoked disapproval of Officer Corps. Resigned from public life in January, 1938.

Bormann, Martin (1900–1945). Member of counterrevolutionary group in 1920. Secretary to Rudolf Hess (1931); enemy of Ernst Röhm (1932). Managed funds for Hitler Donation; built Hitler's *Berghof* in Bavarian Alps. Ardent believer in Nordic religion and violently opposed to traditional religions. Appointed chief of party chancellery in 1941. Systematically extended his influence over the *Gauleiter* and exercised great power in last phase of the Nazi regime. Confidant of Hitler.

Brüning, Heinrich (1885 ——). Active in Christian trade unions in 1920's. Entered parliament in 1924 as member of Catholic party; appointed Chancellor in March, 1930. Governed largely by means of emergency decrees and, as head of a minority government, was only tolerated by parliament. Attempted to fight the Great Depression through deflationary policy. Mainly responsible for re-election of von Hindenburg in 1932; later dismissed from office because he no longer enjoyed the confidence of the aging President. Left Germany in May, 1933; later taught political science in England and the U. S.

Bütefisch, Heinrich. Chief of Leuna plant (in central Germany) of I. G. Farben. Visited Hitler in summer of 1932. Secured contract (signed in December, 1933, by Undersecretary in Ministry of Economics) for supply of synthetic gasoline to Third Reich and granting I. G. Farben a ten-year price guarantee on cost-plus-profits basis. Member of Keppler circle and honorary officer of the SS. Indicted in I. G. Farben trial at Nürnberg, but not sentenced.

Darré, Walther (1895–1953). Agronomist and author of *The Peasant as the Bearer of the Nordic Race* (1928). Joined NSDAP* in 1930 and organized peasant branch of the party. Head of agrarian division at party headquarters and of racial office of the SS (1931–38). Appointed Leader of the Peasants and then (1933) Minister of Agriculture. Father of entailed-estates law and "ordered markets." Supported Four Year Plan for agriculture and introduced German state organizations into occupied countries. Dismissed from office in 1943 by Hitler.

Feder, Gottfried (1883–1941). Trained as engineer; later became charter member of NSDAP. Co-authored party's program and served as member of its central committee. Elected to parliament in 1924. Chairman of the party's economic council, advisor on economic affairs, and head of party's technical branch. Coined "thralldom of interest" slogan and proposed a work-creation program. Demoted by Hitler in Gregor Strasser dispute (1932). Later (1933–34) undersecretary in Ministry of Economics and Commissioner of Resettlements (1934). Dismissed by Schacht after Röhm purge and stripped of his offices in the party. Subsequently appointed to faculty of technological institute in Berlin.

Flick, Friedrich. Formerly head of Mitteldeutsche Stahlwerke A-G and substantial shareholder in Vereinigte Stahlwerke A-G (United Steel Works). Sold his shares of the Gelsenkirchener Bergwerksgesellschaft to the *Reich* in 1932 and contributed two million marks to political parties, including the NSDAP. Regained his sold shares and also exchanged (via Göring) "black" for "brown" coal properties. Member of "Himmler Circle'" and *Reich* negotiator in obtaining the Jewish Petscheck properties (1937). Greatly increased his holdings during Hitler regime. Indicted but acquitted by International Military Tribunal in Nürnberg. Subsequently rebuilt his industrial empire in West Germany.

* National Socialist German Workers' Party.

Frick, Wilhelm (1877–1945). Served with police headquarters in Munich (1922–23). Involved in November revolt in Munich, but released by the court. Member of parliament in 1924, Minister of Education in Thuringia in 1930, *Reichsminister* of Interior in 1933. Opposed "second revolution" and disliked Himmler, but replaced by the latter in 1943 as Minister of the Interior. Administrator of Nürnberg racial laws of 1935. Sentenced to death by International War Crimes Tribunal and executed in Nürnberg (1946).

Fritsch, Colonel-General Freiherr Werner von (1880–1939). Served under General von Seeckt in Russia during World War I and participated in unofficial military expedition to the Baltic. Supported liaison with Russia and in 1928 prepared a plan for the invasion of Poland. Commander of cavalry division in 1930; promoted to Lieutenant-General in 1932. Executed von Papen's decision to remove Prussian government in July, 1932. Appointed Commander-in-Chief of the army in 1934 over Hitler's opposition. Urged rehabilitation of von Schleicher and opposed Hitler's strategy of lightning warfare. Wrongfully accused of homosexuality by Hitler and relieved of command in 1938. Killed in action during invasion of Poland.

Funk, Walther (1890 ———). Resigned as editor of *Berliner Borsenzeitung* in 1931 and joined NSDAP. Served as liaison between party and business leaders and headed party's economic council in 1932 while soliciting funds for the party. Undersecretary in Ministry of Propaganda from 1933 to 1938; member of council of ministers dealing with foreign-exchange crisis (1936); Minister of Economics in 1938; president of the Central Bank in 1939; temporary Plenipotentiary-General of War Economy. His functions gradually absorbed by Albert Speer. Indicted by the International Military Tribunal in Nürnberg and given a life sentence.

Göbbels, Joseph (1897–1945). *Gauleiter* of Berlin and Minister of Propaganda. Participated in the making of several decisions that had economic significance. Organized Chamber of Culture and pressed all cultural professions into compulsory, party-dominated organizations; sided with Hitler against Röhm at the last moment, thereby undermining the position of intransigents in the party; executed attack on Jewish property in November, 1938, on orders from Hitler, thus starting spoliation policy against the Jews. Committed suicide in April, 1945.

Goerdeler, Carl Friedrich (1884–1945). Mayor of Königsberg and then Leipzig, commissioner of price administration in Brüning government, and again price commissioner in 1934–35. Sought return to competitive economy, but was denied extraordinary powers for so orienting economic policy. Opposed Four Year Plan in memorandum to Göring (1936). Resigned in 1937 as mayor of Leipzig in protest against Nazi removal of statue of Mendelssohn and prevented by Hitler from accepting directorship in Krupp organization. Travelled widely in other countries before World War II and later organized circle of resistance of former generals and state officials in attempt to remove Hitler. Condemned to death and executed by Nazis in 1945.

Göring, Reichsmarshall Hermann (1893–1946). Appointed *Reich* Minister of Air Force in Hitler government (1933) and Prussian Minister-President and Minister of Interior. Consistently exhibited extraordinary flair for manipulation of power in economic affairs. Negotiated standstill agreement with Thyssen and Albert Vögler in 1933; used Prussian police to remove Nazi commissioners in business organizations. Deceived Schacht by accepting chairmanship of Commission on Raw Materials and Foreign Exchange (1936) and subsequently outmaneuvered him in long, intricate struggle for control of the economy. Put in charge of Four Year Plan in 1936; founded Herman Göring Works A-G in 1937. Passed on all major economic decisions from 1937 to 1942. Sentenced to death at Nürnberg but committed suicide.

Grauert, Ludwig (1891 ———). Manager of employer association for northwest area of the Ruhr and member of NSDAP. Obtained loan of 200,000 marks for Göring's newspaper in Essen (1931) and campaign funds for NSDAP in spring election of 1932. As undersecretary in Prussian Ministry of Interior, he supervised suppression of Prussian police and was responsible for secret law that transformed SA units into auxiliary police and prepared legal basis for terror election of March, 1933. Subsequently, after political monopoly of NSDAP had been assured, took action against local Nazi terrorists.

Gröner, Lieutenant-General Wilhelm (1867–1939). Chief of field-railway transport 1914–16; in charge of Hindenburg program for war production 1916–17; Chief of Staff to commander of German army of occupation and Quartermaster-General in 1918. Instrumental in abdication of Kaiser (1919), Minister of Transport in 1920, and Minister of Defense in Müller and Brüning governments (1928–32). Dismissed von Blomberg as head of the *Truppenamt* (successor of the General Staff). Attempted to outlaw SS and SA on the strength of secret documents pointing to illegality of these organizations, but later overruled by the *Reichswehr* and forced to resign.

Hess, Rudolf (1894 ——). Joined NSDAP in 1920 and took part in Hitler *Putsch* of 1923. Served as Hitler's private secretary (1926–32); became deputy leader of the party and *Reichsminister* in 1933. Opposed to virtually all forms of middle-class socialism; prevented Labor Front from taking over handicraft organizations and achieving organizational equality with the party. Issued instructions for Nazi revolt in Austria in 1938. Flew to Scotland (May, 1941) in deluded hope of arranging peace settlement. Sentenced to life imprisonment at Nürnberg.

Himmler, Heinrich (1900–1945). *Reich* leader of Blackshirts in 1929, and head of all German police in 1936. Commissioner for resettlement of Germans in other lands in 1939; leader of SS armed forces and Minister of Interior in 1943; Commander-in-Chief of Home Army in 1944. His interest and actions had more indirect than direct economic influence: co-responsible for removal of SA leaders in 1934 and thus helped to defeat economic counterrevolution; used unified police forces and *Gestapo* to frustrate combined actions of Hjalmar Schacht and steel industrialists in 1937; collected annually about one million marks for the SS through business friends in the "Himmler Circle"; transformed concentration camps into industrial work camps under economic administration of the SS. Committed suicide when arrested.

Hitler, Adolf (1889–1945). Chancellor of the *Reich* January 30, 1933; confirmed as *Führer* by referendum August 19, 1934; Supreme Commander of Armed Forces 1934; self-appointed to active command of the army in December, 1941; committed suicide on April 30, 1945, in Berlin. Made relatively few decisions of major economic importance during first phase of regime, but the following actions and policy stances are of interest here: appointed Walther Darré Minister of Agriculture; accepted Minister Schmitt's program in 1933, but made Schacht acting Minister of Economics in the following year; refused to appoint a military man commissioner of oil production in 1934, or a bureaucrat to the same position in 1935; opposed rationing of fat, but favored grain imports; vacillated between Goerdeler and Schacht as future leader of economy; appointed Göring as chairman of Commission on Raw Materials and Foreign Exchange and put him in charge of Four Year Plan (1936).

Hugenberg, Alfred (1865–1951). Director of Krupp Works; member of parliament in 1920; owner of many newspapers and motion-picture and publishing companies. Chairman of German National People's Party (1928–33); put down rebellion against his party leadership in 1930. Campaigned with Nazis against Young Plan in 1929 and formed Harzburg Front with Hitler in 1931. Joined Hitler government as Minister of Economics, Food, and Agriculture in 1933. Failed in struggle with Walther Darré over control of agricultural organizations and rejected Hitler's offer to unite parties. Resigned at the same time that his party was required to "dissolve" itself.

Karmann, General. With von Blomberg, a member of German delegation to disarmament conference of 1932. Became head of army provisioning office and in this capacity was responsible for food policy of Ministry of Defense. Developed close relations with Ministry of Agriculture and agreed to policy of "ordered" farm markets, which he defended against other departments within the Ministry of War.

Keitel, Field-Marshal Wilhelm (1882–1946). Headed political division of Ministry of War in 1934 and later (1938) in charge of Military High Command (OKW), which replaced the Ministry.

As deputy for the Führer in military administration, he rejected all arguments against the leader's military strategy. Worked for full mobilization of the economy as chairman of working committee of Reich Defense Council, and, while head of the OKW, insisted on economic preparation for lightning war. Turned against officers involved in attempt of July, 1944, on Hitler's life. Signed act of unconditional surrender (May, 1945). Sentenced to death at Nürnberg and executed in October, 1946.

Keppler, Wilhelm (1882 ——). Manager of small chemical factory when selected as Hitler's liaison with business leaders. Organized Keppler circle and persuaded Hitler to address it in 1932. Instrumental in arranging meeting between Hitler and von Papen in January, 1933; urged business leaders to petition von Hindenburg for appointment of Hitler as Chancellor. Made economic adviser by Hitler, with instructions to restrain economic actions of party offices during first phase of regime. By sustaining close contact with I. G. Farben and other concerns, helped to prepare the way for Four Year Plan. Also acted as agent for Hitler in Austrian *Anschluss* and "liberation" of Czechoslovakia and served as state secretary, with special duties, in Ministry of Foreign Affairs 1938–45. Sentenced to ten years' imprisonment in "Ministries Trial" (1949).

Krauch, Carl. Well-known chemist and head of Oppau Works of I. G. Farben. Successfully negotiated Air-Force contract for production of synthetic oil. Joined Göring's economic staff in 1936 and became head of research-and-development division. Worked out details for production of synthetic rubber by I. G. Farben and completed preliminary draft of Four Year Plan. Joined Nazi party in 1937. Put in charge of chemical sector of economy in 1938 and directed production of chemical industries while acting as chairman of the board of I. G. Farben.

Krupp von Bohlen und Holbach, Gustav (1870–1950). Minor diplomat when he married eldest daughter of Friedrich Alfred Krupp (1906). Became head of Krupp organization. Not in Hitler's favor prior to von Papen government but later signed petition seeking Hitler's appointment as Chancellor. Obtained one million marks for terror election of March, 1933, and ostentatiously joined forces with Labor Front. Dismissed workers who refused to salute party flag, headed Hitler Donation office, and dissolved *Reichsverband der Deutschen Industrie* (Association of German Industry) at Hitler's wish. Actively collaborated with Nazis during second phase of regime by making pilot plants and skilled workers available to Hermann Göring Works A-G and by providing many of the weapons used by German armies in World War II. Obtained valuable properties in occupied territories and secured passage of law which established his organization as an inseparable estate in inheritance proceedings. Adjudged incompetent to appear before war-crimes tribunal and never stood trial.

Ley, Robert (1890–1946). Early member of Nazi party and doggedly loyal follower of Hitler. *Gauleiter* of Cologne until 1932. First, deputy head and then head of party political organization. After seizure of trade-union buildings, appointed leader of the Labor Front. Authored abortive law of 1934 (issued under Hitler's name) that was intended to organize not only all employers and employees but all business organizations as well under the Labor Front. Later signed Leipzig agreement in attempt to make employers deputy leaders in most of the Labor Front offices, failed to extend influence of his Chambers of Labor in this way. Prevented by Schacht and Göring from incorporating handicraft organizations into Labor Front and by Hess and Göring from making it independent of the party. While using workers' unrest to advance his personal ends, he threatened to have shot any who went on strike. Supported increasing demands of Four Year Plan on workers and used Labor Front as administrative agent in employment of forced labor. Indicted in Nürnberg; took his life during trial.

Ludowici, Johann W. Advocate of Nazi ruralism and author of book on urban resettlement. Deputy to Gottfried Feder as Commissioner of Resettlement and president of Akademie für Landesforschung und Reichplannung. Survived purge of 1934 and later headed Resettlement Office of Labor Front. Dismissed from position when Göring assumed control of construction industry and decreed that home construction would be limited to dwellings for workers considered essential to Four Year Plan.

Mansfield, Werner (1893 ——). First known as corporation lawyer representing employer association of Ruhr iron and steel industry. Member of Sahm committee in 1932, working for re-election of von Hindenburg. As head of wage division of Ministry of Labor in Hitler government, controlled wage policy (via trustees of labor) and participated in formulation of National Labor Law (1934). Later helped to exclude Labor Front from policy decisions affecting wages and worked closely with former associates in employer association. Together with General Georg Thomas, established ceiling (1938) on wages and fringe benefits. Issued wage scale that discriminated against slave labor and worked on racially oriented wage structure for all industries that was to be implemented after German victory.

Papen, Franz von (1879 ——). Politician and diplomat. Military attaché in Mexico, then Washington (1915). Recalled from U. S. because of espionage activities and assigned by German government to service with Turkish army for remainder of World War I. Member of Prussian *Landtag* (1921–32). Succeeded Brüning as Chancellor (1932); then suspended (June, 1932) prohibition against appearance of "Blackshirts" and "Brownshirts" in the streets and created opportunity for riots that led to series of parliamentary crises. With von Hugenberg, von Blomberg, and others prevailed upon von Hindenburg to make Hitler Chancellor. Ambassador to Austria (1936–38), where he supported Nazi movement that culminated in resignation of Kurt Schussnigg and appointment of Seyss-Inquart as Austrian Chancellor. Later acquitted on charge of planning aggressive war by International War Crimes Tribunal at Nürnberg but sentenced to eight years' imprisonment by German denazification court. (Sentence revoked by court of review in 1949.)

Pietzsch, Albert (1874 ——). Active member of Nazi party, economic adviser to Rudolf Hess, and president of Munich industrial chamber. Prior to the Röhm purge, tried to build up the

Industrial Estates, but sidetracked in this attempt by Schacht. One of the few employers who endeavored to live up to the Leipzig agreement, Pietzsch attempted to increase the influence of employers in the party and the Labor Front. Appointed head of National Economic Chamber by Schacht (in recognition of this effort) and used as mediator between Labor Front and handicraft organizations.

Pleiger, Paul. Started as businessman in western Germany; served as economic advisor to his *Gauleiter*. On staff of Wilhelm Keppler when it was incorporated into Göring's Commission on Raw Materials and Foreign Exchange (1936). Combined managerial abilities with ruthlessness; helped to originate the Hermann Göring Works, A-G, of which he later became general manager. Sought to promote the influence of the state in coal and steel industries and in 1942 was appointed plenipotentiary director of the coal industry in occupied countries. Indicted in "Ministries Case" (1949) and sentenced for spoliation of conquered areas.

Poensgen, Ernst (1871 ———). Member of managerial board of Vereinigte Stahlwerke A-G (United Steel Works) at its formation in 1926; in charge of most of the iron and steel cartels and of trade association for Ruhr iron and steel industry. Opposed by *Gauleiter* for the Ruhr area as head of economic groups but confirmed in this position by Schacht (1934) in spite of Nazi protests. Influenced Schacht in latter's decision not to implement Goerdeler's proposal to lower cartel prices. Obtained the right (1936) to formulate Four Year Plan for steel, but unable to prevent founding of Hermann Göring Works A-G. Remained head of iron and steel group until 1942, when his organization was replaced by *Reich* Association created by Speer Ministry.

Pohl, Oswald (——— 1951). Initially a naval officer, later in charge of SS financial office and supervisor of budgets and expenditures. At beginning of World War II helped to transform concentration camps into compulsory work camps and built new camps near industrial centers. Engaged in many quasi-economic activities as chief of Economic Office of the SS, and was responsible for recovery of dental gold from victims of gas chambers. Convicted in "Concentration Camp Case" and sentenced to death. Hanged June 8, 1951, at Nürnberg.

Popitz, Johannes (1884–1944). Well-known scholar in public finance, professor at University of Berlin, and Prussian official during 1920's. Became undersecretary of Finance in Müller government, but forced by Schacht to resign (December, 1929). Joined von Schleicher cabinet (1932) as State Secretary in charge of Prussian Ministry of Finance, retained when Göring became Minister-President of Prussia, and served Third Reich in same position until 1944. In foreign-exchange crisis of 1936, opposed Schacht and presented premium plan (which was not accepted) for export proceeds. As active member of "The Wednesday Club," Popitz reversed his earlier position and favored return to monarchy. Participated in discussions of plans to instigate army revolt, but was excluded from Goerdeler's "shadow government." Subsequently tried before Nazi People's Court and hanged (1945).

Reichenau, Field-Marshal Walther von (1884–1942). Favored use of SA for protection of East Prussia, where he was chief-of-staff to General von Blomberg (1931). Urged inclusion of NSDAP in government of 1932 and received Hitler's ideas on future military policy. Head of political division of Ministry of Defense in 1933; later recommended by Hitler for position of army Commander-in-Chief (first in 1934 and again in 1938), but rejected by the officer corps. Favored war in 1938, but doubtful about Hitler's plan for invasion of the West in 1939. Raised to field-marshal rank because of his part in war against France; defeated by Timoshenko at Rostov in November, 1941. Died of a stroke during Russian campaign (January, 1942).

Reichert, Jakob (1885 ——). General secretary of trade association for iron and steel industry and then of the economic group for the same industry. Effectively represented iron and steel interests and played decisive role in formulation of two cartel bills that were issued as laws by Kurt Schmitt (Minister of Economics) in July, 1933. Ably assisted Ernst Poensgen (*q.v.*) in disputes over Four Year Plan and, with Poensgen, helped to determine steel allocations and formulate plans for economic mobilization prior to and during World War II.

Renteln, Theodor Adrian von (1897 ———). Leader of Hitler Youth and head of *Kampfbund des deutschen Mittelstandes* ("fighting organization of the middle class"). Later (1933) in charge of Estates for Handicraft and Trade and president of Association for German Industry and Trade. Failed to become Prussian Minister of Economics (1933), but appointed chairman of newly created NS Hago, which received its funds from the Labor Front and functioned as an agency of the latter in attempt to take over the handicraft organizations. As chief of staff for Ley, Renteln became president of the disciplinary honor court of Labor Front officials and was thus separated from the organizations of small business.

Röhm, Ernst (1887–1934). Preceded Hitler as member of Nazi party; arrested for participating in *Putsch* (1923). Broke with Hitler over the role of the SA and served for five years as officer in Bolivian army. Recalled by Hitler in 1930 and appointed chief of staff of the SA, which he reorganized along military lines. Both the SA and SS were temporarily outlawed, but the ban was lifted by von Papen in June, 1932. Storm troopers then got control of the streets, and by February, 1933, many SA units had become auxiliary police. Röhm's proposed merger of the SA and the army led to a bitter dispute in the following year between these two forces. Attempts at conciliation failed, and Hitler, acting on proposals made by Göring and Himmler (but also influenced by von Blomberg and von Hindenburg) then staged the purge (June, 1934) that destroyed Röhm and many of his followers.

Schacht, Hjalmar (1877 ———). Entered politics as member of German Democratic party; appointed currency commissioner (November, 1923); twice president of Central Bank (1924–30, 1933–39). First negotiated and then repudiated the Young Plan. Strong supporter of Hitler and a principal speaker at Harzburg Conference. Acting Minister of Economics (August, 1934, to November, 1937); Minister without portfolio from 1937 to 1943.

Turned against Nazis after his defeat by Göring and imprisoned by them after July, 1944, attempt on Hitler's life. Indicted but acquitted by International Military Tribunal in 1946. Author of *Stabilisierung der Mark* (1927), *Das Ende der Reparationen* (1931), *Nationale Kreditwirtschaft* (1934), and autobiography, *Confessions of the Old Wizard* (1956).

Scheer-Hennings, Rudolf. Member of group of intellectuals sponsoring the cause of Nazified small business. As commissioner of steel-products industry in the Ruhr, he proposed to set up a guild-like market organization. This proposal was not accepted, but Scheer was later recalled by Kurt Schmitt (then Minister of Economics) as commissioner and given the figurative title of economic consultant. Later became one of the officers in selling agency of the steel cartels and joined Hermann Göring Works A-G in 1937.

Schleicher, General Kurt von (1882–1934). Outstanding student at military academy; later an officer on the General Staff and liaison between regular army and illicit military formations after World War I. Responsible for political contacts of Ministry of Defense under von Seeckt; appointed head of Ministry political division and acted as power behind the throne, at first selecting Ministers of Defense and then Chancellors. Became Minister of Defense in von Papen government; after fall of the latter made Chancellor by von Hindenburg (1932). Killed (with his wife) in purge of 1934 (at the same time as Ernst Röhm). Later exonerated from charge of treason.

Schmidt-Wiesbaden, Wilhelm (1900 ———). Small-town businessman and head of plumber's guild in Hesse. Member of parliament in 1930 for Nazi party. Appointed leader of Estate of Handicraft in summer of 1934, but ignored by Schacht. Chairman of journeyman division of Labor Front in 1934; resigned his position in 1936 because he did not want to help Ley get control of handicraft organizations.

Schmitt, Kurt (1886 ———). Director-general of Allianz, Germany's largest insurance concern. Appointed Minister of Economics in July, 1933; made public his compromise with Hitler, which ended interference of intransigent Nazis in business. Called a halt to efforts to organize economic estates; issued two cartel laws and a law on the preparation of an "organic" form of economic organization. Later turned against cartels and regulation of imports and delayed payments of subsidies for synthetic oil. Forced to resign in June, 1934, he joined the Himmler circle. Later (1941) opposed nationalization of insurance companies in letter to Martin Bormann.

Schmitz, Hermann. Treasurer of I. G. Farben and later (1934) director-general of same concern. Elected member of parliament in November, 1933, as Nazi representative. Signed gasoline contract in December, 1933. Supported synthetic rubber contract in 1936 and subsequently favored close collaboration with Four Year Plan and its projects, including construction of new plants near Auschwitz.

Schramm, Ferdinand. Party leader in Mecklenburg 1933–35 and regional leader of handicraft organization 1935–38. Mediated in dispute between Schacht and *Gauleiter* Hildebrandt. Appointed by Göring as head of national handicraft organization and fought off attack by Labor Front. Subsequently adapted handicraft organizations to requirements of developing war economy.

Schröder, Freiherr Kurt von (1889 ——). Banker of Cologne, member of Keppler circle, organizer of petition to von Hindenburg urging appointment of Hitler as Chancellor in November, 1932. Invited Hitler and von Papen to meet at his home and clear the way for Hitler government. Member of Himmler circle after 1936 and collector of funds (amounting to one million marks a year) for the SS.

Schuhmann, Walther (1898 ——). Leader of NSBO *(National-sozialistische Betriebszellen Organisation)* and member of parliament. Urged Hitler to seize trade-union buildings (spring, 1933). Insisted upon semi-trade-union function of Labor Front. Removed from office after Röhm purge; appointed trustee of labor in 1936.

Schwarz, Franz Xavier (1875 ——). Early member of Nazi party and party treasurer 1926–45. Examined budgets, audited the expenditures of all party organizations, and supervised finances of auxiliary organizations, but had no control over the finances of the SS or funds received from Hitler donation. Member of *Reichstag* 1933 *et seq.*

Schwerin von Krosigk, Count Lutz (1877 ——). Minister of Finance in governments of von Papen, von Schleicher, and Hitler (1932–45). Acted as Foreign Minister in temporary administration of Admiral Dönitz. Indicted in "Ministries Case" in 1949 and condemned to ten-years' imprisonment.

Seldte, Franz (1882–1947). Magdeburg manufacturer and leader of *Stahlhelm,* an organization of ex-servicemen founded in December, 1918. Formed alliance with Nationalist party and joined "National Front" established at Harzburg Conference. Became Minister of Labor in Hitler government (1933–45) and agreed (1935) to absorption of *Stahlhelm* by SA, which deprived him of any source of influence in spite of his party membership. Died while awaiting trial at Nürnberg.

Speer, Albert (1905 ——). German architect and Nazi politician. Rebuilt Reichschancellery at Berlin according to Hitler's plans and worked with Fritz Todt on *Autobahnen* in 1930's. Became Minister of Munitions and Armaments after Todt's death (1942). Played major part in building of Siegfried Line and construction (1943–44) of Channel defenses. Sentenced (1946) to twenty years' imprisonment by International War Crimes Tribunal at Nürnberg for responsibility in German use of slave labor during World War II.

Strasser, Gregor (1892–1934). Joined Nazi party in 1921 and participated in the Putsch (1923). Head of party's political organization in 1926. Represented moderates in the party, favoring coalition with Catholic party (1930) and participation in von Schleicher's government. Resigned from his offices at end of 1932, when Hitler accused him of disloyalty. Killed in 1934 by the SS during Röhm purge. Author of *Freiheit und Brot* (1928) and *Kampf um Deutschland* (1932).

Strasser, Otto (1897 ——). Joined Nazi party in 1923, influential in it after its reorganization in 1924. Promoted leftist ideas; in conflict with Hitler in latter's attempt to revise party plank on property. Expelled from party in 1930. Subsequently founded nationalist organization known as the Black Front, which fought in exile against Hitler regime. Not permitted to return to West Germany until military occupation had been terminated. Author of *Hitler and I* (1940) and *History in My Time* (1941).

Streicher, Julius (1885–1946). Participated in Hitler *Putsch* (1923). *Gauleiter* of Franconia (1933–40) and editor of anti-Semitic newspaper, *Der Stürmer* (1923–45). Enriched himself in SA pogroms of November, 1938; investigated by Göring and removed from position as *Gauleiter* in 1940. Indicted in Nürnberg and executed.

Thomas, Georg (——— 1945). General-Staff officer and head of economic division of War Ministry. Wrote many important memoranda that prepared for subsequent policy decisions (e.g., on economic dictatorship, June, 1934; foreign-exchange situation, February, 1935, and September, 1936) and contributed many ideas toward realization of goals and policies of original Four Year Plan. Subsequently turned against Hitler's lightning warfare and lost confidence in the regime after von Fritsch affair, but continued to serve until 1943, when his division was absorbed by the Speer Ministry.

Thyssen, Fritz (1873–1951). German industrialist and substantial shareholder in Vereinigte Stahlwerke A-G (United Steel Works). Joined Nazi party in 1931, arranged for Hitler's speech to industrialists in Düsseldorf (1932), signed petition urging von Hindenburg to appoint Hitler as Chancellor (November, 1932). Economic advisor to Ruhr *Gauleiter* (1933). Proposed leadership councils in management of industrial relations (1933); gave estimated one million marks in support of Nazis. Unwilling to vote in parliament for Hitler's plan to invade Poland, Thyssen left Germany. (His holdings were then taken over by Prussian state and managed by Kurt von Schröder in the interest of the government). Later captured by Germans in France, but liberated by U. S. troops (1945). Fined twenty per cent of his property by German denazification court (but Thyssen claimed to be penniless, and no fine was paid).

Todt, Fritz (1891–1942). Construction engineer. Joined the Nazis in 1923. Builder of *Autobahnen* and West Wall, leader of NS-

Technicians (after Gottfried Feder), inspector-general of German highways, and plenipotentiary director of construction industry (1938–42). Later inspector-general for water and power industry, and Minister for Arms and Munitions from 1940 to 1942. Killed in airplane accident February 8, 1942; succeeded by Albert Speer.

Vögler, Albert (1887–1945). First director-general of Vereinigte Stahlwerke A-G (United Steel Works), member of parliament for German People's Party, and German delegate to Young Plan conferences. Resigned in protest against the latter and joined Keppler circle. Signed petition to von Hindenburg urging appointment of Hitler as Chancellor (November, 1932); re-elected to Parliament as Nazi representative (November, 1933). Negotiated with Göring on economic reorganization (1933) and Four Year Plan (1937). Supported Speer's reorganization of steel industry (1942) and acted as economic chief of western Germany in last phase of World War II. Committed suicide at time of arrest by American soldiers.

Wagener, Otto. Retired captain and SA Chief of Staff under Otto von Pfeffer. Member of organizational division of Nazi party (1931–32) and General Commissioner in Economic Affairs (1933). Later removed from his positions in the party and sentenced to short term in concentration camp. On release, he enlisted in German army; had rank of colonel-general at end of World War II.

APPENDIX D

Chronology of Events

March 6   Three junior officers (Scheringer, Ludin, and Wendt) arrested for spreading Nazi propaganda in army.

March 30   Heinrich Brüning appointed Chancellor on recommendation of Gröner and von Schleicher.

July 18   Von Hindenburg dissolved parliament.

Sept. 14   General election brought 107 Nazis to parliament.

Sept. 25   As a witness in the Scheringer trial in Leipzig, Hitler promised not to interfere with the army.

Oct. 5   First secret meeting of Brüning and Hitler.

Oct. 6   Gröner asked Officer Corps to promise allegiance to Weimar Republic.

Oct. 18   Social Democrats decided to "tolerate" Brüning government.

Dec. 30   SA corps estimated at 100,000.

1 9 3 1

March 19   Creation of customs union between Germany and Austria

March 25	Agreement between von Schleicher and Röhm on use of the SA in border control.
April 4	Reorganization of SA and exclusion of Captain Stennes.
May 9	First pocket battleship launched in Kiel.
July 1	Declaration of the Hoover moratorium for one year.
July 15	Failure of Danat and Dresdener banks; subsequent banking holidays.
Sept. ?	International Court of Justice repudiated customs union.
Oct. 9	Brüning became Minister of Foreign Affairs (in addition to serving as Chancellor), and Gröner became Minister of Defense and Interior.
Oct. 11	Conference at Harzburg allying Hitler and Hugenberg, sanctioned by participating business men.
Nov. 25	Boxheim Incident (discovery of secret Nazi documents revealing plans to seize government by force).

1932

Jan. 7	Brüning, Gröner, and von Schleicher met Hitler to negotiate extension of von Hindenburg's term of office.
Jan. 8	Gröner warned Hitler about SA.
Jan. 23	Von Gröner and von Schleicher persuaded von Hindenburg not to dismiss Brüning.
Jan. 27	Hitler spoke to industrialists' club in Düsseldorf.
Feb. 2	General Disarmament Conference opened at Geneva.
April 5	Ministers of the *Länder* demanded suppression of the SA by Gröner.
April 10	Von Hindenburg re-elected President of Germany.
April 13	Brüning government outlawed SA and SS.
April 14	Von Schleicher informed Gröner that army opposed outlawing of SA and SS.
April 26	Brüning reached tentative disarmament agreement at Geneva.
April 28	Von Schleicher met with Hitler secretly.

1 9 3 2 *(cont.)*

May 6	Resignation of Minister of Economics from Brüning government.
May 10	Von Schleicher informed Gröner that he had lost confidence of the army.
May 13	Von Gröner resigned from government.
May 20	Von Schleicher declined offer to become Minister of Defense in Brüning government.
May 30	Brüning dismissed by Hindenburg on suggestion of von Schleicher.
May 31	Hindenburg against "bolshevik confiscation" of landed estates. Von Papen appointed Chancellor, von Schleicher as Defense Minister.
June 16– July 9	Conference at Lausanne accepted end of reparation payments.
June 17	Von Papen government removed ban on SS and SA.
July 17	Nazi riots in Altona (port of Hamburg); 19 killed; 285 wounded.
July 20	Von Papen replaced Prussian government with commissioner.
July 31	Nazis obtained 230 seats in new general election.
"	Total membership in SA and SS: 400,000.
Aug. 5	Von Schleicher met Hitler in Fürstenberg barracks.
Aug. 9	SA murdered worker in Potempa, Silesia.
Aug. 30	Hitler refused to become Vice-Chancellor in von Papen government.
"	Göring elected president of parliament.
Sept. 2	Hitler pledged support to army.
Sept. 12	Overwhelming majority voted down von Papen government in parliament.
"	Five Nazis sentenced to death for Potempa murder. Death sentence commuted to life term as result of Hitler's intervention.
Oct. 20	Beginning of strike by Berlin transportation workers (jointly supported by Nazis and Communists).
Nov. 4	Nazi party lost seats (230 to 196) in general election.

Nov. 16	Hitler refused to join von Papen government.
Nov. 17	Von Hindenburg reluctantly accepted von Papen's resignation.
Nov. 21	Von Hindenburg asked Hitler to form parliamentary government.
Nov. 24	Von Hindenburg refused to appoint Hitler as presidential Chancellor.
Dec. 3	Von Schleicher appointed Chancellor and Minister of Defense.
"	Elections in Thuringia brought 40 per cent drop in Nazi votes.
Dec. 7	Strasser resigned his party offices in dispute with Hitler.
Dec. 15	Von Schleicher presented his recovery program.
Dec. 30	Total unemployed about 7 million.

1933

Jan. 4	Von Papen and Hitler met at home of von Schröder in Cologne.
Jan. 15	Nazis gained 39 per cent of vote in small state of Lippe.
Jan. 28	Von Schleicher resigned Chancellorship.
Jan. 30	Hitler appointed Chancellor in coalition government. Von Blomberg became Minister of Defense; and Neurath, Foreign Minister.
Feb. ?	Two laws passed which permitted recruiting of SA into auxiliary police.
Feb. 20	Hitler government called for new parliamentary election.
"	Hitler met with industrialists and received their promise to finance election.
Feb. 24	Police raided headquarters of Communist party.
Feb. 27	*Reichstag* building went up in flames.
Feb. 28	Hitler government suspended guarantees of individual liberty.
March 5	Nazis obtained 44 per cent of vote in terror election.

1 9 3 3 *(cont.)*

March 6– March 20	Nazi commissioners assumed control of the *Länder*.
March 13	Göbbels appointed as Minister of Propaganda and Enlightenment.
March 18	Hitler government passed a discriminatory tax law.
March 21	Ceremonial meeting of Parliament in church at Potsdam.
March 23	Parliament (surrounded by SS) granted Hitler government the right to rule in disregard of Constitution.
March 27	Göring negotiated with Vögler and Thyssen on economic organizations.
March 28	Nazi party initiated huge anti-Semitic boycott.
April 4	Hitler government accepted secret defense act.
"	Election of Work Councils postponed for six months.
April 7	*Reichsstatthalter* officially introduced in the *Länder*.
April 10	Hitler government announced investigation of banking system.
May 1	First national holiday celebrated.
"	Nazi party imposed embargo on new members.
May 2	Occupation of trade-union buildings by Nazi troopers.
May 3	Proclamation of the Estates for Handicraft and Trade.
May 10	Göring confiscated property of Social Democrats.
May 16	Schacht appointed president of the Central Bank.
May 17	Hitler delivered his "peace speech."
May 19	Trustees of labor made state officials by law.
June 1	Beginning of collections for Hitler Donation.
June 23	Law purged civil service of Social Democrats and Jews.
June 26	Hitler confiscated property of Communist party.
"	Nationalist party dissolved by agreement with Hitler.
June 27	Hugenberg resigned from Hitler government.
July 1	Hitler announced absorption of *Stahlhelm* in SA.
July 4	Bavarian Peoples party forced to dissolve itself.
July 5	Catholic Center party forced to dissolve itself.

July 7	Darré appointed Minister of Agriculture and Food.
"	Hess forbade actions against chain stores and department stores.
July 13	Schmitt revealed his economic program, and Hitler confirmed it.
"	Hitler declared: "Political power must be acquired rapidly. . . . in the economic sphere other principles of development must determine our actions."
July 14	Signing of treaty between Germany and Vatican.
"	Nazi party became the only legally recognized political party in Germany.
July 15	Two cartel laws passed by government.
Aug. 6	Röhm declared that the tasks of the SA had not been accomplished.
Aug. 10	*Kampfbund des deutschen Mittelstandes* ("Fighting Organization of Industrial Middle Class") dissolved by Nazi party.
Sept. 13	Act on the Estate of Agriculture and market control passed.
Sept. 23	Chamber of Culture established by Göbbels.
"	Hitler assured army of Nazi support and expressed gratitude for assistance received.
"	Construction of the *Autobahn* begun.
Sept. 29	Act on inheritance of agricultural land and buildings passed.
Oct. 1	National Organization of German Handicraft was dissolved.
"	Hitler introduced the "Honor Day of the German Peasant."
Oct. 14	Germany left the League of Nations and Disarmament Conference.
"	Feder publicly supported demands of savings banks.
Oct. 20	Von Blomberg insisted upon compulsory business organizations.
Nov. 3	Discriminatory decree wiped out 1,500 publishers.
Nov. 7	Organizations of big and small business celebrated end of Treaty of Versailles.

1933 *(cont.)*

Nov. 12   Plebiscite of the people approving Germany's exit from League of Nations.

Nov. 29   Act on the constitution of the Estate of Handicraft passed.

Dec. 1   Röhm and Hess appointed ministers in Hitler government.

1934

Jan. 20   Publication of National Labor Law.

Jan. 26   Celebration of "historical day" of handicraft; new leader appointed.

"   SA disrupted celebration of Kaiser's birthday in Berlin.

"   Nonaggression pact between Germany and Poland.

Jan. 30   Parliament deprived *Länder* of all rights of sovereignty.

Feb. 1   Von Fritsch replaced Hammerstein as army Commander-in-Chief.

Feb. 17   Britain, France, and Italy assured Austria of independence.

Feb. 21   Hitler offered Anthony Eden two-thirds reduction in size of SA.

Feb. 22   Minister of Labor forbade price increases in construction industry.

Feb. 27   Preliminary law on leadership principle in business organizations.

March 10   Savings banks relieved of liquidity requirements of 1931.

April 1   Himmler appointed head of *Gestapo* in Prussia.

April 4   Armed Forces authorized to draw up their own budgets.

April 16   Offer to reduce size of SA confirmed in note to Great Britain.

April 22   New applications for public-works subsidy not acceptable.

April 26   Public agencies required to have military approval for property use.

April 27	First indication of von Hindenburg's illness.
May 16	Meeting of the generals at Bad Nauheim: Röhm rejected as Defense Minister; succession of von Hindenburg discussed.
"	Schacht and Seldte issued order against rise in prices.
May 20	Von Blomberg complained to Hitler about Schmitt's resistance to oil program.
May 24	Schacht rejected demand for reduction of interest rates.
June 1	Penalty charge of 1,000 marks imposed on visas to Austria.
June 4	Hitler talked to Röhm for five hours about SA.
June 6	One-month furlough (effective July 1) announced for SA.
June 7	Röhm expected SA to return with new vigor: "The SA is Germany's fate."
June 9	Party and SS merged all intelligence functions.
June 13	Hitler met Gregor Strasser and offered him Economic Ministry.
June 14	Hitler visited Mussolini in Venice.
June 15	Second ordinance on the Estate of Handicraft.
June 17	Von Papen delivered provocative speech in Marburg.
June 18	Business group presented proposal for reorganization of "estates."
June 20	Von Papen demanded that Hitler publish his speech in daily press.
"	Von Blomberg requested Hitler to appoint economic dictator.
June 21	Von Hindenburg and von Blomberg demanded action of Hitler in SA dispute.
June 23	Hitler and Schmitt accepted law on economic dictatorship.
June 25	Von Fritsch placed army in state of alert.
June 27	Schmitt resigned as Minister of Economics on account of "illness."
June 28	German Officers' League expelled Röhm from its list.
"	Hitler attended wedding of *Gauleiter* Terboven in Essen.

1934 *(cont.)*

June 29	Von Blomberg explained role of army to Nazi group.
"	Hitler visited labor camps in Westphalia.
June 30	Hitler ordered Röhm's arrest and murder.
July 1	Schacht declared full transfer moratorium for export of capital.
"	Von Hindenburg congratulated Hitler on Röhm purge.
July 3	All officials in handicraft required to be Nazis.
"	Feder published preliminary law on urban resettlement.
"	Cabinet congratulated Hitler on Röhm purge.
July 13	Hitler gave parliament his reasons for Röhm purge.
July 19	Colonel Thomas reminded Keppler of military demands for new economic policy.
July 20	Thirty military officers demanded rehabilitation of von Schleicher.
July 25	Abortive Nazi revolt in Austria and murder of Engelbert Dollfuss.
Aug. 1	Death of von Hindenburg; Hitler became Führer and Chancellor.
Aug. 2	Army took oath to Hitler as Supreme Commander.
"	Schacht's appointment as acting Minister of Economics.
Aug. 6	Hitler's funeral oration in honor of von Hindenburg.
Aug. 7	Schacht forbade all price increases in handicrafts.
Aug. 19	Plebiscite on Hitler's assumption of von Hindenburg's office.
Aug. 20	Schacht cancelled decrees on assignment of workers in industry.
Sept. ?	Schacht's new plan.
Oct. 24	Hitler signed abortive bill on Labor Front.
Nov. 1	Army economic division transferred to Ministry of Defense.
Nov. 4	Goerdeler appointed price commissioner.
Nov. 9	Schacht rescinded order on party membership in handicraft.

Nov. 12   Plebiscite approved Germany's exit from League of Nations.

Nov. 27   Schacht terminated "estates" and established business "groups."

Dec. 4   Supervisory boards engaged in systematic price supervision.

Dec. 17   Law imposed ceiling on dividend payments.

Dec. 22   Banking Act published.

Dec. 30   Number of registered unemployed had fallen to 2.6 million.

1935

Jan. 3   Hitler agreed in secret meeting to exonerate von Schleicher (killed in Röhm purge, June 30, 1934) of charge of treason.

Jan. 13   Saar voted to return to Germany.

Jan. 15   Second settlement act for farmers.

Jan. 18   Third decree on organization of handicraft.

Jan. 28   Göring visited Warsaw.

Feb. 19   Seldte shifted from subsidy to loans for private housing.

Feb. 28   Von Schleicher formally exonerated in meeting of General Staff.

March 9   Existence of Air Force officially announced.

March 16 Reintroduction of compulsory military service.

"   Hitler set military goal at 36 divisions for the army.

March 17 Decree on rules to be followed in bidding for public contracts.

March 23 Instruction to overhaul organization of guilds.

March 26 Goerdeler promulgated rules for examination of cartel prices.

April 11 Britain, France, and Italy denounced German rearmament.

May 3   Schacht's secret letter to Hitler on financing of rearmament.

May 21   Cabinet secretly accepted second Defense Act.

"   Hitler's claim that "Germany is a democracy."

1 9 3 5 *(cont.)*

May 21	Hitler promised not to interfere in internal affairs of Austria.
"	Schacht secretly appointed Plenipotentiary-General of war economy.
"	Law passed on reorganization of consumer cooperatives.
May 25	Second proposal on reform of corporation law.
June 13	Establishment of national and eighteen regional labor chambers.
June 18	Signing of Anglo-German Naval Treaty.
June 28	Imposition of export levy.
July 1	Goerdeler resigned as price commissioner.
July 16	Appointment of a *Reichsminister* for Church Affairs.
Aug. 19	Schacht spoke in Königsberg on capital accumulation and savings.
Sept. 15	Nürnberg race laws on intermarriage and citizenship.
Oct. 3	Italian troops invaded Abyssinia.
Nov. 30	Some six hundred ministers driven from their parishes.
Dec. 15	Von Blomberg demanded 100-per-cent increase in foreign exchange.
Dec. 19	Revision of law regulating textile industry.

1 9 3 6

Feb. 3	Schacht suggested to von Blomberg that rearmament would have to be stretched over a longer period.
Feb. 26	Schacht ruled on penalty for lowering of export prices.
Feb. 27	Franco-Soviet Treaty ratified in Paris.
"	Pietzsch was asked to arbitrate conflict between Labor Front and Handicraft.
March 7	German army reoccupied demilitarized Rhineland zone.
"	Hitler offered France a twenty-five-year nonaggression pact.
March 19	Standstill on organizational disputes decreed.

March 29	Plebiscite approval of reoccupation of Rhineland.
April 1	Von Blomberg promoted to field marshal.
April 3	National Economic Chamber turned against compulsory export cartels.
April 4	Schacht and von Blomberg offered Göring a place on exchange commission.
April 9	Hitler appointed exchange commission, and gave chairmanship to Göring.
"	Law on awarding of public contracts in distressed areas.
June 17	Himmler appointed chief of all police forces.
June 25	Göring expressed gratitude to von Blomberg for his support.
July 7	Schacht issued decree on dues and functions of economic groups.
July 11	Treaty between Germany and Austria signed.
July 22	Hitler granted aid and troops to Franco in Spanish Civil War.
July 27	New Economic Chambers took over functions of the Economic Ministry.
Aug. 15	Göring received preliminary draft of Four Year Plan.
Aug. 20	Schacht demanded decision from Göring on exchange crisis.
Aug. 26	Hitler completed memorandum on Four Year Plan.
Aug. 30	Von Blomberg demanded substantial increase in military funds.
Sept. 2	Goerdeler's memorandum to Göring rejected.
Sept. 4	Göring railroaded Four Year Plan through Cabinet.
Sept. 5	Schacht ordered Chambers to disregard Levy's proclamation.
Sept. 7	Hitler announced Four Year Plan in Nürnberg.
Oct. 17	Göring put in charge of Four Year Plan Office.
Oct. 18	General price ceiling imposed by Göring.
Oct. 20	Schacht ruled in favor of "voluntary" export cartels.
Oct. 25	Berlin-Rome Axis established.
Oct. 31	Schacht gave instructions on training of apprentices.
Nov. 7	Employment offices received right to assign workers in two industries.

1 9 3 6 *(cont.)*

Nov. 12	Decree on relations between cartels and groups.
Nov. 17	Decree on housing policy under Four Year Plan.
Nov. 23	German-Japanese Anti-Comintern agreement signed.
Dec. 17	Göring told industrialists: "Germany is now at war."

1 9 3 7

Jan. 15	Göring informed Mussolini that Austria belonged to Germany.
Jan. 17	Corporation Law published.
Jan. 30	Hitler declared Treaty of Versailles null and void.
March 14	Encyclical of the Pope against Nazi ideology.
April 16	Industrial and Handicraft Chambers signed apprenticeship agreement.
May 11	Schacht threatened to resign if not allowed to speak.
June 24	Von Blomberg outlined military strategy of War Ministry.
July 1	Pastor Niemöller arrested.
Aug. 20– Aug. 21	Meetings of steel industrialists in opposition to Göring Works A-G.
Sept. 5	Schacht ceased to function as Minister of Economics.
Sept. 25	Mussolini visited Hitler.
Nov. 5	Hitler presented plan for lightning warfare.
Nov. 6	Mussolini no longer interested in Austrian independence.
Nov. 7	Lord Halifax saw Hitler in Berchtesgaden.
Nov. 9	Von Fritsch, in meeting with Hitler, expressed opposition to his military strategy.
Nov. 27	Schacht officially resigned as Minister of Economics.
Dec. 5	Göring appointed temporary Minister of Economics.
Dec. 22	Von Blomberg's funeral oration for General Ludendorff.

1 9 3 8

Jan. 12	Von Blomberg married Fräulein Erna Gruhn.
Jan. 24	Von Blomberg resigned under pressure from Officer Corps.

Jan. 25	Von Fritsch accused of homosexuality and sent on leave.
Feb. 3	Hitler assumed functions of War Minister.
Feb. 4	War Ministry transformed into High Command of Armed Forces.
"	Göring appointed field marshal.
"	Brauchitsch appointed Commander-in-Chief of German army.
"	Funk appointed Minister of Economics.
"	Von Neurath dismissed as Foreign Minister.
March 12	German army marched into Austria.
March 13	Wilhelm von Ketteler (German diplomat in Vienna) murdered by *Gestapo*.
March 14	Chamberlain: "Nothing could have saved Austria but force."
March 18	Military Court exonerated von Fritsch.
March 21	Plebiscite on annexation of Austria.
"	Schacht incorporated Austrian bank into German Central Bank.
March 25	Hitler congratulated von Fritsch on his "restored health."
April 21	Hitler considered invasion of Czechoslovakia in case of "incident."
May 16	Concentration of German troops on Czech border.
May 20	Partial mobilization of Czech troops.
May 22	Britain, France, and Moscow gave diplomatic support to Czechoslovakia.
May 23	Foreign Office in Berlin said Germany had no aggressive intentions.
May 28	Hitler ordered preparation for attack to be ready by October 1st.
May 30	Hitler revealed his military intentions to conference of generals.
July 16	General Beck submitted memorandum against aggression to Commander-in-Chief Brauchitsch.
Aug. 4	Beck submitted his memorandum to conference of generals, but no action was taken.

1 9 3 8 *(cont.)*

Aug. 10	Hitler lectured generals on defeatism in answer to Beck.
Aug. 18	Beck resigned as chief of general staff.
Sept. 9	Brauchitsch and Halder advised Hitler against war.
Sept. 13	Hitler argued against defeatism in branches of High Command.
Sept. 28	Hitler gave orders for Czech invasion.
Sept. 30	Britain and France signed Munich agreement which handed Sudetenland to Hitler.
Nov. 4	Von Rundstedt removed from command; Keitel promoted to colonel-general.
Nov. 7	Secretary of German Embassy murdered in Paris.
Nov. 9	Jewish pogrom throughout Germany on Hitler's orders.
Nov. 27	General Wilhelm Adam removed from command in the West.

A SELECTED BIBLIOGRAPHY

i. Handbooks and Documents

Das deutsche Führerlexikon, 1934–35. Berlin, 1934.

Frank, Hans (ed.). *Handbuch für Recht und Gesetzgebung.* Berlin, 1935.

Frankfurter Zeitung: Börsen-und Wirtschaftskalender. Frankfurt, 1933–38 (annual reports).

Institut für Konjunkturforschung. *Konjunktur-Statistisches Handbuch 1936.* Berlin, 1935.

Institut für Konjunkturforschung. *Statistik des Inlandes und Auslandes.* Berlin, 1940.

International Institute for Agriculture. *International Yearbook of Agricultural Statistics.* Rome, 1938.

International Labor Office. *Yearbook of Labor Statistics.* Geneva, 1943.

Jahrbuch des deutschen Handwerks, 1938–39. Munich, 1939.

League of Nations. *Statistical Yearbook, 1938–39.* New York, 1939.

"Miscellaneous German Records Collection" (including those of various ministries). Parts I, II, III, Microcopy T–84. National Archives, Washington, D.C.

Mönckmeier, O. *Jahrbuch der nationalsozialistischen Wirtschaft.* Berlin, 1935.

Müllensiefen, Hans (ed.). *Wirtschaftskartei-Handbuch.* Stuttgart, 1937.

Nazi Conspiracy and Aggression. Selected documents in 10 vols. Washington: U.S. Government Printing Office, 1946.

NSDAP. *Organisationshandbuch der NSDAP.* Munich, 1937, 1940.

Proceedings and Documents in "Flick Case" in Nürnberg before U.S. Military Tribunal. In Law Library of Indiana University, Bloomington.

Proceedings and Documents in "I. G. Farben Case" in Nürnberg before U.S. Military Tribunal. In Law Library of Indiana University, Bloomington.

Proceedings and Documents in "Krupp Case" in Nürnberg before U.S. Military Tribunal. In Westfälisches Wirtschafts-Archiv, Dortmund, Germany.

Proceedings and Documents in the "Ministries Case" in Nürnberg before U.S. Military Tribunal. In Institut für Völkerrecht, Göttingen, Germany.

"Records of Headquarters of the German Army High Command." Parts I, II, III, Microcopy T–84. National Archives, Washington, D.C.

"Records of the National Socialist German Labor Party." Parts I and III, Microcopy T–81. National Archives, Washington.

"Records of the Reich Ministry of Economics." Microcopy T–71. National Archives, Washington.

Reichskreditgesellschaft. *Halbjahresberichte der deutschen Wirtschaft.* Berlin, 1933–38.

Statistisches Handbuch von Deutschland 1928–1944. Munich, 1949.

Statistisches Jahrbuch des Deutschen Reiches. Berlin, 1930–38.

Teschemacher, Hermann (ed.). *Handbuch des Aufbaus der gewerblichen Wirtschaft.* Vol. I. Berlin, 1937.

Trial of the Major War Criminals before the International Military Tribunal, 42 vols. Nürnberg, 1947–49.

Trials of War Criminals before the Nürnberg Military Tribunals. Selected documents in 15 vols. Washington: U.S. Government Printing Office, 1951–52.

Unpublished Files of *Parteikanzlei der NSDAP*. Bundesarchiv, Koblenz, Germany (partly microfilmed as Microcopy T–580, National Archives, Washington).

Unpublished Files of the *Reichskanzlei 1933–1945*. Bundesarchiv, Koblenz, Germany.

Unpublished Files of the *Reichsorganisationsleiter der NSDAP*. Bundesarchiv, Koblenz, Germany (partly mimeographed under Microcopy T–580, National Archives, Washington).

Unpublished Files of *Reichswirtschaftsministerium*. Bundesarchiv, Koblenz, Germany (partly microfilmed under Microcopy T—580, National Archives, Washington).

Unpublished Files of *Reichwerke Hermann Göring A-G*. Bundesarchiv, Koblenz, Germany (partly microfilmed under Microcopy T–580, National Archives, Washington).

Unpublished Papers of Karl Goerdeler. Bundesarchiv, Koblenz, Germany.

Unpublished Papers of Paul Hermberg. Berkeley, California.

ii. Books and Pamphlets

Abel, Theodore. *Why Hitler Came to Power*. New York, 1938.

Angel, Norman. *Peace with Dictators*. New York, 1938.

Angell, L. W. *The Recovery of Germany*. New York, 1929.

Arendt, Hannah. *Origins of Totalitarianism*. New York, 1951.

Ascoli, Max, and Feiler, Arthur. *Fascism for Whom?* New York, 1938.

Ashton, E. B. *The Fascist: His State and His Mind*. New York, 1937.

Baade, Fritz. *Schicksalsjahre der deutschen Landwirtschaft*. Berlin, 1933.

Backe, Herbert. *Das Ende des Liberalismus in der Wirtschaft*. Berlin, 1936.

Barth, E. *Wesen und Aufgaben der Organization der gewerblichen Wirtschaft*. Hamburg, 1939.

Baumont, Fried, and Vermeil (eds.) . *The Third Reich*. London, 1955.

Baynes, Norman (ed.). *The Speeches of Adolt Hitler.* London, 1942.

Beckenrath, Herbert von. *Modern Industrial Organization.* New York, 1933.

Becker, Theodor. "Die Kartellpolitik der Reichsregierung," in *Rechtsfragen der Wirtschaft.* Vol. II, Berlin, 1935.

Bell, Daniel (ed.). *The New American Right.* New York, 1955.

Bendix, Reinhard. *Max Weber—An Intellectual Portrait.* New York, 1960.

Benn, Gottfried. *Der Neue Staat und die Intellektuellen.* Stuttgart, 1933.

Berger, Erhard. *Die Preisbildung der Zwangskartelle im Steinkohlen und Kalibergbau des deutschen Reiches.* Berlin, 1936.

Berger, Ernst. *Arbeitsmarktpolitik.* Berlin, 1926.

Bergson, Abram. *The Real National Income of the Soviet Union since 1928.* Cambridge, Mass., 1961.

Best, Werner. *Die deutsche Polizei.* 2nd ed. Darmstadt, 1941.

Bettelheim, Charles. *L'Economie allemande sous le nazisme. Un aspect de la décadence du capitalisme.* Paris, 1946.

Bewley, Charles. *Hermann Göring.* Göttingen, 1956.

Beyer, Karl. *Der Arbeitseinsatz in der Wehrwirtschaft.* Berlin, 1936.

Bingham, Alfred. *Insurgent America.* New York, 1935.

Bissinger, Edgar (ed.). *Der deutsche Handel-Aufgabe und Zukunft.* Stuttgart, 1936.

Blumer, Herbert. "Collective Behavior," in *New Outline of the Principles of Sociology.* New York, 1946.

Boehm, Franz. *Die Ordnung der Wirtschaft als geschichtliche Aufgabe und rechtsschöpferische Leistung.* Stuttgart, 1937.

Bonn, Franz. *Die Rechtsstellung der Gruppen und ihre Leiter.* Köln, 1938.

Bonnell, A. Th. *German Control over International Economic Relations.* Urbana, Ill., 1940.

Borchmeyer, Joseph (ed.). *Hugenbergs Ringen in deutschen Schicksalsstunden.* Detmold, 1951.

Borgese, G. A. *Goliath: The March of Fascism.* New York, 1937.

Boulding, Kenneth E. *The Skills of the Economist.* Cleveland, 1958.

Bracher, Karl D. *Die Auflösung der Weimarer Republik.* Villingen, 1960.

————, Sauer, Wolfgang, and Schulz, Gerhard. *Die nationalsozialistische Machtergreifung.* Köln, 1960.

Brady, Robert A. *Business As a System Of Power.* New York, 1943.

————. *The Spirit and Structure of German Fascism.* New York, 1937.

Bramstedt, Ernest K. *Dictatorship and Political Police, the Technique of Control by Fear.* New York, 1945.

Brandt, Karl. *The German Fat Plan and Its Economic Setting.* Palo Alto, 1938.

————. *Management of Agriculture and Food of Fortress Europe.* Palo Alto, 1953.

Braun, Otto. *Von Weimar zu Hitler.* Hamburg, 1949.

Brautigam, Harald. *Wirtschaftssystem des Nationalsozialismus.* Berlin, 1932.

Brecht, Arnold. *Prelude to Silence: the End of the German Republic.* New York, 1944.

Breitling, Rupert. *Verbände in der Bundesrepublik.* Meisenheim am Glan. 1955.

Briefs, Götz. "Betriebssoziologie," in *Handwörterbuch der Soziologie.* Stuttgart, 1931.

Brinkmann, Rudolf. *Wirtschaftspolitik aus nationalsozialistische Kraftquelle.* Jena, 1939.

Broszat, Martin. *Der Nationalsozialismus.* Stuttgart, 1960.

Bruck, W. F. *Social and Economic History of Germany, 1888–1938.* Cardiff, 1938.

Buchheim, Hans. *Das Dritte Reich.* München, 1958.

Buchner, Hans. *Grundriss einer nationalsozialistischen Volkswirtschaftstheorie* (Nationalsozialistische Bibliothek, No. 16). 4th ed. München, 1932.

Bullock, Alan. "The Political Ideas of Adolf Hitler," in *The Third Reich* (Baumont, Fried, and Vermeil, eds.).

————. *Hitler—A Study in Tyranny.* London, 1952.

Bülow, Friedrich. *Der deutsche Ständestaat. Nationalsozialistische Gemeinschaftspolitik durch Wirtschaftsorganisation.* Leipzig, 1934.

Butler, Rohan. *The Roots of National Socialism 1783–1933.* London, 1941.

Celovsky, Boris. *Das Münchener Abkommen, 1938.* Stuttgart, 1958.

Child, Frank C. *Theory and Practice of Exchange Control in Germany.* The Hague, 1958.

Craig, Gordon A. *The Politics of the Prussian Army, 1640–1945.* New York, 1955.

Cunio, Hermann. *Führerprinzip und Willensbildung im Aktienrecht.* Leipzig, 1935.

Daeschner, Leon. *Die Deutsche Arbeitsfront.* München, 1934.

Darré, Walther. *Neuadel aus Blut und Boden.* München, 1934.

————. *Das Bauerntum als Lebensquell der nordischen Rasse.* München, 1929.

Decker, Will. *Der deutsche Arbeitsdienst.* 3rd ed. Berlin, 1941.

Deutsches Institut für Bankwissenschaft. *Probleme des deutschen Wirtschaftslebens.* Berlin, 1937.

Dickert, D. *Die Preisüberwachung, 1931–1936.* Berlin, 1937.

Dietrich, Otto. *12 Jahre mit Hitler.* München, 1955.

————. *Mit Hitler an die Macht.* München, 1934.

Dittrich, Manfred. *Die Entstehung der Angestelltenschaft in Deutschland.* Stuttgart, 1939.

Dobbert, Gerhard. *Die faschistische Wirtschaft.* Berlin, 1934.

Drager, Heinrich. *Arbeitsbeschaffung durch produktive Kreditschöpfung.* München, 1932.

Dresdener Bank. *Die grossen Chemie-Konzerne Deutschlands.* Berlin, 1929.

————. *Die Montan-Konzerne.* Berlin, 1929.

Dreyfuss, Carl. *Beruf und Ideologie der Angestellten.* München, 1933.

Drucker, Peter. *The Future of Industrial Man.* New York, 1942.

Ebenstein, William. *The Nazi State.* New York, 1943.

Effer, Franz. *Mittelstand wird Stand.* Düsseldorf, 1934.

Ehrmann, Henry W. *Organized Business in France.* Princeton, 1957.

Eiche, Rudolf. *Warum Aussenhandel.* Berlin, 1937.

Einzig, P. *The Economic Foundations of Fascism.* London, 1933.

Ellis, Howard S. *Exchange Control in Central Europe.* Cambridge, Mass., 1941.

Erbe, Karl. *Die soziale Ehre und die Verstösse gegen-sie.* Zeulenroda, 1936.

Erbe, René. *Die nationalsozialistische Wirtschaftspolitik 1933–39 im Lichte der modernen Theorie.* Zürich, 1958.

Ermath, Fritz. *Theorie und Praxis des faschistisch-korporativen Staates.* Heidelberg, 1932.

Eschenburg, Theodor. *Staat und Gesellschaft in Deutschland.* Stuttgart, 1956.

Eucken, Walter. *The Foundations of Economics.* Chicago, 1951.

Facius, Friedrich. *Wirtschaft und Staat.* Boppard, 1959.

Feder, Gottfried. *Der deutsche Staat auf nationaler und sozialer Grundlage.* 5th ed. München, 1932.

Feder, Gottfried. *Das Manifest zur Brechung der Zinsknechtschaft des Geldes.* München, 1919.

Fey, Walter. *Der künftige Wohnungs-und Siedlungsplan,* Hamburg, 1939.

Fischer, Guido. *Wehrwirtschaft: Ihre Grundlagen und Theorien.* Leipzig, 1936.

Foertsch, Hermann. *Schuld und Verhängnis.* Stuttgart, 1951.

Förster, Wolfgang. *Ein General kämpft gegen den Krieg.* München, 1949.

Franck, Louis. "An Economic and Social Diagnosis of National Socialism," in *The Third Reich* (Baumont, Fried, and Vermeil, eds.). London, 1955.

Fränkel, Ernst. *The Dual State: A Contribution to the Theory of Dictatorship.* New York, 1940.

Fränkel, Heinrich. *The German People* vs. *Hitler.* London, 1940.

Frauendorfer, Max. *Der ständische Gedanke im Nationalsozialismus.* München, 1932.

Frei, Rudolf. *Theoretische Grundlagen der deutschen Währungspolitik während des Nationalsozialismus.* Zürich, 1948.

Fried, Ferdinand. *Die Zukunft des Aussenhandels.* Jena, 1934.

Fried, Hans Ernest. *The Guilt of the German Army.* New York, 1942.

Friedensburg, Ferdinand. *Die Weimarer Republik.* Hannover, 1957.

Friedman, Milton. *Essays in Positive Economics.* Chicago, 1953.

Friedrich, Carl J. (ed.). *Totalitarianism.* Cambridge, 1954.

Friedrich, C. J., and Brzezinski, Z. K. *Totalitarian Dictatorship and Autocracy.* Cambridge, 1956.

Frischauer, Willy. *The Rise and Fall of Hermann Göring.* Boston, 1951.

Fromm, Erich. *Escape from Freedom.* New York, 1941.

Gatzke, Hans W. *Stresemann and the Rearmament of Germany.* Baltimore, 1954.

Geiger, Theodor. *Die soziale Schichtung des deutschen Volkes.* Stuttgart, 1932.

Gerth, Hans, and Mills, C. W. *From Max Weber: Essays in Sociology.* New York, 1946.

Gisevius, Bernd. *To the Bitter End.* Boston, 1947.

Göbbels, Joseph. *Vom Kaiserhof zur Reichskanzlei.* München, 1934.

Görlitz, Walther. *History of the German General Staff, 1657–1945.* New York, 1953.

Grotkopp, Wilhelm. *Die grosse Krise-Lehren aus der Ueberwindung der Wirtschaftskrise 1929–1932.* Düsseldorf, 1954.

Grzesinski, A. C. *Inside Germany.* New York, 1939.

Guerin, Daniel. *Fascism and Big Business.* New York, 1939.

Guillebaud, C. W. *Economic Recovery of Germany.* London, 1939.

————. *The Social Policy of Nazi Germany.* Cambridge (U.K.), 1941.

Gurland, A., Kirchheimer, G., and Neumann, F. *The Fate of Small Business in Germany.* Washington, 1943.

Guth, Karl. *Die Reichsgruppe Industrie.* Berlin, 1941.

Haider, C. *Capital and Labor under Fascism.* New York, 1930.

Hallgarten, George Wolfgang. *Hitler, Reichswehr und Industrie.* Frankfurt, 1955.

Halm, George N. *Economic Systems.* Rev. ed. New York, 1960.

Hamburger, Ludwig. *How Nazi Germany Has Mobilized and Controlled Labor.* Washington, 1940.

Hansen, Alvin H. *Guide to Keynes.* New York, 1953.

Hansen, Alvin H. *Fiscal Policy and Business Cycle.* New York, 1941.

Harms, Bernhard. *Strukturwandlungen der deutschen Volkswirtschaft.* 2 vols. Berlin, 1928.

Harris, C. R. S. *Germany's Foreign Indebtedness.* London, 1935.

Harris, Seymour. *New Economics.* New York, 1947.

Harrod, Roy F. *The Life of John Maynard Keynes.* London, 1951.

Harsch, L. C. *Pattern of Conquest.* New York, 1941.

Hartshorn, Edward Y. *German Universities and National Socialism.* New York, 1940.

Hase, Günther. *Der Werdegang des Arbeitsdienstes.* Berlin, 1940.

Heberle, Rudolf. *From Democracy to Nazism.* Baton Rouge, 1945.

Hedemann, Y. W. *Deutsches Wirtschaftsrecht.* Berlin, 1939.

Heiden, Konrad. *Der Führer.* London, 1944.

_____. *A History of National Socialism.* London, 1934.

Heimann, Eduard. *Communism, Fascism or Democracy.* New York, 1938.

Heimann, Eduard. *Die soziale Theorie des Kapitalismus.* Tübingen, 1929.

Heinrich, Walter. *Das Ständewesen mit besonderer Berücksichtigung der Selbstverwaltung in der Wirtschaft.* Jena, 1932.

Heinrichsbauer, August. *Schwerindustrie und Politik.* Essen, 1948.

Heller, Herman. *Europe und der Faschismus.* Berlin, 1929.

Henri, Ernst. *Hitler over Europe.* Boston, 1933.

Heyde, Ludwig. *Deutsche Gewerbepolitik.* Berlin, 1934.

Hirschman, Albert. *The Strategy of Economic Development.* New Haven, 1958.

Hitler, Adolf. *Mein Kampf.* Munich, 1936.

Hock, Wolfgang. *Deutscher Antikapitalismus.* Frankfurt, 1960.

Hövel, Paul. *Grundfragen deutscher Wirtschaftspolitik.* Berlin, 1935.

Hofer, Walther. *Der Nationalsozialismus, Dokumente 1933–1945.* Frankfurt, 1958.

Holt, Y. B. *German Agricultural Policy*. Chapel Hill, 1936.

Holt, Y. B. *Under the Swastika*. Chapel Hill, 1937.

Hoover, Calvin B. *Economy, Liberty and State*. New York, 1959.

_____. *Dictators and Democracy*. New York, 1937.

_____. *Germany Enters the Third Reich*. New York, 1934.

Hossbach, Friedrich. *Zwischen Wehrmacht und Hitler*. Wolfen-büttel, 1949.

Jöhr, Walter A. *Die ständische Ordnung. Geschichte, Idee und Neuaufblau*. Bern, 1937.

Kaulla, Rudolf. *Staat, Stände und der gerechte Preis*. Wien, 1936.

Kaiser, Joseph H. *Die Representation organisierter Interessen*. Berlin, 1956.

Kersten, Felix. *Memoirs*. New York, 1947.

Keynes, John Maynard. *The General Theory of Employment, Interest and Money*. New York, 1936.

Kielmannsegg, Johann Graf von. *Der Fritsch-Prozess 1938*. Hamburg, 1949.

Kindleberger, Charles P. *The Dollar Shortage*. New York, 1950.

Kirkpatrick, Clifford. *Nazi Germany: Its Women and Family Life*. Indianapolis, 1938.

Klass, Gerd von. *Albert Vögler*. Tübingen, 1957.

Klein, Burton. *Germany's Economic Preparation for War*. Cambridge, Mass., 1959.

Koch, Erich. *Aufbau im Osten*. Breslau, 1934.

Koch, Waldemar. *Die Stattswirtschaft des Faschismus*. Jena, 1935.

Kogon, Eugen. *Der SS-Staat, Das System der deutschen Konzentrationslager*. 3rd ed. Frankfurt, 1948.

Korfes, Otto. *Grundsätze der Wehrwirtschaftslehre*. Hamburg, 1936.

Kraus, Friedrich (ed.). *Gördelers polistisches Testament*. New York, 1945.

Krebs, Albert. *Tendenzen und Gestalten der NSDAP*. Stuttgart, 1959.

Kreutz, Werner. *Die Zwangskartellierung in der gewerblichen Wirtschaft der Gegenwart*. Berlin, 1936.

Kroll, Gerhard. *Von der Wirtschaftskrise zur Staatskonjunktur*. Berlin, 1958.

Kuczynski, Jürgen. *Germany: Economic and Labor Conditions under Fascism*. New York, 1945.

Laswell, Harold D. *The Analysis of Political Behavior*. London, 1948.

Lautenbach, Wilhelm. *Zins, Kredit, und Produktion*. Tübingen, 1952.

Lederer, Emil. *Die Privatangestellten in der modernen Wirtschaftsentwicklung*. Tübingen, 1912.

Lederer, Emil. *State of the Masses*. New York, 1940.

Lederer, Emil, and Marschak, Jacob. "Klassen auf dem Arbeitsmarkt und ihre Organisationen," *Grundriss der Sozialökonomik,* Vol. IX. Tübingen, 1926.

Lederer, Emil, and Marschak, Jacob. "Der Neue Mittelstand," in *Grundriss der Sozialokonomik,* Vol IX. Tübingen, 1926.

Lehmann-Russbueldt, Otto. *Aggression: the Origin of Germany's War Machine*. London, 1942.

Lerner, Daniel. *The Nazi Elite*. Palo Alto, 1951.

Leschnitzer, Adolf. *The Magic Background of Modern Anti-Semitism—An Analysis of the German-Jewish Relationship*. New York, 1956.

Levy, Herman. *Industrial Germany, a Study of its Monopoly Organizations and their Control by the State*. London, 1935.

Ley, Robert. *Deutschland ist schöner geworden*. Berlin, 1936.

Lichtenberger, Henri. *The Third Reich*. New York, 1937.

Lochner, Louis. *Tycoons and Tyrant*. Chicago, 1954.

Luckas, H. *Theorie der Devisenzwangswirtschaft, auf Grund der deutschen und auslandischen Erfahrungen von 1914 bis 1940*. Jena, 1940.

Ludowici, Johann W. *Das Deutsche Siedlungswerk*. 2nd ed. Heidelburg, 1937.

————. *Totale Landesverteidigung*. Oldenburg, 1936.

Luedecke, K. G. W. *I Knew Hitler*. New York, 1937.

Lurie, Samuel. *Private Investment in a Controlled Economy*. New York, 1947.

Mackeroth, Gerhard. *Gewerbepolitik*. Berlin, 1935.

Marbach, Fritz. *Zur Frage der wirtschaftlichen Staatsintervention*. Bern, 1950.

MacIver, Robert M. *Society*. New York, 1937.

Manvell, R., and Fraenkel H. *Dr. Göbbels*. London, 1960.

Marx, Fritz M. *Government in the Third Reich*. New York, 1937.

Mehrens, Bernhard. *Die Marktordnung des Reichsnährstandes*. Berlin, 1938.

Meinck, Gerhard. *Hitler und die deutsche Aufrüstung 1933–1937*. Wiesbaden, 1959.

Meinecke, Friedrich. *Die deutsche Katastrophe*. Wiesbaden, 1946.

Meissner, Otto. *Staatssekretär unter Ebert, Hindenburg und Hitler*. Hamburg, 1950.

Menne, Bernhard. *Krupp or the Lords of Essen*. London, 1939.

Messner, J. *Die berufsständische Ordnung*. Wien, 1936.

Meusel, Alfred. "Revolution and Counterrevolution," in *Encyclopedia of the Social Sciences*, Vol. XIII. New York, 1932.

Michel, Ernst. *Sozialgeschichte der industriellen Arbeitswelt*. Frankfurt, 1948.

Miksch, Leonhard. *Wettbewerb als Aufgabe—Die Grundsätze einer Wettbewerbsordnung*. Stuttgart, 1937.

Mohler, Armin. *Die konservative Revolution in Deutschland*. Stuttgart, 1950.

Mühlen, Norbert. *Die Krupps*. Frankfurt, 1960.

Müllensiefen, Hans. *Gruppeuanfgaben bei Wirtschaftlichkeitsförderung, Marktordnung und Kartellaufsicht*. Stuttgart, 1937.

Müller, Willy. *Das soziale Leben im neuen Deutschland unter besonderer Berücksichtigung der Deutschen Arbeitsfront*. Berlin, 1938.

Münch, Kurt. *Wirtschaftliche Selbstverwaltung*. Hamburg, 1936.

Musgrave, Richard A., and Peacock, Allen T. (eds.). *Classics in the Theory of Public Finance*. New York, 1958.

Nagel, W. *Soziale und Ständische Ehrengerichtsbarkeit*. Berlin, 1939.

Nathan, Otto. *The Nazi Economic System*. Durham, N.C., 1944.

Nathan, Otto. *Nazi War Finance and Banking*. New York, 1944.

Neisser, Hans. *Some International Aspects of the Business Cycle*. Philadelphia, 1935.

Nesse, Gottfried. *Die Nationalsozialistische Deutsche Arbeiterpartei*. Stuttgart, 1935.

_____. *Partei und Staat.* Hamburg, 1936.

Neumann, Franz. *Behemoth: The Structure and Practice of National Socialism.* New York, 1942.

Neumann, Sigmund. *Die deutschen Parteien.* Berlin, 1932.

Neumann, Sigmund. *Permanent Revolution: The Total State in a World at War.* New York, 1942.

Neuordnung des Meisterprüfungswesens. Berlin, 1936.

Nonnenbruch, Fritz. *Die dynamische Wirtschaft.* Berlin, 1936.

Nova, Fritz. *The National Socialist Fuehrerprinzip and Its Background in German Thought.* Philadelphia, 1943.

Oppenheimer-Bluhm, Hilde. *The Standard of Living of German Labor Under Nazi Rule.* New York, 1943.

Oxford University Institute for Statistics. *Economics of Full Employment.* Oxford, 1946.

Papen, Franz von. *Memoirs,* London, 1952.

Pascal, Roy. "Revolutionary Conservatism: Moller van den Bruck," in *The Third Reich.* New York, 1955.

Pigou, A. C. *The Political Economy of War.* New York, 1941.

Poliakov, Leon, and Wulf, Joseph. *Das Dritte Reich und die Juden, Dokumente und Aufsätze.* Berlin, 1955.

Poole, Kenneth. *German Financial Policies, 1932–1939.* Cambridge, Mass., 1940.

Preiser, Erich. *Bildung und Verteilung des Volkseinkommens.* Göttingen, 1957.

Preller, Ludwig. *Sozialpolitik in der Weimarer Republik.* Stuttgart, 1932.

Preiser, Erich. *Bildung und Verteilung des Volkseinkommens.* 1936.

Prinzing, Albert. *Der politische Gehalt internationaler Kartelle.* Berlin, 1938.

Prion W. *Das Deutsche Finanzwunder.* Berlin, 1938.

Ueber die Probleme der deutschen Aussenwirtschaft (Institut für Konjunkturforschung). Berlin, 1936.

Rauscher, E. *Die Umstellung von der Friedens—auf die Kriegsfertigung.* Hamburg, 1937.

Rauschning, Hermann. *Gespräche mit Hitler.* Zürich, 1940.

Raushenbush, S. *The March of Fascism.* New York, 1939.

Rawlins, E. C. D. *Economic Conditions in Germany to March 1936.* London, 1936.

Reimann, Günter. *The Vampire Economy.* New York, 1939.

Reupke, Hans. *Der Nationalsozialismus und die Wirtschaft.* Berlin, 1931.

Reveille, Thomas. *The Spoil of Europe.* New York, 1941.

Reynolds, Lloyd G., and Shister, Joseph. *Job Horizons.* New York, 1949.

Richter-Altschäfer. *Volkswirtschaftliche Theorie der öffentlichen Investitionen.* Leipzig, 1936.

Riemer, Svend. *Upward Mobility and Social Stratification.* New York, 1937.

Ritschl, Hans. *Gemeinwirtschaft und kapitalistiche Marktwirtschaft.* Tübingen, 1931.

Ritter, Gerhard. *Carl Gördeler und die Deutsche Widerstandsbewegung.* Stuttgart, 1954.

Rittig. *Der soziale Preis.* Jena, 1935.

Rocholl, A. *Deutsche Jugend im Beruf.* Hamburg, 1937.

Rosen, Joseph. *Das Existenzminimum in Deutschland.* Zürich, 1939.

Rosenberg, Arthur. *Entstehung und Geschichte der Weimarer Republik.* Frankfurt, 1955.

Rosinski, Herbert. *The German Army.* New York, 1940.

Rothfels, Hans. *Die deutsche Opposition gegen Hitler.* Frankfurt, 1958.

Sauve, Wilhelm. *Reichsnährstandgesetze.* Leipzig, 1935.

Schacht, Hjalmar. *76 Jahre meines Lebens.* Wörishofen, 1953.

Schacht, Hjalmar. *Account Settled.* London, 1949.

Schellenberg, Walter. *Memorien.* Köln, 1956.

Schlange-Schöningen, Hans. *Am Tage Danach.* Hamburg, 1946.

Schmitt, Carl. *Staatsgefüge und Zusammenbruch des zweiten Reiches.* Hamburg, 1934.

Schneider, Herbert. *Führer und Führerrat.* Gelnhausen, 1938.

Schuman, Frederick. *The Nazi Dictatorship.* New York, 1936.

Schumann, Hans-Gerd. *Nationalsozialismus und Gewerkschaftsbewegung.* Hannover, 1958.

Schumpeter, Joseph A. *Business Cycles,* Vol. II. New York, 1939.

Schweitzer, Arthur. "The Nazification of the Lower Middle Class and Peasants," in *The Third Reich* (Baumont, Fried, and Vermeil, eds.). London, 1955.

Schwerin-Krosigk, Lutz von. *Es geschah in Deutschland.* Tübingen, 1952.

————. "Wie wurde der zweite Weltkrieg finanziert?" *Bilanz des zweiten Weltkrieges.* Oldenburg, 1953.

Scolezy, Maxine. *The Structure of the Nazi Economy.* Cambridge, Mass., 1941.

Seltzner, Claus. *Die Deutsche Arbeitsfront, kurzer Abriss.* Berlin, 1935.

Seraphim, Hans-Günther. *Das Politische Tagebuch Alfred Rosenbergs, aus den Jahren 1934–35 und 1939–40.* Göttingen, 1956.

Shirer, William L. *The Rise and Fall of the Third Reich.* New York, 1960.

Siegert, Karl. *Deutsches Wirtschaftsrecht.* Berlin, 1939.

Singer, Hans W. *Standardized Accountancy.* Cambridge (U. K.), 1943.

Sombart, Werner. *Deutscher Sozialismus.* Berlin, 1934.

Sombart, Werner. *Das Wirtschaftsleben im Zeitalter des Hochkapitalismus.* 2 vols. München, 1928.

Sombart, Werner. *Die deutsche Volkswirtschaft im neunzehnten Jahrhundert.* Berlin, 1903.

Splettstösser, Johann. *Der Einzelhandel.* Berlin, 1936.

Stampfer, Friedrich. *Die 14 Jahre der ersten deutschen Republik.* 2nd ed. Offenbach, 1947.

Starcke, Gerhard. *NSBO und Deutsche Arbeitsfront.* Berlin, 1934.

Stark, Werner. *The Sociology of Knowledge.* Glencoe, 1958.

Stewart, J. D. *British Pressure Groups.* Oxford, 1958.

Stocking, George W., and Watkins, Myron W. *Cartels in Action: Case Studies in International Business Diplomacy.* New York, 1946.

Stolper, Gustav. *This Age of Fable.* London, 1943.

————. *German Economy, 1870–1940.* London, 1940.

Strasser, Otto. *Hitler and I.* Boston, 1940.

Stucken, Rudolf. *Deutsche Geld-und Kreditpolitik, 1914–1953.* Tübingen, 1953.

Sweezy, Alan. "Declining Investment Opportunity," in *New Economics.* New York, 1947.

Sweezy, Paul. *The Present as History.* New York, 1953.

Syrup, Friedrich. *Arbeitseinsatz und Arbeitslosenhilfe in Deutschland.* Berlin, 1936.

Tasca, H. Y. *World Trading Systems.* London, 1940.

Taylor, G. W., and Pierson, F. C. *New Concepts in Wage Determination.* New York, 1957.

Taylor, Telford. *Sword and Swastika. The Wehrmacht in the Third Reich.* London, 1953.

Tenenbaum, Joseph. *Race and Reich.* New York, 1956.

Thyssen, Fritz. *I Paid Hitler.* New York, 1941.

Trumann, David. *Governmental Processes.* New York, 1951.

Trivanovitch, Vaso. *Economic Development of Germany under National Socialism.* New York, 1937.

Tschierschky, Siegfried. *Kartell-Organisation.* Berlin, 1928.

Uhlig, Heinrich. *Die Warenhäuser im Dritten Reich.* Köln, 1956.

United States Strategic Bombing Survey. *The Effects of Strategic Bombing on the German War Economy.* Washington, 1945.

Ungern-Sternberg, Roderich von. *Die Planung als Ordnungsprinzip der deutschen Industriewirtschaft.* Stuttgart, 1932.

Vermeil, Edmond. *Doctrinaires de la révolution Allemande.* Paris, 1939.

Vermeil, Edmond. "The Origin, Nature, and Development of German Nationalist Ideology in the 19th and 20th Centuries," in *The Third Reich* (Baumont, Fried, and Vermeil, eds.). London, 1955.

Viner, Jacob. *International Economics.* Glencoe, 1951.

Vogelsang, Otto. *Reichswehr, Staat und NSDAP.* Stuttgart, 1962.

Wagemann, Ernst. *Zwischenbilanz der Krisenpolitik.* Berlin, 1935.

Wagenführ, Horst, *Konjunktur und Kartelle.* Berlin. 1932.

————. *Preise und Preispolitik.* Berlin, 1937.

Wagenführ, Rolf. *Aufstieg und Niedergang der deustchen Rüstung.* Berlin, 1954.

Wallace, Donald H. *Economic Controls and Defense.* New York, 1953.

Weber, Max. *The City.* Glencoe, 1958.

_____. *The Theory of Social and Economic Organization.* New York, 1947.

Weigmann, W. *Selbstkostenrechnung und Preisbildung in der Industrie.* Leipzig, 1939.

Wheeler-Bennett, John W. *Munich: Prologue to Tragedy.* New York, 1948.

_____. *Nemesis of Power.* New York, 1954.

_____. *Wooden Titan: Hindenburg.* New York, 1936.

Wieacker, Franz. *Wandlungen der Eigentumsverfassung.* Hamburg, 1935.

Wittfogel, Karl A. *Oriental Despotism.* New Haven, 1957.

Wunderlich, Frieda. *German Labor Courts.* Chapel Hill, 1946.

Wunderlich, Frieda. *Labor Under German Democracy—Arbitration, 1918–32.* New York, 1940.

Zischka, Anton. *Wissenschaft bricht Monopole.* Leipzig, 1936.

iii. *Articles in Periodicals**

Albrecht, Gerhard. "Geschichte und soziologische Begründung der berufsständischen Sozialordnung." *Jahrbücher für Nationalökonomie und Statistik,* LXXXIII (1940).

Balogh, T. "The National Economy of Germany," *Economic Journal.* (Sept., 1938).

Baster, A. L. Y. "Some Economic Aspects of Rearmament," *"International Labour Review,* XXXVII (1938).

Beckhardt, B. H. "The German Bank Inquiry," *Political Science Quarterly* (1937).

Block, Herbert. "Industrial Combination vs. Small Business: The Trend of Nazi Policy," *Social Research* (May, 1943).

* Materials published in newspapers or in weekly or monthly trade journals can be found in the notes.

Block, Herbert. "German Methods of Allocating Raw Materials," *Social Research* (Sept., 1942).

Block, Herbert. "Subcontracting German Defense Industries," *Social Research* (Feb., 1942).

Brady, R. A. "Policies of Manufacturing Spitzenverbände," *Political Science Quarterly* (1941).

Brandt, Karl. "German Agricultural Policy—Selected Lessons," *Farm Economic Journal* (Feb., 1937).

Braunthal, Gerard. "The German Free Trade Unions during the Rise of Nazism," *Journal of Central European Affairs* (1955).

Brinkmann, Rudolf. "Rechtsgrundlagen der Kapitallenkung," *Zeitschrift der Akademie für deutsches Recht* (1939).

Cole, Taylor. "Italy's Fascist Bureaucracy", *American Political Science Review* (1937).

———. "The Evolution of the German Labor Front," *Political Science Quarterly* (1937).

———. "An Appraisal of Some Theories on National Socialism," *Journal of Politics* (1939).

———. "Cooperative Organization of the Third Reich," *Review of Politics* (1940).

Conze, Werner. "Zum Sturz Brünings," *Vierteljahrshefte für Zeitgeschichte* (1953).

Corey, Lewis. "The Middle Class," *Antioch Review* (1945).

Craig, Gordon. "Briefe Schleichers an Gröner," *Die Welt als Geschichte* (1951).

———. "Reichswehr and National Socialism: The Policy of Wilhelm Gröner, 1928–1932," *Political Science Quarterly* (1949).

Dessauer, Marie. "The German Bank Act of 1934," *Review of Economic Studies* (June, 1935).

Dietze, von Constantin. "Die Bedeutung des preussischen Erbhofrechts für die wirtschaftliche und soziale Entwicklung des Bauerntums," *Soziale Praxis* (1933).

Ebenstein, William. "The Study of Totalitarianism," *World Politics* (1958).

"Employment of Women in Germany under the Nationalist Socialist Regime," *International Labor Review* (Dec., 1941–44).

Eckelt, Ernst. "Der Ausschliesslichkeitsvertrag als Mittel zur Ordnung der gewerblichen Wirtschaft," *Kartell-Rundschau* (1935).

Epstein, Klaus. "Shirer's History of Nazi Germany," *Review of Politics* (1961).

Friedrich Carl J. "The Peasant as Evil Genius of Dictatorship," *Yale Review* (1937).

Gerth, H. "The Nazi Party: Its Leadership and Composition," *Journal of American Sociology* (1940).

Gördeler, Carl. "Deutschland und die Weltwirtschaft," *Deutscher Volkswirt* (June, 1936).

————. "Kleinsiedlung und Wohnungsbau als Politische und wirtschaftliche Notwendigkeit," *Deutscher Volkswirt* (March and April, 1936).

————. "Wirtschaftiche Funktionen der Preise," *Bank* (1936).

————. "Preisbestimmungen durch Gesetz," *Zeitschrift der Akademie für deutsches Recht* (1936).

Grebler, Leo. "Work Creation Policy in Germany, 1932–1935," *International Labor Review* (1937).

"Grenzen kompensatorischer Kreditschöpfung," *Wirtschaftskurve* (1936).

Hamburger, E. "The German Labor Front," *Monthly Labor Review* (Nov., 1944).

Hallgarten, George W. F. "Adolf Hitler and the German Heavy Industry 1931–1933," *Journal of Economic History* (1952).

Hamburger, Ernest. "Significance of Nazi Leisure Time Program," *Social Research* (1945).

Harris, Abram. "Sombart and German National Socialism," *Journal of Political Economy* (1942).

Heberle, Rudolf. "Ecology of Political Parties," *American Sociological Review* (1944).

Hessel, Phillip. "Neuordnung des Wirtschaftsrechts," *Deutsches Handwerksblatt* (1932).

Hirschman, Albert. "Disinflation, Discrimination and the Dollar Shortage," *American Economic Review* (1948).

Huppert, Walter. "Monopol and Konzentration, *Jahrbuch für Sozialwissenschaft* (1950).

Ilau, Hans. "Die Reichswerke A-G Hermann Göring," *Wirtschaftskurve* (1938).

Jasny, Marie P. "Some Aspects of German Agricultural Settlement," *Political Science Quarterly* (1937).

Jacobson, Per. "Le Financement de la Guerre en Allemagne," *Kyklos* (1947).

Junghans-Schramberg, Erwin. "Zur Frage des Kalkulationskartels," *Kartell-Rundschau* (1936).

Keiser, G. "Der Jüngste Konzentrationsprozess," *Wirtschaftskurve* (1939).

Kelsen, Hans. "The Party Dictatorship," *Politica* (1936).

"Kennzeichen für konjunkturelle und inflationäre Preisbewegungen," *Vierteljahrshefte für Konjunktur* (Part A, 1936).

Kerr, Clark. "Labor Markets: Their Character and Consequences" *American Economic Review* (1950).

Kirchheimer, Otto. "Changes in the Structure of Political Compromise," *Studies in Philosophy and Social Science* (1941).

"Die Konversion der Industrieanleihen," *Wirtschaftskurve* (1936).

Kruschwitz, Hans. "Die Deutsche Wohnungswirtschaft seit 1933," *Jahrbuch für Nationalökonomie und Statistik* (1937).

Küch, Otto. "Neugestaltungen der industriellen Fachprüfungen," *Das Junge Deutschland* (1936).

Kühne, Hans. "Der Arbeitseinsatz im Vierjahresplan," *Jahrbuch der Nationalökonomie und Statistik* (1937).

Lachmann, K. "The Hermann Göring Works," *Social Research* (Feb., 1941).

Lautenbach, Wilhelm. "Preisbildung und Produktionselastizität," *Wirtschaftskurve* (1937).

Lederer, Emil. "Economic Doctrine of National Socialism," *Annals* (1937).

Lenich, O. "Die Arbeiten des Kartellausschusses," *Zeitschrift der Akademie für deutsches Recht* (1935).

Lipset, S. M. "Der Faschismus—die Linke, die Rechte und die Mitte," *Kölner Zeitschrift für Soziologie und Sozialphychologie* (1959).

Lütge, F. "Die neuen preispolitischen Eingriffe auf dem Wohnungs-und Bodenmarkt," *Jahrbücher für Nationalökonomie und Statistik* (1938).

Lütge, F. "Der Mietpreis in der Wohnungszwangswirtschaft," *Schmollers Jahrbuch* (1938).

Mann, F. A. "The New German Company Law and its Background," *Journal of Comparative Legislation and International Law* (1937).

Mau, Hermann. "Die Zweite Revolution—Der 30, Juni, 1934," *Vierteljahrshefte für Zeitgeschichte* (1953).

Mayer, Carl. "On the Intellectual Origin of National Socialism," *Social Research,* 1942.

Merlin, Sidney. "Trends in German Economic Control since 1933," *The Quarterly Journal of Economics* (1943).

Miksch, Leonhard. "Kalkulationskartelle wozu?" *Wirtschaft und Arbeit* (1936).

Miksch, Leonhard. "Wo herrscht noch freier Wettbewerb?" *Wirtschaftskurve* (1936).

————— "Kalkulationskartelle und Kalkulationskontrolle," *Wirtschaftskurve* (1937).

Nathan, Otto. "Consumption in Germany during the Period of Rearmament," *Quarterly Journal of Economics* (1942).

Neuling, W. "Wettbewerb, Monopol und Befehl in der heutigen Wirtschaft," *Zeitschrift für die gesamte Staatswissenschaft* (1939).

Nipperdey, H. C. "Wettbewerb und Existenzvernichtung," *Kartell-Rundschau* (1930).

Pauls, H. P. "Das neue Mitteldeutschland," *Wirtschaftskurve* (1939).

Phelps, Reginald H. "Aus den Gröner-Dokumenten, *Deutsche Rundschau* (1951).

Pelcovits, Nathan. "The Social Honor Courts of Nazi Germany," *Poltical Science Quarterly* (1938).

Reynolds, Lloyd G. "Cutthroat Competition," *American Economic Review* (1940).

Rittershausen, H. "Die staatliche Preispolitik auf den deutschen Hauptmärkten der Gegenwart," *Weltwirtschaftliches Archiv* (1940).

Russel, A. "Die Marktordnung im Reichsnährstandsgewerbe," *Zeitschrift für die gesamte Staatswissenschaft* (1935–36).

Russel, C. "Die Praxis des Zwangskartellgesetzes," *Zeitschrift für die gesamte Staatswissenschaft* (1937).

Schaefer, Kurt. "The German Businessmen under Hitler," *Journal of Business* (April, 1941).

Schmidt, W., and Wrede, V. "Konsolidierung und Kreditmechanismus," *Vierteljahrshefte zur Wirtschaftsforschung* (1938).

Schramm, Carl. "Kartellende oder neue Kartellformen?" *Kartell-Rundschau* (1935).

―――――. "Totales Kartell und Fachschaft," *Kartell-Rundschau* (1935).

Schweitzer, Arthur. "Ideological Groups," *American Sociological Review* (1944).

―――――. "The Role of Foreign Trade in the Nazi War Economy," *Journal of Political Economy*, 1943.

―――――. "Big Business and the Nazi Party in Germany," *Journal of Business* (1946).

―――――. "Profits under Nazi Planning," *Quarterly Journal of Economics* (1946).

―――――. "On Depression and War: Nazi Phase," *Political Science Quarterly* (1947).

―――――. "Schacht's Regulation of Money and Capital Markets," *Journal of Finance* (1948).

―――――. "American Competitive Capitalism," *Schweizerische Zeitschrift für Volkswirtschaft und Statistik* (1956).

―――――. "Der ursprüngliche Vierjahresplan," *Jahrbücher für Nationalökonomie und Statistik* (1957).

―――――. "Die wirtschaftliche Wiederaufrüstung Deutschlands von 1934–1936," *Zeitschrift für die gesamte Staatswissenschaft* (1958.)

————. "Organisierter Kapitalismus und Parteidiktatur, 1933–1936," *Schmollers Jahrbuch* (1959).

————. "Labor in Organized Capitalism," *Schweizerische Zeitschrift für Volkswirtschaft und Statistik* (1959).

————. "Business Power in the Nazi Regime," *Zeitschrift für Nationalökonomie* (1960).

————. "The Method of Social Economics," (dittoed paper, Bloomington, 1961).

————. "Ideological Strategy," *Western Political Quarterly* (1962).

————. "Foreign Exchange Crisis of 1936," *Zeitschrift für die gesamte Staatswissenschaft* (1962).

Singer, H. W. "The Sources of War Finance in the German War Economy," *Review of Economic Studies* (1943).

Stigler, George. "The Goals of Economic Policy," *Journal of Business* (1958).

Strauss, Walter. "Die neue deutsche Kartellgesetzgebung," *Kartell-Rundschau* (1933).

————. "Die neue Aenderung der Kartellverordnung," *Kartell-Rundschau* (1934).

Stritzke, Otto. "Die Ordnung des graphischen Gewerbes als Beispiel," *Kartell-Rundschau* (1936).

————. "Das Elektro-Abkommen," *Kartell-Rundschau* (1936).

Sweezy, M. Y. "Distribution of Wealth and Income under the Nazis," *Review of Economic Statistics* (Nov., 1939).

Tauber, Kurt P. "German Nationalists and European Union," *Political Science Quarterly* (1959).

Tern, T. "Hochbetriebe im Baugewerbe," *Wirtschaftskurve* (1938).

Thomas, Georg. "Breite und Tiefe der Rüstung," *Militärwissenschaftliche Rundschau* (1937).

Tschierschky, S. "Kartelrecht und Wettbewerbsrecht," *Kartell-Rundschau* (1933).

————. "Die Kartellfrage als Gegenwartsproblem," *Kartell-Rundschau* (1935).

————. "Wettbewerbsrecht und wirtschaftliche Organisationspolitik," *Kartell-Rundschau* (1935).

V . . ., "The Destruction of Capitalism in Germany," *Foreign Affairs*, 1937.

Völtzer. "Werden des deutschen Sozialismus," *Zeitschrift für die gesamte Staatswissenschaft* (1935).

Waelbraech and Bessling. "German Social Policy under the National Socialist Regime," *International Labor Review* (1941).

Wagenführ, Horst. "Nationalsozialismus und Kartelle," *Kartell-Rundschau* (1933).

————. "Die Entwicklung der Kartellpreise in Deutschland von 1925 zu 1936," *Kartell-Rundschau* (1936).

Wagner, Valentin F. "Geldschöpfung, Wirtschaftskreislauf und Nationalsozialistische Wirtschaftspolitik," *Schweizerische Zeitschrift für Volkswirtschaft und Statistik* (1958).

Wessels, Theodor. "Probleme der Marktordnung in der deutsche Volkswirtschaft," *Schmollers Jahrbuch* (1937).

Winkler, W. "Eine neue Berufsordnung," *Zeitschrift für Nationalökonomie und Statistik* (Vol. 144).

Wunderlich, Frieda. "The National Socialist Agrarian Program," *Social Research* (1946).

Zahn, Friedrich. "Die Lehren der deutschen Preissenkungsaktion," *Jahrbücher für Nationalökonomie und Statistik* (Vol. 83).

Notes

Introduction

1. A brief account of the formerly secret documents is given in Appendix A, pp. 565–71.

2. Max Weber, *The Theory of Social and Economic Organization* (New York: Oxford University Press, 1947), pp. 278 ff.

3. Weber has also a theory of rational capitalism which is not suggestive for our purpose. On the conflict between rational and industrial capitalism see ibid., pp. 211 ff.

4. The new relationship between state and capitalist enterprises became more complex and calls for a more comprehensive interpretation.

5. For a sketch of the current theories of economic systems see Appendix B pp. 572–83.

6. *The Rise and Fall of the Third Reich* (New York: Simon and Schuster, 1960), pp. 206, 259. For an incisive critical review of this book see Klaus Epstein, "Shirer's History of Nazi Germany," *Review of Politics,* April, 1961, pp. 230–45.

Chapter 1

1. Our knowledge of business participation in the formulation of political decisions has been greatly increased through recent studies. See especially David Truman, *Governmental Processes* (New York: Alfred A. Knopf, Inc., 1951) ; J. D. Stewart, *British Pressure Groups* (Oxford: Clarendon Press, 1958); Henry W. Ehrmann, *Organized Business in France* (Princeton, New Jersey: Princeton University Press, 1957); Rupert Breitling, *Verbände in der Bundesrepublik* (Meisenheim am Glan: Hain, 1955).

2. General disapproval of important transactions can have the same effect. When Friedrich Flick sold the shares of the Gelsenkirchen A.G.

in the depth of the depression to the German federal government, giving it the voting majority in the largest steel concern, the universal disapproval was so great that Flick decided to make heavy political contributions. Of the 1.5 million marks paid by him in 1932, about 900,000 marks were spent for the re-election of President von Hindenburg and about 100,000 marks went to the Nazis. See NI-3508.

3. Karl Guth, *Die Reichsgruppe Industrie* (Berlin: Junker und Dünnhaupt, 1941), p. 19.

4. *Nazi Conspiracy and Aggression* (Washington, D.C.: Government Printing Office, 1947), V, 227–28.

5. For further details see ibid., II, 23–91.

6. Cf. ibid., V, 102–12.

7. Ibid., p. 113.

8. Said one Nazi journal: "The work of the new *Reich* leadership of students is based upon the principle that the NS League of Students is the National Socialist nucleus and the leadership organization of the compulsory association of students (*Studentenschaft*). The specific function of the NS League is the comprehensive political-ideological education of the entire student body along the lines laid down by the NSDAP, and it also has to carry out the special professional tasks in accordance with the party line." *Das Dritte Reich,* IV (1936), 360.

9. Reinhard Bendix, *Max Weber—An Intellectual Portrait* (New York: Doubleday, 1960), p. 459.

10. Cf. *Nazi Conspiracy and Aggression,* IV, 411–15.

11. Ibid., IV, 619.

12. J. W. Wheeler-Bennett, *The Nemesis of Power* (New York: The Macmillan Co., 1954), p. 269.

13. R. M. MacIver, *Society* (New York: Long and Smith, 1937), pp. 343 ff.

14. In the spring of 1933 Hermann Göring, in his capacity as Prussian Minister of Police, said: "Whoever did his duty in the service of the State, whoever obeyed my orders and took severe measures against the enemy of the State, whoever ruthlessly made use of his revolver when attacked, could be certain of protection. . . . If one calls this murder, then I am a murderer." Quoted by E. K. Bramstedt, *Dictatorship and Political Police* (London: Oxford University Press, 1945), p. 96.

15. *Nazi Conspiracy and Aggression,* V, 1098.

16. Ibid., IV, 496, and V, 13.

17. Ibid., IV, 196–98.

18. Ibid., IV, 623–26.

19. Ibid., III, 547–50.

20. Ibid., IV, 106–10, 928–29.

21. Himmler said in a speech to the army officers in January of 1937: "As far as I can, I am now bringing the police up to full strength with men leaving the preliminary armed SS and the Death Head units; I am bringing the police officers' corps up to full strength with SS leaders who come from the leader-training schools of the SS" (ibid., IV, 629). It was only in the regular police that some expertness was a reason for hiring people who did not originally come from the SS but who often were accepted as members when they had proven themselves politically reliable.

22. Expulsion of anyone who did not obey or who otherwise failed to live up to the required code of behavior proved to be a very effective weapon in the hands of the leaders. For instance, not less than 60,000 SS men were expelled from 1933 to the end of 1935. (ibid., IV, 619). Students, physicians, and women's associations resisted the pattern of interlocking organizations. (See for instance Edward Y. Hartshorn, *German Universities and National Socialism* [New York: Harvard University Press, 1940] and Clifford Kirkpatrick, *Nazi Germany: Its Women and Family Life* [Indianapolis, Indiana: Bobbs-Merrill, 1938]). Expulsion or punishment by the party court enabled the top leaders to suppress any opposition within the sphere of their monopoly.

23. Herbert Blumer, "Collective Behavior," *New Outline of the Principles of Sociology* (New York: Barnes & Noble, Inc., 1946), p. 242.

24. See the speech of Walter Schuhmann, leader of the Nazi "trade union" in March of 1934. Records of the National Socialist German Labor Party, EAP 250-c-01/7, roll 22, T-81.

25. For details on the origin and extent of the Hitler Donation see Arthur Schweitzer, "Business Power in the Nazi Regime," *Zeitschrift für Nationalökonomie*, December, 1960, pp. 414–42.

26. *Nazi Conspiracy and Aggression*, IV, 481.

27. Ibid., Supplement A, p. 1145.

28. Wheeler-Bennett, op. cit., p. 309.

29. Hitler told Major Buch, judge of the party court, in 1933: "The reason why some revolutions were destroyed or otherwise suffocated by reactionary forces lay in the unrestrained claims of the revolutionaries themselves. It is your task as the highest judge within the party to put a brake upon the revolution." See the speech of Major Walter Buch to officers of the regular army in 1937. Wi/IF 5.2738, roll 380, T-77, p. 9 of the written speech.

30. Alfred Meusel, "Revolution and Counterrevolution," *Encyclopedia of the Social Sciences* (New York: The Macmillan Co., 1932), XIII, 367–76.

31. Wheeler-Bennett, op. cit., pp. 319 ff.

32. *Nazi Conspiracy and Aggression,* IV, 786.

33. "When Otto Strasser asked him what he could do with Krupp if he came to power, Hitler at once replied: 'Of course I would leave him alone. Do you think that I should be so mad as to destroy Germany's economy?' " Alan Bullock, *Hitler—A Study in Tyranny* (New York: Harper and Brothers, 1952), p. 141.

34. *Deutscher Volkswirt,* July 21, 1933.

35. Reichskanzlei, R. 43 II/1602, and Reichsschatzmeister, Box 238, Folder 38, Bundesarchiv, Koblenz.

36. See Schweitzer, "The Method of Social Economics," (Dittoed paper, Bloomington, Indiana, 1961), pp. 1–50.

37. Hans Gerth and C. W. Mills, eds., *From Max Weber: Essays in Sociology* (New York: Oxford University Press, 1946), p. 280.

38. See especially his "Politics as a Vocation," ibid., pp. 77–128.

39. The term "ideology" is used here in the sense of a *Weltanschauung.* Another definition of ideology as "something tainted, something shady, something that ought to be overcome and banished from our mind" (Werner Stark, *The Sociology of Knowledge* [Glencoe, Illinois: Free Press, 1958], p. 48) is not useful for our purpose.

40. Rohan D. O. Butler, *The Roots of National Socialism* (New York: E. P. Dutton and Co., 1942), p. 276. See also Edmond Vermeil, *Doctrinaires de la révolution allemande* (Paris: F. Sorlot, 1939).

41. These groups are nowadays divided into the counterrevolutionary conservatives and Nazis. On the ideas of the former see Armin Mohler, *Die konservative Revolution in Deutschland* (Stuttgart: Vorwerk, 1950); Roy Pascal, "Revolutionary Conservatism: Möller van den Bruck," in *The Third Reich* (compiled by the International Council for Philosophy and Humanistic Studies [London: Weidenfeld and Nicolson, 1955]). See also Wolfgang Hock, *Deutscher Antikapitalismus* (Frankfurt a. M.: Knapp, 1960).

42. The ideals of the party were not identical with the ideals of Hitler's coalition governments, as we shall see presently.

43. There were three such coalition governments. They all were led by Hitler and were formed respectively in January and June of 1933 and in July of 1934. Each one had a different Minister of Economics, namely, Alfred Hugenberg, Kurt Schmitt, and Hjalmar Schacht.

44. See Chapter VII below.

45. Cf. Valentin F. Wagner, "Geldschöpfung, Wirtschaftskreislauf und Nationalsozialistische Wirtschaftspolitik," *Schweizerische Zeitschrift für Volkswirtschaft und Statistik,* No. 1, 1958, p. 20.

46. From Gerth and Mills, op. cit., pp. 168–69. Weber wrote shortly before World War I.

47. The hypothetical form of the discussion on pages 56–58 of this chapter (which was not written until after the other chapters had been completed) was used for the sake of pointing up the issues, although this form is not required by our typological method of research.

Chapter 2

1. Theodor Geiger, *Die Soziale Schichtung des Deutschen Volkes* (Stuttgart: Enke-Verlag, 1932), p. 72.

2. The term "quasi-proletarians" as a sub-section of the middle class was first used by Werner Sombart (*Die Deutsche Volkswirtschaft im Neunzehnten Jahrhundert* [Berlin: Bondi, 1903], p. 531) and is generally accepted by students in the field.

3. Geiger, op. cit., p. 73.

4. For the social composition of the middle class in the United States, based on the census data of 1940, see Lewis Corey, "The Middle Class," *Antioch Review*, Spring, 1945, pp. 56–67.

5. See *25 Jahre Deutscher Handwerks-und Gewerbekammertag* (Hannover, 1927). For detailed studies of the various kinds or organizations of the middle groups see the articles in *Strukturwandlungen der Deutschen Volkswirtschaft* (Berlin: Hobbing, 1928), Vol. II.

6. On the whole problem of salaried employees, their organizations and sentiments, see Emil Lederer and Jacob Marschak, *Der Neue Mittelstand* ("Grundriss der Sozialökonomik," Vol. IX, Part 1 [Tübingen: Mohr-Verlag, 1926]).

7. Sombart, *Das Wirtschaftsleben im Zeitalter des Hochkapitalismus* (München: Duncker und Humblot, 1928), II, 966.

8. This was the main conclusion of Emil Lederer's pioneer study, *Die Privatangestellten in der modernen Wirtschaftsentwicklung* (Tübingen: Mohr-Verlag, 1912). The still-relevant chapters II and III of this book were translated by E. Warburg for the Works Progress Administration, 1937.

9. This policy was severely attacked in the years 1928–32. See especially the extensive discussion in *Die Arbeit*, 1930–32.

10. Although the social composition of the nonvoters cannot be shown statistically, it was a generally accepted political observation that the majority of the nonvoters could be found in the lower groups of the middle class, and the minority belonged to the lowest-paid workers of the

labor class. Most of the latter very likely voted for the Communist Party, which increased its votes by 1.3 million in 1930.

Not only the middle class but also the labor class was thus internally stratified, giving rise to different political beliefs. Such internal stratification lends support to S. M. Lipset's theory that each of the three classes in Germany tended to give rise to a political spectrum of left, middle and right political ideas and groups. See his "Der Faschismus— die Linke, die Rechte und die Mitte," *Kölner Zeitschrift für Soziologie und Sozialpsychologie,* 1959, pp. 401–44.

11. This earlier Nazification of the marginal group reflected itself also in the leadership of the party. As Daniel Lerner has shown, the core leaders were characterized by marginality (*The Nazi Elite* [Stanford, California: Stanford University Press, 1951]). Most of them retained their top positions even after the other segments of the middle class joined the Nazi movement.

Accepting this evidence does not commit us to the thesis that "marginality" tended to dissolve the class structure. The fear of the dependent and marginal groups of being pushed down into the labor class, of being subjected to "proletarization," indicates clearly the vitality of the class structure for most members of the middle class.

12. See the penetrating analysis of the deflation and its relationship to the depression by Hans Neisser, *Some International Aspects of the Business Cycle* (Philadelphia: University of Pennsylvania Press, 1935) chapters II and IV.

13. Compare the conclusive study of the economic status and political affiliation of peasants in northern Germany by Rudolf Heberle, "The Political Movements among the Rural People of Schleswig-Holstein, 1919 to 1932," in *Journal of Politics,* February, 1943. This study is included in Heberle's book, *From Democracy to Nazism* (Baton Rouge: Louisiana State University Press, 1945).

14. See Fritz Baade, *Schicksalsjahre der Deutschen Landwirtschaft* (1933). This book was privately printed and illegally distributed in Nazi Germany. It seems that copies are available only at the libraries of Harvard University and Kiel University.

15. Among the studies dealing with the situation of salaried employees before and during the Great Depression, see especially Carl Dreyfuss, *Beruf und Ideologie der Angestellten* (München: Duncker und Humblot, 1933), and Svend Riemer, *Upward Mobility and Social Stratification,* trans. Howard Lissance (New York: Public Works Project, 1937).

16. A change in the policy of the Social Democrats came in 1927-28. It led, for instance, to the adoption of the agrarian tariff program by the

Social Democrats in 1930. This concession proved to be a wrong choice of method, since tariffs ceased to be an effective means of protection for agriculture because of the fall in aggregate demand for food and a rise of domestic agricultural production. Promotion of price supports by the Social Democratic party would have been much more meaningful.

17. Philipp Hessel, "Neuordnung des Wirtschaftsrechts!" *Deutsche Handwerksblatt* (Hannover), XXVI (1932), 296 ff.

18. Ibid., pp. 415, 421.

19. This summary is derived from the resolutions adopted at the conferences, in the summer of 1932, of the regional and national organizations. See especially *Deutsches Handwerksblatt*, XXVI (1932), 253-54, 270, 292-94, 316, 317.

20. It was not a leader of the guilds but Werner Sombart who coined a name for this new reform program, namely "middle-class socialism." (See his *Deutscher Sozialismus* [Berlin: Buchholz und Weiswange, 1934]). Yet Sombart rejected the other features of Nazi ideology, especially racialism. Those who call him a full-fledged Nazi (Cf. Abram L. Harris, "Sombart and German National Socialism," *Journal of Political Economy*, December, 1942, pp. 805-35) underestimate the breadth of Nazi ideology.

21. Herbert Backe, *Das Ende des Liberalismus in der Wirtschaft* (Berlin: Reichsnährstand Verlag, 1936), p. 16.

22. For a copy of this memorandum of Feder, entitled "Arbeitsbeschaffung," see Records of the National Socialist German Labor Party, EAP-a/14, roll 1, T-81, deposited in the National Archives.

23. The thesis that the Nazis had no program of full employment of their own but had to steal it from a half Jewish businessman, Mr. Robert Friedländer-Prechtl (Gerhard Kroll, *Von der Wirtschaftskrise zur Staatskonjunktur* [Berlin: Duncker und Humblot, 1958] pp. 426-34). overlooks Feder's work-creation program mentioned in the text.

24. An investigating commission was appointed in April, 1933; the issues discussed will concern us in Chapter III below.

25. See H. Reupke, *Der Nationalsozialismus und die Wirtschaft* (Berlin: Elsner, 1931); Hans Aron in *Die Arbeit*, 1931, pp. 137 ff.

26. "Abbau der Regiebetriebe," *Deutsches Handwerksblatt*, XXVI (1932), 296.

27. This was especially true in rural areas. In two districts of Schleswig-Holstein, for instance, the Nazis received 92 and 87 votes out of 100 rural middle-class electors in the November election of 1932. See Heberle, "Ecology of Political Parties," *American Sociological Review*, August, 1944, pp. 401 ff.

28. On the typology of mass movements, dominated by ideologies, see Schweitzer, "Ideological Groups," ibid., pp. 15-26.

29. If limited to the formative period, the theory that interpreted the Nazi party as a movement of the middle class is verified by our findings on the origin of middle-class socialism and the mutual interpenetration of small-business groups and the Nazis. See especially Eduard Heimann, *Communism, Fascism, or Democracy* (New York: W. W. Norton and Company, 1938); Alfred Bingham, *Insurgent America* (New York: Harper & Brothers, 1935); Carl J. Friedrich, "The Peasant as Evil Genius of Dictatorship," *The Yale Review*, XXVI (1937), pp. 724-40.

30. For the evidence on the effects of organized employers deliberately to eliminate the social gains of workers prior to the Nazis, see Ludwig Preller, *Sozialpolitik in der Weimarer Republik* (Stuttgart: Franz Mittelbach, 1949), pp. 391-452.

31. "The Flick Case," Defense Exhibit I, Vol. VI.

32. Sigmund Neumann, *Die Deutschen Parteien* (Berlin: Junker und Dünnhaupt, 1932), p. 56.

33. *Wo für wir kämpfen, Die Gemeinschaftserklärung deutscher Wirtschaftsverbände* (Druckschriften des Hansabundes No. 9 [Berlin, 1931]).

34. George W. F. Hallgarten, "Adolf Hitler and the German Heavy Industry, 1931-33," *Journal of Economic History*, summer, 1952, pp. 222-46.

35. Hans Schlange-Schoenigen, *Am Tage Danach* (Hamburg: Hammerich und Lesser, 1946), pp. 65 ff.

36. "Enteignung statt Osthilfe?" *Deutsche Tageszeitung*, May 5, 1932.

37. Schlange-Schoenigen, op. cit., p. 71.

38. When the danger of compulsory sale had been reduced, not less than 50 per cent of the 13,000 large estates in the East applied for financial support under the revised law. "Wo bleibt das Siedlungsland?" *Tägliche Rundschau*, March 10, 1933.

39. See for instance, the adoption of the slogan by the *Deutsche Allgemeine Zeitung*, which was owned by, and represented adroitly the political and economic views of, big business.

40. Some of the evidence upon which our interpretation is based has been well presented by Karl D. Bracher, *Die Auflösung der Weimarer Republik* (3rd ed.; Villingen: Ring Verlag, 1960).

41. Cf. Friedrich Meinecke, *Die Deutsche Katastrophe* (Wiesbaden: Brockhaus, 1946); Gordon Craig, "Briefe Schleichers an Groener," *Die Welt als Geschichte*, 1951; Reginald H. Phelps, "Aus den Groener—Dokumenten," *Deutsche Rundschau*, January, 1951.

42. Joseph Goebbels, *Vom Kaiserhof zur Reichskanzlei* (München:

Eher, 1934), p. 93. For details of the negotiations see Werner Conze, "Zum Sturz Brünings," *Vierteljahrshefte für Zeitgeschichte* (München), 1953, pp. 27 ff.

43. Otto Braun, *Von Weimar zu Hitler* (2nd ed.; New York: Europa-Verlag, 1940), p. 404.

44. August Heinrichsbauer, *Schwerindustrie und Politik* (Essen: West Verlag, 1948). In spite of an extensive search, no evidence has been found in the captured documents supporting the assertion of Mr. Heinrichsbauer that the subsidy was given to Strasser for splitting the Nazi party.

45. Otto Dietrich, *Mit Hitler an die Macht* (München: Eher, 1934), p. 45.

46. See Kurt Freiherr von Schröder's affidavit on Hitler's speech in NI-7990, "The Krupp Case," Prosecution, Vol. VI.

47. Cross-examination of Keppler in "The Flick Case," VI, 2.

48. Ibid., p. 3.

49. NI-443 and 446.

50. EC-440 in *Nazi Conspiracy and Aggression*, Supplement A, pp. 1194–96.

51. "The Flick Case," VI, 391, 393. The unfavorable publicity created by this sale induced Flick to give also sizeable contributions to other parties, especially in the election of von Hindenburg (ibid., pp. 227, 382–83).

52. NI-8788, the "I. G. Farben Case," Vol. I.

53. NI-391, the "I. G. Farben Case," Prosecution, Vol. II.

54. See D-633 and 634, *Nazi Conspiracy and Aggression*, VII, 106–11.

55. Ibid., pp. 513–14.

56. See Heinrichsbauer's letter of September 20, 1932, to Strasser. Records of the National Socialist German Labor Party, EAP a/14, roll 1, T-81.

57. NI-211 and 212. These two documents disprove the assertion of some defense lawyers at Nürnberg that the petition had never reached the President.

58. See the correspondence between Hitler and Meissner in EAP a/14, roll 1, T-81.

59. See the report of von Schröder in NI-7990.

60. Unwittingly, von Schleicher facilitated the reconciliation between Hitler and von Papen when he tried to split the Nazi party by offering Strasser a post in his cabinet. In ousting Strasser from his party offices, Hitler also dissolved the economic policy department at party headquarters. In doing so, Hitler demoted Feder, who was on the side of

Strasser, and thereby assured the businessmen of the Keppler circle
that he as party leader would not support the economic ideas of the
Strasser-Feder wing. See Feder's reaction to this demotion, as reported
to Bormann, in EAP a/14, roll 1, T-81.

61. Affidavit of Schacht in NI-406, the "I. G. Farben Case," Prosecution, Vol. II.

62. D-203 and 204, *Nazi Conspiracy and Aggression*, VI, 1080-85.

63. EC-439, ibid., VII, 501-2.

64. Lutz Graf von Schwerin-Krosigk, *Es geschah in Deutschland* (3rd ed.; Tübingen: Wunderlich, 1952), pp. 171-79.

65. EAP a/14, roll 1, T-81.

Chapter 3

1. See, for instance, Thilo Keller, "Handwerk und struktureller Wirtschaftsumbau," *Soziale Praxis*, January, 1935, p. 122.

2. Counterrevolutionary opposition against capitalism had nothing
to do with traditional socialism. In a speech on "The Third *Reich* and
Capitalism," Bernhard Köhler, as head of the Nazi bureau on economic
policy, made three points: National Socialism will never change forcefully the foundation of the economy; National Socialism will never lead
to expropriation and nationalization of the means of production; the
demand of laborers for centuries has not been for a new economic order
but for a new justice: the right to work. (Cf. "Was ist deutscher Socialismus?" *Deutscher Volkswirt*, No. 3 [November], 1933, p. 179.) Köhler
thus indirectly recognized that workers did not belong to those who
expected to benefit from middle-class socialism.

3. Heinrich Rainers, "Handwerksarbeit als Grundlage der Handwerkswirtschaft," *Die Form*, March, 1933.

4. *Deutscher Volkswirt*, April 21, 1933, p. 820.

5. Heinrich Schild, "Das Reichsgesetz über den Neuaufbau der
deutschen Handwerksorganisation," *Deutsches Handwerksblatt*, June 15,
1933, pp. 221-24.

6. "Neue Steuervorschriften," *Deutscher Volkswirt*, April 12, 1933,
p. 752.

7. Ibid., June 13, 1933, p. 1032.

8. *Der Tag*, June 7, 1933.

9. *Deutscher Volkswirt*, July 14 and 21, 1933, pp. 1174 and 1206.

10. Ibid., May 19, 1933, p. 939.

11. Ibid., June 16, 1933, p. 1061.

12. "Das Schicksal der Konsumgenossenschaften," *Soziale Praxis*, June,
1935, p. 669.

13. Other Ruhr industrialists worked with the Ministry of Labor, as a result of which one of them was appointed as special plenipotentiary of industrial relations for the Ruhr area, thereby superseding temporarily the trustees of labor.

14. "Parteigenossen in der Wirtschaft," *Deutscher Volkswirt*, July 28, 1933, p. 1216.

15. "Einheitliche Sozialpolitik," ibid., July 21, 1933, p. 1184.

16. "Die wirtschaftlichen Grundsaetze der Reichsregierung," *Soziale Praxis*, July, 1933, pp. 877 ff; NI-472; see also NI-1568 for a speech of Hitler in which he expressed his full support of Schmitt.

17. Reichswirtschaftsministerium, Box 391, Folder 564, Berlin Document Center.

18. "Deutsche Arbeitsfront und staendischer Aufbau," *Soziale Praxis*, July, 1933, pp. 852 ff.

19. Reichswirtschaftsministerium, Box 391, Folder 564, Berlin Document Center; see especially the letters written by Jakob Reichert, of the iron and steel organization, on June 19 and July 11, 1933.

20. J. Jessen, "Zur Kritik der Bankenenquete," *Deutscher Volkswirt*, December 8, 1933, pp. 419 ff.

21. The intransigent wing of the Nazis published its ideas in the new periodical, *Die deutsche Volkswirtschaft*. The bankers and others presented their arguments in the traditional economic press. The *Deutscher Volkswirt*, for instance, published a series of ten articles on the banking investigation.

22. *Die Deutsche Sparkassen-Zeitung*, various issues of October, 1933.

23. *Die Deutsche Volkswirtschaft*, issues of October and November, 1933.

24. "Wilhelm Keppler zur Bankenfrage," *Deutscher Volkswirt*, September 8, 1933, p. 1404. Feder was not a member of the commission; Keppler was.

25. "Die Verstaatlichungsdebatte," *Deutscher Volkswirt*, November 24, 1933, pp. 320 ff.

26. H. Schacht, *Nationale Kreditwirtschaft* (Berlin: Steegemann Verlag, 1934).

27. *Deutsche Sparkassen-Zeitung*, October, 1933, pp. 1117 ff.

28. "Sparkassenentwicklung und Anlagevorschriften," *Deutscher Volkswirt*, March 29, 1934.

29. *Deutsche Sparkassen-Zeitung*, March, 1934.

30. "Widerschein der Bankbilanzen," *Deutscher Volkswirt*, June 15, 1934, pp. 1642 ff.

31. "Wirtschaftsgruppe 10," ibid., April 20, 1934, p. 1258.

32. One commissioner was Dr. Schwarzkopf of Kassel who formerly was undersecretary of the Ministry of Economics under von Papen and von Schleicher. The other was Dr. Rosenkopf of Westphalia, who was an unknown Nazi. *Deutsche Sparkassen-Zeitung,* December 3, 1934.

33. Schwarzkopf, "Umgestaltung des Deutschen Sparkassen-und Giroverbandes," *Deutscher Volkswirt,* April 12, 1935, pp, 1269–71.

34. Friedrich Ernst, "Anlass und Bedeutung der Geldzinssenkung," ibid., March 8, 1935, pp. 1029–31. Ernst was the commissioner for banking and credit who operated under Schacht's instructions.

35. For an analysis of the final act see Marie Dessauer, "The German Bank Act of 1934," *Review of Economic Studies* (London), June, 1935, pp. 214–24.

36. Cf. Walter Heinrich, *Das Staendewesen mit besonderer Beruecksichtigung der Wirtschaft* (Jena: Fischer, 1932), pp. 36 ff.

37. Taylor Cole, "Corporative Organization of the Third Reich," *Review of Politics,* October, 1940, pp. 31 ff.

38. "Organisation des Handwerks," *Deutsches Handwerksblatt,* XXVII (1933), pp. 370–72.

39. "Staende und Verbaende," *Deutscher Volkswirt,* May, 1934, p. 1452.

40. "Umgliederung des Kampfbundes des gewerblichen Mittelstandes," *Deutsches Handwerksblatt,* September 1, 1933, p. 338.

41. "Vereinheitlichung der Spitzenorganisationen des Deutschen Handwerks," ibid., October 15, 1933, pp. 392–93.

42. Heinrich Schild, "Grundsaetzliche Stellung des deutschen Handwerks zur staendischen Wirtschaftsordnung," ibid., November 1, 1933, pp. 402–5.

43. "Gesetz ueber den vorlaeufigen Aufbau des deutschen Handwerks," ibid., 1933, pp. 464–65.

44. H. Schindler, "Das neue Handwerksrecht," *Soziale Praxis,* July 5, 1934, pp. 801–10.

45. "Der historische Tag des deutschen Handwerks," *Deutsches Handwerksblatt,* 1934, pp. 54–55.

46. "Dienstordnung fuer die Landeshandwerksfuehrer," ibid., August 1, 1934, pp. 289–90.

47. "Ausfuehrungsbestimmungen ueber die Errichtung der Handwerkerinnungen durch die Handwerkskammern," ibid., August 1, 1934, pp. 290–91

48 "Einheitliche Fuehrung des deutschen Handwerks in Partei, Arbeitsfront, und Wirtschaft," ibid., June 15, 1934, p. 229.

49. "Aus dem Handwerk: Persönliches," ibid., October 1, 1934, p. 37.

50. "Die Disziplinargerichtsbarkeit im Handwerk," *Deutsches Handwerk,* October 15, 1935, p. 383.

51. "Reichsinnungsverbaende im Handwerk," *Deutscher Volkswirt,* June 7, 1935, p. 1659.

52. "Zu hohe Beiträge," ibid., May 17, 1935, p. 1511.

53. "Beiträge im Handwerk," ibid., October 6, 1935.

54. *National Sozialistische Parteikorrespondenz,* No. 181, 1934; this was a publication of the NSDAP.

55. The major concession of Schacht was his consent to the third decree on the organization of handicraft which laid the cornerstone for the "artisan economy." This series of events will be discussed in the next chapter.

56. See the letter of General von Blomberg and related documents in Wi/IF 5.1260, roll 260, T-77.

57. *Deutscher Volkswirt,* November 27, 1936.

58. Schacht's letter was dated June 26, 1936, and is contained in folder 5.1260, roll 260, T-77.

59. Reichsorganisationsleiter der NSDAP, Box 320, Folder 594, Berlin Document Center.

60. Wi/IF 5.1276, roll 266, T-77.

61. *Amtliches Nachrichtenblatt der DAF,* September 2, 1936. See also *Nazi Conspiracy and Aggression,* IV, 941–43.

62. Wi/IF 5.113, roll 13, T-77.

63. *Völkischer Beobachter,* November 25, 1936.

64. Wi/IF 5.113, roll 13, T-77.

65. Wi/IF 5.383, roll 86, T-77.

66. "Handwerk und Wirtschaftskammern," *Deutscher Volkswirt,* February 27, 1937.

67. Wi/IF 5.1276, roll 266, T-77.

68. Wi/IF 5.1276, roll 266, T-77.

69. Ibid., frames 1088260 ff.

70. See the confidential report of Dr. Wienbeck of the Ministry of Economics to Col. Gutscher of the Ministry of War, dated December 24, 1937, in Wi/IF 5.1274, roll 265, T-77.

71. Wi/IF 5.1276, roll 266, T-77.

Chapter 4

1. See for instance "82 Hauptversammlung des Gewerbevereins für Nassau," *Deutsches Handwerksblatt,* XXVI (1932), 253-54.

2. For a careful assessment of this program see Leo Grebler, "Work

Creation Policy in Germany, 1932–1935," *International Labour Review* (Geneva), March and April, 1937, pp. 329–51 and 505–27.

3. For a survey of the law and its effects see Johannes Splettstoesser, *Der Einzelhandel* (Berlin: Hegmann, 1936), pp. 99–128.

4. "Verteilung der Arbeitskräfte: Frauenarbeit, Schwarzarbeit," *Soziale Praxis,* October, 1933, p. 1242.

5. Über Wege zur Schwarzarbeiterbekämpfung in Königsberg i. P.," ibid., 1936, p. 693.

6. *Wochenbericht,* No. 23 (publication of the Institut für Konjunkturforschung [Berlin, 1934]).

7. "Baumarkt und Arbeitsbeschaffung," *Deutscher Volkswirt,* June 22, 1934, pp. 1681 ff.

8. Gerhard Kutzscher, "Wirtschaftsbelebung durch das Hochbaugewerbe," *Deutscher Volkswirt,* May 18, 1934, pp. 1442–45.

9. The artisan organizations had a conference on January 23, 1935, in Berlin where they celebrated the last two handicraft decrees. The Nazi leader of the Estate of Handicraft, Schmidt-Wiesbaden, welcomed the decrees as putting an end to the 100 years of free trade in handicraft. Schacht, speaking to the same group, insisted strongly that the provisions on training and examination did not destroy the principle of free trade. They merely specified, he said, the conditions under which the principle of free trade would be operating in the handicraft of the future ("Grosser Befähigungsnachweis und Handwerkskarte," *Deutsches Handwerksblatt,* February 11, 1935, pp. 41–42).

10. "Verzeichnis der Handwerksgewerbe," ibid., July 15, 1934, pp. 269–70.

11. "Schutz des Wettbewerbs im Handwerk," *Deutscher Volkswirt,* September 20, 1935, p. 2355.

12. Nathan A. Pelcovits, "The Social Courts of Honor of Nazi Germany," *Political Science Quarterly,* September, 1938, pp. 350–71.

13. *Neuordnung des Meisterprüfungswesens* (Berlin: Handwerker-Verlagshaus, 1936).

14. "Verarbeitungsindustrie und Handel im Reichsnährstand," *Deutscher Volkswirt,* February 23, 1934, p. 894.

15. "Lebensmitteleinzelhandel und Nährstand," ibid., August 24, 1934, p. 2094.

16. "Handwerk-Einzelhandel," ibid., November 27, 1936. A similar agreement defining the line between retail and wholesale trade had been signed six months earlier.

17. "Interne Abgrenzung in der Wirtschaftsorganisation," ibid., June 17, 1936.

18. "Abgrenzungsfragen in der gewerblichen Wirtschaft," ibid., September 11, 1936.

19. "Die handwerklichen Nebenbetriebe," *Soziale Praxis,* September, 1937, p. 677.

20. In a letter to Ley, written on June 26, 1936, Schacht admitted that previously he had "openly criticized the types of organization I inherited but [that] I was always for independent economic organizations of business." Wi/IF 5.113, roll 13, T-77. His implication was that he had originally opposed closed crafts and compulsory membership but failed to reach this goal because of the insistence upon such a type of organization by the generals. Schacht tried to keep these organizations, once they were established, free of party control and to permit the handicraft and trade organizations some forms of interest-representation.

21. "Richtlinien zur Lehrlingsausbildung im Lebensmittelhandel," *Soziale Praxis,* September, 1934, pp. 1168–70.

22. Ernst Hoch, "Die Kaufmannsgehilfenprüfungen," *Deutsche Wirtschaftszeitung,* June 10, 1937, pp. 690–93.

23. Deutsche Arbeitsfront, *Deutsche Arbeitskorrespondenz,* September 8, 1936.

24. Reichsgruppe Industrie, "Facharbeiter und Nachwuchsfrage in der Industrie," pp. 52, 58, contained in Wi/IF 5.1917, roll 322, T-77.

25. Ibid., p. 63.

26. See the memorandum on "Berufsausbildung und Berufserziehung in der gewerblichen Wirtschaft," Wi/IF 5.1276, roll 266, T-77.

27. Otto Küch, "Neugestaltung der industriellen Fachprüfungen," *Das Junge Deutschland,* February, 1936.

28. "Industrielle Berufsausbildung," *Deutscher Volkswirt,* March 13, 1936.

29. Albert Mueller, "Einsatz und Forderung," *Soziale Praxis,* July 25, 1935, pp. 858–68.

30. "Wie soll der Arbeiternachwuchs aussehen?" ibid., August, 1936, pp. 1010–18.

31. "Das erste Leistungsabzeichen für eine vorbildliche Berufserziehungsstätte," ibid., January, 1937, pp. 45–47.

32. Reichgruppe Industrie memorandum on vocational training in Wi/IF 5.1917, roll 322, T-77, p. 68.

33. Wi/IF 5.1260, roll 260, T-77; *Textil-Zeitung,* September 17, 1937.

34. Wi/IF 5.113, roll 13, T-77.

35. See Pietzsch's letter of November 28, 1936, ibid.

36. Wi/IF 5.351, roll 78, T-77.

37. "Ausbildung und Prüfung industrieller Facharbeiter," *Soziale Praxis*, July, 1937, p. 793

38. Schacht, *Abrechnung mit Hitler* (Hamburg: Rowohlt, 1948), p. 14.

39. Wi/IF 5.351, roll 78, T-77.

40. Lessmann, "Gegenwartsfragen des deutschen Handwerks," *Deutsches Handwerksblatt*, XXVIII (November 15, 1933), 421-22.

41. H. Fritzsche, "Die Marktpolitik im Dritten Reich," *Deutscher Volkswirt*, June 1, 1934, pp. 1541-43.

42. Preiskommissar, Box 1, Berlin Document Center.

43. "Grosskampf gegen die Preissteigerung," *Soziale Praxis*, November 15, 1934, pp. 1371-76.

44. "Hamsterpsychose verschwunden," *Berliner Börsen-Zeitung*, December 21, 1934.

45. "Goerdeler's Aufgaben," *Berliner Tageblatt*, November 11, 1934.

46. Ibid.

47. EAP 250-c-18, roll 41, T-81.

48. "Die nächsten Aufgaben des Preiskommissars," *Völkischer Beobachter*, December 5, 1934.

49. "Geordeler über Preisüberwachung," *Deutsche Bergwerks-Zeitung*, March 13, 1935.

50. "Wege und Aufgaben der Preisüberwachung," *Berliner Börsen-Zeitung*, June 18, 1935.

51. "Die Preisbindungen in der Wirtschaft," *Der Deutsche*, November 23, 1934.

52. See *Berliner Tageblatt*, December 25, 1934, and *Berliner Börsen-Zeitung*, December 22, 1934.

53. "Kontrollierte Preisgestaltung in der Bauwirtschaft," *Deutscher Volkswirt*, May 31, 1935.

54. "Preisüberwachung und Vergebung öffentlicher Arbeiten," *Völkischer Beobachter*, April 16, 1935.

55. Reichskanzlei, R. 43/415b and 417, Bundesarchiv, Koblenz.

56. See *Deutsche Bergwerks-Zeitung*, March 13, 1935, and *NS-Landpost*, February 7, 1935.

57. "Goerdelers Aufgaben," *Berliner Tageblatt*, November 9, 1934.

58. "Landwirtschaft und Preisüberwachung," *Kölnische Zeitung*, January 25, 1935.

59. *NS-Landpost*, February 7, 1935.

60. *Economist* (London), July 13, 1935, and January 11, 1936.

61. Wi/IF 5.1568, roll 292, T-77.

62. Gerhard Ritter, *Carl Goerdeler und die Deutsche Widerstandsbewegung* (Stuttgart: Deutsche Verlagsanstalt, 1954), p. 74.

Chapter 5

1. A preliminary inheritance law from Prussia had already been signed on May 15, 1933. Yet one informed observer revealed that Hugenberg himself did not believe in the main provision of the act: to deprive the owner of his right to dispose of his landed property at will or according to common inheritance practice. (Cf. Constantin von Dietze, "Die Bedeutung des preussischen Erbhofrechts fuer die wirtschaftliche und soziale Entwicklung des Bauerntums," *Soziale Praxis*, July, 1933, pp. 897 ff.) The Prussian law was prepared by the *Amt für Agrarpolitik* of the Nazi party and pushed through the cabinet against the opposition of Hugenberg. See K. D. Bracher, W. Sauer, G. Schulz, *Die National-sozialistische Machtergreifung* (Köln: Westdeutscher Verlag, 1960), pp. 572 ff.

2. Wolfgang Luetzow, "Reichserbhofrecht," *Soziale Praxis*, October, 1933, p. 1219.

3. Frieda Wunderlich, "The National Socialist Agrarian Program," *Social Research*, March, 1946, pp. 33–50.

4. Cf. Johann W. Ludowici, *Das Deutsche Siedlungswerk* (2nd ed.; Heidelberg: C. Winter, 1937). From 1933 to 1938 the author of this book headed the program of the party and the Labor Front for building "rurban" communities for laborers.

5. Erich Koch, the Nazi *Gauleiter* and governor of East Prussia, had developed a program of dovetailing industries with agrriculture in his *Der Aufbau im Osten* (Breslau: Gottl, 1934). Koch later became one of the largest owners of industrial properties in the Nazi hierarchy.

6. For a description of the many plans for canal construction, see Kurt Sensemann, "Arbeitsdienst als Mittel zur Krisenueberwindung," *Deutscher Volkswirt*, February 2, 1934, pp. 761–63; August, 1933, pp. 941 ff.

7. "Das Reichsgesetz über die Neubildung deutschen Bauerntums," *Soziale Praxis*, August, 1933, pp. 941 ff.

8. *Vierteljahrshefte zur Statistik des deutschen Reiches* (Berlin), No. 3, 1939.

9. "Kundgebung des Reichssiedlungkommissars," *Deutsches Hand-werksblatt*, June 15, 1934, pp. 236–40.

10. *Preussische Zeitung*, April 4, 1934.

11. *Nationalsozialistische Landpost*, April 6, 1934.

12. Hans Baumgarten, "Siedlung—nicht Siedelei," *Deutscher Volk-swirt*, June 1, 1934, pp. 1546–49.

13. *Deutscher Volkswirt*, November 30 and December 7, 1934, pp. 384 and 430.

14. "Der Siedlungsbeirat des Arbeitsministers," ibid., February 15, 1935, p. 875.

15. "Der Landbedarf der oeffentlichen Hand," *Soziale Praxis,* April, 1935, pp. 485 ff.

16. "Reichsstelle fuer Raumordnung," *Deutscher Volkswirt,* August 2, 1935, p. 2030.

17. *International Yearbook of Agricultural Statistics* (Rome: International Institute of Agriculture, 1934–35, 1938–39).

18. Ludowici, op. cit.

19. "Vorstaedtische Kleinsiedlung," *Deutscher Volkswirt,* March 23, 1934, p. 1075.

20. "Kundgebung des Reichssiedlungskommissars," *Deutsches Handwerksblatt,* June 15, 1934, pp. 236–40.

21. W. Ginsbertz, "Entwicklung und Zukunftsaussichten der Kleinsiedlung," *Soziale Praxis,* August, 1935, pp. 949–56, 978–84.

22. *Deutscher Volkswirt,* August 2, 1935, p. 2055.

23. *Siedlung und Wirtschaft* (Berlin), No. 9, 1938.

24. "Um die Kosten der Siedlung," *Deutscher Volkswirt,* November 20, 1936.

25. Eugen Voegler, "Das Problem der Arbeitersiedlung," ibid., June 24, 1935, pp. 1765–67.

26. "Rund um den Wohnungsbau," *Soziale Praxis,* February, 1939, p. 175.

27. T. Tern, "Hochbetriebe im Baugewerbe," *Wirtschaftskurve,* May, 1938, pp. 131–47.

28. "Totale Landesverteidigung," *Deutscher Volkswirt,* January 22, 1937.

29. Deutsche Arbeitsfront, *Deutsche Arbeitskorrespondenz,* No. 61, 1938.

30. Cf. *Soziale Praxis,* December, 1936, pp. 1511–16; November, 1937, pp. 1361–64; December, 1937, pp. 1517–18.

31. "Die Kreditmaerkte im Konsolidierungsprozess," *Deutscher Volkswirt,* December 24, 1936.

32. "Emmissionssperre und Staatsbedarf," ibid., February 21, 1936.

33. M. Knuettel, "Reserve: Wohnungsbau," ibid., January 31, 1937.

34. Walter Fey, *Der kuenftige Wohnungs-und Siedlungsbau* (Hamburg: Hanseatische Verlagsanstalt, 1939).

35. C. F. Goerdeler, "Deutschland und die Weltwirtschaft," *Deutscher Volkswirt,* June 12, 1936.

36. Goerdeler, "Kleinsiedlung und Wohnungsbau als politische und wirtschaftliche Notwendigkeit," ibid., March 27 and April 3, 1936.

37. *Nazi Conspiracy and Aggression*, VII, 472.

38. "Bau von Arbeiterwohnungen," *Soziale Praxis*, December, 1936, pp. 1434 ff.

39. H. P. Pauls, "Das Neue Mitteldeutschland," *Wirtschaftskurve*, February, 1939, pp. 51–62.

40. "Ordnung im Bauwesen," *Soziale Praxis*, January, 1939, p. 15.

41. For a frank statement of the major ideas of Nazi imperialism see the speech which Hitler addressed to a secret meeting of party leaders and generals on November 5, 1937. *Nazi Conspiracy and Aggression*, III, 295–304.

42. Ibid., Supplement A, pp. 109–11.

43. Wi/IF 5.1276, roll 266, T-77.

44. For a comparison between Nazi and Bolshevik ideological changes see Schweitzer, "Ideological Strategy," *Western Political Quarterly*, March, 1962, pp. 46–66.

45. *Deutsches Handwerk*, May 26, 1939, p. 1.

46. *Jahrbuch des deutschen Handwerks—1938/39* (München: Zeleny-Verlag, 1939), p. 153.

47. Ibid., 1937, pp. 521 ff.

48. "Zur Sicherstellung des Facharbeiternachwuchses im Metall-und Baugewerbe," *Soziale Praxis*, April, 1937, pp. 521–24.

49. *Nazi Conspiracy and Aggression*, III, 827–28.

50. Wi/IF 5.605, roll 148, T-77.

Chapter 6

1. See Bracher, *Die Auflösung der Weimarer Republik*, p. 714.

2. Our summary is based upon the various *Befehlshaberbesprechungen*, on the defense law and its supplements, and on the various speeches made by Hitler and von Blomberg to military audiences from February to September, 1933.

3. Hermann Foertsch, *Schuld und Verhängnis* (Stuttgart: Deutsche-Verlags Anstalt, 1951), pp. 46-47.

4. *Nazi Conspiracy and Aggression*, IV, 936.

5. Hermann Rauschning, *Gespräche mit Hitler* (Zürich: Europa Verlag, 1940), p. 147.

6. See Foertsch, op. cit., p. 47; and *Nazi Conspiracy and Aggression*, IV, 486–88, and V, 458.

7. Hermann Mau, "Die Zweite Revolution—Der 30, Juni, 1934," *Vierteljahrshefte für Zeitgeschichte*, April, 1953, pp. 131–33.

8. Wolfgang Förster, *Ein General kämpft gegen den Krieg* (München: Dom Verlag, 1949).

9. Friedrich Hossbach, *Zwischen Wehrmacht und Hitler* (Wolfen-büttel: Wolfenbütteler Verlagsanstalt, 1949), p. 74.

10. NI-910.

11. See D-157, The "I.G. Farben Case," Vol. II, Exhibit 67.

12. NI-1227 and D-353.

13. NI-1017 and 393.

14. NI-628 and 1568.

15. NIK-12048 and 12372.

16. NIK-11552.

17. Wi/IF 5.604, roll 148, T-77.

18. The letter is available in Wi/IF 5.406, roll 92, T-77.

19. See Wi/IF 5.598, roll 145, T-77. See also "Die Vollmacht für den Reichswirtschaftsminister," *Deutscher Volkswirt*, July 13, 1934.

20. The view that Schmitt "actually left his office because of the pressure and steady accusations of Schacht," (Otto Meissner, *Staatssekretär unter Ebert, Hindenburg, und Hitler* [Hamburg: Hoffmann und Campe, 1950], p. 329) does not take into account the memorandum of General Thomas and the subsequent actions.

21. Wi/IF 5.406, roll 92, T-77.

22. Schacht, *76 Jahre meines Lebens* (Bad Wörishofen: Kindler und Schiermeyer, 1953), p. 411.

23. *Nazi Conspiracy and Aggression*, IV, 934-38, and VI, 464.

24. "Die Organisation der Wirtschaft," *Deutscher Volkswirt*, August, 1934, pp. 2004, 2054.

25. The memorandum was entitled "Beiträge zum Aufbau einer kriegswirtschaftlichen Organisation" (Wi/IF 5.406, roll 92, T-77).

26. See Wi/IF 5.604, roll 148, T-77.

27. "Wirtschaftsgruppe Privates Bankgewerbe," *Deutscher Volkswirt*, September 7, 1934.

28. A case in point was the insistence of the party that the leaders of the iron and steel groups be approved by the *Gauleiter*. Ernst Poensgen, leader of the largest steel concern and acting chairman of the business group for iron and steel, rejected this request, submitted to him by the executive secretary of the *Reichsgruppe Industrie*. Schacht approved the elected business leaders in iron and steel, despite party resistance. Reichswirtschaftsministerium, Box 391, Folder 561, Berlin Document Center.

29. "Die Entwicklung des Unternehmungsbestandes," *Wirtschaft und Statistik*, 1941, p. 187.

30. Kurt Mahn, "Neue Vorschlaege zur Aktienrechtsreform," *Deutscher Volkswirt*, June 22, 1934, pp. 1687-90.

31. Wilhelm Kisskalt, "Zweiter Bericht über die Arbeiten des Aktien-rechtausschusses," *Zeitschrift der Akademie für Deutsches Recht*, 1935, p. 247.

32. "Gehaelter, Tantiemen und Betriebsgemeinschaft," *Der Angriff*, November 19, 1935.

33. Mahn, "Vorstandsmacht im neuen Aktienrecht," *Deutscher Volks-wirt*, June 7, 1935, pp. 1661–63.

34. Partly reprinted in *Schacht in seinen Ausserungen* (publication of the Reichsbank [Berlin, 1937]), p. 97.

35. For details on the act see F. A. Mann, "The New German Company Law and its Background," *Journal of Comparative Legislation and International Law, 1937*, XIX, 220–38.

36. "Anti-Socialistic Socialists," *Economist* (London), December 14, 1935.

37. H. C. Nipperdey, "Wettbewerb und Existenzvernichtung," *Kartell-Rundschau*, March, 1930, pp. 127–52.

38. S. Tschierschky, "Kartellrecht und Wettbewerbsrecht," ibid., February, 1933, pp. 89–106.

39. For a detailed summary of these modifications see E. Schindler, "Aenderungen des Gewerberechts," *Soziale Praxis*, October, 1934, pp. 1190 ff., and January, 1935, pp. 83 ff.

40. "Aus der Kartellrechtspraxis," *Kartell-Rundschau*, October, 1935, pp. 824 ff.

41. Carl Schramm, "Kartellende oder neue Kartellformen?" ibid., February, 1935, pp. 65–67.

42. "Grosskampf gegen die Preissteigerung," *Soziale Praxis,* November 15, 1934, pp. 1374 ff.

43. Reichswirtschaftsministerium, Box 391, Folder 558a, Berlin Document Center.

44. Ibid., Folder 558.

45. See Horst Wagenfuehr, "Die Entwicklung der Kartellpreise in Deutschland von 1925 zu 1936," *Kartell-Rundschau*, August, 1936, pp. 515–19.

46. Reichswirtschaftsministerium, Box 390, Folder 553, Berlin Document Center.

47. "Kontrollierte Preisgestaltung in der Bauwirtschaft," *Deutscher Volkswirt*, May 31, 1935, pp. 1609 ff.

48. Leonhard Miksch, "Kalkulationskartelle und Kalkulationskon-trolle," *Wirtschaftskurve*, August, 1937, pp. 208–21.

49. Erwin Junghans-Schramberg, "Zur Frage des Kalkulationskartells," *Kartell-Rundschau*, June, 1936, pp. 375–77.

50. The economist Leonhard Miksch tried to locate a specific area of free competition but could not find it. "Wo herrscht noch freier Wettbewerb?" *Wirtschaftskurve*, December, 1936, pp. 339–49.

51. Reichswirtschaftsministerium, Box 391, Folder 564, Berlin Document Center.

52. Horst Wagenfuehr, "Nationalsozialismus und Kartelle," *Kartell-Rundschau*, July, 1933, pp. 419–24.

53. O. Lenich, "Die Arbeiten des Kartellausschusses," *Zeitschrift der Akademie für deutsches Recht*, 1935, p. 382.

54. For a detailed analysis of the law, see Walter Strauss, "Die neue deutsche Kartellgesetzgebung," *Kartell-Rundschau*, August, 1933, pp. 497–539. The problem of investment-control contained in the act need not concern us here.

55. Cf. Claire Russell, "Die Praxis der Zwangskartellgesetzgebung," *Zeitschrift für die gesamte Staatswissenschaft*, XCVII (1937), 499–548; and Carl Billich, "Vier Jahre nationalsozialistischer Kartellpolitik," *Deutscher Volkswirt*, September 24, 1937.

56. Otto Stritzke, "Die Ordnung des graphischen Gewerbes als Beispiel," *Kartell-Rundschau*, December, 1936, pp. 829–34.

57. "Zur Kartellfaehigkeit der Kleinstbetriebe," *Deutscher Volkswirt*, April 9, 1937.

58. Strauss, "Die neue Aenderung der Kartellverordnung," *Kartell-Rundschau*, September, 1934, pp. 575–79.

59. "Aus der Kartellrechtspraxis," ibid., January, 1935, pp. 7–12.

60. For instance, 8,000 organized coal dealers once had to face the competition of almost 50,000 unorganized dealers. Under the new law the latter either had to join the dealers' cartel or go out of business.

61. Tschierschky, "Wettbewerbsrecht und wirtschaftliche Organisationspolitik," *Kartell-Rundschau*, December, 1935, pp. 964–73.

62. Hans Fezer, "Zementmarkt in der Schwebe," *Deutscher Volkswirt*, January 11, 1935, pp. 659 ff.

63. For an extensive list of properties that changed hands in this period see Günter Keiser, "Konzernbewegung," *Wirtschaftskurve*, December, 1939.

64. Karl Guth, "Marktordnungsgrundsaetze der Reichsgruppe Industrie," *Deutscher Volkswirt*, June 22, 1935, pp. 1763–65.

65. *Rheinisch-Westfaelische Zeitung*, March 24, 1933.

66. *Deutsche Kohlen-Zeitung*, June 13, 1933.

67. *Deutsche Bergwerks-Zeitung*, July 28, 1934.

68. Ibid., August 3, 1933.

69. Every acceptable dealer had to become a member of the cartel, as if it were a compulsory cartel, established by the government.

70. Carl Schramm, "Totales Kartell und Fachschaft," *Kartell-Rundschau,* January, 1935, pp. 989-96.

71. *Frankfurter-Zeitung,* May 20, 1936.

72. Cf. Ernst Eckelt, "Der Ausschliesslichkeitsvertrag als Mittel zur Ordnung der gewerblichen Wirtschaft," *Kartell-Rundschau,* August, 1935, pp. 635-51.

73. Tschierschky, "Die Kartellfrage als Gegenwartsproblem," ibid., May, 1935, pp. 322-34; June, 1935, pp. 448-55; July, 1935, pp. 521-31.

74. Junghans-Schramberg, "Das deutsche Kartellwesen im Uebergangsstadium," *Deutscher Volkswirt,* December 24, 1936.

75. International cartels were not subject to the supervision of groups. Cf. H. Mullensiefen, *Gruppenaufgaben bei der Wirtschaftlichkeitsfoerderung, Marktordnung, und Kartellaufsicht* (Stuttgart: Forkel, 1937).

76. For an illustration see Stritzke, "Das Elektro-Abkommen," *Kartell-Rundschau,* 1936, pp. 392-95.

77. The theory of the multiple power structure, developed by Otto Kirchheimer in his "Changes in the Structure of Political Compromise" (*Studies in Philosophy and Social Science,* 1941, pp. 264-89), is not applicable to the bilateral power structure in the first period of the Nazi regime.

78. *Nazi Conspiracy and Aggression,* VI, 495.

79. Credit for having developed and applied the theory of a bilateral power structure goes to Ernst Fraenkel (*The Dual State* [New York: Oxford University Press, 1941]). Our findings induce us to accept this theory for the first Nazi period but to give it a more specific expression.

80. See Schacht's letter to Hitler, written in the spring of 1935 (*Nazi Conspiracy and Aggression,* III, 868-70).

81. Wi/IF 5.751, roll 181, and 5.1171, roll 228, T-77.

82. This interaction between property and organizational power is in conflict with the theory of Marx. His strict followers have asserted that in capitalism all power originates from ownership of capital, and that "the ruling class under capitalism is made up of the functionaries of capital" (Paul Sweezy, *The Present as History* [New York: Monthly Review Press, 1953], p. 60). In this view, the Nazi party possessed power only because its leaders became capitalists themselves (p. 61). The party possessed no original base of power but was merely an instrument of monopoly capitalism (p. 238). Neither assertion about leaders and the party can be supported by specific evidence in the formerly secret documents.

83. In total power the ruler "exercises complete administrative, managerial, judicial, military and fiscal authority." For an extensive analysis of total power in the hydraulic society see Karl A. Wittfogel, *Oriental Despotism* (New Haven: Yale University Press, 1957).

Chapter 7

1. Wi/IF 5.406, roll 92, T-77.
2. *Nazi Conspiracy and Aggression*, VI, 539.
3. Ibid., VI, 967, 970, 1017.
4. Ibid., p. 535.
5. Reichsorganisationsleiter der NSDAP, Box 320, Folder 594, Berlin Document Center.
6. *Deutsches Handwerksblatt*, June 1, 1934; and *Berliner Börsen-Zeitung*, May 16, 1934.
7. Fritz Syrup, "Die Verteilung von Arbeitskräften," *Deutscher Volkswirt*, September 14, 1934, pp. 2229-32.
8. Ferdinand Fried, *Die Zukunft des Aussenhandels* (Jena: Diedrich, 1934). This author, who was one of the leaders of the circle that published the periodical *Tat*, drew in this study the same conclusions on foreign trade drawn in his earlier book, *Autarkie* (Jena: Diedrich, 1932). In 1934 Fried was a high official in the Estate of Agriculture.
9. A copy of the New Plan was discovered in Wi/IF 5.1029, roll 205, T-77.
10. "Die Devisenstellen im Neuen Plan," *Deutscher Volkswirt*, September 28, 1934, pp. 2341 ff.
11. The remarkable discrepancy between prices at home and abroad can be seen from the following table, comparing prices as of December, 1934, in reichsmarks per 100 kilograms:

	HOME MARKETS	WORLD MARKETS*
Wheat	20.55	10.41
Rye	16.55	6.58
Oats	14.88	5.29
Fodder barley	15.45	8.17
Maize (Argentine)	15.50	5.84
Cattle	87.00	23.87
Pigs	96.00	28.37
Butter	260.00	121.77
Lard	181.00	66.86
Eggs (per 100)	11.50	4.97
Sugar	44.00	9.17

   * *Börsen-und Wirtschaftskalender* (Frankfurt a. M.: Frankfurter Zeitung, 1934).

12. In the party itself there were devaluers, convinced autarchists, and war economists. For a survey of the arguments used by the various groups

in big business and the party see the regular reports on "Germany" in the *Economist* (London), 1935 and 1936.

13. Economic insulation does not accompany every rearmament boom. It is inevitable for small or poor countries which lack most essential raw materials or foreign exchange to pay for imported raw materials. Large or rich countries, like the United States, may dispense with extensive control of prices, trade, and foreign exchange so long as they possess unused resources for rearmament, including gold reserves for covering the deficit in the balance of payments.

14. "Anlagevorschriften für das Kreditgewerbe," *Deutscher Volkswirt,* November 30, 1934, p. 365. See also the issue of October 19, 1934 (pp. 94 ff.), of the same periodical.

15. *Nazi Conspiracy and Aggression,* VII, 491–92.

16. "Grenzen kompensatorischer Kreditschöpfung," *Wirtschaftskurve,* February, 1936, pp. 237–39.

17. "Die Konversion der Industrieanleihen," ibid., August, 1936, pp. 209–12.

18. "Die Handhabung der Emmissionssperre," *Deutscher Volkswirt,* May 29, 1936.

19. "Die Kreditmärkte im Konsolidierungsprozess," ibid., December 24, 1936.

20. Samuel Lurie, *Private Investment in a Controlled Economy, Germany 1933–39* (New York: Columbia University Press, 1947), pp. 80, 86.

21. For a detailed discussion of how the Central Bank regulated demand and supply of funds and fixed the rates of interest see Schweitzer, "Schacht's Regulation of Money and the Capital Markets," *Journal of Finance,* June, 1948, pp. 1–18.

22. Reprinted in *Nazi Conspiracy and Aggression,* VII, 493.

23. Lurie, op. cit., pp. 126, 135, 137.

24. *Deutschlands wirtschaftliche Lage in der Jahresmitte 1939* (publication of *Reichs-Kredit-Gesellschaft* [Berlin, 1940]), pp. 48 ff.

25. The resulting volume, *Probleme des deutschen Wirtschaftsleben* (Berlin, 1937), published by the *Deutsches Institut für Bankwissenschaft und Bankwesen* in honor of Schacht's sixtieth birthday, is a monument of eulogy.

26. See the *Faserstoffverordnung* of July 19, 1934, in *Reichsgesetzblatt,* July 20, 1934.

27. "Die Lage der Textilindustrie," *Deutscher Volkswirt,* October 25, 1935.

28. "Kontingentierung der Spinnstoffverarbeitung," ibid., December 13, 1935.

29. Joseph Keubel, "Kunstseide und Zellwolle," ibid., April 19, 1936.

30. For details see "Rohstoffbeimischung bei behördlichen Bekleidungs-aufträgen," *Deutscher Volkswirt*, August 10, 1934, pp. 2005 ff.; September 7, 1934, p. 2182; December 6, 1935.

31. Institut für Konjunkturforschung, *Wochenbericht*, October 1, 1938.

32. Joseph Rosen, *Das Existenziminimum in Deutschland* (Zürich: Oprecht, 1939).

33. Testimony of Minister Schwerin von Krosigk in Nürnberg *(Trials of War Criminals*, XII, 607).

34. "Goerdelers Aufgaben," *Berliner Tageblatt*, November 9, 1934.

35. Reichsorganisationsleiter der NSDAP, Box 320, Folder 594, Berlin Document Center.

36. Reichswirtschaftsministerium, Box 320, Folder 520, Berlin Document Center.

37. *Deutscher Volkswirt*, October 19, 1934, p. 112.

38. "Wirtschaftslage der deutschen Textilindustrie," ibid., March 29, 1935, pp. 1183 ff.; July 5, 1935.

39. "Elastische Marktregelung statt starrer Preisbindung," *Berliner Börsen-Zeitung*, December 22, 1934.

40. "Eine zweite und dritte Durchführungsverordnung zum Spinnstoff-gesetz," *Soziale Praxis*, October, 1936, p. 1249.

41. Wi/IF 5.1568, roll 292, T-77.

42. Wi/IF 5.614, roll 151, T-77.

43. Goerdeler reported to Hitler that only 40 per cent of the demand for pork could be satisfied, and that the price of veal had risen so much that by October of 1935 it could no longer be purchased by low-income families. See Wi/IF 5.1568, roll 292, T-77.

44. For details on tax policies see Otto Nathan, *The Nazi Economic System* (Durham, North Carolina: Duke University Press, 1944), chap. 9.

45. See his "Finanzierungsformen in Deutschland 1932–45," Document NI-412. In his testimony in Nürnberg, the Minister of Finance, Schwerin von Krosigk, adopted the same procedure. See *Trials of War Criminals*, XII, 595.

46. A. C. Pigou, *The Political Economy of War* (New York: The Macmillan Co., 1941).

47. Document No. 323 in the defense book of Schwerin-Krosigk, *Trials of War Criminals*, Case XI.

48. Document No. 55, containing the affidavit of Dr. Friedrich Tischbein, in the defense book of Schwerin von Krosigk.

49. *Vierteljahrshefte zur Konjunkturforschung* (Berlin), No. 1, 1937, part A, p. 58.

50. Howard S. Ellis, *Exchange Control in Central Europe* (Cambridge, Mass.: Harvard University Press, 1941), p. 300.

51. Ibid., p. 288.

52. *Balances of Payments, 1938* (League of Nations annual report [Geneva, 1939]), p. 59.

53. Alan Sweezy, "Declining Investment Opportunity," *New Economics* (New York: Alfred A. Knopf, Inc., 1947); and René Erbe, *Die nationalsozialistische Wirtschaftspolitik 1933–39 im Lichte der modernen Theorie* (Zürich: Polygraphischer Verlag, 1958).

54. Wagner, "Geldschöpfung, Wirtschaftskreislauf und die nationalsozialistische Wirtschaftspolitik," *Schweizerische Zeitschrift für Volkswirtschaft und Statistik*, No. 1, 1958.

55. The actual policy of work-creation constituted a compromise between the proposals of business groups, emphasizing subsidies for themselves, and the various proposals of the von Papen and Hitler governments. See Kroll, *Von der Weltwirtschaftskrise zur Staatskonjunktur*, Chap. XII.

56. In a proposal to the Minister of Defense on January 16, 1933, the Reichsverband der deutschen Industrie demanded that Germany insist upon military equality with other powers. The organization of business emphasized that it "must reject any control upon production and trade of military weapons," and it claimed the right to participate in policy decisions of the German government concerning the rearmament negotiations in Geneva. See EC-371.

57. Hermberg, "German Government Finance," p. 5. Profit taxes were paid by individuals while business taxes constituted an obligation for concerns.

58. *Vierteljahrshefte zur Konjunkturforschung*, 1934, p. 78; and *Deutscher Volkswirt*, November 9, 1934, p. 240.

Chapter 8

1. Cf. Donald H. Wallace, *Economic Controls and Defense* (New York: Twentieth Century Fund, 1953), pp. 10–11.

2. Wunderlich, *Labor under German Democracy—Arbitration, 1918–1932* (New York: New School for Social Research, Graduate Faculty of Political and Social Sciences, 1940).

3. Cf. Schweitzer, "American Competitive Capitalism," *Schweizerische Zeitschrift für Volkswirtschaft und Statistik*, April, 1956, pp. 31–51.

4. NI-903.

5. Files of the Rüstungs-und Wirtschaftsstab, Wi/IF 5.326, roll 70, T-77.

6. See Georg Thomas, "Grundlagen für eine Geschichte der deutschen Wehr-und Rüstungswirtschaft" (unpublished study, 1945, deposited in the National Archives), pp. 53, 67, and 90.

7. Mr. Louis Lochner has asserted that director Ernst Poensgen, of the largest steel concern, had publicly protested against the destruction of the trade unions. (*Tycoons and Tyrant* [Chicago: Henry Regnery Co., 1954], p. 61.) Yet no citation is given. Lochner's book is a "white-wash" of big business. Ernst Poensgen actively participated in forming the "Harzburg Front," the political alliance between the Nationalist and Nazi parties, in 1931.

8. Wi/IF 5.406, roll 92, T-77.

9. See the detailed March 3, 1938, report on the Labor Front by Mr. Pietzsch, who was then head of the *Reichswirtschaftskammer*, in Wi/IF 5.1276, roll 266, T-77.

10. Cf. Weber, *The Theory of Social and Economic Organization*, p. 148.

11. The content of the bill was published in *Amtliches Nachrichtenblatt der Deutschen Arbeitsfront*, September 2, 1936, and reproduced in Wi/IF 5.1260, roll 260, T-77.

12. Schacht stated the division of functions publicly (see *Soziale Praxis*, 1935, p. 396) and also privately in a letter written to Ley on June 26, 1936, contained in Wi/IF 5.1260, roll 260.

13. Ernest Hamburger, "Significance of Nazi Leisure Time Program," *Social Research*, May 1945, pp. 227-49.

14. Eduard Heimann, *Theorie des sozialen Kapitalismus* (Tübingen: Mohr-Verlag, 1929).

15. Cf. Götz Briefs, "Betriebssoziologie," *Handwörterbuch der Soziologie* (Stuttgart: Enke-Verlag, 1931), pp. 45 ff.

16. Ernst Michel, *Sozialgeschichte der industriellen Arbeitswelt* (Frankfurt: Knecht-Verlag, 1948), p. 153.

17. Cf. "Streiflichter zur Geschichte der Wahlen im Dritten Reich," *Vierteljahrshefte für Zeitgeschichte*, 1955, p. 315.

18. Karl Erbe, *Die soziale Ehre und die Verstösse gegen sie* (Zeulenroda: Sporn, 1936), pp. 49 ff; Wunderlich, *German Labor Courts* (Chapel Hill: University of North Carolina Press, 1946), pp. 178-79.

19. Among others, Krupp was one of the first business leaders who voluntarily cooperated with the party. See especially the documents of the prosecution in the Krupp trial against the defendants Ihn and Bülow. Many of these Nazi requirements became later a part of the labor law of the state. See for instance, *Reichsarbeitsblatt*, 1935, p. 310.

20. Cf. Clark Kerr, "Labor Markets: Their Character and Consequences," *American Economic Review*, May, 1950, pp. 278-91. Although

the distinction between job and wage markets was derived from American experience, the separation itself had not only become generally recognized during the Weimar period but had led to specific policies, called respectively *Arbeitsmarktpolitik* and *Tarifvertragspolitik*. Cf. Ernst Berger, *Arbeitsmarktpolitik* (Berlin: de Gruyter-Verlag, 1926).

21. For a discussion of local job markets in the United States, see Lloyd G. Reynolds and Joseph Shister, *Job Horizons* (New York: Harper & Brothers, 1949).

22. Ludwig Preller, *Sozialpolitik in der Weimar Republik* (Stuttgart: Mittelbach-Verlag, 1949), pp. 304–10.

23. Monopsonist and absorption powers are not identical. Monopsony lowers the quantity demanded and thereby reduces price and also output. Absorption power deals only with potential and actual job and service offers in markets. Positive absorption power creates jobs or divides the existing volume of employment among more laborers. When enjoying such power, the trade union operates on the demand side of job markets. Yet employers also enjoy power on the demand side when they are able to increase the speed of workers or reduce the number of jobs by innovation. Positive and negative absorption powers are distinguished not by their position in the market but by their impact upon the specific size of the quantities demanded or supplied. This distinction between two powers on the same side of the market overcomes the well-known "independence" handicap of the schedule theory of markets.

24. Lederer and Marschak, *Klassen auf dem Arbeitsmarkt und ihre Organisationen* ("Grundriss der Sozialökonomik," Vol. IX, Part 2 [Tübingen: Mohr-Verlag, 1927]), p. 121.

25. The Nazis even suppressed their own "trade unions," called NSBO. See Hans-Gerd Schumann, *Nationalsozialismus und Gewerkschaftsbewegung* (Hannover: Verlagsanstalt Goedel, 1958), pp. 87-92.

26. "Um die Werkscharen," *Deutscher Volkswirt*, March 13, 1936, p. 1099.

27. C. W. Guillebaud, *The Social Policy of Nazi Germany* (Cambridge: Cambridge University Press, 1941), p. 37.

28. The other two economic policies of the Labor Front—diversions of interests through, say, organized concerts at reduced prices, and sham achievements such as better rest rooms—served the purpose of confusing and mollifying the latent opposition of workers.

29. Since the Spanish *Organisacion Sincical* cannot suppress secret unions, strikes are numerous but fail because the secret police of the Franco regime jail their leaders. See "Spanish Workers Closely Checked," *Christian Science Monitor*, February 2, 1959.

30. Cf. Walter Stothfang, "Die künftige Gestaltung der öffentlichen

Notstandsarbeiten," *Deutscher Volkswirt*, October 11, 1935, pp. 59–61.

31. *Reichsarbeitsblatt*, 1937, p. 13.

32. Stothfang, "Wo bleiben die Abzüge?" *Der Angriff*, March 11, 1934.

33. Guillebaud, op. cit., p. 99.

34. Wi/IF 5.1616, roll 297, T-77.

35. Wi/IF 5.1223, roll 248, T-77.

36. Guillebaud, *The Economic Recovery of Germany* (London: The Macmillan Co., 1939), p. 198.

37. On the distinction between the internal and external structure of labor markets, see the article by John T. Dunlop in *New Concepts in Wage Determination*, ed. G. W. Taylor and F. C. Pierson (New York: McGraw-Hill Book Co., 1957), pp. 117–39.

38. The secret wage census can be found in the files of the Reichskanzlei 43 II/542, Bundesarchiv, Koblenz; and the calculations of the actual cost of living are contained in Wi/IF 5.202, roll 35, T-77.

39. The index of farm selling prices rose from 78 points in 1932 to 100 in 1935. See the report of the Reichskreditanstalt, 1937–38, p. 20. Nazi domination of agriculture was thus economically beneficial for those farmers who produced a significant amount of marketable goods.

40. See the copy of a secret speech delivered by the trustee of labor in Sonneberg on November 17, 1938, in Wi/IF 5.1223, roll 249, T-77.

41. See the 1941 study by Erich Preiser, which has been reprinted in his book *Bildung und Verteilung des Volkseinkommens* (Göttingen: Vandenhoeck & Ruprecht, 1957), pp. 239–83.

42. Quoted by Cole, "The Evolution of the German Labor Front," *Political Science Quarterly*, December, 1937, p. 554.

43. Lloyd G. Reynolds, "Cutthroat Competition," *American Economic Review*, December, 1940, pp. 736–47.

44. Modern economists have discarded this "stickiness" theory. See for instance Alvin H. Hansen, *Guide to Keynes* (New York: McGraw-Hill Book Co., 1953). On pages 176–77 Hansen distinguishes seven possible situations of wage reductions.

45. Per Jacobson, "Le Financement de la Guerre en Allemagne," *Kyklos*, 1947.

Chapter 9

1. In his theory of politically oriented capitalism, Max Weber distinguishes tax farmers, lenders to the state, deliverers to the state, privileged export companies, and colonial plantation or ship owners as capitalist enterprise groups that arose in response to the profit oppor-

tunities created by the state. Cf. *Wirtschaft und Gesellschaft* (Tübingen: Mohr-Verlag, 1956), Vol. II, p. 524 ff.

2. Ellis, *Exchange Control in Central Europe*, p. 180.

3. *Statistisches Jahrbuch für das Deutsche Reich* (Berlin, 1935).

4. Graf von Kalckreuth, "Zwischen den Mühlsteinen des Zinswuchers und des Sozialismus," *Deutsche Tageszeitung*, November 22, 1931.

5. Although the impact of the depression, the credit crisis, deliberate deflation, foreign devaluations, and exchange controls cannot be separated, the following data on foreign trade and monetary reserves suggest that foreign exchange control merely retarded the detrimental influences of the other factors upon the external economy.

6. See the memorandum of February 14, 1933, in Wi/IF 5.370, roll 81, T-77.

7. Hugenberg's letter of February 27, 1933, is also included in Wi/IF 5.370.

8. See the petition of Minister Klagges on behalf of the mines and metal refineries, dated February 14, 1933. Ibid.

9. The Minister's proposed bill, presented on February 28, 1933 (ibid.), thus gave rise to compulsory inter-cartel agreements.

10. For the data on deficit financing, see Chapter VII above.

11. The market price of the new communal bonds fell to 80 per cent of their nominal value and rose gradually to 95 per cent in 1937. See Schacht's speech of September 29, 1937, delivered in Essen. Copy in Wi/IF 5.351, roll 78, T-77.

12. In case of the so-called "classical" conversions, those taking place by voluntary agreement, the bonus was increased to nearly 5 per cent in order to obtain the consent of creditors. Cf. Rudolf Stucken, *Deutsche Geld und Kreditpolitik, 1914–1953* (Tübingen: Mohr-Verlag, 1953), p. 142.

13. See General Thomas' memorandum in Wi/IF 5.370, roll 87, T-77.

14. Acting in the interest of debtors or future borrowers, the economic advisors of the Central Bank could not rely on the liquidity-preference theory. Not only was this theory, at the time, available only in fragmentary form, as Keynes had stated it in his *Treatise on Money* (London; Macmillian, 1930) but to overcome the hoarding tendency of creditors would have required a comprehensive deficit policy that would have come into conflict with the method adopted for financing rearmament. It was thus the support of the power and interest goals of debtors that inevitably prevented the government from accepting the liquidity-preference theory.

15. Erbe, *Die nationalsozialistische Wirtschaftspolitik 1933–1939 im Lichte der modernen Theorie*, p. 63.

16. See Schacht's vigorous defense of saving and self-financing on pages 2 and 12 of his Essen speech (previously cited in n. 11 of this chapter).

17. *Wochenbericht*, 1938, p. 351.

18. R. F. Harrod, *The Life of John Maynard Keynes* (London: The Macmillan Co., 1951), p. 512.

19. The method was well described by Thomas Balogh, "The National Economy of Germany," *Economic Journal* (London), XLVIII (1938), 481 ff.

20. The I. G. Farben had to pay 30 per cent of the gain to the German government for a deal negotiated in 1933. Shortly thereafter, 30 per cent became the general payment to the government.

21. For this accomplishment in economic power politics, Schacht received the admiration of Hitler and became "famous" all over the world. Yet in his recent memoirs, Schacht fails to claim credit for his accomplishment but misrepresents his policy as emergency measures that had to be taken "to secure the necessary goods for the very living of the German people." (See his *76 Jahre meines Lebens*, pp. 415–16.) Why were these "necessary goods" primarily in the form of raw materials for rearmament?

22. See Wi/IF 5.383, roll 86, T-77. A copy of Buecher's proposals was discovered in the office files of General Thomas.

23. For the procedure followed in obtaining foreign currency to purchase foreign bonds see the letter of the Dresden industrialist Witte. Ibid.

24. See the file of the Reichswirtschaftsministerium in microfilm RWM/18/47, roll 86, T-71.

25. Albert O. Hirschman, "Disinflation, Discrimination and the Dollar Shortage," *American Economic Review*, December, 1948, p. 887. See also Charles P. Kindleberger, *The Dollar Shortage* (New York: John Wiley & Sons, 1950), pp. 102–3.

26. Letter from General Thomas to Keppler, dated July 7, 1934. See Wi/IF 5.406, roll 92, T-77.

27. See above, Chap. VI, pp. 250 ff.

28. Wi/IF 5.406, roll 92, T-77.

29. The initiative in planning and implementing the oil program came from the I. G. Farben. See the July 27, 1934, report of Director Krauch to General Thomas, Wi/IF 5.605, roll 148, T-77.

30. The proposal for trading monopolies was presented by the military on April 16, 1934, in order to engage in large-scale barter trade with the Soviet Union. See Wi/IF 5.383, roll 86, T-77.

31. *Vierteljahrshefte zur Wirtschaftsforschung* (publication of the

Institut für Konjunkturforschung [Hamburg: Hanseatische Verlagsanstalt, 1939-40]), pp. 75-77.

32. These direct controls produced almost the opposite effect from that of a monopsonistic policy. A monopsonist reduces the quantity he purchases in order to obtain a lower price. Overissued permits and inconvertible rights produced a steady import surplus on the basis of a rising total volume of trade. The direct controls exerted an influence upon prices only when traders in the other country could sell their goods elsewhere or experienced a decline of stored goods.

33. See the long memorandum of the Dresden industrialist Witte, written on April 3, 1935. Wi/IF 5.383, roll 86, T-77.

34. RWM/18/35, roll 86, T-71.

35. RWM/18/45, roll 88, T-71.

36. The secret documents of the ministries concerned do not verify the conclusion, reached by one eminent economist, that "political aims engulfed the economic calculus." See Howard S. Ellis, *Exchange Control in Central Europe* (Cambridge, Mass.: Harvard University Press, 1941), p. 285.

37. See the report of Undersecretary Rudolf Brinkman to a secret conference of twenty-three political and economic leaders who discussed export policy on May 15, 1936, under the chairmanship of Göring. Wi/IF 5. 203, roll 35, T-77.

Chapter 10

1. For the details of uniform accounting see H. W. Singer, *Standardized Accountancy in Germany* (Cambridge: Cambridge University Press, 1943).

2. The term "state-directed capitalism," as used in this study, signifies an economic system in which the dictatorial state retains most of the essential institutions of private capitalism but adjusts these institutions to the requirements of the dictatorially derived and imposed noneconomic goals. The dictatorial state does not itself become a capitalist but imposes its will primarily through a re-structuring of private markets.

In contrast, the Soviet type of economy constitutes a dictatorial state socialism because the central features of private ownership of the means of production and the private control of markets have been replaced by state ownership and central economic planning.

3. The financial plans exceeded the budgets of the armed forces by the amount of the secret budget as well as the funds spent by civilian agencies for military purposes. On the division and spending of the

funds in the secret budget during the period of rearmament see Wi/IF 5.326, roll 70, T-77.

4. The theory of pre-financing by the device of special bills and subsequent placement of bonds was first worked out by Wilhelm Lautenbach, in September of 1931, when he was an official of the Ministry of Economics. His memoranda, which were secret throughout the Nazi regime, were published later. See his *Zins, Kredit und Produktion,* ed. Wolfgang Stützel (Tübingen: Mohr-Verlag, 1952), pp. 143 ff.

5. Document NI-412.

6. Rudolf Brinkmann, "Rechtsgrundlagen der Kapitallenkung," *Zeitschrift der Akademie für deutsches Recht* (Berlin) No. 6, 1939.

7. Lurie, *Private Investment in a Controlled Economy,* p. 104.

8. Cf. Willi Schmidt and Victor Wrede, "Konsolidierung und Kreditmechanismus," *Vierteljahrshefte zur Wirtschaftsforschung,* No. 4, 1938, pp. 399–416.

9. This happened in Canada in 1958–59 when the increased sale of government bonds led to a higher rate of interest and subsequently to an increase in the money supply, which rose by 12 per cent in one year.

10. Cf. Schweitzer, "Profits under Nazi Planning," *Quarterly Journal of Economics,* November, 1946, pp. 1–25.

11. See W. Prion, *Das deutsche Finanzwunder* (Berlin: Franke, 1938), Chap. III.

12. Evidently fascinated and perhaps frightened by this new development, Mr. Peter Drucker has built a fanciful theory of "the corporation as an autonomous social entity" in which property does not matter, and in regard to which the distinction between capitalism and socialism has become meaningless. (Cf. *The Future of Industrial Man* [New York: L. J. Day Co., 1942], pp. 92 ff.) Why should the rise of interest-free capital constitute a "complete break with the traditional legal and political concept of property?"

13. The same was not true in the United States. During the New Deal, many businessmen did not accept deficit financing as a property-neutral institution. Yet the same opponents often invested their idle funds in government bonds, enjoyed the tax exemption of the interest income, but simultaneously attacked deficit financing as being "socialistic" in nature.

14. See Keiser, "Konzernbewegung."

15. The quantity of German exports fell by 14 per cent in 1932, 7 per cent in 1933, and 15 per cent in 1934. Experts in the Ministry of Economics estimated that four fifths of this decline was attributable to the too high prices and one fifth to the boycott of German goods abroad. See Wi/IF 5.604, roll 148, T-77.

16. About 60 per cent of the German goods exported in 1935 went to the various kinds of clearing countries.

17. See Wi/IF 5.1504, roll 289, T-77.

18. Wi/IF 5.203, roll 35, T-77.

19. In neoclassic competitive theory, "the central banker became a sort of honorary member of the market forces" (Hirschman, *The Strategy of Economic Development* [New Haven: Yale University Press, 1958], p. 64) not because of his monetary quantity decisions but because of his intention to counteract disequilibrium tendencies in markets.

20. In a secret meeting on May 15, 1936, Minister Popitz presented a plan for paying exporters a premium above the prevailing exchange rate of the mark. This plan was uniformly rejected by leaders of government and big business because "premium payments cannot be expected to increase exports appreciably." See Wi/IF 5.203, roll 36, T-77.

21. The "New Plan" was discovered in folder Wi/IF 5.1029, roll 205, T-77. Prior to its adoption a preliminary copy of the plan was approved by the Ministry of War.

22. The head of the *Reich* Chamber of Industries complained bitterly in a letter of July 9, 1935, that some treasonable members had passed on news of the law to representatives of foreign newspapers. See RWM/18/35, roll 86, T-71.

23. Wi/IF 5.1504, roll 289, and 5.420, roll 98, T-77.

24. The principle of supplementary grants was achieved by the Mühlhoff concern which complained of a loss and threatened to dismiss its workers if its subsidy for plowshares was not raised from 33 to 35 per cent. The request was granted when cost and profit data substantiated the firm's claim. See RWM/18/45, roll 88, T-71.

25. See Schacht's speech of November 29, 1938, reproduced in *Nazi Conspiracy and Aggression,* VII, 600.

26. See the affidavit of the I. G. Farben official Kurt Krüger in NI-4928.

27. For details of the difficulties involved in these two balancing decisions see the minutes of the eleven meetings of the heads of the supervisory boards with their superiors in the Ministry of Economics, held during 1934 and 1935. Box 387, Folder 520, Berlin Document Center.

28. See Wi/IF 5.113, roll 14, T-77.

29. Had they been given a free choice, organized business groups would have preferred that planning authority over these markets be transferred to cartels. One economist even translated this proposal into a bill. See Roderich von Ungern-Sternberg, *Die Plannung als Ordnungs-*

prinzip der deutschen Industriewirtschaft, (Stuttgart: Enke-Verlag, 1932).

30. Although a military decision was responsible for the compulsion built into business organizations, the expected assignment of mobilization functions to the economic groups came only in 1938; therefore, we cannot speak of a sustained military influence upon these organizations during the first phase of the regime.

31. Wi/IF 5.2149, roll 339, T-77.

32. Wi/IF 5.598, roll 145, T-77.

33. Ibid. The bill carries the date of August 15, 1934.

34. Wi/IF 5.1276, roll 266, T-77.

35. Jacob Viner, *International Economics* (Glencoe, Illinois: Free Press, 1951), p. 216.

36. As long as we did not have definite information on the duality of the regulated market, we could seek to interpret this market in terms of the monopoly theory (cf. Schweitzer, "The Role of Foreign Trade in the Nazi War Economy," *Journal of Political Economy,* August, 1943, pp. 322–37.) Application of this theory nowadays (cf. Frank C. Child, *Theory and Practice of Exchange Control in Germany* [The Hague: Nyhoff, 1958]) can only prevent us from arriving at a tenable theory of economic statism.

37. See Box 387, Folder 520, Berlin Document Center.

Chapter 11

1. The theory that dictatorial regimes are based upon an "amorphous mass" not only fails to make a careful distinction between the powerful and powerless but also derives the concentrated power of the former from the *Vermassung* of the latter. Neither the mass movement before, nor the monolithic power after, the purge can be explained in terms of this theory.

2. According to Max Weber, it is only when usurpation of office is followed by submission motivated by fear that illegitimate domination arises. The plebs of antiquity and the *popolo* of the Middle Ages formed the counterpart to the modern revolutionary and counterrevolutionary types of illegitimate domination. (See Weber, *The City,* trans. Don Martindale and Gertrude Neuwirth [Glencoe, Illinois: Free Press, 1958], pp. 107 ff.)

3. Carl J. Friedrich and Z. K. Brzezinski, *Totalitarian Dictatorship and Autocracy* (Cambridge, Mass.: Harvard University Press, 1956).

4. Max Weber did not distinguish between charismatic and ideologi-

cal legitimacy. (See Gerth and Mills, *From Max Weber: Essays in Sociology*, pp. 124-25.) He thus deprived himself of the opportunity to suggest a theory of legitimacy for one-party regimes.

5. Quoted by Bullock, "The Political Ideas of Adolf Hitler," in *The Third Reich* p. 352. This study clearly shows the consistency of Hitler's political ideas over a period of time.

6. Wheeler-Bennett, *The Nemesis of Power*, p. 307.

7. Those who interpreted the Soviet regime only in terms of illegitimate power had to accept the economic reforms after 1953 as instances of "economic freedom." Actually, most of the relaxations constituted a shift from physical to mental violence, from illegitimate to ideologically legitimate power. None of these shifts in the method of justifying party rule involved any marked decline in the degree of power enjoyed by the rulers.

8. For a lucid statement of the theory of charismatic leadership see Bendix, *Max Weber—An Intellectual Portrait*, Chap. X.

9. The first *Führerbefehl* in non-ideological matters seems to have been issued to Goebbels who was ordered to cease his love affair with a Czech actress in 1938. See R. Manvell and H. Fraenkel, *Dr. Goebbels* (London: Heinemann, 1960), pp. 170-72.

10. *The Speeches of Adolf Hitler,* ed. Norman Baynes (London: Oxford University Press, 1942), I, 321.

11. *Nazi Conspiracy and Aggression,* IV, 283-88.

12. Akten der Reichskanzlei 43 II/530a and 531, Bundesarchiv, Koblenz.

13. Wi/IF 5.1276, roll 266, T-77.

14. Wi/IF 5.1260, roll 260, T-77.

15. EAP 250-a/1, roll 1, T-81.

16. For the sums involved in these payments, see Schweitzer, "Business Power in the Nazi Regime."

17. *Nazi Conspiracy and Aggression,* IV, 465.

18. Ibid., p. 468. This instruction was issued in 1939 in order to offset the impact of the separation of sexes during war upon the birth of children of the desirable kind.

19. Ibid., p. 563.

20. Among the members of the SS, charismatic belief was associated not only with personal devotion to the Führer but with physical characteristics that were said to be representative of the Aryan race.

21. *Nazi Conspiracy and Aggression,* IV, 559-60.

22. The violence theory of dictatorial (or all) regimes cannot explain

why and how violence produces ideological strength without necessarily resulting in the personal and group debasement of the rulers.

23. This desire for unified interest representation explains why neither business concerns nor Schmitt in the fall of 1933 resisted the declaration of the generals that military plans required a compulsory organization of business.

24. Unified representation of interests and harmony between private and public interests could not be obtained without cost. The total expenses for all economic groups and chambers in 1935 and 1936 amounted to 23 and 34 million marks, respectively, which had to be borne by private concerns. Cf. NI-098, copy in the National Archives.

25. There were unsuccessful attempts to introduce the regulated market and the so-called vertical organization in other sectors of the economy. For a sample see "Bemerkungen zur Frage der Gliederung der deutschen Wirtschaft," microfilm copy TS Germany R350, The Hoover Institution, Stanford University, Stanford, California.

26. We thus accept the concept of authoritarian capitalism, as suggested by George N. Halm in his *Economic Systems* (rev. ed.; New York: Holt, Rinehart and Winston, 1960); but we cannot share the belief that there was only one kind of authority in the Nazi regime.

27. For details see Schweitzer, "The Foreign Exchange Crisis of 1936," *Zeitschrift für die gesamte Staatswissenschaft,* April, 1962, pp. 243-77.

28. See NI-053, NIK-10334, and Wi/IF 5.605, roll 148, T-77.

29. For the correspondence pertaining to this dispute, which occurred in the summer of 1936, see Wi/IF 5.326, roll 70, T-77.

30. Presented first in a memorandum of February 2, 1935 (Wi/IF 5.383, roll 86, T-77) and repeated in many subsequent speeches.

31. *Nazi Conspiracy and Aggression,* III, 881.

32. Reichswirtschaftsministerium Box 397, Folder 646, Berlin Document Center.

33. Ibid., Box 391, Folder 559.

34. See Poensgen's affidavit in Gerd von Klass, *Albert Vögler* (Tübingen: Rainer Wunderlich Verlag, 1957), p. 254. The effect of this telegram is described in the minutes (written by Jakob Reichert) of the meetings in Berlin and Düsseldorf (Box 391, Folder 559).

35. Wi/IF 5.641, roll 151, T-77.

36. Schacht's critique and proposal was communicated to the Minister of War by Captain Drews who was his liaison officer with the Minister of Economics. Ibid.

37. For the relevant memoranda of Karmann and Thomas see Wi/IF 5.614, roll 151, and 5.651, roll 163, T-77.

38. *Nazi Conspiracy and Aggression*, III, 883.

39. In his autobiography Schacht recognized this particular mistake when he said: "that Göring secured a decisive influence in the economy is unfortunately attributable to my own initiative . . . I still believed that men such as Hitler and Göring could be won to a recognition of the principles of law and state." *76 Jahre meines Lebens*, p. 463.

40. For a copy of this agreement see Wi/IF 5.203, roll 35, T-77.

41. Ibid. Bodenschatz was Göring's liaison officer with the Ministry of War.

42. Ibid.

43. Wi/IF 5.433, roll 101, T-77, and RWM/23/25, roll 109, T-71.

44. *Nazi Conspiracy and Aggression*, III, 892–94. Von Blomberg was evidently acting on the assumption that the foreign-exchange crisis could be solved by means of the Four Year Plan.

45. Ibid., IV, 934–38.

46. For details see especially the letter of Count v. d. Goltz to Colonel Friedrich Hossbach, reprinted in the latter's *Zwischen Hitler und Wehrmacht*, pp. 132 ff.

47. Even General Beck did not at first see Hitler's political intent but had to be shown by Colonel Hossbach that the moral charge was only a subterfuge to conceal a political attack. Ibid., pp. 130–31.

48. Methodologically, we are shifting for the next three paragraphs to an ideal typical analysis. The question to be answered is clear. Given their military power, what could the generals have done in order to retain their monopoly over military affairs and restore the power structure of the original coalition?

49. Walter Goerlitz, *Der Deutsche Generalstab* (Frankfurt: Frankfurter Hefte, 1950), p. 457. The leaders of the SS feared an attack by the regular army and were greatly relieved when nothing happened (Walter Schellenberg, *Memoiren*, [Köln: Verlag für Politik und Wirtschaft, 1956] p. 40).

50. The speeches of Gustav Krupp von Bohlen and Carl Krauch leave little doubt on this score. See I. G. Farben Prosecution Documents, Vol. VII, Exhibit 29.

51. If the old principle of co-responsibility of chief and deputy commander had been reintroduced in the army, General Beck would have had the authority to act when von Fritsch resigned.

52. A fascist potential prevails when a lower-middle class is suffering from economic grievances, is fearful of losing its status honor, and attributes all these threats to its ideals and economic interests to one enemy that it hopes to destroy through one supreme effort of concentrated violence.

53. See Kurt P. Tauber, "German Nationalists and European Union," *Political Science Quarterly,* December, 1959, pp. 564–89.

54. If the New Deal had not provided effective support for farmers, it is doubtful whether Richard Hofstadter's inference—economic issues prevail in a depression, while status issues emerge in prosperity—could be accepted as a valid generalization derived from recent American history. (See his article, "The Pseudo-Conservative Revolt," in *The New American Right,* ed. Daniel Bell [New York: Criterion Books, 1955].) The inference does not apply to pre-Nazi Germany, where negative status was coupled with an extensive economic program by a counterrevolutionary movement.

55. In December of 1959, the French army in Algiers at first refused to fight the armed units of the fascist portion of the European settlers. It was only when military units unattached to the cause of the settlers were sent in that the armed insurgents surrendered. The defeat of the para-military fascist troops thus depended only on the availability of a few regiments who were loyal to the non-fascist government.

In 1962 the armed revolt of the OAS was opposed by the regular French army, so the "scorched-earth policy" had no chance of success. The events in Algeria have demonstrated, however, not only the vitality but also the variety of the counterrevolutionary forces in our time. The OAS adopted a different principle of organization. It was not a mass movement controlled by a centralized party but a military organization led primarily by former officers of the regular French army and allied with various fascistically oriented settler groups. Defeat of the OAS could not be assured by a treaty between France and the FLN but required that France be victorious in an open civil war. All kinds of counterrevolutionary groups may thus arise in the future that will fall within the orbit but not necessarily follow the Nazi pattern of partial fascism.

56. In addition to the insufficient knowledge of the early Nazi regime, the major reason for the present incapacity to undercut counterrevolutionary tendencies lay in the chancellor-democracy, which reduced parliament to a rubber stamp, transformed the government party into a mere echo of the chancellor's unilateral decisions, and bred contempt for democracy among many voters.

Appendix B

1. Kenneth E. Boulding, *The Skills of the Economist* (Cleveland, Ohio: Howard Allen, Inc., 1958), Chap. II.

2. George Stigler, "The Goals of Economic Policy," *Journal of Business*, July, 1958, p. 171.

3. *Christian Science Monitor,* January 26, 1960.

4. Cf. Milton Friedman, *Essays in Positive Economics* (Chicago: University of Chicago Press, 1953), p. 34.

5. The work of Professor Hansen is well known. See especially *Fiscal Policy and Business Cycle* (New York: W. W. Norton and Company, 1941), Chap. XX.

6. Hans Ritschl, *Gemeinwirtschaft und Kapitalistische Marktwirtschaft* (Tübingen: Mohr-Verlag, 1931). A brief summary of this book has been recently translated by Richard A. Musgrave and Allen T. Peacock, *Classics in the Theory of Public Finance* (New York: The Macmillan Co., 1958), pp. 233–41.

7. Walter Eucken, *The Foundations of Economics* (Chicago: University of Chicago Press, 1951).

8. Halm, *Economic Systems,* p. 13.

Index

Absorption power: in job markets, 272; negative, 272; positive, 372; operation of, 373; superior positive, 374, 375; originator of work institutions, 374; restricted negative, 375. *See also* Power, suction

Academy of German Law. *See* German Law, Academy of

Accounting, capital: as feature of capitalism, 3, 53

Accounting, uniform cost: demanded by guilds, 63; introduced as measure against cutthroat prices, 264; and establishment of price floor, 264; and small business cartels, 267; for calculation prices, 267; and new function of groups, 285, 286, 287; large firms unaffected by law on, 287; for textile products, 324

Action, threshold of: technique of content analysis, 47. *See also* Typological method

Adenauer, Konrad: and misinterpretation of anti-Fascism, 562; and former Nazis, 562; and misinterpretation of anti-Semitism, 562

Administration: and class administration of controls, 442; private right of participation in, 480; co-responsibility with business, 483, 485; replacement of markets by, 503

Advisory Council. *See* Council, advisory

Aggression, external: as alternative to internal reform, 201; and militant foreign policy, 244. *See also* Foreign policy

Agrarian reform: proposed by Brüning government, 92; opposed by *Junkers*, 92, 93; von Hindenburg's position towards, 92, 93; and resettlement of farmers, 92; falling prices increased significance of, 93;

and dismissal of Brüning government, 93. *See also Junkers*

Agricultural policy: and tariff protection of 1930, 92; and subsidy program of 1931, 92; provided relief from indebtedness, 92; and prevention of compulsory land sale, 93; strongly influenced by Nazis, 124; and peasant socialism, 198 ff.

Agriculture: and inter-industry agreements, 531; and trend towards regulated market, 531

Agriculture, Estate of: and conflict with handicraft estates, 166, 167; and retail in food, 167; and von Blomberg-Hitler deal, 171; opposed more power for Goerdeler, 196; dominated agriculture, 196; as corporative, 198; structure of, 279; cooperated with landowners, 292; blamed for food crises, 325

Agriculture—food supply: and food crisis of 1935, 325; and compulsory milk delivery, 325; and hoarding of butter, 325; fat rationing proposed, 326; rationing rejected by Hitler, 326; imports of fats ordered, 326; and meat famine, 326

Air Force: for expropriation of recalcitrant producers, 498; for public ownership of raw materials plants, 498; proposals for, rejected, 498

Alienation: between big and small business, 78; led to anticapitalism, 78

Alliance: between Nazi party and upper class, 43; supported by some army leaders, 43; preceded by "National Opposition," 96; supported by business groups, 105; led to first Hitler government, 106

683